As Per Latest CBSE Syllabus 2022-23
Issued on 21 April, 2022...

Accountancy

CBSE Class 11

Authors
Parul Jain
Richa Makkar

ARIHANT PRAKASHAN (School Division Series)

ARIHANT PRAKASHAN

School Division Series

卐 ADMINISTRATIVE & PRODUCTION OFFICES

Regd. Office

'Ramchhaya' 4577/15, Agarwal Road, Darya Ganj, New Delhi -110002
Tele: 011- 47630600, 43518550; Fax: 011- 23280316

卐 **Head Office**

Kalindi, TP Nagar, Meerut (UP) - 250002, Tel: 0121-7156203, 7156204

卐 SALES & SUPPORT OFFICES

Agra, Ahmedabad, Bengaluru, Bareilly, Chennai, Delhi, Guwahati, Hyderabad, Jaipur, Jhansi, Kolkata, Lucknow, Nagpur & Pune.

PO No : TXT-XX-XXXXXXX-X-XX

Published By Arihant Publications (India) Ltd.

For further information about the books published by Arihant, log on to www.arihantbooks.com or e-mail at info@arihantbooks.com

Follow us on  

PRODUCTION TEAM

Publishing Managers
Mahendra Singh Rawat & Keshav Mohan

Project Coordinator
Saurabh Gupta

Cover Designer
Bilal Hashmi

Inner Designer
Ankit Saini

Page Layouting
Amit Bansal

Proof Readers
Aarohi, Apoorvi

THE FIRST WORD

TO THE READERS

AllinOne Accountancy Class 11th has been written keeping in mind the needs of students studying in Class 11th CBSE. This book has been made in such a way that students will be fully guided to prepare for the exam in the most effective manner, securing higher grades.

The purpose of this book is to equip every CBSE Student with a sound knowledge of Accountancy at Class 11th Level. It covers the whole syllabus of class 11th Accountancy divided into Section/Chapters as per the NCERT Textbook & CBSE syllabus. This book will give you support during the course as well as guide you on Revision and Preparation for the exam itself. The material is presented in a Clear & Concise form and there are questions for you to practice.

KEY FEATURES

- To make the students understand the chapter completely, each chapter has Detailed Theory, supported by Illustrations, Tables, Flow Charts, etc.
- Each chapter has questions in the format in which they are asked in the examination like Objective Type, Very Short Answer Type, Short Answer Type and Long Answer Type Questions. These questions cover NCERT Questions and other Important Questions from examination point of view.
- To facilitate the easy learning and practice, explanations to all the questions have been given.
- For the students to check their understanding of numerical questions, a small test numerical questions for practice has been given.
- Chapterwise study is not the only feature of this book, after the Chapterwise Study it has a supplement of Sample Project Report (covering 20 marks) and 5 Sample Question Papers.

AllinOne Accountancy for CBSE Class 11th has all the material required for Learning, Understanding, Practice & Assessment and will surely guide the students to the Way of Success.

We are highly thankful to ARIHANT PRAKASHAN, MEERUT for giving us such an excellent opportunity to write this book. Huge efforts have been made from our side to keep this book error free, but inspite of that if any error or whatsoever is skipped in the book then that is purely incidental, apology for the same, please write to us about that so that it can be corrected in the further edition of the book. The role of Arihant DTP Unit and Proof Reading team is praise worthy in making this book. Suggestions for further improvement of the book will also be welcomed.

At the end, we would like to say BEST OF LUCK to our readers!

Authors

01

This introductory chapter of accounting deals with the meaning, characteristics, objectives, advantages, limitations and branches of accounting. It further deals with the accounting information, qualitative characteristics of accounting information, types and users of accounting information and the basic terms used in accounting.

INTRODUCTION TO ACCOUNTING

DETAILED THEORY

To make the student understand the chapter completely, each chapter, each topic has detailed theory, supported by illustrations, tables, flow charts etc.

MEANING OF ACCOUNTING

Accounting is the process of identifying, recording, classifying, summarising, interpreting and communicating financial information relating to an organisation to the interested users for judgement and decision-making.

CHAPTER CHECKLIST

- Meaning of Accounting
- Objectives, Advantages and Limitations of Accounting
- Accounting Information
- Basic Terms in Accounting

Definitions of Accounting

According to *the American Institute of Certified Public Accountants* (AICPA), "Accounting is the art of recording, classifying and summarising in a significant manner and in terms of money, transactions and events which are, in part atleast, of a financial character and interpreting the results thereof."

According to *American Accounting Association* (AAA), "Accounting is the process of identifying, measuring and communicating economic information to permit informed judgements and decisions by users of the information."

According to *Accounting Principles Board of* AICPA, "Accounting is a service activity. Its function is to provide quantitative information, primarily financial in nature about economic entities that is intended to be useful in making economic decisions."

Characteristics of Accounting

The definitions of accounting brings following characteristics (attributes) of accounting

(*i*) **Identification** It involves identification of those transactions and events which are of financial nature and relate to the organisation. It should be remembered that transaction is the process of give and take and event is the end result of the transaction(s).

(*ii*) **Measurement** Only those business transactions and events, which can be quantified or measured in monetary terms, are considered.

(*iii*) **Recording** It is the process of entering business transactions of financial character in the books of original entry in terms of money.

(*iv*) **Classifying** It can be defined as the process of grouping transactions or entries of one nature at one place.

(*v*) **Summarising** It involves presenting the classified data in a manner which is understandable and useful to various users of accounting statements.

(*vi*) **Analysis and Interpretation** Analysing and interpreting the financial data helps users to make a meaningful judgement of the profitability and financial position of the business.

Objectives of Accounting

(*i*) To maintain systematic and complete record of business transactions in the books of accounts.

(*ii*) To ascertain the financial position of the business.

(*iii*) To ascertain the profit earned or loss incurred during a particular accounting period.

(*iv*) To provide useful information to various interested parties.

CONCEPT EXPLANATION

All concepts explained in an easily understandable and effective manner to help in problem solving.

A format of debit voucher is shown below which records purchase of an asset

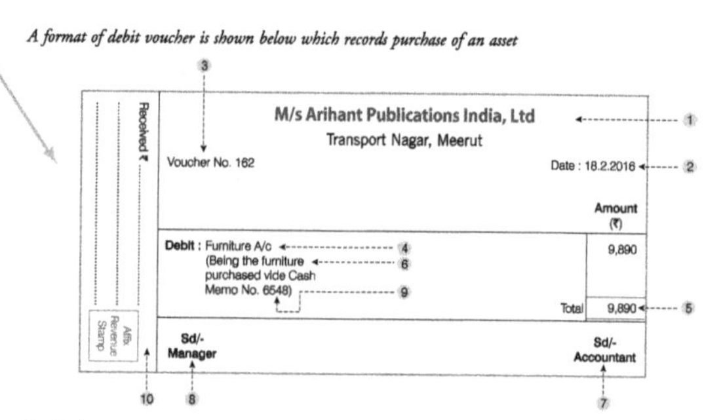

Contents

1. Name and address of the organisation
2. Date of preparing voucher
3. Accounting voucher number
4. Title of the account debited
5. Net amount of transaction
6. Narration (*i.e.*, a brief description of the transaction)
7. Signature of the person preparing it
8. Signature of the authorised signatory
9. Supporting voucher number
10. A document in lieu of supporting voucher

- *If the supporting voucher is not available, then the receipt portion of the debit voucher is filled and is used as supporting voucher.*

DIAGRAMMATIC PRESENTATION

Diagrammatic presentation of concepts to understand the concepts in a better manner.

Accounting Process

Accounting process starts with identifying financial transactions, involves recording, classifying and summarising and ends with interpreting accounting information to various concerned parties.

Accounting process can be explained with the help of the diagram given below

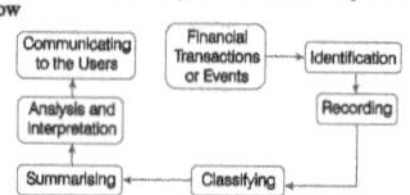

Limitations of Accounting

(*i*) It is historical in nature. It does not reflect the current worth of a business.

(*ii*) The figures given in financial statements ignore the effects of changes in price level.

(*iii*) It ignores qualitative elements.

(*iv*) It may be affected by window dressing.

(*v*) It is not free from personal bias and personal judgement of the people dealing with it.

STEP BY STEP APPROACH

Diagrammatic presentation of concepts to understand the concepts in a better manner. Step by step explanation of practical problem to ease the problem solving process.

Purchased Goods/Fixed Assets on Credit

For example, Ram purchased goods from Shyam on credit for ₹ 15,000.

The transaction is affecting two accounts – **Assets** (Due to purchase, stock/ fixed asset worth ₹ 15,000 will increase) and **Liabilities** (As goods/fixed asset are purchased on credit, creditors will increase by ₹ 15,000).

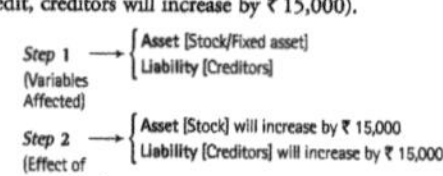

Step 1 (Variables Affected) → **Asset** [Stock]; **Liability** [Creditors]; **Asset** [Cash]

Step 2 (Effect of Transaction) → **Asset** [Stock] will increase by ₹ 5,000; **Liability** [Creditors] will increase by ₹ 2,000; **Asset** [Cash] will decrease by ₹ 3,000

Step 3 (Accounting Equation) → **Assets = Liabilities + Capital**; (3,000) + 5,000 = 2,000 + 0

Sold Goods for Cash

For example, Ajay sold goods costing ₹ 12,000 for cash to Brijesh.

for CBSE Class 11th Examination, it is hoped that this book will reinforce and extend your ideas about the subject and finally will place you in the row of toppers.

CHAPTER PRACTICE

OBJECTIVE TYPE Questions

Multiple Choice Questions

1 Voucher is prepared for NCERT
(a) cash received and paid
(b) cash/credit sale
(c) cash/credit purchase
(d) All of the above

Ans (d) All of the above

2 Voucher is prepare from NCERT
(a) documentary evidence
(b) journal entry
(c) ledger account
(d) All of the above

Ans (a) documentary evidence

3 Which document is issued at the time of purchase return?
(a) Debit note (b) Credit note
(c) ₹1,000 note (d) None of these

Ans (a) When a buyer returns the goods to the seller due to some defect or some other issues, the debit note is issued by buyer to seller as an intimation of amount and quantity being returned and requesting return of money.

4 Identify the transaction for which transfer voucher is prepared?
(a) A payment of ₹ 10,000 towards rent
(b) A receipt of ₹ 15,000 towards professional fee
(c) A credit sale of ₹ 5,000 to Ram
(d) None of the above

Ans (c) The vouchers which are prepared for transactions not involving cash, i.e. non-cash transactions are known as transfer vouchers. There is no cash involvement at the time of credit sale. Hence, transfer/non-cash voucher is prepared in this case

VERY SHORT ANSWER Type Questions

28 Name the source document used for depositing money in the bank.

Ans Pay-in-slip

29 Name the source document which is a written document drawn upon a specified banker and payable on demand.

Ans Cheque

30 Which source document is prepared by the seller for goods sold against cash?

Ans Cash memo

31 Which source document is prepared by the seller for goods sold against credit?

Ans Invoice or bill

32 Name the types of accounting vouchers.

Ans (i) Cash vouchers
(ii) Non-cash vouchers

33 Credit purchases of furniture will be recorded through which voucher?

Ans Transfer voucher

34 Which voucher records transactions with multiple debits and multiple credits?

Ans Complex voucher

35 Which vouchers are prepared for transactions not involving cash?

Ans Transfer vouchers

SHORT ANSWER Type Questions

42 Why is the evidence provided by source documents important to accounting? NCERT

Ans *The evidence provided by source document is important to accounting because of the reasons discussed below.*

NUMERICAL Questions

1 Prepare the debit voucher for furniture purchased for ₹15,000 from Globe Furniture Mart on 2nd January, 2016.

2 Prepare the transfer vouchers from the source vouchers.

2016		Amt (₹)
Nov 10	Purchased goods from M/s Vardhman vide Bill No. 912	15,000

CHAPTER PRACTICE

Each chapter has questions grouped as Objective Type, Very Short Answer Type, Short Answer Type and Long Answer Type Questions. These questions cover whole syllabus and Other Important Questions from examination point of view. To facilitate the easy learning and practice, explanations to all the questions have been given.

PROJECT WORK

Title of the Project : ....
....

Company Chosen for the Project : ....
....

Name : ....
School : ....
Year : 2022-23
Class : XI
Submitted To : ....

Project I Collection of Source Documents, Preparation of Vouchers, Recording of Transactions with the Help of Vouchers

SITUATION

Mr Kartik Makkar, M.Com, started his own business under the name of Kartik Makkar & Sons, at Abulane, Meerut on 1st January, 2016, to deal in a variety of electronic goods. He introduced ₹ 6,00,000 as capital out of which ₹ 1,00,000 was in cash and balance by

Transaction 1

Pay Kartik Makkar & Sons
Rupees Five Lakh Only
₹ 5,00,000/-

SAMPLE PROJECT

After the chapters, a supplement of project work (covering 3 projects) is provided. It covers 20 marks in the examination.

SAMPLE QUESTION PAPER 1

A Highly Simulated Sample Question Paper for CBSE Class XI Examinations

ACCOUNTANCY

GENERAL INSTRUCTIONS
1. This question paper contains two parts A and B.
2. All questions in both the parts are compulsory.
3. All parts of questions should be attempted at one place.
4. Marks for questions are indicated against each questions.
5. Answers should be brief and to the point.

TIME : 3 HOURS MAX. MARKS : 80

Part A

1. If total assets of the business are ₹ 4,50,000 and outside liabilities are ₹ 2,00,000, calculate owner's equity. (1)
(a) ₹ 6,50,000 (b) ₹ 2,50,000 (c) ₹ 4,50,000 (d) ₹ 2,00,000

SAMPLE QUESTION PAPERS

To make the students practice in the real sense, we have provided 5 Sample Question Papers, exactly based on the latest pattern & syllabus of CBSE Examination.

CONTENTS

Accountancy Class 11

PART B

FINANCIAL ACCOUNTING-II

TOP TIPS TO SCORE HIGHEST MARKS in the Class 11th exam.
So, check out and apply these in your exams.

TOP TIPS

to Score the HIGHEST MARKS

ALWAYS FEEL POSITIVE

Positive attitude is the key to solve many of the problems which you face in your life. During exam time, this is an important feature to have in you for success and crack your exams with flying colours. Attitude is important for all students because it reflects your personality as well as your confidence or self-confidence. It always takes you to the top of everything, whether it is for exams or interviews or for your life. Positive attitude will take you through the door of success and make you feel full of self-confidence.

PLAN WELL FOR STUDYING

You must make a schedule for your studies followed by strict implementation of that schedule. Make that schedule detailing days or even hours when your exams are really close or it is high time for your exam.You must interact with your teachers for the important topics or topics which need more hard work or more time than other topics. Use last years' exam papers or sample papers for making a proper schedule for your studies.

You must study more or give more attention to the topics in which you feel you are not up to the mark or which your teachers recommended you to study more. You should study these topics first during your exam preparation.

JUST BEFORE THE EXAM

Never try to read anything or to study or cram just before the exam time, even if your friend asks you for some topic he has missed or left during preparation for the exams. Close your book an hour before the exam starts and feel relaxed and worry free and full of self-confidence. Also get up early in the morning and take another review of the important topics and make yourself filled with confidence, as confidence is the main key to score well. The night before the exam you should sleep as soon as possible to make your brain as well as body relax a bit and to be well prepared for the exams, as our brain too needs a rest to be fresh for the exam.

WAYS TO STAY MOTIVATED

Connect with your classmates

Try having someone to keep you on track in your work, so that you can reap the benefits of being accountable as well.

DISCUSS WHAT YOU LEARN

Find a friend or relative who has similar interests or who would enjoy hearing about your studies and let them know what's going on in your class.

CHART YOUR PROGRESS

Design your map of studying and you would see a certain satisfaction coming after watching your goals being accomplished. When times get hard, you can always turn to your chart and see how far you have reached.

DURING EXAM TIME

Check out all the things you require during exam time i.e., pen, pencil, sketch pens, rubber, sharpener. Each and every thing, whether it is small or big, matters a lot during your exam time. Read all the instructions carefully before starting the paper and keep them in your mind during exam time. Don't make any foolish mistake regarding your exam paper instructions.

ATTEMPTING THE EXAMINATION PAPER

Read out all the questions carefully before writing anything on the answer sheet and always start your answering from the questions which will carry maximum marks as well as which you think are tougher or need much time to think. When you start the exam from small questions, you will always feel the problem of questions left.

So, that's why time management is very much important during exams. You can write small questions even in the last 30 minutes but you will never be able to write enough for the large questions at the end, which will eventually result in sadness.

WHEN YOU FEEL STUCK DURING THE EXAM

There will also come a moment in your exam when you feel stuck with some questions or a single question. You just need to be relaxed and calm, don't panic in that situation and make yourself confident and try to think about the answer with a cool mind.

If you are not feeling like giving that answer at that time, make any sign or mark that question with pen and move on to the next question and try doing that question after you finish your paper but are still left with time. Never try to think about the 'stuck' question when you are writing the answer to any other question. This will reduce your concentration and when you feel no way out, just make a guess and attempt that question. This will leave you with something in the space you left for that question.

ANSWER SHEET SHOULD BE NEAT & CLEAN

Handwriting matters a lot for good or highest marks during your exam, as your writing makes the first impression on the checker's mind and makes your answer sheet more filled with a glow for the examiner or checker of the answer sheet.

Underline the lines you feel important and want to attract the examiner's attention towards so that he/she can be able to make a right mindset about the answer given and also reward you with the full or maximum marks.

AFTER COMPLETION OF EXAM PAPER

When you end the exam paper, don't feel like running out of the examination hall. Sit there and review each and every answer before depositing your answer book with the invigilator. Also, look for the questions you left during answering or in which you got stuck. Search for the mistakes you have done during writing and turn towards the hardest question you think and also feel uncomfortable in answering. Review it and look to add any other important lines you missed in that.

ART OF WRITING ANSWERS : GIVE YOUR BEST SHOT

- One can practice answering in previous test papers or sample papers to get used to the manner in which one has to write answers in the exams.
- Make sure that you answer the question asked and not answer what you hoped or wished the question would be.
- Examiners expect to the point and correct answers. Resist the temptation to write everything or writing beyond limits.
- Keep your answer stepwise. Some of you will be surprised to know that the board gives rather detailed dictates on how to evaluate the answer sheet. Try not to exceed the word limit.
- Write your answers in a logical systematic manner. Use examples, facts, figures, quotations, tables etc wherever necessary to substantiate your answers. Give appropriate heading where necessary.
- Add a touch of class by putting extra information that indicate your being very knowledgeable and put this separately near the end, so that it is read just before giving the marks, especially in an essay type question like new trends etc.

LATEST SYLLABUS

CLASS 11

One Paper | Time: 3 Hours | Total Marks : 80

Units		Periods	Marks
PART A: Financial Accounting-I			
Unit 1	Theoretical Framework	25	12
Unit 2	Accounting Process	115	44
		140	**56**
Part B: Financial Accounting-II			
Unit 3	Financial Statements of Sole Proprietorship	60	24
		60	**24**
Part C: Project Work		**20**	**20**

PART A FINANCIAL ACCOUNTING-I

UNIT 1 Theoretical Frame Work

Units/Topics	Learning Outcomes
Introduction to Accounting • Accounting- concept, meaning, as a source of information, objectives, advantages and limitations, types of accounting information; users of accounting information and their needs. Qualitative characteristics of accounting information. Role of accounting in business. • Basic accounting terms: entity, business transaction, capital, drawings, liabilities (non - current and current); assets (non-current and current), expenditure (capital and revenue), expense, income, profits, gains, losses, purchases, sales, goods, stock, debtors, creditors, vouchers, discount - trade and cash.	After going through this unit, the students will be able to: • describe the meaning, significance, objectives, advantages and limitations of accounting in the modem economic environment with varied types of business and non-business economic entities. • identify / recognise the individual(s) and entities that use accounting information for serving their needs of decision making. • explain the various terms used in accounting and differentiate between different related terms like current and non-current, capital and revenue. • give examples of terms like business transaction, liabilities, assets, expenditure and purchases. • explain that sales/purchases include both cash and credit sales/purchases relating to the accounting year. • differentiate among income, profits and gains.

Theory Base of Accounting

- Fundamental accounting assumptions: GAAP concept.
- Basic accounting concept : Business entity, money measurement, going concern, accounting period, cost concept, dual aspect, revenue recognition, matching, full disclosure, consistency, conservatism, materiality and objectivity.
- System of accounting. Basis of accounting : cash basis and accrual basis.
- Accounting Standards : Applicability in IndAS.
- Goods and Services Tax (GST) : Characteristics and advantages.

- state the meaning of fundamental accounting assumptions and their relevance in accounting.
- describe the meaning of accounting assumptions and the situation in which an assumption is applied during the accounting process.
- explain the meaning, applicability, objectives, advantages and limitations of accounting standards.
- appreciate that various accounting standards developed nationally and globally are in practice for bringing parity in the accounting treatment of different items.
- acknowledge the fact that recording of accounting transactions follows double entry system.
- explain the bases of recording accounting transaction and to appreciate that accrual basis is a better basis for depicting the correct financial position of an enterprise.
- Explain the meaning, advantages, and characteristics of GST.

UNIT 2 Accounting Process

Units/Topics	Learning Outcomes
Recording of Business Transactions • Voucher and Transactions: Source documents and vouchers, preparation of vouchers, accounting equation approach: meaning and analysis, rules of debit and credit. • Recording of Transactions: Books of Original Entry- Journal, Special Purpose books, Cash Book: Simple, cash book with bank column and petty cashbook, Purchases book, Sales book, Purchases return book, Sales return book, journal proper. ***Note: Including trade discount, freight and cartage expenses for simple GST calculations*** • Ledger: Format, posting from journal and subsidiary books, balancing of accounts **Bank Reconciliation Statement** • Need and preparation, Bank Reconciliation Statement **Depreciation, Provisions and Reserves** • Depreciation: Meaning, features, need, causes, factors • Other similar terms: Depletion and Amortisation • Methods of Depreciation: Straight Line Method (SLM), Written Down Value Method (WDV) ***Note: Excluding change of method*** • Difference between SLM and WDV; Advantages of SLM and WDV • Method of recording depreciation Charging to asset account, Creating provision for depreciation/accumulated depreciation account. • Treatment of disposal of asset • Provisions and Reserves: Difference • Types of Reserves: Revenue reserve, Capital reserve, General reserve, Specific reserve, Secret reserve • Difference between capital and revenue reserve	After going through this unit, the students will be able to: • explain the concept of accounting equation and appreciate that every transaction affects either both the sides of the equation or a positive effect on one item and a negative effect on another item on the same side of accounting equation. • explain the effect of a transaction (increase or decrease) on the assets, liabilities, capital, revenue and expenses. • appreciate that on the basis of source documents, accounting vouchers are prepared for recording transaction in the books of accounts. • develop the understanding of recording of transactions in journal and the skill of calculating GST. • explain the purpose of maintaining a Cash Book and develop the skill of preparing the format of different types of cash books and the method of recording cash transactions in Cash book. • describe the method of recording transactions other than cash transactions as per their nature in different subsidiary books. • appreciate that at times bank balance as indicated by cash book is different from the bank balance as shown by the pass book / bank statement and to reconcile both the balances, bank reconciliation statement is prepared. • develop understanding of preparing bank reconciliation statement. • appreciate that for ascertaining the position of individual accounts, transactions are posted from subsidiary books and journal proper into the concerned accounts in the ledger and develop the skill of ledger posting. • explain the necessity of providing depreciation and develop the skill of using different methods for computing depreciation. • understand the accounting treatment of providing depreciation directly to the concerned asset account or by creating provision for depreciation account. • appreciate the method of asset disposal through the concerned asset account or by preparing asset disposal account.

Trial balance and Rectification of Errors

- Trial balance: objectives, meaning and preparation
  (**Scope:** Trial balance with balance method only)
- Errors: classification-errors of omission, commission, principles, and compensating; their effect on Trial Balance.
- Detection and rectification of errors.
  (i) Errors which do not affect trial balance
  (ii) Errors which affect trial balance
- preparation of suspense account.

- appreciate the need for creating reserves and also making provisions for events which may belong to the current year but may happen in next year.
- appreciate the difference between reserve and reserve fund.
- state the need and objectives of preparing trial balance and develop the skill of preparing trial balance.
- appreciate that errors may be committed during the process of accounting.
- understand the meaning of different types of errors and their effect on trial balance.
- develop the skill of identification and location of errors and their rectification and preparation of suspense account.

PART B FINANCIAL ACCOUNTING-II

UNIT 3 Financial Statements of Sole Proprietorship

Units/Topics	Learning Outcomes

Financial statements

- Meaning, Objectives and Importance : revenue receipts and capital receipts. Capital expenditure, revenue expenditure and deferred revenue expenditure. Opening journal entry.
- Trading and profit and loss account: gross profit, operating profit and net profit. Preparation.
- Balance sheet: need, grouping, marshalling of assets and liabilities. Preparation.
- Adjustments in preparation of financial statements : with respect to closing stock, outstanding expenses, prepaid expenses, accrued income, income received in advance, depreciation, bad debts, provision for doubtful debts, provision for discount on debtors, abnormal loss, goods taken for personal use/staff welfare, interest on capital and managers commission.
- Preparation of Trading and Profit and Loss account and Balance Sheet of sole proprietorship with adjustments.

After going through this unit, the students will be able to:

- State the meaning of financial statements and the purpose of preparing them.
- state the meaning of gross profit, operating profit and net profit and develop the skill of preparing trading and profit and loss account.
- explain the need for preparing balance sheet.
- understand the technique of grouping and marshalling of assets and liabilities.
- appreciate that there may be certain items other than those shown in trial balance which may need adjustments while preparing financial statements.
- develop the understanding and skill to do adjustments for items and their presentation in financial statements like depreciation, closing stock, provisions, abnormal loss etc.
- develop the skill of preparation of trading and profit and loss account and balance sheet.

PART C PROJECT WORK (ANY ONE)

1. Collection of source documents, preparation of vouchers, recording of transactions with the help of vouchers.
2. Preparation of Bank Reconciliation Statement with the given cash book and the pass book with twenty to twenty-five transactions.
3. Comprehensive project of any sole proprietorship business. This may state with journal entries and then ledgering, preparation of Trial balance, Trading and Profit and Loss Account and Balance Sheet. Expenses, incomes and profit (loss), assets and liabilities are to be depicted using pie chart / bar diagram.

PART A

FINANCIAL ACCOUNTING-I

01

This introductory chapter of accounting deals with the meaning, characteristics, objectives, advantages, limitations and branches of accounting. It further deals with the accounting information, qualitative characteristics of accounting information, types and users of accounting information and the basic terms used in accounting.

INTRODUCTION TO ACCOUNTING

CHAPTER CHECKLIST

- Meaning of Accounting
- Objectives, Advantages and Limitations of Accounting
- Accounting Information
- Basic Terms in Accounting

MEANING OF ACCOUNTING

Accounting is the process of identifying, recording, classifying, summarising, interpreting and communicating financial information relating to an organisation to the interested users for judgement and decision-making.

Definitions of Accounting

According to *the American Institute of Certified Public Accountants* (AICPA), "Accounting is the art of recording, classifying and summarising in a significant manner and in terms of money, transactions and events which are, in part atleast, of a financial character and interpreting the results thereof."

According to *American Accounting Association* (AAA), "Accounting is the process of identifying, measuring and communicating economic information to permit informed judgements and decisions by users of the information."

According to *Accounting Principles Board of* AICPA, "Accounting is a service activity. Its function is to provide quantitative information, primarily financial in nature about economic entities that is intended to be useful in making economic decisions."

Characteristics of Accounting

The definitions of accounting brings following characteristics (attributes) of accounting

(*i*) **Identification** It involves identification of those transactions and events which are of financial nature and relate to the organisation. It should be remembered that transaction is the process of give and take and event is the end result of the transaction(s).

(*ii*) **Measurement** Only those business transactions and events, which can be quantified or measured in monetary terms, are considered.

(*iii*) **Recording** It is the process of entering business transactions of financial character in the books of original entry in terms of money.

(*iv*) **Classifying** It can be defined as the process of grouping transactions or entries of one nature at one place.

(*v*) **Summarising** It involves presenting the classified data in a manner which is understandable and useful to various users of accounting statements.

(*vi*) **Analysis and Interpretation** Analysing and interpreting the financial data helps users to make a meaningful judgement of the profitability and financial position of the business.

(*vii*) **Communication** It involves communicating the financial statements to the various users *i.e.*, management and other internal and external users.

History and Development of Accounting

The history of accounting is as old as civilisation. The traces of accounting were found in Babylonia, Egypt and Greece.

In India, accounting practices originated twenty three centuries ago when Kautilya, a minister in Chandragupta's kingdom wrote a book named Arthashasthra. This book described how accounting records had to be maintained. Luca Pacioli, an Italian author is considered as the father of modern accounting.

Accounting Process

Accounting process starts with identifying financial transactions, involves recording, classifying and summarising and ends with interpreting accounting information to various concerned parties.

Accounting process can be explained with the help of the diagram given below

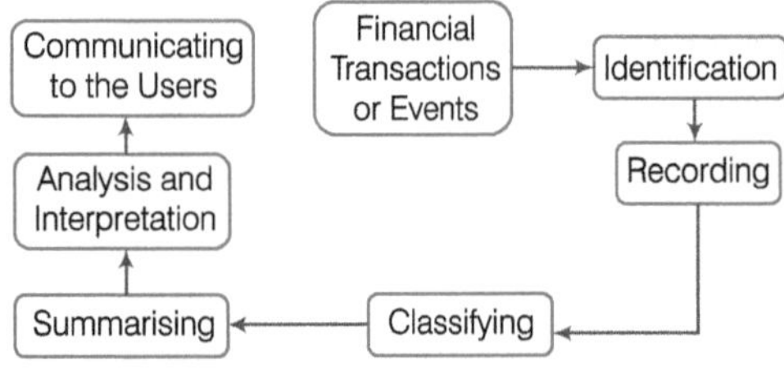

Book-Keeping, Accounting and Accountancy

Book-keeping, accounting and accountancy are different but interrelated terms.

Book-keeping It is an art of recording in the books of accounts, the monetary aspect of commercial and financial transactions.
It is a part of accounting. It is concerned with identifying, recording and classifying economic transactions and events.

Accounting It is a wider concept than book-keeping. It starts where book-keeping ends. It is concerned with summarising the economic transactions, analysis and interpretation of economic transactions and events and communicating the results to the final users.

Accountancy It refers to the entire body of the theoretical knowledge of accounting. It is the theory part of accounting whereas accounting relates to applying the knowledge of accountancy.

Objectives of Accounting

(*i*) To maintain systematic and complete record of business transactions in the books of accounts.

(*ii*) To ascertain the financial position of the business.

(*iii*) To ascertain the profit earned or loss incurred during a particular accounting period.

(*iv*) To provide useful information to various interested parties.

Advantages of Accounting

(*i*) It helps in the preparation of financial statements.

(*ii*) It helps the managers in the decision -making process.

(*iii*) Systematic accounting records act as a valid evidence in the court.

(*iv*) Accounting information is used to compare the result of current year with the previous year to analyse the changes.

(*v*) It helps a firm in the assessment of its correct tax liabilities such as income tax, sales tax, etc.

Limitations of Accounting

(*i*) It is historical in nature. It does not reflect the current worth of a business.

(*ii*) The figures given in financial statements ignore the effects of changes in price level.

(*iii*) It ignores qualitative elements.

(*iv*) It may be affected by window dressing.

(*v*) It is not free from personal bias and personal judgement of the people dealing with it.

Branches of Accounting

Financial, cost and management accounting are the three main branches of accounting.

(*i*) **Financial Accounting** It is concerned with recording of business transactions of finanical nature in a systematic manner, to ascertain the profit or loss of the accounting period and to present the financial position of the business. The end product of financial accounting is trading and profit and loss account and balance sheet.

(*ii*) **Cost Accounting** It is concerned with the ascertainment of total cost and per unit cost of goods/services produced/provided by a business firm.

(*iii*) **Management Accounting** It is concerned with presenting the accounting information in such a manner that helps the management in planning and controlling the operations of a business and in decision-making.

Role of Accounting

The different roles of accounting are as follows

(*i*) **As a Language** Accounting serves as a means of communication. Therefore, it is also referred to as 'language of business'.

(*ii*) **As Current Economic Reality** Accounting is a means to determine the current worth of a business enterprise on the basis of its profit-earning capacity.

(*iii*) **As a Historical Record** Accounting information relates to the past transactions. It records only what has happened.

(*iv*) **As an Information System** Accounting as an information system communicates the accounting information to the users.

ACCOUNTING AS A SOURCE OF INFORMATION

The accounting process begins with the identification of financial transactions, followed by their recording, classification, preparation of financial statements, interpretation and communication. Every step in the process of book-keeping and accounting generates information for different user groups which enables them to take appropriate decisions.

Therefore, accounting acts as a source of information among various users in following ways

(*i*) It provides information to take economic decisions.

(*ii*) Act as principal source of information to end users of accounting service.

(*iii*) It provides information to judge the managerial efficiency.

(*iv*) It provides input to analyse and interprete financial statements.

(*v*) It provides information for inter-firm as well as intra-firm comparison.

(*vi*) It provides information about Corporate Social Responsibility (CSR) of the company.

Qualitative Characteristics of Accounting Information

Qualitative characteristics are the attributes of accounting information which tend to enhance its understandability and usefulness. In order to assess whether accounting information is useful, it must possess the following characteristics

(*i*) **Reliability** It means the users must be able to depend on the information. It must be factual and verifiable. A reliable information should be free from error and bias.

(*ii*) **Relevance** Accounting information presented by financial statements must be relevant to the decision-making needs of the users. To be relevant, information must be available in time, must help in prediction and feedback, and must influence the decisions of users.

(*iii*) **Understandability** It implies that the accounting information provided to the decision-makers must be interpreted by them in the same sense in which it was prepared and conveyed to them.

(*iv*) **Comparability** It means that the users should be able to compare the accounting information. To be comparable, accounting reports must belong to a common period and use common unit of measurement and format of reporting.

Types of Accounting Information

Accounting information can be categorised into the following

(*i*) Information relating to profit or surplus

(*ii*) Information relating to financial position

(*iii*) Information about cash flow

Users of Accounting Information and their Needs

Users of accounting information may be categorised into internal users and external users

1. INTERNAL USERS

These are the persons within the organisation, who are interested in knowing the accounting information of the business. The various internal users are owners, management, employees and workers.

Owners are interested to know about regularity of adequate return on their invested capital in the short run and safety of their capital in the long-run.

Management requires accounting information for the smooth and efficient functioning of the enterprise while **employees and workers** are interested in the accounting information to assess the ability of the enterprise to pay higher and regular payments, bonus, etc.

2. **EXTERNAL USERS**

These are the persons outside the organisation, who are interested in knowing the accounting information of the business. The various external users are

(*i*) Investors and potential investors
(*ii*) Unions and employee groups
(*iii*) Lenders and financial institutions
(*iv*) Suppliers and creditors
(*v*) Customers
(*vi*) Government and other regulators
(*vii*) Social responsibility groups
(*viii*) Competitors

External users like **potential investors** require accounting information to evaluate the earning prospects of the company and safety of their investment.

Lenders and financial institutions need accounting information to know the repayment capacity of loan of the entity and regularity of interest payment on loan. Accounting information is also required by **creditors** as it provides information about the financial soundness of the entity. **Government** requires accounting information to assess the tax liability of the business entity.

BASIC TERMS IN ACCOUNTING

Some basic terms in accounting are as follows

1. Entity

It can be defined as a distinct unit which performs business activity. *e.g.,* Infosys Ltd, Reliance (Company) Kundan Jewellers (Sole proprietorship) Batra and Sons (Partnership) etc are all different forms of business organisations which are treated as a distinct entity from accounting point of view.

2. Business Transaction

It means a financial transaction entered into by various parties and recorded in the books of accounts. It can be a cash transaction or a credit transaction. *e.g.,* purchase of goods, receipt of money from debtors, payment to a creditor, incurring expenses, etc.

3. Assets

Assets are property (movable or immovable) or legal rights owned by an individual or business. These are used by a business to generate cash or income.

Assets can be classified into two types

(*i*) **Current Assets** Current assets are those assets which are held primarily for the purpose of sale or these assets are expected to be converted into cash within a period of one year or within the operating cycle of the business. *e.g.,* Cash in hand, cash at bank, debtors, stock, etc are examples of current assets.

Note *Operating cycle is the time calculated from the point when raw material is purchased, converted into finished goods, sold and cash is realised from the customer.*

(*ii*) **Non-current Assets** These are the assets held by the business not with the purpose to resell but are held either as investment or to facilitate business operations.

Non-current assets are of following types

(*a*) **Tangible Assets** These assets can be touched and seen. Such as machinery, furniture, etc.

(*b*) **Intangible Assets** These assets cannot be touched or seen. Such as goodwill, patents, etc.

4. Liabilities

These are the obligations or debts that an enterprise has to pay at sometime in future. It means the amount owed (payable) by the business to outsiders and to owners. Liabilities towards the outsiders are called external or outside liabilities.

Liabilities towards the owners are called internal liabilities. Liabilities can be classified as

(*i*) **Current Liabilities** These are payable during the course of a year or within the operating cycle of a business.

(*ii*) **Non-current Liabilities** These are payable after one year or beyond the operating cycle of a business.

Note *Generally, the term liabilities refers to external liabilities.*

5. Capital

Capital is the amount invested by the owner in the business. It may be in the form of cash or in the form of assets. The following relationship should be kept in mind relating to assets, liabilities and capital

$$\text{Capital} = \text{Assets} - \text{Liabilities}$$

6. Drawings

It is the amount withdrawn by the owner in cash or assets from the business for personal use. Drawings reduce the capital of the owner in the business.

7. Goods

Goods are the articles in which a business deals. It is a term that applies to all the items held for sale. For a furniture dealer, furniture is goods, for a vehicle dealer, vehicle is goods.

8. Sales

Sales are total revenues from goods or services sold or provided to customers. Sales includes both cash and credit sales.

9. Sales Return

Goods sold when returned by the purchaser are termed as sales return or return inwards.

10. Purchases

The term 'purchases' is used for purchase of goods and not fixed assets. The term 'purchases' includes both cash and credit purchases of goods.

11. Purchases Return

Goods returned are known as purchases return or return outwards. Goods purchased may be returned when they are not as per specification, or are defective or due to any other reason.

12. Stock/Inventory

It is the articles which are held by an enterprise for the purpose of sale in the ordinary course of business or for the purpose of using it in the production of goods meant for sale.

Stock in the beginning of the year is referred to as opening stock and stock at the end of the year is referred to as closing stock. Also stock can be of finished goods, of work-in-progress or of raw material.

13. Expenses

The costs incurred by a business in the process of selling goods or services are known as expenses. It may be in the form of cash payment (salaries, wages, rent), reduction in the value of asset, cost of goods sold, etc.

14. Expenditure

It is the amount spent or liability incurred for acquiring assets, goods and services. Types of expenditures are

(*i*) **Capital Expenditure** It is the expenditure incurred to acquire assets or for improving the quality of existing assets.

(*ii*) **Revenue Expenditure** It is the expenditure on the routine activities of the business *e.g.,* rent paid, salaries paid, etc.

15. Cost

Cost is the amount of expenditure incurred on, or attributable to a specified article, product, or activity.

Cost can be classified as

(*i*) **Direct Cost** This cost is identifiable with the product/service being produced. *e.g.,* for a table, cost of wood is a direct cost.

(*ii*) **Indirect Cost** This cost is not identifiable with the product/service being produced. *e.g.,* for a table, the rent of the factory where the table is being manufactured, is indirect cost.

16. Revenue

It means the money received or receivable in a business. Sources of revenue are sale of goods, rent received, commission received, interest received, dividend received, etc.

17. Receipts

The amount received or receivable by selling assets, goods or services is known as receipts.

The receipts are categorised into two parts

(*i*) **Capital Receipts** The amount received or receivable by selling assets is known as capital receipts.

(*ii*) **Revenue Receipts** The amount which is received or receivable, against the sale of goods or services is known as revenue receipts.

18. Profit

The income earned by the business from its operating activities, is referred to as profit. It is the excess of revenue of a business over its cost.

It can take the following two forms

(*i*) **Gross Profit** It is the excess of revenues over direct cost of the product/service.

(*ii*) **Net Profit** It is the excess of revenues over direct, as well as indirect costs of a product/service.

Note *Operating activity refers to the normal business activity of the firm. For a footwear shop, sale of footwear is operating activity.*

19. Gain

It is a profit of irregular or non-recurring nature. It is a profit that arises from events or transactions which are incidental to business such as sale of fixed assets, winning a court case, etc.

20. Income

The profit earned during an accounting period is referred to as income. It is referred to as the difference between revenue and expense.

21. Loss

The excess of expenses of a period over its related revenues is termed as loss.

22. Discount

It is any type of reduction in the selling price of the goods. Discount is generally of two types

(*i*) **Trade Discount** When the discount is allowed by a seller to its customers at a fixed percentage on the list price of the goods on account of trade practice then it is called trade discount.

(*ii*) **Cash Discount** When discount is allowed to customers for making prompt payment, it is called cash discount.

23. Trade Receivables

The term 'trade receivables' includes the outstanding amount due from the goods sold and services rendered on credit. It includes debtors and bills receivable.

(*i*) **Debtors** These are persons and/or other entities who owe to the business an amount for buying goods and services on credit.

(*ii*) **Bills Receivable** It is a legal document received from a debtor in which he agrees to pay the amount due on a specified future date.

24. Trade Payables

The term 'trade payables' is the amount payable against goods purchased and services availed on credit in the normal course of business. It includes creditors and bills payables.

(*i*) **Creditors** These are persons and/or other entities who have to be paid by the business an amount for providing goods and services on credit.

(*ii*) **Bills Payable** It is a legal document given by the firm to a creditor in which the firm agrees to pay the amount due on a specified future date.

25. Vouchers

Vouchers are documents evidencing a business transaction. A voucher details the accounts that are debited and credited. It is prepared on the basis of source documents such as cash memo, invoice or bill, receipt, etc.

CHAPTER PRACTICE

OBJECTIVE TYPE Questions

Multiple Choice Questions

1 The first step of accounting process is
(a) identifying a transaction
(b) recording a transaction
(c) summarising a transaction
(d) None of the above

Ans (a) Since, only the transaction that have a monetary value is recorded in accounting, so the first step is to identify the nature of transaction whether it has monetary value or not.

2 The purpose(s) of cost accounting is/are
(a) to analyse the expenditure
(b) to ascertain the cost of various products
(c) to fix the price of the products
(d) All of the above

Ans (d) All of the above

3 Who would most likely use an entities financial report to determine whether or not the business entity is eligible for a loan?
(a) Lenders and financial institutions
(b) Debtors
(c) Government (d) Customer

Ans (a) Lenders and financial institutions

4 Accounting serves as a
(a) historical data (b) commodity
(c) language (d) All of these

Ans (d)
(*i*) As a historical record, it is viewed as chronological record of financial transactions of an organisation at actual amounts involved.
(*ii*) As a commodity, specialised information is viewed as a service which is in demand in society, with accountants being willing to and capable of providing it.
(*iii*) As a language, it is perceived as the language of business which is used to communicate information on enterprises.

5 Which of the following is referred to management accounting?
(a) Focuses on estimating future revenues, costs and other measures to forecast activities and their results
(b) Provides information about the company as a whole
(c) Reports information that has occurred in the past that is verifiable and reliable
(d) Provides information that is generally available only on a quarterly or annual basis

Ans (a) In management accounting, the managers plans for future of the entity, these plans are prepared on the basis of previous track record and also after making adjustment for the future possible causes.

6 Cost accounting provides all of the following except
(a) information for management accounting and financial accounting
(b) pricing information from marketing studies
(c) financial information regarding the cost of acquiring resources
(d) non-financial information regarding the cost of operational efficiencies

Ans (d) non-financial information regarding the cost of operational efficiencies

7 Which qualitative characteristic of accounting information is reflected when user of information is able to depend on the information? **NCERT**
(a) Understandability (b) Relevance
(c) Comparability (d) Reliability

Ans (d) Reliability

8 The amount received or receivable by selling assets, goods or services is known as
(a) receipts (b) profit
(c) income (d) gain

Ans (a) receipts

9 Mr Ikram starts business with ₹ 5,00,000, the amount introduced by him is termed as
(a) capital (b) loan
(c) debentures (d) All of these

Ans (a) When the owner of a business introduces something to his business, it is called as capital. So, it can be said that the amount of ₹ 5,00,000 is the capital to business.

10 Deepti wants to buy a building for her business today. What of the following is relevant data for her decision? **NCERT**
(a) Similar business acquired the required building in 2000 for ₹ 10,00,000
(b) Building cost details of 2003
(c) Building cost details of 1998

(d) Similar building cost in August, 2005 for ₹25,00,000

Ans (d) Similar building cost in August, 2005 for ₹25,00,000

11 Use of common unit of measurement and common format of reporting promotes **NCERT**

(a) comparability (b) understandability
(c) relevance (d) reliability

Ans (a) comparability

12 ABC Ltd. deals in selling and purchasing of furniture. Furniture is

(a) goods for ABC Ltd.
(b) asset for ABC Ltd.
(c) intangible assets for ABC Ltd.
(d) None of the above

Ans (a) Goods are the articles in which a business deals. Here, ABC Ltd deals in furniture, hence furniture is goods for ABC Ltd.

13 Trade receivables implies

(a) Debtors + Bills receivables
(b) Debotrs − Bill receivables
(c) Debtors + Bills payable
(d) Debtors − Bills payable

Ans (a) Debtors are those persons who owe to an enterprise an amount for buying goods and services on credit. Bills receivables amount is to be received against B/R (from debtors).

14 Which of these is not a business transaction? **NCERT**

(a) Bought furniture of ₹ 10,000 for business
(b) Paid for salaries of employees ₹ 5,000
(c) Paid sons' fees from her personal bank account ₹ 20,000
(d) Paid sons' fees from business ₹ 2,000

Ans (c) Paid sons' fees from her personal bank account ₹ 20,000

15 Mr A an electronic goods dealer, gifted a TV of value of ₹ 25,000 to his friend Mr B. It will be recorded in books as

(a) drawings (b) expenses
(c) capital (d) sales

Ans (a) Mr A gifted goods to his friend. Thus, this transaction is of personal nature and will be treated as drawings.

16 A firm earns a revenue of ₹ 20,000 and the expenses to earn this revenue are ₹ 12,000. Calculate its income.

(a) ₹ 20,000 (b) ₹ 12,000
(c) ₹ 8,000 (d) Zero

Ans (c) Income = Revenue − Expenses = 20,000 − 12,000 = ₹ 8,000

17 What is the last step of accounting as a source of information?

(a) Recording of data in books of accounts
(b) Preparation of summaries in form of financial statements
(c) Communication of information
(d) Analysis and interpretation of information

Ans (c) Communication of information

Fill in the Blanks

18 Assets having physical existence and which can be seen or felt are ....

Ans tangible assets

19 .... is the excess of revenues over expenses during an accounting period.

Ans Profit

20 Assets which are expected to be converted into cash within one year are ....

Ans current assets

21 .... is concerned with the ascertainment of total cost and per unit cost of goods/services produced/provided by a business firm.

Ans Cost accounting

22 Goods sold when returned by the purchaser are termed as ....

Ans return inwards

State True or False

23 Book-keeping starts where accounting ends.

Ans False. Accounting starts where book-keeping ends.

24 Owners are internal users of accounting information.

Ans True

25 Accounting is historical in nature as it does not reflect the current worth of a business.

Ans True

26 Reliability of information means that the users must be able to depend on the information.

Ans True

Match the Following

27

Column I		Column II
1. Amount invested by the owner in the business	(a)	Drawings
2. Amount withdrawn by the owner	(b)	External users
3. Tax authorities	(c)	Internal users
4. Employees	(d)	Capital

Ans 1-(d), 2-(a), 3-(b), 4-(c)

VERY SHORT ANSWER Type Questions

28 Define accounting. **NCERT**

Ans Accounting is the process of identifying, recording, classifying, summarising, interpreting and communicating financial information relating to an organisation to the interrelated users of such information for judgement and decision-making.

29 Is the basic objective of book-keeping to maintain systematic records or to ascertain net results of operations of financial transactions?

Ans The basic objective of book-keeping is to maintain systematic record of financial transactions.

30 Enumerate main objectives of accounting. **NCERT**

Ans (*i*) To maintain systematic record of business transactions.

(*ii*) To ascertain the financial position of the business.

(*iii*) To provide useful information to interested parties.

31 What is meant by 'window dressing' in accounting?

Ans The term 'window dressing' means manipulation of accounts so as to present the financial statements in a way to show better position than the actual. *e.g.* assets may be overstated and liabilities may be understated.

32 What is meant by qualitative information?

Ans Qualitative information is the information related to the qualitative aspects of business units such as quality of management, reputation of the business, cordial management-labour relations, satisfaction of firm's customers, etc. This information cannot be expressed in monetary terms.

33 Which qualitative characteristics of accounting information is reflected when accounting information is clearly presented?

Ans Understandability

34 State the nature of accounting information required by long-term lenders. **NCERT**

Ans The long-term lenders are interested in knowing, if they are likely to get paid and are interested in knowing whether the business has the ability to repay its debts as they become due.

35 Enumerate information needs of management. **NCERT**

Ans Management needs timely information related to cost of production, sales, profitability, etc that will help the management in planning, controlling and decision-making.

36 Who are external users of information? **NCERT**

Ans External users of information are the individual or organisation who have interest in the business firm, but they are not a part of management.

Some examples of external users are government, tax authorities, labour unions, etc.

37 List any five users who have indirect interest in accounting. **NCERT**

Ans *The five users who have indirect interest in accounting are*

(*i*) Trade associations

(*ii*) Social responsibility groups

(*iii*) Registrar of companies

(*iv*) Government

(*v*) Competitors

38 What are drawings?

Ans It is the amount withdrawn by the owner in cash or assets from the business for personal use.

39 Give any three examples of revenues. **NCERT**

Ans Commission, interest and dividends are examples of revenues.

40 A firm earns a revenue of ₹ 21,000 and the expenses to earn this revenue are ₹ 15,000. Calculate its income.

Ans Income = Revenue − Expense = 21,000 − 15,000 = ₹ 6,000

41 Accounting records business transactions and events which are of financial nature. Is this a limitation of accounting?

Ans Yes, it is a limitation of accounting because there are events which impact business but are not recorded because they are not of financial nature.

42 Name the external user of accounting information from whom the firm purchases goods on credit.

Ans Supplier of goods

43 Confidence and trust that the reported information is a reasonable representation of the actual items and events, that have occurred, indicates which qualitative characteristic of accounting information.

Ans Reliability

44 **Mr Raj, an electronic goods dealer, gifted a microwave of value ₹ 30,000 to his friend Rohan and recorded it in books as drawings. Is he correct?**

Ans Yes, he is correct, it will be treated as drawings and will be recorded in the books.

SHORT ANSWER Type Questions

45 **State the steps involved in the process of accounting.**

Ans *The steps involved in the process of accounting are*

(*i*) Identifying financial transactions
(*ii*) Recording in the books of accounts
(*iii*) Classifying the recorded entries
(*iv*) Summarising
(*v*) Analysis and interpretation of financial statements
(*vi*) Communicating to the users

46 **Explain the accounting process with the help of a diagram.**

Ans Accounting process starts with identifying financial transactions, involves recording, classifying and summarising and ends with interpreting accounting information to various concerned parties.

Accounting process can be explained with the help of the diagram given below

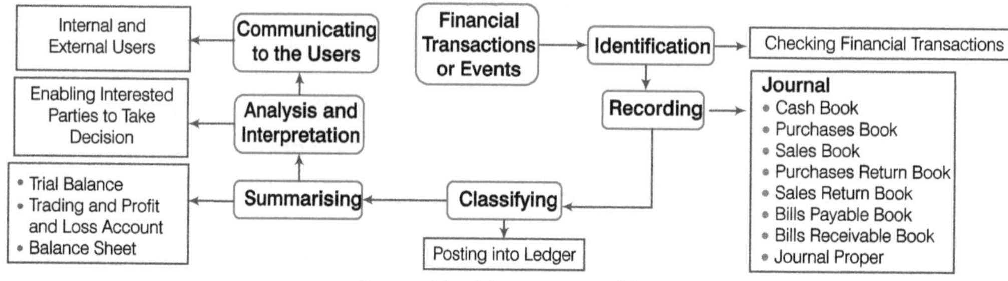

Accounting Process at a Glance

47 **Define book-keeping, accounting and accountancy? With the help of diagram explain the relationship between book-keeping, accounting and accountancy.**

Ans **Book-keeping**

Book-keeping is an art of recording in the books of accounts, the monetary aspect of commercial and financial transactions. It is a part of accounting. It is concerned with identifying, recording and classifying economic transactions and events.

Accounting

Accounting is a wider concept than book-keeping. It starts where book-keeping ends. It is concerned with summarising the economic transactions, analysis and interpretation of economic transactions and events and communicating the results to final users.

Accountancy

'Accountancy refers to the entire body of the theoretical knowledge of accounting. It is the theory part of accounting, whereas accounting relates to applying the knowledge of accountancy. *Diagrammatically, the relationship can be viewed as*

48 **'Non-monetary transactions are not recorded in the books of accounts'. Explain.**

Ans Accounting records only those transactions and events which can be expressed is terms of money such as sale or purchase of goods, salary paid, etc. Non-monetary transactions *i.e.*, those transactions which cannot be expressed in terms of money are not recorded in the books of accounts. Example of such transactions are value of human resources, appointment of a new managing director, etc. These transactions may be important for the business but these are not recorded in the books of accounts because these cannot be measured in monetary terms.

49 **Accounting provides information about the profitability and financial soundness of a concern. In addition, it provides other valuable information also. However, accounting has certain limitations. Explain any three such limitations.**

Ans *The drawbacks or limitations of accounting are as follows*

(*i*) It is historical in nature. It does not reflect the current worth of a business.

(*ii*) The figures given in financial statements ignore the effects of changes in price level.

(*iii*) It is not free from the personal bias and personal judgement of the people dealing with it.

50 Is accounting an art or a science?

Ans Accounting is both an art as well as a science.

Art is the technique of achieving some pre-determined objectives. And accounting is also an art of recording, classifying and summarising financial transactions.

Science is an organised knowledge based on certain basic principles. Therefore, accounting is also a science as it is an organised knowledge based on certain principles.

51 What is the primary reason for business students and others to study accounting discipline? **NCERT**

Ans The primary reason for business students and others to study accounting discipline is to acquire knowledge, which is helpful in understanding accounting information. It is so because accounting information is presented and communicated to various interested parties in the form of financial statements, reports, graphs, charts, etc, which is difficult to understand unless the user has the desired knowledge.

52 'The role of accounting has changed over the period of time'. Do you agree? **NCERT**

Ans Earlier the role of accounting was limited to recording of transactions. Now, it has shifted to providing information to managers and interested parties, to help them take appropriate decision. It is now regarded as an information system.

53 Explain accounting as a source of information.

Ans Every step in the process of accounting generates information for different user groups, such information enables the interested parties to take appropriate decisions. *To be useful, the accounting information should ensure to*

(*i*) Provide information for making economic decisions.

(*ii*) Serve the users who rely on financial statements.

(*iii*) Provide information useful for predicting and evaluating the amount, timing and uncertainty of potential cash flows.

(*iv*) Provide information for judging management's ability to utilise resources effectively in meeting goals.

(*v*) Provide factual and interpretative information.

(*vi*) Provide information on activities affecting the society.

54 Accounting information refers to the financial statements. The information provided by these statements can be categorised into various types. Briefly describe them.

Ans *Accounting information can be categorised into following types*

(*i*) **Information Relating to Profit or Surplus** Information about the profit earned or loss incurred by the business during an accounting period is made available through the income statement *i.e.*, profit and loss account. Trading account provides information about gross profit and profit and loss account provides information about the net profit.

(*ii*) **Information Relating to Financial Position** Information about the financial position of the enterprise is determined through position statement *i.e.*, the balance sheet.

It provides information about the assets and liabilities.

(*iii*) **Information about Cash Flow** Cash flow statement is a statement that shows inflow and outflow of cash during a specific period. It helps in making various decisions like payment of liabilities, payment of dividend and expansion of business, etc as all these are based on availability of cash.

55 'Accounting information should be comparable.' Do you agree with this statement? Give two reasons. **NCERT**

Ans *Yes, accounting information should be comparable because*

(*i*) it helps to make inter-firm comparisons, *i.e.*, to find out how a firm has performed as compared to the other firms.

(*ii*) it helps to make inter-period comparisons, *i.e.*, to find out how it has performed as compared to the previous years.

56 If the accounting information is not clearly presented, which of the qualitative characteristic of the accounting information is violated? **NCERT**

Ans If the accounting information is not clearly presented, it will violate the qualitative characteristic of understandability. Unclear presentation of information makes it difficult for the user to understand it.

57 What are the informational needs of internal users?

Ans (*i*) **Owners** These are interested in knowing about the profit earned or loss suffered by the business, besides the safety of their capital.

(*ii*) **Management** The management requires accounting information for making various decisions such as determination of selling price, cost controls and reduction, investments, etc.

(*iii*) **Employees and Workers** The employees and workers are interested in knowing about the profit earned by an enterprise so that they can demand for bonus or wage hike. Also, whether the firm has deposited its share into the provident fund and employees state insurance, etc.

58 Giving examples, explain each of the following accounting terms **NCERT**

(i) Fixed assets (ii) Gain
(iii) Profit (iv) Revenue
(v) Expenses (vi) Short-term liability
(vii) Capital

Or

How will you define revenue and expenses?

Ans (*i*) **Fixed Assets** It refers to those assets which are held for continued use in the business for the purpose of producing goods and services and not meant for resale *e.g.*, plant and machinery, land and building, etc.

(*ii*) **Gain** It is a profit of irregular or non-recurring nature. It is a profit that arises from events or transactions which are incidental to business *e.g.*, the value of land increased from ₹ 2,00,000 to ₹ 2,50,000.

(*iii*) **Profit** The income earned by the business from its operating activities, is referred to as profit. Excess of revenue of a business over its cost is termed as profit. *e.g.*, A shirt manufacturer had to incur a cost of ₹ 1,00,000 to produce 10,000 shirts. These shirts were sold for ₹ 1,50,000. So, ₹ 50,000 is the profit earned.

(*iv*) **Revenue** It means the amount received from sale of goods or services. *e.g.*, A shirt manufacturer sold 10,000 shirts for ₹ 1,50,000. So, ₹ 1,50,000 is the revenue.

(*v*) **Expenses** The cost incurred by a business in the process of earning revenue are known as expenses. It can be in the form of cash payment. *e.g.*, ABC company paid ₹ 20,000 as salaries, reduction in the value of asset, etc.

(*vi*) **Short-term Liability** Those liabilities which are to be paid within one year are referred to as short-term liability. *e.g.*, PQ Ltd has to pay ₹ 1,00,000 against loan taken from a bank by next month. So, ₹ 1,00,000 is short-term liability for PQ Ltd.

(*vii*) **Capital** It is the amount invested by the owner in the business. It may be in the form of cash or in the form of asset.

59 Name the term associated with the following.

(i) The articles in which a business deals.
(ii) The amount invested by the owner in the business.
(iii) The person who owes amount to the business on account of credit sales of goods or services.
(iv) The person to whom amount is owed on account of credit purchases of goods or services.

Ans (*i*) Goods (*ii*) Capital (*iii*) Debtors (*iv*) Creditors

60 Define inventory or stock. Explain briefly the different kinds of inventory.

Ans It is the articles which are held by an enterprise for the purpose of sale in the ordinary course of business or for the purpose of using it in the production of goods meant for sale. *Inventory are of following kinds*

(*i*) **Inventory of Raw Material** It includes raw material used for manufacturing of goods, *e.g.*, stock of cloth to be used for shirts.

(*ii*) **Inventory of Work-in-progress** It comprises of goods which are in the process of being finished *i.e.*, they are partly finished goods.

(*iii*) **Inventory of Finished Goods** It includes finished goods in saleable condition.

61 Distinguish between debtors and creditors. **NCERT**

Ans *The differences between debtors and creditors are*

Debtors	*Creditors*
Debtors are parties who owes debt towards the company.	Creditors are the parties to whom the company owes a debt.
Payments are received from them.	Payments are made to them.
They are shown as assets in the balance sheet under current assets.	They are shown as liabilities in the balance sheet under current liabilities.

62 Distinguish between trade discount and cash discount.

Ans *The differences between trade discount and cash discount are*

Trade Discount	*Cash Discount*
When discount is allowed by the seller to its customers at a fixed percentage on the list price of the goods, as per the practice of trade, it is called trade discount.	When discount is allowed to customers for making prompt payment, it is called cash discount.
It is allowed to compete with competitors.	It is allowed to facilitate prompt payment.
It is allowed at the time of purchase.	It is allowed at the time of payment.

63 Discuss the various characteristics/attributes of accountancy.

Ans (*i*) **Identification** It involves identification of those transactions, which are of financial nature and relate to the organisation.

(*ii*) **Measurement** Only those business transactions and events, which can be quantified or measured in monetary terms, are considered.

(*iii*) **Recording** Recording is the process of entering business transactions of financial character in the books of original entry.

Once the economic events are identified and measured in financial terms, these are recorded in books of accounts in monetary terms and in a chronological order.

(*iv*) **Classifying** It can be defined as the process of grouping transactions or entries of one nature at one place.

(*v*) **Summarising** It involves presenting the classified data in a manner which is understandable and useful to various users of accounting statements.

(*vi*) **Analysis and Interpretation** Analysing and interpreting the financial data helps users to make a meaningful judgement of the profitability and financial position of the business. It also helps in planning for the future in a better manner.

(*vii*) **Communication** It involves communicating the financial statements to the various users *i.e.*, management and other internal and external users.

LONG ANSWER Type Questions

64 Define accounting and state its objectives. **NCERT**

Ans For definition refer to very short answer Q. No. 28.

The objectives of accounting are as follows

(*i*) **Systematic Recording of Business Transactions** Accounting systematically records all financial transactions and events of the enterprise in the books of accounts. Accounting is done to keep a systematic record of financial transactions, assets and liabilities. The recorded information enables verifiability and acts as an evidence.

(*ii*) **Calculation of Profit or Loss** Another objective of accounting is to ascertain the profit earned or loss sustained by a business during an accounting period. For this purpose trading and profit and loss account or statement of profit and loss (for companies) is prepared. In this account, the revenue and the expenses incurred in the accounting period are recorded, and the comparison of the two shows whether the business has earned profit or incurred loss.

(*iii*) **Ascertainment of Financial Position** Accounting also aims at ascertaining the financial position of the business concern which can be done by preparing a position statement, also called as balance sheet. Balance sheet is a systematic record of various assets (resources owned by the business organisation) and liabilities (claims against such resources).

(*iv*) **Providing Accounting Information to its Users for Decision-making** Another important objective of accounting is to provide accounting information to its users. The accounting information is communicated in the form of reports, statements, graphs, charts, etc.

(*v*) **Assisting the Management** Accounting assists the management by providing financial information to it, which is required by management for decision-making, exercising control, budgeting, forecasting, etc.

(*vi*) **Protecting Business Assets** Accounting helps the management to protect its assets and excercise proper control over them by keeping a record of the assets owned by the business.

65 Explain briefly any six advantages of accounting.

Ans *The various advantages of accounting are as follows*

(*i*) **Financial Information about the Business** Accounting provides the financial information about the business to people, inside and outside the business.

(*ii*) **Replaces Memory** A systematic recording of transactions removes the necessity to remember the transactions. Thus, accounting replaces memory by providing accounting information as and when needed.

(*iii*) **Facilitates Comparative Study** A systematic recording of business transactions enables a businessman to compare current year's results with those of past years. It also helps him to compare the performance of his business with that of other business.

(*iv*) **Facilitates Settlement of Tax Liabilities** A systematic accounting record helps in the settlement of various tax liabilities such as income tax, sales tax, VAT, excise duty, etc.

(*v*) **Facilitates Raising Loans** Accounting makes available the information with respect to performance of the business. Banks and financial institutions grant loans on the basis of this information.

(*vi*) **Acts as an Evidence in Court** Systematic recording of transactions acts as a valid evidence in the court.

66 Explain the factors which necessitated systematic accounting. **NCERT**

Ans *The factors which necessitated systematic accounting are*

(*i*) **To Assess Return on Investment** The owners/shareholders use accounting to see if they are getting a satisfactory return on their investment, and to assess the financial health of their company/business.

(*ii*) **For Making Comparison** The directors/managers use accounting for making both internal and external comparisons in their attempts to evaluate the performance. They may compare the financial analysis of their company with the industry figures in order to ascertain the company's strengths and weaknesses.

(*iii*) **To Know the Paying Ability** The creditors (lenders) want to know if they are likely to get paid and look particularly at liquidity, which is the ability of the company/organisation to pay its debts as they become due.

(*iv*) **To Make Investment** The prospective investors use accounting to assess whether or not to invest their money in the company/organisation.

(*v*) **For Assessing Tax Liability** The government and regulatory agencies such as Registrar of Companies, departments require information for the payment of various taxes such as Value Added Tax (VAT), Income Tax (IT) etc. This necessitated the need for systematic accounting.

67 Discuss the various branches of accounting.

Ans *These are briefly explained below*

(*i*) **Financial Accounting** The process of identifying, measuring, recording, classifying, summarising, analysing, interpreting and communicating the financial transactions and events is known as financial accounting.

The purpose of this branch of accounting is to keep a record of all financial transactions, *so that*

(*a*) The profit earned or loss sustained by the business during an accounting period can be worked out.

(*b*) The financial position of the business as at the end of the accounting period can be ascertained.

(*c*) The financial information required by the management and other interested parties can be provided.

(*ii*) **Cost Accounting** It is the process of ascertaining and controlling the cost of a product, operation or function. The purpose of cost accounting is to analyse the expenditure, so as to ascertain the cost of various products manufactured by the firm and fix the prices. It also helps in controlling the costs and providing necessary costing information to management for decision-making.

(*iii*) **Management Accounting** It is the use of accounting techniques for providing information to help all levels of management in planning and controlling the activities of business to enable decision-making. The purpose of management accounting is to assist the management in taking rational policy decisions and to evaluate the impact of its decisions and actions.

68 Describe the role of accounting in the modern world. **NCERT**

Ans The role of accounting has been changing with the changes in economic development and increasing demands of the society.

The different roles of accounting are as follows

(*i*) **As a Language** Accounting performs a basic function of a language, *i.e.*, to serve as a means of communication.

(*ii*) **As an Information System** Accounting is an information system which communicates the accounting information to the users.

(*iii*) **As current Economic Reality** Accounting is a means to determine the true income of a business namely the change of wealth over time.

(*iv*) **As a Historical Record** Accounting information relates to the past transactions. Accounting records financial transactions of an organisation in the order they happen with the actual amounts.

69 Explain the qualitative characteristics of accounting information. **NCERT**

Ans Qualitative characteristics are the attributes of accounting information which tend to enhance its understandability and usefulness. In order to assess whether accounting information is useful, it must possess the characteristics of reliability, relevance, understandability and comparability. *The qualitative characteristics of accounting information are*

(*i*) **Reliability** It means the users must be able to depend on the information. It must be factual and verifiable. A reliable information should be free from error and bias.

To ensure reliability, the information disclosed must be credible, verifiable by independent parties, must use the same method of measuring and be neutral and faithful.

(*ii*) **Relevance** Accounting information presented by financial statements must be relevant to the decision- making needs of the users. Unnecessary and irrelevant information should not be included. To be relevant, information must be available in time, must help in prediction and feedback, and must influence the decisions of users.

(*iii*) **Understandability** The information provided in financial statements must be understandable by the users. Understandability implies that the accounting information provided to the decision makers must be interpreted by them in the same sense as it was prepared and conveyed to them.

(*iv*) **Comparability** It means that the users should be able to compare the accounting information. To be comparable, accounting reports must belong to a common period and use common unit of measurement and format of reporting.

When accounting information of a period is compared with that of other period, it is known as **intra-firm comparison.** When accounting information of an enterprise is compared with that of other enterprises, it is known as **inter-firm comparison.**

70 Describe the informational needs of external users. **NCERT**

Ans *The various external users and their informational needs are as follows*

(*i*) **Investors and Potential Investors** They require information on the risks and return on investment.

(*ii*) **Unions and Employee Groups** They require information on the stability, profitability and distribution of wealth within the business.

(*iii*) **Lenders and Financial Institutions** They require information on the creditworthiness of the company and its ability to repay loans and pay interest.

(*iv*) **Suppliers and Creditors** They require information on whether amount owed will be repaid when due, and on the continued existence of the business.

(*v*) **Customers** They require information on the continued existence of the business and thus, the probability of a continued supply of products, parts and after sales service.

(*vi*) **Government and Other Regulators** They require information on the allocation of resources and the compliance to regulations.

(*vii*) **Social Responsibility Groups** These groups require information related to the fact that the company is fulfilling its social responsibility or not. e.g. environmental groups require information on the impact of business activities on environment and its protection.

(*viii*) **Competitors** They require information on the relative strengths and weaknesses of their competitors and for comparative and benchmarking purposes.

71 What do you mean by an asset and what are different types of assets? **NCERT**

Ans Assets are property (movable or immovable) or legal rights owned by an individual or business. These are the economic resources of an enterprise that can be expressed in monetary terms. *Assets can be classified into*

(*i*) **Current Assets** These are the assets which are held primarily for the purpose of sale or these assets are expected to be converted into cash within a period of one year or within the operating cycle of the business.

(*ii*) **Non-current Assets** These are the assets held by the business not with the purpose to resell but are held either as investment or to facilitate business operations. *Non-current assets are of following types*

(*a*) **Tangible Assets** These are the assets which have a physical existence *i.e.,* they can be seen or touched. *e.g.* Land, buildings, furniture, vehicle, etc.

(*b*) **Intangible Assets** These are the assets which do not have physical existence *i.e.,* they cannot be seen or touched. *e.g.,* Trademarks, copyrights, patents, goodwill, etc.

72 Explain the meaning of gain and profit. Distinguish between these two terms. **NCERT**

Ans **Meaning of Gain and Profit** Refer to short answer no. 58 (ii) and (iii) part.

The differences between gain and profit are

Gain	*Profit*
It is of irregular or non-recurring nature.	It is of regular or recurring nature.
It arises from non-operating activities, *i.e.,* those activities which are incidental to the main activity of the business.	It arises from operating activity of the business.
Example– Appreciation in value of land by ₹ 1,00,000. So, ₹ 1,00,000 is the gain.	Example– A shirt is sold for ₹ 250. The cost of shirt is 200. So, ₹ 50 is the profit.

73 **Differentiate between book-keeping and accounting.**

Ans *The differences between book-keeping and accounting are*

Basis	*Book-keeping*	*Accounting*
Scope	Book-keeping involves identifying financial transactions, measuring them in money terms, recording them in the books of accounts and classifying them.	Accounting involves summarising the recorded transactions, interpreting them and communicating the results.
Objective	Its objective is to maintain systematic records of financial transactions.	Its objective is to ascertain net results of operations and financial position so as to communicate such information to various interested parties.
Nature of Job	This job is routine in nature.	This job is analytical and dynamic in nature.
Performance	Junior staff performs this function.	Senior staff performs this function.
Relation	Book-keeping provides the basis for accounting.	Accounting begins where book-keeping ends.
Special Skills	Book-keeping does not require special skills.	Accounting requires special skills and ability to analyse and interpret.

74 **Distinguish between financial accounting, cost accounting and management accounting.**

Ans *The differences between financial accounting, cost accounting and management accounting are*

Basis	*Financial Accounting*	*Cost Accounting*	*Management Accounting*
Meaning	The process of identifying, measuring, recording, classifying, summarising, analysing, interpreting and communicating the financial transactions and events is known as financial accounting.	The process of ascertaining and controlling the cost of a product, operation or function is known as cost accounting.	The use of accounting techniques for providing information to help all levels of management in planning and controlling the activities of business to enable decision-making is known as management accounting.
Purpose	To keep record of all financial transactions.	To analyse the expenditure so as to ascertain the cost of various products manufactured by the firm and fix the prices.	To assist the management in taking rational policy decision and to evaluate the impact of its decision and actions.
Data used	Qualitative aspects are not recorded.	Only qualitative aspect is recorded.	Uses both qualitative and quantitative concepts.

75 **Distinguish between book-keeping, accounting and accountancy.**

Ans *The differences between book-keeping, accounting and accountancy are*

Book-keeping	*Accounting*	*Accountancy*
Book-keeping is maintained by junior staff.	Accounting is maintained by senior staff.	Accountancy is maintained by the professionals.
It is the primary stage.	It is the secondary stage.	It is the complete process which includes both, book-keeping and accounting.
It is concerned with recording of day-to-day transactions.	It is based on book-keeping.	It is helpful in decision-making.
It is concerned with identification, recording and classification of financial transactions.	It is concerned with summarising, interpretation and communication of financial results.	It refers to the entire body of the theory and practice of accounting.

02

This chapter deals with various accounting principles. It further deals with the various Accounting Standards issued by Institute of Chartered Accountants of India (ICAI) and International Financial Reporting Standards (IFRS).

THEORY BASE OF ACCOUNTING

Theory base of accounting consists of principles, rules and guidelines. These are developed over a period of time, to bring uniformity and consistency to the process of accounting.

In this way, theory base of accounting brings various financial statements (of various similar business) to a common platform. This enables comparison and provides valuable information regarding the organisation. Apart from these, the ICAI, has issued accounting standards which are expected to be followed, in order to bring consistency in the accounting practices.

CHAPTER CHECKLIST

- Accounting Principles
- System of Accounting
- Basis of Accounting
- Accounting Standards
- IFRS
- Goods and Services Tax (GST)

ACCOUNTING PRINCIPLES

Accounting principles are a uniform set of rules or guidelines which are developed to ensure uniformity and easy understanding of the accounting information. Accounting information is meaningful, useful and is better understood by the users of accounting information, if accounting records and financial statements are prepared by following accounting principles uniformly. Accounting principles may take the form of concepts and conventions.

Generally Accepted Accounting Principles (GAAP)

The term 'principle' has been defined by AICPA (American Institute of Certified Public Accountants) as 'A general law or rule adopted or professed as a guide to action, a settled ground or basis of conduct or practice'. The word 'generally' means 'in a general manner' *i.e.,* pertaining to many persons or cases or occasions.

Thus, GAAP refers to the rules or guidelines adopted for recording and reporting of business transactions, in order to bring uniformity in the preparation and presentation of financial statements. Principles are generally accepted if they are relevant, objective and feasible.

Fundamental Accounting Assumptions/Concepts

The term assumption refers to the economic environment in which accounting exists. It refers to the basic assumptions, rules and principles which work as the basis of recording of business transaction and preparing accounts. The fundamental accounting assumptions/concepts are as follows

(*i*) **Going Concern Concept/Assumption** According to this concept, it is assumed that the business firm would continue its operations for a fairly long period of time and would not be liquidated in the near future. All the transactions are recorded in the books on the assumption that it is a continuing enterprise.

(*ii*) **Consistency Concept/Assumption** According to this concept, accounting policies and practices once chosen and followed, should be applied uniformly and consistently over the years. Accounting policies and practices should not be changed year after year.

(*iii*) **Accrual Concept/Assumption** According to this concept, a transaction is recorded at the time, it takes place and not at the time when settlement is done.

In other words, revenue is recorded when sales are made or services are rendered and it is irrelevant as to when cash is received against such sales. Similarly, expenses are recorded at the time they are incurred and it is irrelevant as to when payment is made in cash for such expenses.

Note *In the course of accounting process, it is assumed that a business is following these concepts. If this is not the case, then the business should disclose this fact in the financial statements alongwith the reasons for not following the concept.*

Accounting Principles : Concepts and Conventions

Concepts refer to the necessary assumptions and ideas which are fundamental to accounting practice and convention denotes customs or traditions as a guide to the preparation of accounting statements. These are the outcome of accounting practices or principles being followed by the enterprises over a period of time.

The various concepts and conventions are discussed below

(*i*) **Business Entity or Accounting Entity** (Separate Entity) **Principle** According to this principle, business is treated as a separate entity distinct from its owners. Thus, for the purpose of accounting, business and its owners are treated as two separate entities. All transactions are recorded from the point of view of business and not from the point of view of businessman.

(*ii*) **Money Measurement Principle** According to this principle, only those transactions which can be expressed in terms of money are recorded in the books of accounts. Non-financial or non-monetary transactions do not find any place in the accounting records.

(*iii*) **Accounting Period Principle** It is also known as periodicity principle or time period principle. According to this principle, the life of a business is divided into smaller periods (usually one year) so that, its performance can be measured on regular basis or intervals.

(*iv*) **Full Disclosure Principle** According to this principle, there should be reporting of all the significant information relating to the economic affairs of the business. As per this principle, financial statements should disclose all significant information relating to an organisation.

(*v*) **Prudence or Conservatism Principle** The principle of conservatism (also called 'prudence') states that 'Do not anticipate profits but provide for all probable losses'.

In other words, this principle suggests that we should make provisions for probable future expenses but ignore any future probable gain, until it actually happens.

This approach of providing for the losses but not recognising the gains until realised is called conservation approach.

(*vi*) **Materiality Principle** According to this principle, only those transactions should be recorded in detail which are material or relevant for the preparation of financial statements. All immaterial facts should be ignored. An information is material, if it has the ability to influence or affect the decision-making of various parties interested in accounting information. Also, it is a matter of judgement to decide whether a particular information is material for a business or not. Also, it depends on the nature and/or amount of that item.

(*vii*) **Cost Concept or Historical Cost Principle** According to this principle, assets are recorded in the books of accounts at their cost price, which includes cost of acquisition, transportation, installation and making the asset ready for use. This cost is the basis for all subsequent accounting of such assets.

Note *It should be remembered that the above principle relates to the treatment of fixed assets. Current assets are shown in the books at cost price or market price, whichever is lower.*

(*viii*) **Matching Cost or Matching Principle** According to this principle, expenses incurred in an accounting period should be matched with revenues of that period.

As per this concept, all revenues earned during the year, whether received during that year or not, and all costs incurred, whether paid during the year or not should be taken into account while ascertaining profit or loss for that year.

(*ix*) **Dual Aspect or Duality Principle** Dual aspect is the foundation or the basic principle of accounting. This concept states that every transaction has a dual or two-fold effect and should therefore be recorded at two places. In other words, as per this principle, each and every transaction in business effects two aspects. *For example*, goods sold for cash will have two effects. One is that cash will increase and the other is that stock of goods will decrease. It is because of this principle that the following accounting equation holds true.

Assets = Liabilities + Capital

(*x*) **Revenue Recognition Principle** (Realisation Principle) This concept requires that the revenue for a business transaction should be included in the accounting records only when it is realised. In other words, it is the sale or change of ownership which decides the revenue and not the actual payment or receipt regarding such sale.

(*xi*) **Verifiable Objective Concept/Objectivity Concept** (Objective by Principle) According to this principle, accounting information should be verifiable and should be free from personal bias. Every transaction should be based on source documents such as cash memo, invoices, sales bills, etc. These evidences should be objective which means that they should state the facts as they are, without any bias towards either side.

Note *Of the above principles, principles of disclosure, conservatism, consistency and materiality are conventions and the rest are concepts.*

SYSTEM OF ACCOUNTING

The system of recording transactions in the books of accounts are generally classified into two types

1. Double Entry System

Double entry system of accounting was developed by *Luca Pacioli* in Italy in 15th century. Double entry system is based on the principle of **dual aspect** which states that every transaction has two aspects *i.e.*, debit and credit.

It is a complete system as both the aspects of a transaction are recorded in the books of accounts. The system is accurate and more reliable as the possibilities of frauds and misappropriations are minimised. The system of double entry can be implemented by big as well as small organisations.

2. Single Entry System

This system is not a complete system of maintaining records of financial transactions. It does not record two-fold effect of each and every transaction. Generally, only cash transactions are recorded and accounts of only debtors and creditors are maintained, under this system, instead of maintaining all the accounts. No uniformity is maintained under this system while recording transactions.

The single entry system is also known as **accounts from incomplete records**. The accounts maintained under this system are incomplete and unsystematic and therefore, not reliable. This system is however, followed by small business firms as it is very simple and flexible.

BASIS OF ACCOUNTING

The most significant function of accounting is to determine profits or losses of a business in an accounting period. Profits or losses of a business can be determined either on cash basis or on accrual (mercantile) basis.

1. Cash Basis of Accounting

Under the cash basis of accounting, entries in the books of accounts are made, when cash is received or paid and not when the receipts or payments become due. Revenue is recognised at the time when cash is received and not at the time of sale. Also, expenses are recorded only at the time of actual payments. As per this basis of accounting, unpaid expenses and unreceived revenues are not recorded in the books of accounts.

2. Accrual Basis of Accounting

Under accrual basis of accounting revenue is recognised when sales take place. It is irrelevant, whether payment for such sales is received or not.

Also, expenses related to a particular period are recorded in the books of accounts, irrespective of the fact whether these expenses have been paid or not paid or whether they have been paid in advance. Accrual basis of accounting is based on realisation and matching principle.

ACCOUNTING STANDARDS

Accounting standards are the written statements consisting of uniform accounting rules and guidelines issued by the accounting body of the country (such as Institute of

Chartered Accountants of India) that are to be followed while preparation and presentation of financial statements.

However, the accounting standards cannot override the provision of applicable laws, custom, usages and business environment in the country.

Note *ICAI is the regulatory body for standardisation of accounting policies in the country.*

Accounting Standards Board

The Institute of Chartered Accountants of India (ICAI) constituted an **Accounting Standards Board** (ASB) in April, 1977 for developing accounting standards.

Its main function is to identify areas in which uniformity in standards is required. It also develops draft standards after wide discussion with representative of the government, public sector undertakings, industry and other organisations.

ASB also gives due consideration to the international accounting standards as India is a member of international account setting body. ASB submits the draft of the standards to the council of the ICAI, which finalises them and notifies them for use in the presentation of the financial statements. ASB also makes a periodic review of the accounting standards.

Objectives of Accounting Standards

(*i*) To promote better understanding of financial statements.

(*ii*) To minimise the diverse accounting policies and practices with the aim to eliminate them to the possible extent.

(*iii*) To enhance reliability of financial statements.

(*iv*) To facilitate meaningful comparison of financial statements of two or more entities.

List of Accounting Standards

The council of the **Institute of Chartered Accountants of India** has so far issued 32 Accounting Standards (AS). These accounting standards are mandatory in the sense that these are binding on the members of the institute. *These standards are as follows*

AS No.	*Title*
AS-1	Disclosure of Accounting Policies
AS-2	Valuation of Inventories (Revised)
AS-3	Cash Flow Statement (Revised)
AS-4	Contingencies and Events Occurring after the Balance Sheet Date (Revised)
AS-5	Net Profit or Loss for the Period, Prior Period and Extraordinary Items and Changes in Accounting Policies
AS-6	Depreciation Accounting (Revised)
AS-7	Accounting for Construction Contracts
AS-8	Accounting for Research and Development (It has been withdrawn.)
AS-9	Revenue Recognition
AS-10	Accounting for Fixed Assets
AS-11	Accounting for the Effect of Changes in Foreign Exchange Rates (Revised)
AS-12	Accounting for Government Grants
AS-13	Accounting for Investments
AS-14	Accounting for Amalgamations
AS-15	Accounting for Retirement Benefits in the Financial Statements of Employers
AS-16	Borrowing Costs
AS-17	Segment Reporting
AS-18	Related Parties Disclosures
AS-19	Leases
AS-20	Earnings Per Share
AS-21	Consolidated Financial Statements
AS-22	Accounting for Taxes on Income
AS-23	Accounting for Investments in Associates in Consolidated Financial Statements
AS-24	Discontinuing Operations
AS-25	Interim Financial Reporting
AS-26	Intangible Assets
AS-27	Financial Reporting of Interests in Joint Venture
AS-28	Impairment of Assets
AS-29	Provisions, Contingent Liabilities and Contingent Assets
*AS-30	Financial Instruments: Recognition and Measurement
*AS-31	Financial Instruments: Presentation
*AS-32	Financial Instruments: Disclosures

* *These standards have been withdrawn by ICAI*

Applicability in Accounting Standards (AS)

AS are applicable to all types of organisations engaged in any industrial and business activity except for purely charitable organisations. These accounting standards are applicable to sole proprietorship firm, partnership firm, societies, trust, Hindu undivided families, cooperatives and companies.

The accounting standards are required to maintain certain level of uniformity at international level so that comparability and analysis of different accounting practices becomes easier. In order to make economy more dynamic, competitive and boost confidence in international circuit, it is important that the financial statements must be prepared in accordance with certain standards.

Due to this reason, accounting standards are being converged with International Financial Reporting Standards (IFRS). In India too, ministry of corporate affairs in callaboration with Institute of Chartered Accountants of India established Indian Accounting Standards (Ind-AS). These are applicable to the certain class of companies under the Companies (Indian Accounting Standards) Rules, 2015 as adopted on 16th February, 2015.

LIST OF IND-AS

The following is the list of Ind AS as follows

AS No.	Title
Ind AS 1	Presentation of Financial Statements
Ind AS 2	Inventories
Ind AS 7	Statement of Cash Flows
Ind AS 8	Accounting Policies, Changes in Accounting Estimates and Errors
Ind AS 10	Events after the Reporting Period
Ind AS 11	Construction Contracts
Ind AS 12	Income Taxes
Ind AS 16	Property, Plant and Equipment
Ind AS 17	Leases
Ind AS 19	Employee Benefits
Ind AS 20	Accounting for Government Grants and Disclosure of Government Assistance
Ind AS 21	The Effects of Changes in Foreign Exchange Rates
Ind AS 23	Borrowing Costs
Ind AS 24	Related Party Disclosures
Ind AS 27	Separate Financial Statements
Ind AS 28	Investments in Associates and Joint Ventures
Ind AS 29	Financial Reporting in Hyper Inflationary Economies
Ind AS 32	Financial Instruments : Presentation
Ind AS 33	Earnings per Share
Ind AS 34	Interim Financial Reporting
Ind AS 36	Impairment of Assets
Ind AS 37	Provisions, Contingent Liablilities and Contingent Assets
Ind AS 38	Intangible Assets
Ind AS 40	Investment Property
Ind AS 41	Agriculture
Ind AS 101	First-time Adoption of Indian Accounting Standards
Ind AS 102	Share-based Payment
Ind AS 103	Business Combinations
Ind AS 104	Insurance Contracts
Ind AS 105	Non-current Assets Held for Sale and Discontinued Operations
Ind AS 106	Exploration for and Evaluation of Mineral Resources
Ind AS 107	Financial Instruments: Disclosures
Ind AS 108	Operating Segments
Ind AS 109	Financial Instruments
Ind AS 110	Consolidated Financial Statements
Ind AS 111	Joint Arrangements
Ind AS 112	Disclosure of Interests in Other Entities
Ind AS 113	Fair Value Measurement
Ind AS 114	Regulatory Deferral Accounts
Ind AS 115	Revenue from Contracts with Customers

INTERNATIONAL FINANCIAL REPORTING STANDARDS

International Financial Reporting Standards (IFRS) are issued by International Accounting Standard Board (IASB). IASB replaced International Accounting Standard Committee (IASC) in 2001. IASC was formed in 1973 to develop International Accounting Standards (IAS) which had global acceptance and made different accounting statements of different countries similar and comparable.

The IFRS foundation is an independent, not for profit private sector organisation working in public interest. Its principal objectives are

(*i*) To develop a single set of high quality, understandable, enforceable and globally accepted international financial reporting standards, through its standard body, the IASB.

(ii) To promote the use and application of those standards.

(*iii*) To take account of the financial reporting needs of emerging economies and small and medium-sized entities.

(*iv*) To bring about convergence of national accounting standards and International Financial Reporting Standards to high quality solutions.

IFRS Issued by the IASB

IFRS No.	Title
IFRS 1	First Time Adoption of International Financial Reporting Standards
IFRS 2	Share Based Payment
IFRS 3	Business Combinations
IFRS 4	Insurance Contracts
IFRS 5	Non-current Assets Held for Sale and Discontinued Operations

IFRS No.	Title
IFRS 6	Exploration for and Evaluation of Mineral Resources
IFRS 7	Financial Instruments : Disclosures
IFRS 8	Operating Segments
IFRS 9	Financial Instruments
IFRS 10	Consolidate Financial Statements
IFRS 11	Jont Arrangements
IFRS 12	Disclosure, of Interest in other Entities
IFRS 13	Fair Value Measurement
IFRS 14	Regulatory Deferral Accounts
IFRS 15	Revenue from Contracts with Customers
IFRS 16	Leases

GOODS AND SERVICES TAX (GST)

The Goods and Services Tax is a value-added tax levied on most goods and services sold for domestic consumption. It is paid by the consumers. However, it is remitted to the government by the businesses selling the goods and services. Goods and Services Tax (GST) provides revenue for the government.

GST has been defined in Article 366 (12A) to mean "any tax on supply of goods or services or both except taxes on supply of the alcoholic liquor for human consumption."

Classification/Categories of list

GST can be classified as under

1. **Central GST (CGST)** Central GST is levied by the Central Government in the course of intra-state sales *i.e.* sales within the state. For example, sale made from lucknow in U.P. to Bareilly in U.P.
2. **State GST** (SGST) State GST is levied by the State Governments in the course of intra-state sales.
3. **Union Territory GST** (UTGST) Union territories such as Chandigarh, Puducherry, etc. levy union territory GST in the course of sales made within the union territory. Students should keep in mind that Cental GST and State/Union Territory GST are charged at half the prescribed rate of GST. So, if the prescribed rate is 18%, then 9% GST will be levied by the Centre and 9% GST will be levied by the State/Union Territory.
4. **Integerated GST** (IGST) Integrated GST is levied in the course of inter-state supply of goods and services. So, if goods are sold from Delhi to Mumbai, then this will attract the levy of Integrated GST. Also, it should be remembered that IGST would be levied and collected by the centre on inter-state supply of goods and services and import of goods and services into India.

Note *CGST, SGST, UTGST, IGST are levied at rates which are to be agreed upon by the centre and the states/union territories under the guidance of GST council.*

Characteristics of GST

The main characteristics/features of GST are as follows

(*i*) GST will be applicable on the 'supply' of goods and services as against the earlier concept of tax on the manufacturing or sale of goods or provision of services.

(*ii*) India has followed a dual GST model *i.e.* centre and states will simultaneously levy tax on a common base.

(*iii*) GST can be charged only by the registered supplier of goods or services or both on the prescribed rate after deducting trade discount and cash discount (if allowed at the time of purchase).

(*iv*) GST paid at the time of purchase is referred to as Input GST and GST collected at the time of sale is referred to as output GST. Input GST can be set off against output GST. Also, it is to be remembered that output GST collected by the supplier is to be remitted by him to the Government and until the time of remittance it is to be treated as his liability. It should be furtuher kept in mind that both input and output GST can be further classified as Centre GST, State/Union Territory GST and Integrated GST.

(*v*) GST is a destination based concept as against the earlier origin based tax. It means tax would accrue to the State/Union Territory where the consumption takes place.

(*vi*) Classification of a supply to be categorised as either supply of goods or supply of services for the purpose of levy of GST.

(*vii*) The GST applies to all the goods other than alcoholic liquor for human consumption and five petroleum products-petroleum crude, motor spirit (petrol), High Speed Diesel (HSD), natural gas and Aviation Turbine Fuel (ATF).

(*viii*) The list of exempted goods and services are common for the centre and the states.

(*ix*) Taxpayers with an aggregate turnover of ₹ 20 lakh (₹ 10 lakh for special category states like north-east and hilly states in a financial year have been exempted from tax.

(*x*) Person doing business in more than one state require separate registration in each state under GST. Person having multiple business verticals within a state may also require separate registration.

(*xi*) Small taxpayers with an aggregate turnover of ₹ 100 lakh (₹ 75 lakh for North Eastern states and Himachal Pradesh) in a financial year shall be eligible for composition key, *i.e.* a taxpayer shall pay tax as a fixed percentage of his turnover during the year without the benefit of Input Tax Credit (ITC).

Objectives of GST

The various objectives of GST are

(*i*) To eliminate classification dispute between goods and services.

(*ii*) To bring uniformity in tax rates and automated compliances.

(*iii*) To ensure availability of input tax credit across the value chain and avoid cascading effect.

(*iv*) To ensure simplification of registration, filing of return, tax administration and compliance.

(*v*) To harmonise tax base, laws and administration procedures across the country.

(*vi*) To minimise tax rate slabs and prevent unhealthy competition among states.

(*vii*) To ensure free movement of goods across the country without any additional tax.

Advantages of GST

There are various advantages of GST, which are as follows

(*i*) The primary benefit of GST is that it abolishes multiple layers of tax levied on goods and services.

(*ii*) It provides an input tax credit structure to eliminate cascading effect.

(*iii*) Under GST regime, their are uniform procedures for registration, filing of returns, payment of taxes as well as tax refunds.

(*iv*) It provides higher efficiency with regards to the neutralisation of taxes so that exports are globally competitive.

(*v*) GST provides a composition scheme for small businesses which gives an option to lower taxes.

(*vi*) Under GST, there is just one unified return which is required to be filed.

CHAPTER PRACTICE

OBJECTIVE TYPE Questions

Multiple Choice Questions

1 .... of accounting are like the foundation pillars on which the structure of accounting is based.
(a) Basic assumption
(b) Basic principles
(c) Basic concept
(d) None of these

Ans (a) Basic assumption

2 Stock-in-trade are to be recorded at cost price or market price whichever is less, it is based on ...... principle.
(a) prudence (b) historical cost
(c) cost benefit (d) business entity

Ans (a) prudence

3 When the information about two different enterprises have been prepared presented in a similar manner the information exhibits the characteristic of **NCERT**
(a) verifiability (b) relevance
(c) reliability (d) None of these

Ans (a) verifiability

4 The primary qualities that make accounting information useful for decision-making are
(a) relevance and freedom from bias **NCERT**
(b) reliability and comparability
(c) comparability and consistency
(d) None of the above

Ans (b) reliability and comparability

5 A trader has made a sale of ₹ 65,500 out of which cash sales amounted to ₹ 25,000. He showed trade receivables on 31st March, 2017 at ₹ 40,500. Which concept is followed by him?
(a) Going concern
(b) Cost
(c) Accrual
(d) Money measurement

Ans (c) Accrual

6 In income measurement and recognisation of assets and liabilities, which of the following concepts goes together?
(a) Periodicity, accrual, matching
(b) Cost, accrual, matching
(c) Going concern, cost, realisation
(d) Going concern, periodicity, reliability

Ans (a) Periodicity, accrual, matching

7 According to which principle, the economic life of an enterprise is artificially split into periodic intervals?
(a) Consistency principle
(b) Accounting period principle
(c) Going concern principle
(d) Accrual principle

Ans (b) Accounting period principle

8 During life time of an entity, accounting produce financial statements in accordance with which basic accounting concept. **NCERT**
(a) Conservatism
(b) Matching
(c) Accounting period
(d) None of the above

Ans (c) Accounting period

9 A concept that a business enterprise will not be sold or liquidated in the near future is known as **NCERT**
(a) going concern (b) economic entity
(c) monetary unit (d) None of these

Ans (a) going concern

10 Identify the incorrect statement.
(a) India has followed dual GST model *i.e.* centre (GST) and state (GST)
(b) Goods and services tax is a value added tax
(c) An integrated tax (GST) would be levied and collected by the center on inter state supply of goods and services
(d) The list of exempted goods and services are different or the centre and the state

Ans (d) India has followed a dual GST model (*i.e.* centre and states) and the list of exempted goods and services are common or the centre and the states.

11 What is the number of categories of GST for accounting purpose?
(a) 5 (b) 6
(c) 7 (d) 4

Ans (b) Input GST and output GST comprises of three categories each. So, total number of categories of GST for accounting purpose is 6.

12 Which principle states that every transaction has a dual or two-fold effect?

(a) Matching principle (b) Historical cost principle
(c) Duality principle (d) Materiality principle

Ans (c) As per duality principle, each and every transaction has a dual effect and therefore recorded at two places.

13 If a piece of land is purchased for ₹ 6,00,000 and its market value is ₹ 9,00,000. At the time of preparing final accounts, the land value is recorded at which value and which concept support this?

(a) ₹ 6,00,000,historical concept
(b) ₹ 6,00,000,matching concept
(c) ₹ 9,00,000,matching concept
(d) ₹ 9,00,000,historical concept

Ans (a) In this case, a piece of land is purchased for ₹ 6,00,000 and its market value is ₹ 9,00,000 at the time of preparing final accounts the land value is recorded only for ₹ 6,00,000 as per historical concept. Thus, the balance sheet does not indicate the price at which the asset could be sold for.

14 Management concealing important financial information violates the ...... principle.

(a) materialtiy (b) full disclosure
(c) consistency (d) None of these

Ans (b) According to full disclosure principle, accounting statements should disclose fully and completely all the significant information. Based on this, decisions can be taken by various interested parties. It involves proper classification and explanations of accounting information which are published in the financial statements.

15 Which board in India developed accounting standard?

(a) Accounting Standard Board
(b) All India Standard Board
(c) Standard Board of India
(d) None of the above

Ans (a) Accounting Standard Board

Fill in the Blanks

16 Double entry system of recording transactions is based on ....

Ans dual aspect concept

17 Personal transactions and business transactions are distinguished according to ....

Ans business entity concept

18 If a firm believes that some of its debtors may default, it should act on this by making sure that all possible losses are recorded in the books. This is an example of the .... concept.

Ans prudence

19 The .... concept states that if straight line method of depreciation is used in one year, then it should also be used in the next year.

Ans consistency

20 Under .... basis of accounting, incomes are recorded when they are earned or accrued, irrespective of the fact whether cash is received or not.

Ans accrual

State True or False

21 Materiality principle is an exception to the 'Full Disclosure Convention'.

Ans True

22 The essence of convention of prudence is to anticipate no profit and provide for all possible losses.

Ans True

23 Accrual concept implies accounting on cash basis.

Ans False. Accrual concept implies accounting done on due or accrual basis.

24 Compliance with accounting standards is mandatory.

Ans True

25 The primary benefit of GST is that it abolishes multiple layers of tax levied on goods and services.

Ans True

Match the Following

26

Column I		Column II	
1.	Ind AS 38	(a)	Agriculture
2.	Ind AS 41	(b)	Employee benefits
3.	Ind AS 12	(c)	Intangible assets
4.	Ind AS 19	(d)	Income Tax

Ans 1-(c), 2-(a), 3-(d), 4-(b)

VERY SHORT ANSWER Type Questions

27 What are accounting principles?

Ans Accounting principles are a set of rules of guidelines which are developed to ensure uniformity and easy understanding of accounting information.

28 What do you mean by accounting concepts?

Ans It refers to the basic assumptions, rules and principles which work as the basis of recording of business transactions and preparing accounts.

29 What do you understand by accounting conventions?

Ans These are the outcome of accounting practices or principles being followed by the enterprises over a period of time. Conventions may undergo a change with time to bring about improvement in the quality of accounting information.

30 Which principle assumes that a business enterprise will not be liquidated in the near future?

Or

Full cost of an asset is not treated as an expense in the year of its purchase because of which principle?

Ans Going concern principle

31 An accountant always charges depreciation on fixed assets @ 20% per annum. Which principle is followed by the accountant?

Or

According to which concept, depreciation is to be charged as per one particular method year after year?

Or

Name the principle which states that if Straight Line Method of depreciation is used in one year, then it should also be used in the next year?

Or

Mr Raghav valued the inventory on FIFO basis and LIFO basis during 2012 and 2013, respectively. Which principle did he violate?

Ans Consistency principle

32 Materiality principle is an exception to which principle?

Or

Due to which principle, contingent liabilities are shown in the balance sheet?

Or

Name the principle which states that the financial statements should disclose all significant information.

Ans Full disclosure principle

33 The cost of a small calculator is accounted as an expense and not shown as a separate asset in financial statements of a business entity due to which principle?

Ans Materiality principle

34 State one limitation of historical cost principle.

Ans During period of inflation, the figure of net profit will be distorted because depreciation based on historical cost will be charged against revenues at current prices.

35 Which principle states that the accounting data should be definite, verifiable and free from the personal bias?

Ans Verifiable objectivity principle

36 Name the basis of accounting, which is recognised under the Companies Act, 2013.

Or

On 1st January, 2016, goods are sold to Aradhya for ₹10,000 and cash is received from her on 1st March, 2016. Identify which basis of accounting is followed if sale is recorded on 1st January itself.

Or

Name the basis of accounting in which outstanding and prepaid expenses are taken into consideration.

Ans Accrual basis of accounting

37 Does cash basis of accounting violates GAAP? If yes, how?

Ans Yes, cash basis of accounting violates GAAP since it does not follow matching and accrual principles of accounting.

38 A company purchased goods for ₹ 10,00,000 and sold 80% of such goods during the year. The market value of remaining goods was ₹ 1,80,000. The company valued the closing stock at ₹ 2,00,000 *i.e.*, cost. Is the treatment correct?

Ans No, the principle of conservatism is being violated. Here the closing stock should have been valued at ₹ 1,80,000 *i.e.*, lower of cost or Net Realisable Value (NRV) whichever is less.

39 Nishant Ltd purchased securities for ₹ 1 crore. At the end of the year, the market value of such securities was ₹ 80 lakh. While preparing the financial statements, the company valued the securities at cost. Is the company following the principle of conservatism?

Ans No, the company is not following the principle of conservatism. It should bring down the value of current assets to its market value otherwise the financial position of the business will be overstated.

40 Due to a labour strike, in a factory the production had to stop for a week. The accountant estimated the loss of production and likely loss of profit and recorded it in the books of accounts. Is the accountant correct?

Ans No, as per the money measurement concept only those transactions and events, which can be recorded in money terms on the basis of documentary evidences are recorded in books of accounts.

41 Vardhman Ltd gets a contract of ₹ 200 crore to build a hospital to be completed in 4 years. The management of the company wants to ascertain profit or loss on this contract only when the contract is completed. Is the management correct?

Ans No, although the true profit or loss can be ascertained only after the completion of the contract but as per accounting period principle the contract period should be divided into time interval of twelve months for the ascertainment of profit of that period.

42 An accountant advised his client, who is a doctor to maintain his accounts on cash basis. Is the advice of accountant correct?

Ans Yes, the advice given by the accountant is correct as cash basis of accounting is more appropriate for a doctor as he receives his fee in cash.

43 Why is it necessary for accountants to assume that business entity will remain a going concern? **NCERT**

Ans The concept of going concern assumes that a business firm would continue to carry out its operations indefinitely. Due to this concept distinction is made between capital and revenue expenditure and thus, assets and liabilities are recognised.

SHORT ANSWER Type Questions

44 Give the advantages of following consistency concept.

Or

Why should a business follow principle of consistency?

Ans A business should follow this principle because of many advantages associated with it.

Advantages of following consistency concept are

(*i*) It helps the financial statements to be more understandable and comparable.

(*ii*) It is important when alternative accounting practices are available.

(*iii*) It eliminates personal bias and helps in achieving results that are comparable.

45 Do you think that the principle of conservatism results in creation of secret reserves?

Ans *Yes,* principle *of conservatism has two effects*

(*i*) Profit and loss account discloses lower profit in comparison to the actual profits.

(*ii*) Balance sheet will disclose understatement of assets and overstatement of liabilities.

These two effects result in creation of secret reserves.

46 How does matching principle apply to depreciation?

Ans Matching principle states that the expenses of an accounting period are matched with the related revenue for correct determination of profit. According to the matching principle, the purchase price of fixed asset is not related to the accounting period because the benefit derived from its use will be spread over a number of years. Therefore, only depreciation related to the accounting period is considered for determination of profit.

47 What is the basic accounting equation? **NCERT**

Ans *The basic accounting equation is given below*

Assets = Liabilities + Capital

or

Assets = Claim of Outsiders + Owner's Equity or Capital

The above equation states that the assets of a business are always equal to the claims of owners and the outsiders.

48 **When should revenue be recognised? Are there exceptions to the general rule?** **NCERT**

Ans Revenue should be recognised only when it is realised.

Only such transactions should be recorded in accounting which have actually taken place not the ones which would take place in future.

Yes, there are certain exceptions to the general rule.

In case of construction projects, revenue is generally realised before the contract is completed. Similarly, when goods are sold on hire purchase, the amount collected in instalments, is treated as realised.

49 **Explain verifiable objective concept or objectivity principle.**

Ans According to this principle, accounting information should be verifiable and should be free from personal bias. Every transaction should be based on source documents such as cash memo, invoices, sales bills, etc. These evidences should be objective which means that they should state the facts as they are, without any bias towards either side.

50 **What is the need for accounting standards?**

Ans *The need for accounting standards arises from the following reasons*

(*i*) They facilitate transparent and meaningful reporting of financial information.

(*ii*) They reduce accounting alternatives to reasonable and practical level.

(*iii*) They enhance comparability of financial statements.

(*iv*) They encourage consistency in accounting practices.

51 **Give any five points highlighting the nature of accounting standards.**

Ans *Following points highlights the nature of accounting standards*

(*i*) Accounting standards are a framework of practices and guidelines which facilitate reliability and comparability to financial statements.

(*ii*) Accounting standards bring uniformity in accounting practices of various business.

(*iii*) Accounting standards design and mould the business environment by prescribing and recommending accounting practices.

(*iv*) Accounting standards cannot violate the prevailing law of the country. If they contradict the law, then law will prevail.

(*v*) Accounting standards are flexible because they provide alternative practices to be followed in different situations.

52 **Niranjan & Co has been charging depreciation @ 20% per annum on Straight Line Method.**

It now wants to change the method to diminishing balance method, the rate of depreciation being 35% per annum. Can the company do so?

Or

As per consistency concept a company cannot change an accounting policy. Does this holds true in all instances? Explain.

Ans Yes, *the method and the rate of depreciation can be changed but only in the following circumstances*

(*i*) The change is to comply with statutory regulations, or

(*ii*) The change would help in better understanding of the true financial position of the business.

Also, the change and its effect on profit should be disclosed in the financial statements of the enterprise.

53 **The realisation concept determines when goods sent on credit to customers are to be included in the sales figure, for the purpose of computing the profit or loss for the accounting period. Which of the following tends to be used in practice to determine when to include a transaction in the sales figure for the period? When the goods have been** **NCERT**

(a) despatched
(b) invoiced
(c) delivered
(d) paid for

Give reason for your answer.

Ans (*b*) The answer to this question would be when the goods have been invoiced. The reason for this is that the revenue is assumed to be realised when a legal right to receive it arises *i.e.*, the point of time when goods have been sold or service has been rendered.

Thus, credit sales are treated as revenue on the day sales are invoiced and not when money is received from buyers or when they are despatched or delivered.

54 **What is the difference between IFRS and Indian GAAP?**

Ans *The two principle differences between IFRS and Indian GAAP or Accounting Standards are as follows*

IFRS	GAAP
IFRS are principle based.	Indian GAAP or accounting standards are rule based.
IFRS are based on fair value concept.	Indian GAAP or accounting standards are based on historical cost concept.

55 Name the accounting concept or convention associated with the following

(i) Assets are recorded at cost, irrespective of the market price.

(ii) Life of a business should be divided into smaller periods.

(iii) Accounting transactions should be free from bias of accountants and others.

Ans (*i*) Historical cost concept.

(*ii*) Accounting period concept.

(*iii*) Verifiable objective concept.

56 Roshan, a Chartered Accountant earned ₹ 12,00,000 during the financial year 2015- 2016, out of which he received ₹ 10,50,000. He incurred expenses of ₹ 5,10,000, out of which ₹ 1,20,000 are outstanding. He also received his fees relating to previous year ₹ 1,35,000 and also paid ₹ 60,000 due on expenses of last year. Find out Roshan's income for 2015-2016 following the cash basis and accrual basis of accounting.

Ans Cash Basis of Accounting

$= 10{,}50{,}000 + 1{,}35{,}000 - 3{,}90{,}000$

$(5{,}10{,}000 - 1{,}20{,}000) - 60{,}000$

$=$ ₹ 7,35,000

Accrual Basis of Accounting

$= 12{,}00{,}000 - 5{,}10{,}000$

$=$ ₹ 6,90,000

57 During the financial year, Rajan had cash sales of ₹ 4,50,000 and credit sales of ₹ 3,00,000. Expenses incurred for the year were ₹ 3,50,000 out of which ₹ 1,50,000 are still to be paid.

Find out Rajan's income following

(i) Cash Basis of Accounting

(ii) Accrual Basis of Accounting.

Ans (*i*) Cash Basis of Accounting

$= 4{,}50{,}000 - 2{,}00{,}000\ (3{,}50{,}000 - 1{,}50{,}000)$

$=$ ₹ 2,50,000

(*ii*) Accrual Basis of Accounting

$= 4{,}50{,}000 + 3{,}00{,}000 - 3{,}50{,}000 =$ ₹ 4,00,000

58 Give the categories of GST.

Ans Refer to text on page no 24.

LONG ANSWER Type Questions

59 Explain the features of accounting principles.

Ans *Features of accounting principles are as follows*

(*i*) **Man-made** Accounting principles are man-made. They are derived by men based on practical experience and reason. However, they lack in universal applicability as they are not laboratory tested like principles of physical and other natural sciences.

(*ii*) **Flexible** Accounting principles are flexible and not rigid. They keep on changing with the passage of time and in response to changes in business practices and government policies. They also change according to the need of users of accounting information.

(*iii*) **Generally Accepted** The general acceptance of the accounting principles or practices depends upon, how well they meet the *following three criteria*

(*a*) **Relevance** A principle is relevant to the extent, it results in information that is meaningful and useful to the user of the accounting information.

(*b*) **Objectivity** A principle is objective to the extent the accounting information is not influenced by personal bias or judgement of those who provide it.

It also implies verifiability which means that there is some way of ascertaining the correctness of the information reported.

(*c*) **Feasibility** A principle is feasible to the extent, it can be implemented without much complexity or cost.

60 The accounting concepts and accounting standards are generally referred to as the essence of financial accounting. Comment. **NCERT**

Ans Financial accounting is concerned with the preparation of financial statements and to provide financial information to various accounting users.

It is performed according to the basic accounting concepts like business entity, money measurement, consistency, conservatism, etc. However, these concepts allow various alternatives to treat the same transaction.

This leads to wrong interpretation of financial results by external users due to the problem of inconsistency and incomparability of financial results among different business entities.

In order to remove inconsistency and incomparability and to bring uniformity in preparation of the financial statements, accounting standards are being issued in India by the Institute of Chartered Accountants of India.

Hence, accounting standards and accounting concepts are referred as the essence of financial accounting.

61 **Explain the going concern concept. Also give the practical implications of this concept.**

Ans According to this concept, it is assumed that the business firm would continue its operations for a fairly long period of time and would not be liquidated in the near future.

All the transactions are recorded in the books on the assumption that it is a continuing enterprise.

For example, if a machinery is purchased which would last, for the next 10 years then, the cost of the machinery will be spread over the next 10 years for calculating the net profit or loss for each year.

The practical implications of this concept are

(*i*) This concept facilitates recording fixed assets on the basis of their cost value and maximum life. Market value of the assets is irrelevant for accounting of these assets.

(*ii*) It is due to this concept, that a distinction is made between capital and revenue expenditure.

(*iii*) It is due to this assumption profits are computed every year so that the performance of a business can be adjudged. Expenses of a business are charged to its revenues, to find out profit.

(*iv*) It is due to this concept, that the total cost of the machinery is not to be treated as an expense in the year of purchase itself.

62 **Why is it important to adopt a consistent basis for the preparation of financial statements? Explain.** **NCERT**

Ans For making the accounting information meaningful to its internal and external users, it is important that such information is reliable as well as comparable.

The comparability of information is required both to make inter-firm comparisons *i.e.*, to see how a firm has performed as compared to the other firms, as well as to make inter-period comparison *i.e.*, how it has performed as compared to the previous years.

This becomes possible only if the information provided by the financial statements is based on consistent accounting policies, principles and practices.

63 **Explain the accrual concept with the help of an example.**

Ans According to this concept, a transaction is recorded at the time, it takes place and not at the time when settlement is done.

In other words, revenue is recorded when sales are made or services are rendered and it is irrelevant as to when cash is received against such sales.

Similarly, expenses are recorded at the time when they are incurred and it is irrelevant as to when payment is made in cash for such expenses.

Thus, to find out correct profit and to show true financial position of an enterprise at the end of accounting period, all expenses and income belonging to that particular accounting period are shown whether cash has been paid or received or not.

Example Goods are sold to Raju on 1st January, 2016 on a credit of 3 months. In this instance, sale will be recorded on 1st January, 2016 although the amount will be received on 1st April, 2016.

64 **'Capital is a liability for the business.' Explain this statement with the principle applied.**

Or

Explain the business entity principle with the help of an example.

Ans According to business entity principle, business is treated as a separate entity distinct from its owners. Accounting information is recorded considering this principle. All transactions are recorded from the point of view of business and not from the point of businessman/owner.

The capital introduced by the owner is treated as a liability from the point of view of business. Business owes money to the owner to the extent of his capital just like it owes money to lenders and creditors.

Due to this reason, interest on capital is treated as a business expense. Also, because of this principle, owner's personal property, investments, expenditures are kept separate from the recording of business transactions in the books.

Example Ram started his business with cash. Purchased stock, machinery and furniture and deposited money into the bank account and also kept some cash in hand. From accounting point of view, cash introduced by Ram is a liability for the business and is referred to as capital.

The assets purchased are of the business and not of the owner. Also, if the owner withdraws some money for his personal use, it will be termed as drawings and it will reduce the cash (assets) and capital at the same time.

65 **What is the money measurement concept? Which one factor can make it difficult to compare the monetary values of one year with the monetary values of another year?** **NCERT**

Or

Explain the money measurement principle.

Ans According to this principle, only those transactions which can be measured and expressed in terms of money are recorded in the books of accounts. Non-financial or non-monetary transactions do not find any place in the accounting records.

For example, sale of goods or payment of expenses or receipt of income, etc will be recorded as these can be expressed in monetary terms.

However, dispute among the owners or managers, appointment of a manager, efficiency of management, quality of product, etc. will not be recorded in the books of accounts simply because it cannot be converted or recorded in terms of money.

The factor which can make it difficult to compare the monetary values of one year with the monetary values of another year is inflation. Due to the changes in price, the value of money does not remain the same over a period of time. The value of rupee today on account of rise in price is much less than what it was, say ten years back.

66 **What is accounting period principle? Who are required to adopt this principle compulsorily?**

Ans Accounting period refers to the span of time at the end of which the financial statements (profit and loss account and balance sheet) of an enterprise are prepared, to know the profitability and financial position of the business.

It is also known as periodicity principle or time period principle. According to this principle, the life of a business is divided into smaller periods (usually one year), so that, its performance can be measured on regular basis or intervals.

According to the amended Income Tax Law, a business has to compulsorily adopt financial year beginning on 1st April and ending on 31st March in the next calendar year, as its accounting period. Apart from this, companies whose shares are listed on the stock exchange, are required to publish quarterly results to ascertain the profitability and financial position at the end of every three months period.

67 **Explain the full disclosure principle. Why should information be fully disclosed?**

Ans According to this principle, there should be reporting of all the significant information relating to the economic affairs of the business and it should be complete and understandable.

For example, reasons for low turnover or destruction of plant and machinery due to natural calamities should be disclosed.

Information should be fully disclosed because

(*i*) Since, one of the objectives of accounting information is to communicate accounting information to various users, it is important to provide complete information to them, so that they can take right decisions at the right time on the basis of the financial statements of the business.

(*ii*) Disclosure of complete and true information projects a correct picture of financial position of the business.

68 **With the help of an example, explain the materiality principle.**

Ans According to this principle, only those transactions should be recorded which are material or relevant for the preparation of financial statements. All immaterial facts should be ignored. An information is material, if it has the ability to influence or affect the decision-making of various parties interested in accounting information, contained in financial statements.

According to American Accounting Association (AAA), an item should be regarded as material if there is a reason to believe that knowledge of it would influence the decision of an informed investor.

Example ₹ 1,00,000 spent on advertising is material for a business having turnover of ₹ 3,00,000 whereas, it is immaterial for a business having turnover of ₹ 30,00,00,000.

69 **Discuss the concept based on the premise 'do not anticipate profits but provide for all losses'.** **NCERT**

Ans The concept of conservatism (also called 'prudence') states that 'Do not anticipate profits but provide for all losses'.

In other words, this principle suggests that we should make provisions for probable future expenses but ignore any future probable gain, until it actually happens.

This approach of providing for the losses but not recognising the gains until realised is called conservation approach.

For example, closing stock is valued at lower of cost or net realisable value, as per this concept only.

The merits of using this concept are

(*i*) It provides guidance for recording transactions in the books of accounts and is based on the policy of playing safe.

(ii) It ensures that the financial statements present a realistic picture of the working affairs of the business and does not present a picture which will mislead the users of accounting information.

However, excess use of this concept leads to creation of secret reserves because liabilities get overstated and assets get understated.

70 **Explain the historical cost concept. How is depreciation and book value of asset calculated as per this concept?**

Ans According to this principle, assets are recorded in the books of accounts at their cost price, which includes cost of acquisition, transportation, installation and making the asset ready for use. This cost is the basis for all subsequent accounting of such assets.

For example, machinery is purchased for ₹ 10,00,000. At the end of the accounting period, it is found that the market value of machinery is ₹ 15,00,000. However, it will be recorded in the books at ₹ 10,00,000 only.

Adoption of historical cost brings objectivity in recording as the cost of acquisition is easily verifiable from the purchase documents.

For calculating depreciation and book value of asset the following points should be considered

(i) Depreciation to be charged on assets is calculated on the basis of cost of asset and market value of such asset is irrelevant for accounting of such assets.

(ii) Book value of the asset in the books of accounts is decided on the basis of cost less depreciation, without giving consideration to its market price.

71 **What is matching concept? Why should a business concern follow this concept? Discuss.** **NCERT**

Ans According to this concept, expenses incurred in an accounting period should be matched with revenues during that period *i.e.*, when a revenue is recognised in a period, then the cost related to that revenue also needs to be recognised in that period to enable calculation of correct profits of the business. *Business concerns should follow this concept because of the following reasons*

(i) Due to this concept, adjustments are made for expenses not paid (outstanding expenses) or for those paid in advance (prepaid expenses).

(ii) This concept should be followed while preparing financial statements to have a true and fair view of the profitability and financial position of a business firm.

72 **Explain the dual aspect principle with the help of an example.**

Ans Dual aspect is the foundation or the basic principle of accounting. According to this principle, every transaction entered by a business affects atleast two aspects of the business. It is because of this principle that the following accounting equation always holds true.

Assets = Liabilities + Capital

or

Assets = Claim of Outsiders + Owner's Equity or Capital

or

Total Assets = Total Equities

Example Yuvraj starts a business with a capital of ₹ 10,00,000. There are two aspects to the transaction. On one hand, the business has an asset of ₹ 10,00,000 (Cash) while on the other hand, it has a liability towards Yuvraj of ₹ 10,00,000 (Capital of Yuvraj). Thus, we can say

Capital (Equities) = Cash (Assets)

₹ 10,00,000 = ₹ 10,00,000

73 **Explain the revenue recognition principle with the help of an example.**

Ans The concept of revenue recognition requires that the revenue for a business transaction should be recorded in the accounts only when it is realised. Revenue is assumed to be realised when a legal right to receive it arises *i.e.*, the point of time when goods have been sold or service has been rendered.

In short, it is the sale or change of ownership which decides the revenue or expense and not the actual payment or receipt regarding such sale or expense.

Example If a business sells goods in January 2016 and receives the amount from such sale in April 2016 then revenue will be considered as recognised in January 2016 when sale is made and not when payments is received from such sale. Similarly, if a business receives advance in January 2016 for a sale to happen in April 2016, then revenue will be recognised when sale takes place *i.e.*, April 2016 and not when money was received.

74 **Explain briefly the various measurement basis on the basis of which the monetary value of assets can be assessed.**

Ans *The various measurement basis are*

(i) **Historical Cost** Assets are recorded at the amount of cash or cash equivalents paid or the fair value of the consideration given to acquire them at the time of their acquisition.

(*ii*) **Current Cost** Assets are carried at the amount of cash or cash equivalents that would have to be paid, if the same or an equivalent asset was acquired currently.

(*iii*) **Realisable** (Settlement) **Value** Assets are carried at the amount of cash or cash equivalents that could currently be obtained by selling the asset in an orderly disposal.

75 Double entry system of accounting is based on the principle of 'dual aspect'. Explain the features of double entry system of accounting and also give its benefits.

Ans *Features of the double entry system are as follows*

(*i*) It maintains a complete record of each transaction.

(*ii*) It recognises atleast two aspects of every transaction *i.e.*, debit and credit.

(*iii*) In this system, one aspect is debited and other aspect is credited as per the rules of debit and credit.

(*iv*) The total of all debits is always equal to the total of all credits.

(*v*) It also helps in establishing arithmetical accuracy of accounting records by preparing the trial balance.

The main advantages of double entry system are

(*i*) Double entry system is a scientific system of recording business transactions. Two sides of a transaction are recorded on the basis of scientific and logical rules due to which there are less chances of errors.

(*ii*) Under the double entry system both sides of a transaction are recorded, which results in presenting correct income or loss, assets and liabilities.

(*iii*) The accuracy of the accounting work can be established by the use of this system, by preparing the trial balance.

(*iv*) The profit earned or loss suffered during a period can be found out by preparing the profit and loss account.

(*v*) The financial position of the business can be ascertained at the end of accounting period by preparing the balance sheet.

76 "Despite many advantages, double entry system also has some disadvantages". In the light of this statement discuss the advantages of double entry system.

Ans *Despite of many advantages, double entry system has some disadvantages which are as follows*

(*i*) Double entry system is complex and hard to understand.

(*ii*) It involves time, labour and money, so it is not possible for small business to keep accounts under this system.

(*iii*) It requires expert knowledge to keep accounts under this system.

(*iv*) As the system is complex, there is greater possibility of committing errors and mistakes.

77 What are the advantages and disadvantages of cash basis of accounting?

Ans *The advantages of cash basis of accounting are*

(*i*) It is very simple because no adjustments are required for advance and outstanding incomes and expenses.

(*ii*) It is an objective approach.

(*iii*) This approach suits the organisations which mostly have cash transactions.

The disadvantages of cash basis of accounting are

(*i*) It does not provide true and fair view of the financial position of the enterprise because it does not record advance and outstanding incomes and gains.

(*ii*) It ignores matching principle, accrual concept and revenue recognition principles of accounting.

(*iii*) This system does not differentiate between capital and revenue items.

78 Discuss the advantages and disadvantages of accrual basis of accounting.

Ans *Following are the advantages of accrual basis of accounting*

(*i*) It is more scientific as compared to cash basis of accounting.

(*ii*) It shows true and fair view of financial statements by taking in consideration all advances and outstanding incomes and expenses.

(*iii*) It shows correct profit or loss of an enterprise.

(*iv*) It is recognised by Companies Act, 2013.

Following are the disadvantages of accrual basis of accounting

(*i*) It is complicated as compared to cash basis. There are adjustments which need to be carried out while preparing final accounts.

(*ii*) It is a time-consuming process to prepare financial statements under accrual basis of accounting.

79 Explain any six points highlighting the utility of accounting standards.

Ans *Accounting standards serve the following purposes*

(*i*) **Basis of Preparing Financial Statements** Accounting standards provide the norms or guidelines on the basis of which financial statements should be prepared.

(*ii*) **Uniformity in Accounting Methods** Uniformity in the preparation and presentation of financial statements can be ensured by accounting standards.

(*iii*) **Sense of Confidence to Various Users** Accounting standards create a sense of confidence amongst various users of accounting information.

(*iv*) **Help to Auditors** Accounting standards help auditors in auditing the accounts by providing them standards to judge the financial statements.

(*v*) **Simplifying Accounting Information** Accounting standards simplify the accounting information in financial statements.

(*vi*) **Render Reliability to Financial Statements** Accounting standards render reliability to financial statements by providing common platform for preparation of financial statements.

80 **What do you mean by International Accounting Standard Board. (IASB). State any four objectives of IASB.**

Ans IASB is an independent, private sector body that develops and approves the IFRSs. The IASB operates under the oversight of IFRS foundation. The IASB was formed in 2001 to replace the International Accounting Standard Committee. At present, IASB has 14 members. All meetings of the IASB are held in public and webcast. The IASB engages closely with the stakeholders around the world, including investors, analyst, regulators, business leaders, accounting standard setters and the accountancy profession. *The objectives of IASB are as follows*

(*i*) To issue accounting standards which facilitate transparency and comparability to facilitate right decisions.

(*ii*) To promote use of these standards.

(*iii*) To look into the concerns of small and medium enterprises having difficulties in implementation of IFRS.

(*iv*) To bring uniformity in national accounting standards and IFRS.

81 **International Financial Reporting Standards (IFRS) provide a number of benefits. Explain any four.**

Ans IFRS are very useful for multinational or global business enterprises. *IFRS are useful in the following manner*

(*i*) **Helpful to Global Enterprises** IFRS unify accounting practices worldwide which helps enterprises operating in different countries in consolidation of financial statements of their different units of different countries.

(*ii*) **Helpful to Investors** IFRS help investors by facilitating financial statements prepared on common set of accounting standards which enhances their quality, reliability and comparability.

(*iii*) **Helpful to Industry** Following IFRS makes it easier for business to obtain funds globally.

(*iv*) **Helpful to Accounting Professionals** Accounting professionals will be able to provide better services to global business enterprises following IFRS.

82 **Differentiate between accrual basis and cash basis of accounting.**

Ans *The differences between accrual and cash basis of accounting are*

Basis	*Accrual Basis of Accounting*	*Cash Basis of Accounting*
Nature of Transactions	Both cash and credit transactions are recorded.	Only cash transactions are recorded.
Advance/ Outstanding Incomes and Expenses	These are adjusted in profit and loss account and shown in balance sheet.	These are not adjusted in profit and loss account nor shown in balance sheet.
Reliability of Profits	Correct profit or loss is ascertained because it records both cash and credit transactions.	Correct profit or loss is not ascertained because it records only cash transactions.
Accounting Knowledge	The accrual basis of accounting requires accounting knowledge, as many adjustments of advance, outstanding, capital and revenue are to be carried out in financial statements.	It does not require much of accounting knowledge, as only cash receipts and cash payments are considered for financial statements.
Legal Position	Accrual basis of accounting is recognised by the Companies Act, 2013.	Cash basis of accounting is not recognised by the Companies Act, 2013.

Basis	Accrual Basis of Accounting	Cash Basis of Accounting
Acceptability	Accrual basis of accounting is more acceptable in business, as it reveals correct income and expense besides assets and liabilities.	Cash basis of accounting is not acceptable in business as it does not reveal the required information.
Suitability	This basis is suitable for business.	This basis is suitable for not-for-profit organisation and professionals like, doctors, lawyers, Chartered Accountants, etc.

83 **Explain the concept of Goods and Service Tax (GST).**

Ans Refer to text on page no. 24

84 **Give the characteristies of GST.**

Ans The main characteristics/features of GST are as follows

(*i*) GST will be applicable on the 'supply' of goods and services as against the earlier concept of tax on the manufacturing or sale of goods or provision of services.

(*ii*) India has followed a dual GST model *i.e.* centre and states will simultaneously levy tax on a common base.

(*iii*) GST can be charged only by the registered supplier of goods or services or both on the prescribed rate after deducting trade discount and cash discount (if allowed at the time of purchase).

(*iv*) GST paid at the time of purchase is referred to as Input GST and GST collected at the time of sale is referred to as output GST. Input GST can be set off against output GST. Also, it is to be remembered that output GST collected by the supplier is to be remitted by him to the Government and until the time of remittance it is to be treated as his liability. It should be furtuher kept in mind that both input and output GST can be further classified as Centre GST, State/Union Territory GST and Integrated GST.

(*v*) GST is a destination based concept as against the earlier origin based tax. It means tax would accrue to the State/Union Territory where the consumption takes place.

(*vi*) Classification of a supply to be categorised as either supply of goods or supply of services for the purpose of levy of GST.

(*vii*) The GST applies to all the goods other than alcoholic liquor for human consumption and five petroleum products-petroleum crude, motor spirit (petrol), High Speed Diesel (HSD), natural gas and Aviation Turbine Fuel (ATF).

03

This chapter deals with the various types of source documents and the preparation of vouchers. It further deals with how to develop an accounting equation.

SOURCE DOCUMENTS AND ACCOUNTING EQUATION

|TOPIC 1|
Source Documents and Preparation of Vouchers

CHAPTER CHECKLIST

- Source Documents and Preparation of Vouchers
- Accounting Equation
- Effect of Transactions on Accounting Equation

In a business, various transactions are made everyday such as sale and purchase of goods and services, payment or receipt of cash, etc.

All these financial transactions recorded in the books of accounts are usually evidenced by an appropriate document. The document which provides evidence of the transaction is called source document or voucher.

SOURCE DOCUMENTS

Source documents are written documents which contain details of the transactions and are prepared at the time, a transaction is entered into. They are also referred to as supporting documents.

Source documents are of prime importance, as they are the evidences of business transactions which provide information about the nature of the transaction, parties involved, date and the amount involved in it.

Examples of source documents are, bills of purchases, invoices for sales, debit and credit notes, etc.

The most common source documents are as follows

(*i*) **Cash Memo** It is a written document prepared by the seller, for goods sold against cash. Cash memo acts as an evidence for both the seller and the purchaser of goods. It contains details of goods sold, quantity, rate, total amount received, date of transaction, etc.

(*ii*) **Invoice or Bill** It is prepared by the seller, for goods sold against credit. It contains details such as party to whom goods are sold, goods sold and the total sale amount.

The original copy of the sales invoice is sent to the purchaser which acts as an evidence for the purchaser. A duplicate copy of this invoice or bill is retained by the seller as an evidence for the sales made, for recording in the books of accounts and for future reference.

(*iii*) **Pay-in-slip** It is used for depositing cash or cheques into bank. It is a form which is available from a bank having a counterfoil which is returned to the depositor with cashier's signature and bank's stamp as receipt. The counterfoil gives details regarding the date and the amount (in cash or cheque) deposited.

(*iv*) **Cheque** It is a document in writing drawn upon a specified banker and payable on demand. A cheque must be dated and signed by the drawer.

(*v*) **Debit Note** When a buyer returns goods to the seller, he sends a debit note to the seller as an intimation of the amount and quantity being returned and requesting return of money. A debit note is sent to inform about the debit made in the account of the seller alongwith the reasons mentioned in it.

(*vi*) **Credit Note** When a seller receives goods returned from the buyer, he prepares and sends a credit note as an intimation to the buyer showing that the money for the related goods is being returned in the form of a credit note. A credit note is sent to inform about the credit made in the account of the buyer alongwith the reasons mentioned in it.

Note *The specimens of various source documents are given ahead in the topic.*

VOUCHERS

Vouchers are documents evidencing a business transaction. A voucher details the accounts that are debited and credited. It is prepared on the basis of source documents such as cash memo, invoice or bill, receipt, pay-in-slip, cheque, debit and credit notes, etc.

Preparation of Vouchers

There is no set format of a voucher. The design of the voucher depends upon the nature, requirement and convenience of the business. To distinguish various vouchers, different colour papers and different fonts of printing are used.

However, a standard voucher must contain the following essential elements

(*i*) It should be printed on a good quality paper.

(*ii*) Name of the firm must be printed on the top.

(*iii*) Date of transaction should be entered. Date of recording the transaction is irrelevant.

(*iv*) The number of the voucher should be in a serial order.

(*v*) Name of the account to be debited or credited should be mentioned.

(*vi*) Debit or credit amount should be written in figures against the amount.

(*vii*) Description of the transaction should be given account wise.

(*viii*) The person who prepares the voucher must mention his name alongwith signature.

(*ix*) The name and signature of the authorised person are to be mentioned on the voucher.

Types of Vouchers

Basically, vouchers may be classified into two categories as follows

1. SUPPORTING VOUCHERS

These are the documents which come into existence when a transaction is entered into. These are also known as source vouchers or source documents.

For example, issue of cash memo on cash sales, issue of credit memo (invoice) on credit sales, issue of receipt on receipt of rent and so on.

2. ACCOUNTING VOUCHERS

Accounting vouchers are the secondary vouchers. These vouchers are a written document prepared on the basis of supporting vouchers for accounting and recording purposes, prepared by an accountant and countersigned by an authorised person. The accounting vouchers are prepared for cash as well as non-cash transactions.

Types of Accounting Vouchers

Accounting vouchers may be classified into cash vouchers and non-cash vouchers.

CASH VOUCHERS

These are prepared for cash transactions only, *i.e.*, cash receipts and cash payments. It includes receipt and payment through cheques.

Cash vouchers can further be classified as debit vouchers and credit vouchers

Debit Vouchers These are prepared to record the transactions involving cash payments.

For example, for cash payment of expenses, for cash purchases of goods, for cash purchases of fixed assets, for cash purchases of investments, for cash payment to creditors, for granting loans and advances to employees or other persons, for repayment of loans and advances already taken, for deposit of cash into the bank.

A format of debit voucher is shown below which records purchase of an asset

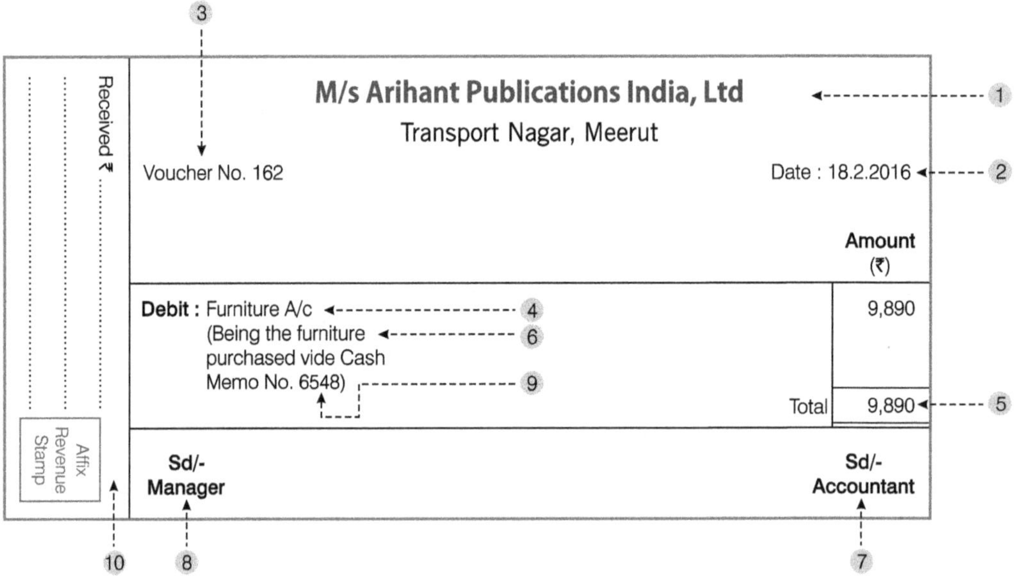

Contents

1. Name and address of the organisation
2. Date of preparing voucher
3. Accounting voucher number
4. Title of the account debited
5. Net amount of transaction
6. Narration (*i.e.*, a brief description of the transaction)
7. Signature of the person preparing it
8. Signature of the authorised signatory
9. Supporting voucher number
10. A document in lieu of supporting voucher

- *If the supporting voucher is not available, then the receipt portion of the debit voucher is filled and is used as supporting voucher.*

ILLUSTRATION |1| The following transactions took place in M/s Vardhman Furniture Traders, Agra. Prepare the debit vouchers.

2016		Amt (₹)
Jan 8	Wages paid for the month of December, 2016 vide Wage Sheet No. 68	8,000
Jan 25	Paid cash to Radha & Sons account for purchase of 2 sewing machines vide Cash Memo No. 1,560	10,000

Sol. (*i*)

Received ₹ .... / Affix Revenue Stamp	**M/s Vardhman Furniture Traders** Agra Voucher No. 1	Date : 8.1.2016 Amount (₹)
	Debit : Wages A/c (Being wages paid for December, 2015 vide Wage Sheet No. 68)	8,000
		8,000
	Sd/ Manager	Sd/ Accountant

(*ii*)

Received ₹ .... / Affix Revenue Stamp	**M/s Vardhman Furniture Traders** Agra Voucher No. 2	Date : 25.1.2016 Amount (₹)
	Debit : Machinery A/c (Being the amount paid for 2 sewing machines purchased for cash vide Cash Memo No. 1,560)	10,000
		10,000
	Sd/ Manager	Sd/ Accountant

Credit Vouchers These are prepared to record the transactions involving cash receipts *i.e.*, when cash is received. *For example,* for cash receipt of income (say interest), for cash sales of goods, for cash sales of fixed assets, for cash sales of investments, for cash received from debtors, for taking loans and advances, for receipt of repayment of loans and advances already granted, for withdrawal of cash from the bank. *A format of credit voucher is shown below*

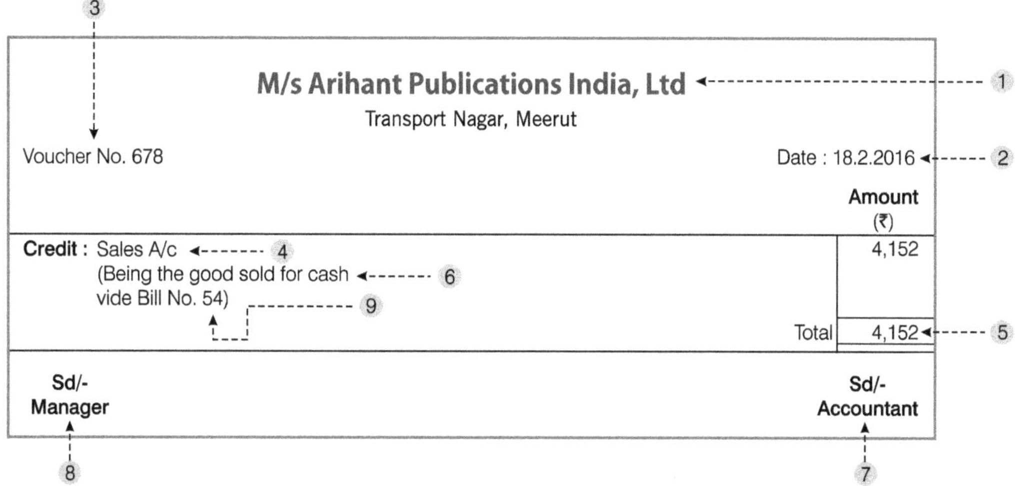

M/s Arihant Publications India, Ltd Transport Nagar, Meerut Voucher No. 678	Date : 18.2.2016 **Amount** (₹)
Credit : Sales A/c (Being the good sold for cash vide Bill No. 54)	4,152
Total	4,152
Sd/- **Manager**	**Sd/-** **Accountant**

Contents

1. Name and address of the organisation
2. Date of preparing the voucher
3. Accounting voucher number
4. Title of the account credited
5. Net amount of transaction
6. Narration (*i.e.*, a brief description of the transaction)
7. Signature of the person preparing it
8. Signature of the authorised signatory
9. Supporting voucher number

ILLUSTRATION |2| Prepare the credit vouchers from the following information, gathered from supporting vouchers of M/s Varun Garment Store, Lucknow.

2016		Amt (₹)
May 10	Commission received vide Cash Receipt No. 925	1,500
May 20	Sold two old sewing machines wide Cash Memo No. 5678	5,000

Sol. (*i*)

M/s Varun Garment Store Lucknow	
Voucher No. 1	Date : 10.5.2016 Amount (₹)
Credit : M/s Raj & Co. (Being the amount of commission received vide Cash Receipt No. 925)	1,500
	1,500
Sd/ Manager	Sd/ Accountant

(*ii*)

M/s Varun Garment Store Lucknow	
Voucher No. 2	Date : 20.5.2016 Amount (₹)
Credit : Sewing Machine A/c (Being two old sewing machines sold for cash vide Cash Memo No. 5678)	5,000
	5,000
Sd/ Manager	Sd/ Accountant

NON-CASH VOUCHERS OR TRANSFER VOUCHERS

The vouchers which are prepared for transactions not involving cash *i.e.*, non-cash transactions are known as non-cash vouchers or transfer vouchers.

For example, for credit sales of goods, for credit sales of fixed assets, for credit sales of investments, for return of goods sold, for return of goods purchased, for writing off depreciation, for writing off bad debts.

A format of non-cash voucher or transfer voucher is shown below

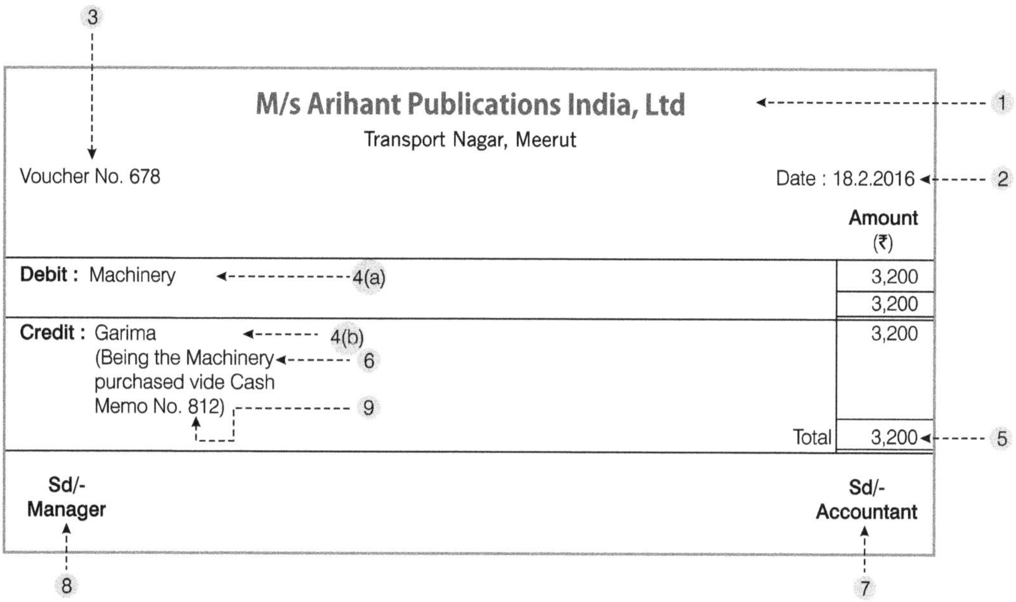

M/s Arihant Publications India, Ltd
Transport Nagar, Meerut

Voucher No. 678 (3)

Date : 18.2.2016 (2)

	Amount (₹)
Debit : Machinery (4(a))	3,200
	3,200
Credit : Garima (4(b)) (Being the Machinery (6) purchased vide Cash Memo No. 812) (9)	3,200
Total	3,200 (5)

Sd/- **Manager** (8)

Sd/- **Accountant** (7)

Contents

1. Name and address of the organisation
2. Date of preparing voucher
3. Accounting voucher number
4. (a) Title of account to be debited (b) Title of account to be credited
5. Net amount of transaction
6. Narration (*i.e.*, a brief description of the transaction)
7. Signature of the person preparing it
8. Signature of the authorised signatory
9. Supporting voucher number

ILLUSTRATION |3| Prepare the transfer vouchers from the source vouchers based on the following transactions.

2016		Amt (₹)
Aug 3	Purchased goods from M/s Raj & Sons vide Bill No. 990	8,600
Aug 10	Sold goods to M/s Vidya vide Bill No. 65432	6,000

Sol. (*i*)

Firm's Name

Voucher No.....

Date : 3.8.2016

		Amount (₹)
Debit:	Purchases A/c	8,600
		8,600
Credit:	M/s Raj & Sons (Being the goods purchased from M/s Raj & Sons vide Bill No. 990)	8,600
		8,600

Sd/
Manager

Sd/
Accountant

(ii)

Firm's Name

Voucher No..... Date : 10.8.2016

		Amount (₹)
Debit:	M/s. Vidya	6,000
		6,000
Credit:	Sales A/c (Being the amount of credit sales vide Bill No. 65432 to M/s. Vidya)	6,000
		6,000

Sd/ Manager — Sd/ Accountant

ILLUSTRATION |4| Prepare the transfer voucher from the following supporting voucher.

Krishan Mohan & Sons
Meerut

Sale Bill No. 9999 Date : 13.4.2016
To
M/s Bihari Lal & Sons

Quantity	Particulars	Rate (₹)	Amount (₹)
20 Nos.	Chairs	200	4,000
10 Nos.	Tables	4,000	40,000
			44,000

Sd/ Manager — Sd/ Ram Ratan & Sons

Sol.

Krishan Mohan & Sons
Meerut

Voucher No. 1 Date : 13.4.2016

		Amount (₹)
Debit :	M/s Bihari Lal & Sons	44,000
		44,000
Credit :	Sales A/c (Being the amount of credit sales vide Bill No. 9999 to M/s Bihari Lal & Sons)	44,000
		44,000

Sd/ Manager — Sd/ Accountant

IMPORTANT SPECIMENS OF SOURCE DOCUMENTS

SPECIMEN OF A CASH MEMO

Cash Memo Tanishq Jewellers
225, M.G. Road, Mumbai

No. .. Date : 10th February, 2016

Quantity	Descriptions	Rate (₹)	Amount	
			₹	P
1	Silver Anklet	3,000	3,000	...
2	Gold Rings	15,000	30,000	...
			33,000	...
	(+) VAT @ 14%		4,620	...
			37,620	...
	No. 340 Debit Purchases Credit Cash			

Goods once sold will not be taken back For Tanishq Jewellers

SPECIMEN OF AN INVOICE OR A BILL

Heman Electric Suppliers Ltd.
222, Begum Bridge, Meerut Cantt, 250001

No. 3978 Date : 10th February, 2016

Vikram Enterprises
Lodhi Road, Delhi ....Dr

Quantity	Particulars	Rate (₹)	Amount	
			₹	P
1	Air Conditioner	30,000	30,000	...
2	Microwave	20,000	40,000	...
			70,000	...
	(+) VAT @ 14%		9,800	...
			79,800	...
	(+) Forwarding and Delivery Charges		1,000	...
	Total		80,800	...

Rupees Eighty Thousand Eight Hundred Only
E.&.O.E. Sales Manager

SPECIMEN OF A RECEIPT

Vardhman Computers & Peripherals
Abulane, Meerut

No. 15137 Date : 15.2.2016

Received with thanks from M/s Arihant Publications India Ltd, Meerut a sum of

Rupees Fifty Two Thousand Eight Hundred Seventy Four only in Cash/

Cheque No. 446546 dated 5.2.2016 drawn on State Bank of India, Baghpat Road, Meerut on

account of Invoice No. 54564 dated 3.2.2016

Note : Cheque are subject to realisation. **Authorised Signatory**

SPECIMEN OF A PAY-IN-SLIP

शाखा / Branch:..........................
दिनांक / Date:..........................
AXIS BANK
जमा के लिए / For the credit of SB / CA / CC / RD / TD
खाता संख्या Account No.
पैन सं. PAN No.
(₹ 50000 या अधिक नकद जमा करने पर / For Cash Deposit ₹ 50000 and above)
नाम / Name

	₹	P.
कुल / Total		

₹ (शब्दों में)
₹ (In words) ____________

जमाकर्ता के हस्ताक्षर Signature of the Depositor..................
बैंक अधिकारी के हस्ताक्षर Bank Official's Signature..................
Please See Overleaf For Conditions

जमा पर्ची / PAY-IN-SLIP

Please use separate slips for Local, Outstation Cheques and Cash
जमा के लिए / For the credit of SB / CA / CC / RD / TD
AXIS BANK
Account No.
शाखा / Branch: ....
PAN No.
दिनांक / Date
(₹ 50000 या अधिक नकद जमा करने पर / For Cash Deposit ₹ 50000 and above)
नाम / NAME ....
फोन नंबर / Mobile / Tel No.

चेक का विवरण / Details Of Cheques			नकद जमा / Cash Deposit		₹	P
बैंक / Bank	शाखा / Branch	चेक सं. / Cheque No.	मूल्यवर्ग / Deno.	संख्या / Pieces		
			1000 x			
			500 x			
			100 x			
			50 x			
			20 x			
			10 x			
			5 x			
			x			
₹ (शब्दों में) .... ₹ (In Words)			कुल / Total			

जमाकर्ता के हस्ताक्षर / Signature of the Depositor
(FOR OFFICE USE) Tran. ID No. .... Entered Verified

SPECIMEN OF A CHEQUE

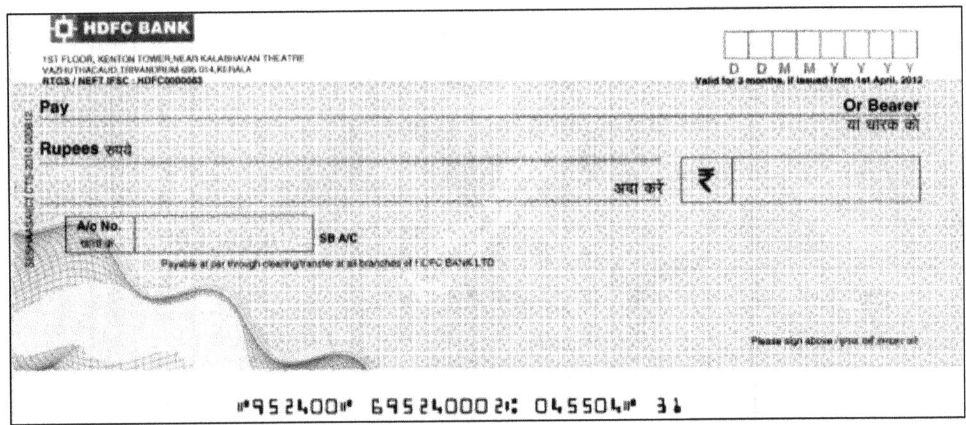
HDFC BANK
1ST FLOOR, KENTON TOWER, NEAR KALABHAVAN THEATRE
VAZHUTHACAUD, TRIVANDRUM 695 014, KERALA
RTGS / NEFT IFSC : HDFC0000063
D D M M Y Y Y Y
Valid for 3 months, if issued from 1st April, 2012
Pay Or Bearer
या धारक को
Rupees रुपये
अदा करें ₹
A/c No. खाता क्र. SB A/C
Payable at par through clearing/transfer at all branches of HDFC BANK LTD
Please sign above
⑈952400⑈ 695240002⑆ 045504⑈ 31

SPECIMEN OF A DEBIT NOTE

M/s Arihant Publications (India) Ltd
Transport Nagar,
Meerut

No. : 5456

DEBIT NOTE

21st February, 2016

Against : **M/s Book Mart, New Delhi**
Goods returned as per delivery
Challan No. 387
Rupees Six Thousand Two Hundred Thirty Five Only

₹ 6,235
TR Mani
Manager

SPECIMEN OF A CREDIT NOTE

M/s Arihant Publications (India) Ltd
Transport Nagar,
Meerut

No. : 879

CREDIT NOTE

22nd February, 2016

To
M/s Unique Books, Chandigarh
Goods received as per delivery challan
No. 4655 dated 22.2.2016 valued
at Rupees Eighteen Thousand Six Hundred Seventy Only

₹ 18,670
TR Mani
Manager

NUMERICAL Questions for Practice

1 The following transactions took place in M/s Starbucks Readymade Clothes Shop. Prepare the debit vouchers.

2016		Amt (₹)
Sep 1	Bought readymade clothes for cash vide Cash Memo No. 886	11,000
Sep 10	Wages paid for the month of December 2016 vide Wage Sheet No. 57	10,000
Sep 20	Paid for conveyance	100

2 Prepare the credit vouchers from the source vouchers of M/s Raghav Jain & Company based on the following transactions.

2016		Amt (₹)
Apr 10	Sold old furniture for cash vide Cash Receipt No. 422	2,700
Apr 20	Received cash from M/s Raj & Company on account vide Cash Receipt No. 555	8,000
Apr 25	Sold goods for cash vide Cash Memo No. 80	36,000
Apr 30	Withdrawn cash from bank for office use vide Cheque No. 15698	8,500

3 Prepare the transfer voucher from the source voucher based on the following transaction.

2016		Amt (₹)
Sep 8	Sold goods to M/s Radha Mohan vide Bill No. 45678	15,920
Sep 11	Purchased goods from M/s Kartik & Sons vide Bill No. 119	14,100

4 The following transactions took place in M/s Vardhman Computers. Prepare the accounting vouchers .

2016		Amt (₹)
Mar 1	Bought Computer Mouse (4 Nos.) vide Cash Memo No. 777	12,000
Mar 8	Wages paid for the month of December, 2015 vide Wage Sheet No. 67	20,000
Mar 12	Purchased two Desktop Computers from M/s Computech for cash vide Cash Memo No. 190	65,000
Mar 25	Paid cash to Rajeev & Sons vide Receipt No. 104 for repairs.	2,000
Mar 28	Paid cartage	400
Mar 30	Cash withdrawn from bank	20,000

5 Prepare the accounting vouchers for the following transactions.

2016	
July 1	Started business with cash ₹ 40,000
July 1	Purchased furniture for ₹ 2,000 vide Cash Memo No. 410
July 5	Opened a bank account in AXIS Bank with ₹ 12,000
July 10	Purchased garments on credit from M/s Rajasthan Store for ₹ 2,000 vide Bill No. 390
July 12	Sold two shirts to Vishwajeet on credit ₹ 1,000 vide Bill No. 2
July 15	Sold shirts for cash ₹ 1,400 vide Cash Memo No. 2
July 20	Withdrew ₹ 4,000 from bank for office use by Cheque No. 64421
July 27	Withdrew ₹ 1,000 for personal use by Cheque No. 72501

|TOPIC 2|
Accounting Equation

A mathematical expression, which shows that the **assets** and **liabilities** of a firm are equal is known as accounting equation. An accounting equation is based on **dual aspect concept** which states that every transaction has two aspects. This equation signifies that the assets of a business are always equal to the total of its liabilities and capital (owner's equity). Accounting equation may be expressed as

$$\boxed{\text{Assets} = \text{Capital} + \text{Liabilities}}$$

The above equation can also be presented in the following forms

$$\text{Capital} = \text{Assets} - \text{Liabilities}$$

or

$$\text{Liabilities} = \text{Assets} - \text{Capital}$$

Accounting equation is also known as **balance sheet equation**, as it depicts the fundamental relationship among the components of balance sheet. An accounting equation always holds true with every change that occurs due to a transaction entered into due to the reason that it is based on the dual aspect concept of accounting.

A transaction may affect either both sides of the equation by the same amount or one side of the equation only, by both increasing or decreasing it by equal amounts.

PRACTICAL STEPS INVOLVED IN DEVELOPING AN ACCOUNTING EQUATION

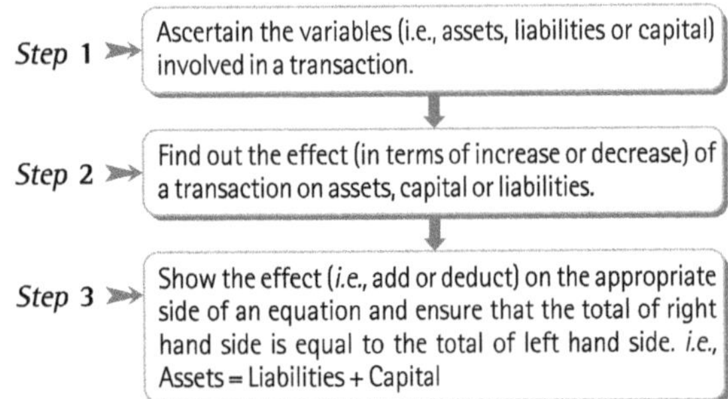

Step 1
Ascertain the variables (i.e., assets, liabilities or capital) involved in a transaction.
Step 2
Find out the effect (in terms of increase or decrease) of a transaction on assets, capital or liabilities.
Step 3
Show the effect (i.e., add or deduct) on the appropriate side of an equation and ensure that the total of right hand side is equal to the total of left hand side. i.e., Assets = Liabilities + Capital

EFFECT OF VARIOUS TRANSACTIONS ON ACCOUNTING EQUATION

Commenced Business with Cash

For example, Rajeev started business with cash ₹ 50,000.

The transaction is affecting two accounts—**Capital** (As owner is bringing cash into the business, capital will increase by ₹ 50,000) and **Asset** (Cash will also increase by ₹ 50,000).

Step 1 (Variables Affected) ⟶ **Capital**; **Asset** [Cash]

Step 2 (Effect of Transaction) ⟶ **Capital** will increase by ₹ 50,000; **Asset** [Cash] will increase by ₹ 50,000

Step 3 (Accounting Equation) ⟶

Assets	=	**Liabilities**	+	**Capital**
50,000	=	0	+	50,000

Cash Withdrawn for Personal Use

For example, Withdrawn cash ₹ 2,000 for personal use. It involves two accounts—**Capital** (As drawings are made by the proprietor, it will reduce the capital by ₹ 2,000) and **Asset** (Cash will decrease by ₹ 2,000 due to drawings).

Step 1 (Variables Affected) ⟶ **Asset** [Cash]; **Capital**

Step 2 (Effect of Transaction) ⟶ **Asset** [Cash] will decrease by ₹ 2,000; **Capital** will decrease by ₹ 2,000

Step 3 (Accounting Equation) ⟶

Assets	=	**Liabilities**	+	**Capital**
(2,000)	=	0	+	(2,000)

- *In case, goods are withdrawn instead of cash, stock will reduce instead of cash.*

Purchased Goods/Fixed Assets for Cash

For example, Rahul purchased goods/furniture for cash ₹ 20,000. The transaction is affecting two accounts—**Asset** (Due to purchase, stock/furniture worth ₹ 20,000 will increase) and **Asset** (Cash will reduce by ₹ 20,000 due to purchase).

Step 1 (Variables Affected) ⟶ **Asset** [Cash]; **Asset** [Stock/Furniture]

Step 2 (Effect of Transaction) ⟶ **Asset** [Cash] will decrease by ₹ 20,000; **Asset** [Stock/Furniture] will increase by ₹ 20,000

Step 3 (Accounting Equation) ⟶

Assets	=	**Liabilities**	+	**Capital**
(20,000) + 20,000	=	0	+	0

Purchased Goods/Fixed Assets on Credit

For example, Ram purchased goods from Shyam on credit for ₹ 15,000.

The transaction is affecting two accounts – **Assets** (Due to purchase, stock/ fixed asset worth ₹ 15,000 will increase) and **Liabilities** (As goods/fixed asset are purchased on credit, creditors will increase by ₹ 15,000).

Step 1 (Variables Affected) ⟶ {
Asset [Stock/Fixed asset]
Liability [Creditors]

Step 2 (Effect of Transaction) ⟶ {
Asset [Stock] will increase by ₹ 15,000
Liability [Creditors] will increase by ₹ 15,000

Step 3 (Accounting Equation) ⟶ {
Assets = Liabilities + Capital
15,000 = 15,000 + 0

Depreciation on Fixed Assets

For example, Depreciation on machinery provided ₹ 10,000.

It involves two accounts–**Asset** (Value of machinery will reduce by ₹ 10,000 due to depreciation) and **Capital** (Capital will decrease due to expenses).

Step 1 (Variables Affected) ⟶ {
Asset [Machinery]
Capital

Step 2 (Effect of Transaction) ⟶ {
Asset [Machinery] will reduce by ₹ 10,000
Capital will decrease by ₹ 10,000

Step 3 (Accounting Equation) ⟶ {
Assets = Liabilities + Capital
(10,000) = 0 + (10,000)

Purchased Some Goods for Cash and Some on Credit

For example, B purchased goods, worth ₹ 2,000 on credit and ₹ 3,000 for cash.

The transaction is affecting three accounts—**Asset** (Due to purchases stock will increase by ₹ 5,000 **Liability** (As goods worth ₹ 2,000 are purchased on credit, creditors will increase by ₹ 2,000) **Asset** (Due to cash purchases of goods worth ₹ 3,000, cash will reduce by ₹ 3,000)

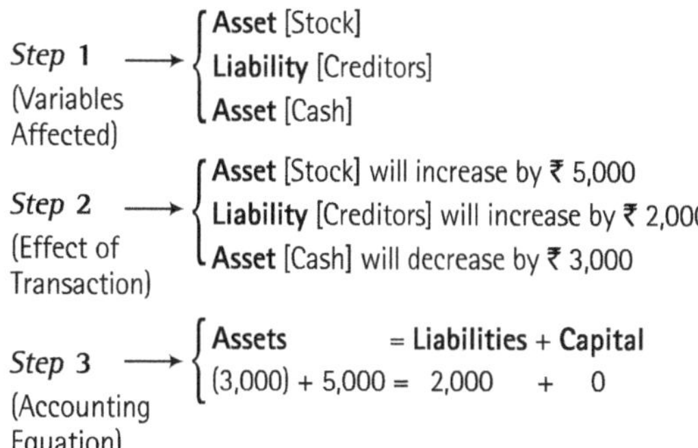
Step 1 (Variables Affected) ⟶ {
Asset [Stock]
Liability [Creditors]
Asset [Cash]

Step 2 (Effect of Transaction) ⟶ {
Asset [Stock] will increase by ₹ 5,000
Liability [Creditors] will increase by ₹ 2,000
Asset [Cash] will decrease by ₹ 3,000

Step 3 (Accounting Equation) ⟶ {
Assets = Liabilities + Capital
(3,000) + 5,000 = 2,000 + 0

Sold Goods for Cash

For example, Ajay sold goods costing ₹ 12,000 for cash to Brijesh.

The transaction is affecting two accounts–**Asset** (Sale of goods to Ajay will decrease the stock by ₹ 12,000) and **Asset** (Sale of goods for cash will increase the cash by ₹ 12,000).

Step 1 (Variables Affected) ⟶ {
Asset [Cash]
Asset [Stock]

Step 2 (Effect of Transaction) ⟶ {
Asset [Cash] will increase by ₹ 12,000
Asset [Stock] will decrease by ₹ 12,000

Step 3 (Accounting Equation) ⟶ {
Assets = Liabilities + Capital
12,000 + (12,000) = 0 + 0

- *In case, goods are sold on credit, debtors will increase, instead of cash, rest will remain the same.*

Sold Goods for Cash at a Profit

For example, Sold goods costing ₹ 2,500 on cash for ₹ 4,000.

It involves three accounts – **Asset** (Stock will decrease by ₹ 2,500 due to sale of goods), **Asset** (Cash will increase by ₹ 4,000 due to cash sales) and **Capital** (Goods costing ₹ 2,500 were sold for ₹ 4,000 so, profit of ₹ 1,500 (4,000 – 2,500) will increase the capital).

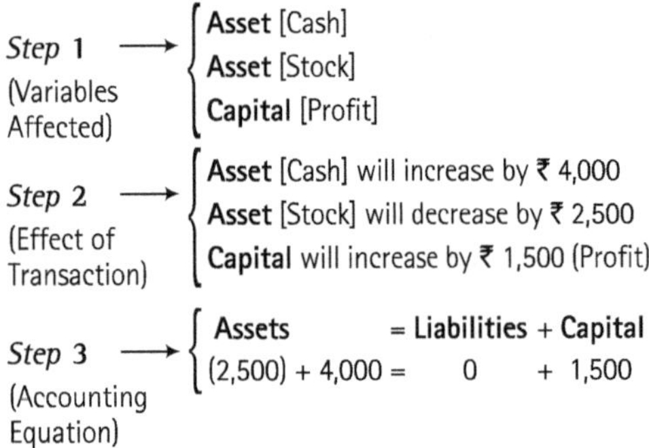
Step 1 (Variables Affected)
Asset [Cash]
Asset [Stock]
Capital [Profit]
Step 2 (Effect of Transaction)
Asset [Cash] will increase by ₹ 4,000
Asset [Stock] will decrease by ₹ 2,500
Capital will increase by ₹ 1,500 (Profit)
Step 3 (Accounting Equation)
Assets = Liabilities + Capital
(2,500) + 4,000 = 0 + 1,500

- *In case, goods are sold at a loss instead of profit, capital will decrease with the amount of loss.*
- *In case, goods are sold on credit, debtors will increase instead of cash.*

Sold Some Goods for Cash and Some on Credit

For example, Sold goods, worth ₹ 1,000 on credit and ₹ 2,000 for cash.

The transaction is affecting three accounts–**Assets** (Due to sale, stock will reduce by ₹ 3,000), **Asset** (Due to credit sales of ₹ 1,000 debtors will increase by ₹ 1,000), **Asset** (Due to cash sales worth ₹ 2,000, cash will increase by ₹ 2,000)

Step 1 → (Variables Affected)
- **Asset** [Cash]
- **Asset** [Stock]
- **Asset** [Debtors]

Step 2 → (Effect of Transaction)
- **Asset** [Cash] will increase by ₹ 2,000
- **Asset** [Stock] will decrease by ₹ 3,000
- **Asset** [Debtors] will increase by ₹ 1,000

Step 3 → (Accounting Equation)

Assets	= **Liabilities** + **Capital**
2,000 + (3,000) + 1,000 =	0 + 0

Return of Goods by a Customer

For example, Vijay received return of goods from a customer to whom goods costing ₹ 5,000 were sold for ₹ 6,250.

It involves three accounts – **Asset** (Stock will increase by ₹ 5,000 due to sales return), **Asset** (Debtors will decrease by ₹ 6,250) and **Capital** (Earlier profit arising from sale of goods *i.e.*, ₹ 1,250 (6,250 – 5,000) will no more exist, due to sales return, so capital will decrease by ₹ 1,250).

Step 1 → (Variables Affected)
- **Asset** [Stock]
- **Asset** [Debtors]
- **Capital**

Step 2 → (Effect of Transaction)
- **Asset** [Stock] will increase by ₹ 5,000
- **Asset** [Debtors] will decrease by ₹ 6,250
- **Capital** will decrease by ₹ 1,250

Step 3 → (Accounting Equation)

Assets	= **Liabilities** + **Capital**
5,000 + (6,250) =	0 + (1,250)

Return of Goods to a Supplier

For example, Ashwani returned goods costing ₹ 5,000 to supplier of goods.

It involves two accounts—**Asset** (Stock will reduce by ₹ 5,000 due to purchase return) and **Liabilities** (Creditors will decrease by ₹ 5,000).

Step 1 → (Variables Affected)
- **Asset** [Stock]
- **Liability** [Creditors]

Step 2 → (Effect of Transaction)
- **Asset** [Stock] will decrease by ₹ 5,000
- **Liability** [Creditors] will decrease by ₹ 5,000

Step 3 → (Accounting Equation)

Assets	= **Liabilities**	+ **Capital**
(5,000) =	(5,000)	+ 0

Goods Destroyed by Fire

For example, Goods worth ₹ 5,000 were destroyed by fire.

It involves two accounts–**Asset** (Stock will reduce by ₹ 5,000) and **Capital** (Capital will decrease by ₹ 5,000 due to loss).

Step 1 → (Variables Affected)
- **Capital**
- **Asset** [Stock]

Step 2 → (Effect of Transaction)
- **Capital** will decrease by ₹ 5,000
- **Asset** [Stock] will decrease by ₹ 5,000

Step 3 → (Accounting Equation)

Assets =	**Liabilities**	+ **Capital**
(5,000) =	0	+ (5,000)

Payment Received from a Customer to Whom Cash Discount was Allowed

For example, Gagan received cash from a customer ₹ 19,800 and allowed him discount ₹ 200.

It involves three accounts – **Asset** (Cash will increase by ₹ 19,800 due to the amount received from a customer), **Asset** (Debtors will decrease by ₹ 20,000) and **Capital** (Discount allowed 200 = 20,000 – 19,800) to the customer will decrease the capital).

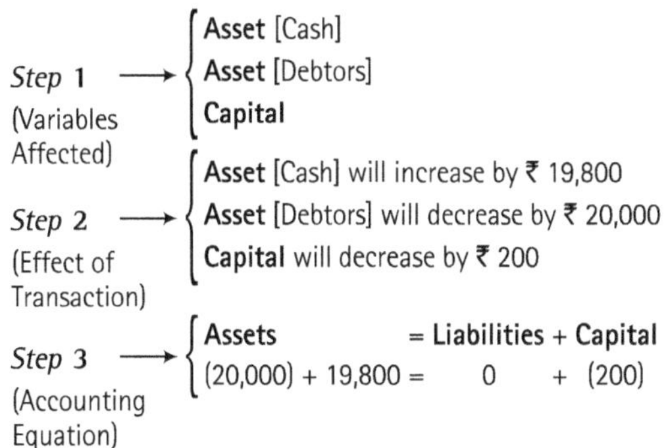

Payment Made to a Supplier who Allowed Cash Discount

For example, Creditors of ₹ 1,000 accepted ₹ 900 and allowed discount of ₹ 100.

It involves three accounts – **Asset** (Cash will decrease by ₹ 900 due to payment to creditors), **Liabilities** (Creditors will decrease by ₹ 1,000) and **Capital** (Capital will increase by (100 = 1,000 – 900) due to discount received on payment to creditor).

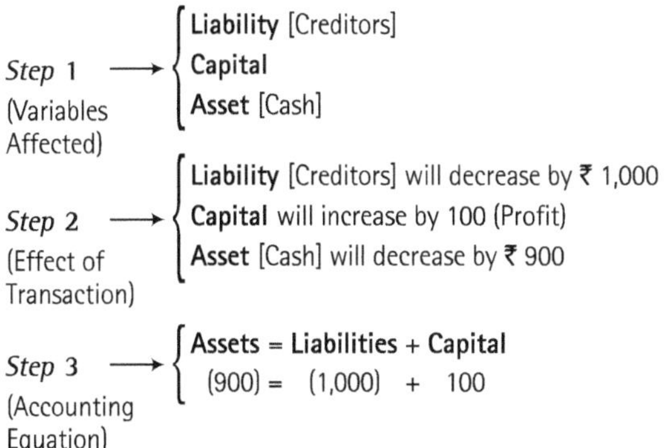

Loan Taken

For example, Ram borrowed ₹ 5,000 from Shyam.

It involves two accounts – **Asset** (Cash will increase by ₹ 5,000 due to borrowings) and **Liability** (Due to amount payable to Shyam, liability will increase by ₹ 5,000).

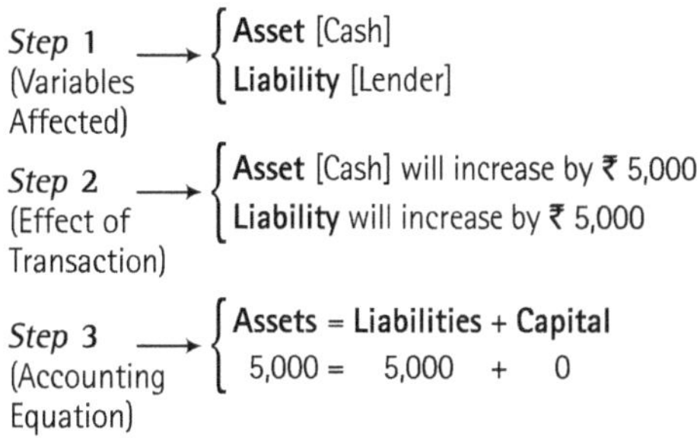

Repayment of Loan

For example, Daksh repaid loan of ₹ 10,000 alongwith interest of ₹ 100.

It involves three accounts – **Asset** (Cash will reduce by ₹10,100 due to repayment of loan), **Liability** (Loan will reduce by ₹ 10,000) and **Capital** (Payment of interest will reduce the capital).

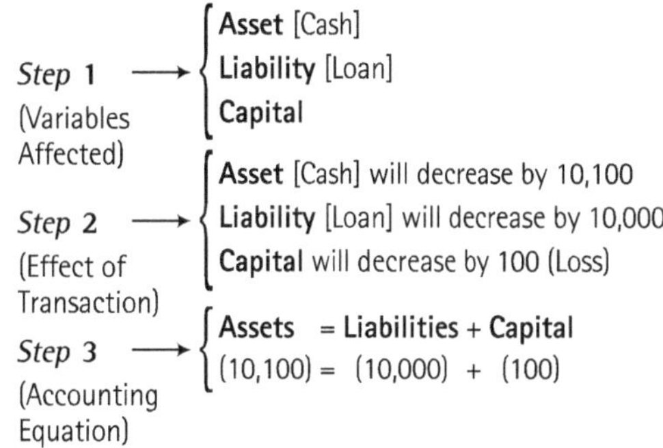

- *Profit are added to capital e.g., discount received, interest received and margin on sales, etc and losses are deducted from capital e.g., discount allowed, interest paid, bad debts, depreciation, etc.*

Expenses Paid

For example, Rent paid ₹ 2,000.

It involves two accounts—**Asset** (Cash will decrease by ₹ 2,000 on payment of rent) and **Capital** (Payment of rent in cash will reduce the capital).

Step 1 (Variables Affected) → **Asset** [Cash]
Capital

Step 2 (Effect of Transaction) → **Asset** [Cash] will decrease by ₹ 2,000
Capital will decrease by ₹ 2,000

Step 3 (Accounting Equation) → **Assets = Liabilities + Capital**
(2,000) = 0 + (2,000)

- Expenses tend to decrease the profit of a business. Profit is the part of capital. It is because of this that expenses are deducted from capital.

Outstanding Expenses (Expenses due but not Paid)

For example, Rent outstanding ₹ 1,000.

It involves two accounts—**Liability** (Outstanding rent will increase the liability) and **Capital** (Capital will decrease by ₹ 1,000 due to expenses).

Step 1 (Variables Affected) → **Liabilities** [Outstanding rent]; **Capital**

Step 2 (Effect of Transaction) → **Liabilities** [Outstanding rent] will increase by ₹ 1,000; **Capital** will decrease by ₹ 1,000

Step 3 (Accounting Equation) → **Assets** = **Liabilities** + **Capital**
0 = 1,000 + (1,000)

- *Outstanding rent is treated as a liability because these are expenses which are due to be paid, but are not yet paid.*

Prepaid Expenses (Paid in Advance)

For example, Prepaid Insurance ₹ 5,000.

It involves two accounts–**Asset** (Cash will decrease by ₹ 5,000 due to payment) and **Asset** (Prepaid insurance will increase).

Step 1 (Variables Affected) → **Assets** [Cash]; **Asset** [Prepaid insurance]

Step 2 (Effect of Transaction) → **Assets** [Cash] will decrease by ₹ 5,000; **Asset** [Prepaid insurance] will increase by ₹ 5,000

Step 3 (Accounting Equation) → **Assets** = **Liabilities** + **Capital**
5,000 + (5,000) = 0 + 0

- *Prepaid expense is treated as an asset because prepaid expense is expense paid in advance but which has not yet been incurred.*

Income Received

For example, Rent received ₹ 2,000.

It involves two accounts–**Asset** (Cash will increase due to the amount received for rent) and **Capital** (Amount received for rent will increase the capital).

Step 1 (Variables Affected) → **Asset** [Cash]; **Capital**

Step 2 (Effect of Transaction) → **Assets** [Cash] will increase by ₹ 2,000; **Capital** will increase by ₹ 2,000

Step 3 (Accounting Equation) → **Assets** = **Liabilities** + **Capital**
2,000 = 0 + 2,000

Accrued Income (Income due but not Received)

For example, Interest accrued but not received ₹ 1,000

It involves two accounts—**Asset** (Accrued income will increase) and **Capital** (Capital will increase due to increase in income).

Step 1 (Variables Affected) → **Asset** [Accrued Income]; **Capital**

Step 2 (Effect of Transaction) → **Asset** [Accrued Income] will increase by ₹ 1,000; **Capital** will increase by ₹ 1,000

Step 3 (Accounting Equation) → **Assets** = **Liabilities** + **Capital**
1,000 = 0 + 1,000

Income Received in Advance

For example, Commission received in advance ₹ 1,000.

It involves two accounts–**Asset** (Cash will increase by ₹ 1,000 due to commission received) and **Liability** (Income received in advance will increase the liability).

Step 1 (Variables Affected) → **Assets** [Cash]; **Liability** [Income received in advance]

Step 2 (Effect of Transaction) → **Assets** will increase by ₹ 1,000; **Liability** will increase by ₹ 1,000

Step 3 (Accounting Equation) → **Assets** = **Liabilities** + **Capital**
1,000 = 1,000 + 0

Interest on Drawings

For example, Interest on drawings charged ₹ 250.

It involves two accounts—**Capital** (Capital will decrease by ₹ 250) and **Capital** (Capital will increase by ₹ 250)

Step 1 (Variables Affected) → { **Capital** / **Capital** }

Step 2 (Effect of Transaction) → { **Capital** will increase by ₹ 250 / **Capital** will decrease by ₹ 250 }

Step 3 (Accounting Equation) → { **Assets** = **Liabilities** + **Capital** / 0 = 0 + 250 + (250) }

- *Interest on drawings is an income for the firm and is an expense for the proprietor.*

Interest on Capital

For example, Interest on capital ₹ 10,000.

It involves two accounts–**Capital** (Capital will increase by ₹ 10,000) and **Capital** (Capital will decrease by ₹ 10,000).

Step 1 (Variables Affected) → { **Capital** / **Capital** }

Step 2 (Effect of Transaction) → { **Capital** will increase by ₹ 10,000 / **Capital** will decrease by ₹ 10,000 }

Step 3 (Accounting Equation) → { **Assets** = **Liabilities** + **Capital** / 0 = 0 + 10,000 + (10,000) }

- *Interest on capital is an expense for the firm and is an income for the proprietor.*

Bad Debts on Insolvency of a Debtor

For example, Raj who owed us ₹ 1,000 became insolvent.

It involves two accounts–**Debtors** (Debtors will decrease due to non-payment) and **Capital** (Capital will decrease due to loss).

Step 1 (Variables Affected) → { **Assets** [Debtors] / **Capital** }

Step 2 (Effect of Transaction) → { **Asset** [Debtors] will decrease by ₹ 1,000 / **Capital** will decrease by ₹ 1,000 }

Step 3 (Accounting Equation) → { **Assets** = **Liabilities** + **Capital** / (1,000) = 0 + (1,000) }

ILLUSTRATION |5| The capital of a business is ₹ 4,00,000 and outside liabilities are ₹ 3,00,000. Calculate the total assets of the business.

Sol. Assets = Capital + Outside Liabilities

= 4,00,000 + 3,00,000 = ₹ 7,00,000

ILLUSTRATION |6| If total assets of the business are ₹ 4,50,000 and outside liabilities are ₹ 2,00,000, calculate owner's equity.

Sol. Assets = Owner's Equity + Liabilities

4,50,000 = Owner's Equity + 2,00,000

Owner's Equity = ₹ 2,50,000.

ILLUSTRATION |7| A commenced his cloth business on 1st April, 2015 with a capital of ₹ 60,000. On 31st March, 2016, his assets were ₹ 1,00,000 and liabilities were ₹ 20,000. Find out his closing capital and profits earned during the year.

Sol. Total Assets = Capital + Liabilities

1,00,000 = Capital + 20,000

Closing Capital = 1,00,000 – 20,000 = 80,000

Profit = Closing Capital – Opening Capital

= 80,000 – 60,000 = ₹ 20,000.

ILLUSTRATION |8| On 31st March, 2016, the total assets and external liabilities were ₹ 2,00,000 and ₹ 6,000 respectively. During the year, the proprietor had introduced additional capital of ₹ 20,000 and had withdrawn ₹ 12,000 for personal use. He made a profit of ₹ 20,000 during the year. Calculate the capital as on 1st April, 2015.

Sol. Closing Capital = Closing Assets – Closing External Liabilities

= 2,00,000 – 6,000 = ₹ 1,94,000

Opening Capital = Closing Capital + Drawings – Additional Capital – Profits

= 1,94,000 + 12,000 – 20,000 – 20,000

= ₹ 1,66,000

ILLUSTRATION |9| If total assets of a business are ₹ 2,60,000 and capital is ₹ 1,60,000, calculate the outside liabilities.

Sol. Outside Liabilities = Total Assets – Capital

= 2,60,000 – 1,60,000

= ₹ 1,00,000

ILLUSTRATION |10| From the following information, calculate the total assets of the business.

Capital ₹ 8,00,000, creditors ₹ 6,00,000, revenue earned during the period ₹ 15,00,000, expenses incurred during the period ₹ 4,00,000 and value of unsold stock ₹ 4,00,000.

Sol. Total Assets = Creditors + Capital + Profit
= 6,00,000 + 8,00,000 + 11,00,000 (15,00,000 − 4,00,000)
= ₹ 25,00,000 (including ₹ 4,00,000 closing stock).

ILLUSTRATION |11| Calculate the total equity if

(i) Owner's equity in the beginning is ₹ 1,20,000.
(ii) Equity of creditors at the end is ₹ 1,00,000.
(iii) Revenue during the period is ₹ 1,40,000.
(iv) Expenses during the same period are ₹ 1,30,000.

Also calculate the amount of owner's equity at the end.

Sol. Total Equity = Owner's Equity + Creditors' Equity
= (Opening Owner's Equity + Revenue − Expenses) + Creditors' Equity
= (1,20,000 + 1,40,000 − 1,30,000) + 1,00,000
= 1,30,000 + 1,00,000 = 2,30,000
Owner's equity at the end = ₹ 2,30,000

ILLUSTRATION |12| Monika has the following assets and liabilities as on 31st March, 2016. Ascertain her capital.

Cash ₹ 50,000, bank ₹ 95,000, debtors ₹ 36,000, creditors ₹ 44,000, plant and machinery ₹1,60,000, building ₹ 4,00,000, furniture ₹48,000, bills receivable ₹ 1,13,000, bills payable ₹ 47,000.

Sol. Assets = Liabilities + Capital
Capital = Assets − Liabilities
Capital = (Cash + Bank + Debtors + Plant and Machinery + Building + Furniture + Bills Receivable) − (Creditors + Bills Payable)
= (50,000 + 95,000 + 36,000 + 1,60,000 + 4,00,000 + 48,000 +1,13,000) − (44,000 + 47,000)
= 9,02,000 − 91,000 = ₹ 8,11,000.

Monika's capital = ₹ 8,11,000

ILLUSTRATION |13| Raja started a business on 1st April, 2015 with a capital of ₹ 1,00,000 and a loan of ₹ 50,000 borrowed from Ram. During 2015-16, he had introduced additional capital of ₹ 50,000 and had withdrawn ₹ 30,000 for personal use. On 31st March, 2016, his assets were ₹ 3,00,000. Find out his capital as on 31st March, 2016 and profit made or loss incurred during the year 2015-16.

Sol. Closing Capital = Closing Assets − Closing Liabilities (*i.e.*, Ram's Loan)
= 3,00,000 − 50,000
= ₹ 2,50,000

Profit = Closing Capital + Drawings − Additional Capital − Opening Capital
= 2,50,000 + 30,000 − 50,000 − 1,00,000
= ₹ 1,30,000.

ILLUSTRATION |14| Calculate the amount of total assets and capital as on 31st December, 2016 in each of the following cases :

(a) Z started a business on 1st April, 2015 with a capital ₹ 20,000 and a loan of ₹ 10,000 borrowed from Y. During the year, he made a profit of ₹ 10,000.

(b) If in the preceeding case the proprietor had introduced additional capital of ₹ 10,000 and had withdrawn ₹ 6,000 for personal use.

(c) If in the preceeding case, apart from loan, Z owes ₹ 5,000 to a supplier of goods on 31st March, 2016.

Sol. (*a*) Closing Capital = Opening Capital + Additional Capital + Profit − Drawings
= 20,000 + 0 + 10,000 − 0 = ₹ 30,000

Closing Assets = Closing Capital + Closing Liabilities
= 30,000 + 10,000
= ₹ 40,000

(*b*) Closing Capital = Opening Capital + Additional − Capital + Profit − Drawings
= 20,000 + 10,000 + 10,000 − 6,000
= ₹ 34,000

Closing Assets = Closing Capital + Closing Liabilities
= 34,000 + 10,000 = ₹ 44,000

(*c*) Closing Capital = Opening Capital + Additional Capital + Profit − Drawings
= 20,000 + 10,000 + 10,000 − 6,000
= ₹ 34,000

Closing Assets = Closing Capital + Closing Liabilities
= 34,000 + 10,000 + 5,000
= ₹ 49,000

ILLUSTRATION |15| Calculate the amount of external equities as on 31st March, 2016 in each of the following alternatives cases

(a) On 31st, March, 2016, total assets and capital were ₹ 1,00,000 and ₹ 70,000 respectively.

(b) On 1st April, 2015, A started a business with a capital of ₹ 20,000 and a loan of ₹ 10,000 borrowed from a freind. During 2015-2016, he earned a profit of ₹ 10,000. On 31st March, 2016, the total assets were ₹ 1,00,000.

(c) On 1st April, 2015, Shyam started a business with a capital of ₹ 20,000 and a loan of ₹ 10,000 borrowed from a friend. During 2015-2016, he earned a profit of ₹ 10,000 introduced an additional capital of ₹ 12,000 and had withdrawn ₹ 6,000 for his personal use. On 31st March, 2016 the total assets were ₹ 10,000.

Sol. (*a*) External Equities = Assets − Capital = 1,00,000 − 70,000 = 30,000

(*b*) Closing Capital = Opening Capital + Additional Capital + Profit − Drawings

= 20,000 + 0 + 10,000 − 0 = ₹ 30,000

External Equities = Assets − Capital = 1,00,000 − 30,000 = ₹ 70,000

(*c*) Closing Capital = Opening Capital + Additional Capital + Profit − Drawings

= 20,000 + 12,000 + 10,000 − 6,000 = ₹ 36,000

External Equities = Assets − Capital = 1,00,000 − 36,000 = ₹ 64,000

ILLUSTRATION |16| Goods costing ₹ 20,000 have been sold for cash for ₹ 25,000. How will you show the transaction in the accounting equation?

Sol. Increase cash by ₹ 25,000, decrease stock by ₹ 20,000 and increase capital by ₹ 5,000 (profit)

ILLUSTRATION |17| Mohit has the following transactions, prepare accounting equation. **NCERT**

	Amt (₹)
(i) Business started with cash	1,75,000
(ii) Purchased goods from Rohit	50,000
(iii) Sold goods on credit to Manish (costing ₹ 17,500)	20,000
(iv) Purchased furniture for office use	10,000
(v) Cash paid to Rohit (Creditor) in full settlement	48,500
(vi) Cash received from Manish	20,000
(vii) Rent paid	1,000
(viii) Cash withdrew for personal use	3,000

Sol.

Accounting Equation

Transaction	Assets				=	Liabilities +	Capital
	Cash +	Stock +	Debtors +	Furniture	=	Creditors +	Capital
(i) Business started with cash	1,75,000 +	0 +	0 +	0	=	0 +	1,75,000
New equation	1,75,000 +	0 +	0 +	0	=	0 +	1,75,000
(ii) Purchased goods from Rohit	0 +	50,000 +	0 +	0	=	50,000 +	0
New equation	1,75,000 +	50,000 +	0 +	0	=	50,000 +	1,75,000
(iii) Sold goods on credit to Manish	0 +	(17,500) +	20,000 +	0	=	0 +	2,500
New equation	1,75,000 +	32,500 +	20,000 +	0	=	50,000 +	1,77,500
(iv) Purchased furniture for office use	(10,000) +	0 +	0 +	10,000	=	0 +	0
New equation	1,65,000 +	32,500 +	20,000 +	10,000	=	50,000 +	1,77,500
(v) Cash paid to Rohit in full settlement	(48,500) +	0 +	0 +	0	=	(50,000) +	1,500
New equation	1,16,500 +	32,500 +	20,000 +	10,000	=	0 +	1,79,000
(vi) Cash received from Manish	20,000 +	0 +	(20,000) +	0	=	0 +	0
New equation	1,36,500 +	32,500 +	0 +	10,000	=	0 +	1,79,000
(vii) Rent paid	(1,000) +	0 +	0 +	0	=	0 +	(1,000)
New equation	1,35,500 +	32,500 +	0 +	10,000	=	0 +	1,78,000
(viii) Cash withdrew for personal use	(3,000) +	0 +	0 +	0	=	0 +	(3,000)
Final equation	1,32,500 +	32,500 +	0 +	10,000	=	0 +	1,75,000

ILLUSTRATION |18| Prove that the accounting equation is satisfied in all the following transactions of Sudhir.

(i) Started business with cash ₹ 1,00,000 and goods ₹ 40,000.
(ii) Bought goods on cash ₹ 30,000 and on credit for ₹ 20,000.
(iii) Goods costing ₹ 48,000 sold at a profit of $33\frac{1}{3}$% to Pranav. Half the payment received in cash.
(iv) Purchased furniture for office use ₹ 12,000 and for household use ₹ 8,000.
(v) Received cash from Pranav (Customer) ₹ 25,500 and allowed him a discount ₹ 500.
(vi) Creditors of ₹ 5,000 accepted ₹ 4,000 and allowed a discount of ₹ 1,000.

Sol.

Accounting Equation

Transaction	Assets							=	Liabilities	+	Capital
	Cash	+	Stock	+	Debtors	+	Furniture	=	Creditors	+	Capital
(i) Started business with cash ₹ 1,00,000 and goods ₹ 40,000.	1,00,000	+	40,000	+	0	+	0	=	0	+	1,40,000
New equation	1,00,000	+	40,000	+	0	+	0	=	0	+	1,40,000
(ii) Bought goods on cash ₹ 30,000 and on credit for ₹ 20,000.	(30,000)	+	50,000	+	0	+	0	=	20,000	+	0
New equation	70,000	+	90,000	+	0	+	0	=	20,000	+	1,40,000
(iii) Goods costing ₹ 48,000 sold at a profit of 33.33%. Half the payment received in cash. (W.N.)	32,000	+	(48,000)	+	32,000	+	0	=	0	+	16,000
New equation	1,02,000	+	42,000	+	32,000	+	0	=	20,000	+	1,56,000
(iv) Purchased furniture for office use ₹ 12,000 and for household use ₹ 8,000.	(20,000)	+	0	+	0	+	12,000	=	0	+	(8,000)
New equation	82,000	+	42,000	+	32,000	+	12,000	=	20,000	+	1,48,000
(v) Received cash from Pranav ₹ 25,500 and allowed him a discount of ₹ 500	25,500	+	0	+	(26,000)	+	0	=	0	+	(500)
New equation	1,07,500	+	42,000	+	6,000	+	12,000	=	20,000	+	1,47,500
(vi) Creditors of ₹ 5,000 accepted ₹ 4,000 and allowed discount of ₹ 1,000	(4,000)	+	0	+	0	+	0	=	(5,000)	+	1,000
Final equation	1,03,500	+	42,000	+	6,000	+	12,000	=	15,000	+	1,48,500

Working Note

Cost price of goods = ₹ 48,000, Profit on sale of goods = $33\frac{1}{3}\% = 48,000 \times 33\frac{1}{3}\%$ = ₹ 16,000, Sale price = 48,000 + 16,000 = ₹ 64,000

Payment received in cash = $64,000 \times \frac{1}{2}$ = ₹ 32,000

ILLUSTRATION |19| Show the effect of the following transactions on assets, liabilities and capital through accounting equation.

	Amt (₹)
(i) Started business with cash	1,20,000
(ii) Rent received	10,000
(iii) Invested in shares	50,000
(iv) Received dividend	5,000
(v) Purchased goods on credit from Ragani	35,000
(vi) Paid cash for household expenses	7,000
(vii) Sold goods for cash (costing ₹ 10,000)	14,000
(viii) Cash paid to Ragani	35,000
(ix) Deposited into bank	20,000
(x) Goods destroyed by fire	1,000
(xi) Returned goods to a supplier of goods	2,000
(xii) Received return of goods from a customer Raghav to whom goods costing ₹ 2,000 were sold for	4,560

Sol.

Accounting Equation

Transaction	Assets					=	Liabilities	+	Capital
	Cash +	Stock +	Investment +	Bank +	Debtors	=	Creditors	+	Capital
(i) Started business with cash	1,20,000 +	0 +	0 +	0 +	0	=	0	+	1,20,000
New equation	1,20,000 +	0 +	0 +	0 +	0	=	0	+	1,20,000
(ii) Rent received	10,000 +	0 +	0 +	0 +	0	=	0	+	10,000
New equation	1,30,000 +	0 +	0 +	0 +	0	=	0	+	1,30,000
(iii) Invested in shares	(50,000) +	0 +	50,000 +	0 +	0	=	0	+	0
New equation	80,000 +	0 +	50,000 +	0 +	0	=	0	+	1,30,000
(iv) Received dividend	5,000 +	0 +	0 +	0 +	0	=	0	+	5,000
New equation	85,000 +	0 +	50,000 +	0 +	0	=	0	+	1,35,000
(v) Purchased goods on credit from Ragani	0 +	35,000 +	0 +	0 +	0	=	35,000	+	0
New equation	85,000 +	35,000 +	50,000 +	0 +	0	=	35,000	+	1,35,000
(vi) Paid cash for household expenses	(7,000) +	0 +	0 +	0 +	0	=	0	+	(7,000)
New equation	78,000 +	35,000 +	50,000 +	0 +	0	=	35,000	+	1,28,000
(vii) Sold goods for cash	14,000 +	(10,000) +	0 +	0 +	0	=	0	+	4,000
New equation	92,000 +	25,000 +	50,000 +	0 +	0	=	35,000	+	1,32,000
(viii) Cash paid to Ragani	(35,000) +	0 +	0 +	0 +	0	=	(35,000)	+	0
New equation	57,000 +	25,000 +	50,000 +	0 +	0	=	0	+	1,32,000
(ix) Deposited into bank	(20,000) +	0 +	0 +	20,000 +	0	=	0	+	0
New equation	37,000 +	25,000 +	50,000 +	20,000 +	0	=	0	+	1,32,000
(x) Goods destroyed by fire	0 +	(1,000) +	0 +	0 +	0	=	0	+	(1,000)
New equation	37,000 +	24,000 +	50,000 +	20,000 +	0	=	0	+	1,31,000
(xi) Returned goods to a supplier of goods	0 +	(2,000) +	0 +	0 +	0	=	(2000)	+	0
New equation	37,000 +	22,000 +	50,000 +	20,000 +	0	=	(2000)	+	1,31,000
(xii) Received return of goods from Raghav	0 +	2,000 +	0 +	0 +	(4,560)	=	(2000)	+	(2,560)
Final equation	37,000 +	24,000 +	50,000 +	20,000 +	(4,560)	=	(2000)	+	1,28,440

ILLUSTRATION |20| Prepare accounting equation from the following

(i) Started business with cash ₹ 1,00,000 and machinery ₹ 80,000.

(ii) Purchased goods for cash ₹ 20,000 and on credit ₹ 30,000.

(iii) Sold goods for cash costing ₹ 10,000 and on credit costing ₹ 15,000 both at a profit of 20%.

(iv) Cash withdrawn for personal use ₹ 10,000.

(v) Accrued interest ₹ 2,000.

(vi) Rent received in advance ₹ 1,000.

(vii) Interest on capital @ 10% (only on cash introduced as capital).

(viii) Interest on drawings charged @ 5% (Total drawings till now is ₹ 10,000).

(ix) Depreciation on machinery provided @ 10%.

(x) Rent paid in cash ₹ 1,000 and rent outstanding ₹ 500.

(xi) Prepaid insurance ₹ 1,000.

(xii) Bad debts written off ₹ 1,000.

Sol.

Accounting Equation

Transaction	Assets						=	Liabilities		+	Capital
	Cash +	Stock +	Machinery +	Debtors +	Prepaid Expenses +	Accrued Income	=	Creditors +	Outstanding Expenses +	Unearned Income +	Capital
(i) Started business with cash ₹ 1,00,000 and machinery ₹ 80,000	1,00,000	0	80,000	0	0	0	=	0	0	0	1,80,000
New equation	1,00,000	0	80,000	0	0	0	=	0	0	0	1,80,000
(ii) Purchased goods for cash ₹ 20,000 and on credit ₹ 30,000	(20,000)	50,000	0	0	0	0	=	30,000	0	0	0
New equation	80,000	50,000	80,000	0	0	0	=	30,000	0	0	1,80,000
(iii) Sold goods for cash costing ₹ 10,000 and on credit costing ₹ 15,000 both at a profit of 20%	12,000	(25,000)	0	18,000	0	0	=	0	0	0	5,000
New equation	92,000	25,000	80,000	18,000	0	0	=	30,000	0	0	1,85,000
(iv) Cash withdrawn for personal use	(10,000)	0	0	0	0	0	=	0	0	0	(10,000)
New equation	82,000	25,000	80,000	18,000	0	0	=	30,000	0	0	1,75,000
(v) Accrued interest	0	0	0	0	0	2,000	=	0	0	0	2,000
New equation	82,000	25,000	80,000	18,000	0	2,000	=	30,000	0	0	1,77,000
(vi) Rent received in advance	1,000	0	0	0	0	0	=	0	0	1,000	0
New equation	83,000	25,000	80,000	18,000	0	2,000	=	30,000	0	1,000	1,77,000
(vii) Interest on capital $\left(1,00,000 \times \frac{10}{100}\right)$	0	0	0	0	0	0	=	0	0	0	10,000 + (10,000)
New equation	83,000	25,000	80,000	18,000	0	2,000	=	30,000	0	1,000	1,77,000
(viii) Interest on drawings charged @ 5%	0	0	0	0	0	0	=	0	0	0	500 + (500)
New equation	83,000	25,000	80,000	18,000	0	2,000	=	30,000	0	1,000	1,77,000
(ix) Depreciation on machinery @ 10% $\left(80,000 \times \frac{10}{100}\right)$	0	0	(8,000)	0	0	0	=	0	0	0	(8,000)
New equation	83,000	25,000	72,000	18,000	0	2,000	=	30,000	0	1,000	1,69,000
(x) Rent paid in cash ₹ 1,000 and rent outstanding ₹ 500	(1,000)	0	0	0	0	0	=	0	500	0	(1,000) + (500)
New equation	82,000	25,000	72,000	18,000	0	2,000	=	30,000	500	1,000	1,67,500
(xi) Prepaid insurance	(1,000)	0	0	0	1,000	0	=	0	0	0	0
New equation	81,000	25,000	72,000	18,000	1,000	2,000	=	30,000	500	1,000	1,67,500
(xii) Bad debts written off ₹ 1,000	0	0	0	(1,000)	0	0	=	0	0	0	(1,000)
Final equation	81,000	25,000	72,000	17,000	1,000	2,000	=	30,000	500	1,000	1,66,500

Working Note

(*i*) Goods costing ₹ 10,000 sold at a profit of 20%.

Profit = $10{,}000 \times \frac{20}{100}$ = ₹ 2,000, sale price 10,000 + 2,000 = ₹12,000.

(*ii*) Goods costing ₹ 15,000 sold at a profit of 20%.

Profit = $15{,}000 \times \frac{20}{100}$ = ₹ 3,000, sale price 15,000 + 3,000 = ₹ 18,000.

(*iii*) Profit on sale = 2,000 + 3,000 = ₹5,000 is added to capital.

ILLUSTRATION |21| Show the effect of following transaction on the accounting equation **NCERT**

		Amt (₹)
(i)	Manoj started business with	
	(a) Cash	2,30,000
	(b) Goods	1,00,000
	(c) Building	2,00,000
(ii)	Purchased goods for cash	50,000
(iii)	Sold goods (costing ₹ 20,000)	35,000
(iv)	Purchased goods from Rahul	55,000
(v)	Sold goods to Varun (costing ₹ 52,000)	60,000
(vi)	Paid cash to Rahul in full settlement	53,000
(vii)	Salary paid by him	20,000
(viii)	Received cash from Varun in full settlement	59,000
(ix)	Rent outstanding	3,000
(x)	Prepaid insurance	2,000
(xi)	Commission received by him	13,000
(xii)	Amount withdrawn by him for personal use	20,000
(xiii)	Depreciation charged on building	10,000
(xiv)	Fresh capital invested	50,000
(xv)	Purchased goods from Rakhi	6,000
(xvi)	Rent received in advance	5,000

Sol.

Accounting Equation

Transaction	Assets					= Liabilities			+ Capital
	Cash +	Stock +	Building +	Debtors +	Prepaid Expenses =	Creditors +	Outstanding Expenses +	Unearned Income +	Capital
(i) Manoj started business with Cash, Goods and Building	2,30,000 +	1,00,000 +	2,00,000 +	0 +	0 =	0 +	0 +	0 +	5,30,000
New equation	2,30,000 +	1,00,000 +	2,00,000 +	0 +	0 =	0 +	0 +	0 +	5,30,000
(ii) Purchased goods for cash	(50,000) +	50,000 +	0 +	0 +	0 =	0 +	0 +	0 +	0
New equation	1,80,000 +	1,50,000 +	2,00,000 +	0 +	0 =	0 +	0 +	0 +	5,30,000
(iii) Sold goods (costing ₹ 20,000)	35,000 +	(20,000) +	0 +	0 +	0 =	0 +	0 +	0 +	15,000
New equation	2,15,000 +	1,30,000 +	2,00,000 +	0 +	0 =	0 +	0 +	0 +	5,45,000
(iv) Purchased goods from Rahul	0 +	55,000 +	0 +	0 +	0 =	55,000 +	0 +	0 +	0

Transaction	Assets					=	Liabilities			+ Capital
New equation	2,15,000 +	1,85,000 +	2,00,000 +	0 +	0	=	55,000 +	0 +	0 +	5,45,000
(v) Sold goods to Varun (costing ₹ 52,000)	0 +	(52,000) +	0 +	60,000 +	0	=	0 +	0 +	0 +	8,000
New equation	2,15,000 +	1,33,000 +	2,00,000 +	60,000 +	0	=	55,000 +	0 +	0 +	5,53,000
(vi) Paid cash to Rahul in full settlement	(53,000) +	0 +	0 +	0 +	0	=	(55,000) +	0 +	0 +	2,000
New equation	1,62,000 +	1,33,000 +	2,00,000 +	60,000 +	0	=	0 +	0 +	0 +	5,55,000
(vii) Salary paid by him	(20,000) +	0 +	0 +	0 +	0	=	0 +	0 +	0 +	(20,000)
New equation	1,42,000 +	1,33,000 +	2,00,000 +	60,000 +	0	=	0 +	0 +	0 +	5,35,000
(viii) Received cash from Varun in full settlement	59,000 +	0 +	0 +	(60,000) +	0	=	0 +	0 +	0 +	(1,000)
New equation	2,01,000 +	1,33,000 +	2,00,000 +	0 +	0	=	0 +	0 +	0 +	5,34,000
(ix) Rent outstanding	0 +	0 +	0 +	0 +	0	=	0 +	3,000 +	0 +	(3,000)
New equation	2,01,000 +	1,33,000 +	2,00,000 +	0 +	0	=	0 +	3,000 +	0 +	5,31,000
(x) Prepaid insurance	(2,000) +	0 +	0 +	0 +	2,000	=	0 +	0 +	0 +	0
New equation	1,99,000 +	1,33,000 +	2,00,000 +	0 +	2,000	=	0 +	3,000 +	0 +	5,31,000
(xi) Commission received by him	13,000 +	0 +	0 +	0 +	0	=	0 +	0 +	0 +	13,000
New equation	2,12,000 +	1,33,000 +	2,00,000 +	0 +	2,000	=	0 +	3,000 +	0 +	5,44,000
(xii) Amount withdrawn by him for personal use	(20,000) +	0 +	0 +	0 +	0	=	0 +	0 +	0 +	(20,000)
New equation	1,92,000 +	1,33,000 +	2,00,000 +	0 +	2,000	=	0 +	3,000 +	0 +	5,24,000
(xiii) Depreciation charged on building	0 +	0 +	(10,000) +	0 +	0	=	0 +	0 +	0 +	(10,000)
New equation	1,92,000 +	1,33,000 +	1,90,000 +	0 +	2,000	=	0 +	3,000 +	0 +	5,14,000
(xiv) Fresh capital invested	50,000 +	0 +	0 +	0 +	0	=	0 +	0 +	0 +	50,000
New equation	2,42,000 +	1,33,000 +	1,90,000 +	0 +	2,000	=	0 +	3,000 +	0 +	5,64,000
(xv) Purchased goods from Rakhi	0 +	6,000 +	0 +	0 +	0	=	6,000 +	0 +	0 +	0
New equation	2,42,000 +	1,39,000 +	1,90,000 +	0 +	2,000	=	6,000 +	3,000 +	0 +	5,64,000
(xvi) Rent received in advance	5,000 +	0 +	0 +	0 +	0	=	0 +	0 +	5,000 +	0
Final equation	2,47,000 +	1,39,000 +	1,90,000 +	0 +	2,000	=	6,000 +	3,000 +	5,000 +	5,64,000

NUMERICALS Questions for Practice

1 (a) Vansh started a business on 1 April, 2015 with a capital of ₹ 20,000 and a loan of ₹10,000 borrowed from Bharat. On 31st March, 2016 his assets were ₹ 60,000. Find out his capital as on 31st March, 2016 and profits made or losses incurred during the year 2015-2016.

(b) If in the above part (a) during 2015-16 the proprietor had introduced additional capital of ₹ 10,000 and had withdrawn ₹6,000 for personal purposes then find out the profit.

(c) If in the above part (a) on 31st, March, 2016 apart from loan, Vansh owes ₹ 5,000 to a suplier of goods, find out his capital as on 31.03.2016 and profit.

Ans (*a*) Closing Capital = ₹ 50,000; Profit = ₹ 30,000
(*b*) Profit = ₹ 26,000
(*c*) Closing Capital = ₹ 45,000; Profit = ₹ 25,000

2 Prove that accounting equation is satisfied in all the following transactions of Swati Goyal.

(i) Started business with cash ₹ 3,00,000.
(ii) Paid rent in advance ₹ 9,000.
(iii) Purchased goods for cash ₹ 1,50,000 and credit ₹ 60,000.
(iv) Sold goods for cash ₹ 2,40,000 costing ₹ 1,20,000.
(v) Paid salary in cash ₹ 13,500 and salary outstanding ₹ 3,000.
(vi) Bought motor cycle for personal use ₹ 90,000.

Ans **Assets = Liabilities + Capital**
3,76,500 = 63,000 + 3,13,500

3 Rohit has the following transactions. **NCERT**

		Amt (₹)
(i)	Commenced business with cash	1,50,000
(ii)	Purchased machinery on credit	40,000
(iii)	Purchased goods for cash	20,000
(iv)	Purchased car for personal use	80,000
(v)	Paid to creditors in full settlement	38,000
(vi)	Sold goods for cash costing ₹ 5,000	4,500
(vii)	Paid rent	1,000
(viii)	Commission received in advance	2,000

Prepare the accounting equation to show the effect of the above transactions on the assets, liabilities and capital.

Ans **Assets = Liabilities + Capital**
73,500 = 2,000 + 71,500

4 Show the accounting equation on the basis of the following transactions.

		Amt (₹)
(i)	Udit started business with	
	(a) Cash	5,00,000
	(b) Goods	1,00,000
(ii)	Purchased building for cash	2,00,000
(iii)	Purchased goods from Himani	50,000
(iv)	Sold goods to Ashu (cost ₹ 25,000)	36,000
(v)	Paid insurance premium	3,000
(vi)	Rent outstanding	5,000
(vii)	Depreciation on building	8,000
(viii)	Cash withdrawn for personal use	20,000
(ix)	Rent received in advance	5,000
(x)	Cash paid to Himani on account	20,000
(xi)	Cash received from Ashu	30,000
(xii)	Received interest	1,000

Ans **Assets = Liabilities + Capital**
6,16,000 40,000 + 5,76,000

5 Prepare the accounting equation on the basis of the following.

(i) Started business with cash ₹ 40,000 and machinery ₹ 25,000.
(ii) Purchased goods from Vivek ₹ 5,000.
(iii) Accrued interest ₹ 1,000
(iv) Commission received in advance ₹ 500
(v) Interest on capital @ 10% (only on cash introduced as capital).
(vi) Proprietor paid the fee of his son ₹ 2,500 (withdrawn from business).
(vii) Sold goods on credit (costing ₹ 5,000) for ₹ 6,000 to Puneet.
(viii) Bought furniture from Aakash ₹ 7,500 and paid ₹ 2,500 in cash and for the balance, bill was accepted.

Ans **Assets = Liabilities + Capital**
75,000 = 10,500 + 64,500

6 Prepare the accounting equation on the basis of the following.

(i) Started business with cash ₹ 15,000 ; goods ₹ 6,000 ; machinery ₹ 10,000 and furniture ₹ 5,000.
(ii) 1/3 of the above goods sold at a profit of 10% on cost and half of the payment is received in cash.
(iii) Cash withdrawn for personal use ₹ 1,000.
(iv) Interest on drawing charged @ 5%.
(v) Depreciation on machinery provided @ 10%.
(vi) Goods sold to Rohan for ₹ 1,000 and received a bill receivable for the same for 3 months.
(vii) Received ₹ 1,000 from Rohan against the bill receivable on maturity.
(viii) Rent received in advance ₹ 500.

Ans **Assets = Liabilities + Capital**
34,700 = 500 + 34,200

CHAPTER PRACTICE

OBJECTIVE TYPE Questions

Multiple Choice Questions

1 Voucher is prepared for **NCERT**

(a) cash received and paid
(b) cash/credit sale
(c) cash/credit purchase
(d) All of the above

Ans (d) All of the above

2 Voucher is prepare from **NCERT**

(a) documentary evidence
(b) journal entry
(c) ledger account
(d) All of the above

Ans (a) documentary evidence

3 Which document is issued at the time of purchase return?

(a) Debit note (b) Credit note
(c) ₹1,000 note (d) None of these

Ans (a) When a buyer returns the goods to the seller due to some defect or some other issues, the debit note is issued by buyer to seller as an intimation of amount and quantity being returned and requesting return of money.

4 Identify the transaction for which transfer voucher is prepared?

(a) A payment of ₹ 10,000 towards rent
(b) A receipt of ₹ 15,000 towards professional fee
(c) A credit sale of ₹ 5,000 to Ram
(d) None of the above

Ans (c) The vouchers which are prepared for transactions not involving cash, *i.e.* non-cash transactions are known as transfer vouchers. There is no cash involvement at the time of credit sale. Hence, transfer/non-cash voucher is prepared in this case.

5 At the time of preparing voucher of sales, the accountant of Arihant publication requires original copy of sales bill. Identify the correct statement from the following.

(a) No, the accountant is not correct with his stand
(b) Yes, the accountant is correct with his stand
(c) Somehow the accountant is correct
(d) None of the above

Ans (a) The accountant is not correct as the original copy of sales bill is handed over to purchaser at the time of sales. Only duplicate is available for recording the same.

6 Identify the following voucher.

M/S Mesaxis Pvt Ltd Jani Khurd Meerut	
Voucher No. 67	Date 07-01-2018
Credit : Sales A/c	5,000
(Being the goods sold for cash vide B.N. 50)	
Total	5,000
Sd/Manager	Sd/Accountant

(a) Cash voucher (b) Cash memo
(c) Non-cash voucher (d) All of these

Ans (a) Cash voucher

7 Ramdas purchases goods worth ₹ 15,000 from Rahimdas and received a invoice of the same, the payment of these goods are payable after one month. Identify the correct statement from the following.

(a) Ramdas issued credit memo of ₹ 15,000 to Rahimdas
(b) Rahimdas issued a credit memo of ₹ 15,000 to Ramdas
(c) Rahimdas issued a cash memo of ₹ 15,000 to Ramdas
(d) None of the above

Ans (b) As the payment of the goods is payable after one month that implies that the goods are sold on credit basis by Rahimdas to Ramdas, so the credit memo has been issued.

8 Which of the following is correct? **NCERT**

(a) Liabilities = Assets + Capital
(b) Assets = Liabilities – Capital
(c) Capital = Assets – Liabilities
(d) Capital = Assets + Liabilities

Ans (c) Capital = Assets – Liabilities

9 Mohit has the following assets and liabilities as on 31st March, 2017. Ascertain his capital. Cash ₹ 50,000, Bank ₹ 95,000, Debtors ₹ 36,000, Creditors ₹ 44,000, Plant and machinery ₹ 1,60,000, Building ₹ 4,00,000, Furniture ₹ 48,000, Bills receivable ₹ 1,13,000, Bills payable ₹ 47,000.

(a) ₹ 8,11,000 (b) ₹ 1,50,000
(c) ₹ 8,10,000 (d) ₹ 9,50,000

Ans (a) Assets = Liabilities + Capital

Capital = Assets – Liabilities

Capital = (Cash + Bank + Debtors + Plant and machinery + Building + Furniture + Bills receivable) – (Creditors + Bills payable)

= (50,000 + 95,000 + 36,000 + 1,60,000 + 4,00,000 + 48,000 + 1,13,000) – (44,000 + 47,000)
= 9,02,000 – 91,000 = ₹ 8,11,000

(Questions 10-11 are based on this paragraph)

Deva has started a business on 1st April, 2015 with a capital of ₹ 10,000 and loan of ₹ 5,000 borrowed from Ramesh. During 2016-17, he had introduced additional capital of ₹ 7,500 and had withdrawn ₹ 2,500 for personal use. On 31st March, 2017 his assets were ₹ 30,000.

10 What is the status of his capital as on 31st March, 2017?

(a) ₹ 25,000 (b) ₹ 20,000
(c) ₹ 27,500 (d) ₹ 30,000

Ans (a) Closing capital = Closing assets – Closing liabilities
= 30,000 – 5,000 = ₹ 25,000

11 Ascertain the profit or loss incurred during the year 2016-17.

(a) ₹ 10,000 (b) ₹ 15,000
(c) ₹ 16,000 (d) ₹ 12,500

Ans (a) Profit = Closing capital + Drawings – Additional capital – Opening capital
= 25,000 + 2,500 – 7,500 – 10,000 = ₹ 10,000

12 In June, Company 'X' receives ₹ 5,000. Which account of company 'X' is affected?

(a) Assets
(b) Liability
(c) Owner equity
(d) No effect

Ans (d) While the amount received, then there is an increase in cash and on the same time decrease in debtors. Hence, overall no effect on assets and also this transaction has no connection with owner equity and liability.

13 On 31st March, 2017, the total assets and external liabilities were ₹ 2,00,000 and ₹ 6,000, respectively. During the year, the proprietor had introduced additional capital of ₹ 20,000 and had withdrawn ₹ 12,000 for personal use. He made a profit of ₹ 20,000 during the year. Calculate the capital as on 1st April, 2016.

(a) ₹ 1,66,000 (b) ₹ 1,76,000
(c) ₹ 1,94,000 (d) ₹ 2,24,000

Ans (a) Closing capital = Closing assets – Closing external liability = 2,00,000 – 6,000 = ₹ 1,94,000

Opening capital = Closing capital + Drawings – Additional capital – Profit
= 1,94,000 + 12,000 – 20,000 – 20,000
= ₹ 1,66,000

14 The company purchases equipment in cash. Identify the correct statement.

(a) There is an increase in assets
(b) There is an increase in owner's equity
(c) There is a decrease in assets
(d) There is no effect on assets

Ans (d) When the equipment purchased for cash then, there is inflow of equipment and also at the same time outflow of cash. So, overall there is no increase or decrease in the net position of assets.

15 "The company repays its bank loan". In the light of this statement, all the given statements are correct except one. Identify that wrong statement.

(a) There is decrease in assets
(b) There is decrease in liability
(c) There is no effect on owner's equity
(d) There is increase in equity

Ans (d) While bank loan is paid then the cash (assets) is decreased and also loan (liability) is decreased, thus there is no effect on owner's equity as well.

16 A creditor of ₹9,500 is settled by a final payment of ₹ 9,000. How will it effect the capital?

(a) Increase by ₹ 9,500
(b) Decrease by ₹ 500
(c) Increase by ₹ 500
(d) Decrease by ₹ 9,500

Ans (c) ₹ 500 (₹ 9,500 – ₹ 9,000) is the amount of discount received (profit), which will be added to the capital. So, capital will increase by ₹ 500.

Fill in the Blanks

17 A document which provides evidence of the transaction is called the ....

Ans source document

18 Transactions are recorded in a .... order.

Ans chronological

19 Every business transaction affects at least .... accounts.

Ans two

20 A .... is an order in writing drawn upon a bank to pay a specified sum to the bearer or the person named in it.

Ans cheque

21 .... is prepared by the seller of goods when he sells goods on credit.

Ans Invoice or bill

22 .... ensures the truthfulness of the recorded transactions.

Ans Source documents

State True or False

23 A credit note is sent to inform about the credit made in the account of the buyer along with the reasons mentioned in it.

Ans True

24 Supporting vouchers are the secondary vouchers.

Ans False, Accounting vouchers are the secondary vouchers which are prepared on the basis of supporting vouchers.

25 Transfer vouchers are prepared for transactions not involving cash.

Ans True

26 Accounting equation is also known as balance sheet equation, as it depicts the fundamental relationship among the components of balance sheet.

Ans True

Match the Following

27

	Column I		Column II
1.	Cash memo	(a)	Liability
2.	Pay-in-slip	(b)	Asset
3.	Loan	(c)	Supporting vouchers
4.	Debtors	(d)	Depositing money in the bank

Ans 1-(c), 2-(d), 3-(a), 4-(b)

VERY SHORT ANSWER Type Questions

28 Name the source document used for depositing money in the bank.

Ans Pay-in-slip

29 Name the source document which is a written document drawn upon a specified banker and payable on demand.

Ans Cheque

30 Which source document is prepared by the seller for goods sold against cash?

Ans Cash memo

31 Which source document is prepared by the seller for goods sold against credit?

Ans Invoice or bill

32 Name the types of accounting vouchers.

Ans (*i*) Cash vouchers
(*ii*) Non-cash vouchers

33 Credit purchases of furniture will be recorded through which voucher?

Ans Transfer voucher

34 Which voucher records transactions with multiple debits and multiple credits?

Ans Complex voucher

35 Which vouchers are prepared for transactions not involving cash?

Ans Transfer vouchers

36 How is an accounting equation fundamental?

Ans Accounting equation is fundamental in the sense that it gives foundation to the double entry book keeping.

37 Give the formula for computing owner's equity at the end of the year.

Ans Owner's equity at the end of a year can be computed by using the given formula
Owner's Equity = Amount Invested by the Owner (Cash + Assets) – Drawings + Profit on Sale of Goods – Loss on Sale of Goods – Expenses + Incomes

38 When proprietor withdraws cash for his/her personal use, what will be the effect on capital?

Ans Decrease in capital

39 Which document evidenced that the credit has been granted to the named person for the reason stated their in?

Ans Credit note

40 If machinery is purchased for cash, indicate how accounting equation will be affected?

Ans It will result in cash being reduced and machinery being increased.

41 Do you think that a transaction can break the accounting equation?

Ans No, a transaction can change the accounting equation but cannot break it.

SHORT ANSWER Type Questions

42 Why is the evidence provided by source documents important to accounting? **NCERT**

Ans *The evidence provided by source document is important to accounting because of the reasons discussed below.*

(*i*) It provides evidence that a transaction has actually occurred.

(*ii*) It provides important and relevant information about date, amount, parties involved and other details of a particular transaction.

(*iii*) It acts as a proof in the court of law.

(*iv*) It helps in verifying transactions during the auditing process.

43 What is a compound voucher? What are its types?

Ans Vouchers which record transactions with multiple debits/credits and one credit/debit are called compound vouchers.

Compound vouchers are of two types

(*i*) **Debit Voucher** Voucher showing transactions that contain multiple debits and one credit is called debit voucher.

(*ii*) **Credit Voucher** Voucher showing transactions that contain multiple credits but one debit is called credit voucher.

44 State the features of supporting vouchers.

Ans *Features of supporting voucher are as follows*

(*i*) It is a written document.

(*ii*) It contains complete detail of the transaction.

(*iii*) It is a proof of a transaction having taken place.

(*iv*) It is generally for a business transaction.

(*v*) It is signed by the maker.

45 State the features of accounting vouchers.

Ans *Features of accounting voucher are as follows*

(*i*) It is a written document.

(*ii*) It is prepared on the basis of evidence of the transaction.

(*iii*) It is an analysis of a transaction.

(*iv*) It is prepared and signed usually by an accountant and countersigned by the authorised signatory.

(*v*) In the case of cash/bank voucher, it is a receipt.

46 Give two basic purposes of accounting equation.

Ans *The two basic purposes of an accounting equation are*

(*i*) As the accounting equation is always equal, it ensures the accuracy in recording the business transaction.

(*ii*) It helps in the preparation of balance sheet.

47 If a transaction has the effect of decreasing an asset, is the decrease recorded as a debit or as a credit? If the transaction has the effect of decreasing a liability, is the decrease recorded as a debit or as a credit? **NCERT**

Ans If a transaction has the effect of decreasing an asset, the decrease will be recorded as credit because all the assets have debit balance. So, if asset decreases, it is credited.

For example, when an asset is decreased because of depreciation, in that case asset account is credited.

On the other hand, if a transaction has the effect of decreasing a liability, the decrease will be recorded as debit because all the liabilities have credit balance. So, if the liability decreases, it is debited.

For example, when capital is decreased because of the withdrawal by the proprietor, drawing account is debited.

48 Accounting equation (A = L + C) always holds good under all circumstances. Explain.

Or

Accounting equation remains intact under all circumstances. Justify the statement with the help of an example. **NCERT**

Ans An accounting equation always remains intact with every change that occurs due to a transaction *i.e.,* under all the circumstances. It is because dual aspect concept of accounting says that, every transaction simultaneously, has two effects of equal amount. A transaction may affect either both sides of the equation by the same amount or one side of the equation only, by both increasing or decreasing it by equal amounts.

However, in any case, the equality of total assets with the total claims of the business (sum of capital and liabilities) is not disturbed. This equality is algebraically represented as

Assets = Liabilities + Capital

49 Give an example for each of the following types of transaction.

(i) Increase in one asset, decrease in another asset.

(ii) Increase in asset, increase in liability.

(iii) Increase in asset, increase in owner's capital.

(iv) Decrease in asset, decrease in liability.

(v) Decrease in asset, decrease in owner's capital.

(vi) Decrease in liabilities, increase in owner's capital.

(vii) Increase in one liability, decrease in another liability.

(viii) Increase in liabilities, decrease in owner's capital.

Ans (*i*) Purchase of furniture for cash—Increase in furniture and decrease in cash.

(*ii*) Purchase of furniture on credit—Increase in furniture and increase in creditors.

(*iii*) Capital introduced by proprietor—Increase in cash and increase in capital.

(*iv*) Payment to creditors—Decrease in cash and decrease in creditors.

(*v*) Cash withdrawn by proprietor—Decrease in cash and decrease in capital.
(*vi*) Conversion of partner's loan into capital—Increase in capital and decrease in loan.
(*vii*) Bills payable accepted—Increase in bills payable and decrease in creditors.
(*viii*) Outstanding expenses provided—Increase in creditors for outstanding expenses and decrease in capital.

50 **What is the difference between source documents and vouchers?** **NCERT**

Ans *Difference between source documents and vouchers are*

Source Documents	*Vouchers*
It is a support to the voucher.	Voucher is supported by source document.
It is not prepared to record transactions.	It is prepared for the purpose of recording of transactions.
It contains full details of a transaction.	It puts emphasis on which account is to be debited and which account is to be credited.
It is evidence of the transaction.	It is a document of correct recording of a transaction.

NUMERICAL Questions

1 **Prepare the debit voucher for furniture purchased for ₹ 15,000 from Globe Furniture Mart on 2nd January, 2016.**

2 **Prepare the transfer vouchers from the source vouchers.**

2016		Amt (₹)
Nov 10	Purchased goods from M/s Vardhman vide Bill No. 912	15,000
Nov 20	Sold goods to M/s Eva vide Bill No. 12345	10,000

3 **Prepare the accounting vouchers for the following transactions.**

2016	
Oct 1	Started business with cash ₹ 40,000
Oct 5	Opened a bank account in Axis Bank with ₹ 20,000
Oct 10	Purchased a computer on credit from M/s Raju Stores for ₹ 10,000

4 **If total assets of a business are ₹ 2,60,000 and net worth is ₹ 1,60,000. Calculate the creditors.**

Ans Creditors = ₹ 1,00,000.

5 **If the capital of a business is ₹ 2,40,000 and outside liabilities are ₹ 40,000. Calculate total assets of the business.**

Ans Total Assets = ₹ 2,80,000.

6 **Calculate total equity if**

(i) Owner's equity in the beginning ₹ 60,000.
(ii) Equity of creditors at the end ₹ 50,000.
(iii) Revenue during the period is ₹ 70,000.
(iv) Expenses during the same period are ₹ 65,000.

Also calculate amount of owner's equity at the end.

Ans Total Equity = ₹ 1,15,000, Owner's Equity = ₹ 65,000.

7 **Calculate the total assets if**

(i) Capital is ₹ 40,000.
(ii) Creditors are ₹ 25,000.
(iii) Revenue during the period is ₹ 50,000.
(iv) Expenses during the period are ₹ 40,000.

Ans Total Assets = ₹ 75,000.

8 **On 31st March, 2016 the total assets and external liabilities were ₹ 6,00,000 and ₹ 18,000 respectively. During the year, the proprietor had introduced capital of ₹ 60,000 and withdrawn ₹ 36,000 for personal use.**

He made a profit of ₹ 60,000 during the year. Calculate the capital as on 1st April, 2015.

Ans Opening Capital = ₹ 4,98,000.

9 **A commenced his cloth business on 1st April, 2015 with a capital of ₹ 60,000. On 31st March, 2016, his assets were worth ₹ 1,00,000 and liabilities of ₹ 20,000. Find out his closing capital and profits earned during the year.**

Ans Capital = ₹ 80,000, Profit = ₹ 20,000.

10 **Prepare an accounting equation on the basis of the following transactions.**

(i) Started business with cash ₹ 70,000.
(ii) Credit purchase of goods ₹ 18,000.
(iii) Payment made to creditors in full settlement ₹ 17,500.
(iv) Purchase of machinery for cash ₹ 20,000.
(v) Depreciation on machinery ₹ 2,000.

Ans Assets = ₹ 68,500, Liabilities = Nil and Capital = ₹ 68,500.

11 **Show effect of the following transactions on accounting equation.**

		Amt (₹)
(i)	Started business with cash amounting to ₹ 1,05,000 and goods ₹ 45,000	
(ii)	Salaries paid	6,000
(iii)	Wages outstanding	600

		Amt (₹)
(iv)	Prepaid insurance	2,100
(v)	Interest due but not paid	300
(vi)	Rent paid in advance	450

Ans Assets = ₹ 1,44,000, Liabilities ₹ 900 and Capital = ₹ 1,43,100.

12 Prove that the accounting equation is satisfied in all the following transactions of Preeti Gupta.

(i) Started business with cash ₹ 10,000.
(ii) Paid rent in advance ₹ 300.
(iii) Purchased goods for cash ₹ 5,000 and credit ₹ 2,000.
(iv) Sold goods for cash ₹ 8,000 costing ₹ 4,000.
(v) Paid salary ₹ 450 and salary outstanding being ₹ 100.
(vi) Bought motorcycle for personal use ₹ 3,000.

Ans Assets = ₹ 12,550, Liabilities = ₹ 2,100 and Capital = ₹ 10,450.

13 Prepare accounting equation from the following

(i) Raghu started business with cash ₹ 4,50,000.
(ii) Bought goods for cash ₹ 2,40,000 and on credit for ₹ 1,20,000.
(iii) Goods costing ₹ 2,25,000 sold at a profit of $33\frac{1}{3}$%. Half the payment received in cash.
(iv) Goods costing ₹ 30,000 sold for ₹ 36,000 on credit.
(v) Paid for rent ₹ 6,000 and for salaries ₹ 12,000.
(vi) Goods costing ₹ 60,000 sold for ₹ 55,500 for cash.

Ans Assets = ₹ 6,28,500, Liabilities = ₹ 1,20,000 and Capital = ₹ 5,08,500

14 Vanishka had the following transactions. Use accounting equation to show their effect on her assets, liabilities and capital.

(i) Invested ₹ 30,000 in cash as capital.
(ii) Purchased furniture for cash ₹ 15,000.
(iii) Purchased a building for ₹ 30,000, giving ₹ 10,000 in cash and the balance through a loan.
(iv) Sold furniture costing ₹ 2,000 for ₹ 3,000.
(v) Purchased an old car for ₹ 5,600 cash.
(vi) Received cash as rent ₹ 7,200.
(vii) Paid cash ₹ 1,000 for loan and ₹ 600 for interest.
(viii) Paid cash for household expenses ₹ 600.
(ix) Received cash for dividend on securities ₹ 400.

Ans Assets = ₹ 56,400, Liabilities = ₹ 19,000 and Capital = ₹ 37,400

15 Vishnu had the following transactions.

(i) Commenced business with cash ₹ 60,000.
(ii) Purchased goods for cash ₹ 24,000 and credit ₹ 36,000.
(iii) Sold goods for cash ₹ 48,000 costing ₹ 36,000.
(iv) Rent paid ₹ 600.
(v) Rent outstanding ₹ 120.
(vi) Bought furniture ₹ 6,000 on credit.
(vii) Bought refrigerator for personal use ₹ 6,000.
(viii) Purchased building for cash ₹ 24,000.

Use accounting equation to show the effect of the above transactions on his assets, liabilities and capital and also show his balance sheet.

Ans Assets = ₹ 1,07,400, Liabilities = ₹ 42,120 and Capital = ₹ 65,280.

16 Show the accounting equation on the basis of the following transactions and present a balance sheet on the last new equation balances.

		Amt (₹)
(i)	Kartik commenced business with cash	1,40,000
(ii)	Purchased goods on credit	28,000
(iii)	Withdrew for private use	3,400
(iv)	Goods purchased for cash	20,000
(v)	Paid wages	600
(vi)	Paid to creditors	20,000
(vii)	Sold goods on credit	30,000
(viii)	Sold goods for cash (cost price was ₹ 6,000)	8,000
(ix)	Purchased furniture	1,000

Ans Assets = ₹ 1,46,000, Liabilities = ₹ 8,000 and Capital = ₹ 1,38,000.

17 Show the accounting equation on the basis of the following transactions and present a balance sheet on the last new equation balances. Varun and Raj entered into a partnership agreement to deal in furniture. They contributed ₹ 2,10,000 and ₹ 1,50,000 as capital respectively. Other transactions were as under

		Amt (₹)
(i)	Timber purchased by them	1,20,000
(ii)	Wages paid to carpenters	90,000
(iii)	Furniture sold (costing ₹ 1,20,000)	1,50,000
(iv)	Furniture sold on credit (costing ₹ 27,000)	30,000

		Amt (₹)
(v)	Amount received from debtors Discount allowed	29,700 300
(vi)	Timber purchased on credit	18,000
(vii)	Furniture purchased	15,000
(viii)	Payment to creditors ₹ 17,850 in full settlement	
(ix)	Amount withdrawn	
	Varun	6,000
	Raj	3,000

Ans Assets = ₹ 3,83,850, liabilities = Nil and Capital = ₹ 3,83,850.

18 Analyse the effect of each transaction and prove that the accounting equation (A = L + C) always remains balanced.

(i) Introduced ₹ 4,00,000 as cash and ₹ 25,000 by stock.

(ii) Purchased plant for ₹ 1,50,000 by paying ₹ 7,500 in cash and balance at a later date.

(iii) Deposited ₹ 3,00,000 into the bank.

(iv) Purchased office furniture for ₹ 50,000 and made payment by cheque.

(v) Purchased goods worth ₹ 40,000 for cash and for ₹ 17,500 on credit.

(vi) Goods amounting to ₹ 22,500 was sold for ₹ 30,000 on cash basis.

(vii) Goods costing to ₹ 40,000 was sold for ₹ 62,500 on credit basis.

(viii) Cheque issued to the supplier of goods worth ₹ 17,500.

(ix) Cheque received from customer amounting to ₹ 37,500.

(x) Withdrawn by owner for personal use ₹ 12,500.

Ans Assets = ₹ 5,97,500, Liabilities ₹ 1,42,500 and Capital = ₹ 4,55,000.

19 Raghav started a real estate agency business with a cash investment of ₹ 42,000. The following business transactions have been recorded

(i) Paid 3 months advance rent for office accommodation ₹ 2,520.

(ii) Bought car for office ₹ 25,200.

(iii) Purchased office furniture ₹ 8,400.

(iv) Bought office typewriter from Comprehensive Company ₹ 3,600.

(v) Sold extra office furniture at cost to Amar for ₹ 1,200. Amar paid ₹ 720 in cash and accepted a bill at 3 months for the balance.

(vi) Veer paid the amount of the bill at maturity and Amar paid half the amount he owed to Comprehensive Company.

(vii) Collected ₹ 7,200 as commission.

(viii) Paid telephone bill amounting ₹ 180.

Ans Assets = ₹ 50,820, Liabilities = ₹ 1,800 and Capital = ₹ 49,020.

04

After studying this chapter, students will learn the rules of debit and credit, the process of journalising, format of journal, steps in journalising, simple and compound journal entries and recording in journal.
The students will further learn the concept of ledger, posting of journal entries to ledger accounts and how to balance an account.

JOURNAL AND LEDGER

On the basis of source documents prepared, business transactions are recorded in the books of accounts. Normally, transactions are recorded in two sets of books *i.e.,* journal and ledger.

Transactions are firstly recorded in the journal in a systematic manner and thereafter these transactions are posted into the ledger. This sequence causes the journal to be called as the book of original entry and the ledger as the book of principal or final entry.

CHAPTER CHECKLIST

- Journal
- Rules for Journalising
- Recording in Journal
- Ledger
- Balancing of Accounts

|TOPIC 1|

Journal

The word 'journal' has been derived from the French word 'Jour' meaning daily records. Journal is a book in which transactions are recorded in chronological order, *i.e.,* date-wise, in the order in which they occur. The process of recording a transaction in a journal is called **journalising**. An entry made in the journal is called a **journal entry**. If the size of the business is small, then it is convenient to record all the transactions in the journal. But for large businesses recording all the transactions in the journal is a time-consuming and tedious process.

Because of this, the journal is divided into a number of books, referred to as subsidiary books or sub-journals, which are enumerated below

(*i*) Cash book (For cash transactions)

(*ii*) Other day books or subsidiary books (For non-cash transactions)

(*a*) Purchases book (*b*) Sales book (*c*) Purchase returns book

(*d*) Sales return book (*e*) Bills receivable book (*f*) Bills payable book

(*iii*) Journal proper

Note *In this chapter, only the process of journalising and then posting into ledger has been discussed. Subsidiary books have been discussed in the subsequent chapter.*

Format of Journal

The format of journal is given below

JOURNAL

Date (1)	Particulars (2)	LF (3)	Amt (Dr) (4)	Amt (Cr) (5)

The information to be contained in each of the column of the journal has been explained below

1. **Date Column** The first column in a journal records the date on which the transaction occur.
2. **Particulars Column** In this column, the journal entry is recorded. The account to be debited is written on the first line beginning from the left hand corner and the word 'Dr' is written at the end of the column.

   The account to be credited is written on the second line leaving sufficient margin on the left side with a prefix 'To'.

   Below the journal entry a brief description of the transaction is given, which is called **narration.** Having written the narration, a line is drawn in the particulars column which indicates the end of recording the specific journal entry.
3. **Ledger Folio** (LF) **Column** It records the page number of the ledger book on which the relevant account appears. This column is filled up at the time of posting and not at the time of making journal entry.
4. **Debit Amount Column** The amount to be debited is entered in this column.
5. **Credit Amount Column** The amount to be credited is entered in this column.
   - *It may be noted that transactions are recorded in a number of pages in the journal book, hence, at the end of each page of the journal book, the amount columns are totalled and carried forward (c/f) to the next page where such amounts are recorded as brought forward (b/f) balances. (Illustration 8)*

Rules of Journalising

The rules of journalising can be studied under two approaches.

1. TRADITIONAL APPROACH

Under this system, accounts are classified as

(i) Personal Accounts

These are the accounts which relate to persons *i.e.*, individuals, firms, companies, debtors/creditors, etc.

Personal accounts can be classified into three categories

(*a*) **Natural Personal Accounts** These accounts record transactions of individual human beings *e.g.*, Kartik's account, Aroha's account, etc.

(*b*) **Artificial Personal Accounts** These accounts include accounts of corporate bodies or institutions which are recognised as artificial persons in business dealings *e.g.*, the account of a limited company or a cooperative society.

(*c*) **Representative Personal Accounts** These accounts represent a particular person or group of persons indirectly. *e.g.*, capital account represents the contribution made by the owner.

For personal accounts, the rule for passing the journal entry is

"Debit the receiver, credit the giver."

EXAMPLE Sohan received ₹ 5,000 from Rohan and paid ₹ 10,000 to Mohan. Identify the accounts to be debited and credited in Sohan's book.

Sol. Mohan's account will be debited in Sohan's book by ₹ 10,000 as he is the receiver.
Rohan's account will be credited in Sohan's book by ₹ 5,000 as he is the giver.

(ii) Impersonal Account

These are the accounts which are not personal such as cash account, machinery account, rent account, etc.

Impersonal accounts can be classified into two categories

(*a*) **Real Accounts** These are the accounts which relate to both tangible and intangible assets of the firm.

For example, Tangible assets - Plant and machinery, land, building, stock, cash, etc.
Intangible assets - Goodwill, patents, trademark, etc.

For real accounts, the rule for passing the journal entry is

"Debit what comes in and credit what goes out".

EXAMPLE Sohan purchased machinery for ₹ 50,000 and paid for the same in cash. Identify the accounts to be debited and credited in Sohan's book.

Sol. In the given example, machinery has been purchased for cash. So, machinery is coming in, therefore machinery account will be debited. Cash is going out, therefore cash account will be credited.

(*b*) **Nominal Accounts** These are the accounts which relate to expenses, losses, revenue, gain, etc. *e.g.,* salary account, purchases account, interest paid account, commission received account, sales account, etc.

For nominal accounts, the rule for passing the journal entry is

"Debit all expenses and losses and credit all incomes and gains".

EXAMPLE Sohan paid the rent for the month of November, ₹ 8,000. He also received commission ₹ 5,000. Identify the accounts to be debited and credited in Sohan's book.

Sol. In the given example, Sohan has paid rent ₹ 8,000. This is an expense. Hence, rent account will be debited. By paying rent cash (real account) is going out of the business, therefore cash account will be credited.

Also, in the given example, Sohan has received commission ₹ 5,000. This is an income. So, commission account will be credited. On receiving commission, cash (real account) is coming in, therefore cash account will be debited.

Note *Students should keep in mind that when any prefix or suffix is added to a nominal account, it becomes a personal account.*

For example, Nominal Account : Commission account. Personal Account : Outstanding commission account, Prepaid commission account.

- It should also be kept in mind that a transaction can involve two different categories of account. In such a case, the rule of each individual category should be applied.
- While recording expenses and incomes, it should be kept in mind that expenses and incomes should be stated and not the name of the individuals to whom those expenses are paid or from whom incomes are received. So, if salary is paid to Dinaram then salary account will be debited and not Dinaram.

Rules for Debit and Credit According to Traditional Approach
(A summarised view)

Type of Accounts	*Rule for Debit*	*Rule for Credit*
Personal Accounts	Debit the receiver	Credit the giver
Real Accounts	Debit what comes in	Credit what goes out
Nominal Accounts	Debit all expenses and losses	Credit all incomes and gains

2. **MODERN APPROACH OR ACCOUNTING EQUATION BASED APPROACH**

According to the modern approach, accounts are classified as follows

(*i*) **Assets Accounts** The accounts of assets and properties are termed as assets accounts. *e.g.*, building, plant and machinery, land, patents, inventory, etc.

(*ii*) **Liabilities Accounts** The accounts of lenders, creditors for goods and expenses are termed as liabilities accounts. *e.g.*, lender account, creditors for goods account, etc.

(*iii*) **Capital Accounts** The accounts of the partners or the proprietors, who have invested money in the business are termed as capital accounts.

(*iv*) **Revenue/Gains Accounts** These are the accounts of income and gains that the business has earned by selling its goods and services. *e.g.*, sales, interest received, etc.

(*v*) **Expenses/Losses Accounts** The accounts which show the amount spent or lost in carrying on the business operations are termed as expenses/losses accounts. *e.g.*, purchases, wages paid, etc.

Rules for Debit and Credit According to Modern Approach or Accounting Equation Based approach (A summarised view)

Type of Accounts	*Rule for Debit*	*Rule for Credit*
Assets Accounts	Debit the increase	Credit the decrease
Liabilities Accounts	Debit the decrease	Credit the increase
Capital Accounts	Debit the decrease	Credit the increase
Revenue Accounts	Debit the decrease	Credit the increase
Expenses Accounts	Debit the increase	Credit the decrease

Steps in Journalising

The main steps involved in journalising are

Step 1 Identify the accounts involved in a transaction.

Step 2 Identify the nature of accounts involved.

Step 3 Identify the rules of debit and credit that are applicable for each of the accounts involved.

Step 4 Identify which account is to be debited and which account is to be credited.

Step 5 Pass the necessary journal entry in the journal and also record the date and amount of transaction in the respective columns of the journal.

Simple and Compound Journal Entries

The journal entry is the basic record of a business transaction. It may be classified as

I. SIMPLE JOURNAL ENTRY

When only two accounts are involved to record a transaction, it is called a simple journal entry. In this, one account is debited and another account is credited with an equal amount.

For example, Salary paid ₹ 1,00,000 on 2nd December, 2016. It involves only two accounts—Salary account (nominal) and cash account (real).

JOURNAL

Date	Particulars		LF	Amt (Dr)	Amt (Cr)
2016 Dec 2	Salary A/c	Dr		1,00,000	
	To Cash A/c				1,00,000
	(Being salary paid)				

II. COMPOUND JOURNAL ENTRY

When the number of accounts to be debited or credited is more than one, entry made for recording the transaction is called compound journal entry. In other words, it involves more than two accounts.

For example, office furniture is purchased 4th July, 2016 for ₹ 25,000. On the same date, machinery is also purchased for ₹ 75,000.

This transaction involves three accounts. It increases furniture (real) by ₹ 25,000, increases machinery (real) by ₹ 75,000 and reduces cash (real) by ₹ 1,00,000.

JOURNAL

Date	Particulars		LF	Amt (Dr)	Amt (Cr)
2016 Jul 4	Office Furniture A/c	Dr		25,000	
	Machinery A/c	Dr		75,000	
	To Cash A/c				1,00,000
	(Being purchases of office furniture and machinery)				

Entries of Some Common Transactions

(i) Vijay Started Business with Cash

The transaction affects two accounts : Cash and Capital

Cash is a real (Asset) account. As per the traditional approach, the rule of real account *i.e.*, debit what comes in will apply; since cash is coming in, it will be debited. Similarly, as per the modern approach, the rule of asset account *i.e.*, debit the increase in asset will apply; since cash is increasing, it will be debited.

Capital is a personal (Capital) account. As per the traditional approach, the rule of personal account. *i.e.*, credit the giver, will apply; since Vijay is the giver, capital will be credited. Similarly, as per the modern approach, the rule of capital account *i.e.*, credit the increase in capital, will apply; since capital is increasing, it will be credited.

Accounts Involved and Effect as per Traditional/Modern Rule	Nature of Accounts and Traditional Rule	Nature of Accounts and Modern Rule	Entry	
Cash (It is coming in/Increase)	Real— Debit what comes in	Asset— Debit the increase in asset	Cash A/c	Dr
Capital (Vijay is the giver/Increase)	Personal— Credit the giver	Capital— Credit the increase in capital	To Capital A/c	

Note *The explanation of the subsequent transactions can be easily understood with the help of the tables given below.*

(ii) Purchased Goods for Cash

Accounts Involved and Effect as per Traditional/Modern Rule	Nature of Accounts and Traditional Rule	Nature of Accounts and Modern Rule	Entry	
Purchases (It is an expense /Increase)	Nominal— Debit all expenses and losses	Expenses— Debit the increase in expenses	Purchases A/c	Dr
Cash (It is going out /Decrease)	Real— Credit what goes out	Asset— Credit the decrease in asset	To Cash A/c	

(iii) Purchased Goods from Kartik on Credit

Accounts Involved and Effect as per Traditional/Modern Rule	Nature of Accounts and Traditional Rule	Nature of Accounts and Modern Rule	Entry	
Purchases (It is an expense /Increase)	Nominal— Debit all expenses and losses	Expenses— Debit the increase in expenses	Purchases A/c	Dr
Kartik's (Kartik is the giver /Increase)	Personal— Credit the giver	Liability— Credit the increase in liability	To Kartik	

(iv) Sold Goods for Cash

Accounts Involved and Effect as per Traditional/Modern Rule	Nature of Accounts and Traditional Rule	Nature of Accounts and Modern Rule	Entry	
Cash (It is coming in /Increase)	Real— Debit what comes in	Asset— Debit the increase in asset	Cash A/c	Dr
Sales (It is a revenue /Increase)	Nominal— Credit all revenue and income	Revenue— Credit the increase in revenue	To Sales A/c	

(v) Sold Goods to Aroha on Credit

Accounts Involved and Effect as per Traditional/Modern Rule	Nature of Accounts and Traditional Rule	Nature of Accounts and Modern Rule	Entry	
Aroha (She is the receiver /Increase)	Personal— Debit the receiver	Asset (Debtor)— Debit the increase in asset	Aroha	Dr
Sales (It is a revenue /Increase)	Nominal— Credit all revenue and income	Revenue— Credit the increase in revenue	To Sales A/c	

(vi) Purchased Asset (Furniture) for Cash

Accounts Involved and Effect as per Traditional/Modern Rule	Nature of Accounts and Traditional Rule	Nature of Accounts and Modern Rule	Entry	
Furniture (It is coming in /Increase)	Real— Debit what comes in	Asset— Debit the increase in asset	Furniture A/c	Dr
Cash (It is going out /Decrease)	Real— Credit what goes out	Asset— Credit the decrease in asset	To Cash A/c	

(vii) Purchased Furniture from Kartik on Credit

Accounts Involved and Effect as per Traditional/Modern Rule	Nature of Accounts and Traditional Rule	Nature of Accounts and Modern Rule	Entry	
Furniture (It is coming in /Increase)	Real— Debit what comes in	Asset— Debit the increase in asset	Furniture A/c	Dr
Kartik (Kartik is the giver /Increase)	Personal— Credit the giver	Liability (Creditors)—Credit the increase in liability	To Kartik	

Note *In case of transactions related to sale and purchase of goods or assets, the following points should be kept in mind.*

- *If the name of seller or purchaser is given and it is not stated whether it is a cash or credit transaction, it is considered to be a credit transaction e.g., goods sold to Raj.*
- *If the name of seller or purchaser is given alongwith cash, it is considered as a cash transaction e.g., goods sold to Raj for cash.*
- *If the name of the seller or purchaser is not given, it is considered as a cash transaction e.g., goods sold for ₹ 50,000.*

(viii) Cash Received from Rohan

Accounts Involved and Effect as per Traditional/Modern Rule	Nature of Accounts and Traditional Rule	Nature of Accounts and Modern Rule	Entry	
Cash (It is coming in /Increase)	Real— Debit what comes in	Asset— Debit the increase in asset	Cash A/c	Dr
Rohan (Rohan is the giver /Decrease)	Personal— Credit the giver	Asset (Debtor)— Credit the decrease in asset	To Rohan	

(ix) Cash Withdrawn for Personal Use

Accounts Involved and Effect as per Traditional/Modern Rule	Nature of Accounts and Traditional Rule	Nature of Accounts and Modern Rule	Entry	
Drawings (Vijay is the receiver /Decrease)	Personal— Debit the receiver	Capital— Debit the decrease in capital	Drawings A/c	Dr
Cash (It is going out /Decrease)	Real— Credit what goes out	Asset— Credit the decrease in assets	To Cash A/c	

- *When cash is withdrawn for personal use, it is termed as drawings.*

Note *If cash is withdrawn from bank for personal use, bank account will be credited in place of cash account.*

ILLUSTRATION |1| Journalise the following transactions

2016		Amt (₹)
Jan 1	Rajesh started business with cash ₹ 1,00,000 and a building valued at ₹ 5,00,000	
Jan 3	Purchased goods amounting to ₹ 2,00,000 out of which goods of ₹ 1,80,000 were purchased on credit from Smith	
Jan 5	Sold goods to Anil	44,000
Jan 9	Goods returned by Anil	4,000
Jan 11	Goods purchased from Karan	63,000
Jan 15	Goods returned to Karan	3,000
Jan 22	Purchased goods for cash	2,000
Jan 22	Paid cartage	100
Jan 30	Paid interest on loan	1,000

Sol. JOURNAL

Date	Particulars		LF	Amt (Dr)	Amt (Cr)
2016					
Jan 1	Cash A/c	Dr		1,00,000	
	Building A/c	Dr		5,00,000	
	To Capital A/c				6,00,000
	(Being the business started with cash and building)				
Jan 3	Purchases A/c	Dr		2,00,000	
	To Cash A/c				20,000
	To Smith				1,80,000
	(Being the goods purchased for cash ₹ 20,000 and on credit from Smith for ₹ 1,80,000)				
Jan 5	Anil	Dr		44,000	
	To Sales A/c				44,000
	(Being the goods sold to Anil)				
Jan 9	Sales Return A/c	Dr		4,000	
	To Anil				4,000
	(Being the goods returned by Anil)				
Jan 11	Purchases A/c	Dr		63,000	
	To Karan				63,000
	(Being the goods purchased from Karan)				
Jan 15	Karan	Dr		3,000	
	To Purchases Return A/c				3,000
	(Being the goods returned to Karan)				
Jan 22	Purchases A/c	Dr		2,000	
	To Cash A/c				2,000
	(Being the goods purchased against cash)				
Jan 22	Cartage A/c	Dr		100	
	To Cash A/c				100
	(Being the cartage paid)				
Jan 30	Interest on Loan A/c	Dr		1,000	
	To Cash A/c				1,000
	(Being the payment of interest on loan)				
	Total			9,17,100	9,17,100

ILLUSTRATION |2| Transactions of Sunil for the month of April are given below. Journalise them.

2016		Amt (₹)
Apr 1	Sunil started business with cash	3,00,000
Apr 3	Bought goods for cash	15,000
Apr 13	Sold goods to Aditya	4,500
Apr 20	Bought goods from Sunny	6,750
Apr 24	Received from Aditya	4,500
Apr 28	Paid cash to Sunny	6,450
Apr 30	Cash sales for the month	24,000
Apr 30	Paid salary to Ram	9,000
Apr 30	Goods were returned to Abhishek	10,000

Sol.

JOURNAL

Date	Particulars		LF	Amt (Dr)	Amt (Cr)
2016 Apr 1	Cash A/c To Capital A/c (Being the amount invested by Sunil in the business as capital)	Dr		3,00,000	3,00,000
Apr 3	Purchases A/c To Cash A/c (Being the goods purchased for cash)	Dr		15,000	15,000
Apr 13	Aditya To Sales A/c (Being the goods sold to Aditya on credit)	Dr		4,500	4,500
Apr 20	Purchases A/c To Sunny (Being the goods bought from Sunny on credit)	Dr		6,750	6,750
Apr 24	Cash A/c To Aditya (Being the cash received from Aditya)	Dr		4,500	4,500
Apr 28	Sunny To Cash A/c (Being the amount paid to Sunny)	Dr		6,450	6,450
Apr 30	Cash A/c To Sales A/c (Being the goods sold for cash)	Dr		24,000	24,000
Apr 30	Salaries A/c To Cash A/c (Being the amount paid for salary)	Dr		9,000	9,000
Apr 30	Abhishek To Purchases Return A/c (Being the goods return to Abhishek)	Dr		10,000	10,000
	Total			3,80,200	3,80,200

NUMERICAL Questions for Practice

1 Enter the following transactions in the Journal of Ram Das

2016		Amt (₹)
Jan 1	Ram Das started business with cash	60,000
Jan 2	Purchased furniture for cash	10,000
Jan 4	Purchased goods for cash	25,000
Jan 5	Bought goods from Raju	15,000
Jan 6	Sold goods for cash	36,000
Jan 8	Sold goods to Ramesh	30,000
Jan 10	Paid cash to Raju	15,000
Jan 14	Received cash from Ramesh	18,000
Jan 16	Purchased goods from Kapil	6,000
Jan 18	Purchased goods from Kapil for cash	8,000
Jan 20	Paid rent for the office	1,000
Jan 26	Received commission	750
Jan 27	Paid salary to Prashant	1,200
Jan 28	Received cash from Ramesh	12,000
Jan 29	Withdrew cash from office for personal use	4,000
Jan 30	Wages paid	7,200
Jan 30	Bought machinery for cash	8,000

Ans Total of Journal = ₹ 2,57,150

2 Journalise the following transactions in the books of Gopi Chand.

2016		Amt (₹)
Aug 1	Gopi Chand commenced business with cash	50,000
Aug 2	Purchased goods for cash	10,000
Aug 5	Purchased goods from Hari on credit	6,000
Aug 7	Paid into bank	5,000
Aug 10	Purchased furniture	2,000
Aug 15	Sold goods for cash	7,000
Aug 20	Sold goods to Ram on credit	5,000
Aug 25	Cash sales	3,500
Aug 27	Paid to Hari on account	3,000
Aug 28	Paid wages	100
Aug 30	Paid rent	1,200
Aug 31	Paid salaries	2,800
Aug 31	Rejected and returned 10% of goods supplied by Hari.	

Ans Total of Journal = ₹ 96,200

Hint : Goods returned by Hari ₹ 600 (6,000×10%)

3 Give journal entries for the following transactions

(i) Vishal started business by investing cash ₹ 50,00,000. He bought goods of ₹ 4,00,000 and furniture of ₹ 5,00,000.

(ii) Purchased building for ₹ 10,00,000.

(iii) Purchased goods for cash ₹ 3,00,000.

(iv) Purchased goods on credit from Varun ₹ 25,000.

(v) Paid cartage ₹ 2,000.

(vi) Sold goods for cash ₹ 2,55,000.

(vii) Sold goods for cash Vivek ₹ 24,000.

(viii) Sold goods to Viren on credit ₹ 46,500.

(ix) Cash withdrawn by Vishal for personal use ₹ 5,000.

Ans Total of Journal = ₹ 75,57,500

GST Transactions

GST, as we have already learned, is an indirect tax which is collected by the supplier and remitted to the government. It is an important tax and one that we encounter daily in our life.

The journal entries related to GST transactions are discussed ahead.

(i) Purchase of Goods and GST Paid

This transaction affects the following accounts:

Purchases, GST (CGST, SGST, IGST) and Cash/Bank/Creditor.

Purchases As per traditional approach, rule of nominal account, debit all expenses will apply. So, purchases account will be debited. Similarly, as per the modern approach, the rule of expenses account, i.e. debit the increase in expenses will apply and purchases account will be debited.

GST Input GST (either CGST, SGST or IGST) will be required to be paid by the purchaser. Hence, GST paid will be an expense for him. So, as per traditional approach, rule of nominal account, i.e. debit all expenses, will apply and GST will be debited. Similarly, as per the modern approach, the rule of expenses account, i.e. debit increase in expenses, will apply and hence GST account will be debited.

Cash/Bank/Creditor If purchases are made in cash or through cheque, then as per traditional approach, the rule of real account, i.e. credit what goes out, will apply and cash or bank account will be credited. However, if purchases are made on credit, then the rule of personal account, i.e. credit the giver, will apply and creditor's account will be credited. As per the modern approach, if purchases are made in cash or through cheque, then the rule of asset account, i.e. credit account will be credited. However, if purchases are been made on credit, then the rule of liability account, i.e. credit increase in liabilities, will apply and creditor's account will be credited.

Accounts involved and effect as per Traditional/Modern Rule	Nature of Account and Traditional Rule	Nature of Account and Modern Rule	Entry
Purchase (It is an expense/increase)	Nominal-Debit all expenses	Expenses-Debit the increase in expenses	For Intra-state Purchase Purchases A/c Dr
GST (It is an expense/increase)	Nominal-Debit all expenses	Expenses-Debit the increase in expenses	Intput CGST A/c Dr Intput SGST/UTGST A/c Dr To Cash/Bank/Creditor
Cash/Bank (It is going out/decrease)	Real-Credit what goes out	Asset-Credit the decrease in asset	**For Inter-state Purchase**
Creditor (He is the giver/increase)	Personal-Credit the giver	Liability-Credit the increase in liability	Purchase A/c Dr Input IGST A/c Dr To Cash/Bank/Creditor

(ii) Goods Purchased Returned

Accounts involved and effect as per Traditional/Modern Rule	Nature of Account and Traditional Rule	Nature of Account and Modern Rule	Entry
Dinesh (Dinesh is the receiver/decrease)	Personal-Debit the receiver	Liability-Debit the decrease in liability	**For Return of Intra-state Purchase** Creditor's/Cash/Bank A/c Dr To Purchases Return A/c To Input CGST A/c To Input SGST A/c **For Return of Inter-state Purchase**
GST (GST in an expense/decrease)	Nominal-Credit all gains	Expenses-Credit the decrease in expense	Creditor's/Cash/Bank A/c Dr To Purchases Return A/c To Input IGST A/c
Purchases Return (It is an expense/decrease)	Nominal-Credit all gains	Expenses-Credit the decrease in expenses	

(iii) Purchase of Asset for Cash

Accounts involved and effect as per Traditional/Modern Rule	Nature of Account and Traditional Rule	Nature of Account and Modern Rule	Entry
Machinery (It is coming in/increase)	Real-Debit what comes in	Asset-Debit the increase in asset	**In Case of Intra-state Purchase**
GST (It is an expense/increase)	Nominal-Debit all expenses	Expenses-Debit the increase in expenses	Asset A/c Dr Input CGST A/c Dr Input SGST A/c Dr To Vendor's/ Bank A/c **In Case of Inter-state Purchase**
Cash (It is going out/decrease)	Real-credit what goes out	Asset-Credit the decrease in asset	Asset A/c Dr Input IGST A/c Dr To Vendor's/Bank A/c

Note *If the asset is purchased on credit, then vendor's account will be credited.*

(iv) Sold Goods for Cash GST Collected from the Customer

Accounts involved and effect as per Traditional/Modern Rule	Nature of Account and Traditional Rule	Nature of Account and Modern Rule	Entry
Cash (It is coming in/increase)	Real-Credit what comes in	Asset-Debit the increase in asset	**For Intra-state Sale** Cash/Bank/A/c Dr To Sales A/c To Output CGST A/c To Output SGST A/c
Sales (It is revenue/increase)	Nominal-Credit all revenue and income	Revenue-Credit the increase in revenue	**For Inter-state Sale** Cash/Bank A/c Dr To Sales A/c To Output IGST A/c
GST (It is revenue/increase)	Nominal-Credit all revenue and income	Revenue-Credit the increase in revenue	

Note *If goods are sold on credit, then instead of cash/bank, debtor's account will be debited.*

(v) Goods Sold are Returned

Accounts involved and effect as per Traditional/Modern Rule	Nature of Account and Traditional Rule	Nature of Account and Modern Rule	Entry
Sales Return (It is a revenue/decrease)	Nominal-Debit decrease in revenue	Income-Debit the decrease in income	**For Return of Intra-state Sale** Sales Return A/c Dr Output CGST A/c Dr Output SGST A/c Dr To Debtor's/Cash/Bank A/c
GST (It is an expense/increase)	Nominal-Debit all expenses	Expenses-Debit the increase in expenses	**For Return of Inter-state Sale** Sales Return A/c Dr Output IGST A/c Dr To Debtor's/Cash/Bank A/c
Cash/Bank (It is going out/decrease)	Real-Credit what goes out	Asset-Debit the decrease in asset	

Note *In case of credit sale, debtor's account will be credited.*

ILLUSTRATION |3| Transactions of Sukhwinder of Mumbai for April, 2019 are given below. Journalise them.

2019	Particulars	Amt (₹)
April 1	Sukhwinder started business and brought capital in cash	2,00,000
April 3	Bought goods for ₹ 10,000 *plus* CGST and SGST @ 9% each	
April 13	Sold goods to Sangeet for ₹ 3,000 *plus* CGST and SGST @ 9% each	
April 20	Bought goods from Karamveer for ₹ 6,000 *plus* CGST and SGST @ 9% each	
April 24	Cash received from Sangeet	
April 24	Sold goods to Ramanpreet for ₹ 20,000 *plus* CGST and SGST @ 9% each. She paid the due amount immediately and availed cash discount @ 2%	3,540
April 28	Cash paid to Karamveer	4,300
	Discount allowed by him	100
April 30	Cash sales for the month ₹ 16,000 *plus* CGST and SGST @ 9% each	

Sol. **JOURNAL**

Date	Particulars		LF	Amt (Dr)	Amt (Cr)
2019					
Apr 1	Cash A/c	Dr		2,00,000	
	To Capital A/c				2,00,000
	(Being the amount bought in by Sukhwinder in the business as capital)				
Apr 3	Purchases A/c	Dr		10,000	
	Input CGST A/c	Dr		900	
	Input SGST A/c	Dr		900	
	To Cash A/c				11,800
	(Being the goods purchased for cash, paid CGST and SGST @ 9% each)				
Apr 13	Sangeet	Dr		3,540	
	To Sales A/c				3,000
	To Output CGST A/c				270
	To Output SGST A/c				270
	(Being the goods sold to Sangeet on credit, charged CGST and SGST @ 9%)				
Apr 20	Purchases A/c	Dr		6,000	
	Input CGST A/c	Dr		540	
	Input SGST A/c	Dr		540	
	To Karamveer				7,080
	(Being the goods bought from Karamveer on credit, CGST and SGST payable @ 9% each)				
Apr 24	Cash A/c	Dr		3,540	
	To Sangeet				3,540
	(Being the cash received from Sangeet)				
Apr 24	Bank A/c	Dr		23,138	
	Discount Allowed A/c	Dr		472	
	To Sales A/c				20,000
	To Output CGST A/c				1,800
	To Output SGST A/c				1,800
	(Being the goods sold against cash payment, charged CGST and SGST @ 9% each and allowed 2% cash discount)				
Apr 28	Karamveer	Dr		4,500	
	To Cash A/c				4,300
	To Discount Received A/c (W.N.)				200
	(Being the discount allowed by Karamveer on payment being made to him)				
Apr 30	Cash A/c	Dr		18,880	
	To Sales A/c				16,000
	To Output CGST A/c				1,440
	To Output SGST A/c				1,440
	(Being the goods old for cash, charged CGST and SGST @ 9% each)				

Working Note *Discount allowed by others is a gain thus, it is credited.*

ILLUSTRATION |4| Pass the journal entries for the following transactions:

(i) Purchased goods from Kavya of ₹ 20,000 *plus* IGST @ 18% at 10% trade discount and 2.5% cash discount. Paid amount at the time of purchase itself.

(ii) Purchased goods from Divij of ₹ 20,000 *plus* IGST @ 18% at 10% trade discount and 3% cash discount. Half of the amount paid at the time of purchase.

(iii) Sold goods to Raunak for ₹ 10,000 *plus* CGST and SGST @ 9% each, allowed him 10% trade discount and 3% cash discount. Received half of the amount of cash and balance half by cheque immediately.

(iv) Sold goods to Vardaan for ₹ 25,000 *plus* CGST and SGST @ 9% each fallowing 10% trade discount and 2% cash discount. Half of the amount received by cheque immediately.

(v) Sold goods costing ₹ 40,000 to Ayaan against a current dated cheque at a profit of 25% on cost *less* 20% trade discount *plus* IGST @ 18%. Cash discount is allowed @ 2%.

Sol.

JOURNAL

Date	Particulars		LF	Amt (Dr)	Amt (Cr)
(i)	Purchases A/c	Dr		18,000	
	Input IGST A/c	Dr		3,240	
	To Cash/Bank A/c				20,709
	To Discount Received A/c [2.5% (₹ 18,000 + 3,240)]				531
	(Being the goods purchased, paid IGST @ 18% at 10% trade discount and 2.5% cash discount) (W.N. 1)				
(ii)	Purchases A/c	Dr		18,000	
	Input IGST A/c	Dr		3,240	
	To Divij				10,620
	To Cash/Bank A/c				10,301.5
	To Discount Received A/c				318.5
	(Being the goods purchased, paid IGST @ 18% at 10% trade discount and 3% cash discount, half of the amount paid) (W.N. 2)				
(iii)	Cash A/c	Dr		5,150.5	
	Bank A/c	Dr		5,150.5	
	Discount Allowed A/c	Dr		319	
	To Sales A/c				9,000
	To Output CGST A/c				810
	To Output SGST A/c				810
	(Being the goods sold, charged CGST and SGST @ 9% each. Half the amount received in cash and balance by cheque. Allowed trade discount @ 10% and cash discount @ 3%) (W.N. 3)				
(iv)	Vardaan	Dr		13,275	
	Bank A/c	Dr		10,009.5	
	Discount Allowed A/c	Dr		265.5	
	To Sales A/c				22,500
	To Output CGST A/c				2,025
	To Output SGST A/c				2,025
	(Being the goods sold, charged CGST and SGST @ 9% each. Allowed trade discount @ 10% and cash discount @ 2%. Half the amount received) (W.N. 4)				
(v)	Bank A/c	Dr		23,128	
	Discount Allowed A/c	Dr		472	
	To Sales A/c				20,000
	To Output IGST A/c				3,600
	(Being the goods sold by cheque, charged IGST @ 18%) (W.N. 5)				

Working Notes

	Particulars			Amt (₹)
1.	Cost			20,000
	(–) Trade Discount 10%			(2,000)
				18,000
	(+) IGST @ 18%			3,240
	Invoice Price			21,240
	(–) Cash Discount 2.5%			(531)
				20,709
2.	Cost			20,000
	(–) Trade Discount 10%			(2,000)
				18,000
	(+) IGST @ 18%			3,240
				21,240
	Credit Transaction			10,620
	Cash Transaction			10,620
	(–) Cash Discount 3%			(318.5)
				10,301.5
3.	Sale Value (Gross)			10,000
	(–) Trade Discount 10%			(1,000)
				9,000
	(+) CGST @ 9%			810
	SGST @ 9%			810
				10,620
	By Cheque	5,310	By Cash	5,310
	(–) Cash Discount 3%	(159.5)		(159.5)
		5,150.5		5150.5
4.	Sales Value (Gross)			25,000
	(–) Trade Discount 10%			(2,500)
				22,500
	(+) CGST @ 9%			2,025
	SGST @ 9%			2,025
				26,550
	Cash Transaction (1/2 of ₹ 26,550)			13,275
	(–) Cash Discount			(265.5)
				13,004.5
	Credit Transaction			13,275
5.	Cost			20,000
	(+) Profit 25% on Cost			5,000
				25,000
	(–) Trade Discount @ 20%			(5,000)
	Invoice Price			20,000
	(+) IGST @ 18%			3,600
	Total Invoice Value			23,600
	(–) Cash Discount 2%			(472)
	Net Amount Received			23,178

Numerical Questions for Practice

1 Journalise the following transactions in the books of Sukumar of Kolkata:

(i) Sold goods to Sonu of Delhi at the list price ₹ 60,000 less trade discount 10% *add* CGST and SGST @ 9% each, and allowed cash discount 5%. He paid the amount immediately.

(ii) Supplied goods costing ₹ 18,000 to Teetu of Delhi issued invoice at 10% above cost *less* 5% trade discount *plus* IGST @ 18%.

(iii) Sold goods costing ₹ 3,00,000 to Sweety of Delhi at a profit of 20% on sales *less* 20% trade discount *plus* CGST and SGST @ 9% each and paid cartage ₹ 250 (Not to be charged from customer).

Ans Total of Journal = ₹ 4,39,907

2 Journalise the following transactions in the books of Amit of Mumbai:

(i) He started business contributing ₹ 40,000 in cash, ₹ 20,00,000 in cheque and a building valued at ₹ 20,00,000.

(ii) Purchased goods from Darshan Lal, Kanpur for ₹ 8,00,000 out of which cheque was issued for ₹ 2,40,000.

(iii) Sold goods on credit to Raman of Mumbai for ₹ 6,40,000.

(iv) Received ₹ 7,39,200 by cheque from Raman in full settlement of his account.

(v) Paid ₹ 6,96,000 to Darshan Lal in full settlement of amount due to him.

(vi) A new machine of ₹ 9,60,000 was purchased from Sewing Tools Ltd., Delhi in exchange of an old machine valued at ₹ 2,00,000. He gave a cheque of ₹ 4,00,000 from his savings account and balance from firm's account.

(vii) Purchased machinery from Ravinder and Sons, Mumbai for ₹ 2,00,000 on credit.

CGST and SGST @ 9% each to be levied on intra-state (within the state purchase and sale) while IGST is to be levied @ 18% on inter-state transactions.

Ans Total of Journal = ₹ 96,28,000

Banking Transactions

In the present economic scene of demonetisation, banking transactions are of utmost importance.

Examples of banking transactions are payment by cheque, cheque received, cash deposited into bank, bank charges/ interest charged by bank, etc. To record a banking transaction, a bank account is opened. As per the traditional classification, bank account is a personal account and as per the modern classification it is an asset account.

Some common banking transactions have been explained below.

(i) Deposited Cheque into Bank/Deposited into Bank/Cash Deposited for Opening an Account

The transaction affects two accounts : Bank and Cash

Bank As per the traditional approach, rule of personal account debit the receiver will apply; since bank is the receiver, bank account will be debited. Similarly as per the modern approach, the rule of assets account *i.e.*, debit the increase in asset, will apply; since bank balance is increasing, bank account will be debited.

Cash is a real (Asset) account. As per the traditional approach, the rule of real account *i.e.*, credit what goes out, will apply; since cash is going out, it will be credited. Similarly, as per the rule of asset account credit the decrease in asset, will apply; since cash is decreasing, it will be credited.

Accounts Involved and Effect as per Traditional/Modern Rule	Nature of Accounts and Traditional Rule	Nature of Accounts and Modern Rule	Entry
Bank (Bank is the receiver /Increase)	Personal— Debit the receiver	Asset— Debit the increase in asset	Bank A/c Dr
Cash (It is going out /Decrease)	Real— Credit what goes out	Asset— Credit the decrease in asset	To Cash A/c

Note *The explanation of the subsequent transactions can be easily understood with the help of the tables given below.*

(ii) Paid Rahul (Creditor) by Cheque

Accounts Involved and Effect as per Traditional/Modern Rule	Nature of Accounts and Traditional Rule	Nature of Accounts and Modern Rule	Entry
Rahul (Rahul is the receiver /Decrease)	Personal— Debit the receiver	Liability— Debit the decrease in liability	Rahul Dr
Bank (Bank is the giver /Decrease)	Personal— Credit the giver	Asset— Credit the decrease in asset	To Bank A/c

(iii) Withdrawn from Bank/Withdrawn from Bank for Office Use

Accounts Involved and Effect as per Traditional/Modern Rule	Nature of Accounts and Traditional Rule	Nature of Accounts and Modern Rule	Entry
Cash (It is coming in /Increase)	Real— Debit what comes in	Asset— Debit the increase in asset	Cash A/c Dr
Bank (Bank is the giver /Decrease)	Personal— Credit the giver	Asset— Credit the decrease in asset	To Bank A/c

(iv) Bank Charges-Interest/Interest on Overdraft Charged by Bank

Accounts Involved and Effect as per Traditional/Modern Rule	Nature of Accounts and Traditional Rule	Nature of Accounts and Modern Rule	Entry
Bank charges/ Interest (It is an expense /Increase) Bank (Bank is the giver /Decrease)	Nominal— Debit all expenses Personal— Credit the giver	Expenses— Debit the increase in expenses Asset— Credit the decrease in asset	Bank Charges/Interest A/c Dr To Bank A/c **It GST is specified** Bank Charges A/c Dr Input CGST A/c Dr Input SGST A/c Dr To Bank A/c

(v) Interest Allowed by Bank

Accounts Involved and Effect as per Traditional/Modern Rule	Nature of Accounts and Traditional Rule	Nature of Accounts and Modern Rule	Entry
Interest allowed (it is an income/increase) Bank (Bank is the receiver/increase)	Nominal—Credit all incomes Personal—Debit the receiver	Income—Credit the increase in incomes Asset—Debit the increase in asset	Bank A/c Dr To Interest A/c

(vi) Paid Expenses (Rent) by Cheque

Accounts Involved and Effect as per Traditional/Modern Rule	Nature of Accounts and Traditional Rule	Nature of Accounts and Modern Rule	Entry
Rent (It is an expense /Increase) Bank (Bank is the giver /Decrease)	Nominal— Debit all expenses Personal— Credit the giver	Expenses— Debit the increase in expenses Asset— Credit the decrease in asset	**If GST is not specified** Rent A/c Dr To Bank A/c **If GST is specified** Rent A/c Dr Input CGST A/c Dr Input SGST A/c Dr To Cash/Bank/ Outstanding Rent A/c

ILLUSTRATION |5| Journalise the following transactions

2016		Amt (₹)
Jan 1	Paid into bank for opening a current account	10,000
Jan 3	Withdrew from bank	1,500
Jan 4	Withdrew from bank for private use	1,000
Jan 5	Placed in fixed deposit account at bank by transfer from current account	2,500
Jan 10	Goods purchased and amount paid by cheque	1,250

Sol. **JOURNAL**

Date	Particulars	LF	Amt (Dr)	Amt (Cr)
2016				
Jan 1	Bank A/c Dr		10,000	
	To Cash A/c			10,000
	(Being the cash deposited into the bank)			
Jan 3	Cash A/c Dr		1,500	
	To Bank A/c			1,500
	(Being the cash withdrawn for office use)			
Jan 4	Drawings A/c Dr		1,000	
	To Bank A/c			1,000
	(Being the cash withdrawn from bank for personal use)			
Jan 5	Fixed Deposit A/c Dr		2,500	
	To Bank A/c			2,500
	(Being the transfer from current account to fixed deposit account)			
Jan 10	Purchases A/c Dr		1,250	
	To Bank A/c			1,250
	(Being the goods purchased and payment made through cheque)			
	Total		16,250	16,250

ILLUSTRATION |6| On 1st January, 2016, Gyan Singh opened a bank account by depositing ₹24,000 in cash. All remittances are to be paid into bank on the same day on which they are received and all payments are made by cheques. Enter the following transactions in the journal.

2016

Jan 2 Goods sold to Pritam for cash ₹ 1,000.

Jan 5 Settled Arjun's account of ₹ 800.

Jan 7 Received from Vinay a cheque for ₹ 3,000.

Jan 10 Purchased a typewriter for ₹ 800 and spend ₹ 200 on its repairs.

Jan 12 Vinay's cheque was returned dishonoured.

Jan 15 Received a money order for ₹ 100 from Arjun.

Jan 20 Vinay settled his account by means of a cheque for ₹ 3,020, ₹ 20 being for interest charged and ₹ 5 each for Input SGST and CGST.

Jan 27 Purchased machinery from Sunil for ₹ 20,000 and paid him by means of a bank draft purchased from bank for ₹ 20,020.

Sol. **JOURNAL**

Date	Particulars		LF	Amt (Dr)	Amt (Cr)
2016					
Jan 1	Bank A/c	Dr		24,000	
	To Cash A/c				24,000
	(Being the cash deposited into bank and current account opened)				
Jan 2	Cash A/c	Dr		1,000	
	To Sales A/c				1,000
	(Being the goods sold for cash)				
Jan 2	Bank A/c	Dr		1,000	
	To Cash A/c				1,000
	(Being the cash deposited into bank)				
Jan 5	Arjun's A/c	Dr		800	
	To Bank A/c				800
	(Being Arjun's account settled)				
Jan 7	Bank A/c	Dr		3,000	
	To Vinay's A/c				3,000
	(Being Vinay's account settled)				
Jan 10	Typewriter A/c	Dr		1,000	
	To Bank A/c (800 + 200)				1,000
	(Being a typewriter purchased for ₹ 800 and spend ₹ 200 on its repairs)				
Jan 12	Vinay's A/c	Dr		3,000	
	To Bank A/c				3,000
	(Being Vinay's cheque returned dishonoured)				
Jan 15	Cash A/c	Dr		100	
	To Arjun's A/c				100
	(Being a money order of ₹ 100 received from Arjun)				
Jan 15	Bank A/c	Dr		100	
	To Cash A/c				100
	(Being the cash deposited into bank)				
Jan 20	Bank A/c	Dr		3,030	
	To Vinay's A/c				3,000
	To Interest A/c				20
	To Input CGST A/c				5
	To Input SGST A/c				5
	(Being Vinay's account settled and ₹ 20 being for interest charged and ₹ 10 for CGST and SGST)				
Jan 27	Machinery A/c	Dr		20,000	
	Draft Commission A/c	Dr		20	
	To Bank A/c				20,020
	(Being a machinery purchased by means of a bank draft and draft commission being paid)				
	Total			57,040	57,040

NUMERICAL Questions for Practice

1 Pass journal entries for the following

2016		Amt (₹)
Jan 1	Paid into bank for opening a current account	25,000
Jan 5	Goods purchased and payment made by cheque	10,000
Jan 8	Cash sales ₹ 40,000, out of this amount ₹ 30,000 deposited in bank	
Jan 10	Withdrawn for private use	5,000
Jan 15	Withdrawn from bank	12,000
Jan 20	Placed on fixed deposit account at bank by transferring from current account	20,000

Ans Total of Journal = ₹ 1,42,000

2 Journalise the following transactions

(i) Deposited cash into bank ₹ 90,000.
(ii) Withdrew from the bank ₹ 50,000 for office use.
(iii) Withdrew from the bank ₹ 30,000 for private use.
(iv) Paid life insurance premium by cheque ₹ 1,000.
(v) Bank charges ₹ 200.
(vi) Interest allowed by bank ₹ 1,000.

Ans Total of Journal = ₹ 1,72,200

3 Pass necessary entries for the following transactions

(i)	Opened current account in Punjab National Bank	15,000
(ii)	Purchased for office by cheque	
	Stationery	100
	Furniture	5,000
(iii)	Withdrew from bank	
	For office use	1,000
	For private use	5,000
(iv)	Received a cheque from Goyal Bros	2,000
(v)	Sold goods to a customer and received a cheque in payment	1,200
(vi)	Sent a cheque to New General Insurance Co. for premium	3,000
(vii)	Paid rent by cheque Applicable rate of GST is 9%.	2,000
(viii)	Paid salary to an employee by cheque	5,000

Ans Total of Journal = ₹ 39,336

Entries of Some Specific Transactions

Entries of some specific transactions are summarised as follows

(i) Rohan became bankrupt (insolvent) and was able to pay only 60% of the amount due from him

This transaction affects three accounts : Cash, Bad Debts and Rohan's account

Cash As per the traditional approach, the rule of real account *i.e.*, debit what comes in will apply; since cash is coming in (Rohan is paying 60%) it will be debited. Similarly, as per the modern approach, the rule of asset account *i.e.*, debit the increase in asset will apply; since cash is increasing, it will be debited.

Bad debts is a nominal (loss) account. As per the traditional approach, the rule of nominal account *i.e.*, debit all expenses and losses will apply; since bad debts is a loss it will be debited (Rohan is not paying 40%). Similarly, as per the modern approach, the rule of expense/loss account *i.e.*, debit the increase in expense/loss will apply; since loss is increasing due to bad debts, it will be debited.

Rohan's account As per the traditional approach, rule of personal account credit the giver, will apply; since Rohan (Debtor) is a giver, his account will be credited. As per the modern approach, the rule of asset account credit the decrease in asset will apply; since debtors are decreasing, Rohan's account will be credited.

Accounts Involved and Effect as per Traditional/Modern Rule	Nature of Accounts and Traditional Rule	Nature of Accounts and Modern Rule	Entry	
Cash (It is coming in /Increase)	Real— Debit what comes in	Asset— Debit the increase in asset	Cash A/c	Dr
			Bad Debts A/c	Dr
Bad Debts (It is a loss /Increase)	Nominal— Debit all losses	Expense— Debit the increase in loss	To Rohan	
Rohan (He is the giver/Decrease)	Personal— Credit the giver	Asset (Debtor)— Credit the decrease in asset		

Note *The explanation of subsequent transactions can be easily understood with the help of the tables given below.*

(ii) Recovered from Rohan, an old amount written-off as bad debt.

Accounts Involved and Effect as per Traditional/Modern Rule	Nature of Accounts and Traditional Rule	Nature of Accounts and Modern Rule	Entry	
Cash (It is coming in /Increase)	Real— Debit what comes in	Asset— Debit the increase in asset	Cash A/c	Dr
Bad Debts Recovered (It is a gain/Increase)	Nominal— Credit all income and gains	Revenue— Credit the increase in revenue	To Bad Debts Recovered A/c	

Note *When the amount previously written-off as bad debts is received (partly or fully), it is termed as bad debts recovered.*

(iii) Goods withdrawn by Vijay for personal use.

Accounts Involved and Effect as per Traditional/Modern Rule	Nature of Accounts and Traditional Rule	Nature of Accounts and Modern Rule	Entry	
Drawings (Vijay is the receiver/Decrease)	Personal— Debit the receiver	Capital— Debit the decrease in capital	Drawings A/c	Dr
Purchases (It is going out/Decrease)	Real— Credit what goes out	Asset— Credit the decrease in asset	To Purchases A/c	

Note *Students should note, that purchase account is treated both as an expense (nominal) and asset (real) account When goods are purchased—It is treated as an expense and when goods are decreasing (i.e., when goods are withdrawn for personal use, goods are given as charity or are distributed as free samples or are loss by theft or fire) it is treated as an asset.*

(iv) Suresh distributed goods as charity

Accounts Involved and Effect as per Traditional/Modern Rule	Nature of Accounts and Traditional Rule	Nature of Accounts and Modern Rule	Entry
Charity (It is an expense /Increase) Purchases (It is going out/Decrease)	Nominal— Debit all expenses Real— Credit what goes out	Expense— Debit the increase in expenses Asset— Credit the decrease in asset	**If GST is not specified** Charity A/c Dr To Purchases A/c **If GST is Specified** *If goods were purchased intra-state* Donation/charity A/c Dr To Purchases A/c To Input CGST A/c To Input SGST A/c *If goods were purchased inter-state* Donation/Charity A/c To Purchases A/c To Input IGST A/c

(v) Sheenu distributed goods as free samples

Accounts Involved and Effect as per Traditional/Modern Rule	Nature of Accounts and Traditional Rule	Nature of Accounts and Modern Rule	Entry
Free Samples/ Advertisement (It is an expense /Increase) Purchases (It is going out/Decrease)	Nominal— Debit all expenses Real— Credit what goes out	Expense— Debit the increase in expenses Asset— Credit the decrease in asset	**If GST is not specified** Advertisement/Free Sample A/c Dr To Purchases A/c **If GST is specified** *If goods were purchased intra-state* Advertisement/Samples A/c Dr To Purchases A/c To Input CGST A/c To Input SGST A/c *If goods were purchased inter-state* Advertisement/Samples A/c Dr To Purchases A/c To Input IGST A/c

Note *A free sample account/advertisement account is opened to record goods distributed as free and sample.*

(vi) Shilpa had to bear loss due to theft/fire

Accounts Involved and Effect and Analysis as per Traditional/Modern Rule	Nature of Accounts and Traditional Rule	Nature of Accounts and Modern Rule	Entry
Loss by Theft/Fire (It is a loss/Increase)	Nominal— Debit all losses	Expense— Debit the increase in losses	**If GST is not specified** Loss by Theft/Fire A/c Dr
Purchases (It is going out /Decrease)	Real— Credit what goes out	Asset— Credit the decrease in asset	To Purchases A/c **If GST is specified** *In case goods were purchased intra-state* Loss of Goods by Fire/Theft A/c Dr To Purchases A/c To Input CGST A/c To Input SGST A/c *In case goods were purchased inter-state* Loss of Goods by Fire/Theft A/c Dr To Purchases A/c To Input IGST A/c

(vii) Kavya purchased machinery and paid installation expenses.

Accounts Involved and Effect as per Traditional/Modern Rule	Nature of Accounts and Traditional Rule	Nature of Accounts and Modern Rule	Entry
Machinery (It is coming in /Increase)	Real— Debit what comes in	Asset— Debit the increase in asset	**If GST is not specified** Machinery A/c Dr
Cash (It is going out /Decrease)	Real— Credit what goes out	Asset— Credit the decrease in asset	To Cash A/c

Note
- *When an asset is purchased, then asset account is debited and not purchases account. Purchases account is debited when goods are purchased with an intention to resell.*
- *Installation expenses will be added to the purchase price of machinery. They will not be shown separately.*

(viii) Karishma paid sundry expenses related to postage and conveyance

Accounts Involved and Effect as per Traditional/Modern Rule	Nature of Accounts and Traditional Rule	Nature of Accounts and Modern Rule	Entry
Sundry Expenses (It is an expense /Increase)	Nominal— Debit all expenses	Expenses— Debit the increase in expenses	Sundry Expenses A/c Dr
Cash (It is going out /Decrease)	Real— Credit what goes out	Asset— Credit the decrease in asset	To Cash A/c

Note *Business often incurs petty expenses such as refreshment, postage, conveyance, etc. To record all such expenses, an account named sundry expenses account is opened.*

(ix) Chhotey Lal, a timber dealer, used wood from his godown to make tables for office use.

Accounts Involved and Effect as per Traditional/Modern Rule	Nature of Accounts and Traditional Rule	Nature of Accounts and Modern Rule	Entry
Assets (It is coming in /Increase)	Real— Debit what comes in	Asset— Debit the increase in asset	Assets A/c Dr
Purchases (It is going out /Decrease)	Real— Credit what goes out	Asset— Credit the decrease in asset	To Purchases A/c

(x) X sold goods to Z, allowed him 10% trade discount and 10% cash discount.

Accounts Involved and Effect as per Traditional/Modern Rule	Nature of Accounts and Traditional Rule	Nature of Accounts and Modern Rule	Entry
Cash (It is coming in /Increase)	Real— Debit what comes in	Asset— Debit the increase in asset	Cash A/c Dr
Cash Discount Allowed (It is an expense /Increase)	Nominal— Debit all expenses	Expenses— Debit the increase in expenses	Discount Allowed A/c Dr
Sales (It is a revenue/Increase)	Nominal— Credit all revenue	Revenue— Credit the increase in revenue.	To Sales A/c

Note *It may be noted, if both trade discount and cash discount are allowed, firstly, trade discount is allowed and thereafter, cash discount is allowed. However, in the journal entry, only cash discount is shown.*

Opening Entry

An opening entry is a journal entry by the means of which the various balances related to assets, liabilities and capital of the previous accounting period are brought forward in the books of current accounting period. While passing an opening entry, all assets account are debited and all liabilities account are credited. If the amount of capital is not mentioned, then the difference between the total of assets and total of liabilities is treated as capital. Also if the total of liabilities and capital exceed the total of assets, then the difference between the two is treated as goodwill and the goodwill account is debited in the opening entry.

ILLUSTRATION |7| Following balances appear in the books of Keshav Ram & Sons as on 31st March, 2016

Assets :

Cash in hand ₹ 430; cash at bank ₹ 2,675; sundry debtors ₹ 7,495; closing stock ₹ 9,000; machinery and equipments ₹ 6,000

Liabilities & Capital :

Creditor ₹ 5,600 (CSI & Sons);
Capital ₹ 25,000
Pass the opening entry as on 1st April, 2016.

Sol.

Date	Particulars		LF	Amt (Dr)	Amt (Cr)
2016					
Apr 1	Cash A/c	Dr		430	
	Bank A/c	Dr		2,675	
	Sundry Debtors A/c	Dr		7,495	
	Closing Stock A/c	Dr		9,000	
	Machinery and Equipment A/c	Dr		6,000	
	Goodwill A/c	Dr		5,000	
	To CSI & Sons				5,600
	To Capital A/c				25,000
	(Being the balances brought forward)				

ILLUSTRATION |8| Journalise the following transactions in the journal of Shri Padukone.

	Amt (₹)
(i) Paid cash to Anil	2,400
and discount received from him	100
(ii) Received cash from Vijay	1,225
and discount allowed to him	25
(iii) Goods sold to Ravish	7,500
Ravish returned goods	500
Received cash from Ravish ₹ 6,875 in full settlement of his account.	

(iv) Sold goods to Rohan of the list price of ₹ 15,000 at 10% trade discount.
(v) Purchased goods from Bindu of the list price of ₹ 5,000 at 15% trade discount.
(vi) Purchased furniture worth ₹ 20,000 and tools worth ₹ 4,000.
(vii) Paid to Nishant out of business funds for repair of Shri Padukone's house ₹ 8,000.
(viii) Supplied goods costing ₹ 12,000 to Peter, issued invoice at 10% above cost less 5% trade discount.

Sol.

JOURNAL

Date	Particulars		LF	Amt (Dr)	Amt (Cr)
(i)	Anil	Dr		2,500	
	To Cash A/c				2,400
	To Discount Received A/c				100
	(Being cash paid to Anil and discount received)				
(ii)	Cash A/c	Dr		1,225	
	Discount Allowed A/c	Dr		25	
	To Vijay				1,250
	(Being cash received from Vijay and discount allowed)				
(iii)	Ravish	Dr		7,500	
	To Sales A/c				7,500
	(Being goods sold to Ravish)				
	Sales Return A/c	Dr		500	
	To Ravish				500
	(Being goods returned by Ravish)				
	Cash A/c	Dr		6,875	
	Discount Allowed A/c	Dr		125	
	To Ravish				7,000
	(Being cash received from Ravish and discount allowed to him)				
	Balance c/f			18,750	18,750

Date	Particulars	LF	Amt (Dr)	Amt (Cr)
	Balance b/f		18,750	18,750
(iv)	Rohan Dr		13,500	
	To Sales A/c			13,500
	(Being goods of the list price of ₹ 15,000 sold at 10% trade discount)			
(v)	Purchases A/c Dr		4,250	
	To Bindu			4,250
	(Being goods of the list price of ₹ 5,000 purchased at 15% trade discount)			
(vi)	Furniture A/c Dr		20,000	
	Tools A/c Dr		4,000	
	To Cash A/c			24,000
	(Being furniture and tools purchased)			
(vii)	Drawings A/c Dr		8,000	
	To Cash A/c			8,000
	(Being amount paid for repairs of Shri Padukones' residential house)			
(viii)	Peter Dr		12,540	
	To Sales A/c (W.N)			12,540
	(Being goods sold to Peter at 10% above cost and allowed 5% discount)			
	Total		81,040	81,040

In the given illustration, the total of one page has been carried forward to the subsequent page for the understanding of the student.

Working Note

Cost of goods	12,000
(+) 10% of 12,000	1,200
	13,200
(–) Trade discount 5%	(660)
	₹ 12,540

ILLUSTRATION |9| Pass the journal entries for the following

(i) Proprietor withdrew for his personal use cash ₹ 10,000 and goods worth ₹ 5,000.

(ii) Goods worth ₹ 25,000 were given away as charity (sale price ₹ 30,000).

(iii) Goods worth ₹ 12,500 were distributed as free samples. Applicable GST rate was 9%.

(iv) Goods worth ₹ 25,000 and cash ₹ 10,000 were stolen by an employee.

(v) Goods worth ₹ 50,000 were destroyed by fire. Insurance company admitted and paid claim for 60% amount.

Sol.

JOURNAL

Date	Particulars	LF	Amt (Dr)	Amt (Cr)
(i)	Drawings A/c Dr		15,000	
	To Cash A/c			10,000
	To Purchases A/c			5,000
	(Being cash and goods taken away by proprietor for personal use)			
(ii)	Charity A/c Dr		29,500	
	To Purchases A/c			25,000
	To Input CGST A/c			2,250
	To Input SGST A/c			2,250
	(Being goods given away as charity)			

Date	Particulars		LF	Amt (Dr)	Amt (Cr)
(iii)	Advertisement Expenses A/c	Dr		12,500	
	To Purchases A/c				12,500
	(Being goods distributed as free samples)				
(iv)	Loss by Theft A/c	Dr		35,000	
	To Purchases A/c				25,000
	To Cash A/c				10,000
	(Being goods and cash stolen by an employee)				
(v)	Loss by Fire A/c	Dr		50,000	
	To Purchases A/c				50,000
	(Being goods destroyed by fire)				
	Insurance Company A/c	Dr		50,000	
	To Loss by Fire A/c				50,000
	(Being insurance claim lodged with the insurance company)				
	Bank A/c	Dr		30,000	
	Profit and Loss A/c	Dr		20,000	
	To Insurance Company A/c				50,000
	(Being insurance claim of ₹ 50,000, accepted and received at ₹ 30,000 *i.e.*, 60% of 50,000)				
	Total			2,37,500	2,37,500

ILLUSTRATION |10| Journalise the following transactions in the books of Shree Nimesh.

(i) Goods sold to Sweety list price ₹ 10,000, trade discount 10% and cash discount 5%. The cash discount was availed by Sweety.

(ii) Manu who owed us ₹ 5,000 is declared insolvent and 65 paise in a rupee is received from his estate.

(iii) ₹ 1,000 due from Rohit are now bad debts.

(iv) Goods worth ₹ 2,000 were used by the proprietor.

(v) Paid income tax ₹ 5,000.

Sol.

JOURNAL

Date	Particulars		LF	Amt (Dr)	Amt (Cr)
(i)	Cash A/c	Dr		8,550	
	Discount Allowed A/c (9,000 × 5%)	Dr		450	
	To Sales A/c [10,000 – (10,000 × 10%)]				9,000
	(Being goods of list price ₹ 10,000 sold at 10% trade discount and 5% cash discount)				
(ii)	Cash A/c (5,000×.0.65)	Dr		3,250	
	Bad Debts A/c	Dr		1,750	
	To Manu				5,000
	(Being cash received and bad debts written-off)				
(iii)	Bad Debts A/c	Dr		1,000	
	To Rohit (Debtor)				1,000
	(Being ₹ 1,000 due from Rohit is bad debts now)				
(iv)	Drawings A/c	Dr		2,000	
	To Purchases A/c				2,000
	(Being goods worth ₹ 2,000 used by the proprietor)				
(v)	Drawings A/c	Dr		5,000	
	To Cash A/c				5,000
	(Being the income tax paid)				
	Total			22,000	22,000

ILLUSTRATION |11| Record the following transactions in a journal

(i) Received cash from Jaya for a bad debt written-off last year ₹ 400.

(ii) Bought goods at the list price of ₹ 1,00,000 from Rani less 20% trade discount and 2% cash discount and paid 40% by cheque.

(iii) Sold goods to Preeti at the list price of ₹ 2,00,000 less 20% trade discount and 2% cash discount and paid 50% by cheque.

(iv) Sold goods to Tanu for ₹ 40,000, allowing her a trade discount of 5% and a cash discount of 10%. She paid 1/4th of the amount in cash at the time of purchase.

Sol.

JOURNAL

Date	Particulars		LF	Amt (Dr)	Amt (Cr)
(i)	Cash A/c	Dr		400	
	To Bad Debts Recovered A/c				400
	(Being the bad debts written-off last year, now recovered)				
(ii)	Purchases A/c	Dr		80,000	
	To Rani				80,000
	(Being the goods purchased from Rani at a trade discount of 20%)				
	Rani	Dr		32,000	
	To Bank A/c				31,360
	To Discount Received A/c (W.N. 1)				640
	(Being the 40% payment made to Rani under a cash discount of 2%)				
	In place of the two entries, one single entry can also be passed.				
	Purchases A/c	Dr		80,000	
	To Bank A/c				31,360
	To Discount Received A/c				640
	To Rani				48,000
(iii)	Preeti	Dr		1,60,000	
	To Sales A/c				1,60,000
	(Being the goods sold to Preeti at a trade discount of 20%)				
	Bank A/c	Dr		78,400	
	Discount Allowed A/c	Dr		1,600	
	To Preeti (W.N. 2)				80,000
	(Being the 50% payment made by Preeti under a cash discount of 2%)				
	In place of two entries, one single entry can also be passed				
	Bank A/c	Dr		78,400	
	Discount Allowed A/c	Dr		1,600	
	Preeti	Dr		80,000	
	To Sales A/c				1,60,000
(iv)	Tanu	Dr		28,500	
	Cash A/c	Dr		8,550	
	Discount Allowed A/c	Dr		950	
	To Sales A/c (W.N. 3)				38,000
	(Being the goods sold to Tanu at terms of 5% trade discount and 10% cash discount and received 1/4th in cash)				
	Total			3,90,400	3,90,400

Working Note 1

Gross value of purchases	1,00,000
(–) Trade discount @ 20%	20,000
	80,000
Cash payment $= 80{,}000 \times 40\%$	32,000
(–) Discount received $= 32{,}000 \times 2\%$	640
Cash received	31,360
Balance amount payable to Rani $= 80{,}000 - 32{,}000$	48,000

Working Note 2

Gross value of sales	2,00,000
(–) Trade discount @ 20%	40,000
	1,60,000
Cash to be received $= 1{,}60{,}000 \times 50\%$	80,000
(–) Discount given $= 80{,}000 \times 2\%$	1,600
Cash received	78,400

Balance amount to be received from Preeti = 1,60,000 – 80,000 = ₹ 80,000

Working Note 3

Gross value of sales	40,000
(–) Trade discount @ 5%	2,000
	₹ 38,000

Cash transaction amount $= 38{,}000 \times \frac{1}{4} =$ ₹ 9,500

Credit transaction amount $= 38{,}000 \times \frac{3}{4} =$ ₹ 28,500

Cash discount allowed $= 9{,}500 \times 10\% =$ ₹ 950

Cash received from cash transaction $= 9{,}500 - 950 =$ ₹ 8,550

ILLUSTRATION |12| Journalise the following transactions in the books of Madan.

2016

Sep 2 Sold goods costing ₹ 45,000 to Suresh at a profit of $33\frac{1}{3}\%$ on cost less 20% trade discount and paid carriage ₹ 400 (to be charged from the customer).

Sep 5 Spent ₹ 300 for refreshment of a customer.

Sep 7 Machinery purchased ₹ 10,000 paid installation expenses ₹ 2,500.

Sep 9 Sold goods costing ₹ 40,000 to Prateek for cash at a profit of 25% on cost less 20% trade discount and paid cartage ₹ 200 (not to be charged from the customer).

Sep 19 Paid life insurance premium ₹ 5,000.

Sol.

JOURNAL

Date	Particulars		LF	Amt (Dr)	Amt (Cr)
2016					
Sep 2	Suresh A/c	Dr		48,400	
	To Sales A/c (W.N.1)				48,000
	To Carriage Outwards A/c				400
	(Being goods sold to Suresh on credit)				
Sep 5	Sundry Expenses A/c	Dr		300	
	To Cash A/c				300
	(Being amount spent for refreshment of customer)				
Sep 7	Machinery A/c	Dr		12,500	
	To Cash A/c (10,000 +2,500)				12,500
	(Being machinery purchased and installation expenses paid ₹ 2,500)				
Sep 9	Cash A/c	Dr		40,000	
	To Sales A/c (W.N. 2)				40,000
	(Being goods sold for cash)				
	Cartage Outwards A/c	Dr		200	
	To Cash A/c				200
	(Being the cartage paid)				
Sep 19	Drawings A/c	Dr		5,000	
	To Cash A/c				5,000
	(Being the life insurance premium paid)				
	Total			1,06,400	1,06,400

Working Note

1. List Price	45,000
(+) Profit (45,000 × 33.33%)	15,000
	60,000
(–) Trade Discount (60,000 × 20%)	(12,000)
	48,000
2. List Price	40,000
(+) Profit (40,000 × 25%)	10,000
	50,000
(–) Trade Discount (50,000 × 20%)	(10,000)
	40,000

ILLUSTRATION |13| Journalise the following transactions in the books of Shrinath Apte.

(i) Opened bank account with PNB ₹ 10,000.

(ii) Cash sent to bank ₹ 50,000.

(iii) Bought shares in 'Birla Ltd' for ₹ 5000 and brokerage paid @ 2%. The payment is made by cheque.

(iv) Received cheque for ₹ 1,56,000 from John in full settlement of his account of ₹ 1,60,000.

(v) Paid ₹ 1,78,000 to Smith in full settlement of ₹ 1,80,000 due to him by cheque.

(vi) A cheque from a customer amounted to ₹ 5,000 deposited in the bank was returned dishonoured.

(vii) Bought furniture for office use by cheque for ₹ 18,000.

(viii) Sold goods to Kaushal of the list price of ₹ 12,500 less 20% trade discount and 2% cash discount and paid 40% by cheque.

(ix) Sold goods to Kaushal of the list price of ₹ 1,25,000 less 20% trade discount and received dated cheque under a cash discount of 2%.

Sol.

JOURNAL

Date	Particulars		LF	Amt (Dr)	Amt (Cr)
2016					
(i)	Bank A/c	Dr		10,000	
	To Cash A/c				10,000
	(Being amount deposited in PNB)				
(ii)	Bank A/c	Dr		50,000	
	To Cash A/c				50,000
	(Being amount deposited into bank)				
(iii)	Investment A/c [(5,000 + 100 (5,000 × 2%)]	Dr		5,100	
	To Bank A/c				5,100
	(Being investment in shares of Birla Ltd for ₹ 5,000 and brokerage paid @ 2%)				
(iv)	Bank A/c	Dr		1,56,000	
	Discount Allowed A/c	Dr		4,000	
	To John				1,60,000
	(Being cheque received from John and allowed him discount of ₹ 4,000)				
(v)	Smith	Dr		1,80,000	
	To Bank A/c				1,78,000
	To Discount Received A/c				2,000
	(Being cheque issued to Smith in full settlement of his dues ₹ 1,80,000)				
(vi)	Customer A/c	Dr		5,000	
	To Bank A/c				5,000
	(Being cheque deposited into bank dishonoured)				
(vii)	Furniture A/c	Dr		18,000	
	To Bank A/c				18,000
	(Being furniture bought and paid by cheque)				
(viii)	Kaushal	Dr		10,000	
	To Sales A/c				10,000
	(Being goods sold to Kaushal at a trade discount of 20%)				
	Bank A/c (W.N.1)	Dr		3,920	
	Discount Allowed A/c	Dr		80	
	To Kaushal				4,000
	(Being 40% payment made by Kaushal under a cash discount of 2%)				
(ix)	Bank A/c (W.N. 2)	Dr		98,000	
	Discount Allowed A/c	Dr		2,000	
	To Sales A/c				1,00,000
	(Being goods sold against a current dated cheque at a trade discount of 10% and cash discount of 2%)				
	Total			5,42,100	5,42,100

Working Note 1

(40% of ₹ 10,000)	4,000
(–) Cash discount [2% of ₹ 4,000]	(80)
Net payment made	3,920

Working Note 2

List Price	1,25,000
(–) Trade discount (20%)	(25,000)
	1,00,000
Cash discount (2%)	(2,000)
	98,000

NUMERICAL Questions for Practice

1 Journalise the following transactions

(i) Paid customs duty ₹ 11,000 in cash on import of a new machinery.

(ii) Goods sold costing ₹ 10,000 to M/s. Abbas & Sons at a invoice price 10% above cost less 10% trade discount.

(iii) Goods worth ₹ 50,000 and cash ₹ 20,000 were stolen by an employee.

(iv) Goods costing ₹ 10,000 were returned to Ram Bros. as the goods were hazardous for the health of the consumers.

(v) Received ₹ 9,500 from Sohan in full settlement of his account for ₹ 10,000.

(vi) Received ₹ 9,500 from Shyam on his account for ₹ 10,000.

(vii) Paid ₹ 4,800 to Mohan in full settlement of his account for ₹ 5,000.

(viii) Paid ₹ 4,800 to Ashok on his account for ₹ 5,000.

(ix) Sold goods to Kitty at a list price of ₹ 20,000. Sales subject to 10% trade discount and 5% cash discount if payment is made immediately. Kitty availed cash discount.

(x) Supplied goods costing ₹ 60,000 to Shyam. Issued invoice at 10% above cost less 5% Trade discount.

Ans Total of Journal = ₹ 2,10,900

2 Pass journal entries for the following transactions

(i) Received cash ₹ 2,000 for bad-debts written off last year.

(ii) Kabir was declared bankrupt. He owed ₹ 5,000 to us. Nothing could be recovered from his estate.

(iii) Purchased furniture for ₹ 12,000 for the proprietor and paid the amount by cheque.

3 Prepare journal from the transactions given below

(i) Proprietor withdrew for private use ₹ 20,000 from bank.

(ii) Goods costing ₹ 1,00,000 were burnt by fire.

(iii) Purchased machinery for cash ₹ 3,00,000 and paid ₹ 4,000 on its installation.

(iv) Gaurav is declared insolvent. A compensation of 25 paise in the rupee is received from his estate out of ₹ 5,000.

Ans Total of Journal = ₹ 4,29,000

4 Journalise the following transactions

(i) Sold goods to Brijesh of the list price of ₹ 10,000 at trade discount of 5%. Received full payment in cash.

(ii) Goods given away as charity ₹ 1,000.

(iii) Received commission ₹ 5,000 half of which is in advance.

(iv) Cash embezzeled by an employee ₹ 1,000.

(v) ₹ 5,000 due from Raj are now bad debts.

(vi) ₹ 50,000 cash sales (of goods costing ₹ 40,000).

Ans Total of Journal = ₹ 71,500

5 Journalise the following transactions

(i) Goods for ₹ 50,000 were destroyed by fire.

(ii) Goods worth ₹ 18,000 were distributed as free samples and ₹ 20,000 were given away as charity in cash.

(iii) Goods worth ₹ 25,000 and cash ₹ 40,000 were taken away by the proprietor for his personal use.

(iv) Goods worth ₹ 20,000 and cash ₹ 5,000 were given away as charity.

(v) Cash ₹ 1,00,000 were stolen from the iron safe of trader.

(vi) Goods sold for a list price of ₹ 50,000, trade discount allowed 10%, cash discount allowed 10%.

Ans Total of Journal = ₹ 3,18,500

Adjustment Entries

These entries are passed at the end of the year to make necessary adjustments in accounts, so that final accounts show true and fair view of the results of the business.

(*i*) **Closing Stock** The goods lying unsold at the end of the year is termed as closing stock. It is valued at cost or net realisable value whichever is lower. It is given as additional information and not in trial balance. It should be brought into the books. In order to calculate the correct gross profit or gross loss.

Entry	
Closing Stock A/c	Dr
To Trading A/c	

(*ii*) **Depreciation** The value of fixed assets decreases every year due to efflux of time or obsolescence or use. This decrease in value is called depreciation. It is an expense hence, a loss.

Entry	
Depreciation A/c	Dr
To Assets A/c	

(*iii*) **Interest on Capital** Interest may be allowed on proprietor's/ partner's capital. It is an expense for the firm.

Entry	
Interest on Capital A/c	Dr
To Capital A/c	

(*iv*) **Interest on Drawings** Withdrawal of cash or goods for personal use by the owner is termed as drawings. If interest is charged on drawings, it is an income.

Entry	
Drawings A/c	Dr
To Interest on Drawings A/c	

(*v*) **Outstanding Expenses** The expenses that relate to the current year but have not been paid till the end of the year are outstanding expenses. They are treated as expenses and also payable.

Entry	
Expenses A/c	Dr
To Outstanding Expenses A/c	

(*vi*) **Prepaid Expenses** Those expenses which have been paid during the current accounting period but the benefit of which will accrue in the subsequent accounting period or periods like insurance, rent of shop, etc.

Entry	
Prepaid Expenses A/c	Dr
To Expenses A/c	

(*vii*) **Accrued Income or Income Accrued but not Due** Accrued income is the income which is earned but not received. It is an asset for the firm. *e.g.,* interest on investment has become due but not received.

Entry	
Accrued Income A/c	Dr
To Income A/c	

(*viii*) **Income Received in Advance or Unearned Income** Income received in advance is the income received but not earned during the accounting period. It is a liability for the firm.

Entry	
Concerned Income A/c	Dr
To Income Received in Advance A/c	

ILLUSTRATION |14| Journalise the following transactions

(i) Paid rent of building ₹ 30,000, half of the building is used by the proprietor for residential use.
(ii) Paid fire insurance of the above building ₹ 2,500.
(iii) Salary due to clerk ₹ 1,250.
(iv) Charge depreciation on furniture @ 10% per annum for 1 month (furniture ₹ 30,000).
(v) Provide interest on capital (₹ 1,50,000) at 15% per annum for 6 months.
(vi) Charge interest on drawings (₹ 25,000) at 18% per annum for 6 months.
(vii) Interest on loan from Ram (₹ 2,50,000) at 18% per annum for 2 months is outstanding.
(viii) Interest on loan to Shyam (₹ 5,00,000) at 18% per annum for 2 months is outstanding.
(ix) Received commission ₹ 2,500 half of which is in advance.
(x) Brokerage due to us ₹ 1,250.
(xi) Salaries remaining unpaid ₹ 15,000 and rent due to landlord ₹ 2,000.

Sol. **JOURNAL**

Date	Particulars		LF	Amt (Dr)	Amt (Cr)
(i)	Rent A/c	Dr		30,000	
	To Cash A/c				30,000
	(Being the rent paid for building)				
	Drawings A/c (30,000 × 50%)	Dr		15,000	
	To Rent A/c				15,000
	(Being the rent for half building charged to proprietor)				
	In place of the two entries, one single entry can also be passed.				
	Rent	Dr		15,000	
	Drawings A/c	Dr		15,000	
	To Cash A/c				30,000
(ii)	Fire Insurance Premium A/c	Dr		2,500	
	To Cash A/c				2,500
	(Being the fire insurance premium paid for building)				
	Drawings A/c	Dr		1,250	
	To Fire Insurance Premium A/c				1,250
	(Being the fire Insurance premium for half building charged to proprietor)				
	In place of two entries, one single entry can also be passed.				
	Drawings A/c	Dr		1,250	
	Fire Insurance Premium A/c	Dr		1,250	
	To Cash A/c				2,500
(iii)	Salary A/c	Dr		1,250	
	To Outstanding Salary A/c				1,250
	(Being salary due to clerk)				

Date	Particulars		LF	Amt (Dr)	Amt (Cr)
(iv)	Depreciation on Furniture A/c $\left(30{,}000 \times \frac{10}{100} \times \frac{1}{12}\right)$	Dr		250	
	To Furniture A/c				250
	(Being the depreciation on furniture provided)				
(v)	Interest on Capital A/c $\left(1{,}50{,}000 \times \frac{15}{100} \times \frac{6}{12}\right)$	Dr		11,250	
	To Capital A/c				11,250
	(Being the interest on capital provided @ 15% per annum for 6 months)				
(vi)	Capital A/c	Dr		2,250	
	To Interest on Drawings A/c $\left(25{,}000 \times \frac{18}{100} \times \frac{6}{12}\right)$				2,250
	(Being the interest on drawings charged @ 18% per annum for 2 months)				
(vii)	Interest on Loan from Ram A/c $\left(2{,}50{,}000 \times \frac{18}{100} \times \frac{2}{12}\right)$	Dr		7,500	
	To Outstanding Interest on Loan from Ram A/c				7,500
	(Being the interest on loan from Ram provided @ 18% per annum for 2 months)				
(viii)	Accrued Interest on Loan to Shyam A/c	Dr		15,000	
	To Interest on Loan to Shyam A/c $\left(5{,}00{,}000 \times \frac{18}{100} \times \frac{2}{12}\right)$				15,000
	(Being the interest on loan to Shyam charged @ 18% per annum 2 months)				
(ix)	Cash A/c	Dr		2,500	
	To Commission A/c				2,500
	(Being the commission received)				
	Commission A/c	Dr		1,250	
	To Commission Received in Advance A/c (2,500 × 50%)				1,250
	(Being the commission received in advance adjusted)				
(x)	Accrued Brokerage A/c	Dr		1,250	
	To Brokerage A/c				1,250
	(Being the brokerage due to us adjusted)				
(xi)	Salaries A/c	Dr		15,000	
	To Outstanding Salaries A/c				15,000
	(Being salaries due)				
	Rent A/c	Dr		2,000	
	To Outstanding Rent A/c				2,000
	(Being rent due)				
	Total			1,08,250	1,08,250

Comprehensive Illustration

ILLUSTRATION |15| Journalise the following transactions.

		Amt (₹)
(i)	Commenced business with cash	25,000
(ii)	Purchased furniture for cash	2,000
(iii)	Stationery purchased	150
(iv)	Cash paid for installation of machine	500
(v)	Goods given as charity	2,000
(vi)	Drawings by the proprietor for household expenses	400
(vii)	Bought from Salil	2,600
(viii)	Interest charge on capital @ 7% per annum when total capital were	70,000
(ix)	Received ₹ 1,200 of a bad debts written-off last year	
(x)	Sold to Mathur on credit	4,000
(xi)	Goods destroyed by fire	2,000
(xii)	Cash paid to Salil after deduction of discount ₹ 130	2,470
(xiii)	Rent outstanding	1,000
(xiv)	Interest on drawings	900
(xv)	Purchase of office equipment for cash	1,250
(xvi)	Mathur returned goods	200
(xvii)	Sudhir Kumar who owed me ₹ 3,000 has failed to pay the amount. He pays me a compensation of 45 paise in a rupee.	
(xviii)	Salary paid to clerk	2,000
(xix)	Commission received in advance	7,000

Sol.

JOURNAL

Date	Particulars		LF	Amt (Dr)	Amt (Cr)
(i)	Cash A/c To Capital A/c (Being amount brought in as capital)	Dr		25,000	25,000
(ii)	Furniture A/c To Cash A/c (Being furniture purchased for cash)	Dr		2,000	2,000
(iii)	Stationery A/c To Cash A/c (Being stationery purchased)	Dr		150	150
(iv)	Machinery A/c To Cash A/c (Being ₹ 500 installation charges for machinery paid)	Dr		500	500
(v)	Charity A/c To Purchases A/c (Being goods given as charity)	Dr		2,000	2,000
(vi)	Drawings A/c To Cash A/c (Being drawings in cash made by proprietor)	Dr		400	400
(vii)	Purchases A/c To Salil (Being goods purchased from Salil)	Dr		2,600	2,600
(viii)	Interest on Capital A/c (70,000 × 7%) To Capital A/c (Being interest @ 7% charged on capital of ₹ 70,000)	Dr		4,900	4,900

Date	Particulars		LF	Amt (Dr)	Amt (Cr)
(ix)	Cash A/c	Dr		1,200	
	To Bad Debts Recovered A/c				1,200
	(Being ₹ 1,200 bad debts recovered)				
(x)	Mathur	Dr		4,000	
	To Sales A/c				4,000
	(Being sales to Mathur on credit)				
(xi)	Loss by Fire A/c	Dr		2,000	
	To Purchases A/c				2,000
	(Being goods destroyed by fire)				
(xii)	Salil	Dr		2,600	
	To Cash A/c				2,470
	To Discount Received A/c				130
	(Being cash paid to Salil and discount received from him)				
(xiii)	Rent A/c	Dr		1,000	
	To Outstanding Rent A/c				1,000
	(Being outstanding rent recorded in books)				
(xiv)	Drawings A/c	Dr		900	
	To Interest on Drawings A/c				900
	(Being interest on drawings charged)				
(xv)	Office Equipment A/c	Dr		1,250	
	To Cash A/c				1,250
	(Being equipment purchased for cash)				
(xvi)	Sales Return A/c	Dr		200	
	To Mathur				200
	(Being goods returned by Mathur)				
(xvii)	Cash A/c (3,000×0.45)	Dr		1,350	
	Bad Debts A/c	Dr		1,650	
	To Sudhir				3,000
	(Being 45 paise in a rupee received from Sudhir who owed ₹ 3,000)				
(xviii)	Salary A/c	Dr		2,000	
	To Cash A/c				2,000
	(Being salary paid)				
(xix)	Cash A/c	Dr		7,000	
	To Commission Received in Advance A/c				7,000
	(Being commission received in advance)				
	Total			62,700	62,700

NUMERICAL Questions for Practice

1 **Enter the following transactions in the journal of Vaibhav who trades in readymade garments.**

2016		Amt (₹)
Jan 1	Suresh paid into bank as capital	60,000
Jan 2	He bought goods and paid by means of a cheque	24,000
Jan 3	Sold to Vishal & Co.	6,700
Jan 4	Sold goods for cash	10,900
Jan 5	Paid sundry expenses in cash	3,000
Jan 6	Cash sent to bank	15,000
Jan 7	Received cheque from Vishal & Co.	6,500
	Discount allowed	200
Jan 8	Paid wages in cash	1,000
Jan 8	Paid for office furniture and fittings by cheque	4,000

2016		Amt (₹)
Jan 9	Bought goods from Karunesh and Bros.	10,600
Jan 10	Sold to Mahendra	18,700
Jan 11	Returned goods to Karunesh & Bros.	1,500
Jan 12	Sent cheque to Karunesh & Bros. in full settlement	9,000
Jan 14	Sold goods for cash	4,900
Jan 14	Paid into bank	4,000
Jan 15	Drew cash from office for personal use	500
Jan 30	Bank charged interest	200
Jan 30	Paid cash for stationery	300
Jan 30	Bought goods from Rahul & Co. Ltd.	10,000
Jan 30	Received from Kartik on account	6,000
Jan 30	Sold household furniture and paid the money into business	20,000
Jan 30	Sold goods costing ₹ 50,000 to Aarav for cash at profit of 20% on cost less 20% trade discount.	

Ans Total of Journal = ₹ 2,65,000

2 **Journalise the following transactions of Kunal Gupta.**

2016		Amt (₹)
Dec 1	Kunal Gupta started business with cash	1,00,000
Dec 2	Paid into bank	60,000
Dec 3	Bought goods from M/s. Gaurav & Co. on credit	20,000
Dec 4	Purchased furniture	2,000
Dec 4	Purchased adding machine	8,000
Dec 4	Purchased typewriter	6,000
	(Payment in all cases made by cheque)	
Dec 6	Paid for postage	150
Dec 8	Sold goods for cash	4,000
Dec 9	Sold goods on credit to M/s. Rastogi & Co.	10,000
Dec 15	Paid to M/s Gaurav & Co.	19,500
	Discount allowed by them	500
Dec 25	Sold goods to M/s. Singh & Co.	5,600
Dec 27	Received cheque from M/s Rastogi & Co. in full settlement of amount due from them	9,750
Dec 31	Paid for electricity charges	100
Dec 31	Paid salary	1,500
Dec 31	Paid rent of building by cheque, half of the building is used by the proprietor for residential use	5,000
Dec 31	Drew for private use	3,500

Ans Total of Journal = ₹ 2,55,850

3 **Record the following transactions in the journal of Rawal Furniture Traders.**

2016		Amt (₹)
July 1	Started business with cash	4,00,000
July 2	Deposited into bank	3,50,000
July 10	Purchased machinery (issued cheque for the same)	1,00,000
July 15	Paid installation charges for machinery	2,000
July 20	Purchased timber from Bisla & Co. at the list price of ₹ 20,000.	
	He allowed 10% trade discount	
July 25	Timber costing ₹ 5,000 was used for furnishing the office	
July 31	Sold furniture to Rakesh on the list price of ₹ 10,000 and allowed him 10% trade discount	
Aug 10	Sent cheque to Bisla & Co. in full settlement	17,500
Aug 15	Received from Rakesh in full and final settlement	8,750
Aug 20	Paid wages	15,000
Aug 25	Issued a cheque for ₹ 5,000 in favour of the landlord for rent of August	

Ans Total of Journal = ₹ 9,31,000

4 Journalise the following transactions in the books of M/s. Chandra Mohan.

(i) Vishal who owed ₹ 5,000 was declared insolvent and 60 paise in a rupee are received as final compensation.
(ii) Out of insurance paid this year, ₹ 3,000 is related to next year.
(iii) Provide depreciation @ 10% on furniture costing ₹ 10,000 for 9 months.
(iv) Paid customs duty ₹ 11,000 in cash on import of a new machinery.
(v) Goods sold costing ₹ 10,000 to M/s. Bhardwaj & Sons at a invoice price 10% above cost less 10% trade discount.
(vi) Received a cheque from Rajesh ₹ 5,450. Allowed him discount ₹ 150.
(vii) Returned goods to Simran of the value of ₹ 350.
(viii) Issued a cheque in favour of M/s. Rajveer Timber Company on account of the purchase of timber worth ₹ 7,500.
(ix) Sold goods to Sunny, list price ₹ 4,000, trade discount 10% and cash discount 5%. He paid the amount on the same day and availed the cash discount.
(x) Received an order from Gauri & Co. for supply of goods of the list price ₹ 1,00,000 with an advance of 10% of list price.
(xi) Received commission ₹ 5,000 half of which is in advance.
(xii) Cash embezzled by an employee ₹ 1,000.

Ans Total of Journal = ₹ 1,07,950

5 Journalise the following transactions.

(i) Started business with cash ₹ 1,50,000 and goods worth ₹ 10,000.
(ii) Goods purchased from M/s Garg. & Sons ₹ 4,000 and from Peterson ₹ 1,000.
(iii) Goods uninsured worth ₹ 2,000 were destroyed by fire.
(iv) Supplied goods costing ₹ 1,000 to Gavaskar issued at 10% above cost less 5% trade discount.
(v) Issued a cheque in favour of M/s. Garg & Sons on account of purchase of goods worth ₹ 4,000.
(vi) Outstanding salary at the end of the year ₹ 650
(vii) Paid to Peterson ₹ 990 in full settlement of ₹ 1,000.
(viii) Paid insurance premium ₹ 13,000.
(ix) Out of insurance paid this year, ₹ 1,000 is related to next year.
(x) Provide depreciation @ 10% per annum on furniutre costing ₹ 20,000 for 9 months.

Ans Total of Journal = ₹ 1,89,195

6 Journalise the following transactions.

(i) Goods drawn by proprietor for own use ₹ 1,000.
(ii) Goods given as charity costing ₹ 501.
(iii) Income tax paid ₹ 2,500.
(iv) Goods costing ₹ 300 given as samples.
(v) College fee of proprietor's son paid ₹ 650.
(vi) Provide interest on capital (₹ 50,000) at 6% for six months.
(vii) Received interest on loan from the debtor ₹ 25,000.
(viii) Stock in hand at the end of the year ₹ 20,000.

Ans Total of Journal = ₹ 51,451

7 On 31st March, 2016, Kushal's assets and liabilities stood as under

Assets: Building ₹ 30,000, machinery ₹ 10,000, furniture ₹ 2,000, bill receivable ₹ 5,000, sundry debtors ₹ 12,000, stock ₹ 9,000, cash at bank ₹ 15,000, cash in hand ₹ 2,000.

Liabilities: Bills payable ₹ 4,000, Twinkle's loan ₹ 15,000, sundry creditors ₹ 20,000

Make an opening entry on 1st April, 2016.

Ans Capital (Balancing figure) = ₹ 46,000

8 Journalise the following transactions in the books of Kunal Kapoor, a trader.

Balance as on 1st April, 2016

Debit Balances : Cash in hand ₹ 18,000; cash at bank ₹ 25,600; stock of goods ₹ 50,000; furniture ₹ 10,000; and building ₹ 4,51,400.

Debtors : Amit ₹ 2,700; Manpreet ₹ 1,500; Zoya ₹ 2,000; Verma ₹ 1,800; and Sona ₹ 5,000.

Credit Balances : Sharma ₹ 5,400; Gupta & Co. ₹ 77,000; Shekhar Kapoor ₹ 52,000; and Mrs. Kanika's Loan ₹ 1,00,000.

2016

Sep 1 Purchased goods of ₹ 50,000 less 20% trade discount and 5% cash discount.

Sep 3 ₹ 2,646 received from Amit and allowed him discount ₹ 54.

Sep 5 Bought 100 shares in Patanjali Ltd. @ ₹ 15 per share brokerage paid ₹ 30.

Sep 8 Goods costing ₹ 500 were damaged in transit; a claim was made on the railway authorities for the same.

Sep 10 Cash ₹ 5,292 paid to Sharma and discount allowed by him ₹ 108.

Sep 13 Received cash from the railway in full settlement of claim for damaged in transit.

Sep 15 Verma is declared insolvent and a dividend of 50 paise in the rupee is received from him in full settlement.

Sep 18 Sold 40 shares in Patanjali Ltd. @ ₹ 18 per share, brokerage paid ₹ 15.

Sep 20 Bought an auto rickshaw for ₹ 21,000 to deliver goods to coustomers.

Sep 22 Paid for : Charity ₹ 501
Postage ₹ 200
Stationery ₹ 199

Sep 30 One month's interest on Mrs. Kanika's loan @ 12% per annum became due but could not be paid.

Sep 30 The auto rickshaw bought on Sep 20 met with an accident was sold as scrap for ₹ 5,000.

Sep 30 Received from salesman ₹ 3,000 for goods sold by him after deducting his travelling expenses ₹ 150.

Sep 30 Paid for: Salaries ₹ 3,500
Rent ₹ 1,500

Sep 30 Sold goods for ₹ 12,000 less 10% trade discount.

Ans Total of Journal = ₹ 6,83,985

A Quick Glance of Some Important Journal Entries

Transactions	Journal Entry	
1. Cash brought into the business as capital	Cash/Bank A/c	Dr
	To Capital A/c	
2. Cash and other assets brought into business	Building A/c	Dr
	Plant and Machinery/Furniture A/c	Dr
	Cash A/c	Dr
	To Capital A/c	
3. Goods purchased on cash	Purchases A/c	Dr
	To Cash/Bank A/c	
4. Goods purchased on credit	Purchases A/c	Dr
	To Supplier's A/c	
5. Cash sales	Cash A/c	Dr
	To Sales A/c	
6. Sales of goods on Credit	Customer A/c	Dr
	To Sales A/c	
7. Opening a bank account	Bank A/c	Dr
	To Cash A/c	

	Transactions	Journal Entry	
8.	Purchase of assets for cash	Assets A/c To Cash/Bank A/c	Dr
9.	Depreciation charged on assets	Depreciation A/c To Asset A/c	Dr
10.	Sale or disposal of any old asset at a loss	Cash/Bank A/c Loss on Sale of Assets A/c To Asset A/c	Dr Dr
11.	Sale or disposal of any old asset at a profit	Cash/Bank A/c To Asset A/c To Profit on Sale of Assets A/c	Dr
12.	Cash withdrawn for personal use	Drawings A/c To Cash A/c	Dr
13.	Goods withdrawn for personal use	Drawings A/c To Purchases A/c	Dr
14.	Goods given as chairty	Charity A/c To Purchases A/c	Dr
15.	Goods returned by the customer	Return Inwards A/c To Customer	Dr
16.	Goods returned to the supplier	Supplier's A/c To Return Outwards A/c	Dr
17.	Withdrawal of cash from bank	Cash A/c (Office Cash) Drawings A/c (Personal use) To Bank A/c	Dr Dr
18.	Collection of cash/cheque from customers (and discount allowed, if any)	Cash/Bank A/c (Net amount) Discount Allowed A/c (Discount) To Customer	Dr Dr
19.	For payment of cash/cheque to suppliers (and discount received, if any)	Supplier's A/c To Cash/Bank A/c (Net Amount) To Discount Received A/c (Discount)	Dr
20.	For abnormal loss of goods (Fire/Stolen)	Bank A/c (Insurance claim received) or Insurance Claim A/c (Insurance claim admitted) Abnormal Loss A/c (Loss) To Purchases A/c	Dr Dr Dr
21.	Bad debts	Bed Debts A/c To Customer	Dr
22.	Recovery of bad debts	Cash/Bank A/c To Bad Debts Recovered A/c	Dr
23.	Drawing a bill of exchange on debtor	Bills Receivable A/c To Debtor	Dr
24.	Acceptance of a bill of exchange	Creditor To Bills Payable A/c	Dr
25.	Bank charges/Interest etc charged by bank	Bank Charges/Interest A/c To Bank A/c	Dr
26.	Paid expenses by cheque	Expenses A/c To Bank A/c	Dr

|TOPIC 2|
Ledger

A ledger is the principal book of accounting system which contains all the accounts related to assets, liabilities, revenues, expenses. All the transactions recorded in the journal are transferred to ledger.

Ledger is called the **principal book/book of final entry** as trial balance is prepared from it and thereafter financial statements are prepared. It contains a summarised, classified and permanent record of all the business transactions.

A ledger may be in the form of bound register or cards or separate sheets may be maintained in a loose leaf binder. In the ledger, each account is opened preferably on separate page or card.

Utility of Ledger

(*i*) The net result of all transactions in respect of a particular account on a given date can be ascertained only from the ledger.

(*ii*) Ledger facilitates preparation of final accounts.

(*iii*) Accounts are opened in the ledger in some definite order for easy posting and location. Index is also provided in the beginning of ledger book. This ensures easy accessibility to accounting information.

(*iv*) Ledger provides complete information about all the accounts in one book.

Format of Ledger Account

Each ledger account is the summary of transactions at one place, relating to a particular head. It records not only the amount of transactions but also their effect and direction. The account is divided into two parts; the left hand side is the debit side and the right hand side is the credit side. The statement is prepared in 'T' shape, therefore sometimes it is called as 'T' account.

Dr **Name of the Account** Cr

Date	Particulars	JF	Amt (₹)	Date	Particulars	JF	Amt (₹)

A brief description of account is given below

(*i*) **Title of the Account** The name of the item is written at the top of the format as the title of the account. The title of the account ends with suffix 'account'.

(*ii*) **Dr/Cr** Dr means debit side of the account *i.e.*, left side and Cr means credit side of the account *i.e.*, right side.

(*iii*) **Date** Year, month and date of transactions are posted in chronological order in this column.

(*iv*) **Particulars** Name of the item with reference to the original book of entry is written on debit/credit side of the account. An account is debited or credited according to the rules of debit and credit.

(*v*) **Journal Folio** (JF) It records the page number of the original book of entry on which relevant transaction is recorded. This column is filled up at the time of posting.

(*vi*) **Amount** This column records the amount in numerical figure, corresponding to what has been entered in the amount column of the original book of entry.

POSTING THE ENTRIES

The process of transferring the entries from the books of original entry (journal) to the ledger is referred to as posting. Posting is the grouping of all the transactions, in respect to a particular account at one place, which facilitates meaningful conclusion. As per the requirements and convenience of the business, posting may be done periodically, weekly, fortnightly or monthly. But now-a-days, through accounting softwares, posting process is done automatically as the journal entry is passed.

Process of Posting from Journal to Ledger

The steps for posting of an account debited in a journal entry are

Step 1 Identify the account to be debited in the ledger.

Step 2 Enter the date of transaction in the date column on the debit side.

Step 3 In the 'particulars' column, write the name of the account credited in the journal on the debit side as "To...(name of the account credited)".

Step 4 Record the page number of the journal where the entry exists, in the 'Journal Folio (JF)'column.

Step 5 Enter the relevant amount in the 'amount' column on the debit side.

The steps for posting of an account credited in a journal entry are

Step 1 Identify the account to be credited in the ledger.

Step 2 Enter the date of transaction in the date column on the credit side.

Step 3 In the 'particulars' column, write the name of the account debited in the journal on the credit side as "By...(name of the account debited)".

Step 4 Record the page number of the journal where the entry exists, in the 'Journal Folio (JF)' column.

Step 5 Enter the relevant amount in the 'amount' column on the credit side.

Note *An account is opened only once in the ledger and all the entries relating to a particular account are posted on the debit or credit side, as the case may be.*

ILLUSTRATION |16| **Machinery of ₹ 1,00,000 is purchased from NTPC Ltd on 6th January, 2016.**

Sol. *Journal entry will be*

Machinery A/c	Dr	1,00,000	
To NTPC Ltd			1,00,000
(Being the machinery purchased on credit from NTPC Ltd.)			

The process of posting will be

In the Machinery account, we shall write 'To NTPC Ltd' in the particulars column of the debit side. In the account of NTPC Ltd, we shall write 'By Machinery Account' in the particulars column of the credit side. *The accounts will appear as under*

Dr **Machinery Account** Cr

Date	Particulars	JF	Amt (₹)	Date	Particulars	JF	Amt (₹)
2016 Jan 6	To NTPC Ltd.		1,00,000				

Dr **NTPC Ltd** Cr

Date	Particulars	JF	Amt (₹)	Date	Particulars	JF	Amt (₹)
				2016 Jan 6	By Machinery A/c		1,00,000

Note *Students should keep in mind that the account credited in the journal entry is entered on the debit side of the ledger account debited in the journal entry. Also, the account debited in the journal entry will be entered on the credit side of the ledger account credited in the journal entry.*

Posting an Opening Entry

While passing an opening entry, all assets account are debited and all liabilities account are credited. So, in case of an account, which has been debited, it will be written on the debit side as 'To balance b/d' and in case of an account, which has been credited, it will be written on the credit side as 'By balance b/d'.

ILLUSTRATION |17| Pass the opening entry as on 1st April, 2016. Also, post the opening entry.

1st April, 2016	Amt (₹)
Cash in Hand	36,000
Cash at Bank	51,200
Stock of Goods	1,00,000
Furniture	20,000
Building	9,02,800
Sundry Debtors	26,000
Sundry Creditors	4,68,800

Sol.

JOURNAL

Date	Particulars		LF	Amt (Dr)	Amt (Cr)
2016 Apr 1	Cash in Hand A/c	Dr		36,000	
	Cash at Bank A/c	Dr		51,200	
	Stock A/c	Dr		1,00,000	
	Furniture A/c	Dr		20,000	
	Building A/c	Dr		9,02,800	
	Sundry Debtors A/c	Dr		26,000	
	To Sundry Creditors A/c				4,68,800
	To Capital A/c (Balancing figure)				6,67,200
	(Being balances carried forward from last year)				

Dr **Cash Account** Cr

Date	Particulars	JF	Amt (₹)	Date	Particulars	JF	Amt (₹)
2016 Apr 1	To Balance b/d		36,000				

Dr **Bank Account** Cr

Date	Particulars	JF	Amt (₹)	Date	Particulars	JF	Amt (₹)
2016 Apr 1	To Balance b/d		51,200				

Dr **Stock Account** Cr

Date	Particulars	JF	Amt (₹)	Date	Particulars	JF	Amt (₹)
2016 Apr 1	To Balance b/d		1,00,000				

Dr **Furniture Account** Cr

Date	Particulars	JF	Amt (₹)	Date	Particulars	JF	Amt (₹)
2016 Apr 1	To Balance b/d		20,000				

Dr **Building Account** Cr

Date	Particulars	JF	Amt (₹)	Date	Particulars	JF	Amt (₹)
2016 Apr 1	To Balance b/d		9,02,800				

Dr **Sundry Debtors Account** Cr

Date	Particulars	JF	Amt (₹)	Date	Particulars	JF	Amt (₹)
2016 Apr 1	To Balance b/d		26,000				

Dr **Sundry Creditors Account** Cr

Date	Particulars	JF	Amt (₹)	Date	Particulars	JF	Amt (₹)
				2016 Apr 1	By Balance b/d		4,68,800

Dr **Capital Account** Cr

Date	Particulars	JF	Amt (₹)	Date	Particulars	JF	Amt (₹)
				2016 Apr 1	By Balance b/d		6,67,200

BALANCING OF ACCOUNTS

Balancing of an account is the process of ascertaining the difference between the total of debits and total of credits appearing in an account. In other words, balancing of an account suggests totalling both the sides of an account, finding the difference in total of the two sides and writing the difference on the side whose total is less. The difference of amount will be recorded as 'Balance c/d'. It may be a debit balance or a credit balance or a nil balance.

Balancing of an account is necessary to ascertain the net effect of all the transactions posted to that account during a given period.

Generally, personal and real accounts are balanced and nominal accounts are closed by transferring the balance to trading or profit and loss account. However, considering the scope of the present chapter, even nominal accounts have been balanced in subsequent illustration.

Procedure for Balancing a Ledger Account

The basic procedure for balancing a ledger account is as follows

Step 1 Total both the sides of a ledger account (i.e., the debit amount and credit amount column) and find out the difference in the totals.

Step 2 If the debit side total is more than the credit side total, write the difference on the credit side as 'By balance c/d'. If the credit side total is more than the debit side total, write the difference on the debit side as 'To balance c/d'.

Step 3 Make the total of the debit side equal to the credit side and draw a double line after the totals.

Step 4 Bring forward the balance on the next date. If debit balance, write on the debit side as 'To Balance b/d'. If credit balance, write on the credit side as 'By balance b/d'.

Balancing of a ledger account can be explained from the given ledger account

Dr **Kartik's Account** Cr

Date	Particulars	JF	Amt (₹)	Date	Particulars	JF	Amt (₹)
2016				2016			
Jan 6	To Purchase Return A/c		16,000	Jan 1	By Purchases A/c		2,00,000
Jan 26	To Cash A/c		40,000				
Jan 31	To Bank A/c		60,000				
Jan 31	To Discount A/c		2,000				
Jan 31	To Balance c/d		82,000				
			2,00,000				2,00,000
				Feb 2016	By Balance b/d		82,000

3 1 5 4 2

Contents

1. Total the debit side = ₹ 1,18,000.
2. Total the credit side = ₹ 2,00,000.
3. Find out the difference = ₹ 82,000 (2,00,000 – 1,18,000).
   As the credit side total is more than the debit side total, write the difference on the debit side as 'To balance c/d' 82,000.
4. Make the total of the debit side equal to the credit side and draw a double line after the totals
5. Bring forward the balance on the next date and since it is a credit balance, write on the credit side as 'By balance b/d' 82,000.

ILLUSTRATION |18| Journalise the following transactions, post them in ledger accounts and balance them.

2016		Amt(₹)
Aug 1	Vimal started business with cash	2,50,000
Aug 2	Bought goods for cash	76,250
Aug 3	Opened bank account with cash	1,25,000
Aug 4	Sold goods for cash	1,00,000
Aug 7	Bought goods from Jaya on credit	75,000
Aug 10	Sold goods to Prateek on credit	62,500
Aug 15	Purchased plant and machinery and payment is made by cheque	41,500
Aug 19	Paid to Jaya in cash	25,000
Aug 21	Received loan from Vineet and deposited the same into bank	20,000
Aug 23	Goods returned to Jaya	2,500
Aug 26	Withdrew from bank for personal use	12,500
Aug 27	Paid to Jaya by cheque	20,000
Aug 29	Received cash from Prateek	25,000
Aug 30	Purchased stationery by cash	500
Aug 30	Paid wages and salaries	25,000

Sol.

JOURNAL

Date	Particulars	LF	Amt (Dr)	Amt (Cr)
2016 Aug 1	Cash A/c Dr		2,50,000	
	To Capital A/c			2,50,000
	(Being the business started with capital of ₹ 2,50,000 brought in cash)			
Aug 2	Purchases A/c Dr		76,250	
	To Cash A/c			76,250
	(Being the goods purchased for cash)			

Date	Particulars		LF	Amt (Dr)	Amt (Cr)
Aug 3	Bank A/c	Dr		1,25,000	
	To Cash A/c				1,25,000
	(Being the bank account opened by depositing cash into bank)				
Aug 4	Cash A/c	Dr		1,00,000	
	To Sales A/c				1,00,000
	(Being the goods sold for cash)				
Aug 7	Purchases A/c	Dr		75,000	
	To Jaya				75,000
	(Being the goods purchased on credit from Jaya)				
Aug 10	Prateek	Dr		62,500	
	To Sales A/c				62,500
	(Being the goods sold to Prateek on credit)				
Aug 15	Plant and Machinery A/c	Dr		41,500	
	To Bank A/c				41,500
	(Being the plant and machinery purchased by cheque)				
Aug 19	Jaya	Dr		25,000	
	To Cash A/c				25,000
	(Being the amount paid to Jaya in cash)				
Aug 21	Bank A/c	Dr		20,000	
	To Vineet's Loan A/c				20,000
	(Being the loan from Vineet received and deposited into bank)				
Aug 23	Jaya	Dr		2,500	
	To Return Outwards A/c				2,500
	(Being the goods returned to Jaya)				
Aug 26	Drawings A/c	Dr		12,500	
	To Bank A/c				12,500
	(Being the amount withdrawn from bank for personal use)				
Aug 27	Jaya	Dr		20,000	
	To Bank A/c				20,000
	(Being the amount paid to Jaya by cheque)				
Aug 29	Cash A/c	Dr		25,000	
	To Prateek				25,000
	(Being the cash received from Prateek)				
Aug 30	Stationery A/c	Dr		500	
	To Cash A/c				500
	(Being the stationery purchased for cash)				
Aug 30	Wages and Salaries A/c	Dr		25,000	
	To Cash A/c				25,000
	(Being the wages and salaries paid in cash)				
	Total			8,60,750	8,60,750

LEDGER

Dr **Cash Account** Cr

Date	Particulars	JF	Amt (₹)	Date	Particulars	JF	Amt (₹)
2016				2016			
Aug 1	To Capital A/c		2,50,000	Aug 2	By Purchases A/c		76,250
Aug 4	To Sales A/c		1,00,000	Aug 3	By Bank A/c		1,25,000
Aug 29	To Prateek		25,000	Aug 19	By Jaya		25,000
				Aug 30	By Stationery A/c		500
				Aug 30	By Wages and Salaries A/c		25,000
				Aug 30	By Balance c/d		1,23,250
			3,75,000				3,75,000

Dr **Capital Account** Cr

Date	Particulars	JF	Amt (₹)	Date	Particulars	JF	Amt (₹)
2016				2016			
Aug 30	To Balance c/d		2,50,000	Aug 1	By Cash A/c		2,50,000
			2,50,000				2,50,000

Dr **Purchases Account** Cr

Date	Particulars	JF	Amt (₹)	Date	Particulars	JF	Amt (₹)
2016				2016			
Aug 2	To Cash A/c		76,250	Aug 30	By Balance c/d		1,51,250
Aug 7	To Jaya		75,000				
			1,51,250				1,51,250

Dr **Bank Account** Cr

Date	Particulars	JF	Amt (₹)	Date	Particulars	JF	Amt (₹)
2016				2016			
Aug 3	To Cash A/c		1,25,000	Aug 15	By Plant and Machinery A/c		41,500
Aug 21	To Vineet's Loan A/c		20,000	Aug 26	By Drawings A/c		12,500
				Aug 27	By Jaya		20,000
				Aug 30	By Balance c/d		71,000
			1,45,000				1,45,000

Dr **Sales Account** Cr

Date	Particulars	JF	Amt (₹)	Date	Particulars	JF	Amt (₹)
2016				2016			
Aug 30	To Balance c/d		1,62,500	Aug 4	By Cash A/c		1,00,000
				Aug 10	By Prateek		62,500
			1,62,500				1,62,500

Dr **Jaya's Account** Cr

Date	Particulars	JF	Amt (₹)	Date	Particulars	JF	Amt (₹)
2016				2016			
Aug 19	To Cash A/c		25,000	Aug 7	By Purchases A/c		75,000
Aug 23	To Return Outwards A/c		2,500				
Aug 27	To Bank A/c		20,000				
Aug 30	To Balance c/d		27,500				
			75,000				75,000

Dr **Prateek's Account** Cr

Date	Particulars	JF	Amt (₹)	Date	Particulars	JF	Amt (₹)
2016				2016			
Aug 10	To Sales A/c		62,500	Aug 29	By Cash A/c		25,000
				Aug 30	By Balance c/d		37,500
			62,500				62,500

Dr **Plant and Machinery Account** Cr

Date	Particulars	JF	Amt (₹)	Date	Particulars	JF	Amt (₹)
2016				2016			
Aug 15	To Bank A/c		41,500	Aug 30	By Balance c/d		41,500
			41,500				41,500

Dr **Vineet's Loan Account** Cr

Date	Particulars	JF	Amt (₹)	Date	Particulars	JF	Amt (₹)
2016				2016			
Aug 30	To Balance c/d		20,000	Aug 21	By Bank A/c		20,000
			20,000				20,000

Dr **Return Outwards Account** Cr

Date	Particulars	JF	Amt (₹)	Date	Particulars	JF	Amt (₹)
2016				2016			
Aug 30	To Balance c/d		2,500	Aug 23	By Jaya		2,500
			2,500				2,500

Dr **Drawings Account** Cr

Date	Particulars	JF	Amt (₹)	Date	Particulars	JF	Amt (₹)
2016				2016			
Aug 26	To Bank A/c		12,500	Aug 30	By Balance c/d		12,500
			12,500				12,500

Dr **Stationery Account** Cr

Date	Particulars	JF	Amt (₹)	Date	Particulars	JF	Amt (₹)
2016				2016			
Aug 30	To Cash A/c		500	Aug 30	By Balance c/d		500
			500				500

Dr **Wages and Salaries Account** Cr

Date	Particulars	JF	Amt (₹)	Date	Particulars	JF	Amt (₹)
2016				2016			
Aug 30	To Cash A/c		25,000	Aug 30	By Balance c/d		25,000
			25,000				25,000

ILLUSTRATION |19| (With GST) Journalise the following transactions of Adhiraj, Delhi for April, 2019, post them in ledger accounts and balance them:

Date	Particulars	Amt (₹)
2019		
Apr 1	Adhiraj started business with cash*	2,00,000
Apr 2	Bought goods for cash	60,000
Apr 3	Opened Bank account with cash*	1,00,000
Apr 4	Sold goods for cash	80,000
Apr 7	Bought goods from Amrit Kanpur on credit	60,000
Apr 10	Solds goods to Aryan, Delhi on credit	50,000
Apr 15	Purchased machinery costing ₹ 20,000 from Bhalla Bros, Patiala (Punjab) and payment is made by cheque	
Apr 19	Paid to Amrit in cash on account*	40,000
Apr 23	Goods returned to Amrit	10,000
Apr 27	Paid to Amrit by cheque in full settlement*	15,000
Apr 29	Received cash from Aryan*	20,000

CGST & SGST is leived @ 6% each on intra-state transactions and IGST @12% on inter-state transactions. GST is not levied on transactions marked with (*).

Sol.

In the Books of Adhiraj, Delhi

JOURNAL

Date	Particulars		LF	Amt (Dr)	Amt (Cr)
2019					
Apr 1	Cash A/c	Dr		2,00,000	
	To Capital A/c				2,00,000
	(Being the business started with capital of ₹ 2,00,000 brought in cash)				
Apr 2	Purchases A/c	Dr		60,000	
	Input CGST A/c	Dr		3,600	
	Input SGST A/c	Dr		3,600	
	To Cash A/c				67,200
	(Being the intra-state purchase of goods for cash, paid CGST and SGST @ 6% each)				
Apr 4	Cash A/c	Dr		89,600	
	To Sales A/c				80,000
	To Output CGST A/c				4,800
	To Output SGST A/c				4,800
	(Being the intra-state of goods, charged CGST and SGST @ 6% each)				
Apr 7	Purchases A/c	Dr		60,000	
	Input IGST A/c	Dr		7,200	
	To Amrit				67,200
	(Being the inter-state purchase of goods on credit from Amrit plus IGST @ 12%)				
Apr 10	Aryan	Dr		56,000	
	To Sales A/c				50,000
	To Output CGST A/c				3,000
	To Output SGST A/c				3,000
	(Being the intra-state sale of goods on credit to Aryan, charged CGST and SGST @ 6% each)				

Date	Particulars		LF	Amt (Dr)	Amt (Cr)
Apr 15	Machinery A/c	Dr		40,000	
	Input IGST A/c			4,800	
	To Bank A/c				44,800
	(Being the machinery purchased, plus IGST @ 12% and payment made by cheque)				
Apr 19	Amrit	Dr		40,000	
	To Cash A/c				40,000
	(Being the amount paid to Surya in Cash)				
Apr 23	Amrit	Dr		11,200	
	To Returns Outward A/c				10,000
	To Input IGST A/c				1,200
	(Being the goods returned to Amrit, input IGST reversed)				
Apr 27	Amrit	Dr		16,000	
	To Bank A/c				15,000
	To Discount Received A/c				1,000
	(Being the amount paid to Amrit by cheque and discount received)				
Apr 29	Cash A/c	Dr		20,000	
	To Aryan				20,000
	(Being the cash received from Aryan)				

LEDGER

Dr **Cash Account** Cr

Date	Particulars	JF	Amt (₹)	Date	Particulars	JF	Amt (₹)
2019				2019			
Apr 1	To Capital A/c		2,00,000	Apr 2	By Purchases A/c		60,000
Apr 4	To Sales A/c		80,000	Apr 2	By Input CGST A/c		3,600
Apr 4	To Output CGST A/c		4,800	Apr 2	By Input SGST A/c		3,600
Apr 4	To Output SGST A/c		4,800	Apr 3	By Bank A/c		1,00,000
Apr 29	To Aryan		20,000	Apr 19	By Amrit		40,000
				Apr 30	By Balance c/d		1,02,400
			3,09,600				3,09,600
May 1	To Balance b/d		1,02,400				

Dr **Capital Account** Cr

Date	Particulars	JF	Amt (₹)	Date	Particulars	JF	Amt (₹)
2019				2019			
Apr 30	To Balance c/d		2,00,000	Apr 1	By Cash A/c		2,00,000
			2,00,000				2,00,000
				May 1	By Balance b/d		2,00,000

Dr **Purchases Account** Cr

Date	Particulars	JF	Amt (₹)	Date	Particulars	JF	Amt (₹)
2019				2019			
Apr 2	To Cash A/c		60,000	Apr 30	By Balance c/d		1,20,000
Apr 7	To Amrit		60,000				
			1,20,000				1,20,000
May 1	To Balance b/d		1,20,000				

Dr **Bank Account** Cr

Date	Particulars	JF	Amt (₹)	Date	Particulars	JF	Amt (₹)
2019				2019			
Apr 3	To Cash A/c		1,00,000	Apr 15	By Machinery A/c		40,000
				Apr 15	By Input IGST A/c		4,800
				Apr 27	By Amrit		15,000
				Apr 30	By Balance c/d		40,200
			1,00,000				1,00,000
May 1	To Balance b/d		40,200				

Dr **Sales Account** Cr

Date	Particulars	JF	Amt (₹)	Date	Particulars	JF	Amt (₹)
2019				2019			
Apr 30	To Balance c/d		1,30,000	Apr 4	By Cash A/c		80,000
				Apr 10	By Aryan		50,000
			1,30,000				1,30,000
				May 1	By Balance b/d		1,30,000

Dr **Amrit's Account** Cr

Date	Particulars	JF	Amt (₹)	Date	Particulars	JF	Amt (₹)
2019				2019			
Apr 19	To Cash A/c		40,000	Apr 7	By Purchases A/c		60,000
Apr 23	To Returns Outward A/c		10,000	Apr 7	By Input IGST A/c		7,200
Apr 23	To Input IGST A/c		1,200				
Apr 27	To Bank A/c		15,000				
Apr 27	To Discount Received A/c		1,000				
			67,200				67,200

Dr **Aryan's Account** Cr

Date	Particulars	JF	Amt (₹)	Date	Particulars	JF	Amt (₹)
2019				2019			
Apr 10	To Sales A/c		50,000	Apr 29	By Cash A/c		20,000
Apr 10	To Output CGST A/c		3,000	Apr 30	By Balance c/d		36,000
Apr 10	To Output SGST A/c		3,000				
			56,000				56,000
May 1	To Balance b/d		36,000				

Dr **Machinery Account** Cr

Date	Particulars	JF	Amt (₹)	Date	Particulars	JF	Amt (₹)
2019				2019			
Apr 15	To Bank A/c		40,000	Apr 30	By Balance c/d		40,000
			40,000				40,000
May 1	To Balance b/d		40,000				

Dr **Returns Outward Account** Cr

Date	Particulars	JF	Amt (₹)	Date	Particulars	JF	Amt (₹)
2019				2019			
Apr 30	To Balance c/d		10,000	Apr 23	By Amrit		10,000
			10,000				10,000
				May 1	By Balance b/d		10,000

Dr **Input CGST Account** Cr

Date	Particulars	JF	Amt (₹)	Date	Particulars	JF	Amt (₹)
2019				2019			
Apr 2	To Cash A/c (Purchases)		3,600	Apr 30	By Balance c/d		3,600
			3,600				3,600

Dr **Input SGST Account** Cr

Date	Particulars	JF	Amt (₹)	Date	Particulars	JF	Amt (₹)
2019				2019			
Apr 2	To Cash A/c (Purchases)		3,600	Apr 30	By Balance c/d		3,600
			3,600				3,600

Dr **Output CGST Account** Cr

Date	Particulars	JF	Amt (₹)	Date	Particulars	JF	Amt (₹)
2019				2019			
Apr 30	To Balance c/d		7,800	Apr 4	By Cash A/c (Sales)		4,800
				Apr 10	By Aryan (Sales)		3,000
			7,800				7,800

Dr **Output SGST Account** Cr

Date	Particulars	JF	Amt (₹)	Date	Particulars	JF	Amt (₹)
2019				2019			
Apr 30	To Balance c/d		7,800	Apr 4	By Cash A/c (Sales)		4,800
				Apr 10	By Aryan (Sales)		3,000
			7,800				7,800

Dr **Input IGST Account** Cr

Date	Particulars	J.F	Amt (₹)	Date	Particulars	JF	Amt (₹)
2019				2019			
Apr 7	To Amrit (Purchases)		7,200	Apr 23	By Amrit (Returns Outward)		1,200
Apr 15	To Bank A/c (Machinery)		4,800	Apr 30	By Balance c/d		10,800
			12,000				12,000

Dr **Discount Received Account** Cr

Date	Particulars	JF	Amt (₹)	Date	Particulars	JF	Amt (₹)
2019				2019			
Apr 30	To Balance c/d		1,000	Apr 27	By Amrit		1,000

NUMERICAL Questions for Practice

1 Journalise the following transactions and post them into ledger.

		Amt (₹)
(i)	Business started with	
	(a) Cash	1,50,000
	(b) Goods	50,000
(ii)	Purchased computers and paid by cheque	2,50,000
(iii)	Goods returned to Ritika	2,000
(iv)	Stationery purchased for cash	3,000
(v)	Goods returned by Krishna	2,000
(vi)	Cheque given to Ritika	28,000
(vii)	Cheque received from Krishna	8,000
(viii)	Cash deposited into bank	20,000
(ix)	Goods given as charity	2,000
(x)	Paid sundry expenses	200
(xi)	Cash paid to Harish in full settlement of account (amount due ₹ 15,000)	14,700
(xii)	Cartage paid	200

2 The following balances appeared in the ledger of M/s Khullar Traders on 1st April, 2016.

	Amt (₹)
Cash in hand	6,000
Sambhav (Cr)	3,000
Ashutosh (Dr)	9,700
Cash at bank	12,000
Stock (Goods)	5,400
Arjun (Dr)	10,000
Bills receivable	7,000
Bills payable	2,000

Transactions during the month were

April		Amt (₹)
1	Goods sold to Vikas	3,000
2	Purchased goods from Sambhav	8,000
3	Received cash from Ashutosh in full settlement	9,200
5	Cash received from Arjun on account	4,000
6	Paid to Sambhav by cheque	6,000
8	Rent paid by cheque	1,200
10	Cash received from Vikas	3,000
12	Cash sales	6,000
14	Goods returned to Sambhav	1,000
15	Cash paid to Sambhav in full settlement (Discount received ₹ 300)	3,700
18	Goods sold to Ranveer	10,000
20	Paid trade expenses	200
21	Drew for personal use	1,000
22	Goods returned from Ranveer	1,200
24	Cash received from Ranveer	6,000
26	Paid for stationery	100
27	Postage charges	60
28	Salary paid	2,500
29	Goods purchased from Seema Traders	7,000
30	Sold goods to Kamal	6,000
30	Goods purchased from Ravi Traders	5,000

Journalise the above transactions, post them to the ledger and balance the accounts.

3 Vishwas of Delhi started business on 1st April, 2019 with building of ₹ 12,00,000 and machinery of ₹ 3,00,000. He purchased these assets from Delhi and paid by cheque from his savings account. He introduced capital of ₹ 3,00,000 in cash. Journalise the following transactions for the month of April, prepare the ledger accounts and balance them:

Date	Particulars	Amt (₹)
2019		
Apr 1	Purchased goods for cash from Ram, Delhi	55,000
Apr 4	Purchased goods from Naresh, Gurugram (Haryana)	40,000
Apr 5	Sold goods for cash	70,000
Apr 12	Cash depoisted into bank*	80,000
Apr 14	Purchased machinery costing ₹ 10,000 for cash	
Apr 15	Solds goods to Garg Bros., Delhi	30,000
Apr 16	Returned goods to Naresh	2,000
Apr 28	Paid salary for the month of April*	10,000
Apr 30	Received bank interest*	400
Apr 30	Paid for courier charges	1,000

CGST and SGST is levied @ 6% each on intra-state transactions and @ 12% on inter-state transactions excepts transactions marked With (*).

CHAPTER PRACTICE

OBJECTIVE TYPE Questions

Multiple Choice Questions

1 The journal entry to record the sale of services on credit should include **NCERT**

(a) debit to debtors and credit to capital
(b) debit to cash and credit to debtors
(c) debit to fees income and credit to debtors
(d) debit to debtors and credit to fees income

Ans (d) debit to debtors and credit to fees income

2 The ledger folio column of journal is used to **NCERT**

(a) record the date on which amount posted to a ledger account
(b) record the number of ledger account to which information is posted
(c) record the number of amounts posted to ledger account
(d) record the page number of ledger account

Ans (d) record the page number of ledger account

3 When a entry is made in journal **NCERT**

(a) assets are listed first
(b) accounts to be debited listed first
(c) accounts to be credited listed first
(d) accounts may be listed in any order

Ans (b) accounts to be debited listed first

4 If a transaction is properly analysed and recorded **NCERT**

(a) only two accounts will be used to record the transaction
(b) one account will be used to record transaction
(c) one account balance will increase and another will decrease
(d) total amount debited will equal total amount credited

Ans (d) total amount debited will equal total amount credited

5 Trial balance is prepared from

(a) Journal (b) Ledger
(c) Ledger folio (d) Journal folio

Ans (b) Ledger

6 The book in which all accounts are maintained is known as **NCERT**

(a) Cash book (b) Journal
(c) Purchases book (d) Ledger

Ans (b) Journal

7 Each journal entry is followed by

(a) narration (b) description
(c) sequence (d) random

Ans (a) narration

8 Recording of transactions in journal is called **NCERT**

(a) Costing (b) Posting
(c) Journalising (d) Recodrly

Ans (c) Journalising

9 Balancing of account means **NCERT**

(a) total of debit side
(b) total of credit side
(c) difference in total of debit and credit
(d) None of the above

Ans (c) difference in total of debit and credit

10 Which of the following is a rule for debit of nominal account?

(a) Debit the receiver
(b) Debit what comes in
(c) Debit all expenses and losses
(d) All of the above

Ans (c) Debit all expenses and losses

11 The journal entry to record purchase of equipment for ₹ 2,00,000 cash and a balance of ₹ 8,00,000 due in 30 days include **NCERT**

(a) debit equipment for ₹ 2,00,000 and credit cash ₹ 2,00,000
(b) debit equipment for ₹ 10,00,000, credit cash ₹ 2,00,000 and creditors ₹ 8,00,000
(c) debit equipment ₹ 2,00,000 and credit debtors ₹ 8,00,000
(d) debit equipment ₹ 10,00,000 and credit cash ₹ 10,00,000

Ans (b) debit equipment for ₹ 10,00,000, credit cash ₹ 2,00,000 and creditors ₹ 8,00,000

12 Each account in ledger is opened on separate

(a) register (b) book
(c) journal (d) page

Ans (d) page

13 The journal entry to record payment of monthly bill will include **NCERT**

(a) debit monthly bill and credit capital
(b) debit capital and credit cash

(c) debit monthly bill and credit cash
(d) debit monthly bill and credit creditors

Ans (c) debit monthly bill and credit cash

14 Journal entry to record salaries will include **NCERT**

(a) debit salaries, credit cash
(b) debit capital, credit cash
(c) debit cash, credit salary
(d) debit salary, credit creditors

Ans (c) debit cash, credit salary

15 The amount due from customers which could not be recovered and requires to be written-off is booked into

(a) bad debt recovered account
(b) cash withdrawal
(c) goods withdrawn
(d) bad debts account

Ans (d) bad debts account

16 Cash withdrawn by proprietor should be credited to **NCERT**

(a) Drawings account
(b) Capital account
(c) Profit and loss account
(d) Cash account

Ans (a) Drawings account

17 A purchase of machine for cash should be debited to **NCERT**

(a) Cash account (b) Machine account
(c) Purchase account (d) None of the above

Ans (b) Machine account

18 A firm has interest on investment becoming due but not yet received. What will be the entry in this situation?

(a) Income A/c Dr
To Accrued Income A/c
(b) Accrued Income A/c Dr
To Assets A/c
(c) Accrued Income Ac Dr
To Purchases A/c
(d) Accrued Income A/c Dr
To Income A/c

Ans (d) Accrued Income A/c Dr
To Income A/c

Fill in the Blanks

19 Accounts related to an individual, firm, company or an institution are called .... accounts.

Ans personal

20 Rule for recording a transaction in personal accounts is ....

Ans "Debit the receiver and credit the giver"

21 All the transactions are first recorded in a primary book called ....

Ans journal

22 Debit what comes in and credit what goes out is applicable to ....

Ans real account

23 The ledger is the .... book of account.

Ans principal

24 The transfer of journal entry to a ledger account is called ....

Ans posting

State True or False

25 Trademarks account is an intangible real account.

Ans True

26 Wages paid for erection of machinery are debited to profit and loss account.

Ans False. Wages paid for erection of machinery are debited to machinery account, being a capital expenditure.

27 Outstanding expenditure account is a nominal account.

Ans False. Outstanding expenditure represents a liability due to some person. Hence, it is a personal account.

28 In a journal, it is not necessary to record every transaction in a chronological order.

Ans False. Transactions are recorded in a chronological order.

29 The word account is not required to be used with personal account.

Ans True

Match the Following

30

	Column I		Column II
1.	Capital Account	(a)	Trading Account
2.	Furniture Account	(b)	Personal Account
3.	Salary Account	(c)	Real Account
4.	Freight	(d)	Nominal Account

Ans 1-(b), 2-(c), 3-(d), 4-(a)

31

	Column I		Column II
1.	Book of second entry	(a)	Journal
2.	Book of original entry	(b)	Posting

Column I		Column II
3. Account stand automatically closed	(c)	Ledger
4. Transferring an entry from journal to ledger	(d)	Zero balance

Ans 1-(c), 2-(a), 3-(d), 4-(b)

Journalise the Following

32 **Withdrew cash from office for personal use ₹ 2,000.**

Ans

Drawings A/c	Dr	2,000	
To Cash A/c			2,000
(Being cash withdrawn for personal use)			

33 **Goods of the list price of ₹ 1,00,000 sold to Mukta at 20% trade discount and 5% cash discount. Charged CGST and SGST @ 6% each. 80% of the amount received by cheque immediately.**

Ans

Bank A/c	Dr	68,480	
Discount Allowed A/c	Dr	3,200	
Mukta	Dr	17,920	
To Sales A/c			80,000
To Output CGST A/c			4,800
To Output SGST A/c			4,800
(Being goods sold to Mukta at 20% TD and 5% CD and charged CGST and SGST @ 6% each)			

Working Note

List price of goods sold	1,00,000
Less : Trade discount @ 20%	(20,000)
	80,000
Add: SGST @ 6% each	4,800
Add : CGST @ 6% each	4,800
	89,600
Cash transaction 80% of ₹ 89,600	71,680
Less : Cash discount (80,000 × 80% × 5%)	(3,200)
Amount received by cheque	68,480

Credit transaction 20% of ₹ 89,600 = ₹ 17,920

34 **Received cash from Arjun ₹ 3,850 and discount allowed to him ₹ 150.**

Ans

Cash A/c	Dr	3,850	
Discount Allowed A/c	Dr	150	
To Arjun			4,000
(Being cash received from Arjun and discount allowed)			

35 **Paid Life Insurance Premium of the proprietor by cheque ₹ 8,000.**

Ans

Drawings A/c	Dr	8,000	
To Bank A/c			8,000
(Being LIC paid by cheque)			

36 **Business started with cash ₹ 10,000. Furniture ₹ 4,000 and goods ₹ 6,000.**

Ans

Cash A/c	Dr	10,000	
Furniture A/c	Dr	4,000	
Purchase A/c	Dr	6,000	
To Capital A/c			20,000
(Being business started with cash, furniture and goods)			

37 **When a cheque received from the customer is not sent to bank on the same day.**

Ans

Cheque-in-hand A/c	Dr	—	
To Customer's Personal A/c			—
(Being cheque received but not deposited in bank on the same day)			

38 **When a cheque received from X previously deposited into the bank is dishonoured.**

Ans

X's A/c	Dr	—	
To Bank A/c			—
(Being cheque received and deposited in a bank is dishonoured)			

VERY SHORT ANSWER Type Questions

39 **Is journal a book of original entry?**

Ans Yes, journal is a book of original entry because it is the primary book of accounts in which transactions are first recorded in a chronological order.

40 **Are debits or credits listed first in journal entries? Are debits or credits indented?** **NCERT**

Ans Debits are listed first in journal entries. Credits are indented in the journal entries, it means the account title to be credited is written on the second line leaving sufficient margin on the left side with a prefix 'To'.

41 Journal records the transactions of the firm in which order?

Ans Chronological order

42 What is compound journal entry?

Ans Compound journal entry is the entry in which more than one account is debited or credited.

43 Should a transaction be first recorded in a journal or ledger? Why? **NCERT**

Or

Why are transactions first entered in a journal rather than directly into the ledger?

Ans A transaction should be recorded in journal first because the journal entry is the basic record of business transaction and contains all important information relating to a transaction. On the other hand, a ledger contains only the summary.

44 State whether a capital account is a personal account? If yes give reasons.

Ans Yes, a capital account is a personal account, because it is the amount due to the proprietor by the firm.

45 State when is a capital account credited.

Ans A capital account is credited, when the proprietor introduces further capital and with the amount of profit.

46 Why is ledger called the book of final entry or the principal book of accounts?

Ans A ledger is the principal book or book of final entry. As the ledger is the ultimate destination of all the transactions, the ledger is called the book of final entry.

47 Name the process of transferring the debit and credit items from a journal to their respective accounts in the ledger.

Ans Posting

48 What technique is used to find the net balance of an account after considering the totals of both debits and credits appearing in the account?

Ans Balancing of an account

49 Name the category of accounts that is not balanced.

Ans Expenses and revenue accounts are not balanced. They are totalled and transferred to trading and profit and loss account at the end of the accounting year.

50 When an account is said to have a debit balance and credit balance?

Ans An account is said to have a debit balance if the total of its debit side is more than the total of its credit side. While an account is said to have a credit balance if the total of its credit side is more than the total of its debit side.

51 Rohan purchased goods from Rajasthan traders for ₹ 2,00,000. As per the terms, if Rohan made full payment within 21 days, he will get cash discount at 2.5%. Rohan paid ₹ 1,50,000 within the stipulated time. How much discount will he get?

Ans Rohan will not get any discount because he has not paid the full amount.

52 What does debit balance of a nominal account indicates?

Ans It indicates loss or expenses.

53 Vishal purchased from Karan Sports Ltd 200 balls @ ₹ 50 each on which he is given 20% trade discount. He is further given 2% cash discount as he made payment for the purchases immediately. Determine the amount that Vishal will debit to purchases account?

Ans Vishal will debit ₹ 8,000 [$200 \times 50 - (10{,}000 \times 20\%)$] *i.e.*, the amount of purchases after trade discount.

54 Does debit always mean increase and credit always mean decrease?

Ans No, it is not true. Debit does not always mean increase and credit does not always mean decrease. It depends upon the accounts involved.

SHORT ANSWER Type Questions

55 Give the characteristics of Journal.

Ans *The characteristics of journal are*

(*i*) It contains day-to-day transactions in a chronological order.

(*ii*) It shows complete details of a transaction in one entry.

(*iii*) It records both the debit and credit aspects of a transaction according to the double entry system of book-keeping.

(*iv*) Each entry in the journal is followed by a narration which is a brief explanation of the transactions.

56 State the need for sub-division in a journal.

Ans When the size of the business is large then it is a tedious and time consuming job to record all the transactions in the journal. Because of this, *the journal is sub-divided into a number of books of original entry as follows*

(*i*) Cash book (*ii*) Other day books

(*iii*) Journal proper

(*a*) Purchases (journal) book

(*b*) Sales (journal) book

(*c*) Purchases return (journal) book

(*d*) Sales returns (journal) book

(*e*) Bills receivable (journal) book

(*f*) Bills payable (journal) book

57 Give the advantages of a journal.

Ans *The advantages of journal are*

(*i*) Possibility of omission of a transaction is reduced, as transactions are entered in journal, as and when they take place.

(*ii*) It becomes easy to locate a particular transaction, as they are recorded in chronological order.

(*iii*) Journal facilitates posting into the ledger by analysing each transaction into debit and credit aspects.

(*iv*) It helps in cross checking of ledger, in case a trial balance does not agree.

(*v*) From legal point of view, journal is more reliable evidence of business transactions than ledger.

58 Despite a number of advantages, a journal also suffers from various limitations. Give any four such limitations.

Ans *The limitations of journal are*

(*i*) As the number of transactions are large, journal becomes bulky and voluminous.

(*ii*) Journal does not provide information on prompt basis.

(*iii*) As the journal can only be handled by one person, it does not facilitate the installation of an internal check system.

(*iv*) Cash transactions are usually recorded in a separate book called 'cash book'. Such transactions are not recorded in journal.

59 What is the purpose of posting JF numbers that are entered in the journal at the time entries are posted to the accounts? **NCERT**

Ans Journal Folio (JF) column in the ledger records the page number of the journal from which posting to the ledger has been made.

The purpose of posting JF numbers at the time entries are posted to the accounts, is that it provides a reference for locating/tracking the page of the journal from where the entry has been posted.

60 Why are the rules of debit and credit same for both liability and capital? **NCERT**

Ans According to the business entity concept, the owner is considered to be an outsider for the business firm and the capital invested by the proprietor, is treated as liability for the business.

It is assumed that the amount invested by the proprietor as capital is also required to be returned, in the same manner as liabilities are required to be paid off. It is because of this that the rule of debit and credit are same for capital and liability.

61 What do you understand by trade discount and cash discount.

Ans (*i*) **Trade Discount** The discount which is usually on the list price to increase the sales of the business is referred to as trade discount. This discount is offered to all the customers, as per the practice of the trade. It is not shown in the books of account and sale is recorded at net amount *i.e.*, sale less trade discount.

(*ii*) **Cash Discount** The discount which is allowed by the supplier for immediate payment or payment before its due date, is known as cash discount. Cash discount is usually allowed as a percentage of the amount received. Cash discount is shown in the books of accounts.

62 What entry (debit or credit) would you make to

(i) increase revenue (ii) decrease in expense

(iii) record drawings

(iv) record the fresh capital introduced by the owner **NCERT**

Ans *The following entry will be made in the above case*

(*i*) Increase Revenue—Credit entry will be made in this case.

(*ii*) Decrease in Expense—Credit entry will be made in this case.

(*iii*) Record Drawings—Debit entry will be made in this case.

(*iv*) Record the Fresh Capital Introduced by the Owner—Credit entry will be made in this case.

63 State the features of a ledger.

Ans *The features of ledger are*

(*i*) Ledger is prepared from journal.

(*ii*) Trial balance is prepared from ledger accounts.

(*iii*) Financial statements *i.e.*, trading, profit and loss account, and balance sheet are also prepared from ledger accounts.

(*iv*) Ledger is the master record of all the transactions of a business firm.

64 Describe how accounts are used to record information about the effects of transactions. **NCERT**

Ans Each account is the summary of transactions at one place, relating to a particular head. It records not only the amount of transactions but also their effect and direction. The account is divided into two parts, the left hand side is the debit side and the right hand side is the credit side. The statement is prepared is 'T' shape, therefore it is also called 'T' account.

The effect of transaction related to assets, liabilities, capital, expenses/losses and income/gains is recorded in the account in the following manner

Assets		Liabilities		Capital		Expenses/Losses		Revenues/Gains	
Increase	Decrease	Decrease	Increase	Decrease	Increase	Increase	Decrease	Decrease	Increase
+	–	–	+	–	+	+	–	–	+
Debit	Credit	Debit	Credit	Debit	Credit	Debit	Credit	Debit	Credit

LONG ANSWER Type Questions

65 Describe how debits and credits are used to analyse transactions. **NCERT**

Ans The system of double entry book-keeping is founded upon the truth that every transaction affects two accounts. As per the traditional approach, there are three classes of accounts. *The general rule for debit and credit for each class and their use in analysing a transaction has been explained below*

Traditional Classification of Accounts

(i) **Personal Accounts**	Debit the receiver, credit the giver. **Use in analysing a transaction** If in a journal entry, Dinesh's account has been debited and cash account has been credited, then on the basis of the above rule, it can be easily concluded that Dinesh has received cash from the business. Also, if in a journal entry, Mahesh's account has been credited, and cash account has been debited, then it can be concluded that Mahesh has given cash to the business.
(ii) **Real Accounts**	Debit what comes in, credit what goes out. **Use in analysing a transaction** If in a journal entry, furniture account has been debited, then it can be safely concluded that furniture is coming into the business, or in other words the value of furniture is increasing in the business. Also, if in a journal entry, machinery account has been credited, then it can be safely concluded that machinery is going out of the business, or in other words the value of machinery is decreasing in the business.
(iii) **Nominal Accounts**	Debit expenses or losses, credit incomes and gains. **Use in analysing a transaction** If in a journal entry, salary account has been debited, then it can be concluded that salary is an expense for the business. Also, if in a journal entry, commission account has been credited, then it can be concluded that commission is an income for the business.

66 Distinguish between cash discount and trade discount.

Ans *The differences between trade discount and cash discount are*

Basis	*Trade Discount*	*Cash Discount*
Meaning	It is a reduction granted by a supplier from the list price of goods or services on business considerations other than for prompt payment.	A reduction granted by a supplier in consideration of immediate payment or payment within a stipulated period.
Purpose	It is allowed to all the customers with an intention to increase sales.	It is allowed with the purpose of encouraging prompt payment.
Nature of Transaction	It is allowed on both credit and cash transactions.	It is allowed only on cash transactions.

Basis	Trade Discount	Cash Discount
Recording	It is not recorded in the books of accounts.	It is recorded in the books of accounts.
Deduction from	It is deducted from the invoice.	It is not deducted from the amount payable.
Time when Allowed	It is allowed on purchase of goods.	It is allowed on immediate payment or payment within a specified period.

67 Distinguish between journal and ledger.

Ans The journal and the ledger are the most important books of the double entry mechanism of accounting and are indispensable for an accounting system. *The differences between journal and ledger are*

Basis	Journal	Ledger
Nature of Book	The journal is the book of first entry (original entry).	The ledger is a book of secondary or final entry.
Chronological/ Analytical Record	The journal is the book for chronological record.	The ledger is the book for analytical record.
Format	A journal has five columns— Date, Particulars, Ledger Folio, Debit Amount, Credit Amount.	Ledger has four identical columns on debit and credit side— Date, Particulars, Journal Folio, Amount.
Classification	Transaction is the basis of classification of data within the journal.	Account is the basis of classification of data within the ledger.
Process of Recording	Process of recording in the journal is called journalising.	The process of recording in the ledger is known as posting.

NUMERICAL Questions

1 Journalise the following transactions.

2016		Amt (₹)
Mar 1	Raju started business with cash	1,00,000
	Bought goods from Bobby for cash	80,000
Mar 13	Sold goods to Gudiya for cash	96,000
Mar 14	Bought goods from Rano	12,000
Mar 15	Sold goods to Guddu	14,400
Mar 26	Received from Guddu	14,000
	Allowed him discount	400
Mar 27	Paid Rano cash	11,400
	Discount allowed	600
Mar 28	Purchased furniture	20,000
Mar 30	Paid office expenses	2,000

Ans Total of Journal = ₹ 3,50,800

2 Pass journal entries for the following transactions.

(i) Provide depreciation on furniture ₹ 2,000 and on machinery ₹ 8,000.

(ii) Received cash ₹ 4,000 for bad debts written-off last year.

(iii) Ajay was declared bankrupt. He owed ₹ 10,000 to us. This amount was written-off as bad.

(iv) ₹ 80,000 for wages and ₹ 16,000 for salaries are outstanding.

(v) Purchased furniture for ₹ 24,000 for the proprietor and paid the amount by cheque.

(vi) Provide 9% interest on capital amounting to ₹ 8,00,000.

(vii) Charge interest on drawings ₹ 4,000.

Ans Total of Journal = ₹ 2,20,000

3 Pass journal entries for the following transactions.

2016	
Jan 6	Sold goods to Meetu of the list price of ₹ 2,00,000 at trade discount of 20%.
Jan 8	Meetu returned goods of the list price of ₹ 5,000.
Jan 15	Received from Meetu the full payment under a cash discount of 4%.

Ans Total of Journal = ₹ 3,20,000

4 Pass journal entries for the following transactions.

(i) Bought goods from Raj of the list price of ₹ 30,000 at 15% trade discount.
(ii) Settled the account of Raj by paying cash, under a discount of 4%.
(iii) Bought goods for cash of the list price of ₹ 1,50,000 at 20% trade discount and 5% cash discount.
(iv) Sold goods for cash of the list price of ₹ 60,000 at 10% trade discount and 3% cash discount.

Ans Total of Journal = ₹ 2,25,000

5 Journalise the following transactions.

2016		Amt (₹)
Mar 3	Sold goods to Mohan	50,000
Mar 5	Received from Mohan in full settlement of his account	49,000
Mar 6	Sold goods to Chintamani	40,000
Mar 8	Chintamani returned goods	500
Mar 15	Received from Chintamani in full settlement of his account	39,100
Mar 16	Received cash from Shaurya	9,750
	and discount allowed	250
Mar 20	Paid cash to Swastik	2,350
	and discount received from him	150
Mar 25	Sold goods to Hemant of the list price of ₹ 12,500 at 20% trade discount.	

Ans Total of Journal = ₹ 2,02,500

6 Journalise the following entries.

(i) Goods worth ₹ 500 given as charity.
(ii) Received ₹ 975 from Harikrishna in full settlement of his account for ₹ 1,000.
(iii) Received the first and final dividend of 60 paise in a rupee from the official receiver of Rajan, who owed us ₹ 1,000.
(iv) Charged depreciation on plant ₹ 1,000.
(v) Interest on capital ₹ 300.
(vi) Paid ₹ 250 as wages on installation of a new machine.
(vii) Supplied goods costing ₹ 600 to Mohan issued at 10% above cost less 5% trade discount.

Ans Total of Journal = ₹ 4,677

7 Journalise the following transactions.

(i) Paid ₹ 2,500 in cash as wages on installation of a machinery.
(ii) Issued a cheque in favour of M/s Parmatma Singh & Sons on account of purchase of goods worth ₹ 7,500.
(iii) Goods sold costing ₹ 6,000 to M/s Kalu & Sons at an invoice price 10% above cost less 5% trade discount.
(iv) Goods worth ₹ 500 were used by the proprietor for domestic purposes.
(v) Goods uninsured worth ₹ 3,000 were destroyed by fire.

Ans Total of Journal = ₹ 19,770

8 **Record the following transactions in the journal of Sunder.**

2016

Apr 1	Sunder started business with cash ₹ 1,50,000, goods ₹ 60,000 and furniture ₹ 10,000.
Apr 2	Sold goods to Walia of the list price of ₹ 20,000 at trade discount of 10%.
Apr 5	Walia returned goods of the list price ₹ 2,000.
Apr 10	Received from Walia ₹ 16,000 in full settlement of his account.
Apr 12	Purchased furniture for ₹ 12,000.
	Purchased goods from Kharbanda for ₹ 50,000 less trade discount 12%.
Apr 15	Returned goods to Kharbanda goods of the list price of ₹ 4,000.
Apr 16	Cleared the account of Kharbanda by paying cash, under a discount of 5%.
Apr 17	Sold goods to Amar ₹ 20,000 and Akbar ₹ 32,000.
Apr 20	Received cash from Amar ₹19,600 in full settlement of his account.
	Paid insurance premium ₹ 1,500.
Apr 22	Paid for Sunder's life insurance premium ₹ 2,400.
Apr 24	Purchased goods for ₹ 16,000 for cash at a trade discount of 10% and cash discount of 2%.
Apr 25	Received cash from Akbar at a cash discount of 5% in full settlement of his account.
Apr 30	Paid rent ₹ 1,600, advertisement 2,000, and salaries ₹ 8,000.
Apr 30	Received commission ₹ 1,000.

Ans Total of Journal = ₹ 4,90,900

9 **Pass journal entries for the following.**

2016

Sep 2	Purchased an Iron safe for business for 80,000.
Sep 3	Purchased filing cabinet for office use ₹ 32,000 and paid ₹ 160 as cartage on it.
Sep 4	Purchased a portable typewriter ₹ 64,000.
Sep 5	Purchased an electric fan for ₹ 16,000.
Sep 6	Purchased a 'Horse' for business for ₹ 1,20,000.
Sep 7	Purchased post cards for ₹ 200, envelopes for ₹ 400 and stamps for ₹ 800.
Sep 8	Purchased office stationery for ₹ 3,200.
Sep 15	Gave as charity–cash ₹ 1,600 and goods ₹ 3,200.
Sep 20	The horse bought on 6th September died , is carcass was sold for ₹ 8,000.
Sep 25	Sold household furniture for ₹ 80,000 and paid the money into business.
Sep 31	Paid to landlord ₹ 96,000 for rent. One third of the building is occupied by the proprietor for residential use.

Ans Total of Journal = ₹ 6,17,560

10 **Give the journal entries of M/s Sumit Traders. Post them to ledger from the following transactions.**

2016		Amt (₹)
Jan 1	Commenced business with cash	2,20,000
Jan 2	Opened bank account with SBI	1,00,000
Jan 3	Purchased furniture	40,000
Jan 7	Bought goods for cash from M/s Riya traders	60,000
Jan 8	Purchased goods from M/s Priya traders	84,000
Jan 10	Sold goods for cash	60,000
Jan 14	Sold goods on credit to M/s Sharma traders	24,000
Jan 16	Rent paid	8,000
Jan 18	Paid trade expenses	2,000
Jan 20	Received cash from Sharma traders	24,000
Jan 22	Goods returned to Priya traders	4,000
Jan 23	Cash paid to Priya traders	80,000
Jan 25	Bought postage stamps	200
Jan 30	Paid salary to Karan	8,000

11 **Give journal entries related to the transactions given below in the books of M/s Punjab Jewellers.**

2017	
Jan 2	Sold jewellery costing ₹ 1,40,000 to Smita for cash at a profit of 25% on cost less 20% trade discount and charged 8% making charges.
Jan 5	Rajneesh, an employee, stole jewellery costing ₹ 10,000 sale price ₹ 12,500.
Jan 6	Received ₹ 10,375 from a customer in full settlement of his account of ₹10,500.
Jan 10	Received a first and final dividend of 70 paise in the rupee from the official receiver of Mr. Jagdish, who owed the firm ₹2,75,000.
Jan 11	Paid into ICICI bank ₹ 25,000 for opening a current account.
Jan 15	Withdrew from bank ₹5,000.
Jan 16	Placed on fixed deposit account at bank by transfer from current account ₹10,000.
Jan 20	Purchased 50 war Bonds of ₹ 100 each at ₹ 96 and paid for them by cheque.
Jan 25	Salary due to salesman ₹5,000.

Ans Total of Journal = ₹4,96,500

12 **Journalise the following transactions**

(i) Paid rent of the building ₹20,000. Half of the building is used by the proprietor for residential use.

(ii) Paid fire insurance of the above building in advance ₹5,000.

(iii) Paid life insurance premium ₹2,500 charge depreciation on furniture @ 15% per annum for two months (furniture ₹50,000).

(iv) Charge interest on capital @ 10% per annum for six months (capital ₹2,50,000).

(v) Charge interest on drawings @ 12% per annum for six months (drawings ₹ 50,000).

(vi) Provide interest on loan from Raj at 15% per annum for three months (loan ₹75,000).

(vii) Received commission ₹2,500, half of which is in advance.

Ans Total of Journal = 65,812.5

13 **Journalise the following transactions in the books of Rachna and post them into the ledger.**

2016		Amt (₹)
Dec 1	Cash in hand	18,000
	Cash at bank	1,65,000
	Stock of goods	1,20,000
	Due to X	18,000
	Due from Y	30,000
Dec 3	Sold goods to Z	45,000
Dec 4	Cash sales	30,000
Dec 6	Goods sold to S	15,000
Dec 8	Purchased goods from T	90,000
Dec 10	Goods returned from Z	6,000
Dec 14	Cash received from Z	39,000
Dec 15	Cheque given to X	18,000
Dec 16	Cash received from S	9,000
Dec 20	Cheque received from Y	30,000
Dec 22	Cheque received from S	6,000
Dec 25	Cash given to T	54,000
Dec 26	Paid cartage	3,000
Dec 27	Paid salary	24,000
Dec 28	Cash sales	21,000
Dec 29	Cheque given to T	36,000
Dec 30	Rachna took goods for personal use	12,000
Dec 31	Paid general expenses	1,500

14 Journalise the following transactions in the journal of M/s Goel Brothers and post them to the ledger. **NCERT**

2016		Amt (₹)
Jan 1	Started business with cash	1,65,000
Jan 2	Open bank account in PNB	80,000
Jan 4	Goods purchased from Tara	22,000
Jan 5	Goods purchased for cash	30,000
Jan 8	Goods sold to Naman	12,000
Jan 10	Cash paid to Tara	22,000
Jan 15	Cash received from Naman	11,700
	Discount allowed	300
Jan 16	Paid wages	200
Jan 18	Furniture purchased for office use	5,000
Jan 20	Withdrawn from bank for personal use	4,000
Jan 22	Issued cheque for rent	3,000
Jan 23	Goods issued for household purpose	2,000
Jan 24	Drawn cash from bank for office use	6,000
Jan 26	Commission received	1,000
Jan 27	Bank charges	200
Jan 28	Cheque given for insurance premium	3,000
Jan 29	Paid salary	7,000
Jan 30	Cash sales	10,000

15 Pass journal entries and prepare necessary ledger accounts for the following transactions:

(i) Purchased goods from M/s Batra Electricals, Delhi ₹ 50,000 *less* 10% trade discount. Cheque was issued immediately and availed 2% cash discount on purchase price.

(ii) Gave goods costing ₹ 5,000 as charity. These goods were purchased from Kolkata.

(iii) In a competition held by the RWA where the shop is located an electric iron costing ₹ 2,500 was given as an award. It had been purchased from Batra Electricals, Delhi.

(iv) A debt of ₹ 50,000 that was written-off as bad debt in the past was received*.

(v) Salaries amounting to ₹ 75,000 provided in the books for the month of March, 2019 were paid through cheque*.

(vi) Sales for the month were: cash sales ₹ 75,00,000 (Intra-state) and credit sales ₹ 15,00,000 (Inter-state).

(vii) Purchases for the month were: cash purchase ₹ 5,00,000 (Intra-state) and credit purchases (Inter-state) ₹ 45,00,000.

Inter-state transactions are subject to levy of IGST @ 12% and Intra-state transactions are subject to levy of CGST and SGST @ 6% each. GST is not levied on transactions marked with (*).

05

After studying this chapter, the students will be able to familiarise with the various kinds of cash book, techniques to prepare the cash book and how to balance them. The students will further understand the meaning and the kinds of other subsidiary books.

SPECIAL PURPOSE BOOKS

CHAPTER CHECKLIST

- Types of Special Purpose Books
- Cash Book
- Other Special Purpose Books

For a small business, it is easy to record all its transactions in one book only *i.e.*, the journal. But as the business expands and the number of transactions become large, it may become difficult and complex to journalise each and every transaction. For quick, efficient and accurate recording of business transactions, journal is required to be sub-divided into special journals. These special journals are also called **day books** or **subsidiary books** or **special purpose books**. Each subsidiary book is meant for recording transactions of similar nature. *e.g.*, all cash transactions are recorded in one book, all credit in another.

Types of Special Purpose Books

It is difficult to record all the transactions in only one book of prime entry. Therefore, the journal is divided into a number of special purpose books. There are as follows

(*i*) **Cash Book** To record all cash transactions.

(*ii*) **Purchases Book** To record credit purchase of goods only.

(*iii*) **Sales Book** To record credit sales of goods only.

(*iv*) **Purchase Return Book** To record return of goods purchased earlier on credit from suppliers.

(*v*) **Sales Return Book** To record return of goods from customers earlier sold on credit.

(*vi*) **Journal Proper** To record all other transactions which could not be recorded in any of the above specified journals.

Note *Cash book, purchase book, sales book, purchase return book and sales return book are referred to as special journals and journal proper is referred to as general journal.*

|TOPIC 1|
Cash Book

Cash book is a special journal which is used for recording only cash transactions *i.e.*, all cash receipts and cash payments. Cash book is a book of **prime entry/original entry** since transactions (all cash and bank transactions) are recorded in it for the first time from the source documents in a chronological order. It has two sides *i.e.*, debit and credit. Debit side records all receipts of cash (including cheques). Credit side records all payments of cash (including cheques).

In the case of cash book, there will always be debit balance because cash payments can never exceed the sum of cash receipts and cash in hand at the beginning of the period.

Cash Book—Both a Subsidiary Book (Journal) **and a Principal Book** (Ledger)

Cash book serves both purposes i.e., of a subsidiary book (book of original entry) and of a principal book. Cash transactions are first recorded in cash book and thereafter ledger posting is done from cash book. This is the reason due to which it is called a **subsidiary book** or book of original entry. When a cash book is prepared, there is no need to prepare a cash account because cash book in itself serves the purpose of cash account. Therefore, the cash book is also a part of ledger. Hence, it is also a **principal book.**

TYPES OF CASH BOOK

There are three types of cash book

1. Single column cash book or simple cash book
2. Double column or two column cash book
3. Petty cash book

1. Single Column Cash Book or Simple Cash Book

The single column cash book records all cash transactions of the business in a chronological order. It has one column on each side. All cash receipts are recorded on the debit side and all cash payments on the credit side. Single column cash book is nothing but a cash account.

Format of single column cash book is shown below

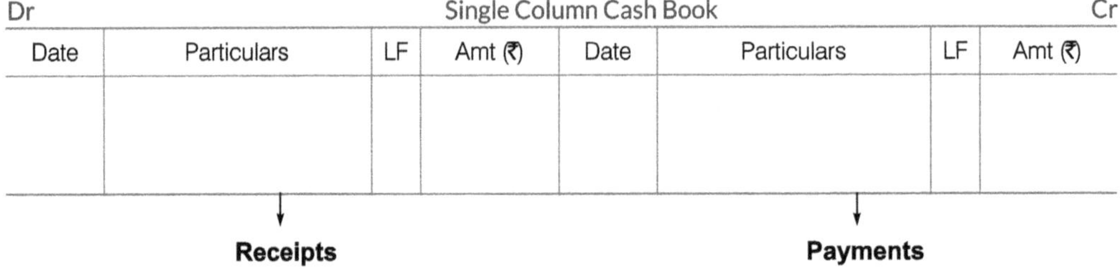

Dr Single Column Cash Book Cr

Date	Particulars	LF	Amt (₹)	Date	Particulars	LF	Amt (₹)

Columns on either side of cash book are

(*i*) **Date** This column records the date of transaction.

(*ii*) **Particulars** This column records the name of the account under which cash has been received and paid.

(*iii*) **Ledger Folio** (LF) This column records the page number of the ledger where the amount has been posted in the account.

(*iv*) **Amount** (₹) This column records amount received (on debit side) and amount paid (on credit side).

BALANCING OF SINGLE COLUMN CASH BOOK

The cash book is balanced in the same way as an account is balanced in the ledger. The total of the receipts column (debit side) will always be greater than the total of the payments column (credit side). The difference will be written on the credit side as 'By Balance c/d'. This will make the total of the two sides equal and the total will be written in the two columns opposite one another. The closing balance becomes opening balance of cash in hand at the beginning of the next period and is written on the debit side as 'To Balance b/d'.

Note *Cash column in a cash book cannot have a credit balance because actual payments (credit side) of cash cannot exceed actual cash available (debit side) with the business.*

LEDGER POSTING FROM SINGLE COLUMN CASH BOOK

Posting of debit side and credit side of cash book is carried out as follows

Debit Side The left side or debit side of the cash book shows the receipts of the cash. The accounts appearing on the debit side of the cash book are credited to their respective ledger accounts by writing 'By Cash' in the particulars column because cash has been received in respect of them.

Credit Side The right side or credit side of the cash book shows all the payments made in cash. The accounts appearing on the credit side of the cash book are debited to the ledger accounts by entering 'To Cash' in the particulars column as cash/cheque has been paid in respect of them.

ILLUSTRATION |1| **Prepare single column cash book for the month of April 2016 of Lalit, a trader, from the following particulars and also post them into ledger.**

2016	Particulars	Amt (₹)
Apr 1	Cash in hand	75,000
Apr 2	Cash sales	7,80,000
Apr 3	Deposited cash into bank	6,00,000
Apr 3	Paid cheque to creditors of ₹ 1,49,700 after deducting cash discount of	9,300
Apr 4	Wages paid in cash	67,500
Apr 4	Cash sales of ₹ 5,40,000 of which ₹ 4,50,000 were banked on 7th April	
Apr 9	Paid cash to transport corporation of India ₹ 13,500 against their bill number 265	
Apr 15	Cash sales ₹ 4,50,000 of which ₹ 3,60,000 were banked on 16th April	
Apr 17	Paid to cleaner in cash	10,800
Apr 19	Cash sales	3,42,000
Apr 20	Deposited cash into bank	2,25,000
Apr 20	Paid cash for window cleaning	5,400
Apr 21	Purchased goods on credit	45,000
Apr 25	Paid cash for rates	1,08,000
Apr 26	Cash sales	5,76,000
Apr 28	Paid cash to Dharma, a creditor after deducting discount ₹ 1,500	28,500
Apr 29	Paid electricity bill in cash	27,000
Apr 30	Cash collected from Karun (debtor) ₹ 1,35,000 after allowing discount of ₹ 7,500	

Sol. Dr **Cash Book** (Single Column) Cr

Date	Particulars	LF	Amt (₹)	Date	Particulars	LF	Amt (₹)
2016				2016			
Apr 1	To Balance b/d		75,000	Apr 3	By Bank A/c		6,00,000
Apr 2	To Sales A/c		7,80,000	Apr 4	By Wages A/c		67,500
Apr 4	To Sales A/c		5,40,000	Apr 7	By Bank A/c		4,50,000
Apr 15	To Sales A/c		4,50,000	Apr 9	By Transport Corporation of India		13,500
Apr 19	To Sales A/c		3,42,000				

Date	Particulars	LF	Amt (₹)	Date	Particulars	LF	Amt (₹)
Apr 26	To Sales A/c		5,76,000	Apr 16	By Bank A/c		3,60,000
Apr 30	To Karun		1,35,000	Apr 17	By Office Expenses A/c		10,800
				Apr 20	By Bank A/c		2,25,000
				Apr 20	By Office Expenses A/c		5,400
				Apr 25	By Rates A/c		1,08,000
				Apr 28	By Dharma		28,500
				Apr 29	By Electricity Expenses A/c		27,000
				Apr 30	By Balance c/d		10,02,300
			28,98,000				28,98,000
May 1	To Balance b/d		10,02,300				

LEDGER POSTING OF SINGLE COLUMN CASH BOOK

Dr **Wages Account** Cr

Date	Particulars	JF	Amt (₹)	Date	Particulars	JF	Amt (₹)
2016 Apr 4	To Cash A/c		67,500				

Dr **Sales Account** Cr

Date	Particulars	JF	Amt (₹)	Date	Particulars	JF	Amt (₹)
				2016			
				Apr 2	By Cash A/c		7,80,000
				Apr 4	By Cash A/c		5,40,000
				Apr 15	By Cash A/c		4,50,000
				Apr 19	By Cash A/c		3,42,000
				Apr 26	By Cash A/c		5,76,000

Dr **Transport Corporation Account** Cr

Date	Particulars	JF	Amt (₹)	Date	Particulars	JF	Amt (₹)
2016 Apr 9	To Cash A/c		13,500				

Dr **Office Expenses Account** Cr

Date	Particulars	JF	Amt (₹)	Date	Particulars	JF	Amt (₹)
2016							
Apr 17	To Cash A/c		10,800				
Apr 20	To Cash A/c		5,400				

Dr **Rates Account** Cr

Date	Particulars	JF	Amt (₹)	Date	Particulars	JF	Amt (₹)
2016							
Apr 25	To Cash A/c		1,08,000				

Dr **Dharma's Account** Cr

Date	Particulars	JF	Amt (₹)	Date	Particulars	JF	Amt (₹)
2016							
Apr 28	To Cash A/c		28,500				

Dr **Electricity Expenses Account** Cr

Date	Particulars	JF	Amt (₹)	Date	Particulars	JF	Amt (₹)
2016 Apr 29	To Cash A/c		27,000				

Dr **Karun's Account** Cr

Date	Particulars	JF	Amt (₹)	Date	Particulars	JF	Amt (₹)
				2016 Apr 30	By Cash A/c		1,35,000

Working Note

(i) *Credit purchases are not recorded in the cash book since the cash book is maintained to record only cash transactions.*

(ii) *Cheque issued to creditors ₹1,49,700 on 3rd April, is not recorded in single column cash book.*

(iii) *Cheque deposited into bank is not a cash transaction.*

(iv) *Discount allowed to Karun ₹ 7,500 and discount received from Dharma ₹ 1,500 shall be recorded through journal entry in the following manner.*

			Dr (₹)	Cr (₹)
(a)	Dharma	Dr	1,500	
	To Discount Received A/c			1,500
	(Being the cash discount received from Dharma)			
(b)	Discount Allowed A/c	Dr	7,500	
	To Karun			7,500
	(Being the discount allowed to Karun)			

ILLUSTRATION |2| (With GST) Enter the following transactions in a Single Column Cash Book and post them into the Ledger:

Date	Particulars	Amt (₹)
2019		
Apr 1	Cash in hand	1,00,000
Apr 5	Cash purchases of ₹ 20,000 *plus* CGST and SGST @ 6% each	
Apr 8	Cash sales of ₹ 16,000 *plus* CGST and SGST @ 6% each	
Apr 15	Purchased furniture for ₹ 10,000 *plus* CGST and SGST @ 6% each	
Apr 25	Received commission ₹ 2,000 *plus* CGST and SGST @ 6% each	
Apr 30	Paid rent ₹ 12,000 *plus* CGST and SGST @ 6% each	

Sol.

Dr **Cash Book** Cr

Date	Particulars	V. No.	LF	Amt (₹)	Date	Particulars	V.No.	LF	Amt (₹)
2019					2019				
Apr 1	To Balance b/d			1,00,000	Apr 5	By Purchases A/c			20,000
Apr 8	To Sales A/c			16,000	Apr 5	By Input CGST A/c			1,200
Apr 8	To Output CGST A/c			960	Apr 5	By Input SGST A/c			1,200
Apr 8	To Output SGST A/c			960	Apr 15	By Furniture A/c			10,000
Apr 25	To Commission Received A/c			2,000	Apr 15	By Input CGST A/c			600
Apr 25	To Output CGST A/c			120	Apr 15	By Input SGST A/c			600
Apr 25	To Output SGST A/c			120	Apr 30	By Rent A/c			12,000
					Apr 30	By Input CGST A/c			720
					Apr 30	By Input SGST A/c			720
					Apr 30	By Balance c/d			73,120
				1,20,160					1,20,160

Dr **Purchases Account** Cr

Date	Particulars	JF	Amt (₹)	Date	Particulars	JF	Amt (₹)
2019 Apr 5	To Cash A/c		20,000				

Dr **Sales Account** Cr

Date	Particulars	JF	Amt (₹)	Date	Particulars	JF	Amt (₹)
				2019 Apr 8	By Cash A/c		16,000

Dr **Furniture Account** Cr

Date	Particulars	JF	Amt (₹)	Date	Particulars	JF	Amt (₹)
2019 Apr 15	To Cash A/c		10,000				

Dr **Commission Received Account** Cr

Date	Particulars	JF	Amt (₹)	Date	Particulars	JF	Amt (₹)
				2019 Apr 25	By Cash A/c		2,000

Dr **Rent Account** Cr

Date	Particulars	JF	Amt (₹)	Date	Particulars	JF	Amt (₹)
2019 Apr 30	To Cash A/c		12,000				

Dr **Input CGST Account** Cr

Date	Particulars	JF	Amt (₹)	Date	Particulars	JF	Amt (₹)
2019							
Apr 5	To Cash A/c (Purchase)		1,200				
Apr 15	To Cash A/c (Furniture)		600				
Apr 30	To Cash A/c (Rent)		720				
			2,520				

Dr **Input SGST Account** Cr

Date	Particulars	JF	Amt (₹)	Date	Particulars	JF	Amt (₹)
2019							
Apr 5	To Cash A/c (Purchase)		1,200				
Apr 15	To Cash A/c (Furniture)		600				
Apr 30	To Cash A/c (Rent)		720				
			2,520				

Dr **Output CGST Account** Cr

Date	Particulars	JF	Amt (₹)	Date	Particulars	JF	Amt (₹)
				2019			
				Apr 8	By Cash A/c (Sales)		960
				Apr 25	By Cash A/c (Commission Received)		120
							1,080

Dr **Output SGST Account** Cr

Date	Particulars	JF	Amt (₹)	Date	Particulars	JF	Amt (₹)
				2019			
				Apr 8	By Cash A/c (Sales)		960
				Apr 25	By Cash A/c (Commission)		120
							1,080

2. Double Column or Two Column Cash Book (Cash Book with Cash and Bank Column)

Double column cash book is a cash book which has two columns on each side; one for cash and one for bank. It represents two accounts *i.e.,* cash account and bank account. Hence, there is no need to open these accounts in the ledger.

As cash and bank account are both asset account (as per modern classification), therefore cash and bank transactions are recorded in the cash and bank column respectively, following the rule 'debit the increase in asset and credit the decrease in asset'. All the cash receipts/deposits into the bank are recorded on debit side and all cash payments/withdrawals from bank are recorded on credit side.

Format of double column cash book is shown below

Dr **Double Column Cash Book** Cr

Date	Particulars	LF	Cash (₹)	Bank (₹)	Date	Particulars	LF	Cash (₹)	Bank (₹)

↓ **Receipts** ↓ **Payments**

SOME IMPORTANT POINTS RELATED TO DOUBLE COLUMN CASH BOOK

(*i*) Cash discount allowed or received is recorded by means of a journal entry

(*a*) Cash discount may be received/allowed when payment is made/received by cheque/cash.

For Discount Allowed

Discount Allowed A/c	Dr
To Debtors A/c	

For Discount Received

Creditors A/c	Dr
To Discount Received A/c	

(*b*) In case cheque is dishonoured, discount received/allowed is also written back by passing a entry in journal proper.

For Reversal of Discount Allowed

Debtors A/c	Dr
To Discount Allowed A/c	

For Reversal of Discount Received

Discount Received A/c	Dr
To Creditors A/c	

(*ii*) **Contra Entries** Contra entries mean entries that are made on both sides of cash book.

In a double column cash book, there are some transactions that relate to both cash and bank. Such transactions are entered on both sides of the cash book. Such entries are known as contra entries and are not posted into the ledger.

Against such entries, the letter 'C' is written in the LF column to indicate that these are contra transactions and are not posted into the ledger account.

Contra entries are required to be passed in the following cases

(*a*) Cash deposited into bank

Bank A/c	Dr
To Cash A/c	

(*b*) Cash withdrawn from bank for office use

Cash A/c	Dr
To Bank A/c	

Let us understand it in detail

Example : Cash deposited into bank ₹ 50,000

Entry

Bank A/c	Dr	50,000	
To Cash A/c			50,000

As the cash book with cash and bank columns is a combined cash and bank account, both the aspects of the transaction will be entered in the same book. On the debit side, 'To Cash A/c' will be entered in the particulars column and the amount will be entered in the bank column, signifying increase in bank balance.

On the credit side, 'By Bank A/c' will be entered in the particulars column and the amount will be entered in the cash column signifying decrease in cash in hand.

Dr **Cash Book** Cr

Date	Particulars	LF	Cash (₹)	Bank (₹)	Date	Particulars	LF	Cash (₹)	Bank (₹)
	To Cash A/c	C		50,000		By Bank A/c	C	50,000	

Example : Cash withdrawn from bank ₹ 15,000

Entry

Cash A/c	Dr	15,000	
To Bank A/c			15,000

In double-column cash book, on the debit side, 'To Bank A/c' will be entered in the particulars column and the amount will be entered in cash column, signifying increase in cash in hand.

On the credit side, 'By Cash A/c' will be entered in the particulars column and the amount will be entered in the bank column, signifying decrease in bank balance.

Dr **Cash Book** Cr

Date	Particulars	LF	Cash (₹)	Bank (₹)	Date	Particulars	LF	Cash (₹)	Cash (₹)
	To Bank A/c	C	15,000			By Cash A/c	C	15,000	

(*iii*) **Cheques Received Deposited into Bank on Same Date**

If a business firm receives cheques and deposits the same into bank on the same day, then the following entry is passed

Bank A/c	Dr
To Debtors	

It is recorded in the debit side of cash book in the bank column.

Example : Cheque of ₹ 2,000 is received from Raj and is deposited into the bank on the same day.

Entry

Bank A/c	Dr	2,000	
To Raj			2,000

Dr **Cash Book** Cr

Date	Particulars	LF	Cash (₹)	Bank (₹)	Date	Particulars	LF	Cash (₹)	Bank (₹)
	To Raj		—	2,000					

(*iv*) **Cheques Received and Deposited on Different Dates**

If a business firm receives cheques but does not deposit it into bank on the same day, then the following entries are passed

When cheque is received

Cheques in Hand A/c	Dr
To Debtors	

Note : *This entry will not be recorded in cash book*

When cheque received is deposited

Bank A/c	Dr
To Cheques in Hand A/c	

It is recorded on the debit side of cash book in the bank column.

In this manner, the balance in cheques in hand account will become nil.

Example : A cheque is received from Laksh for ₹ 5,000 on 16th August, 2016 and this cheque is deposited into the bank on 20th August, 2016.

Entry

2016 Aug 16	Cheques in Hand A/c	Dr		5,000	
	To Laksh				5,000
Aug 20	Bank A/c	Dr		5,000	
	To Cheques in Hand A/c				5,000

Dr **Cash Book** Cr

Date	Particulars	LF	Cash (₹)	Bank (₹)	Date	Particulars	LF	Cash (₹)	Bank (₹)
2016 Aug 20	To Cheques in Hand A/c		—	5,000					

An Alternate Treatment Alternately, the following accounting treatment can be done.

When Cheque is Received When cheque is received, it is treated as equivalent of cash and the following entry is made.

Cash A/c	Dr
To Debtor	

In the cash book, it will be recorded on the debit side in the cash column.

When Cheque is Deposited When cheque received is deposited in bank, then it is assumed that cash is being deposited in bank, and the following entry is made.

Bank A/c	Dr
To Cash A/c	

In the cash book, it is recorded as a contra entry.

However, in the present times, this method is not much preferred due to increase in the number of banking transactions.

Note *In case a question is silent as to the deposit date of the cheque, it will be assumed that the cheque has been deposited into the bank on same date.*

(*v*) Cheque Received, Endorsed in Favour of a Creditor

In case a business firm endorses the cheque received from a debtor in favour of a creditor, then the following entries are passed

When Cheque is Received

Cheques in Hand A/c	Dr
To Debtor	

When cheque is endorsed

Creditor	Dr
To Cheques in Hand A/c	

These entries will not be recorded in cash book.

Note *Alternatively, cash can be debited when cheque is received and at the time of endorsement, cash can be credited. However, it is not a preferred treatment.*

Example : A cheque for ₹ 10,000 is received from Sita on 2nd January, 2016 and it is endorsed to Geeta on 5th January, 2016.

Entry

2016				
Jan 2	Cheques in Hand A/c	Dr	10,000	
	To Sita			10,000
Jan 5	Geeta	Dr	10,000	
	To Cheques in Hand A/c			10,000

(*vi*) **Cheque Deposited into Bank Dishonoured**

There can be two possible conditions

(*a*) The cheque which is dishonoured was deposited in bank on the day on which it was received. In this case the following entry is passed

Debtor	Dr
To Bank A/c	

It is recorded on the credit side of cash book in the bank column.

Example : A cheque of ₹ 2,000 received from Kumar is dishonoured. It was deposited in the bank on the same day of receipt.

Entry

Kumar	Dr	2,000	
To Bank A/c			2,000

Dr **Cash Book** Cr

Date	Particulars	LF	Cash (₹)	Bank (₹)	Date	Particulars	LF	Cash (₹)	Bank (₹)
						By Kumar		—	2,000

(*b*) The cheque which is dishonoured was not deposited in bank on the day on which it was received.

In this case the following entries are passed

Cheques in Hand A/c	Dr
To Bank A/c	

Debtor	Dr
To Cheques in Hand A/c	

It is recorded on the credit side of cash book in the bank column.

Example A cheque, of ₹ 5,000 which was received from Diksha on 9th February and deposited on 12th February was dishonoured.

Entry

Cheques in Hand A/c	Dr	5,000	
To Bank A/c			5,000
Diksha	Dr	5,000	
To Cheques in Bank A/c			5,000

Dr Cr

Date	Particulars	LF	Cash (₹)	Bank (₹)	Date	Particulars	LF	Cash (₹)	Bank (₹)
						By Cheques-in-hand		—	5,000

BALANCING OF DOUBLE COLUMN CASH BOOK

Cash columns are balanced in the same manner as in case of single column cash book. Cash column will always have a nil or debit balance which will be shown on the assets side of balance sheet. The process for balancing the bank column is also the same. However, it is possible that the bank column may either have a debit or credit balance which will be shown on the assets or liabilities side of balance sheet respectively. Debit balance indicates bank balance and credit balance indicates bank overdraft.

Note *Bank overdraft is a facility provided by the bank in which the bank allows the customer to withdraw more money than the cash deposited or lying with bank.*

LEDGER POSTING OF DOUBLE COLUMN CASH BOOK

Posting of debit side and credit side of two column cash book is carried out as follows

Debit Side The left side or debit side of the cash book shows the receipt of cash. Transactions written in the cash and bank column on debit side are credited to their respective ledger account by writing 'By Cash' (for cash transactions) and 'By Bank' (for bank transactions) in the particulars column. 'Amount column' records the amount of the transaction. Discount allowed is individually posted to the credit of debtor's account and to the debit of discount allowed account.

Credit Side The right side or credit side of the cash book shows all the payments made in cash.

Transactions written in cash and bank column on credit side are debited to their respective ledger accounts by writing 'To Cash' (for cash transactions) and 'To Bank' (for bank transactions) in the particulars column. 'Amount column' records the amount of transaction.

Discount received is individually posted to the debit of creditor's account and to the credit of discount received account.

ILLUSTRATION |3| **Prepare two column cash book from the following transactions of M/s Raj Mohan for the month of April, 2016. Also prepare any five related ledger accounts and pass journal entries related to discount received and discount allowed.**

2016	Particulars	Amt (₹)
Apr 1	Cash in hand	70,000
	Bank overdraft	66,000
Apr 2	Cash purchases ₹ 8,000 less trade discount @ 10%	
Apr 3	Sold goods to Raja on credit	4,000
	Purchased goods on credit from Rajesh	8,000
Apr 4	Wages paid	7,000
Apr 5	Cash sales	85,000
Apr 7	Purchased goods from Manisha for ₹ 61,250 paid by cheque in full settlement	60,000
Apr 9	Purchased furniture for cash	50,000
Apr 10	Cash paid to Sarika discount received ₹ 500	25,000
Apr 11	Cheque issued to Manisha was dishonoured	
Apr 13	Cash sales	22,500
Apr 16	Bank charged interest on overdraft	2,500
Apr 18	Deposited into bank	35,000
Apr 20	Paid telephone bill by cheque	3,000
Apr 25	Sold goods for ₹ 1,17,500 to Sachin and received cheque in full settlement (Deposited same day)	1,15,000
Apr 27	Paid rent	4,000
Apr 29	Drew cash for personal use	5,000
Apr 30	Paid salary	10,000
Apr 30	Interest collected by bank	12,500

Sol.

Dr Cash Book Cr

Date	Particulars	LF	Cash (₹)	Bank (₹)	Date	Particulars	LF	Cash (₹)	Bank (₹)
2016					2016				
Apr 1	To Balance b/d		70,000	—	Apr 1	By Balance b/d		—	66,000
Apr 5	To Sales A/c		85,000	—	Apr 2	By Purchases A/c		7,200	—
Apr 11	To Manisha		—	60,000	Apr 4	By Wages A/c		7,000	—
Apr 13	To Sales A/c		22,500	—	Apr 7	By Manisha		—	60,000
Apr 18	To Cash A/c	C	—	35,000	Apr 9	By Furniture A/c		50,000	—
Apr 25	To Sachin		—	1,15,000	Apr 10	By Sarika		25,000	—
Apr 30	To Interest A/c		—	12,500	Apr 16	By Interest on Bank Overdraft A/c		—	2,500
					Apr 18	By Bank A/c	C	35,000	—
					Apr 20	By Telephone Expenses A/c		—	3,000
					Apr 27	By Rent A/c		4,000	—
					Apr 29	By Drawings A/c		5,000	—
					Apr 30	By Salary A/c		10,000	—
					Apr 30	By Balance c/d		34,300	91,000
			1,77,500	2,22,500				1,77,500	2,22,500
May 1	To Balance b/d		34,300	91,000					

Note *Trade discount is not recorded separately in the books of accounts. Net amount 8,000 – 800 = ₹ 7,200 is credited to cash account and debited to purchases account. Transactions of 3rd April are not recorded being credit transactions.*

JOURNAL

Date	Particulars		LF	Amt (Dr)	Amt (Cr)
2016					
Apr 7	Manisha	Dr		1.250	
	To Discount Received A/c				1,250
	(Being the cash discount received from Manisha)				
Apr 10	Sarika	Dr		500	
	To Discount Received A/c				500
	(Being the cash discount received from Sarika)				
Apr 11	Discount Received A/c	Dr		1,250	
	To Manisha				1,250
	(Being the discount received reversed on cheque being dishonoured)				
Apr 25	Discount Allowed A/c	Dr		2,500	
	To Sachin				2,500
	(Being the cash discount allowed to Sachin)				

Dr **Wages Account** Cr

Date	Particulars	JF	Amt (₹)	Date	Particulars	JF	Amt (₹)
2016							
Apr 4	To Cash A/c		7,000				

Dr **Sales Account** Cr

Date	Particulars	JF	Amt (₹)	Date	Particulars	JF	Amt (₹)
				2016			
				Apr 5	By Cash A/c		85,000
				Apr 13	By Cash A/c		22,500

Dr **Manisha's Account** Cr

Date	Particulars	JF	Amt (₹)	Date	Particulars	JF	Amt (₹)
2016				2016			
Apr 7	To Bank A/c		60,000	Apr 11	By Bank A/c		60,000
Apr 7	To Discount Received A/c		1,250	Apr 25	By Discount Allowed A/c		2,500

Dr **Discount Allowed Account** Cr

Date	Particulars	JF	Amt (₹)	Date	Particulars	JF	Amt (₹)
2016							
Apr 25	To Sachin		2,500				

Dr **Discount Received Account** Cr

Date	Particulars	JF	Amt (₹)	Date	Particulars	JF	Amt (₹)
2016				2016			
Apr 11	To Manisha		1,250	Apr 7	By Manisha		1,250
				Apr 10	By Sarika		500

ILLUSTRATION |4| Prepare a double column cash book (Cash and Bank) from the following transactions. Also pass the necessary journal entries.

2016

Aug 1 Cash in hand ₹ 1,200; overdraft at bank ₹ 15,000.

Aug 3 Further capital introduced ₹ 20,000 out of which ₹ 16,000 deposited in the bank.

Aug 4 Purchased goods from Vrijesh Traders amounting to ₹ 3,000 and they allowed trade discount ₹ 200. The amount was paid by cheque.

Aug 4 Goods purchased for cash ₹ 4,000.

Aug 5 Sold goods to Varun on credit ₹ 5,000.

Aug 6 Received cheque from Siddhartha ₹ 2,450. Allowed him discount ₹ 50.

Aug 10 Cheque received from Siddhartha deposited into bank.

Aug 11 Settled the account of Superstar Printers ₹ 750 by paying cash ₹ 680.

Aug 12 Cash received from Varun ₹ 4,750 in full settlement of his account of ₹ 5,000.

Aug 16 An amount of ₹ 1,000 due from Kartik Brothers written off as bad debts in the previous year, now recovered.

Aug 17 Received from Kunal on behalf of Karan ₹ 200.

Aug 19 Received a cheque for ₹ 800 from Adarsh, which was endorsed to Parth on 24th August.

Aug 20 Sale of old furniture, payment received in cash for ₹ 720.

Aug 25 Cashed a cheque for ₹ 3,000

Aug 25 Drew from bank for household expenses ₹ 1,000 and for income tax ₹ 500.

Aug 28 Amit who owed ₹ 400 became bankrupt and paid 60 paise in a rupee.

Aug 28 Received repayment of a loan ₹ 3,000 and deposited out of it ₹ 2,500 into the bank.

Aug 30 Interest debited by bank ₹ 375.

Aug 30 Deposited with the bank the entire balance after retaining ₹ 2,000 at office.

Sol. Dr **Cash Book** Cr

Date	Particulars	LF	Cash (₹)	Bank (₹)	Date	Particulars	LF	Cash (₹)	Bank (₹)
2016					2016				
Aug 1	To Balance b/d		1,200		Aug 1	By Balance b/d			15,000
Aug 3	To Capital A/c		4,000	16,000	Aug 4	By Purchases A/c (₹ 3,000– ₹ 200)			2,800
Aug 10	To Cheques in Hand A/c			2,450	Aug 4	By Purchases A/c		4,000	
Aug 12	To Varun		4,750		Aug 11	By Superstar Printers		680	
Aug 16	To Bad Debts Recovered A/c		1,000		Aug 25	By Cash A/c	C		3,000
					Aug 25	By Drawings A/c (₹ 1,000+ ₹ 500)			1,500
Aug 17	To Karan		200						
Aug 20	To Furniture A/c		720		Aug 30	By Interest A/c			375
Aug 25	To Bank A/c (Note iii)	C	3,000		Aug 30	By Bank A/c (Note iv)	C	8,930	
					Aug 30	By Balance c/d		2,000	7,205
Aug 28	To Amit		240						
Aug 28	To Loan A/c		500	2,500					
Aug 30	To Cash A/c (Note iv)	C		8,930					
			15,610	29,880				15,610	29,880
Sep 1	To Balance b/d		2,000	7,205					

JOURNAL

Date	Particulars		LF	Amt (Dr)	Amt (Cr)
2016					
Aug 6	Cheques in Hand A/c	Dr		2,450	
	Discount Allowed A/c	Dr		50	
	To Siddhartha's A/c				2,500
	(Being the cheque received from Siddhartha's and allowed him discount. Cheque received was not deposited the same day)				
Aug 11	Superstar Printers	Dr		70	
	To Discount Received A/c				70
	(Being the discount received on payment made to Superstar Printers)				
Aug 12	Discount Allowed A/c	Dr		250	
	To Varun				250
	(Being the cash discount allowed to Varun against payment received)				
Aug 19	Cheques in Hand A/c	Dr		800	
	To Adarsh				800
	(Being the cheque received from Adarsh not deposited but endorsed) (Note ii)				
Aug 24	Parth	Dr		800	
	To Cheques in Hand A/c				800
	(Being the cheque received from Adarsh endorsed in favour of Parth) (Note ii)				

Working Note

(i) Goods sold to Varun on 5th August, will not be recorded in the cash book, it being credit sale.

(ii) When a cheque is received but endorsed in favour of a creditor, the transaction is recorded through a journal entry. It is recorded through the journal and not cash book because cheque has neither been deposited in the bank nor has been issued to the third party. In this case, we shall pass two entries one for receiving cheque from Adarsh on 19th August, 2016 and later for endorsing the cheque in favour of Parth on 24th August, 2016.

(iii) On 25th August, a cheque encashed for ₹ 3,000 is treated as cash withdrawn from bank for business.

(iv) ₹ 15,610 – (₹ 4,000 + ₹ 680 + ₹ 2,000) = ₹ 8,930.

(v) ₹ 8,930 is deposited into bank after retaining ₹ 2,000 at office on 30th August, 2016.

ILLUSTRATION |5| (With GST) Record the following transactions of Subramaniam of Chennai in a Two-column Cash Book and balance the book on 31st January, 2019:

Date	Particulars	Amt (₹)	Date	Particulars	Amt (₹)
2019			2019		
Jan 1	Cash Balance	30,000	Jan 16	Bought goods, including IGST @ 12%	13,440
Jan 1	Bank Balance	39,000			
Jan 3	Purchased goods from Raunak ₹ 26,000 plus CGST and SGST @ 6% each and paid by cheque ₹ 28,000 in full settlement		Jan 24	Cash Sales, including CGST and SGST @ 6% each	3,808
			Jan 28	Issued cheque for cash purchases including IGST @ 12%	4,480
Jan 14	Purchased stationery for cash ₹ 3,000 plus CGST and SGST @ 6% each		Jan 30	Paid rent ₹ 4,000 by cheque plus CGST and SGST @ 6% each	

Sol. **In the Books of Subramaniam, Chennai**

Two-Column Cash Book

Dr | Cr

Date	Particulars	LF	Cash (₹)	Bank (₹)	Date	Particulars	LF	Cash (₹)	Bank (₹)
2019					2019				
Jan 1	To Balance b/d		30,000	39,000	Jan 3	By Purchases A/c (₹ 26,000 – ₹ 1,120)			24,880
Jan 24	To Sales A/c		3,400		Jan 3	By Input CGST A/c			1,560
Jan 24	To Output CGST A/c		204		Jan 3	By Input SGST A/c			1,560
Jan 24	To Output SGST A/c		204		Jan 14	By Stationery A/c		3,000	
					Jan 14	By Input CGST A/c		100	
					Jan 14	By Input SGST A/c		180	
					Jan 16	By Purchases A/c		12,000	
					Jan 16	By Input IGST A/c		1,440	
					Jan 28	By Purchases A/c			4,000
					Jan 28	By Input IGST A/c			480
					Jan 30	By Rent A/c			4,000
					Jan 30	By Input CGST A/c			240
					Jan 30	By Input SGST A/c			240
					Jan 31	By Balance c/d		13,768	2,040
			33,808	39,000				33,808	39,000
Feb 1	To Balance b/d		8,004	62,120					

CASH BOOK FOR MORE THAN ONE BANK ACCOUNT

In case a firm has more than one bank account, the bank column of cash book is divided to record bank transactions through different banks separately.

Cash Book

Dr | Cr

Date	Particulars	LF	Cash (₹)	Bank		Date	Particulars	LF	Cash (₹)	Bank	
				PNB (₹)	SBI (₹)					PNB (₹)	SBI (₹)

ILLUSTRATION |6| From the following particulars provided by Rishi, prepare a cash book with suitable columns.

2016		Amt (₹)
Mar 1	Cash in hand	85,000
	Bank balance with ICICI Bank	2,50,000
	Overdraft with Axis Bank	1,75,000
Mar 3	Cash sales	70,000
Mar 5	Paid salary to staff by cheque on ICICI Bank	1,00,000
Mar 8	Cheque received from Raj deposited with Axis Bank	90,000
Mar 10	Cash deposited into ICICI Bank	50,000
Mar 12	Amount transferred from ICICI Bank to Axis Bank by cheque	30,000
Mar 15	Cash withdrew from ICICI Bank	80,000

Sol.

Dr **Cash Book** Cr

Date	Particulars	LF	Cash (₹)	Bank		Date	Particulars	LF	Cash (₹)	Bank	
				ICICI (₹)	Axis (₹)					ICICI (₹)	Axis (₹)
2016						2016					
Mar 1	To Balance b/d		85,000	2,50,000	—	Mar 1	By Balance b/d		—	—	1,75,000
Mar 3	To Sales A/c		70,000	—	—	Mar 5	By Salaries A/c		—	1,00,000	—
Mar 8	To Raj		—	—	90,000	Mar 10	By ICICI	C	50,000	—	—
Mar 10	To Cash A/c	C	—	50,000	—	Mar 12	By Axis	C	—	30,000	—
Mar 12	To ICICI	C	—	—	30,000	Mar 15	By Cash A/c	C	—	80,000	—
Mar 15	To ICICI	C	80,000	—	—	Mar 15	By Balance c/d		1,85,000	90,000	—
Mar 15	To Balance c/d		—	—	55,000				—	—	—
			2,35,000	3,00,000	1,75,000				2,35,000	3,00,000	1,75,000
Mar 16	To Balance b/d		1,85,000	90,000	—	Mar 31	By Balance b/d		—	—	55,000

3. Petty Cash Book

Petty cash book is the book which is used for the purpose of recording the payment of petty cash expenses. It is prepared by the petty cashier to record petty expenses (of small amounts). This book is prepared to save valuable time of chief (head) cashier from bothering about small and irrelevant cash expenses. For transferring cash to petty cash account, cash account is credited and petty cash account is debited.

SYSTEM OF PETTY CASH BOOK

Petty cash book may be maintained by following systems

(*i*) **Ordinary System** In this system, petty cashier is given a certain appropriate amount of cash and after spending the whole amount, he submits the accounts to the cashier.

(*ii*) **Imprest System** Under this system, the petty cashier is given a fixed sum of money at the beginning of a certain period. This amount is called **imprest amount.** The petty cashier makes all small payments out of this imprest amount. The amount spent in a particular period is reimbursed from the head cashier. Thus, he again has the full imprest amount in the beginning of the next period. The reimbursement may be made on a weekly, fortnightly or monthly basis, depending on the frequency of small payments.

For example, ₹ 1,000 is given to a petty cashier on 1st January, 2016, during the month he spent ₹ 700, at the end of the month *i.e.*, 31st January, 2016, he had ₹ 300 balance. On 1st February, he will be paid ₹ 700 again so that his balance again becomes ₹ 1,000.

TYPES OF PETTY CASH BOOK

Following are the types of petty cash book

Simple Petty Cash Book

A simple petty cash book is similar to a cash book. Cash received by the petty cashier is recorded on the debit side(receipt column) and cash paid out is recorded on the credit side (payment column). Simple petty cash book is balanced like a ledger account.

Format of simple petty cash book is shown below

Dr **Simple Petty Cash Book** Cr

Amount Received	Cash Book Folio	Date	Particulars	Voucher No.	Amount Paid
Amount Received	....	....	.... Head of Expenses	....	....

↓ **Receipts** ↓ **Payments**

ILLUSTRATION |7| From the following particulars, prepare a petty cash book for the month of June 2016.

Date	Particulars	Amt (₹)
2016		
June 1	Received petty cash	2,000
June 3	Paid for postage	300
June 5	Paid for telephone	40
June 8	Paid for cartage	140
June 9	Paid for postage	200
June 12	Paid for sundries	100
June 27	Paid for taxi fare	240

If the imprest amount is ₹ 2,000, show what amount the petty cashier would be entitled to draw in the beginning of the next month.

Sol. Dr Petty Cash Book Cr

Amount Received (₹)	Cash Book Folio	Date	Particulars	Voucher No.	Amount Paid (₹)
		2016			
2,000		June 1	To Bank A/c		
		June 3	By Postage A/c		300
		June 5	By Telephone A/c		40
		June 8	By Cartage A/c		140
		June 9	By Postage A/c		200
		June 12	By Sundry Expenses A/c		100
		June 27	By Travelling Expenses A/c		240
		June 30	By Balance c/d		980
2,000					2,000
980		July 1	To Balance b/d		
1,020		July 1	To Bank A/c		

Analytical Petty Cash Book

This cash book has one amount column on its debit side and a number of columns on its credit side relating to most common petty expenses. Since this book analyses the expenses into a number of head of expenses, the name given to it is analytical petty cash book. Each payment is recorded on it twice, one on total amount column and next on individual expense column. Analytical petty cash book is balanced on the basis of impress system of petty cash. The total amount column is balanced and individual expense columns are totalled. The total of different columns for payments equals the totals in the 'total payment column'. Format of analytical petty cash book is shown below

Dr **Analytical Petty Cash Book** Cr

Receipts		Payments								
Receipts (₹)	Date	Voucher No.	Particulars	Total Payment (₹)	Postage/ Telegram (₹)	Conveyance /Travelling (₹)	Staff Welfare/ Entertainment (₹)	Cartage (₹)	Printing and Stationery (₹)	Misce-llaneous Items (₹)

POSTING THE PETTY CASH BOOK

(*i*) Entries in the petty cash book are posted into the ledger accounts at the end of the specified period *i.e.,* monthly or quarterly or as the case may be.

(*ii*) Petty cash book is not posted directly in the ledger. For posting the petty cash book, a petty cash account is opened in the ledger.

(*iii*) When petty cash is advanced to the petty cashier the following journal entry is passed

Petty Cash A/c	Dr
To Cash A/c	

It is recorded by the chief cashier on the credit side of petty cash book as 'By Petty Cash A/c'.

(*iv*) At the end of specified period, the following journal entry is first prepared on the basis of the petty cash book, debiting each expense account individually as per the total shown by respective columns and crediting the petty cash account with the total expenditure incurred during the period.

Expenses A/c	Dr
To Petty Cash A/c	

(Each expense is debited separately with the expenditure incurred during the period as shown by the petty cash book).

Thus, in the ledger, there is a petty cash account as well as separate ledger account for each expense.

Thereafter, posting is made to the debit of each expense account by writing 'To Petty Cash A/c.'

ILLUSTRATION |8| Prepare analytical petty cash book for the following transactions. The imprest amount is ₹ 2,000. **NCERT**

		Amt (₹)
Jan 1	Paid cartage	50
Jan 2	STD charges	40
Jan 2	Bus fare	20
Jan 3	Postage	30
Jan 4	Refreshment for employees	80
Jan 6	Courier charges	30
Jan 8	Refreshment of customer	50

Jan 10	Cartage	35
Jan 15	Taxi fare to manager	70
Jan 18	Stationery	65
Jan 20	Bus fare	10
Jan 22	Fax charges	30
Jan 25	Telegram charges	35
Jan 27	Postage stamps	200
Jan 29	Repair of furniture	105
Jan 30	Laundry expenses	115
Jan 31	Miscellaneous expenses	100

Sol.

Dr **Petty Cash Book** Cr

Amount Received	Date	Particulars	Voucher No.	Total Payment	Cartage	Postage	Telephone & Telegram	Conveyance	Stationery	Miscella-neous
2,000	Jan 1	To Cash Received		—	—	—	—	—	—	—
	Jan 1	By Cartage		50	50	—	—	—	—	—
	Jan 2	By STD Charges		40	—	—	40	—	—	—
	Jan 2	By Bus Fare		20	—	—	—	20	—	—
	Jan 3	By Postage		30	—	30	—	—	—	—
	Jan 4	By Refreshment for Employees		80	—	—	—	—	—	80
	Jan 6	By Courier Charges		30	—	30	—	—	—	—
	Jan 8	By Refreshment of Customer		50	—	—	—	—	—	50
	Jan 10	By Cartage		35	35	—	—	—	—	—
	Jan 15	By Taxi Fare		70	—	—	—	70	—	—
	Jan 18	By Stationery		65	—	—	—	—	65	—
	Jan 20	By Bus Fare		10	—	—	—	10	—	—
	Jan 22	By Fax Charges		30	—	—	30	—	—	—
	Jan 25	By Telegram Charges		35	—	—	35	—	—	—
	Jan 27	By Postage Stamps		200	—	200	—	—	—	—
	Jan 29	By Repair of Furniture		105	—	—	—	—	—	105
	Jan 30	By Laundry Expenses		115	—	—	—	—	—	115
	Jan 31	By Miscellaneous Expenses		100	—	—	—	—	—	100
				1,065	85	260	105	100	65	450
	Jan 31	By Balance c/d		935						
2,000				2,000						
935	Feb 1	To Balance b/d								
1,065	Feb 1	To Cash A/c								

LEDGER POSTING OF PETTY CASH BOOK

Dr **Cartage Account** Cr

Date	Particulars	JF	Amt (₹)	Date	Particulars	JF	Amt (₹)
Jan 31	To Petty Cash A/c		85				

Dr **Postage Account** Cr

Date	Particulars	JF	Amt (₹)	Date	Particulars	JF	Amt (₹)
Jan 31	To Petty Cash A/c		260				

Dr **Telephone and Telegram Account** Cr

Date	Particulars	JF	Amt (₹)	Date	Particulars	JF	Amt (₹)
Jan 31	To Petty Cash A/c		105				

Dr **Conveyance Account** Cr

Date	Particulars	JF	Amt (₹)	Date	Particulars	JF	Amt (₹)
Jan 31	To Petty Cash A/c		100				

Dr **Stationery Account** Cr

Date	Particulars	JF	Amt (₹)	Date	Particulars	JF	Amt (₹)
Jan 31	To Petty Cash A/c		65				

Dr **Miscellaneous Expenses Account** Cr

Date	Particulars	JF	Amt (₹)	Date	Particulars	JF	Amt (₹)
Jan 31	To Petty Cash A/c		450				

Dr **Petty Cash Account** Cr

Date	Particulars	JF	Amt (₹)	Date	Particulars	JF	Amt (₹)
2016				2016			
Jan 1	To Cash A/c		2,000	Jan 31	By Cartage A/c		85
				Jan 31	By Postage A/c		260
				Jan 31	By Telephone and Telegram A/c		105
				Jan 31	By Conveyance A/c		100
				Jan 31	By Stationery A/c		65
				Jan 31	By Miscellaneous Expenses A/c		450
				Jan 31	By Balance c/d		935
			2,000				2,000
Feb 1	To Balance b/d		935				
Feb 1	To Cash A/c		1,065				

NUMERICAL Questions for Practice

1 Enter the following transactions in a single column cash book and post them into a ledger.

2016		Amt (₹)
Mar 1	Commenced business with cash	10,000
Mar 2	Bought goods for cash	2,500
Mar 5	Sold goods for cash	2,000
Mar 10	Goods purchased from Vinay on credit	5,000
Mar 13	Paid to Vinay	3,500
Mar 15	Cash sales	4,000
Mar 18	Purchased furniture for office	3,000
Mar 20	Paid wages	190
Mar 24	Paid rent	200
Mar 26	Received commission	300
Mar 28	Withdrew for personal expenses	500
Mar 31	Paid salary	450

Ans Cash Balance = ₹ 5,960

2 Compile simple cash book from the following transactions and post them into ledger.

Date	Particulars	Amt (₹)	Date	Particulars	Amt (₹)
2016 Jan 1	Mr Banarsi Das commenced		2016 Jan 17	Paid for miscellaneous expenses	450
	business with cash	65,000	Jan 19	Received cash from Mr. Kishor Lal	4,850
Jan 3	Bought goods for cash	6,850	Jan 22	Purchased a radio set	2,500
Jan 4	Paid to Mr Radhey Shyam cash	950	Jan 22	Paid salary	4,000
Jan 6	Deposited in Bank	40,000	Jan 25	Paid rent	900
Jan 6	Paid for office furniture in cash	4,650	Jan 28	Paid electricity bill	350
Jan 9	Sold goods for cash	30,000	Jan 29	Paid for advertising	400
Jan 12	Paid wages in cash	1,200	Jan 31	Paid into bank	25,000
Jan 13	Paid for stationery	400			
Jan 15	Sold goods for cash	25,000			

Ans Cash Balance = ₹ 37,200

3 Write a two-column cash book with cash and bank columns from the following transactions and post them into ledger. Also pass necessary journal entries related to discount allowed and discount received.

2016

Mar 1 Cash in hand ₹ 30,000

Mar 3 Purchased goods for cash ₹ 12,000

Mar 5 Deposited in bank ₹ 10,000

Mar 8 Cash sales ₹ 20,000

Mar 10 Cash withdrew from bank for office use ₹ 4,000

Mar 12 Received cash from Daksh ₹ 6,000 and allowed him discount of ₹ 200

Mar 15 Received cheque from Kanika ₹ 4,000 and deposited in the bank on the same day, allowed her discount ₹ 150

Mar 18 Received cheque from Sakshi for ₹ 10,000 (not banked)

Mar 19	Cheque received from Sakshi deposited in the bank
Mar 24	Paid to Simran by cheque ₹ 5,000, she allowed discount ₹ 250
Mar 27	Withdrew from bank for personal use ₹ 3,000
Mar 28	Sold goods on credit to Deeksha ₹ 8,000
Mar 30	Purchased goods on credit from Simran ₹ 10,000
Mar 31	Received cheque from Deeksha ₹ 4,000 and deposited in the bank
Mar 31	Bank charges for the month ₹ 200

Ans Cash Balance = ₹ 38,000, Bank Balance = ₹ 15,800

4 From the following cash and bank transactions of Mr Pulkit, owner of Pulkit Stationery House, prepare a two column cash book and post them into ledger.

2016		Amt (₹)
Apr 1	Cash in hand	22,000
	Cash at bank	27,500
Apr 3	Purchased goods from M/s Arun for ₹ 3,500 and paid by cheque GST applicable is 6%	
Apr 9	Cash purchases ₹ 4,000 less trade discount 5%	
Apr 10	Purchased postage stamps	250
Apr 12	Proceeds of cash sales of ₹ 25,000 deposited into bank	
Apr 14	Drew cash for personal use	2,050
Apr 15	Received from Manan cash ₹ 1,500 and cheque ₹ 2,500, both deposited into bank allowed ₹ 250 as cash discount	
Apr 15	Withdrew from bank for office use	4,000
Apr 16	Paid wages ₹ 1,500 and rent ₹ 2,500	
Apr 19	Paid M/s Vrijesh by cheque, cash discount allowed by him ₹ 500	12,000
Apr 23	Received a cheque from Nitin for sale of old goods	4,000
Apr 25	Paid M/s Arun cash ₹ 3,750 and ₹ 1,800 by a cheque, received cash discount ₹ 125	
Apr 26	Karan, a customer, deposited into bank	3,000
Apr 29	Withdrew from bank for personal use	1,000
Apr 30	Bank charged commission	500
Apr 30	Withdrew from bank for paying income tax	2,500

Ans Cash Balance = ₹ 12,150, Bank Balance = ₹ 38,200

5 Miss Manya Rai maintains cash book with two bank columns. Enter the following transactions of 5th May, 2016 in the cash book and balance the same

	Amt (₹)
(i) Balance in the beginning of the day	
Cash	11,500
Canara Bank	3,50,000
Punjab National Bank (Overdraft)	30,000

(ii) Received a cheque of ₹ 53,500 from Khan Bros., in full settlement of invoice for ₹ 55,000 The cheque was deposited in Punjab National Bank, which charged ₹100 as collection charges.

(iii) Cash purchases ₹ 1,00,000. Paid bearer cheque on Punjab National Bank.

(iv) Transferred ₹ 50,000 from Canara Bank to Punjab National Bank.

(v) Withdrew ₹ 50,000 from Canara Bank; ₹ 30,000 for office use and ₹ 20,000 for personal use.

(vi) Paid advance salary to Manager ₹ 10,000 by bearer cheque on Punjab National Bank.

Ans Cash in Hand = ₹ 41,500; Cash at Canara Bank = ₹ 2,50,000;
Overdraft at Punjab National Bank = ₹ 36,600

6 A petty cashier in a firm received ₹ 3,000 as the petty cash imprest on 4th June, 2016. During the week, his expenses were as follows

2016		Amt (₹)
Mar 4	Conveyance charges for Manager's trip to the city	100
Mar 4	Wages to casual labourers	300
Mar 5	Bus fare to workmen sent to customer's premises	40
Mar 5	Stationery purchased	200
Mar 6	Sent documents to head office by registered post	80
Mar 6	Postage stamps purchased	200
Mar 6	Revenue stamps for payment of wages	100
Mar 7	Repair to typewriter	80
Mar 7	Paid electric lighting bill	340
Mar 8	Wages paid to coolies for shifting furniture, etc	80
Mar 8	Taxi fare to Assistant Manager	100
Mar 8	Letters by registered post sent to different suppliers	200
Mar 8	Locks purchased	160
Mar 8	Stationery purchased	80
Mar 8	Refreshments to customers	40

Write up the analytical petty cash book and draft the necessary journal entries for the payments made.

Ans Petty Cash Balance = ₹ 900

7 Raja Ram maintains a columnar petty cash book on the imprest system. The imprest amount is ₹ 50,000. From the following information, show how his petty cash book would appear for the week ended 12th August, 2016.

2016		Amt (₹)
Aug 7	Balance in Hand	13,490
	Received Cash Reimbursement to Make up the Imprest	36,510
	Postage	1,230
	Stationery	3,210
	Entertainment	540
Aug 8	Travelling and Conveyance	1,260
	Miscellaneous Expenses	110
	Entertainment	720
Aug 9	Repairs	1,567
Aug 10	Postage	1,740
	Entertainment	1,270
	Travelling	6,730
Aug 11	Stationery	410
	Entertainment	120
Aug 12	Miscellaneous Expenses	2,010
	Travelling	510
	Postage	4,830
	Repairs	300

Ans Petty Cash Balance = ₹ 23,443, Reimbursement = ₹ 26,557

|TOPIC 2|
Other Special Purpose Books

In addition to cash transactions there are a number of non-cash transactions. These non–cash transactions can be recorded in separate books popularly known as 'other special purpose books' such as—purchases book, purchases return book, sales book, sales return book, bills receivable book, bills payable book and journal proper. It is not necessary for every business to maintain all the above mentioned subsidiary books. Depending on the need of the business, it may prepare any of the above books.

Note *Bills payable and bills receivable books are not in syllabus.*

Purchases Book

Purchases book records all credit purchases of goods (*i.e.*, goods in which the enterprise deals in). Cash purchases, purchases of assets (for cash or on credit) and purchase of stationery for office use (for cash or on credit) are not recorded in purchases book. This book is prepared on the basis of invoices or bills received by the firm from the suppliers of the goods with the amount net of trade discount/quantity discount. Purchases book is also known as invoice book/bought book/purchase day book/purchase journal/supplier's journal.

Format of a purchases book is shown below

Purchases Book

Date	Particulars/Name of the Suppliers (Account to be credited)	Invoice No.	LF	Details (₹)	Total Amt (₹)

The purchases book has six columns

(*i*) **Date** In the first column, the transaction date is written.

(*ii*) **Particulars** In this column, the name of the supplier, name of the articles and quantities purchased are written.

(*iii*) **Invoice Number** Invoice number of the goods purchased is written.

(*iv*) **LF** When the purchases book is posted to the ledger, the page number of the ledger is written.

(*v*) **Details** The amount in respect of each article is written in this column. If the seller has allowed a trade discount, it is also deducted in this column itself. It is shown as follows

Quantity × Price per Article	...
(–) Trade Discount	(...)

(*vi*) **Total Amount** The net amount of the invoice is recorded in the extreme right hand column. The total in this column will show the 'total credit purchases' made in a period.

Treatment of Some Important Items in Purchases Book

(*i*) **Goods and Services Tax** (GST) GST is the tax levied on most goods and services (GST) sold for domestic consumption. It is paid by the consumer but is remitted to the government by the business selling the goods and services.

Treatment It is essential that a separate column be provided in the purchases book for GST paid. The total of GST paid column is posted to the debit of GST paid account' in the ledger.

(*ii*) **Freight/Packing and Forwarding Charges** At the time of sending goods, supplier may include freight/cartage/packing and forwarding expenses in the invoice.

Treatment A separate column is maintained to record such freight/packing and forwarding expenses. The total invoice price is divided among cost, freight/packing and forwarding expenses. The total of cost column is debited to purchases account and total of freight/packing and forwarding expenses are debited to freight/packing and forwarding account. Total of invoice price is credited to supplier's account.

LEDGER POSTING FROM PURCHASES BOOK

The individual entries and the total of the purchases book are posted into the ledger as follows

(*i*) Individual amounts are daily posted to the credit of supplier's accounts by writing 'By Purchases A/c' in the particulars column.

(*ii*) Periodic total is posted to the debit of purchases account by writing 'To Sundries as per Purchases Book' in the particulars column.

ILLUSTRATION |9| Record the following transactions in purchases book and prepare purchases account and M/s Neema Electronics' account.

2016

Aug 04 Purchased from M/s Neema Electronics (Invoice no. 3250). 20 mini-size TV @ ₹ 2,000 per piece, 15 tape recorders @ ₹ 12,500 per piece. Trade discount @ 20%.

Aug 10 Bought from M/s Pawan Electronics (Invoice no. 8260). 10 video cassettes @ ₹ 150 per piece, 20 tape recorders @ ₹ 1,650 per piece. Trade discount @ 10%.

Aug 18 Purchased from M/s Northern Electronics (Invoice no. 4256). 15 northern stereos @ ₹ 4,000 per piece, 20 northern colour TV @ ₹14,500 per piece. Trade discount @ 2.5%.

Aug 26 Purchased from M/s Neema Electronics (Invoice no. 3294). 10 mini-size TV @ ₹ 1,000 per piece, 5 colour TV @ ₹ 12,500 per piece. Trade discount @ 20%.

Aug 29 Bought from M/s Pawan Electronics (Invoice No. 8281). 20 video cassettes @ 150 per piece, 25 tape recorders @ ₹ 1,600 per piece. Trade discount @ 10%.

Sol.

Purchases Book

Date	Particulars	Invoice No.	LF	Details (₹)	Total Amt (₹)
2016					
Aug 04	**Neema Electronics**	3250			
	20 Mini-Size TV @ ₹ 2,000 per Piece			40,000	
	15 Tape Recorders @ ₹ 12,500 per Piece			1,87,500	
				2,27,500	
	(–) Trade Discount @ 20%			(45,500)	1,82,000
Aug 10	**Pawan Electronics**	8260			
	10 Video Cassettes @ ₹ 150 per Piece			1,500	
	20 Tape Recorders @ ₹ 1,650 per Piece			33,000	
				34,500	
	(–) Trade Discount @ 10%			(3,450)	31,050

Date	Particulars	Invoice No.	LF	Details (₹)	Total Amt (₹)
Aug 18	**Northern Electronics**	4256			
	15 Northern Stereos @ ₹ 4,000 per Piece			60,000	
	20 Northern Colour TV @ 14,500 per Piece			2,90,000	
				3,50,000	
	(–) Trade Discount @ 12.5%			(43,750)	3,06,250
Aug 26	**Neema Electronics**	3294			
	10 Mini-Size TV @ ₹ 1,000 per Piece			10,000	
	5 Colour TV @ ₹ 12,500 per Piece			62,500	
				72,500	
	(–) Trade Discount @ 20%			(14,500)	58,000
Aug 29	**Pawan Electronics**	8281			
	20 Video Cassettes @ ₹ 150 per Piece			3,000	
	25 Tape Recorders @ ₹ 1,600 per Piece			40,000	
				43,000	
	(–) Trade Discount @ 10%			(4,300)	38,700
Aug 31	**Purchases A/c** **Dr**				6,16,000

LEDGER POSTING OF PURCHASES BOOK

Dr **Neema Electronics Account** Cr

Date	Particulars	JF	Amt (₹)	Date	Particulars	JF	Amt (₹)
				2016			
				Aug 04	By Purchases A/c		1,82,000
				Aug 26	By Purchases A/c		58,000

Dr **Purchases Account** Cr

Date	Particulars	JF	Amt (₹)	Date	Particulars	JF	Amt (₹)
2016							
Aug 31	To Sundries as per Purchases Book		6,16,000				

ILLUSTRATION |10| (With GST) From the following information of M/s. Makkar and Co., Delhi, prepare the Purchases Book for the month of February, 2019

2019

Feb 1 Purchased from M/s. Black and Co., Kolkata
5 Gross pencils @ ₹ 600 per gross
2 dozen registers @ ₹ 250 per dozen
Less Trade Discount @ 10%

Feb 5 Purchased for cash from the Student Mart
20 dozen exercise books @ ₹ 150 per dozen

Feb 10 Purchased from The Paparika Co., Delhi
8 reams of white paper @ ₹ 250 per ream
10 reams of ruled paper @ ₹ 300 per ream
Less Trade Discount @ 10%

Feb 20 Purchased 80 Reynolds Pens @ ₹ 10 each from M/s. Sharma Bros., Delhi
CGST and SGST is levied @ 2.5% each and IGST is levied @ 5%.

Sol.

Purchases Book

Date	Particulars	Invoice No.	LF	Details (₹)	Cost (₹)	Input CGST (₹)	Input SGST (₹)	Input IGST (₹)	Total (₹)
2019									
Feb 1	**M/s. Black and Co. Kolkata**								
	5 gross Pencils @ ₹ 600 per gross			3,000					
	2 dozen Registers @ ₹ 250 per dozen			500					
				3,500					
	Less : Trade Discount @ 10%			(350)					
				3,150					
	Add : IGST @ 5%			158					
				3,308	3,150	....	....	158	3,308
Feb 5	**The Paparika Co., Delhi**								
	8 reams White Paper @ ₹ 250 each			2,000					
	10 reams Ruled Paper @ ₹ 300 each			3,000					
				5,000					
	Less : Trade Discount @ 10%			(500)					
				4,500					
	Add : CGST @ 2.5%			122					
	SGST @ 2.5%			123					
				4,725	4,500	122	123	....	4,725
Feb 20	**M/s. Sharma Bros., Delhi**								
	80 Reynolds Pens @ ₹ 10 each			800					
	Add : CGST @ 2.5%			20					
	SGST @ 2.5%			20					
				840	800	20	20	....	840
Feb 28	Purchases A/c Dr				8,450	142	143	158	8,873

Sales Book

Sales book records all credit sales of merchandise (*i.e.*, the goods in which the firm deals in). It does not record the cash sales of goods and sale of fixed assets (for cash or on credit). The source documents for recording entries in the sales journal are sales invoice or bill issued by the firm to the customers with the amount net of trade discount/quantity discount. Sales book is also known as sales day book/sales journal/customer journal.

Format of a sales book is shown below

Sales Book

Date	Particulars/Name of the Customer (Account to be debited)	Invoice No.	LF	Details (₹)	Total Amt (₹)

Note *The format of the sales book is similar to the purchases book.*

Treatment of Some Important Items in Sales Book

(i) **Goods and Services Tax** (GST) As the seller is liable to deposit GST in the government account, a separate column to record the GST charged is provided in the sales book. Periodically, the total of the column for GST is credited to GST account.

(ii) **Freight/Packing and Forwarding Charges** Sometimes freight paid/packing charges on sending the goods is charged from the customer along with sale proceeds. In the sales book, a separate column is maintained to record such recoveries. They are recorded in a separate column because it is not a part of sales proceeds and thus, are shown separately in the final accounts. Monthly total of the freight and packing charges column is credited to freight and packing charges recovered account, while the customer is debited with the cost of goods (Sales value) plus GST and freight and packing charges.

LEDGER POSTING FROM SALES BOOK

The individual entries and the total of the sales book are posted into the ledger as follows

(*i*) Individual amounts are daily posted to the debit of customer's accounts by writing 'To Sales A/c' in the particulars column.

(*ii*) Periodic total is posted to the credit of sales account by writing 'By Sundries as per Sales Book' in the pariculars column.

ILLUSTRATION |11| M/s Koina sold on credit

(i) 2 water purifiers @ ₹ 2,100 each and 5 buckets @ ₹ 130 each to M/s Raman Traders (Invoice no. 178 dated 6th April, 2016) Less trade discount @ 10%.

(ii) 5 road side containers @ ₹ 4,200 each to M/s Nutan Enterprises (Invoice No. 180 dated 9th April, 2016).

(iii) 100 big buckets @ ₹ 850 each to M/s Raman Traders (Invoice No. 209, dated 28th April, 2016).

(iv) Sold old furniture to Rajesh & Co on credit ₹ 1,000.

Record the above transactions in sales book and prepare sales account and Raman Trader's account.

Sol.

Sales Book

Date	Particulars	Invoice No.	LF	Details (₹)	Total Amt (₹)
2016					
Apr 06	**Raman Traders**	178			
	2 Water Purifiers @ ₹ 2,100 each			4,200	
	5 Buckets @ ₹ 130 each			650	
				4,850	
	(–) Trade Discount @ 10%			485	4,365
Apr 09	**Nutan Enterprises**	180			
	5 Road Side Containers @ ₹ 4,200 each				21,000
Apr 28	**Raman Traders**	209			
	100 Big Buckets @ ₹ 850 each				85,000
Apr 30	**Sales A/c** Cr				1,10,365

LEDGER POSTING OF THE SALES BOOK

Dr Raman Traders Account Cr

Date	Particulars	JF	Amt (₹)	Date	Particulars	JF	Amt (₹)
2016							
Apr 06	To Sales A/c		4,365				
Apr 28	To Sales A/c		85,000				

Dr **Sales Account** Cr

Date	Particulars	JF	Amt (₹)	Date	Particulars	JF	Amt (₹)
				2016 Apr 30	By Sundries as per Sales Book		1,10,365

Working Note

Sale of old furniture is not recorded in the sales book as the firm does not deal in furniture.

ILLUSTRATION |12| (With GST) From the following transactions of M/s. Moon Moon Sales, Kolkata, prepare Sales Book.

2019

March 1 Sold to M/s. Mahima Tea, Darjeeling, vide Invoice No. 1008, 3 chests of tea ₹ 15,000 per chest less Trade discount @ 5% and IGST is charged @ 12%.

March 4 Sold to M/s. Madhurkar and Sons, Kolkata vide Invoice No. 1010, 20 kg Amul Butter @ ₹ 750 per kg less Trade discount @ 5% and charged CGST and SGST @ 6% each.

March 5 Sold to M/s. Samuel Sons, Delhi vide Invoice No. 1012, 20 kg Assam Tea @ ₹ 1,800 per kg less Trade discount @ 5%, charged IGST @ 12%. Freight and packing charges were separately charged in the invoice at ₹ 4,800.

Sol

M/s. Moon Moon Sales, Kolkata
Sales Book

Date	Particulars	Invoice No.	LF	Details (₹)	Sale Value (₹)	Output CGST (₹)	Output SGST (₹)	Output IGST (₹)	Freight And Packing Charges (₹)	Total (₹)
2019										
Mar 1	**M/s. Mahima Tea, Assam**	1008								
	3 Chests Tea @ ₹ 15,000 per chest			45,000						
	Less :Trade Discount @ 5%			(2,250)						
				42,750						
	Add : IGST @ 12%			5,130						
				47,880	42,750	....	....	5,130	....	47,880
Mar 4	**M/s. Madhurkar and Sons, Kolkata**	1010								
	20 kg Amul Butter @ ₹ 750 per kg			15,000						
	Less : Trade Discount @ 5%			(750)						
				15,250						
	Add : CGST @ 6%			855						
	SGST @ 6%			855						
				15,960	15,250	855	855	....	....	15,960

Date	Particulars		Invoice No.	LF	Details (₹)	Sale Value (₹)	Output CGST (₹)	Output SGST (₹)	Output IGST (₹)	Freight And Packing Charges (₹)	Total (₹)
Mar 5	**M/s. Samuel Sons, Delhi**		1012								
	20 kg Assam Tea @ ₹ 600 per kg				36,000						
	Less : Trade Discount @ 5%				(1,800)						
					34,200						
	Add : IGST @ 12%				4,104						
					38,304						
	Add : Freight and Packing Charges				4,800						
					43,104	34,200	....	....	4,104	4,800	43,104
Mar 31	Sales A/c	Cr				92,200	285	855	9,234	4,800	1,06,944

Purchases Return Book

Goods may be returned due to various reasons such as the goods are not of required quality or are defective or are not according to sample, etc. In this book, purchases return of goods are recorded. It does not record the returns of goods purchased on cash basis nor the returns of purchases other than the goods in which the firm deals in. The entries are usually made in the purchases return book on the basis of debit notes issued to the suppliers and credit notes received from the suppliers. Purchases return book is also known as return outwards book.

Format of a purchases return book is shown below

Purchases Return Book

Date	Particulars/Name of the Suppliers (Account to be debited)	Debit Note No.	LF	Details (₹)	Total Amt (₹)

Note *The format of a purchases return book is similar to the purchases book except that instead of a column for 'Invoice No.' it has a column for 'Debit Note No.'.*

LEDGER POSTING FROM PURCHASES RETURN BOOK

(*i*) Individual amounts are debited to the supplier's account by writing 'To Purchases Return A/c' in the particulars column.

(*ii*) Periodic total is credited to the purchases return account by writing 'By Sundries as per Purchases Returns Book' in the particulars column.

ILLUSTRATION |13| Record the following transactions in purchases return book

(i) 2 Banarsi sarees @ ₹ 2,000 each and 2 Kanjivaram sarees @ ₹ 12,500 each were bought from Neema Mills, trade discount on all items @ 20%. However, on delivery these sarees were found defective and were returned back with debit note no. 03/2016.

(ii) Returned to Payal Mills, Surat-5 polyster sarees @ ₹ 200 each
Trade discount @ 10% (Debit Note No. 101)

(iii) Garg Mills, Kota accepted the returns of goods (which were purchased for cash) from us, 5 Kota sarees @ ₹ 80. (Debit Note No. 102)

(iv) Returned to Mittal Mills, Bangalore, 5 Silk sarees @ ₹ 520 each
Trade discount @ 10% (Debit Note No. 103)

(v) Returned one typewriter (being defective)@ ₹ 7,000 to Bansal & Co

Also prepare purchase return account and Neema Mills account.

Sol.

Purchases Return Book

Date	Particulars	Debit Note No.	LF	Details (₹)	Total Amt (₹)
	Neema Mills	03/2016			
	2 Banarsi Sarees @ ₹ 2,000 each			4,000	
	2 Kanjivaram Sarees @ ₹ 12,500 each			25,000	
				29,000	
	(–) Trade Discount @ 20%			5,800	23,200
	Payal Mills, Surat	101			
	5 Polyster Sarees @ 200 each			1,000	
	(–) Trade Discount @ 10%			100	900
	Mittal Mills, Bangalore	103			
	5 Silk Sarees @ 520 each			2,600	
	(–) Trade Discount @ 10%			260	2,340
	Purchases Return A/c **Cr**				26,440

Note *Return of Kota sarees will be recorded in the cash book and return of typewriter will be recorded in the general journal (journal proper) since in the purchases return book, only the return of merchandise purchased on credit are recorded.*

LEDGER POSTING

Dr **Neema Mills Account** Cr

Date	Particulars	JF	Amt (₹)	Date	Particulars	JF	Amt (₹)
	To Purchases Return A/c		23,200				

Dr **Purchases Return Account** Cr

Date	Particulars	JF	Amt (₹)	Date	Particulars	JF	Amt (₹)
					By Sundries as per Purchases Return Book		26,440

ILLUSTRATION |14| (With GST) Record the following in Purchases Return Book.

2019

March 10 Returned 2 washing machines purchased from M/s. Sudhakar Electronics at the list price of ₹ 21,000 per machines *less* Trade Discount 20%, CGST and SGST was paid @ 6% each.

March 24 Returned 6 pendrives to M/s. Monika Electronics purchased @ ₹ 3,000 each *plus* IGST @ 12%

Sol.

Purchases Return Book

Date	Particulars	Invoice No.	LF	Details (₹)	Cost (₹)	Input CGST (₹)	Input SGST (₹)	Input IGST (₹)	Total (₹)
2019									
March 10	**M/s. Sudharkar Electronics**								
	2 Washing Machines @ ₹ 21,000 each			42,000					
	Less : Trade Discount @ 20%			(8,400)					
				33,600					
	Add : CGST @ 6%			2,016					
	SGST @ 6%			2,016					
				37,632	33,600	2,016	2,016	....	37,632

Date	Particulars		Invoice No.	LF	Details (₹)	Cost (₹)	Input CGST (₹)	Input SGST (₹)	Input IGST (₹)	Total (₹)
March 24	**M/s. Monika Electronics**									
	6 Pendrives @ ₹ 3,000 each				18,000					
	Add : IGST @ 12%				2,160					
					19,160	18,000	.....	.....	2,160	19,160
March 31	Purchase Return A/c	Cr				51,600	2,016	2,016	2,160	56,792

Sales Return Book

This subsidiary book is used to record return of goods by customers that had been sold on credit. It does not record the return of goods sold on cash basis nor the return of any asset other than the goods in which the firm deals in.

The source documents for recording entries in the sales return journal are the credit notes issued to the customers or debit notes issued by the customers. Sales return book is also known as return inwards book.

Format of a sales return book is shown below

Sales Return Book

Date	Particulars/Name of the Customers (Account to be credited)	Credit Note No.	LF	Details (₹)	Total Amt (₹)

Note *The format of a sales return book is similar to the sales book except that instead of a column for 'Invoice No.' it has a column for 'Credit Note No.'.*

LEDGER POSTING FROM SALES RETURN BOOK

(*i*) Individual amounts are credited to the customer's accounts by writing 'By Sales Returns A/c' in the particulars column.

(*ii*) Periodic total is debited to the sales return account by writing 'To Sundries as per Sales Return Book' in the particular column.

ILLUSTRATION |15| Record the following transactions in the sales return book.

Two water purifiers were sold to M/s Raman Traders for ₹ 2,100 each, out of which one purifier was returned back due to the manufacturing defect (Credit Note No. 10/2016).

Other transactions were

(i)	M/s Gupta Traders returned the purifiers	1,500
(ii)	Purifiers returned from M/s Harish Traders	800
(iii)	M/s Rahul Traders returned the purifiers not as per specifications	1,200
(iv)	Purifiers returned from M/s Sushil Traders	1,000

Also prepare sales return account and M/s Raman Traders account.

Sol.

Sales Return Book

Date	Particulars	Credit Note No.	LF	Details (₹)	Total Amt (₹)
	Raman Traders	10/2016			
	1 Water Purifier @ ₹ 2,100 each				2,100
	M/s Gupta Traders				1,500
	M/s Harish Traders				800
	M/s Rahul Traders				1,200
	M/s Sushil Traders				1,000
	Sales Return A/c Dr				6,600

Dr **M/s Raman Traders Account** Cr

Date	Particulars	JF	Amt (₹)	Date	Particulars	JF	Amt (₹)
					By Sales Return A/c		2,100

Dr **Sales Return Account** Cr

Date	Particulars	JF	Amt (₹)	Date	Particulars	JF	Amt (₹)
	To Sundries as per Sales Return Book		6,600				

ILLUSTRATION |16| (With GST) Prepare Sales Return Book in the Books of Lal and Co., Delhi from the following transactions,

2019

Aril 6 Goods returned by Komalika and Co., Delhi

2 Table Fans @ ₹ 5,000 each

Less : Trade Discount 15%

Add : CGST and SGST @ 6% each

April 12 Sehgal Electricals, Agra returned defective Room Cooler ₹ 21,250 plus IGST @ 12%.

Sol.

Sales Return Book

Date	Particulars	Credit Note No.	LF	Details (₹)	Value (₹)	Output CGST (₹)	Output SGST (₹)	Output IGST (₹)	Total (₹)
2019									
April 6	**Komalika and Co., Delhi**								
	2 Table Fans @ ₹ 5,000 each			10,000					
	Less : Trade Discount @ 15%			(1,500)					
				8,500					
	Add : CGST @ 6%			510					
	SGST @ 6%			510					
				9,520	8,500	510	510	....	9,520
April 12	**Sehgal Electricals, Agra**								
	1 Room Cooler			21,250					
	Add : IGST @ 12%			2,550					
				23,800	21,250	....	....	2,550	23,800
April 30	Sales Return A/c Dr				29,750	510	510	2,550	33,320

Journal Proper

Journal proper is a book that records transactions which cannot be recorded in any other subsidiary book such as cash book, purchases book, sales book, purchases return book, sales return book. In other words, a book maintained to record transactions which do not find place in special journals, is known as journal proper or journal residual.

Following transactions are recorded in journal proper

(*i*) **Opening Entry** The opening entry is passed in the journal in the beginning of a financial year to open the books by bringing the balances of various assets, liabilities and capital appearing in the balance of the previous accounting period.

(It has been discussed in detail in the fourth chapter Journal and Ledger).

(*ii*) **Closing Entries** The closing entries are passed in the journal for closing the nominal accounts by transferring them to trading and profit and loss account. These entries are passed at the end of the year at the time of preparation of final accounts.

(It will be discussed in detail in the chapter Final Accounts).

(*iii*) **Adjustment Entries** Adjusting entries are passed in the journal in order to bring into books of accounts certain unrecorded items or in order to update ledger accounts on accrual basis. Such entries are made at the end of the accounting period *e.g.*, closing stock, depreciation on fixed assets, outstanding and prepaid items.

(It has been discussed in detail in fourth chapter Journal and Ledger).

(*iv*) **Rectification Entries** To rectify errors in recording transactions in the books of original entry and their posting to ledger accounts, journal proper is used.

(It will be discussed in detail in the chapter Rectification of Entries).

(*v*) **Transfer Entries** Transfer entries are passed in the journal for transferring an amount from one account to another account.

(*vi*) **Dishonour and Endorsement of Bills** Bills of exchange and promissory note not honoured on due date are known as dishonoured bills. Endorsement of bills of exchange means transfer of bills of exchange or promissory note to another person.

(*vii*) **Other Entries** In addition to the above mentioned entries, recording of the following transactions is also done in the journal proper

- (*a*) Discount received or discount allowed.
- (*b*) Purchase/Sale of items on credit other than goods.
- (*c*) Goods withdrawn by the owner for personal use.
- (*d*) Goods distributed as samples for sales promotion.
- (*e*) Loss of goods by fire/theft/spoilage.

ILLUSTRATION |17| Record the following transactions in the 'journal proper' of Shree Tarun Talpade.

2016

(i) An old machinery was sold to Rajesh for ₹ 20,000 on credit.

(ii) Anil who owed us ₹ 50,000 was declared insolvent and 40% is received as full and final payment.

(iii) Goods worth ₹ 80,000 were destroyed by fire.

(iv) Insurance company admitted a fire insurance claim of ₹ 50,000.

(v) Proprietor withdrew for personal use cash ₹ 10,000 and goods ₹ 8,000.

(vi) A bill receivable for ₹ 20,000 was endorsed to Mr Sharma.

(vii) Debtors include ₹ 5,000 due from Ajay, whereas creditors include ₹ 2,000 due to Ajay.
(viii) Salary and wages of ₹ 10,000 remain outstanding.
(ix) Insurance is prepaid to the extent of ₹ 1,000.
(x) Provide depreciation on furniture for ₹ 2,000.
(xi) Interest accrued on investment ₹ 400.

Sol

JOURNAL

Date	Particulars		LF	Amt (Dr)	Amt (Cr)
2016					
(i)	Rajesh	Dr		20,000	
	To Machinery A/c				20,000
	(Being old machinery sold on credit)				
(ii)	Bad Debts A/c	Dr		30,000	
	To Anil				30,000
	(Being bad debts written off on Anil's insolvency)				
(iii)	Loss by Fire A/c	Dr		80,000	
	To Purchases A/c				80,000
	(Being goods destroyed by fire)				
(iv)	Insurance Company	Dr		50,000	
	To Loss by Fire A/c				50,000
	(Being insurance claim admitted by insurance company)				
(v)	Drawings A/c	Dr		8,000	
	To Purchases A/c				8,000
	(Being goods withdrawn for personal use)				
(vi)	Mr Sharma	Dr		20,000	
	To Bills Receivable A/c				20,000
	(Being bills receivable endorsed to Mr Sharma)				
(vii)	Creditors A/c	Dr		2,000	
	To Debtor's A/c				2,000
	(Being amount transferred from creditor to debtor account)				
(viii)	Salaries and Wages A/c	Dr		10,000	
	To Outstanding Salaries and Wages A/c				10,000
	(Being adjustment of salaries due but not paid)				
(ix)	Prepaid Insurance A/c	Dr		1,000	
	To Insurance A/c				1,000
	(Being adjustment of prepaid insurance premium)				
(x)	Depreciation on Furniture A/c	Dr		2,000	
	To Furniture A/c				2,000
	(Being depreciation provided on furniture)				
(xi)	Accrued Interest A/c	Dr		400	
	To Interest A/c				400
	(Being interest accrued on investment)				

Comprehensive Illustration

ILLUSTRATION |18| Enter the following transactions in the proper subsidiary books, post them into a ledger and balance the ledger account. The accounts are to be closed on 31st March, 2016.

The following balances existed in the books of Khandelwal & Sons on 1st March, 2016

Assets : Cash in hand ₹ 1,00,000; Cash at bank ₹ 1,10,000; Debtors (Karun ₹ 90,000; Geeta ₹ 50,000); Stock ₹ 3,20,000 and Machinery ₹ 4,00,000.

Liabilities : Creditors: Avinash & Co. ₹ 70,000.

The following transactions took place during the month of March, 2016

Jan 2	Deposited into bank ₹ 30,000.
Jan 4	Purchased from Raghav goods of the list price of ₹ 70,000 at 10% trade discount.
Jan 5	Returned to Raghav goods worth ₹ 8,000.
Jan 7	Issued a cheque to Raghav in full settlement of their account after deducting cash discount @ 5%.
Jan 10	Sold to Dishant goods worth ₹ 80,000.
Jan 12	Received cash ₹ 60,000 and cheque ₹ 8,000 from Dishant. The cheque was sent to bank on the same day. Discount allowed ₹ 1,000.
Jan 14	Purchased machinery from Ronak & Co. on credit for ₹ 50,000.
Jan 16	Khandelwal withdrew goods for his personal use ₹ 20,000
Jan 18	Sold to Anuj goods valued ₹ 32,000.
Jan 19	Issued cheque to Ronak & Co. ₹ 50,000.
Jan 20	Returned by Anuj goods worth ₹ 4,000.
Jan 21	Purchased goods from Gaurav for ₹ 80,000. Trade discount 10%.
Jan 22	Accepted a bill drawn by Gaurav for ₹ 72,000 at 1 month.
Jan 27	Received from Anuj ₹ 20,000. Discount allowed ₹ 100.
Jan 27	Goods purchased for cash ₹ 60,000.
Jan 28	Withdrew from bank ₹ 40,000.
Jan 29	Paid salaries by cheque ₹ 10,000.
Jan 30	Paid rent ₹ 5,600.
Jan 31	Received commission in cash ₹ 3,200.

Sol.

Cash Book

Date	Particulars	LF	Cash (₹)	Bank (₹)	Date	Particulars	LF	Cash (₹)	Bank (₹)
2016					2016				
Jan 1	To Balance b/d		1,00,000	1,10,000	Jan 2	By Bank A/c	C	30,000	
Jan 2	To Cash A/c	C		30,000	Jan 7	By Raghav (Note)			52,250
Jan 12	To Dishant		60,000	8,000	Jan 19	By Ronak & Co.			50,000
Jan 27	To Anuj		20,000		Jan 27	By Purchases A/c		60,000	
Jan 28	To Bank A/c	C	40,000		Jan 28	By Cash A/c	C		40,000
Jan 31	To Commission A/c		3,200		Jan 29	By Salaries A/c			10,000
Jan 31	To Balance c/d			4,250	Jan 30	By Rent A/c		5,600	
					Jan 31	By Balance c/d		1,27,600	
			2,23,200	1,52,250				2,23,200	1,52,250
Feb 1	To Balance b/d		1,27,600		Feb 1	By Balance b/d			4,250

Working Note	***Amt*** (₹)
List Price	70,000
(–) Trade Discount	7,000
Net Price	63,000
(–) Goods Returned	8,000
	55,000

Cash Discount = 55,000 × 5/100 = ₹ 2,750

Net Amount Paid = 55,000 – 2,750 = ₹ 52,250

Purchases Book

Date	Particulars		Invoice No.	LF	Details (₹)	Total Amt (₹)
2016						
Jan 4	Raghav				70,000	
	(–) Trade Discount @ 10%				7,000	63,000
Jan 21	Gaurav				80,000	
	(–) Trade Discount @ 10%				8,000	72,000
Jan 31	**Purchases A/c**	**Dr**				1,35,000

Sales Book

Date	Particulars		Invoice No.	LF	Details (₹)	Total Amt (₹)
2016						
Jan 10	Dishant					80,000
Jan 18	Anuj					32,000
Jan 31	**Sales A/c**	**Cr**				1,12,000

Purchases Return Book

Date	Particulars		Debit Note No.	LF	Details (₹)	Total Amt (₹)
2016						
Jan 5	Raghav					8,000
Jan 31	**Purchases Return A/c**	**Cr**				8,000

Sales Return Book

Date	Particulars		Credit Note No.	LF	Details (₹)	Total Amt (₹)
2016						
Jan 20	Anuj					4,000
Jan 31	**Sales Return A/c**	**Dr**				4,000

Journal Proper

Date	Particulars		LF	Amt (Dr)	Amt (Cr)
2016					
Jan 1	Cash A/c	Dr		1,00,000	
	Bank A/c	Dr		1,10,000	
	Karun	Dr		90,000	
	Geeta	Dr		50,000	
	Stock A/c	Dr		3,20,000	
	Machinery A/c	Dr		4,00,000	
	To Avinash & Co.				70,000
	To Capital A/c (Balancing Figure)				10,00,000
	(Being the last year's balances brought forward)				

Date	Particulars		LF	Amt (Dr)	Amt (Cr)
Jan 7	Raghav	Dr		2,750	
	To Discount Received A/c				2,750
	(Being the discount received on payment made to Raghav)				
Jan 12	Discount Allowed A/c	Dr		1,000	
	To Dishant				1,000
	(Being the discount allowed to Dishant against payment received)				
Jan 14	Machinery A/c	Dr		50,000	
	To Ronak & Co.				50,000
	(Being the machinery purchased on credit)				
Jan 16	Drawings A/c	Dr		20,000	
	To Purchases A/c				20,000
	(Being the goods withdrawn by the proprietor for personal use)				
Jan 22	Ganesh	Dr		72,000	
	To Bills Payable A/c				72,000
	(Being the bills accepted for 1 month tenure)				
Jan 27	Discount Allowed A/c	Dr		100	
	To Anuj				100
	(Being the discount allowed to Anuj against payment received)				

LEDGER POSTING

Dr **Karun's Account** Cr

Date	Particulars	JF	Amt (₹)	Date	Particulars	JF	Amt (₹)
2016				2016			
Jan 1	To Balance b/d		90,000	Jan 31	By Balance c/d		90,000
			90,000				90,000
Feb 1	To Balance b/d		90,000				

Dr **Geeta's Account** Cr

Date	Particulars	JF	Amt (₹)	Date	Particulars	JF	Amt (₹)
2016				2016			
Jan 1	To Balance b/d		50,000	Jan 31	By Balance c/d		50,000
			50,000				50,000
Feb 1	To Balance b/d		50,000				

Dr **Stock Account** Cr

Date	Particulars	JF	Amt (₹)	Date	Particulars	JF	Amt (₹)
2016				2016			
Jan 1	To Balance b/d		3,20,000	Jan 31	By Balance c/d		3,20,000
			3,20,000				3,20,000

Dr **Machinery Account** Cr

Date	Particulars	JF	Amt (₹)	Date	Particulars	JF	Amt (₹)
2016				2016			
Jan 1	To Balance b/d		4,00,000	Jan 31	By Balance c/d		4,50,000
Jan 14	To Ronak & Co.		50,000				
			4,50,000				4,50,000
Feb 1	To Balance b/d		4,50,000				

Dr **Avinash & Co** Cr

Date	Particulars	JF	Amt (₹)	Date	Particulars	JF	Amt (₹)
2016				2016			
Jan 31	To Balance c/d		70,000	Jan 1	By Balance b/d		70,000
			70,000				70,000
				Apr 1	By Balance b/d		70,000

Dr **Capital Account** Cr

Date	Particulars	JF	Amt (₹)	Date	Particulars	JF	Amt (₹)
2016				2016			
Jan 31	To Balance c/d		10,00,000	Jan 1	By Balance b/d		10,00,000
			10,00,000				10,00,000
				Feb 1	By Balance b/d		10,00,000

Dr **Raghav's Account** Cr

Date	Particulars	JF	Amt (₹)	Date	Particulars	JF	Amt (₹)
2016				2016			
Jan 5	To Purchases Return A/c		8,000	Jan 4	By Purchases A/c		63,000
Jan 7	To Bank A/c		52,250		(₹ 70,000 – ₹ 7,000)		
Jan 7	To Discount Received A/c		2,750				
			63,000				63,000

Dr **Dishant's Account** Cr

Date	Particulars	JF	Amt (₹)	Date	Particulars	JF	Amt (₹)
2016				2016			
Jan 10	To Sales A/c		80,000	Jan 12	By Cash A/c		60,000
				Jan 12	By Bank A/c		8,000
				Jan 12	By Discount Allowed A/c		1,000
				Jan 31	By Balance c/d		11,000
			80,000				80,000
Feb 1	To Balance b/d		11,000				

Dr **Ronak & Co.** Cr

Date	Particulars	JF	Amt (₹)	Date	Particulars	JF	Amt (₹)
2016				2016			
Jan 19	To Sales A/c		50,000	Jan 14	By Machinery A/c		50,000
			50,000				50,000

Dr **Discount Received Account** Cr

Date	Particulars	JF	Amt (₹)	Date	Particulars	JF	Amt (₹)
2016				2016			
Jan 31	To Balance c/d		2,750	Jan 31	By Sundries as per Cash Book		2,750
			2,750				2,750

Dr **Discount Allowed Account** Cr

Date	Particulars	JF	Amt (₹)	Date	Particulars	JF	Amt (₹)
2016				2016			
Jan 31	To Sundries as per Cash Book		1,100	Jan 31	By Balance c/d		1,100
			1,100				1,100

Anuj's Account

Dr Date	Particulars	JF	Amt (₹)	Date	Particulars	JF	Amt (₹) Cr
2016				2016			
Jan 18	To Sales A/c		32,000	Jan 20	By Sales Return A/c		4,000
				Jan 27	By Cash A/c		20,000
				Jan 27	By Discount Allowed A/c		100
				Jan 31	By Balance c/d		7,900
			32,000				32,000
Feb 1	To Balance b/d		7,900				

Gaurav's Account

Dr Date	Particulars	JF	Amt (₹)	Date	Particulars	JF	Amt (₹) Cr
2016				2016			
Jan 22	To Bills Payable A/c		72,000	Jan 21	By Purchases A/c		72,000
			72,000				72,000

Drawings Account

Dr Date	Particulars	JF	Amt (₹)	Date	Particulars	JF	Amt (₹) Cr
2016				2016			
Jan 16	To Purchases A/c		20,000	Jan 31	By Balance c/d		20,000
			20,000				20,000
Feb 1	To Balance b/d		20,000				

Purchases Account

Dr Date	Particulars	JF	Amt (₹)	Date	Particulars	JF	Amt (₹) Cr
2016				2016			
Jan 27	To Cash A/c		60,000	Jan 16	By Drawings A/c		20,000
Jan 31	To Sundries as per Purchases Book		1,35,000	Jan 31	By Balance c/d		1,75,000
			1,95,000				1,95,000

Purchases Return Account

Dr Date	Particulars	JF	Amt (₹)	Date	Particulars	JF	Amt (₹) Cr
2016				2016			
Jan 31	To Balance c/d		8,000	Jan 31	By Sundries as per Purchases Return Book		8,000
			8,000				8,000

Sales Account

Dr Date	Particulars	JF	Amt (₹)	Date	Particulars	JF	Amt (₹) Cr
2016				2016			
Jan 31	To Balance c/d		1,12,000	Jan 31	By Sundries as per Sales Book		1,12,000
			1,12,000				1,12,000

Dr **Sales Return Account** Cr

Date	Particulars	JF	Amt (₹)	Date	Particulars	JF	Amt (₹)
2016				2016			
Jan 31	To Sundries as per Sales Return Book		4,000	Jan 31	By Balance c/d		4,000
			4,000				4,000

Dr **Bills Payable Account** Cr

Date	Particulars	JF	Amt (₹)	Date	Particulars	JF	Amt (₹)
2016				2016			
Jan 31	To Balance c/d		72,000	Jan 22	By Gaurav		72,000
			72,000				72,000
				Feb 1	By Balance b/d		72,000

Dr **Salaries Account** Cr

Date	Particulars	JF	Amt (₹)	Date	Particulars	JF	Amt (₹)
2016				2016			
Jan 29	To Bank A/c		10,000	Jan 31	By Balance c/d		10,000
			10,000				10,000

Dr **Rent Account** Cr

Date	Particulars	JF	Amt (₹)	Date	Particulars	JF	Amt (₹)
2016				2016			
Jan 30	To Cash A/c		5,600	Jan 31	By Balance c/d		5,600
			5,600				5,600

Dr **Commission Account** Cr

Date	Particulars	JF	Amt (₹)	Date	Particulars	JF	Amt (₹)
2016				2016			
Jan 31	To Balance c/d		3,200	Jan 31	By Cash A/c		3,200
			3,200				3,200

NUMERICAL Questions for Practice

1 Enter the following transactions in the purchase journal (book) of M/s Gupta Traders of July, 2019.

Jul 1 Bought from Rahul Traders as per Invoice No. 20041
40 Registers @ ₹ 60 each
80 Gel pens @ ₹ 15 each
50 Note books @ ₹ 20 each
Trade discount @ 10%.

Jul 15 Bought from Global Stationers as per Invoice No. 1132
40 Ink pads @ ₹ 8 each

50 Files @ ₹ 10 each
20 Colour books @ ₹ 20 each
Trade discount @ 5%.

Jul 23 Purchased from Lamba Furniture as per Invoice No. 3201
2 Chairs @ ₹ 600 per chair
1 Table @ 1,000 per table

Jul 25 Bought from Mumbai Traders as per Invoice No. 1111
10 Paper rim @ ₹ 100 per rim
400 Drawing sheets @ 3 each
20 Packet water colour @ 40 per packet

Jul 26 Bought from Mona Lamp, Saket, for cash (Invoice No. 705)
5 Electric irons @ ₹ 175 each

Jul 28 Bought from Innovation Furniture Co Kankerkhera, on credit
(Invoice No. 3450)
12 Chairs @ ₹ 200 each
2 Tables @ 1,000 each
CGST and SGST are to be
charged @ 6% each and IGST @ 12%

Ans Total Purchases = ₹ 8,299

2 Following balances appeared in the balance sheet of Ganpati Stores on 31st March, 2015. Pass the necessary journal entries for opening the books for the year 2015-16.

Debit Balances : Furniture ₹ 8,000; Machinery ₹ 40,000; Debtors ₹ 10,000; Bills receivable ₹ 23,600; Cash ₹ 28,400

Credit Balances : Capital ₹ 60,000; Bills payable ₹ 30,000; Creditors ₹ 20,000

3 Prepare a purchases return book from the following transactions for January, 2016.

2016		
Jan 5	Return goods to M/s Kartik Traders	1,200
Jan 10	Goods returned to Sahil Pvt Ltd as the goods were inferior in quality	2,500
Jan 17	Goods returned to M/s Kohinoor Traders for list price ₹ 2,000 less 10% trade discount	
Jan 28	Return outwards to M/s Handa traders	550
Jan 29	Allowance claimed from Gajendra on account of mistake in invoice ₹ 1,000 (Debit Note 145)	

Ans Total of Purchases Return Book = ₹ 6,050

4 Following transactions are of M/s Ramesh & Sons for the month of June, 2019. Prepare their sales book.

2019

Jun 3 Sold to M/s Daya & Abhishek on credit
40 shirts @ ₹ 200 each 15 trousers @ ₹ 400 each
(–) Trade discount @ 10%.

Jun 10 Sold old furniture to M/s Singhal & Co on credit ₹ 800

Jun 20 Sold 50 shirts on credit to M/s Vijay & Sons @ ₹ 200 each

Jun 23 Sold on credit to M/s Ravi & Kavi
100 shirts @ ₹ 225 each
10 overcoats @ 650 each
(–) Trade discount @ 10%
CGST and SGST are to be
charged @ 6% each and IGST @ 12%

Ans Total Sales = ₹ 48,700

5 Enter following transactions in the sales return books of Evergreen Stores.

2016	
Sep 1	Naman and Sons returned 50 bags of wheat, rate ₹ 130 per bag
Sep 2	Anil and Sons returned 60 bags of rice, rate ₹ 150 per bag
Sep 20	Naveen returned 10 tins of refined oil, rate ₹ 120 per tin
Sep 25	Kamlesh returned goods of the value of ₹ 200
Sep 26	Goods returned by Rajan worth ₹ 200 which were sold for cash

Ans Total of Sales Return Book = ₹ 16,900

6 Prepare return inwards and return outwards books from the following transactions.

2016

Jun 1 Gupta Bros., Rajasthan, returned
5 pairs of canvas shoes for being defective @ ₹ 500 per pair
Less: Trade discount 10%

Jun 5	Returned to Banglore Leather Private Ltd., Banglore
	100 pairs of ladies chappals being not up to the approved sample
	@ ₹ 150 per pair
	Less : Trade discount 15%
Jun 12	Sethi Shoes Co., Agra, returned 12 pairs of chappals
	₹ 200 per pair
	Less : Trade discount 10%
Jun 20	Returned to Liberty Shoes Pvt. Ltd., Meerut
	100 pairs shoes @ 175 per pair
	Less: Trade discount 15%
Jun 24	Jain Bros., Delhi, returned 10 pairs ladies sandals
	@ ₹ 250 per pair

Ans Total of Return Outwards Book = ₹ 27,625; Total of Return Inwards Book = ₹ 6,910

7 Prepare sales book and purchases book of M/s Ramlal from the following transactions.

2016	
Jun 7	Purchased from Deepa and Co., Shimla
	10 Chairs @ ₹ 200 each
	1 Table for ₹ 600
	Trade discount 10%
Jun 10	Sold to Sudhir Furniture Co., Faridabad
	1 Almirah @ ₹ 2,000
	Less: 15% trade discount
Jun 12	Sold to Mohan Mart for cash
	10 Tables @ ₹ 1,000 each
Jun 15	Purchased from Gopal Das and Sons for cash 15 Chairs @ ₹ 350 each
Jun 16	Purchased from Sultan Chand & Co., Modinagar 5 Chairs @ ₹ 180 each
Jun 25	Sold to Manveer, Kanpur
	2 Dining tables @ ₹ 6,000 each
	Less: 10% trade discount

Ans Total of Purchases Book = ₹ 3,240; Sales Book = ₹ 12,500

8 From the following information available on 31st March, 2016, pass the necessary adjustment entries in the journal for the year ending on that date.

(i) Interest accrued ₹ 5,000.
(ii) Wages for March 2016 outstanding ₹ 20,000.
(iii) Insurance prepaid ₹ 3,000.
(iv) Rent for April 2016 received in advance ₹ 6,000.
(v) Depreciation on furniture ₹ 10,000.
(vi) Commission due to Manager 6% on net profit after charging such commission. The profit before charging such commission was ₹ 2,12,000.
(vii) Interest due on loan but not paid. Loan of ₹ 3,00,000 was taken at 9% per annum; 9 months before end of the year.

Ans Commission Due to Manager = ₹ 12,000; Interest Due on Loan = ₹ 20,250

9 Enter the following transactions in journal proper of Komal Sharma (Proprietor).

(i) Rent not paid (Rent outstanding) ₹ 1,000.
(ii) Goods withdrawn by proprietor for personal use ₹ 5,000.
(iii) Purchase of machine on credit for ₹ 10,000 from Ram sons.
(iv) Depreciate motor car with book value ₹ 1,00,000 @ 10% per annum for one year.

10 Enter the following transactions in proper subsidiarv books of Balram.

2016		Amt (₹)
Jan 1	Sold goods to Ramesh	21,000
	Bought from Hari Ram	31,200
Jan 2	Ramesh returned goods	3,000
	Sold to Dina Nath	22,000
Jan 2	Purchased goods from Mangal	28,000
Jan 4	Returned goods to Mangal	4,000
Jan 4	Bought from Devi Dayal	13,000
Jan 4	Sold to Zakir Hussain	14,000
Jan 5	Zakir Hussain returned goods	1,800
Jan 6	Sold to Ram Saran	20,000
Jan 6	Sold to Ghanshyam	12,000
Jan 7	Ram Saran returned goods	2,000
Jan 7	Bought from Devi Dayal	28,000
Jan 8	Returned goods to Devi Dayal	3,000
Jan 9	Purchased goods from Raghu Nath subject to a trade discount of 10%	40,000
Jan 10	Sold to Raja Ram goods subject to trade discount of 5%	20,000

Ans Total of Purchases Book = ₹ 1,36,200
Total of Sales Book = ₹ 1,08,000
Total of Purchases Return Book = ₹ 7,000
Total of Sales Return Book = ₹ 6,800

CHAPTER PRACTICE

OBJECTIVE TYPE Questions

Multiple Choice Questions

1 When a firm maintains a cash book, it does not need to maintain **NCERT**
(a) Journal Proper
(b) Purchases (Journal) Book
(c) Sales (Journal) Book
(d) Bank and cash account in the ledger

Ans (d) Bank and cash account in the ledger

2 Double column cash book records **NCERT**
(a) all transactions
(b) cash and bank transactions
(c) only cash transactions
(d) only credit transactions

Ans (b) cash and bank transactions

3 Which cash book is prepared to book small amounts by cashier to save valuable time of main cashier?
(a) Three column cash book
(b) Two column cash book
(c) Petty cash book
(d) None of the above

Ans (c) Petty cash book

4 Purchase book is also known as
(a) invoice book
(b) bought book
(c) sales book
(d) Both (a) and (b)

Ans (d) Purchase book records all invoices or bills received by the firm. All the goods bought on credit are recorded in this book.

5 Goods purchased on cash are recorded in the **NCERT**
(a) Purchases (Journal) Book
(b) Sales (Journal) Book
(c) Cash Book
(d) Purchases return (Journal book)

Ans (c) Cash Book

6 Cash book does not record transaction of **NCERT**
(a) cash nature
(b) credit nature
(c) cash and credit nature
(d) None of the above

Ans (b) credit nature

7 Total of these transactions is posted in purchase account **NCERT**
(a) purchase of furniture
(b) cash and credit purchase
(c) purchases return
(d) purchase of stationery

Ans (b) cash and credit purchase

8 When there is return of goods in a journal, then a debit note is prepared and sent to supplier, what type of journal is used for this purpose?
(a) Sale return journal
(b) Purchase return journal
(c) Cash sale journal
(d) Cash purchase journal

Ans (b) Purchase return journal

9 The periodic total of purchases return journal is posted to **NCERT**
(a) purchase account
(b) profit and loss account
(c) purchase returns account
(d) furniture account

Ans (c) purchase returns account

10 The periodic total of sales return journal is posted to **NCERT**
(a) sales account
(b) goods account
(c) purchases return account
(d) sales return account

Ans (d) sales return account

11 Where would a second hand motor car purchased on credit from Mr XYZ be recorded?
(a) Purchase return book
(b) Purchase book
(c) Journal proper
(d) Cash book

Ans (c) Journal proper is a book that records transactions which cannot be recorded in any other subsidiary book, *i.e.* cash book, purchase book, sales book, etc. Purchase/sale of items on credit other than goods are recorded into journal proper only.

12 Which is not a special subsidiary book?
(a) Journal proper (b) Sales book
(c) Purchase book (d) None of these

Ans (d) None of these

13 How many columns are there in a purchase book?
(a) 4 (b) 5
(c) 6 (d) 7

Ans (c) 6

14 Credit balance of bank account in cash book shows **NCERT**
(a) overdraft
(b) cash deposited in our bank
(c) cash withdrawn from bank
(d) None of the above

Ans (a) overdraft

15. M/s ABC & Sons sold 40 ink pads @ ₹ 8 each, 50 files @ ₹ 10 each, 20 colour books @ ₹ 20 each to Global Stationers and provided 5% trade discount. GST of 5% is applicable on stationery product. How this transaction will be recorded in Global Stationers account?
(a) To Sales A/c 1,216.95
(b) By Sales A/c 1,216.95
(c) By Sales A/c 1,220
(d) To Sales A/c 1,159

Ans (a)

40 ink pads @ ₹ 8 each	320.000
50 files @ ₹ 10 each	500.000
20 colour books @ ₹ 20 each	400.000
	1,220.000
(−) Trade discount	61.000
	1,159.000
(+) Central GST 2.5%	28.975
(+) State GST 2.5%	28.975
Amount recorded in Global stationers A/c	1,216.95

Journal Entry in the Books of M/s ABC & sons

Global Stationers A/c	Dr	1,216.95	
To Sales A/c			1,216.95

Fill in the Blanks

16 When a firm maintains a cash book, it need not to maintain .... account.

Ans cash

17 Entries which are recorded on both sides of the cash book are called .... entries.

Ans contra

18 If we withdraw money from bank for office use, cash column of cash book will be............ and bank column will be............ .

Ans debited, credited

19 In Returns Outward Book, we record return of goods which was .... earlier.

Ans bought

20 Debit side of cash book represents .... and credit side represents .... of cash transactions.

Ans receipts, payments

State True or False

21 Cash book is both a subsidiary book and a ledger account.

Ans True

22 A contra entry is one which does not require posting to the ledger.

Ans True

23 The bank column of the cash book always shows a debit balance.

Ans False. The balance of bank column may be debit or credit.

24 Cash discount allowed on receipt of cash is debited.

Ans True

25 Closing entries are recorded in journal proper.

Ans True

Match the Following

26

	Column I		Column II
1.	Defective goods returned by Taksh	(a)	Journal proper
2.	Providing interest on capital	(b)	Purchase Return Book
3.	Bill accepted by proprietor from creditor	(c)	Sales Return Book
4.	Received credit note from Khushi	(d)	Bills Payable Book

Ans 1-(c), 2-(a), 3-(d), 4-(b)

VERY SHORT ANSWER Type Questions

27 Name the various books of original entries.

Ans *The various books of original entries are*
(*i*) Cash book (*ii*) Purchases book
(*iii*) Sales book (*iv*) Purchases return book
(*v*) Sales return book (*vi*) Journal proper

28 A cheque received and deposited into bank the same day will be recorded in cash book in which column and on which side.

Ans Bank column, debit side

29 What is the purpose of contra entry? **NCERT**

Ans The purpose of contra entry is to indicate the transactions that effect both cash and bank balances. This entry does not affect the financial position of a business.

30 What do you understand by imprest amount in petty cash book? **NCERT**

Ans Amount, which is given to the petty cashier by the head cashier in the beginning of a period is called the imprest amount.

31 Give one point of distinction between purchases book and purchases account.

Ans Purchases book is a part of journal whereas purchases account is a part of ledger.

32 Is it correct to say that sales book is a record prepared from invoices issued to customers?

Ans Yes, as the source documents for recording entries in the sales book are invoices or bills issued to customers.

33 The periodic total of purchase return journal is posted to which account? **NCERT**

Ans Purchases return account

34 The periodic total of sales return journal is posted to which account? **NCERT**

Ans Sales return account

35 For what purposes is a journal proper used?

Ans Journal proper is a residuary book which is used for recording those transactions which are not recorded in any of the other books of original entry.

36 Give two examples of entries which appear in a 'journal proper'.

Ans Credit purchase of plant and machinery, credit sales of fixed assets.

37 In which book of original entry will

(i) The partial recovery from Mr Ajay of an amount of ₹ 4,000 earlier written off as bad be recorded?

(ii) In which book of original entry, a discount of ₹50 offered for an early payment of cash of ₹1,050 be recorded?

Ans (*i*) Cash book (*ii*) Journal proper

38 Can there be a credit balance in simple cash book? State with reasons.

Ans Cash column in a cash book cannot have credit balance because actual payments (credit side) of cash cannot exced actual cash available (debit side) with the business.

39 To which side of the ledger account are the transactions on the payments side of the cash book posted?

Ans They are posted on the debit side of the respective ledger account.

40 Is the balance of petty cash book an asset or income?

Ans Balance of petty cash book in an asset for the firm.

SHORT ANSWER Type Questions

41 What are special purpose books? **NCERT**

Ans Special purpose subsidiary books are those books in which the transactions of similar nature are recorded. For a large business organisation it is not possible to journalise each transaction, thus, journal is sub-divided into subsidiary books in which transactions of similar nature are recorded.

These books are also called books of original entry as ledger accounts are prepared from the transactions recorded in these books and for these transactions journal entry is not passed. All the transactions of purchases, sales, cash are recorded in their respective books, such as purchase book, sales book etc.

42 Explain the need for drawing up the special purpose books. **NCERT**

Ans *The needs for drawing up the special purpose books are as follows*

(*i*) **Quick and Efficient Recording** It is a time consuming process to record all the transactions in a journal. If there are separate books, then recording of transactions can be done more efficiently and timely. So, the need of special purpose books arises.

(*ii*) **Repetitive Nature** In every business, some transactions are similar and repetitive in nature. It will be more convenient to record all similar transactions at one place. *e.g.*, all credit sales are recorded in the sales book.

(*iii*) **Economical** It is more economical as recording through the special purpose books saves time and also enhances the efficiency of accountants and clerks.

(*iv*) **Easy Posting** If similar transactions are recorded at one place, positing becomes easier.

(*v*) **Complete Information at One Place** All information related to purchases, sales, cash receipts, payments, etc are easily available.

43 Describe the advantages of sub-dividing the journal. **NCERT**

Ans *The various advantages of sub-dividing the journal are*

(*i*) **Division of Work** In place of one journal, many special journals are prepared. This results in division of work among various executives.

(*ii*) **Specialisation** If a particular task is handled by a particular executive, then this leads to specialisation and increases efficiency.

(*iii*) **Time Saving** Dividing journal into different categories means different executives can work simultaneously on different journals. This will increase the speed of work and will save time.

(*iv*) **Easy Access to Desired Information** Transactions are recorded on the basis of their nature *i.e.*, purchase transactions in purchase book, sales transactions in sales book, etc. This facilitates easy and quick accessibility to particular type of transactions.

(*v*) **Quick Checking** In case of errors in recording, it is easier to find out the reasons of errors.

44 Define the purposes of maintaining subsidiary journal. **NCERT**

Ans *The purposes of maintaining subsidiary journal are given below*

(*i*) It saves time and efforts in recording.

(*ii*) It enables division of work, leading to an enhancement of efficiency and effectiveness, as particular accountant takes care of particular books.

(*iii*) It also makes each accountant more responsible and accountable for the books assigned to them.

(*iv*) It records routine and repetitive transactions at one place, which leads to easy accessibility of information.

45 Briefly state how the cash book is both journal and a ledger. **NCERT**

Or

Explain the statement 'Cash book is a journalised ledger'.

Ans Cash book is a journal since the transactions are recorded in it for the first time from the source documents and from there these are posted to the respective accounts in the ledger. The cash book is also a ledger in the sense that it serves the purpose of a cash account also. When a cash book is prepared, no separate cash account is opened in the ledger. As such, the cash book is a journal, as well as, a ledger and hence it may be called a journalised ledger.

46 How does a cash book serves a dual purpose?

Or

Cash book is both a subsidiary book and principal book.

Ans Cash book achieves a dual purpose. It is both a subsidiary book (book of original entry) and principal book. When a cash book is maintained, transactions of cash are not recorded in the journal. As all the cash transactions are recorded for the first time in the cash book, it is therefore a book of original entry.

Also, when a cash book is prepared, cash account in the ledger is not prepared. In this way, cash book represents the cash accounts and hence, becomes the principal book of accounts. As such, the cash book is a subsidiary book as well as principal book.

47 State any four essential features of cash book.

Ans *Four features of cash book are as follows*

(*i*) It records only cash transactions.

(*ii*) Cash and cheques received are recorded on debit side and cash and cheques paid are recorded on credit side.

(*iii*) Transactions are recorded in a chronological order.

(*iv*) It performs the function of both journal and ledger.

48 Give the similarities of cash book with ledger.

Ans (*i*) Form of cash book closely resembles to a ledger account. It has two equally divided sides having identical column. The left side (receipts side) is the debit side and the right side (payment side) is the credit side.

(*ii*) Cash book itself serves as a cash account also and as such when a cash book is maintained, cash account is not opened in the ledger. The cash book, hence is a part of ledger also.

(*iii*) Just like a ledger account, the words 'To' and 'By' are used in a cash book also.

(*iv*) It is balanced just like a ledger account.

49 Give the similarities of cash book with journal.

Ans (*i*) Just like a journal, transactions in the cash book are recorded for the first time from source documents.

(*ii*) Just like a journal, transactions in the cash book are recorded datewise *i.e.,* in a chronological order, as and when they take place.

(*iii*) Just like a journal, transactions from cash book are posted to the relevant accounts (except cash account) in the ledger.

(*iv*) Just like a journal, a cash book also contains a ledger folio column.

50 What are the advantages of having a cash book?

Ans (*i*) Both cash and bank transactions can be entered in the cash book.

(*ii*) It enables a businessman to know the balance of cash in hand and at bank at any point of time.

(*iii*) It gives information about daily receipts, payments and the closing cash and bank balance at the end of each day.

(*iv*) Since cash account is not opened in the ledger, it prevents the size of ledger from becoming two voluminous.

51 What is contra entry? How can you deal with this entry while preparing cash book? **NCERT**

Ans Contra entries mean entries that are made on both sides of cash book. In a two-column cash book, there are some transactions that relate to both cash and bank. Such transactions are entered on both sides of the cash book. Such entries are known as contra entries and are not posted into the ledger.

Against such entries, the letter 'C' is written in the LF column to indicate that these are contra transactions. *e.g.,* cash deposited into the bank.

As the cash book with cash and bank columns is a combined cash and bank account, both the aspects of the transaction will be entered in the same book. On the debit side 'To Cash A/c' will be entered in the particulars column and the amount will be entered in the bank column.

On the credit side 'By Bank A/c' will be entered in the particulars column and the amount will be entered in the cash column.

52 What is petty cash book? How is it prepared? **NCERT**

Ans It is the book which is used for the purpose of recording the payment of petty cash expenses.

Petty cash book is prepared by petty cashier to record petty expenses (expenses of small amounts).
This book is prepared to save valuable time of main (head) cashier from bothering about small and irrelevant cash expenses. Petty cash book can be prepared according to the ordinary system or according to the imprest system.

53 Write the advantages of petty cash book. **NCERT**

Ans *Some advantages of petty cash book are as follows*

(*i*) Maintaining petty cash book is simple and does not require any specialised knowledge of accounting.

(*ii*) Petty cash book is maintained by the petty cashier, therefore efforts and time of the chief/head cashier is saved.

(*iii*) The chances of fraud minimises, as each petty expense is supported by a voucher.

(*iv*) Petty expenses are maintained within the limit of imprest amount so the petty cashier can never spend more than the available petty cash with him.

(*v*) Head cashier can keep a close watch time to time on the amount paid to petty cashier and all payment made by him.

54 Name the books of original entry where the following transactions will be recorded with reasons thereof

(i) Goods purchased from Ram Lal for ₹ 5,000 on credit.

(ii) Provision for doubtful debts created @ 5% on debtors with books value of ₹ 10,000.

(iii) Defective goods sold to Babita on credit worth ₹ 4,000 were returned by her.

(iv) Purchased furniture on credit from Mr Ratan Singh for ₹ 15,000 for use in the business.

Ans (*i*) Purchases book because it is credit purchase of goods.

(*ii*) Journal proper because it will not be recorded in any other subsidiary books.

(*iii*) Sales return book because it is return of goods sold.

(*iv*) Journal proper because it is credit purchase of asset.

55 Mention the subsidiary books in which following transactions are recorded along with reason thereof

(i) Purchase of furniture on credit for use in shop

(ii) Sale of goods on credit

(iii) Goods returned by debtors

(iv) Purchase of stock on credit

(v) Providing for interest on capital to proprietor

(vi) Goods returned to creditors

(vii) Sale of goods for cash

Ans (*i*) Journal proper because purchase of fixed assets on credit is recorded in journal proper.

(*ii*) Sales book because sales book records credit sales of goods.

(*iii*) Sales return book because goods returned by customer are recorded in sales return book.
(*iv*) Purchases book because purchases book records credit purchases of goods.
(*v*) Journal proper because it is an adjustment entry and adjustment entries are recorded in journal proper.
(*vi*) Purchases return book because it records goods returned by the firm to its suppliers.
(*vii*) Cash book because cash book records cash receipts and cash payments.

56 Is it correct that individual accounts of customers is debited by the respective amount and the total of the sales book is posted to the credit side of the sales account in the general ledger?

Ans Yes, sale is revenue account and therefore, following the rule 'increase in revenue is credited' sales account is credited. Since, the sales book contains records of credit sales, the purchaser's account (being debtors) is debited following the rule applicable to asset accounts *i.e.*, 'increase in assets is debited'.

57 Is it correct that total of the purchase invoices recorded in the purchases book is posted to debit side of the purchases account in the ledger and credited to the accounts of suppliers?

Ans Yes, purchase is an expense account therefore, following the rule 'increase in expenses is debited', purchases account is debited. Since, the purchases book contains records of credit purchases, the suppliers account is credited following the rule applicable to liabilities accounts *i.e.*, 'increase in liabilities is credited'.

58 Distinguish between purchases book and purchases account.

Ans *The differences between purchases book and purchases account are*

Purchases Book	*Purchases Account*
Purchases book is a part of a journal.	Purchases account is a part of a ledger.
Purchases book does not have debit and credit columns like ledger account.	Purchases account has debit and credit columns.
In a purchases book, only credit purchase of goods dealt in or consumed for production are recorded.	In a purchases account, credit as well as cash purchase of goods dealt in or consumed for production are recorded.
Total of purchases book is posted to the purchases account.	Balance in the account is transferred to the trading account.

59 Distinguish between sales book and sales account.

Ans *The differences between sales book and sales account are*

Sales Book	*Sales Account*
Sales book is a part of journal book.	Sales account is a part of a ledger.
Sales book does not have debit and credit columns like a ledger account.	Sales account has debit and credit columns.
In a sales book, only credit sales of goods are recorded.	In a sales account, credit as well as cash sales of goods are recorded.
Total amount of sales book is posted to the sales account periodically.	Balance in the sales account is transferred to the trading account.

60 Distinguish between special journal and general journal.

Ans *The differences between special journal and general journal are*

Special Journal (Subsidiary Books)	*General Journal (Journal Proper)*
It records transactions of similar nature *e.g.*, purchase book records only credit purchase.	It does not record transactions of a similar nature.
It is in the form of a statement.	It is in the form of a journal.

Special Journal (Subsidiary Books)	*General Journal (Journal Proper)*
A business unit may not have a special journal.	A business unit must have a journal proper.
Each transaction is not recorded in the ledger separately.	Each transaction is recorded in the ledger separately.
A mistake in the journal proper is not recitified by a special journal.	A mistake in a special journal is recitified by the journal proper.

61 Write the difference between return inwards and return outwards. **NCERT**

Ans *The differences between return inwards and return outwards are*

Basis	*Return Inwards*	*Return Outwards*
Meaning	Goods sold to customers, are returned by them.	Goods purchased are returned to the suppliers.
Balance	It has debit balance.	It has credit balance.
Treatment	It is deducted from sales in the trading account.	It is deducted from purchases in trading account.
Issued	Credit note is prepared by the seller.	Debit note is prepared by the buyer.
Reduction	It reduces the payment from the debtors.	It reduces the payment made to the creditors.
Term	It is also termed as sales return.	It is also termed as purchases return.

62 Distinguish between cash account and cash book.

Ans *The differences between cash account and cash book are*

Cash Account	*Cash Book*
It is an account in the ledger.	It is a separate book maintained for recording cash transactions.
It records only one aspect of a transaction *i.e.,* cash.	It records both the aspects of a transaction.
Cash account is opened in the ledger and posting is done in this account from journal.	It is a book of original entry because all cash transactions are first of all recorded in cash book and then posted from cash book to various accounts in the ledger.
When transactions of cash are recorded in journal, it is necessary to open a cash account in the ledger.	When transactions of cash are recorded in cash book, there is no necessity to open a cash account in the ledger.

LONG ANSWER Type Question

63 What is cash book? Explain the types of cash book. **NCERT**

Ans Cash book is a special journal which is used for recording only cash transactions *i.e.*, all cash receipts and cash payments. Cash book is a book of **prime entry/original entry** since transactions (all cash and bank transactions) are recorded in it for the first time from the source documents in a chronological order. It has two sides *i.e.*, debit and credit. Debit side records all receipts of cash (including cheques). Credit side records all payments of cash (including cheques).

It may be noted that in the case of cash book there will always be debit balance, because cash payments can never exceed cash receipts and cash in hand at the beginning of the period.

There are two types of cash book

(*i*) **Single Column Cash Book or Simple Cash Book** The single column cash book has one column on each side. All cash receipts are recorded on the debit side and all cash payments on the credit side. Single column cash book is nothing but a cash account.

(ii) **Two Column or Double Column Cash Book** (Cash Book with Cash and Bank Column) Two column cash book is a cash book which has two columns on each side. One for cash, one for bank.

In other words, it can be said that two column cash book represents two accounts *i.e.,* cash account and bank account. Hence, there is no need to open these accounts in the ledger. Cash and bank transactions are recorded in the cash and bank column respectively.

All the cash receipts, deposits into the bank are recorded on debit side and all cash payments, withdrawals from bank are recorded on credit side.

(iii) **Petty Cash Book** Petty cash book is the book which is used for the purpose of recording the payment of petty cash expenses. It is prepared by petty cashier to record petty expenses (of small amounts). This book is prepared to save valuable time of chief (head) cashier from bothering about small and irrelevant cash expenses. For transferring cash to petty cash account, cash account is credited and petty cash account is debited.

NUMERICAL Questions

1 Enter the following transaction in single column cash book .

2016		Amt (₹)
Jan 1	Mr Vijay commenced business with cash	3,50,000
Jan 2	Bought goods for cash	22,000
Jan 6	Purchased goods from Raja & Co on credit	20,000
Jan 8	Cash sales	75,000
Jan 10	Paid rent	1,200
Jan 18	Purchased building	3,00,000
Jan 21	Sold goods for cash	9,900
Jan 22	Sold goods to Kishan on credit	20,000
Jan 25	Paid salaries	10,000
Jan 28	Paid wages	5,500
Jan 30	Received from Kishan	12,000

Ans Cash Balance = ₹ 1,08, 200

2 Prepare single column cash book from the following transactions for the month of April 2016.

2016		Amt (₹)
Apr 1	Cash balance	25,000
Apr 2	Paid to Y in full settlement of ₹ 5,000	4,750
Apr 4	Received from Z, allowing him discount of ₹ 400	9,600
Apr 7	Cash purchases	10,000
Apr 11	Cash sales	15,000
Apr 15	Received from X, allowed him discount ₹ 500	19,500
Apr 21	Paid to W against his dues of ₹ 7,500	7,000
Apr 25	Paid into bank	20,000
Apr 31	Withdrew for personal use	5,000
Apr 31	Paid salary and wages	15,000

Ans Cash Balance = ₹ 7,350

3 Enter the following transaction in a cash book with cash and bank columns.

2016		Amt (₹)
Dec 1	Started business with cash	50,000
Dec 2	Pays into bank	29,000
Dec 3	Received cheque from Raja & Co	800
Dec 5	Withdrew cash from bank for private use	240
Dec 14	Received cheque from Kamla	395
	Discount allowed	15
Dec 16	Kamla's cheque endorsed to Bala in full settlement of her account of ₹ 425	
Dec 29	Paid bills payable by cheque	1,000
Dec 30	Deposited into bank, balance of cash in excess of ₹ 450	

Ans Cash Balance = ₹ 450; Bank Balance = ₹ 49,110; Cash Deposited into Bank = ₹ 20,550

4 Verma Bros. carry on business as wholesale cloth dealers. Prepare purchases book to record the following transactions entered into by them.

Apr 3	Purchased on credit from M/s Birla Mills
	100 pieces long cloth @ ₹ 80 each
	50 pieces shirting @ ₹ 100 each
Apr 8	Purchased for cash from M/s Ambika Mills
	50 pieces muslin @ ₹ 120 each
Apr 15	Purchased on credit from M/s Arvind Mills
	20 pieces of coats @ ₹ 1,000 each
	10 pieces shirting @ ₹ 90 each
Apr 20	Purchased on credit from M/s Bharat Typewriters Ltd
	5 typewriters @ ₹ 1,400 each

Ans Total of Purchases Book = ₹ 33,900

5 Prepare the purchases return book of Abdulla Stores from the following transactions.

2016	
Mar 10	Returned to Rizwan & Sons
	1 Orient fan 36″ @ ₹ 1,250
	Trade discount 10%
Mar 25	Returned to Ram & Co
	1 Dozen lamp-holders @ ₹ 200 per dozen
Mar 27	Returned to Prem & Co
	4 Fancy light @ ₹ 50 each
	The lights were purchased in cash

Ans Total of Purchases Return Book = ₹ 1,325

6 Record the following transactions in the sales book of Chrome Furnishing Stores. Also open the necessary ledger accounts, including sales account and post the transactions.

2016		Rate per piece
Aug 1	Sold to M/s Gupta's Furniture Co	Amt (₹)
	2 Coffee tables	1,000
Aug 6	Sold to M/s Ghansham & Co	
	1 Dinning table	1,300
	2 Chairs	800
Aug 12	Sold to M/s. Ultimate Ltd	
	2 Centre tables	1,800
	3 Side corner tables	1,100
Aug 20	Sold to M/s Gupta's Furnishing Co	
	3 Stools	380
	3 Lamp tables	300
Aug 29	Sold to M/s Ultimate Ltd	
	3 Cabinets	1,650

Ans Total of Sales Book = ₹ 18,790

7 Prepare sales return book of Anand Singh from the following transactions and post them into ledger.

2016	
Feb 10	Bhardwaj stores returned
	1 Dozen Osram lamps 25W @ ₹ 160 per dozen
	Reason–Breakage due to bad packing
Feb 20	Ram Mohan & Co. returned
	1 Ranjit fan 48" AC @ ₹ 1,400
	Reason–Being out of order

Ans Total of Sales Return Book = ₹ 1,560

8 Enter the following transactions in the 'journal proper' of Bharat Gupta.

2016	
Jan 1	Purchased furniture on credit from Rawal Furniture Store for ₹ 15,000.
Jan 5	Goods for ₹ 6,000 given away as charity.
Jan 12	Goods worth ₹ 8,000 and cash ₹ 4,000 were stolen by an employee.
Jan 15	Gurmeet who owed us ₹ 20,000 was declared insolvent and nothing was received from him.
Jan 18	Proprietor withdrew for his personal use cash ₹ 5,000 and goods worth ₹ 10,000.
Jan 31	Provide interest on capital of ₹ 5,00,000 at 6% per annum for full year.
Jan 31	Out of the rent paid this year, ₹ 5,000 is related to the next year.
Jan 31	Salaries due to clerks ₹ 12,000.

Hint Interest on capital = ₹ 30,000

9 Enter the following transactions into Karanveer and Sons cash book with cash and bank columns.

2016		Amt (₹)	2016		Amt (₹)
Jan 1	Opening cash balance	22,500	Jan 17	Received cash from Gautam	26,500
	Bank overdraft	40,000		allowed him discount	500
Jan 2	Cash sales ₹ 50,000 out of which deposited in Bank	15,000	Jan 18	Brought furniture from Rohan and paid him by cheque	30,000
Jan 3	Paid to Karan by cheque	14,000	Jan 19	Drew from Bank	9,000

2016		Amt (₹)	2016		Amt (₹)
Jan 5	Received cheque from Varun and sent it to Bank	80,000	Jan 20	Paid advertisement expenses	5,000
Jan 6	Paid wages	24,500	Jan 21	Received cheque from Swami	25,500
Jan 6	Cash purchases	11,000		Allowed him discount	500
Jan 8	Paid office expenses by cheque	16,000	Jan 24	Deposited the above cheque into the bank	
Jan 9	Cash sales	20,000	Jan 25	Paid salary	15,500
Jan 10	Paid rent	12,000	Jan 25	Swami's cheque was returned dishonoured	
Jan 12	Received cheque from		Jan 26	Paid octroi by cheque	1,000
	Arun in full settlement of		Jan 27	Cash deposited in Bank	10,000
	his account of ₹ 37,000 and deposited it in Bank	36,000	Jan 29	Withdrew by cheque for domestic expenses	4,000
Jan 15	Paid to Mohan by cheque	16,500			
	He allowed us discount	500			

Ans Bank Balance = ₹ 10,500, Cash Balance = ₹ 45,000

10 Mr Yadav, the petty cashier of M/s Tripati Traders received ₹ 5,000 on 1st April, 2016 from the head cashier. Following were the petty expenses during the month of April.

2016		Amt (₹)
Apr 2	Taxi fare	440
Apr 3	Refreshments	180
Apr 5	Registered postal chargers	76
Apr 5	Telegram	70
Apr 8	Auto fare	100
Apr 9	Courier charges	130
Apr 12	Postal stamps	300
Apr 14	Eraser/sharpener/pencils	420
Apr 17	Speed post charges	180
Apr 20	Cartage	140
Apr 20	Computer stationery	400
Apr 22	STD call charges	90
Apr 24	Bus fare	20
Apr 25	Office sanitation	360
Apr 26	Refreshments	120
Apr 28	Loading charges	150
Apr 30	Photostatting charges	108
Apr 30	Fax charges	160

You are required to prepare a petty cash book.

Ans Petty Cash Balance = ₹ 1,556; Postage = ₹ 686; Telephone and Telegram = ₹ 320; Conveyance = ₹ 560; Stationery = ₹ 820, Miscellaneous Expenses = ₹ 1,058

11 Prepare the purchases book and sales book from the following transactions.

2016	
Jan 1	Bought from M/s SCS, Bangalore, on credit
	100 Pilot pens @ ₹ 80 each
	100 Gel pens @ ₹ 50 each
Jan 2	Sold Shri Manvendra
	24 Pilot pens @ ₹ 85 each
	25 Gel pens @ ₹ 57 each
Jan 8	Bought from D Anand, Delhi
	40 Fountain pens @ ₹ 80 each
	Less: 15% trade discount
Jan 12	Sold to Dass Bros
	20 Fountain pens @ ₹ 80 each
Jan 18	Sold to Gopi Nath
	20 pilot pens @ ₹ 85 each
Jan 22	Bought from Delhi
	100 Lunar pens @ ₹ 45 each
	Less : Trade discount 20%
Jan 25	Bought from Kishori Lal, Meerut
	50 Highlighter pens @ ₹ 50 each
	Less : 15% trade discount
Jan 31	Sold to Rishi Kumar
	25 Luxar pens @ 45 each

Ans Total of Purchases Book = ₹ 21,445
Total of Sales Book = ₹ 7,890

12 Prepare return inwards and return outwards books from the following.

2016	
Jan 3	Returned to HCL Co.,
	50 metre of cotton cloth being not up to the approved sample @ ₹ 42 per metre
	Less : Trade discount 20%
Jan 10	APL & Co., Faridabad, returned to us
	10 metre of silk cloth, for being defective @ ₹ 120 per metre
	Less : Trade discount 10%
Jan 15	Returned to PBR Co.
	20 metre of woollen cloth @ ₹ 36 per metre
	Less : Trade discount 15%
Jan 22	ISC Co., Gujarat, returned to us
	50 metre of georgette cloth @ ₹ 85 per metre
	Less : Trade discount 5%
Jan 27	ABC Co., Delhi, returned to us
	20 metre of chiffon cloth @ ₹ 85 per metre
Jan 31	Returned to XYZ Co. defective cloth worth ₹ 1,200.

Ans Total of Return Outwards Book = ₹ 3,492
Total of Return Inwards Book = ₹ 6,817.5

13 From the following information, prepare the necessary subsidiary books of M/s Hira Lal.

2016		Amt (₹)
Feb 1	Goods sold to Sen	10,000
Feb 4	Purchased from Kamal	4,960
Feb 6	Sold to Manas	4,200
Feb 7	Sen returned goods	1,200
Feb 8	Return to Kamal	560
Feb 10	Sold to Mohan	6,600
Feb 14	Purchased from Ram	10,400
Feb 17	Bought from Rakesh	8,120
Feb 20	Return to Ram	400
Feb 22	Return inwards from Mohan	500
Feb 24	Purchased goods from Kirti (−) 10% trade discount	11,400
Feb 25	Sold to Chand (−) 5% trade discount	13,200
Feb 26	Sold to Vinod	8,000
Feb 28	Return outwards to Kirti (−) 10% trade discount	2,000
Feb 28	Return from Vinod	1,000

Ans Purchases Book = ₹ 33,740; Sales Book = ₹ 41,340; Purchases Return Book = ₹ 2,760
Sales Return Book = ₹ 2,700.

14 Enter the following transactions in the subsidiary books and post them into the ledger and balance the ledger account.

2016		Amt (₹)
Sep 1	Mr Vineet started a business with	6,00,000
Sep 4	Furniture purchased from Erotic Furniture worth	50,000
Sep 5	Purchased goods for cash (Plus CGST and SGST @ 6% each)	1,00,000
Sep 8	Purchased goods from Muneer Khan & Co. for ₹ 1,50,000, trade discount 20%	
Sep 9	Opened a bank account by depositing	1,50,000
Sep 10	Sold goods for cash (Plus CGST and SGST @ 6% each)	2,00,000
Sep 10	Purchased stationery worth ₹ 5,000 from R.S. Mart	
Sep 11	Sold goods to Ankush Verma worth	1,00,000
Sep 14	Goods returned by Ankush Verma worth	20,000
Sep 15	Payment to Muneer Khan & Co. by cheque after discount of ₹ 1,000	50,000
Sep 20	Goods purchased on credit from Namish Gupta & Co worth	1,00,000
Sep 25	Goods returned to Namish Gupta & Co worth	10,000
Sep 28	Paid electricity bill	1,000
Sep 29	Cash sales	90,000
Sep 30	Withdrew ₹ 10,000 for private use from bank	

06

After studying this chapter, students will be familiarise with the meaning, objectives and methods of preparation of trial balance.
Students will also learn the format and steps to prepare a trial balance and also the various rules to be followed while preparing a trial balance.

TRIAL BALANCE

CHAPTER CHECKLIST

- Meaning of Trial Balance
- Objectives of Preparing a Trial Balance
- Steps to Prepare a Trial Balance

MEANING OF TRIAL BALANCE

After recording the transactions in journal and subsidiary books and posting them into the ledger, it is necessary to check the accuracy of the transactions recorded and posted to ledger. For this purpose, trial balance is prepared. It is a statement which incorporates the balances of ledger accounts. A trial balance consists of debit column which records debit balances of ledger accounts and a credit column which records credit balances of ledger accounts. If the total of the debit column equals that of the credit column, then this proves the arithmetical accuracy of the accounts maintained.

So, on the basis of the above discussion, it can be concluded that trial balance is a statement prepared with the help of ledger balances, at the end of a specific period, to find out whether debit total agrees with credit total.

Objectives of Preparing a Trial Balance

The trial balance is prepared to fulfil the following objectives

(*i*) To ascertain the arithmetical accuracy of ledger accounts.

(*ii*) To help in identifying errors.

(*iii*) To help in the preparation of financial statements (Trading account, profit and loss account and balance sheet).

Methods of Preparation of Trial Balance

There are three methods used for the preparation of a trial balance

(*i*) Total method (*ii*) Balance method

(*iii*) Total cum-balance method

Note *As per the syllabus only balance method is discussed.*

Balance Method of Preparing Trial Balance

Balance method is the most commonly used method of preparing trial balance. Under this method, the balances of all the accounts (including cash and bank account) are incorporated in the trial balance. The debit and credit columns of the trial balance are totalled and they must be equal.

It may be noted that trial balance can be prepared under balance method, only when all the ledger accounts have been balanced. The account balances are used because the balance summarises the net effect of all transactions relating to an account and helps in the preparation of financial statements.

FORMAT OF TRIAL BALANCE

Trial Balance
as on ...

Name of Accounts (1)	LF (2)	Debit Balance (₹) (3)	Credit Balance (₹) (4)
Total			

Different columns of trial balance are explained below

1. **First Column** The name of the account is written.
2. **Second Column** Ledger Folio (LF) *i.e.*, the page number of the ledger where the balance appears, is written.
3. **Third Column** The debit balance (if any) is entered.
4. **Fourth Column** The credit balance (if any) is written.

LIMITATIONS OF TRIAL BALANCE

Limitations of a trial balance are as follows

(*i*) Trial balance only confirms that the total of all debit balances matches the total of all credit balances.

(*ii*) A trial balance gives only condensed information of each account.

(*iii*) Trial balance total may agree inspite of errors. There are certain errors which are not disclosed by a trial balance.

These are

(*a*) Errors of complete omission
(*b*) Errors of principles
(*c*) Compensating errors
(*d*) Incorrect amount entered in the journal
(*e*) Posting to the wrong account
(*f*) An entry posted twice in the ledger

STEPS TO PREPARE A TRIAL BALANCE

Step 1 The balances of each account in the ledger are ascertained. The balance of an account is the difference between the total of the debit entries and the total of the credit entries in an account. If the total of debit entries is greater, it is called debit balance. Likewise, if the total of credit entries is greater, it is called credit balance.

Step 2 List each account and place its balance in the debit or credit column (If an account does not have a balance, it is ignored).

Step 3 Compute the total of debit balances column.

Step 4 Compute the total of the credit balances column.

Step 5 Verify that the sum of the debit balances equals the sum of credit balances. If they do not tally, it indicates, that there are some errors. So, one must check the correctness of the balances of all accounts.

Rules for Preparing the Trial Balance from the Given List of Ledger Balances

Following rules should be taken into care

(*i*) The balances of all (a) assets accounts (b) expenses and losses accounts (c) drawings (d) cash and bank balances (e) purchases (f) sales return are placed in the debit column of the trial balance.

(*ii*) The balances of all (a) liabilities accounts (b) income and profit accounts (c) capital (d) sales (e) purchases return are placed in the credit column of the trial balance.

(*iii*) Generally, closing stock does not appear in the trial balance. It is usually given outside the trial balance as an additional information or adjustment.

In case, it appears in the trial balance, it means that it has already been adjusted through purchases.

(*iv*) The amount due from all the debtors is shown collectively under the head 'Sundry Debtors'.

(*v*) The amount due to all the creditors is shown collectively under the head 'Sundry Creditors'.

ILLUSTRATION |1| Given below is a ledger extract relating to the business of Viren & Co as on 31st March, 2019. You are required to prepare the trial balance by balance method.

Dr **Cash Account** Cr

Date	Particulars	JF	Amt (₹)	Date	Particulars	JF	Amt (₹)
	To Capital A/c		1,00,000		By Furniture A/c		30,000
	To Veer		2,50,000		By Salaries A/c		25,000
	To Sales A/c		5,000		By Arjun		2,10,000
					By Purchases A/c		10,000
					By Capital A/c		5,000
					By Balance c/d		75,000
			3,55,000				3,55,000

Dr **Furniture Account** Cr

Date	Particulars	JF	Amt (₹)	Date	Particulars	JF	Amt (₹)
	To Cash A/c		30,000		By Balance c/d		30,000
			30,000				30,000

Dr **Salaries Account** Cr

Date	Particulars	JF	Amt (₹)	Date	Particulars	JF	Amt (₹)
	To Cash A/c		25,000		By Balance c/d		25,000
			25,000				25,000

Dr **Arjun's Account** Cr

Date	Particulars	JF	Amt (₹)	Date	Particulars	JF	Amt (₹)
	To Cash A/c		2,10,000		By Purchases A/c (Credit purchases)		2,50,000
	To Purchases Return A/c		5,000				
	To Balance c/d		35,000				
			2,50,000				2,50,000

Dr **Purchases Account** Cr

Date	Particulars	JF	Amt (₹)	Date	Particulars	JF	Amt (₹)
	To Cash A/c		10,000		By Balance c/d		2,60,000
	To Arjun (as per purchases book-credit purchases)		2,50,000				
			2,60,000				2,60,000

Dr **Purchases Return Account** Cr

Date	Particulars	JF	Amt (₹)	Date	Particulars	JF	Amt (₹)
	To Balance c/d		5,000		By Arjun (as per purchases return book)		5,000
			5,000				5,000

Veer's Account

Dr Date	Particulars	JF	Amt (₹)	Date	Particulars	JF	Cr Amt (₹)
	To Sales A/c (Credit sales)		3,00,000		By Sales Return A/c		1,000
					By Cash A/c		2,50,000
					By Balance c/d		49,000
			3,00,000				3,00,000

Sales Account

Dr Date	Particulars	JF	Amt (₹)	Date	Particulars	JF	Cr Amt (₹)
	To Balance c/d		3,05,000		By Cash A/c		5,000
					By Veer (as per sales book-credit sales)		3,00,000
			3,05,000				3,05,000

Sales Return Account

Dr Date	Particulars	JF	Amt (₹)	Date	Particulars	JF	Cr Amt (₹)
	To Veer (as per sales return book)		1,000		By Balance c/d		1,000
			1,000				1,000

Capital Account

Dr Date	Particulars	JF	Amt (₹)	Date	Particulars	JF	Cr Amt (₹)
	To Cash A/c		5,000		By Cash A/c		1,00,000
	To Balance c/d		95,000				
			1,00,000				1,00,000

- *Students should keep in mind that balancing amount on the credit side signifies debit balance and balancing amount on the debit side signifies credit balance.*

Sol.

Trial Balance
as on 31st March, 2019

Name of Accounts	LF	Debit Balance (₹)	Credit Balance (₹)
Cash A/c		75,000	
Furniture A/c		30,000	
Salaries A/c		25,000	
Arjun's A/c			35,000
Purchases A/c		2,60,000	
Purchases Return A/c			5,000
Veer's A/c		49,000	
Sales A/c			3,05,000
Sales Return A/c		1,000	
Capital A/c			95,000
Total		4,40,000	4,40,000

ILLUSTRATION |2| From the following list of balances extracted from the books of Shri Sahiram. Prepare a trial balance as on 31st March, 2016.

Name of Accounts	Amt (₹)	Name of Accounts	Amt (₹)
Stock on 1st April, 2015	22,000	Discount Received	20,000
Purchases	2,57,500	Long-term Borrowings	1,70,000
Sales	3,61,800	Provision for Doubtful Debts	5,000
Carriage Inwards	300	Provision for Depreciation on Machinery	5,000
Carriage Outwards	120	Bad Debts	600
Return Inwards	23,500	Stationery	420
Return Outwards	2,000	Insurance	340
Debtors	32,000	Wages and Salaries	18,500
Creditors	17,400	Investment	30,000
Leasehold Premises	1,60,000	Interest on Investment	2,700
Equipment	2,00,000	Cash and Bank Balance	1,240
Repairs to Equipment	2,000	Premises	60,000
Depreciation	8,000	Furniture and Fixtures	14,000
Bills Receivable	840	Miscellaneous Expenses	520
Bills Payable	480	Miscellaneous Income	140
Bank Overdraft	1,50,000	Loan from Axis Bank	25,000
Interest on Overdraft	640	Interest on above Loan	3,000
Purchases Return	50,000	Capital	70,000
Discount Allowed	4,000	Proprietor's Withdrawals (Drawings)	6,000
Salaries	10,000	Computers	9,000
		Goodwill	15,000
		Stock on 31st March, 2016 (not adjusted)	31,000

Sol.

Trial Balance
as on 31st March, 2016

Name of Accounts	LF	Debit Balance (₹)	Credit Balance (₹)
Stock on 1st April, 2015		22,000	
Purchases		2,57,500	
Sales			3,61,800
Carriage Inwards		300	
Carriage Outwards		120	
Return Inwards		23,500	
Return Outwards			2,000
Debtors		32,000	
Creditors			17,400
Leasehold Premises		1,60,000	
Equipment		2,00,000	
Repairs to Equipment		2,000	
Depreciation		8,000	
Bills Receivable		840	
Bills Payable			480
Bank Overdraft			1,50,000
Interest on Overdraft		640	
Purchases Return			50,000
Discount Allowed		4,000	

Name of Accounts	LF	Debit Balance (₹)	Credit Balance (₹)
Salaries		10,000	
Discount Received			20,000
Long-term Borrowings			1,70,000
Provisions for Doubtful Debts			5,000
Provision for Depreciation on Machinery			5,000
Bad Debts		600	
Stationery		420	
Insurance		340	
Wages and Salaries		18,500	
Investment		30,000	
Interest on Investment			2,700
Cash and Bank Balance		1,240	
Premises		60,000	
Furniture and Fixtures		14,000	
Miscellaneous Expenses		520	
Miscellaneous Income			140
Loan from Axis Bank			25,000
Interest on above Loan		3,000	
Capital			70,000
Proprietor's Withdrawals (Drawings)		6,000	
Computers		9,000	
Goodwill		15,000	
Total		8,79,520	8,79,520

- *Closing stock will not be shown in trial balance because it has not yet been adjusted.*

ILLUSTRATION |3| (With GST) Prepare trial balance from the following information of Bansal & Sons as on 31st December, 2021. Capital of the firm is the balancing figure.

Name of Accounts	Amt (₹)	Name of Accounts	Amt (₹)
Stock (1st January, 2021)	50,800	Discount Allowed	6,000
Purchases	2,20,000	Cash at Bank	16,000
Sales	2,80,000	Bad Debts	6,000
Carriage	12,000	Debtors	44,400
Cash	16,000	Creditors	49,000
Furniture	36,000	Provision for Doubtful Debts	2,800
Depreciation	8,000	Input CGST	9,000
Drawings	13,000	Output CGST	10,000
Return Outwards	6,400	Input SGST	9,000
Return Inwards	4,000	Output SGST	10,000

Sol.

Trial Balance

as on 31st December, 2021

Name of Accounts	LF	Debit Balance (₹)	Credit Balance (₹)
Stock on (1st January, 2021)		50,800	
Purchases		2,20,000	
Sales			2,80,000
Carriage		12,000	
Input CGST		9,000	

Name of Accounts	LF	Debit Balance (₹)	Credit Balance (₹)
Input SGST		9,000	
Cash		16,000	
Furniture		36,000	
Depreciation		8,000	
Drawings		13,000	
Output CGST			10,000
Output SGST			10,000
Return Outwards			6,400
Return Inwards		4,000	
Discount Allowed		6,000	
Cash at Bank		16,000	
Bad Debts		6,000	
Debtors		44,400	
Creditors			49,000
Provision for Doubtful Debts			2,800
Capital (Balancing Figure)			92,000
Total		4,50,200	4,50,200

ILLUSTRATION |4| The following trial balance has been prepared by an inexperienced accountant. You are required to identify the errors and prepare the trial balance in a correct form.

Name of Accounts	LF	Debit Balance (₹)	Credit Balance (₹)
Cash in Hand		10,000	
Fixed Assets			12,500
Capital			38,600
Purchases		22,500	
Sales		10,250	
Discount Allowed			250
Return Inwards			500
Return Outwards		700	
Wages and Salaries		5,000	
Debtors		1,340	
Creditors			4,700
Drawings			1,000
Discount Received			350
Bills Receivable		1,170	
Bills Payable			2,160
Rent		1,500	
Interest Paid			1,000
Total		52,460	61,060

Sol. *Following errors are identified in the above trial balance*

(*i*) Fixed assets are shown in the credit column, which is wrong. Assets have a debit balance and as such, they should be shown in the debit column.

(*ii*) Sales have been shown in the debit column. Sales are revenue for a business and therefore should be shown in the credit column.

(*iii*) Discount allowed has been shown in the credit column, which is wrong. Discount allowed is an expense for the business and should therefore be shown in the debit column.

(*iv*) Return inwards have been entered in the credit column and return outwards have been entered in the debit column, which is not correct. Return inwards should be recorded in debit column and return outwards in the credit column.

(*v*) Drawings have been recorded in the credit column, which is wrong. Drawings reduce the capital and should therefore be recorded in the debit column.

(*vi*) Interest paid has been recorded in the credit column. This is not correct. Interest paid is an expense for the business and should therefore be recorded in debit column.

Redrafted trial balance is given below

Trial Balance
as on...

Name of Accounts	LF	Debit Balance (₹)	Credit Balance (₹)
Cash in Hand		10,000	
Fixed Assets		12,500	
Capital			38,600
Purchases		22,500	
Sales			10,250
Discount Allowed		250	
Return Inwards		500	
Return Outwards			700
Wages and Salaries		5,000	
Debtors		1,340	
Creditors			4,700
Drawings		1,000	
Discount Received			350
Bills Receivable		1,170	
Bills Payable			2,160
Rent		1,500	
Interest Paid		1,000	
Total		56,760	56,760

ILLUSTRATION |5| Following is the trial balance of Sudhir Chaudhary as on 31st March, 2021.

Name of Accounts	LF	Debit Balance (₹)	Credit Balance (₹)
Capital			10,00,000
Plant and Machinery		13,40,000	
Furniture		2,40,000	
Cash in Hand		60,000	
Bank Overdraft			1,10,000
Purchases		22,40,000	
Sales			34,80,000
Debtors		10,20,000	
Creditors			5,00,000
Rent		1,76,000	
General Expenses		14,000	
Total		50,90,000	50,90,000

Following transactions were entered into but were not recorded in the books of accounts

(*i*) Goods worth ₹ 30,000 were purchased on credit.

(*ii*) Received a cheque of ₹ 48,000 from a debtor in full settlement of his account of ₹ 50,000.

(*iii*) Goods amounting to ₹ 6,000 were returned by a customer.

(*iv*) Paid rent for the month ₹ 16,000 by cheque.

Required

(*i*) Pass journal entries for the above mentioned transactions and post them into the ledger.

(*ii*) Redraft the trial balance.

Sol.

JOURNAL

Date	Particulars		LF	Amt (Dr)	Amt (Cr)
(i)	Purchases A/c	Dr		30,000	
	To Creditors A/c				30,000
	(Being goods purchased on credit)				
(ii)	Bank A/c	Dr		48,000	
	Discount Allowed A/c	Dr		2,000	
	To Debtors A/c				50,000
	(Being amount received from debtors and discount allowed)				
(iii)	Sales Return A/c	Dr		6,000	
	To Debtors A/c				6,000
	(Being goods returned by a debtor)				
(iv)	Rent A/c	Dr		16,000	
	To Bank A/c				16,000
	(Being rent paid by cheque)				

Ledger

Dr **Purchases Account** Cr

Date	Particulars	JF	Amt (₹)	Date	Particulars	JF	Amt (₹)
	To Balance b/d		22,40,000		By Balance c/d		22,70,000
	To Creditors A/c		30,000				
			22,70,000				22,70,000

Dr **Creditors Account** Cr

Date	Particulars	JF	Amt (₹)	Date	Particulars	JF	Amt (₹)
	To Balance c/d		5,30,000		By Balance b/d		5,00,000
					By Purchases A/c		30,000
			5,30,000				5,30,000

Dr **Bank Account** Cr

Date	Particulars	JF	Amt (₹)	Date	Particulars	JF	Amt (₹)
	To Debtors A/c		48,000		By Balance b/d		1,10,000
	To Balance c/d		78,000		By Rent A/c		16,000
			1,26,000				1,26,000

Dr **Discount Allowed Account** Cr

Date	Particulars	JF	Amt (₹)	Date	Particulars	JF	Amt (₹)
	To Debtors A/c		2,000		By Balance c/d		2,000
			2,000				2,000

Dr **Debtors Account** Cr

Date	Particulars	JF	Amt (₹)	Date	Particulars	JF	Amt (₹)
	To Balance b/d		10,20,000		By Bank A/c		48,000
					By Discount Allowed A/c		2,000
					By Sales Return A/c		6,000
					By Balance c/d		9,64,000
			10,20,000				10,20,000

Sales Return Account

Date	Particulars	JF	Amt (₹)	Date	Particulars	JF	Amt (₹)
	To Debtors A/c		6,000		By Balance c/d		6,000
			6,000				6,000

Rent Account

Date	Particulars	JF	Amt (₹)	Date	Particulars	JF	Amt (₹)
	To Balance b/d		1,76,000		By Balance c/d		1,92,000
	To Bank A/c		16,000				
			1,92,000				1,92,000

Trial Balance
as on 31st March, 2021

Name of Accounts	LF	Debit Balance (₹)	Credit Balance (₹)
Capital			10,00,000
Plant and Machinery		13,40,000	
Furniture		2,40,000	
Cash in Hand		60,000	
Bank Overdraft			78,000
Purchases		22,70,000	
Discount Allowed		2,000	
Sales			34,80,000
Debtors		9,64,000	
Creditors			5,30,000
Sales Return		6,000	
Rent		1,92,000	
General Expenses		14,000	
Total		50,88,000	50,88,000

CHAPTER PRACTICE

OBJECTIVE TYPE Questions

Multiple Choice Questions

1 A trial balance is prepared **NCERT**

(a) after preparation financial statement
(b) after rewarding transactions in subsidiary books
(c) after posting to ledger is complete
(d) after posting to ledger is complete and accounts have been balanced

Ans (d) after posting to ledger is complete and accounts have been balanced

2 Trial balance shows the

(a) final position of accounts
(b) standard position of accounts
(c) working position of accounts
(d) None of the above

Ans (a) Trial balance is an important statement as it shows the final position of all accounts and helps in the preparation of financial statements.

3 Trial balance is considered as the connecting link between accounting records and preparation of financial statements. It provides a basis for

(a) auditing accounting reports
(b) accuracy of the ledger account
(c) further processing of accounting data
(d) All of the above

Ans (c) further processing of accounting data

4 Agreement of trial balance is affected by **NCERT**

(a) one sided errors only
(b) two sided errors only
(c) Both (a) and (b)
(d) None of the above

Ans (a) one sided errors only

5 What will be the effect on trial balance if ₹ 2,000 received as rent and correctly entered in the cash book but not posted to rent account?

(a) Debit side of trial balance will exceed by ₹ 2,000
(b) Debit side of trial balance will decrease by ₹ 2,000
(c) Credit side of trial balance will decrease by ₹ 2,000
(d) Credit side of trial balance will exceed by ₹ 2,000

Ans (a) In this situation, one account has been posted correctly, i.e. cash account but one account has been left to be posted i.e. rent account.

Rent received is an income, thus debit side of trial balance will exceed by ₹ 2,000 due to effect on cash account.

6 If the trial balance agrees, it implies that **NCERT**

(a) there is no error in books
(b) there may be two sided errors in the book
(c) there may be one sided error in the books
(d) there may be both two sided and one sided errors in the books]

Ans (b) there may be two sided errors in the book

7 Which is not a trial balance method?

(a) Balance method
(b) Total method
(c) Balance cum total method
(d) Grand total method

Ans (d) Grand total method

8 Under which method of trial balance, the balance of each account is extracted and written against each account?

(a) Balance method of trial balance
(b) Total method of trial balance
(c) Balance total method of trial balance
(d) None of the above

Ans (a) Balance method of trial balance

9 One of the trader is preparing trial balance and it has maintained all the books of accounts properly. What is the best method you suggest to prepare trial balance?

(a) Balance total method
(b) Total method
(c) Balance method
(d) None of the above

Ans (c) Trader should use the balance method for preparing trial balance for its business because in this method, balances summarise the net effect of all transactions relating to an account which help in ascertaining the correctness of the ledger account.

10 Trial balance can be prepared under balance method, only when

(a) all the entries are made in journal
(b) all the subsidiary books are maintained
(c) all the ledger accounts have been balanced

(d) all the balances have been transferred to final accounts

Ans (c) all the ledger accounts have been balanced

11 A trader has prepared the trial balance and total doesn't tie. Which approach the trader should follow?

(a) Firstly, he should recheck all the ledger
(b) He should recheck the total of trial balance
(c) He should open the suspense account
(d) All of the above

Ans (d) All of the above

12 Balance method is the most commonly used method of preparing trial balance as it facilitates the preparation of final account where

(a) all ledger accounts are showcased
(b) debit/credit column are totalled
(c) balances are transferred
(d) Both (a) and (b)

Ans (d) In balance method of trial balance, it is ascertained that all debit and credit balances are equal and it assures their correctness. Account balances are used because the balance summaries the net effect of all transactions relating to an account and help in pren paring final accounts.

Fill in the Blanks

13 A trial balance is a ....

Ans statement

14 Input GST has .... balance while output GST has..........balance.

Ans debit, credit

15 The trial balance can be prepared under balance method, only when all the .... have been balanced.

Ans ledger accounts

State True or False

16 The trial balance ensures the arithmetical accuracy of the books.

Ans True

17 Closing stock will never appear in the trial balance.

Ans False. When cost of goods sold or gross profit is given in trial balance, closing stock will appear in the trial balance.

18 The balances of all liabilities accounts are placed in the credit column of the trial balance.

Ans True

Match the Following

19

Column I		Column II	
1.	First Column	(a)	Account name
2.	Second Column	(b)	Debit balance is entered
3.	Third Column	(c)	Ledger Folio
4.	Fourth Column	(d)	Credit balance is entered

Ans 1–(a), 2–(c), 3–(b), 4–(d)

VERY SHORT ANSWER
Type Questions

20 State the meaning of a trial balance. **NCERT**

Ans Trial balance is a statement, prepared with the debit and credit balances of ledger accounts to test the arithmetical accuracy of the books.

21 Give two objectives of preparing a trial balance.

Ans *The two objectives of preparing a trial balance are*

(*i*) To verify the arithmetical accuracy of ledger accounts.
(*ii*) To help in locating errors.

22 Is the preparation of trial balance compulsory or optional?

Ans It is optional.

23 What is the reason for the agreement of a trial balance?

Ans Under the double entry system, each transaction is recorded two times, once on the debit side of an account and again on the credit side of another account. It is because of this reason that the trial balance always agree.

24 Is trial balance prepared for a particular period?

Ans No, it is prepared on a particular date.

25 State the accounts, which are not considered while preparing trial balance by balance method.

Ans Accounts having no balance or zero balance are not considered while preparing the trial balance.

26 Is trial balance an account or a statement?

Ans Trial balance is a statement, showing the names and balances of all the accounts in the ledger and cash book.

27 Is it correct to say that trial balance facilitates the preparation of financial statements?

Ans Yes, trial balance helps in preparing the financial statements by making available the balances of all the accounts at one place.

28 When is the closing stock shown in the trial balance?

Ans The closing stock is shown in the trial balance when it is adjusted against purchases.

29 Is it correct to say that a trial balance is only a prima facie evidence of arithmetical accuracy of records?

Ans Yes, if totals of both the sides of a trial balance are equal then it is proved that books are atleast arithmetically correct.

30 What will be the effect on trial balance if purchases return of ₹ 10,000 has been wrongly posted to the debit of sales return account but correctly entered in the customers account?

Ans The debit side of the trial balance will be more by ₹ 10,000.

31 What will be the effect on trial balance if ₹ 2,000 received as rent and correctly entered in the cash book is not posted to rent account?

Ans Debit side of trial balance will exceed by ₹ 2,000.

SHORT ANSWER Type Questions

32 State any four functions of a trial balance.

Or Describe the purpose for the preparation of a trial balance. **NCERT**

Or What are the objectives or functions or importance of a trial balance?

Ans *The objectives/functions/purpose of a trial balance are*

(*i*) **Ascertain the Arithmetical Accuracy of the Ledger Accounts** The trial balance ensures the arithmetical accuracy of the ledger accounts. When the debit and credit balances in the trial balance are equal, it is assumed that the posting to the ledger accounts is arithmetically correct *i.e.*, all debits and corresponding credit have been properly recorded in the ledger.

(*ii*) **Helps in Locating Errors** A trial balance helps in the detection or location of errors. However, all the errors are not disclosed, but only arithmetical errors are disclosed.

(*iii*) **Summary of the Ledger Accounts** Trial balance offers a summary of the ledger. It enables to know the assets, liabilities, expenses, incomes, etc.

(*iv*) **Helps in the Preparation of Final Accounts** Trial balance is considered as the connecting link between accounting records and the preparation of financial statements. As trial balance is a list of summary of all ledger accounts, it provides a basis for, preparation of final accounts (trading and profit and loss account and balance sheet).

33 State the characteristics/features of a trial balance.

Ans *The characteristics/features of a trial balance are as follows*

(*i*) Trial balance contains a list of all ledger accounts including cash account.

(*ii*) It is a statement, not an account.

(*iii*) It is just a working paper, it is not a part of the double entry system of book-keeping.

(*iv*) It can be prepared at any time during the accounting period, *i.e.*, at the end of any chosen period which may be monthly, quarterly, half-yearly or annually depending upon the requirements.

(*v*) It is prepared to check the arithmetical accuracy of the ledger accounts.

(*vi*) It is not an absolute proof of the accuracy of accounting records.

(*vii*) It is always prepared on a particular date and not for a particular period.

34 State whether the balance of the following accounts should be placed in the debit or the credit columns of the trial balance.

(i) Plant and machinery
(ii) Discount allowed (iii) Bank overdraft
(iv) Sales (v) Interest paid
(vi) Bad debts

Ans (*i*) Debit (*ii*) Debit (*iii*) Credit
(*iv*) Credit (*v*) Debit (*vi*) Debit

35 State the limitations of trial balance. **NCERT**

Ans Refer to text on Pg. No. 193.

36 Trial balance is a link between the ledger and final accounts. Explain.

Ans Trial balance is a connecting link between the accounting records and the preparation of financial statements. The availability of a tallied trial balance is the first step in the preparation of financial statements, as it contains the balances of all the accounts. All revenue and expenses account, which appear in the trial balance are transferred to the trading and profit and loss account and all liabilities, capital and assets accounts are transferred to the balance sheet.

NUMERICAL Questions

1 From the following ledger balances, prepare trial balance.

Capital ₹ 20,800; rent outstanding ₹ 1,420; amount due to Param, ₹ 15,000; drawings ₹ 2,800; goodwill ₹ 12,000; interest received ₹ 2,000; discount received ₹ 1,580; amount due from Deepan ₹ 26,000.

Ans Trial Balance Total = ₹ 40,800

2 Prepare a correct trial balance from the following trial balance in which there are certain mistakes.

Name of Accounts	LF	Debit Balance (₹)	Credit Balance (₹)
Cost of Goods Sold		75,000	
Closing Stock			20,000
Debtors			30,000
Creditors			15,000
Fixed Assets		25,000	
Opening Stock		30,000	
Expenses			10,000
Sales			1,00,000
Capital		45,000	
Total		1,75,000	1,75,000

Ans Trial Balance Total = ₹ 1,60,000;
Purchases = ₹ 65,000

Hint: *Purchases = Cost of Goods Sold + Closing Stock – Opening Stock*
= 75,000 + 20,000 – 30,000
= ₹ 65,000

3 From the following information, draw up a trial balance in the books of Shri Parminder Singh as on 31st March, 2016.

Capital ₹ 56,000; purchases ₹ 14,400; discount allowed ₹ 480; carriage inwards ₹ 3,480; carriage outwards ₹ 920; sales ₹ 24,000; return inwards ₹ 120; return outwards ₹ 280; rent and taxes ₹ 480; plant and machinery ₹ 32,280; stock on 1st April, 2015 ₹ 6,200; sundry debtors ₹ 8,080; sundry creditors ₹ 4,800; investments ₹ 1,440; commission received ₹ 720; cash in hand ₹ 40; cash at bank ₹ 4,040; motor cycle ₹ 13,840 and stock on 31st March, 2016 (not adjusted) ₹ 8,200.

Ans Total of Trial Balance = ₹ 85,800

4 Following balances were extracted from the books of Shri A Jadeja on 31st March, 2016. You are required to prepare a trial balance. The amount required to balance the trial balance should be entered as capital.

Name of Accounts	Amt (₹)	Name of Accounts	Amt (₹)
Purchases	2,12,500	Drawings	9,625
Stock (1st April, 2015)	30,000	Return Inwards	4,375
Sales	1,31,250	Premises	6,60,000
Sundry Debtors	29,750	Sundry Creditors	20,125
Discount Received	4,375	Discount Allowed	3,500
Carriage Outwards	875	Carriage Inwards	1,750

Name of Accounts	Amt (₹)	Name of Accounts	Amt (₹)
Cash in Hand	4,375	Cash at Bank	21,875
Machinery	1,55,625	General Expenses	2,625
Provision for Depreciation on Machinery	30,250	Bad Debts Written off	3,065
		Provision for Doubtful Debts	2,975

Ans Total of Trial Balance = ₹ 11,39,940 ; Capital = ₹ 9,50,965

5 **Prepare trial balance from the following information of Ankur & Sons as on 31st March, 2021. Capital of the firm is the balancing figure.**

Name of Accounts	Amt (₹)	Name of Accounts	Amt (₹)
Stock (Opening)	8,400	Bad Debts	1,500
Sales	35,100	Discount Allowed	1,000
Cash	4,000	Discount Received	750
Printing and Stationery	2,000	Debtors	12,000
Bank Overdraft	4,500	B/P	4,000
Return Inwards	2,000	Creditors	11,000
Purchases	25,000	B/R	4,500
Drawings	3,250	Provision for Doubtful Debts	1,000
Return Outwards	500	Provision for Depreciation	800
Salary	4,500	Rent	2,500
Furniture	10,000	Input SGST	1,500
Advertisement	2,500	Output SGST	1,750
Input CGST	1,500		
Output CGST	1,750		

Ans Capital = ₹ 25,000; Total of Trial Balance = ₹ 86,150

6 **The following trial balance has been prepared by an unexperienced accountant. Redraft it in a correct form.**

Name of Accounts	LF	Debit Balance (₹)	Credit Balance (₹)
Cash in Hand		4,000	
Machinery		25,000	
Purchases		66,000	
Sundry Debtors		24,000	
Carriage Inwards		2,000	
Carriage Outwards			1,000
Wages		18,000	
Rent and Taxes		5,000	
Sundry Creditors			15,500
Discount Allowed			1,000
Return Outwards		2,500	
Return Inwards			10,000
Capital		30,000	
Drawings			6,000
Bank Loan		10,000	
Interest on Loan		1,500	
Opening Stock			26,000
Sales			1,30,000
Discount Received		1,500	
Total		1,89,500	1,89,500

Ans Total of Redrafted Trial Balance = ₹ 1,89,500

7 **Enter the following transactions in the subsidiary books, post them into the ledger and prepare a trial balance.**

Date	Particulars	Amt (₹)
2016		
Jan 1	Kamlesh commenced business with cash	2,00,000
Jan 4	Bought furniture from Rawat Furniture House	10,000
Jan 5	Purchased goods for cash	20,000
Jan 8	Purchased goods from Dhar & Co for ₹ 30,000. Trade discount 10%	
Jan 9	Opened a bank account by depositing	30,000
Jan 10	Sold goods for cash	40,000
Jan 10	Purchased stationery from V Mart	1,000
Jan 11	Sold goods to Vishal Bhardwaj	26,000
Jan 14	Goods returned by Vishal Bhardwaj	6,000
Jan 15	Payment to Dhar & Co by cheque	10,000
Jan 20	Goods purchased on credit from Sujit & Co	20,000
Jan 25	Goods returned to Sujit & Co	2,000
Jan 28	Paid electricity bill	400
Jan 29	Cash sales	20,000
Jan 30	Withdrew for private use from the bank	4,000

Ans Total of Trial Balance = ₹ 3,34,000

8 **Following is the trial balance of Raj Nayak as on 31st March, 2016.**

Name of Accounts	LF	Debit Balance (₹)	Credit Balance (₹)
Capital			6,40,000
Fixed Assets		3,60,000	
Drawings		1,20,000	
Debtors		4,80,000	
Creditors			3,60,000
Purchases		14,20,000	
Sales			21,00,000
Bank Balance		90,000	
Cash in Hand		60,000	
Salaries		3,30,000	
Rent		2,40,000	
Total		31,00,000	31,00,000

Having prepared the trial balance, it was discovered that following transactions remained unrecorded

(i) Goods were sold on credit amounting to ₹ 80,000.
(ii) Paid to creditors ₹ 44,000 by cheque.
(iii) Goods worth ₹ 14,000 were returned to a supplier.
(iv) Paid salary ₹ 30,000 by cheque.

Required

(i) Pass journal entries for the above mentioned transactions and post them into ledger.
(ii) Redraft the trial balance.

Ans Total of Trial Balance = ₹ 31,36,000

07

After studying this chapter, the students will be able to understand the meaning, need and importance of bank reconciliation statement.
Students will learn the various reasons of difference between cash book and passbook balance.
Students will further learn the preparation of an reconciliation statement under various situations.

BANK RECONCILIATION STATEMENT

CHAPTER CHECKLIST

- Meaning of Bank Reconciliation Statement
- Need of Bank Reconciliation Statement
- Reasons of Difference between Cash Book and Passbook Balances
- Preparation of Bank Reconciliation Statement

Banking transactions are recorded by the business firms as well as the banks. Business firms prepare cash book with bank column to record banking transactions while banks prepare **passbook.** As both the books are related to one individual entity and same transactions are recorded in both the books so the balance of both the books should match. When these balances do not match, then it becomes necessary to reconcile them by preparing a statement which is called bank reconciliation statement.

Bank Passbook (Bank Statement) is a copy of the customer's account in the books of a bank. This statement is usually prepared by the bank to keep a record of customer's transactions with the bank and to ascertain the balance in the account of the customer.

MEANING OF BANK RECONCILIATION STATEMENT

Bank reconciliation statement is a statement which is prepared mainly to reconcile (tally) the difference between the bank balance as shown by the cash book and passbook.

Need of Bank Reconciliation Statement

(*i*) It helps in locating any error, that may have been committed either in the cash book or in the passbook.

(*ii*) It helps in bringing out the unnecessary delay in the collection of cheques by the bank.

(*iii*) It helps in avoiding embezzlements or misappropriation of funds by regular periodic reconciliation.

(*iv*) It helps to assure the customer about the correctness of the bank balance shown by the passbook.

(*v*) It helps the management to keep a track of cheques, which have been sent to the bank for collection.

Reasons of Difference between Cash Book and Passbook Balances

The difference between cash book and passbook balances is caused by following reasons

1. DIFFERENCE DUE TO TIMING ON RECORDING ANY TRANSACTION

When a comparison is made between the balance of the cash book with the balance of the passbook, there is often a difference which is caused due to the time gap in recording the transactions relating either to payments or receipts.

The transactions affecting time gap includes

(i) Cheques Issued by the Customer but not yet Presented for Payment

When cheques are issued for payment by the firm to the suppliers/creditors of the firm, they are immediately credited in the bank column of the cash book.

However, it is recorded by the bank only when it is presented for payment. Hence, there may be a gap between the issue of a cheque and its presentation to the bank, which may cause the difference.

(ii) Cheques Paid/Deposited into the Bank but not yet Collected

When a firm receives cheques from its customers (debtors), it immediately enters them in the debit side of cash book, which increases the balance as per the cash book. However, the banks credits the firm's account when they have received the payment from the other bank *i.e.,* when the cheques have been cleared.

This leads to a difference between the bank balance shown by the cash book and the balance shown by the passbook.

2. TRANSACTIONS RECORDED BY THE BANK

There are some transactions, which are recorded by the bank but are not known to the customer/account holder. The account holder comes to know about such transactions after receiving the bank passbook.

These transactions lead to a difference between the balance as per cash book and passbook

Examples of such transactions are

(i) Direct Debits Made by the Bank on Behalf of the Customer

The bank deducts/debits a certain amount also known as bank charges for various services, it renders to its customers.

Such deductions include cheque collection charges, incidental charges, interest on overdraft etc.

As a result, the balance as per passbook will be less than the balance as per cash book.

(ii) Amounts Directly Deposited in the Bank Account by the Customer

Sometimes, the debtor (customer) may directly deposit the amount into the firm's bank account, about which the firm will come to know only after receiving the passbook.

As a result, the balance shown in the passbook will be more than the balance shown in the firm's cash book.

(iii) Interest and Dividend Collected by the Bank

Sometimes, the bank collects interest and dividend on customer's behalf which is immediately credited by the bank to the customer's account but it will be known to the customer only after he receives the passbook. Till then the balance in passbook will be higher than the balance in the cash book.

(iv) Direct Payments Made by the Bank on Behalf of the Customers

Sometimes, a standing instruction is given by account holder/customer to the bank to make some payments regularly on stated days to the third parties *e.g.,* insurance premium, telephone bills, rent, taxes, etc.

When the payment is made by the bank, it debits the account holder's account, about which the account holder comes to know only after receiving the passbook.

As a result, the balance as per bank passbook will be less than the balance in the cash book.

(v) Interest Credited by the Bank But not Recorded in the Cash Book

When interest is allowed by the bank to the account holder/customer, bank credits the customer's account but the account holder will record the same, when he receives the passbook.

As a result, the balance of passbook will be higher than the balance in cash book.

(vi) Cheque Deposited/Bills Discounted Dishonoured

If a cheque deposited by the firm is dishonoured or a bill of exchange, discounted with the bank is dishonoured on the date of maturity, then the same is debited to customer's account by the bank.

As this information is not available to the firm immediately, there will be no entry in the firm's cash book regarding the above items. This will be known to the firm when it receives a statement from the bank. As a result, the balance as per the passbook will be less than the cash book balance.

3. **DIFFERENCES CAUSED BY ERRORS**

Sometimes, there may be difference between the balance as per cash book and the balance as per passbook on account of an error on the part of the bank or an error in the cash book of the business.

Examples of such errors are

(i) Errors Committed in Recording Transactions by the Firm

There are various errors committed by the firm while recording entries in the cash book. This causes difference between cash book and passbook balance. *For example*, omission or wrong recording of transactions relating to cheques issued, cheques deposited and wrong totalling, etc.

(ii) Errors Committed in Recording Transactions by the Bank

Errors like omission or wrong recording of transactions relating to cheques deposited and wrong totalling, etc are committed by the bank while posting entries in the passbook. This also causes difference between passbook and cash book.

PREPARATION OF BANK RECONCILIATION STATEMENT

After identifying the causes of difference, a bank reconciliation statement can be prepared by taking the balance as per cash book or the balance as per passbook as the starting point. If the starting point is balance as per cash book, the answer arrived at will be the balance as per pass book and *vice-versa.*

The simplest and most common format is given below

Bank Reconciliation Statement
as on... ...

Particulars	Plus (₹)	Minus (₹)

Note *Students should keep in mind that bank reconciliation statement is prepared only on a particular date.*

There may be four different situations while preparing the bank reconciliation statement.

These are as follows

(*i*) When debit balance (favourable balance) as per cash book is given and the balance as per passbook is to be ascertained. Debit balance of cash book implies that deposits in bank account are more than the withdrawls made from the bank account.

(*ii*) When credit balance (favourable balance) as per passbook is given and the balance as per cash book is to be ascertained. Credit balance of passbook means that the deposits made in the bank account, as per the passbook, are more than the withdrawls made from the bank account.

(*iii*) When credit balance as per cash book (unfavourable balance/overdraft balance) is given and the balance as per passbook is to ascertained. Credit balance of cash book implies that the withdrawls made from the bank account exceed the deposits in the account.

(*iv*) When debit balance as per pass book (unfavourable balance/overdraft balance) is given and the balance as per cash book is to ascertained. Debit balance of passbook means that the withdrawls made from the bank account, as per the passbook, exceeds the deposits made in the account.

Preparation of BRS when Balance of Cash Book is given

While preparing BRS when debit (favourable) balance as per cash book or credit (unfavourable) balance as per cash book is given, then following steps should be followed

(*i*) If the starting point is the debit balance as per cash book, then it should be entered in the plus column. If the starting point is the credit balance as per cash book, then it should be entered in the minus column.

(*ii*) Amounts corresponding to the following items should be entered in the plus column

Items	Reason for entering it in plus column
Cheques issued but not yet presented for payment.	This transaction reduces the cash book balance, but the passbook balance is more. Therefore it should be entered in the plus column to reconcile the cash book with the passbook.
Credit made by the bank. or Amount directly deposited by the customer in firm's bank account. or Interest and dividend collected by the bank. or Cheques paid into bank, but omitted to be recorded in the cash book.	These transactions increase the balance at bank, but the cash book balance is less. Therefore, the amount corresponding to these transactions should be entered in the plus column to reconcile the cash book with the passbook.

(*iii*) Amounts corresponding to the following items should be entered in the minus column

Items	Reason for entering it in minus column
Cheques sent to bank for collection but not yet credited by the bank. or Cheques sent to bank for collection are dishonoured.	These transactions increase the cash book balance, but the passbook balance is less. Therefore, amounts corresponding to these transactions should be entered in the minus column to reconcile the cash book with the passbook.
Direct payment made by the bank on behalf of customers. or Debits made by the bank for bank charges, interest etc. or Cheques issued but omitted to be recorded in the cash book.	These transactions reduce the passbook balance, but the cash book balance is more. Therefore, amounts corresponding to these transactions should be entered in the minus column to reconcile the cash book with the passbook.

(*iv*) The total of the plus and minus columns should be ascertained. If the total of the 'plus column' exceeds that of 'minus column', then the difference between the two is termed as favourable balance as per passbook and entered in the 'minus column'. If the total of the 'minus column' exceeds that of 'plus column', then the difference between the two is termed as unfavourable balance as per passbook and is entered in the 'plus column'. Both the columns are then added showing the same total.

ILLUSTRATION |1| (*When favourable i.e., debit balance as per cash book is given*)

Prepare a bank reconciliation statement from the following particulars on 31st March, 2020.

	Amt (₹)
(i) Debit balance as per bank column of the cash book	3,72,000
(ii) Cheques issued to creditors but not yet presented to the bank for payment	72,000
(iii) Dividend received by the bank but not entered in the cash book	5,000
(iv) Interest allowed by the bank	1,250
(v) Cheques deposited into bank for collection but not collected by bank upto this date	15,400
(vi) Bank charges	200
(vii) A cheque deposited into bank was dishonoured but no intimation was received	320
(viii) Bank paid house tax on our behalf but no information received from bank in this connection	350

Sol.

Bank Reconciliation Statement
as on 31st March, 2020

Particulars	Plus (₹)	Minus (₹)
Debit/Favourable Balance as per Cash Book	3,72,000	
Add Cheques issued but not yet presented for payment	72,000	
Dividend received by the bank not entered in the cash book	5,000	
Interest allowed by the bank not entered in the cash book	1,250	
Less Cheques deposited into bank but not collected by bank upto this date		15,400
Bank charges not entered in the cash book		200
Cheque deposited into bank but dishonoured		320
Payment of house tax by bank on our behalf not entered in the cash book		350
Credit/Favourable Balance as per Passbook		4,33,980
	4,50,250	4,50,250

ILLUSTRATION |2| On comparing the cash book with passbook of Naman, it is found that on 31st March, 2016, bank balance of ₹ 40,960 showed by the cash book differs from the bank balance with regard to the following

(i) Bank charges ₹ 100 on 31st March, 2016, are not entered in the cash book.

(ii) On 21st March, 2016, a debtor paid ₹ 2,000 into Naman's bank account in settlement of his dues, but no entry was made in the cash book in respect of this.

(iii) Cheques totalling ₹ 12,980 were issued by Naman and duly recorded in the cash book before 31st March, 2016 but had not been presented at the bank for payment upto that date.

(iv) A bill for ₹ 6,900 discounted with the bank is entered in the cash book without recording the discount charges of ₹ 800.

(v) ₹ 3,520 is entered in the cash book as paid into bank on 31st March, 2016 but not credited by the bank until the following day.

(vi) No entry has been made in the cash book to record the dishonour on 15th March, 2016 of a cheque for ₹ 650 received from Bhanu.

Prepare a reconciliation statement as on 31st March, 2016. **NCERT**

Sol.

Bank Reconciliation Statement
as on 31st March, 2016

Particulars	Plus (₹)	Minus (₹)
Debit/Favourable Balance as per Cash Book	40,960	
Add Cash deposit by debtor directly in bank account	2,000	
Cheque issued but not presented for payment	12,980	
Less Bank charges not entered in cash book		100
Discount charges recorded in bank		800
Cash deposited in bank but not credited		3,520
Cheque of Bhanu dishonoured		650
Credit/Favourable Balance as per Passbook		50,870
	55,940	55,940

ILLUSTRATION |3| *(When credit balance/overdraft as per cash book is given)*

On 31st December, 2016, the cash book of Mittal Bros showed an overdraft of ₹ 6,920. From the following particulars, prepare a bank reconciliation statement and ascertain the balance as per passbook.

(i) Debited by bank ₹ 200 on account of interest on overdraft and ₹ 50 on account of charges for collecting bills.

(ii) Cheque drawn but not encashed before 31st December, 2016 for ₹ 4,000.

(iii) The bank has collected interest and has credited ₹ 600 in passbook.

(iv) A bill receivable for ₹ 700 previously discounted with the bank, had been dishonoured and debited in the passbook.

(v) Cheque paid into bank but not collected and credited before 31st December, 2016 amounted to ₹ 6,000.

NCERT

Sol.

Bank Reconciliation Statement
as on 31st December, 2016

Particulars	Plus (₹)	Minus (₹)
Overdraft/Credit/Unfavourable Balance as per Cash Book		6,920
Add Cheque issued but not presented for payment	4,000	
Interest collected by bank has not been credited in cash book	600	
Less Interest and collection charges debited by bank (200 + 50)		250
Bill discounted with bank dishonoured		700
Cheque sent to the bank for collection but not collected and credited by the bank		6,000
Overdraft/Debit/Unfavourable Balance as per Passbook	9,270	
	13,870	13,870

ILLUSTRATION |4| On 30th September, 2016 my cash book (bank column of account number 1) showed a bank overdraft of ₹ 98,700. On going through the bank passbook for reconciling the balance, I found the following

(i) Out of cheques drawn on 26th September, those for ₹ 7,400 were cashed by the bankers on 2nd October.

(ii) A crossed cheque for ₹ 1,500 given to Abdul was returned by him and a bearer cheque was issued to him in lieu on 1st October.

(iii) Cash and cheques amounting to ₹ 6,800 were deposited in the bank on 29th September, but cheques worth ₹ 2,600 were cleared by the bank on 1st October and one cheque for ₹ 500 was returned by them as dishonoured on the latter date.

(iv) According to my standing instructions, the bankers have on 30th September, paid ₹ 640 as interest to my creditors, paid quarterly premium on my policy amounting to ₹ 320 and have paid a second call of ₹ 1,200 on shares held by me and lodged with the bankers for safe custody. They have also received ₹ 300 as dividend on my shares and recovered an insurance claim of ₹ 1,600 and their charges and commission on the above being ₹ 30. On receipt of information of the above transactions, I have passed necessary entries in my cash book on 1st October.

(v) My bankers seem to have given me a wrong credit for ₹ 1,000 paid in by me in account number 2 and a wrong debit in respect of a cheque for ₹ 600 drawn against my account number 2.

Prepare a bank reconciliation statement as on 30th September, 2016.

Sol.

Bank Reconciliation Statement
as on 30th September, 2016

Particulars		Plus (₹)	Minus (₹)
Overdraft/Credit/Unfavourable Balance as per Cash Book			98,700
Add Cheques issued but not presented for payment		7,400	
Crossed cheque issued to Abdul not presented for payment		1,500	
Amounts collected by the bank on my behalf but not entered in the cash book			
Dividend	300		
Insurance claim (1600-30)	1570	1,870	
Amount paid in account number 2 credited by the bank wrongly to this account		1,000	
Less Cheques deposited in the bank but not cleared (₹ 2,600 + ₹ 500)			3,100
Payments made by the bank on my behalf but not entered in the cash book			
Interest	640		
Premium	320		
Second call	1,200		2,160
Cheques issued against account number 2 but wrongly debited by the bank to this account			600
Overdraft/Debit/Unfavourable Balance as per Passbook		92,790	
		1,04,560	1,04,560

ILLUSTRATION |5| (*When two accounts are given*)

Raja has two accounts (A and B) with PNB. On 31st December, 2016, his ledger shows a balance of ₹ 10,000 in account 'A' and an overdraft of ₹ 4,500 in account 'B'. On verification of the ledger entries with the respective bank statement, the following mistakes were noticed

(i) Deposit of ₹ 3,000 made in account 'A' on 20th December has been entered in the ledger in account 'B'.

(ii) Withdrawal of ₹ 1,000 from account 'A' on 20th November, has been entered in the ledger in account 'B'.

(iii) Two cheques of ₹ 1,000 and ₹ 1,500 deposited in account 'A' on 1st December, (and entered in the books in account 'B') have been dishonoured by the bankers. The entries for dishonour of these cheques have been entered in the books in account 'B'.

(iv) In accounts 'A' and 'B', Raja has issued on 29th December, cheques for ₹ 20,000 and ₹ 2,000 respectively, and these have not been encashed till 31st December.

(v) Incidental charges of ₹ 20 and ₹ 50 charged in accounts 'A' and 'B' respectively, have not been entered in the books.

(vi) The bank has credited interest of ₹ 100 for account 'A' and has charged interest of ₹ 550 for account 'B', which have not been recorded in the books.

(vii) Deposits of ₹ 10,000 and ₹ 7,000 made into accounts 'A' and 'B' respectively, both on 30th December, have not been credited by the bank till 31st December.

Prepare a bank reconciliation statement for the above accounts.

Sol.

Bank Reconciliation Statement of Account 'A'
as on 31st December, 2016

Particulars	Plus (₹)	Minus (₹)
Debit/Favourable Balance as per Cash Book	10,000	
Add Cheque deposited but entered in account 'B'	3,000	
Cheques issued but not presented	20,000	
Interest credited by bank	100	
Less Incidental charges		20
Cheques deposited but not credited		10,000
Withdrawn from account 'A' but entered in account 'B'		1,000
Credit/Favourable Balance as per Passbook		22,080
	33,100	33,100

Bank Reconciliation Statement of Account 'B'
as on 31st December, 2016

Particulars	Plus (₹)	Minus (₹)
Overdraft/Credit/Unfavourable Balance as per Cash Book		4,500
Add Withdrawal from A's account but entered in Account 'B'	1,000	
Cheque issued but not presented	2,000	
Less Cheque deposited with account 'A' but entered in Account 'B'		3,000
Incidental charges		50
Interest charged by bank		550
Cheques deposited but not credited		7,000
Overdraft/Debit/Unfavourable Balance as per Passbook	12,100	
	15,100	15,100

Note *No entry is necessary for two cheques of ₹ 1,000 and ₹ 1,500 deposited in account 'A' on 1st December, as by mistake these deposits were entered into the columns of account B and again the entries for dishonour were passed through the column of account 'B' thereby cancelling the two entries passed in the columns of account 'B'.*

Preparation of BRS when Balance of Passbook is Given

While preparing BRS when credit (favourable) balance as per passbook or debit (unfavourable) balance as per passbook is given, then following steps should be followed

(*i*) If the starting point is the credit balance as per passbook, then it should be entered in the plus column. If the starting point is the debit balance as per passbook, then it should be entered in the minus column.

(*ii*) Amounts corresponding to the following items should be entered in the plus column

Items	Reason for entering it in plus column
Cheques sent to bank for collection but not yet credited by the bank. or Cheques sent to bank for collection are dishonoured.	These transactions increase the cash book balance, but passbook balance is less. Therefore, the amount corresponding to these transactions are entered in the plus column, so that the passbook balance increases and gets reconciled with cash book balance.
Direct payment made by the bank on behalf of customers. or Debits made by the bank for bank charges, interest etc. or Cheques issued but omitted to be recorded in cash book.	These transactions reduce the passbook balance, but the cash book balance is more. Therefore, amounts corresponding to these transactions are entered in the plus column, so that the passbook balance increases and gets reconciled with cash book balance.

(*iii*) Amounts corresponding to the following items should be entered in the minus column.

Items	Reason for entering it in minus column
Cheques issued but not yet presented for payment.	This transaction reduces the cash book balance but the passbook balance is more. Therefore, the amount corresponding to this transaction is entered in the minus column so that passbook balance is reduced and it gets reconciled with cash book balance.
Credit made by the bank. or Amount directly deposited by the customer in firm's bank account. or Interest and dividend collected by the bank. or Cheques paid into bank but omitted to be recorded in the cash book.	These transactions increase the passbook balance, but the cash book balance is less. Therefore, the amount corresponding to these transactions should be entered in the minus column, so that the passbook balance is reduced and gets reconciled with cash book balance.

(*iv*) The total of the plus and minus columns should be ascertained. If the total of the 'plus column' exceeds that of 'minus column', then the difference between the two is termed as favourable balance as per cash book and entered in the minus column'. If the total of 'minus column' exceeds that of 'plus column', then the difference between the two is termed as unfavourable balance as per cash book and is entered in the plus column.

Both the columns are then added, showing the same total.

Note *Students should keep in mind that the treatment of items is reversed when balance as per passbook is the starting point.*

ILLUSTRATION |6| (*When favourable i.e., credit balance as per passbook is given*)

Prepare a bank reconciliation statement as on 30th September, 2016 from the following particulars.

		Amt (₹)
(i)	Bank balance as per passbook	10,000
(ii)	Cheque deposited into the bank but no entry was passed in the cash book	500
(iii)	Cheque received and entered in the cash book but not sent to bank	1,200
(iv)	Credit side of the cash book bank column cast short	200
(v)	Insurance premium paid directly by the bank under the standing advice	600
(vi)	Bank charges entered twice in the cash book	20
(vii)	Cheque issued but not presented to the bank for payment	500
(viii)	Cheque received entered twice in the cash book	1,000
(ix)	Bill discounted dishonoured, not recorded in the cash book	5,000

Sol.

Bank Reconciliation Statement
as on 30th September, 2016

Particulars	Plus (₹)	Minus (₹)
Credit/Favourable Balance as per Passbook	10,000	
Add Cheque received and recorded in the cash book but not sent to bank	1,200	
Credit side of the cash book bank column cast short	200	
Insurance premium not recorded in the cash book	600	
Cheque received entered twice in the cash book	1,000	
Bill discounted dishonoured, not recorded in the cash book	5,000	

Particulars	Plus (₹)	Minus (₹)
Less Cheque deposited into the bank but not recorded in the cash book		500
Bank charges entered twice in the cash book		20
Cheque issued but not presented for payment		500
Debit/Favourable Balance as per Cash Book		16,980
	18,000	18,000

ILLUSTRATION |7|

(i) On 31st March, 2016 the bank passbook of Radha showed a balance of ₹ 15,000 to her credit.

(ii) Before that date, she had issued cheques amounting to ₹ 8,000 out of which cheques amounting to ₹ 3,200 have so far been presented for payment.

(iii) A cheque of ₹ 2,200 deposited by her into the bank on 26th March, 2016 is not yet credited in the passbook.

(iv) She had also received a cheque of ₹ 500 which although entered by her in the bank column of cash book, was omitted to be paid into the bank.

(v) On 30th March, 2016 a cheque of ₹ 1,570 received by her was paid into bank but the same was omitted to be entered in the cash book.

(vi) There was a credit of ₹ 150 for interest on current account and a debit of ₹ 25 for bank charges.

Draw up a bank reconciliation statement.

Sol.

Bank Reconciliation Statement
as on 31st March, 2016

Particulars	Plus (₹)	Minus (₹)
Credit/Favourable Balance as per the Passbook	15,000	
Add Cheque deposited but not yet credited	2,200	
Cheque received but omitted to be deposited into bank	500	
Bank charges	25	
Less Cheques issued but not presented for payment (8,000 – 3,200)		4,800
Cheque received was paid into bank but not entered in the cash book		1,570
Interest credited on current account		150
Debit/Favourable Balance as per Cash Book		11,205
	17,725	17,725

ILLUSTRATION |8| (*When debit balance/overdraft as per passbook is given*)

From the following information supplied by Sanjay, prepare his bank reconciliation statement as on 31st December, 2016.

		Amt (₹)
(i)	Bank overdraft as per passbook	16,500
(ii)	Cheques issued but not presented for payment	8,750
(iii)	Cheques deposited with the bank but not collected	10,500
(iv)	Cheques recorded in the cash book but not sent to the bank for collection	2,000
(v)	Payment received from customers directly by the bank	3,500
(vi)	Bank charges debited in the passbook	200
(vii)	Premium on life policy of Sanjay paid by the bank on standing advice	1,980
(viii)	A bill for ₹ 3,000 (discounted with the bank in November), dishonoured on 31st December, 2016 and noting charges paid by the bank	100

Sol.

Bank Reconciliation Statement
as on 31st December, 2016

Particulars	Plus (₹)	Minus (₹)
Overdraft/Debit/Unfavourable Balance as per Passbook		16,500
Add Cheques deposited with the bank but not yet collected	10,500	
Cheques recorded in the cash book but not sent to the bank for collection	2,000	
Bank charges debited in the passbook	200	
Premium on life policy paid by the bank	1,980	
Dishonoured bill (including noting charges) (3,000 + 100)	3,100	
Less Cheques issued but not yet presented for payment		8,750
Payments received from customers directly by the bank		3,500
Overdraft/Credit/Unfavourable Balance as per Cash Book	10,970	
	28,750	28,750

ILLUSTRATION |9| On 31st January, 2016 the passbook of Shri ML Gupta shows a debit balance of ₹ 41,000. Prepare a bank reconciliation statement from the following particulars

(i) Cheques amounting to ₹ 15,600 were drawn on 27th January, 2016. Out of which cheques for ₹ 11,000 were encashed upto 31st January, 2016.
(ii) A wrong debit of ₹ 800 has been given by the bank in the passbook.
(iii) A cheque for ₹ 200 was credited in the passbook but was not recorded in the cash book.
(iv) Cheques amounting to ₹ 21,000 were deposited for collection. But out of these, cheques for ₹ 7,400 have been credited in the passbook on 5th February, 2016.
(v) A cheque for ₹ 1,000 was returned dishonoured by the bank and was debited in the passbook only.
(vi) Interest on overdraft and bank charges amounted to ₹ 100 were not entered in the cash book.
(vii) A cheque of ₹ 500 debited in the cash book was omitted to be banked.

Sol.

Bank Reconciliation Statement
as on 31st January, 2016

Particulars	Plus (₹)	Minus (₹)
Overdraft/Debit/Unfavourable Balance as per Passbook		41,000
Add Wrong debit given by bank in the passbook	800	
Cheques deposited but not credited upto January, 2016	7,400	
Cheque deposited but dishonoured	1,000	
Interest on overdraft and bank charges charged by bank	100	
Cheque debited in the cash book but omitted to be banked	500	
Less Cheques drawn but not encashed upto 31st January, 2016 (15,600 – 11,000)		4,600
Cheque credited in the pass book but not recorded in the cash book		200
Overdraft/Credit/Unfavourable Balance as per Cash Book	36,000	
	45,800	45,800

ILLUSTRATION |10| The following particulars relate to the business of Varun on 31st March, 2016.

	Amt (₹)
(i) Cheques issued but not presented for payment	34,500
(ii) Cheques paid into the bank but not yet collected	7,500
(iii) Interest credited by the bank but not entered in the cash book	1,650
(iv) Bank charges debited in the pass book but not entered in the cash book	105
(v) Credit balance as shown by the pass book	1,06,590
(vi) Debit balance as shown by the cash book	78,045

Prepare (a) Statement reconcillng the bank balance as per cash book with that shown by the bank pass book as on 31st March, 2016. (b) Statement reconciling the bank balance as per pass book with that shown by the cash book as on 31st March, 2016.

Sol. *(a)*

Bank Reconciliation Statement
as on 31st March, 2016

Particulars	Plus (₹)	Minus (₹)
Debit/Favourable Balance as per Cash Book	78,045	
Add Cheques issued but not presented for payment	34,500	
Interest credited in the pass book	1,650	
Less Cheques paid to the bank but not yet cleared		7,500
Bank charges debited in pass book		105
Credit/Favourable Balance as per Passbook		1,06,590
	1,14,195	1,14,195

(b)

Bank Reconciliation Statement
as on 31st March, 2016

Particulars	Plus (₹)	Minus (₹)
Credit/Favourable Balance as per Passbook	1,06,590	
Add Cheques paid to the bank but not yet cleared	7,500	
Bank charges debited in the pass book	105	
Less Cheques issued but not presented for payment		34,500
Interest credited in the pass book		1,650
Debit/Favourable Balance as per Cash Book		78,045
	1,14,195	1,14,195

A summarised view of transactions related to BRS

Items	Balance as per		Overdraft as per	
	Cash Book	Passbook	Cash Book	Passbook
1. Cheques issued but not yet presented for payment	+	−	−	+
2. Cheques etc. sent to the bank for collection but not yet collected	−	+	+	−
3. Interest allowed by the bank but not written in the cash book	+	−	−	+
4. Bank charges and interest on overdraft charged by the bank but not written in the cash book	−	+	+	−
5. Payment received by bank but not written in the cash book	+	−	−	+
6. Payments made by the bank but not written in the cash book	−	+	+	−
7. Money directly deposited by a customer in our bank account	+	−	−	+
8. Cheques etc. sent to the bank for collection but dishonoured	−	+	+	−
9. Cheques etc. debited in the cash book but not sent to the bank	−	+	+	−
10. Cheques issued and dishonoured but no entry made in cash book for dishonour	+	−	−	+
11. Any wrong entry in debit side of the passbook	−	+	+	−
12. Any wrong entry in credit side of the passbook	+	−	−	+
13. Interest or dividend collected by bank from investment	+	−	−	+
14. Cheque deposited into bank but not written in cash book	+	−	−	+

CHAPTER PRACTICE

OBJECTIVE TYPE Questions

Multiple Choice Questions

1 A bank reconciliation statement is prepared by **NCERT**

(a) creditors (b) bank
(c) account holder in bank (d) debtors

Ans (c) account holder in bank

2 A bank reconciliation statement is prepared with the balance of **NCERT**

(a) passbook (b) cashbook
(c) Both (a) and (b) (d) None of these

Ans (c) Both (a) and (b)

3 Passbook is a copy of **NCERT**

(a) customer account
(b) bank column of cash book
(c) cash column of cash book
(d) receipts and payments

Ans (a) customer account

4 In case when balance of cash book is given, first item in bank reconciliation statement will be balance as per

(a) cash (b) bank
(c) bank book (d) cash book

Ans (d) When cash book balance is given, then starting point in the bank reconciliation statement is balance which is given as per cash book and that is to be shown on the plus side when dealing with favourable balances.

5 In which approach, balance as per cash book or balance as per passbook is taken as starting item?

(a) In case of with adjusting cash book
(b) In case of after adjusting cash book
(c) In case of without adjusting cash book
(d) None of the above

Ans (c) In case of without adjusting cash book

6 A book reconciliation statement is mainly prepared for **NCERT**

(a) reconcile the cash balance of cash book
(b) reconcile the difference between bank balance shown by cash book and bank passbook
(c) Both (a) and (b)
(d) None of the above

Ans (b) reconcile the difference between bank balance shown by cash book and bank passbook

7 There are various errors committed by the bank, while recording entries. Which of the following is an example of error?

(a) Omission of recording transaction
(b) Statement printout error
(c) Less data error
(d) None of the above

Ans (a) Omission of recording transaction

8 Cheque deposited by firm is recorded in the books and bank records when the cheque has been cleared. Which kind of gap is that?

(a) Recording of transaction gap
(b) Firm and bank gap
(c) Timing gap
(d) Receipt and payment gap

Ans (c) Timing gap

9 Unfavourable bank balance means **NCERT**

(a) credit balance in passbook
(b) credit balance in cash book
(c) debit balance in cash book
(d) None of the above

Ans (b) credit balance in cash book

10 Favourable bank balance means **NCERT**

(a) credit balance in cash book
(b) credit balance in passbook
(c) debit balance in cash book
(d) Both (b) and (c)

Ans (d) Both (b) and (c)

11 A cheque is deposited by a firm but cheque got dishonoured due to insufficient balance in firm's account. What will be the reason for variance between firm and bank?

(a) Cheque entry in bank but not in firm
(b) Cheque entry in firm but not in bank
(c) Cheque entry in firm and bank
(d) No variance will be there

Ans (b) There will be a variance because when cheque is deposited by firm, then firm made an entry into the cash book but cheque got dishonoured and no entry is entered in the bank. Hence, there will be a variance in the cash and bank book.

12 An auto debit transaction is made by bank for which firm has given approval in advance. It is causing a variance between cash book and bank book. What should be the reason for the variance?

(a) Transaction in bank but not in firm
(b) Transaction in firm but not in bank
(c) Transaction in firm and in bank
(d) Transaction not in firm and not in bank

Ans (a) A transaction auto debited on behalf of customer will have a variance between cash book and passbook because bank recorded the transaction but firm will record the same when it will compare with bank statement. Hence, there will be a variance.

13 M/s Suresh & Sons is preparing bank reconciliation statement. Debit balance as per cash book was ₹ 3,72,000. One cheque deposited in bank but not collected by bank for ₹ 15,400. ₹ 5,000 received as dividend (no entry in cash book). What will be the balance as per passbook?

(a) ₹ 3,72,000 (b) ₹3,77,000
(c) ₹ 3,92,400 (d) ₹3,61,600

Ans (d)

Particulars	Plus (₹)	Minus (₹)
Debit balance as per cash book	3,72,000	
(+) Dividend received (not in cash book)	5,000	
(–) Cheque deposited into bank but not collected by bank		15,400
Credit balance as per passbook		3,61,600
	3,77,000	3,77,000

14 Kumar finds that the bank balance by his cash book on 31st December, 2021 is ₹ 90,600 (credit) but the passbook shows difference due to the following reason

A cheque (post dated) for ₹ 1,000 has been debited in bank column of cash book but not presented for payment. Cheque totalling ₹ 1,500 deposited in bank yet not collected. What will be the balance as per passbook?

(a) ₹ 93,580 (b) ₹ 93,100
(c) ₹ 88,100 (d) ₹ 90,100

Ans (b)

Particulars	Plus (₹)	Minus (₹)
Credit balance as per cash book		90,600
(–) Cheque posted in debit column of cash book not presented for payment		1,000
(–) Cheque deposit in bank for collection but not collected		1,500
Debit balance as per passbook	93,100	
	93,100	93,100

Fill in the Blanks

15 Bank Pass book is given by .... to its ....

Ans bank, customer

16 Cheque issued but not presented for payment will .... the balance of pass book

Ans not reduce

17 Debit balance of pass book refers to ....

Ans bank overdraft

18 BRS helps the management to keep a ...., which have been sent to the bank for collection.

Ans track of cheques

State True or False

19 Bank statement is a copy of the customer's account in the books of a bank.

Ans True

20 If the starting point is the debit balance as per cash book, then it should be entered in the minus column.

Ans False. If the starting point is the debit balance as per cash book, then it should be entered in the plus column.

21 If the starting point is the credit balance as per passbook, then it should be entered in the plus column.

Ans True

22 Errors like omission or wrong recording of transactions relating to cheques deposited and wrong totalling, etc are committed by the bank while posting entries in the passbook.

Ans True

Match the Following

23

	Column I		*Column II*
1.	Pass book is a copy of	(a)	Bank Overdraft
2.	Credit balance of cash book shows	(b)	Customer's A/c
3.	Credit balance of pass book shows	(c)	Negative balance
4.	Debit balance of pass book means	(d)	Favourable balance

Ans 1-(b), 2-(c), 3-(d), 4-(a)

VERY SHORT ANSWER Type Questions

24 By whom is the bank statement prepared?

Ans It is prepared by the bank.

25 State whether bank reconciliation statement is a statement or an account.

Ans Bank reconciliation statement is a statement which reconciles the balance as per cash book with the balance as per pass book, by showing all the causes of difference between the two.

26 State the causes of difference occurred due to time lag. **NCERT**

Ans *The causes of difference occurred due to time lag are*

(*i*) Cheques issued by the bank but not yet presented for payment.

(*ii*) Cheques paid into the bank but not yet collected.

27 What is a bank overdraft? **NCERT**

Ans When a firm withdraws more than its deposits from the bank, it is bank overdraft.

28 Bank reconciliation statement is prepared only once *i.e.*, at the end of the year? Comment.

Ans No, bank reconciliation can be prepared at any time of the year *e.g.*, every month or every quarter or half yearly or yearly.

29 Name two items which are written in minus column while starting with credit balance of passbook.

Ans (*i*) Interest and dividend collected by the bank.

(*ii*) Cheques issued but not yet presented for payment.

30 In which column (Plus or Minus) you will write the following while preparing bank reconciliation statement from the credit balance of cash book.

(i) Cheques paid into the bank but not collected.

(ii) Interest on bank overdraft.

Ans (*i*) Minus (*ii*) Minus

31 Which account is credited in addition to debit to bank account when a customer directly deposits an amount in the bank.

Ans Debtor's personal account will be credited.

32 Is bank reconciliation statement, a part of double entry system?

Ans No, it is not a part of double entry system. It is a method to reconcile the balances.

33 When bank column of a cash book shows a debit balance, what does it mean?

Ans It means balance lying with the bank or the deposits made by the firm are more than its withdrawals.

SHORT ANSWER Type Questions

34 State the reasons when the cash book balance will be higher than the passbook balance.

Ans *The reasons when cash book balance will be higher than the passbook balance are*

(*i*) Cheques paid into the bank but not yet collected.

(*ii*) Direct debits made by the bank on behalf of the customers.

(*iii*) Direct payment made by the bank on behalf of the customers.

(*iv*) Cheques deposited/bill discounted dishonoured.

35 Briefly explain the term favourable balance as per cash book. **NCERT**

Ans The favourable balance as per cash book means, balance of deposits held at the bank. It is also known as debit balance as per the cash book.

Such a balance will be a credit balance as per passbook. This type of balance exist when the deposits made by the firm are more than its withdrawals.

36 Briefly explain the statement 'wrongly debited by the bank' with the help of an example. **NCERT**

Ans Amount wrongly debited by the bank implies a situation when the bank wrongly debits a passbook. *For example* a firm issued a cheque of ₹ 1,500 to its creditor and it is presented for payment and paid by the bank but in place of ₹ 1,500 bank debited it wrongly by ₹ 15,000.

The above error may be opposite too but in every situation, the balance of cash book and passbook will not tally. The term used for it will be wrongly debited by the bank. It generally happens at the time of posting the transaction.

LONG ANSWER Type Questions

37 What is bank reconciliation statement? Why is it prepared? **NCERT**

Or

State the need for the preparation of bank reconciliation statement. **NCERT**

Ans Bank reconciliation statement is a statement which is prepared mainly to reconcile (tally) the difference between the bank balance as shown by the cash book and **bank passbook**.

In day to day affairs, an individual or organisation makes numerous transactions through bank. Along with the copy of bank statement (*i.e.*, the passbook), an individual or organisation needs to maintain a separate book (cash book) for recording the banking transactions.

Bank reconciliation statement is important for many reasons.

They are listed as below

(*i*) It helps in locating any error, that may have been committed either in the cash book or in the passbook.

(*ii*) It helps in bringing out the unnecessary delay in the collection of cheques by the bank.

(*iii*) Misappropriation of funds are avoided by regular periodic reconciliation.

(*iv*) The customer is assured of the correctness of the bank balance shown by the passbook, by preparing a bank reconciliation statement.

(*v*) It helps the management to keep a track of cheques, which have been sent to the bank for collection.

38 Explain the reasons where the balance shown by the passbook does not agree with the balance as shown by the bank column of the cash book. **NCERT**

Ans *The reasons where the balance shown by the pass book does not agree with the balance as shown by the bank column of the cash book are as follows*

(*i*) **Differences Due to Timing on Recording Any Transaction** When a comparison is made between the balance of the cash book with the balance of the bank passbook, there is often a difference which is caused due to the time gap in recording the transactions relating either to payments or receipts. *The transactions affecting time gap includes*

(*a*) Cheques issued by the bank but not yet presented for payment.

(*b*) Cheques paid/deposited into the bank but not yet collected.

(*ii*) **Transactions Recorded by the Bank** There are transactions, which are recorded by the bank and are not known to the customer/account holder.

The account holder comes to know about such transactions after receiving the bank passbook. *Such transactions can take the following forms*

(*a*) Direct debits made by the bank on behalf of the customer.

(*b*) Amounts directly deposited in the bank account by the customer.

(*c*) Interest and dividend collected by the bank.

(*d*) Direct payments made by the bank on behalf of the customers.

(*e*) Interest credited by the bank but not recorded in the cash book.

(f) Cheque deposited/bills discounted dishonoured.

(*iii*) **Differences Caused by Errors** Sometimes, there may be a difference between the balance as per cash book and the balance as per passbook on account of an error on the part of the bank or an error in the cash book of the business.

(*a*) Errors committed in recording transactions by the firm.

(*b*) Errors committed in recording transactions by the bank.

NUMERICAL Questions

1 The balance (debit) at bank in Rahul's cash book on 30th April, 2016 is ₹ 37,380. However a cheque for ₹ 43,410 received from Mahesh and a cheque for ₹ 5,220 paid to Aman appear in the cash book, but not on the bank statement. Also, bank charges of ₹ 13,500 have not been entered in the cash book. What will be the balance as per pass book?

Ans Debit/Unfavourable Balance as per Passbook = ₹ 14,310

2 The cash book of Rahul shows ₹ 16,728 as the balance at bank as on 31st December, 2016 but you find that this does not agree with the balance as per the bank passbook. On scrutiny, you find the following discrepancies

(*i*) On 15th December, the payments side of the cash book was undercast by ₹ 200.

(*ii*) A cheque for ₹ 262 issued on 25th December, was recorded in the cash column.

(*iii*) One deposit of ₹ 300 in the bank was recorded in the cash book as if there is no bank column therein.

(*iv*) On 18th December, the debit balance of ₹ 3,052 on the previous day, was brought forward as a credit balance.

(*v*) Of the total cheques amounting to ₹ 23,028 drawn in the last week of December, cheques aggregating ₹ 15,630 were encashed in December.

(*vi*) Dividends of ₹ 500 collected by the bank and subscription of ₹ 200 paid by it were not recorded in the cash book.

(*vii*) One out-going cheque of ₹ 700 was recorded twice in the cash book.

Prepare a bank reconciliation statement as on 31st December, 2016.

Ans Credit/Favourable Balance as per Passbook = ₹ 31,068

3 From the following particulars, prepare a bank reconciliation statement as on 31st March, 2021.

(*i*) Bank balance as per cash book is ₹ 1,00,000.

(ii) A cheque for ₹ 10,000 deposited but not recorded in the cash book. Bank has collected and credited this cheque.

(iii) A bank deposit of ₹ 2,000 was recorded in the cash book as if there is no bank column therein.

(iv) A cheque issued for ₹ 2,500 was recorded as ₹ 2,050 in the cash column. Bank has made the payment of this cheque.

(v) The debit balance of ₹ 15,000 as on the previous day was brought forward as a credit balance.

(vi) The payment side of the cash book (bank column) was undercast by ₹ 1,000.

(vii) A cash discount allowed of ₹ 1,120 was recorded as ₹ 1,210 in the bank column.

(viii) A cheque of ₹ 5,000 received from a debtor was recorded in the cash book but not deposited in the bank for collection.

(ix) One outgoing cheque of ₹ 3,000 was recorded twice in the cash book.

Ans Credit/Favourable Balance as per Passbook = ₹ 1,35,290

4 Prepare a bank reconciliation statement from the following particulars on 30th June, 2016, when bank statement showed a favourable balance of ₹ 9,214.

(i) On 29th June, 2016 the bank credited the sum of ₹ 1,650 in error.

(ii) Certain cheques, valued at ₹ 4,500 issued before 29th June, 2016 were not cleared.

(iii) A hire purchase payment of ₹ 950, made by a standing order was not entered in the cash book.

(iv) A cheque of ₹ 600 received, deposited and credited by bank, was accounted as a receipt in the cash column of the cash book.

(v) Other cheques for ₹ 8,500 were deposited in June but cheques for ₹ 6,000 only were cleared by the bankers.

Ans Debit/Favourable Balance as per Cash Book = ₹ 5,914

5 On 30th June, 2016, the cash book of Galaxy Ltd, showed a balance of ₹ 400 at bank. They had sent cheques amounting to ₹ 2,000 to the bank before 30th June but it appears from the pass book that cheques worth only ₹ 800 had been credited before that date. Similarly, out of cheques of ₹ 1,000 issued during the month of June, cheques for ₹ 50 were presented and paid in July.

The passbook also showed the following payments

(i) ₹ 64 as premium on the life policy according to standing instructions.

(ii) ₹ 400 against a pro-note, as per instructions.

The passbook showed that the bank had collected ₹ 120 as interest on government securities. The bank had charged interest ₹ 10 and bank charges ₹ 4. There was no entry in the cash book for the payments, interest, etc. Prepare the bank reconciliation statement as on 30th June, 2016.

Ans Overdraft Balance as per Passbook = ₹ 1,108.

6 Overdraft as per cash book is ₹ 10,000. Cheques deposited but not credited ₹ 2,500. Cheques issued but not encashed ₹ 3,500. What is the balance as per passbook?

Ans Debit/Unfavourable balance as per Pass Book = ₹ 9,000

7 The credit balance as per cash book is ₹ 1,500. Cheques for ₹ 400 were deposited but were not collected. The cheques issued but not presented were of ₹ 100, ₹ 125 and ₹50. What will be the balance as per passbook?

Ans Debit/Unfovourable Balance as per Passbook = ₹ 1,625

8 Prepare a bank reconciliation statement.

(i) Overdraft shown as per cash book on 31st December, 2016, ₹ 30,000.

(ii) Bank charges for the above period also debited in the passbook, ₹ 300.

(iii) Interest on overdraft for six months ending 31st December, 2016, ₹ 1,140 debited in the passbook.

(iv) Cheques issued but not encashed prior to 31st December, 2016 amounted to ₹ 6,450.

(v) Interest on investment collected by the bank and credited in the passbook, ₹ 1,800.

(vi) Cheques paid into bank but not cleared before 31st December, 2016 were ₹ 3,300.

Ans Balance as per Passbook (Debit) = ₹ 26,490

9 On 31st December, 2016, the cash book of Rohan showed an overdraft of ₹ 5,600. From the following particulars make out a bank reconciliation statement.

(i) Cheques drawn but not cashed before 31st December, 2016 amounted to ₹ 3,946.

(ii) Cheques paid into the bank but not credited before 31st December, 2016 amounted to ₹ 4,891.

(iii) A bill receivable for ₹ 520 previously discounted with the bank had been dishonoured and bank charges debited in the passbook amounted to ₹ 55.

(*iv*) Debit is made in the passbook for ₹ 120 on account of interest on overdraft.

(*v*) The bank has collected interest on investment and credited ₹ 760 in the passbook.

Ans Overdraft/Debit/Unfavourable Balance as per Passbook = ₹ 6,480

10 The following facts relate to the business of Roshan who requires you to reconcile his cash book with the passbook balance.

	Amt (₹)
Balance as per cash book (Credit)	2,800
Unpresented cheques	3,440
Uncredited cheques	2,260

Additional Information

(*i*) The debit side of the cash book (bank column) has been undercast by ₹ 500.

(*ii*) A cheque of ₹ 200 paid to a creditor has been entered by mistake in the cash column.

(*iii*) Bank charges ₹ 80 have not been entered in the cash book.

Ans Debit/Overdraft/Unfavourable Balance as per Passbook = ₹ 1,400

11 The bank account of Noddy was balanced on 31st March, 2016. It showed an overdraft of ₹ 2,000. The bank statement of Noddy showed a credit balance of ₹ 30,700. Prepare a bank reconciliation statement taking the following into account.

(*i*) Cheques issued but not presented for payment till 31st March, ₹ 4,800.

(*ii*) Cheques deposited but not collected by bank till 31st March, ₹ 8,000.

(*iii*) Interest on term loan ₹ 4,000 debited by bank on 31st March but not accounted in Noddy's books.

(*iv*) Bank charge ₹ 100 was debited by bank during March but not accounted in the books of Noddy on 4th April.

(*v*) An amount of ₹ 40,000 representing collection of Noddy's cheque was wrongly credited to the account of Noddy by the bank in their bank statement.

Ans Balance (Credit) as per Passbook = ₹ 30,700

12 From the following particulars, prepare the bank reconciliation statement of Arun as on 31st March, 2016.

(*i*) Balance as per passbook is ₹ 10,000.

(*ii*) Bank collected a cheque of ₹ 500 on behalf of Arun but wrongly credited it to Varun account (another customer).

(*iii*) Bank recorded a cash deposit of ₹ 1,589 as ₹ 1,598.

(*iv*) Withdrawal column of the passbook undercast by ₹ 100.

(*v*) The credit balance of ₹ 1,500 on page 5 of the passbook was recorded on page 6 as the debit balance.

(*vi*) The payment of a cheque of ₹ 350 was recorded twice in the passbook.

(*vii*) The passbook showed a credit for a cheque of ₹ 1,000 deposited by Shri Kishan (another customer of the bank).

Ans Debit/Favourable Balance as per Cash Book = ₹ 12,741

13 Prepare a bank reconciliation statement in the books of Bharti as on 31st January, 2016

(*i*) Balance as per passbook as on 31st January, 2016 was ₹ 62,500.

(*ii*) Cheque of ₹ 17,800 was issued by her on 28th January, 2016 but this was not presented for payment till 31st January, 2016.

(*iii*) A cheque of ₹ 4,000 issued to Mr Rahim, was taken in the cash column.

(*iv*) A cheque of ₹ 15,000 was paid into bank but was omitted to be entered in the cash book.

(*v*) The bank has charged ₹ 55 as its commission and has allowed interest ₹ 50.

Ans Debit Balance as per Cash Book = ₹ 33,705

14 (*i*) On 31st March, 2016 bank passbook of Mohan showed a balance on ₹ 15,000 to his credit.

(*ii*) Before that date, he had issued cheques amounting to ₹ 8,000, of which cheques amounting to ₹ 3,200 have so far been presented for payment.

(*iii*) A cheque of ₹ 2,200 paid by him into the bank on 26th March, is not yet credited in the passbook.

(*iv*) He had also received a cheque for ₹ 500 which although entered by him in the bank column of cash book, was omitted to be paid into the bank.

(*v*) On 30th March, a cheque for ₹ 1,570 received by him was paid into the bank but the same was omitted to be entered in the cash book.

(*vi*) There was a credit of ₹ 150 for interest on current account and a debit of ₹ 25 for bank charges.

Draw up a reconciliation statement.

Ans Balance (Debit) as per Cash Book = ₹ 11, 205

15 Find out bank balance as per cash book from the following particulars

(*i*) Overdraft as per passbook ₹ 5,000.

(*ii*) Cheques deposited into bank but not credited ₹ 2,000.

Ans Credit/Unfavourable Balance as per Cashbook ₹ 3,000

16 On 31st March, 2016 passbook of Shri Rajendra shows a debit balance of ₹ 10,000. From the following, prepare a bank reconciliation statement.

(*i*) Cheques amounting to ₹ 8,000 drawn on 25th March, 2016 of which cheques of ₹ 5,000 were encashed on 2nd April, 2016.

(*ii*) Cheques paid into the bank for collection ₹ 5,000 but cheques of ₹ 2,200 could only be collected in March, 2016.

(*iii*) Bank charges ₹ 25 and dividend of ₹ 350 on investments collected by the bank could not be shown in the cash book.

(*iv*) A bill of ₹ 10,000 was retired by the bank under rebate of ₹ 150 but the full amount was credited in the cash book.

(*v*) The payment of a cheque for ₹ 550 was recorded twice in the passbook.

(*vi*) Withdrawal column of the passbook undercast by ₹ 200.

(*vii*) ₹ 500 in respect of dishonoured cheque were entered in the passbook but not in the cash book.

Ans Overdraft/Credit/Unfavourable Balance as per Cash Book = ₹ 11,825

17 Following information has been given by Rajendra. Prepare a bank reconciliation statement as on 31st December, 2015, showing balance as per cash book.

(*i*) Debit balance shown by the passbook ₹ 17,800.

(*ii*) Cheques of ₹ 21,600 were issued in the last week of December but only cheques of ₹ 14,800 were presented for payment.

(*iii*) Cheques of ₹ 10,750 were presented to the bank. Out of them, a cheque of ₹ 4,200 was credited in the first week of January, 2016.

(*iv*) A cheque of ₹ 1,200 was debited in the cash book but was not presented in the bank.

(*v*) Insurance premium paid by the bank ₹ 1,450.

(*vi*) A bills of exchange of ₹ 6,200 which was discounted with the bank was returned dishonoured but no entry was made in the cash book.

(*vii*) Bank charges and interest charged by the bank are ₹ 350.

Ans Credit/Overdraft/Unfavourable Balance as per Cash Book = ₹ 11,200

18 On checking the bank passbook it was found that it showed an overdraft of ₹ 5,220 as on 31st December, 2016, while as per ledger it was different to bank debit. The following differences were noted

(*i*) Cheques deposited but not yet credited by bank ₹ 6,000.

(*ii*) Cheques dishonoured and debited by bank but not given effect to it in the ledger ₹ 800.

(*iii*) Bank charges debited by bank but debit memo not received from bank ₹ 50.

(*iv*) Interest on overdraft excess credited in the ledger ₹ 200.

(*v*) Wrongly credited by bank to account, deposit of some other party ₹ 900.

(*vi*) Cheques issued but not presented for payment ₹ 400.

Ans Debit Balance as per Cash Book = ₹ 130

19 On 31st December, 2016, the bank passbook of Taneja & Co showed an overdraft of ₹ 7,700. On the basis of the following particulars, prepare a bank reconciliation statement.

(*i*) Cheques issued before 31st December, 2016 but not yet presented for payment amounted to ₹ 3,500.

(*ii*) Cheques paid into the bank but a cheque amounting to ₹ 2,600, has not been collected yet.

(*iii*) Interest on loan amounting to ₹ 554 directly debited by the bank did not appear in the cash book.

(*iv*) ₹ 4,800 directly deposited by the customer entered in the passbook but not in cash book.

Ans Balance (Credit) as per Cash Book = ₹ 12,846

20 Prepare a bank reconciliation statement of Mr Careless on 31st December, 2016

(*i*) The payment of cheques for ₹ 1,100 was recorded twice in the passbook.

(*ii*) Withdrawal column of the passbook undercast by ₹ 400.

(*iii*) A cheque of ₹ 400 has been debited in the bank column of the cash book but it was not sent to bank at all.

(*iv*) A cheque of ₹ 600 debited to bank account of the passbook has been omitted to be recorded in cash book.

(*v*) ₹ 1,000 in respect of dishonoured cheque were entered in the passbook but not in the cash book.
Overdraft as per passbook is ₹ 40,000.

Ans Balance as per Cash Book (Credit) = ₹ 37,300

08

After studying this chapter, students will be able to understand the meaning, features, causes and need of depreciation. Students will further learn the factors affecting the amount of depreciation, methods of calculating depreciation–straight line and written down value method, accounting treatment for recording depreciation. They will further learn the meaning, features, objectives, types and accounting treatment of provisions and reserves.

DEPRECIATION, PROVISIONS AND RESERVES

|TOPIC 1|

Introduction to Depreciation

The word depreciation has been derived from the Latin word 'Depretium' which means 'decline in price or value'. Therefore, **depreciation means decline in the value of fixed assets on account of usage and various other factors such as passage of time or obsolescence.** Fixed assets such as machinery, furniture, etc are used in business operations. These assets lose their value due to constant use. The loss in value of these assets is termed as depreciation.

CHAPTER CHECKLIST

- Introduction to Depreciation
- Accounting Treatment of Depreciation
- Creating Provision for Depreciation Account/ Accumulated Depreciation Account
- Provisions and Reserves

Definitions of Depreciation

According to *Institute of Cost and Management Accounting, London* (ICMA), "Depreciation is the diminution in intrinsic value of the asset due to use and/or lapse of time".

According to *Accounting Standard-6 Issued by the Institute of Chartered Accountants of India* (ICAI), "Depreciation is a measure of the wearing out, consumption or other loss of value of **depreciable asset** arising from use, effluxion of time or obsolescence through technology and market changes. Depreciation is allocated so as to charge a fair proportion of the **depreciable amount** in each accounting period during the expected useful life of the asset. Depreciation includes amortisation of assets whose **useful life** is pre-determined."

Note *Depreciable asset is the fixed asset which is loosing its value on account of use.*

Other Terms related to Depreciation

(i) **Depletion**

The term depletion is used in relation to natural resources or wasting assets such as mines, oil wells, timber, trees etc. As the resource is extracted or removed, its asset value will be reduced or exhausted. This reduction in value or expiration of cost of asset resulting from production is called depletion.

(ii) **Amortisation**

Amortisation refers to the process of writing-off the cost of an intangible asset over a future period covering its expected useful life. This applies to patents, goodwill, copyrights etc.

Features/Characteristics of Depreciation

(*i*) Depreciation is a decline in the value of fixed assets (except land).

(*ii*) Depreciation is a continuing process.

(*iii*) Depreciation is a non-cash expense.

(*iv*) Depreciation is an expired cost, *i.e.,* cost which has already been borne, and hence, must be deducted for ascertaining correct profits.

(*v*) Depreciation includes loss of value due to effluxion of time, usage or obsolescence.

(*vi*) The term depreciation is used only for tangible fixed assets.

Causes of Depreciation

Various causes of depreciation, are as follows

(*i*) **Constant use** Constant use of asset leads to wear and tear of asset which results in decline in the value of asset.

(*ii*) **Passage of Time** Even if the assets are not put to use, their value decreases due to the expiry or passage of time, especially when the assets are exposed to adverse weather, rains, etc.

(*iii*) **Expiry of Legal Rights** Value of intangible assets like patents, copyrights, trademarks, leases, etc becomes nil after a pre-determined period. Expiry of legal rights is also referred to as **amortisation.**

(*iv*) **Obsolescence** In simple words, obsolescence means 'out of date'. When old asset becomes out dated, then it loses its value. It can be due to

(*a*) Technological changes

(*b*) Change in market demand

(*c*) Improved production methods

(*d*) Legal or other causes

Assets can become obsolete even when they can be physically used.

(*v*) **Depletion of Assets** It is the decrease in the value of natural assets such as mines, oil-wells etc, due to constant extraction of raw materials from them.

(*vi*) **Abnormal Reasons** Assets may lose their value due to abnormal reasons like fire, floods or other natural calamities and also due to accidents.

Need for Depreciation

(*i*) **To Ascertain True Net Profit or Net Loss** Correct profit or loss can be ascertained when all the expenses and losses incurred (for earning revenues) are charged to profit and loss account. Assets are used for earning revenues and their cost is charged in the form of depreciation from profit and loss account.

(*ii*) **Consideration of Tax** Depreciation is allowed as an expense in income tax. Hence, it reduces the tax burden on the firm.

(*iii*) **True and Fair Financial Position** Balance sheet will not show the correct financial position of the business, if depreciation is not provided on assets as the assets will remain overvalued.

(*iv*) **Compliance with the Law** Apart from the tax regulations, it is necessary to charge depreciation to comply with the provisions of the Companies Act.

Factors Affecting the Amount of Depreciation

The determination of depreciation depends on the following parameters

I. **ORIGINAL** (HISTORICAL) **COST OF THE ASSETS**

It includes all the cost incurred on acquisition, installation, freight and transportation, insurance charges, etc upto the point the asset is ready for use.

In case a second hand asset is purchased, it will also include the initial repair cost to put the asset in a workable condition. The given formula is used to calculate the original cost of the assets.

Original Cost = Purchase Price + Freight + Installation Cost

II. **EXPECTED USEFUL LIFE**

Useful life of an asset is the estimated economic or commercial life of an asset. Generally, it is expressed in number of years but can also be expressed in other units. *For example,* number of units of output (in case of mines) or number of working hours.

III. **ESTIMATED NET RESIDUAL VALUE/SCRAP VALUE/SALVAGE VALUE**

It is estimated net selling price of the asset at the end of its useful life. The expenses related to sale of asset should be deducted from the selling price to arrive at net selling price. *For example,* if selling price of an asset after 10 years is ₹ 10,000 but expenses relating to disposal/sale of asset are ₹ 2,000 then net selling price will be ₹ 8,000.

IV. **DEPRECIABLE COST/DEPRECIABLE AMOUNT**

Depreciable cost of an asset is equal to its cost less net scrap value. It is the depreciable cost which is distributed and charged as depreciation expense over the useful life. Formula of depreciable cost is as follows

Amount to be Written-off or Depreciable Cost = Cost of Asset – Residual Scrap Value

Note *It should be noted that the total amount of depreciation charged over the useful life of the asset must be equal to the depreciable cost.*

Methods of Calculating Depreciation

There are several methods of calculating depreciation. Some of them are named below

(*i*) Straight line method
(*ii*) Written down value method
(*iii*) Annuity method
(*iv*) Depreciation fund method
(*v*) Insurance policy method
(*vi*) Sum of years digit method
(*vii*) Double declining method etc.

However as per syllabus, only first two methods have been discussed in subsequent topics.

STRAIGHT LINE METHOD (SLM)

Under this method, a fixed and equal amount in the form of depreciation is charged every year during the life time of the asset. It is called a straight line because if the amount of depreciation and corresponding time period is plotted on a graph, it will result in a straight line parallel to the X-axis.

As the amount of depreciation remains equal from year to year, it is also called as fixed or equal instalment method.

Calculation of the Amount of Depreciation

Depreciation under this method can be calculated in the following two ways

(I) **BY USING FORMULA**

The given formula is used to calculate the amount of depreciation

$$\text{Depreciation} = \frac{\left[\begin{array}{l}\text{Acquisition Cost of Asset} \\ - \text{Estimated Scrap Value / Residual Value}\end{array}\right]}{\text{Estimated Useful Life of the Asset}}$$

Note *The variables used in the above formula are the factors affecting the amount of depreciation. Also, the depreciation so computed relates to the whole year.*

ILLUSTRATION |1| The original cost of the asset is ₹ 2,50,000. The freight and installation charges amounted to ₹ 25,000. The useful life of the asset is 10 years and net residual value is estimated to be ₹ 50,000. Calculate the amount of depreciation to be charged every year under straight line method for the year ended 31st December 2016, in each of the following conditions.

(*i*) When the asset has been purchased on 1st January, 2016.

(*ii*) When the asset has been purchased on 1st April, 2016.

Sol. (*i*) Annual Depreciation Amount

$$= \frac{\text{Acquisition Cost of Asset} - \text{Estimated Net Residual Value}}{\text{Estimated Life of Asset}}$$

$$= \frac{2{,}75{,}000 - 50{,}000}{10} = ₹\ 22{,}500$$

So, if the asset was purchased on 1st, January, 2016, then depreciation charged will be ₹ 22,500.

(*ii*) Annual depreciation = ₹ 22,500

∴ Depreciation for the period from 1st April, 2016 to 31st December, 2016, *i.e.*, for a period of 9 months $= 22{,}500 \times \frac{9}{12} = ₹\ 16{,}875$

(II) **AS A PERCENTAGE OF ORIGINAL COST**

It is computed in the following manner

$$\text{Depreciation} = \text{Cost of Acquisition} \times \frac{\text{Rate of Depreciation}}{100}$$

While calculating depreciation as a percentage of original cost, following points should be kept in mind

(*a*) If the percentage is defined for a year, *e.g.*, 10% per annum. In such a case, the time period for which the asset is being used during the concerned year, should be kept in mind while calculating the depreciation for the year.

(*b*) If the percentage is not defined for a year, *e.g.*, 10%. In such a case, the time period for which the asset is being used during the concerned year has no relevance.

ILLUSTRATION |2| Sudarshan Ltd. purchased a machinery of ₹ 1,00,000 and spent ₹ 10,000 on its installation. The estimated useful life of the asset is 10 years. Calculate depreciation for the year ending 31st March, 2016 in each of the following instances.

(i) Depreciation is to be charged @ 10% per annum and the machinery was purchased on 1st April, 2015.

(ii) Depreciation is to be charged @ 10% per annum and the machinery was purchased on 1st October, 2015.

(iii) Depreciation is to be charged @ 10% and the machinery was purchased on 1st January, 2016.

Sol. (*i*) Depreciation $= 1{,}10{,}000 \times \frac{10}{100} = ₹\ 11{,}000$

Note *Depreciation has been charged for full year.*

(*ii*) Depreciation $= 1{,}10{,}000 \times \frac{10}{100} \times \frac{6}{12} = ₹\ 5500$

Note *Depreciation has been charged for a 6-month period.*

(*iii*) Depreciation $= 1{,}10{,}000 \times \frac{10}{100} = ₹\ 11{,}000$

Note *Time period will not be considered, as depreciation is not defined with reference to a year.*

Calculating Rate of Depreciation

If the annual depreciation amount is given then we can calculate the rate of depreciation with the following formula

Rate of Depreciation

$$= \frac{\text{Annual Depreciation Amount}}{\text{Cost of Asset}} \times 100$$

ILLUSTRATION |3| The cost of acquisition of an asset is ₹ 2,50,000 and the annual depreciation amounts to ₹ 20,000. Calculate the rate of depreciation.

Sol. The rate of depreciation will be calculated as

Rate of Depreciation

$$= \frac{\text{Annual Depreciation Amount}}{\text{Acquisition Cost}} \times 100$$

The annual depreciation amounts to ₹ 20,000.

Thus, the rate of depreciation will be

$$= \frac{₹\ 20{,}000}{₹\ 2{,}50{,}000} \times 100 = 8\%$$

Advantages of Straight Line Method

(*i*) It is a simple method of calculating depreciation.

(*ii*) Assets can be depreciated fully or upto the scrap value over the life of the asset.

(*iii*) Since, the depreciation amount is same every year hence, there is a same effect on the profit and loss account every year.

Limitations of Straight Line Method

(*i*) This method assumes that asset is utilised consistently over the life of asset which is practically not correct in most cases.

(*ii*) This method reduces the book value of an asset to zero although the asset may still be in existence.

(*iii*) If some additions are made to the asset, fresh calculations are to be made.

(*iv*) As the depreciation remains equal year after year, the repair and renewals goes on increasing, as the asset turns older.

(*v*) It does not take into account, the interest on investment in fixed assets.

(*vi*) Determination of scrap value on a future date is practically very difficult.

Suitability This method of depreciation is suitable for assets in which the repair charges are less, the possibility of obsolescence is less and for those assets whose useful life can be predicted accurately.

WRITTEN DOWN VALUE METHOD (WDV)

Under this method, depreciation is charged at a fixed rate on the book value (Written Down Value) of the asset rather than original cost. The amount of depreciation goes on reducing, year after year. As the book value keeps on reducing, it is also known as **reducing balance method or diminishing balance method.** For the first year, the book value is the cost of acquisition. For subsequent years, the book value or the Written Down Value is the value of the asset subsequent to charging depreciation.

For example, if an asset is purchased for ₹ 1,00,000 and depreciation is to be charged @ 10% on WDV method, then depreciation for first year will be ₹ 10,000 (1,00,000 × 10%), and for the second year the depreciation charged will be ₹ 9,000 [(1,00,000 – 10,000) × 10%].

Calculation of the Amount of Depreciation

Under the Written Down Value method, the annual depreciation can be calculated by using the given formula.

Annual Depreciation

$$= \text{Book Value of the Asset} \times \frac{\text{Rate of Depreciation}}{100}$$

The following points should be kept in mind while calculating depreciation by this method

(*i*) The book value of the asset and not the original cost should be considered for the purpose of calculating depreciation.

Book Value = Original Cost – Depreciation

(*ii*) If the percentage is defined for a year, *e.g.* 10% per annum, then the time period for which the asset is being used in the concerned year, should be kept in mind while calculating the annual depreciation.

(*iii*) If the percentage is not defined for a year, *e.g.* 10%, then the time period for which the asset is used during the concerned year has no relevance.

ILLUSTRATION |4| Original cost of an asset is ₹ 2,00,000 and depreciation is charged at written down value. Calculate the amount of depreciation for the next 4 years, if the year ending is 31st December in each of the following conditions

(i) The rate of depreciation is 10% per annum and the asset was purchased on 1st January.

(ii) The rate of depreciation is 10% per annum and the asset was purchased on 1st April.

(iii) The rate of depreciation is 10% and the asset was purchased on 1st October.

Sol. (*i*)

Year	Depreciation Amount	Book Value WDV (Year End)
Ist Year	$2,00,000 \times \frac{10}{100}$ = ₹ 20,000	2,00,000 – 20,000 = ₹ 1,80,000
IInd Year	$1,80,000 \times \frac{10}{100}$ = ₹ 18,000	1,80,000 – 18,000 = ₹ 1,62,000
IIIrd Year	$1,62,000 \times \frac{10}{100}$ = ₹ 16200	1,62,000 – 16200 = ₹ 1,45,800
IVth Year	$1,45,800 \times \frac{10}{100}$ = ₹ 14,580	1,45,800 – 14,580 = ₹ 1,31,220

(*ii*)

Year	Depreciation Amount	Book Value/WDV (Year End)
Ist Year	$2,00,000 \times \frac{10}{100} \times \frac{9}{12}$ = ₹ 15,000	2,00,000 – 15,000 = ₹ 1,85,000
IInd Year	$1,85,000 \times \frac{10}{100}$ = ₹ 18,500	1,85,000 – 18,500 = ₹ 1,66,500
IIIr Year	$1,66,500 \times \frac{10}{100}$ = ₹ 16,650	1,66,500 – 16,650 = ₹ 1,49,850
IVth Year	$1,49,850 \times \frac{10}{100}$ = ₹ 14,985	1,49,850 – 14,985 = ₹ 1,34,865

(*iii*) Depreciation will be the same as calculated in (*i*) because rate of depreciation is not defined with reference to time period.

Calculating Rate of Depreciation

Under the Written Down Value method, the rate of depreciation is computed by using the following formula,

$$R = \left[1 - \sqrt[n]{\frac{S}{C}}\right] \times 100.$$

Where, R = Rate of depreciation

n = Expected useful life

S = Scrap value

C = Cost of an asset

ILLUSTRATION |5| Original cost of machine is ₹ 4,00,000 with a scrap value of ₹ 25,000 after 4 years. Calculate rate of depreciation.

Sol. Rate of Depreciation

$$R = \left[1 - \sqrt[4]{\frac{25,000}{4,00,000}}\right] \times 100$$

$$= \left[1 - \sqrt[4]{\frac{625}{10,000}}\right] \times 100$$

$$= \left[1 - \left(\frac{5^4}{10^4}\right)^{\frac{1}{4}}\right] \times 100$$

$$= \left[1 - \left[\left(\frac{5}{10}\right)^4\right]^{\frac{1}{4}}\right] \times 100$$

$$= \left[1 - \frac{5}{10}\right] \times 100$$

$= 0.5 \times 100 = 50\%$ per annum.

Advantages of Written Down Value Method

(i) It is an approved method of depreciation by income tax authorities.

(ii) Under this method, the asset can never be reduced to zero.

(iii) As a large portion of cost is written-off in earlier years, loss due to obsolescence gets reduced.

Limitations of Written Down Value Method

(i) Even if the asset loses its utility, it appears in the books of accounts.

(ii) It is difficult to calculate the rate of depreciation.

Suitability This method of depreciation is suitable for those assets that have a long life and require more repair with passage of time.

NUMERICAL Questions for Practice

1 A machinery was purchased on 1st January, 2016 for ₹ 3,50,000. Transportation and installation expenses amounted to ₹ 50,000. The scrap value at the end of an estimated life of 19 years in ₹ 20,000. Find the amount of depreciation to be charged under straight line method.

Ans ₹ 20,000

2 On the basis of the information given in Question 1, calculate the amount of depreciation for 2016 if the machinery was purchased on 1st July, 2016. What will be the depreciation charged in subsequent years?

Ans Depreciation for 2016 = ₹ 10,000
Depreciation for subsequent years = ₹ 20,000

3 Sigma Limited purchased a truck on 1st April, 2016 for ₹ 4,50,000. Registration charges amounted to ₹ 25,000. Depreciation is to charged @ 15% per annum on fixed instalment method.

Calculate the amount of depreciation

(i) if Sigma Limited closes its books on 31st March, 2016.

(ii) if Sigma Limited closes its books on 31st December, 2016.

Ans (i) ₹ 71,250 (ii) ₹ 53,437.5

4 Yudhister imported a machinery to pack forzen foods for ₹ 12,00,000 from Germany. ₹ 3,00,000 were spend for transportation and ₹ 1,00,000 custom duty was paid. As per income tax rules, Yudhister decided to charge depreciation as per written down value method. He closes his books on 31st March, every year. Calculate the amount of depreciation to be charged in first two years, if

(i) the rate of depreciation is 15% per annum, and the machine was purchased on 1st April.

(ii) the rate of depreciation is 15% per annum, and the machine was purchased on 1st September.

(iii) the rate of depreciation is 15% and the machine was purchased on 15th July.

Ans (i) Depreciation for Ist year = ₹ 2,40,000
Depreciation for IInd year = ₹ 2,04,000

(ii) Depreciation for Ist year = ₹ 1,40,000
Depreciation for IInd year = ₹ 2,19,000

(iii) Depreciation for Ist year = ₹ 2,40,000
Depreciation for IInd year = ₹ 2,04,000

5 Book value of machine as on 31st March, 2016 is ₹ 2,91,600. This machine was purchased on 1st April, 2013. Depreciation is charged at 10% on written down value method. What is the original cost of machine?

Original Cost = ₹ 4,00,000

Ans

Let the Cost of Machine on 1st April, 2013	100
∴ Depreciation for Ist year (2013-14) =	10
Written down value	90
Depreciation for II year (2014-15)	9
Written down value	81
Depreciation for III year (2015-16)	8.1
Written down value	72.9

When, WDV is 72.9 cost is = ₹ 100

When, WDV is 2,91,600 cost is

$$= ₹ \frac{100}{72.9} \times 2{,}91{,}600$$

= ₹ 4,00,000

|TOPIC 2|
Accounting Treatment of Depreciation

The accounting treatment of depreciation is same under the straight line method and written down value method. Only the amount of depreciation differs.

In the books of account, there are two types of arrangements for recording depreciation of fixed assets. These are

(*i*) Charging depreciation to asset account.

(*ii*) Creating provision for depreciation/accumulated depreciation account.

This topic discusses the first method. The second method is discussed in subsequent topic.

Charging Depreciation to Asset Account

Under this method, every year the value of the asset is reduced with the amount of depreciation. The depreciation, being an expense, is then transferred to profit and loss account.

The following journal entries are passed in this method to record purchase of asset and to provide for depreciation.

Journal Entries

(i) To Record Purchase of Asset	Asset A/c To Cash/Bank A/c (Being the asset purchased)	Dr
(ii) To Provide Depreciation	Depreciation A/c To Asset A/c (Being the depreciation provided)	Dr
(iii) To Transfer Depreciation	Profit and Loss A/c To Depreciation A/c (Being the transfer of depreciation to profit and loss account)	Dr

BALANCE SHEET TREATMENT

Under this method, the fixed asset appear at its net book value/written down value (*i.e.*, cost less depreciation charged till date) on the assets side of balance sheet and not at its cost of acquisition.

Balance Sheet

Liabilities	Amt (₹)	Assets		Amt (₹)
		Asset	...	
		(–) Depreciation	(...)	...

ILLUSTRATION |6| (Straight Line Method, when estimated working life of the asset is given). On 1st July, 2014 Ashok Ltd purchased a machine for ₹ 1,08,000 and spent ₹ 12,000 on its installation. At the time of purchase, it was estimated that the effective commerical life of the machine will be 12 years and after 12 year, its salvage value will be ₹ 12,000.

Pass necessary journal entries and prepare machinery account and depreciation account in the books of Ashok Ltd for first 3 years, if depreciation is written-off according to straight line method. The accounts are closed on 31st December, every year. **NCERT**

Sol.

Date	Particulars		LF	Amt (Dr)	Amt (Cr)
2014 July 1	Machinery A/c To Bank A/c (Being machinery purchased for ₹ 1,08,000 and ₹ 12,000 spent on its installation)	Dr		1,20,000	1,20,000
Dec 31	Depreciation A/c To Machinery A/c (Being depreciation charged to machinery account)	Dr		4500*	4,500
Dec 31	Profit and Loss A/c To Depreciation A/c (Being depreciation transferred to profit and loss account)	Dr		4,500	4,500
2015 Dec 31	Depreciation A/c To Machinery A/c (Being depreciation charged to machinery account)	Dr		9,000	9,000
Dec 31	Profit and Loss A/c To Machinery A/c (Being depreciation transferred to profit and loss account)	Dr		9,000	9,000
2016 Dec 31	Depreciation A/c To Machinery A/c (Being depreciation charged to machinery account)	Dr		9,000	9,000
Dec 31	Profit and Loss A/c To Machinery A/c (Being depreciation transferred profit and loss account)	Dr		9,000	9,000

Dr **Machinery Account** Cr

Date	Particulars	JF	Amt (₹)	Date	Particulars	JF	Amt (₹)
2014				2014			
Jul 1	To Bank A/c (1,08,000 + 12,000)		1,20,000	Dec 31	By Depreciation A/c		4,500*
				Dec 31	By Balance c/d		1,15,500
			1,20,000				1,20,000
2015				2015			
Jan 1	To Balance b/d		1,15,500	Dec 31	By Depreciation A/c		9,000
				Dec 31	By Balance c/d		1,06,500
			1,15,500				1,15,500
2016				2016			
Jan	To Balance b/d		1,06,500	Dec 31	By Depreciation A/c		9,000
				Dec 31	By Balance c/d		97,500
2017			1,06,500				1,06,500
Jan 1	To Balance b/d		97,500				

Dr **Depreciation Account** Cr

Date	Particulars	JF	Amt (₹)	Date	Particulars	JF	Amt (₹)
2014				2014			
Dec 31	To Machinery A/c		4,500	Dec 31	By Profit and Loss A/c		4,500
			4,500				4,500
2015				2015			
Dec 31	To Machinery A/c		9,000	Dec 31	By Profit and Loss A/c		9,000
			9,000				9,000
2016				2016			
Dec 31	To Machinery A/c		9,000	Dec 31	By Profit and Loss A/c		9,000
			9,000				9,000

Working Note

Computation of Annual Amount of Depreciation $= \frac{(1,08,000 + 12,000 - 12,000)}{12} =$ ` 9,000

* *For the first year, machine has been used for half year that's why half year depreciation has been charged i.e.* ₹ *4,500.*

ILLUSTRATION |7| (Straight Line Method, on the basis of percentage) Evergreen Traders purchased a machine on 1st April, 2012 at a cost of ₹ 8,000 and spent ₹ 2,000 on its installation. The firm writes off depreciation @ 10% per annum by fixed instalment method.

Show the machine account for 4 years in the books of Evergreen Traders. The books are closed on 31st March every year.

Sol. Dr **Machinery Account** Cr

Date	Particulars	Amt (₹)	Date	Particulars	Amt (₹)
2012 Apr 1	To Bank A/c (8,000 + 2,000)	10,000	2013 Mar 31	By Depreciation A/c (10% on ₹ 10,000)	1,000
			Mar 31	By Balance c/d	9,000
		10,000			10,000
2013 Apr 1	To Balance b/d	9,000	2014 Mar 31	By Depreciation A/c	1,000
			Dec 31	By Balance c/d	8,000
		9,000			9,000
2014 Apr 1	To Balance b/d	8,000	2015 Mar 31	By Depreciation A/c	1,000
			Mar 31	By Balance c/d	7,000
		8,000			8,000
2015 Apr 1	To Balance b/d	7,000	2016 Mar 31	By Depreciation A/c	1,000
			Mar 31	By Balance c/d	6,000
		7,000			7,000
2016 Apr 1	To Balance b/d	6,000			

LLUSTRATION |8| (Written Down Value Method) On 1st July, 2014, Ashwani purchased a machine for ₹ 2,00,000 on credit from Dushyant. Installation expenses ₹ 25,000 are paid by cheque. Depreciation is to be charged on written down value method @ 10% per annum. Prepare necessary ledger accounts for first three years, assuming that Ashwani closes his books on 31st December.

Sol. Dr **Machinery Account** Cr

Date	Particulars	JF	Amount	Date	Particulars	JF	Amount
2014 July 1	To Dushyant		2,00,000	2014 Dec 31	By Depreciation A/c		11,250
	To Bank A/c		25,000	Dec 31	By Balance c/d		2,13,750
2015			2,25,000	2015			2,25,000
Jan 1	To Balance b/d		2,13,750	Dec 31	By Depreciation A/c		21,375
				Dec 31	By Balance c/d		1,92,375
2016			2,13,750	2015			2,13,750
Jan 1	To Balance b/d		1,92,375	Dec 31	By Depreciation A/c		19,237.5
				Dec 31	By Balance c/d		1,73,137.5
2017			1,92,375				1,92,375
Jan 1	To Balance b/d		1,73,137.5				

Dr Depreciation Account Cr

Date	Particulars	JF	Amt (₹)	Date	Particulars	JF	Amt (₹)
2014 Dec 31	To Machinery A/c		11,250	2014 Dec 31	By Profit and Loss A/c		11,250
			11,250				11,250
2015 Dec 31	To Machinery A/c		21,375	2015 Dec 31	By Profit and Loss A/c		21,375
			21,375				21,375
2016 Dec 31	To Machinery A/c		19,237.5	2015 Dec 31	By Profit and Loss A/c		19,237.5
			19,237.5				19,237.5

Note *Depreciation for 2014* $= 2{,}25{,}000 \times \frac{10}{100} \times \frac{6}{12} = 11{,}250.$

ILLUSTRATION |9| (More than one machine is being purchased) A machine was purchased on 1st April, 2014 for ₹ 10,00,000. On 1st October, 2014 another machine was purchased for ₹ 6,00,000. Estimated scrap values were ₹ 40,000 and ₹ 20,000 respectively. Depreciation is to be provided @ 10% per annum on the machines under the fixed instalment method.

(i) Show the machinery account for the year ended 31st March, 2015 and 2016.

(ii) Show how the machinery account will appear in the balance sheet as at 31st March, 2016.

Sol.

Dr Machinery Account Cr

Date	Particulars	JF	Amt (₹)	Date	Particulars		JF	Amt (₹)
2014 Apr 1	To Bank A/c (Mach. A)		10,00,000	2015 Mar 31	By Depreciation A/c			
					Mach. A	1,00,000		
					Mach. B	30,000		1,30,000
Oct 1	To Bank A/c (Mach. B)		6,00,000	Mar 31	By Balance c/d			
					Mach. A	9,00,000		
					Mach. B	5,70,000		14,70,000
			16,00,000					16,00,000
2015 Apr 1	To Balance b/d			2016 Mar 31	By Depreciation A/c (WN 1)			
	Mach. A 9,00,000				Mach. A	1,00,000		
	Mach. B 5,70,000		14,70,000		Mach. B	60,000		1,60,000
				Mar 31	By Balance c/d			
					Mach. A	8.00,000		
					Mach. B	5,10,000		13,10,000
			14,70,000					14,70,000
2016 Apr 1	To Balance b/d							
	Mach. A 8,00,000							
	Mach. B 5,10,000		13,10,000					

Balance Sheet (Extract)
as at 31st March, 2016

Liabilities	Amt (₹)	Assets		Amt (₹)
		Machinery		
		A	8,00,000	
		B	5,10,000	13,10,000

Working Note

Depreciation on Machinery A $= 10{,}00{,}000 \times \frac{10}{100} =$ ₹ 1,00,000

Depreciation on Machinery B

(a) For year ended 2015 $= 6{,}00{,}000 \times \frac{10}{100} \times \frac{6}{12} =$ ₹ 30,000

(b) For subsequent year $= 6{,}00{,}000 \times \frac{10}{100} =$ ₹ 60,000

ILLUSTRATION |10| A machine was purchased on 1st April, 2015 for ₹ 10,00,000. On 1st October, 2015 another machine was purchased for ₹ 6,00,000. Estimated scrap values were ₹ 40,000 and ₹ 20,000 respectively. Depreciation is to be provided @ 10% per annum on the machines under the reducing balance system.

(i) Show the machinery account for the year ended 31st March, 2016 and 2017.

(ii) Show how the machinery account will appear in the balance sheet as at 31st March, 2017.

Sol. (i) Dr **Machinery Account** Cr

Date	Particulars		JF	Amt (₹)	Date	Particulars		JF	Amt (₹)
2015					2016				
Apr 1	To Bank A/c (Mach. A)			10,00,000	Mar 31	By Depreciation A/c (WN)			
Oct 1	To Bank A/c (Mach. B)			6,00,000		Mach. A	1,00,000		
						Mach. B	30,000		1,30,000
					Mar 31	By Balance c/d			
						Mach. A	9,00,000		
						Mach. B	5,70,000		14,70,000
				16,00,000					16,00,000
2016					2017				
Apr 1	To Balance b/d				Mar 31	By Depreciation A/c (WN)			
	Mach. A	9,00,000				Mach. A	90,000		
	Mach. B	5,70,000		14,70,000		Mach. B	57,000		1,47,000
						By Balance c/d			
						Mach. A	8,10,000		
						Mach. B	5,13,000		13,23,000
				14,70,000					14,70,000
2017									
Apr 1	To Balance b/d								
	Mach. A	8,10,000							
	Mach. B	5,13,000		13,23,000					

Working Note

Table showing calculation of depreciation on machinery

Machinery Date of Acquistion	1st 1st April, 2015	2nd 1st October, 2015	Total Depreciation
Cost	10,00,000	6,00,000	
(–) Depreciation for 2015-16 @ 10% per annum	1,00,000	30,000*	1,30,000
WDV (or book value) on 1st April, 2016	9,00,000	5,70,000	
(–) Depreciation for 2016-17 @ 10% per annum	90,000	57,000	1,47,000
WDV on 1st April, 2017	8,10,000	5,13,000	

* *Depreciation for half year, i.e.,* $6,00,000 \times 10/100 \times 6/12 = 30,000$

(ii) **Balance Sheet** (Extract)
as at 31st March, 2017

Liabilities	Amt (₹)	Assets		Amt (₹)
		Machinery		
		A	8,10,000	
		B	5,13,000	13,23,000

Note *In balance sheet, the balance of machinery account as on 31st March, 2017 will be shown.*

Students Should Keep in Mind

When more than one asset is being purchased, then it is preferable to show depreciation and balance of each asset individually.

When rate of depreciation is given, then scrap value and useful life of an asset should be ignored.

ILLUSTRATION |11| (Additions made to an existing asset) On 1st April, 2013, a merchant purchased a furniture costing ₹ 55,000. It is estimated that its life is 10 years at the end of which it will be sold for ₹ 5,000. Additions are made on 1st April, 2014 and 1st April, 2016 to the value of ₹ 9,500 and ₹ 8,800 (Residual values ₹ 500 and ₹ 400 respectively). Show the furniture account for the first four years, if depreciation is written off according to the straight line method, and the merchant closes his books on 31st March, every year, assuming that

(i) the additions made to the furniture are an integral part of the furniture and will lose their utility with the expiration of the useful life of the original furniture.

(ii) the additions have their separate identity and their estimated useful life is 10 years each.

Sol. (i) Dr **Furniture Account** Cr

Date	Particulars	JF	Amt (₹)	Date	Particulars	JF	Amt (₹)
2013				2014			
Apr 1	To Bank A/c		55,000	Mar 31	By Depreciation A/c		5,000
					By Balance c/d		50,000
			55,000				55,000
2014				2015			
Apr 1	To Balance b/d		50,000	Mar 31	By Depreciation A/c		6,000
Apr 11	To Bank A/c		9,500		(5,000 + 1,000)		
					By Balance c/d		53,500
					(45,000 + 8,500)		
			59,500				59,500
2015				2016			
Apr 1	To Balance b/d		53,500	Mar 31	By Depreciation A/c		6,000
					(5,000 + 1,000)		
				Mar 31	By Balance c/d		47,500
					(40,000 + 7,500)		
			53,500				53,500
2016				2017			
Apr 1	To Balance b/d		47,500	Mar 31	By Depreciation A/c		7,200
Apr 1	To Bank A/c		8,800		(5,000 + 1,000 + 1,200)		
				Mar 31	By Balance c/d		49,100
					(35,000 + 6,500 + 7,600)		
			56,300				56,300

Working Note

Depreciation charged on furniture purchased on 1st April, 2013 = $\frac{55,000 - 5,000}{10}$ = ₹ 5,000

Depreciation charged on addition made on 1st April, 2014 = $\frac{9,500 - 500}{9*}$ = ₹ 1,000

*The estimated life is taken as 9 years because one year has elapsed since the purchase of original furniture.

Depreciation charged on addition made on 1st April, 2016 = $\frac{8,800 - 400}{7*}$ = 1,200

*The estimated life is taken as 7 years because three years have elapsed since the purchase of original furniture.

(ii) Dr **Furniture Account** Cr

Date	Particulars	JF	Amt (₹)	Date	Particulars	JF	Amt (₹)
2013				2014			
Apr 1	To Bank A/c		55,000	Mar 31	By Depreciation A/c		5,000
				Mar 31	By Balance c/d		50,000
			55,000				55,000
2014				2015			
Apr 1	To Balance b/d		50,000	Mar 31	By Depreciation A/c		5,900
					(5,000 + 900)		
Apr 11	To Bank A/c		9,500	Mar 31	By Balance c/d		53,600
					(45,000 + 8,600)		
			59,500				59,500

Date	Particulars	JF	Amt (₹)	Date	Particulars	JF	Amt (₹)
2015 April 1	To Balance b/d		53,600	2016 March 31	By Depreciation A/c (5,000 + 900)		5,900
				March 31	By Balance c/d (40,000 + 7,700)		47,700
			53,600				53,600
2016 April 1	To Balance b/d		47,700	2017 March 31	By Depreciation A/c (5,000 + 900 + 840)		6,740
April 1	To Bank A/c		8,800	March 31	By Balance c/d (35,000 + 6,800 + 7,960)		49,760
			56,500				56,500

Working Note

Depreciation on addition made on 1st April, 2014 = $\frac{9,500 - 500}{10}$ = ₹ 900

Depreciation on addition made on 1st April, 2016 = $\frac{8,800 - 400}{10}$ = ₹ 840

EFFECT OF ANY ADDITION OR EXTENSION TO THE EXISTING ASSET

AS-6 (Revised) mentions that

(*i*) Any addition or extension to an existing asset which is of capital nature and which becomes an integral part of the existing asset is depreciated over the remaining useful life of the original asset.

(*ii*) Where an addition or extension retains a separate identity and is capable of being used after the existing asset is disposed off, then it is depreciated independently on the basis of its own useful life.

NUMERICAL Questions for Practice

1 On 1st April, 2016, Chaman Lal purchased a machinery costing ₹ 40,000 and spent ₹ 5,000 on its erection. The estimated effective life of the machinery is 10 years with a scrap value of ₹ 5,000. Calculate the depreciation on the straight line method and show the machinery account of first three years. Accounting year ends on 31st march every year.

[Balance of Machinery Account = ₹ 33,000]

[***Hint*** : Depreciation = (₹ 40,000 + ₹ 5,000 – ₹ 5,000)/10 = ₹ 4,000 per annum]

2 A boiler was purchased from abroad on 1st July, 2014 for ₹ 20,000; shipping and forwarding charges ₹ 4,000, Import duty ₹ 14,000 and expenses of installation amounted to ₹ 2,000. Depreciation is charged @ 10% on diminishing balance method. Prepare boiler account and depreciation account for four years, assuming that books are closed on 31st March every year.

[***Hint:*** Depreciation; 1st year = 4,000; 2nd year = ₹ 3,600; 3rd year = ₹ 3240; 4th year = ₹ 2,916
Balance of Boiler Account = ₹ 26,244]

3 From the following transactions of a concern, prepare the machinery account for the year ended 31st March, 2016

1st April, 2015	:	Purchased a second-hand machinery for ₹ 40,000.
1st April, 2015	:	Spent ₹ 10,000 on repairs for making it serviceable.
30th September, 2015	:	Purchased additional new machinery for ₹ 20,000.
31st December, 2015	:	Repairs and renewals of machinery ₹ 3,000.
31st March, 2016	:	Depreciate the machinery at 10% per annum

[Balance of Machinery Account– ₹ 64,000]

[***Hint:*** The amount spent on repairs and renewals of machinery ₹ 3,000 on 31st December, is of revenue nature and not of capital nature and hence not debited to the machinery account. Also, depreciation for the first year will be the same, irrespective of the method of depreciation.]

DISPOSAL OF ASSET

Disposal of the asset means that the asset has been sold or has been discarded.

The following journal entries are passed in this regard

(i)	To Record Depreciation upto the Date of Sale	Depreciation A/c Dr To Asset A/c (Being depreciation charged)
(ii)	To Record Sale of Asset	Cash/Bank A/c Dr To Asset A/c (Being the asset sold)
(iii)	To Record Profit/Loss on Sale (a) In Case of Profit	Asset A/c Dr To Profit and Loss A/c (Being the transfer of profit on sale of asset)
	(b) In Case of Loss	Profit and Loss A/c Dr To Asset A/c (Being the transfer of loss on sale of asset)
(iv)	To Transfer Depreciation	Profit and Loss A/c Dr To Depreciation A/c (Being depreciation transferred to profit and loss account)

The following conditions related to disposal of an asset should be kept in mind

1. **IF THE ASSET IS SOLD/DISCARDED AT THE END OF THE YEAR**

   In this case the depreciation on asset sold/discarded will be charged for the full year in the year of sale. The amount realised from the sale of asset should be credited to the asset account and the balance of the asset account is transferred to profit and loss account. A debit balance indicates profit on sale of asset and a credit balance indicates loss on sale of asset.

ILLUSTRATION |12| **(Depreciation is charged by straight line method). RS Ltd purchased a vehicle for ₹ 4,00,000. After 4 year its salvage value is estimated at ₹ 40,000. Find out the amount of depreciation to be charged every year based on straight line basis, and also show the vehicle account as would appear for four years assuming it is sold for ₹ 50,000 at the end of the fourth year when depreciation is charged to asset account. Prepare the ledger in the books of account of RS Ltd.** **NCERT**

Sol. Dr **Vehicle Account** Cr

Date	Particulars	JF	Amt (₹)	Date	Particulars	JF	Amt (₹)
I Year	To Bank A/c		4,00,000	end of year	By Depreciation A/c By Balance c/d		90,000 3,10,000
			4,00,000				4,00,000
II Year	To Balance b/d		3,10,000	end of year	By Depreciation A/c By Balance c/d		90,000 2,20,000
			3,10,000				3,10,000
III Year	To Balance b/d		2,20,000	end of year	By Depreciation A/c By Balance c/d		90,000 1,30,000
			2,20,000				2,20,000
IV Year	To Balance b/d To Profit and Loss A/c (Profit on Sale of Vehicle)		1,30,000 10,000	end of year	By Depreciation A/c By Bank A/c		90,000 50,000
			1,40,000				1,40,000

Working Note

(*i*) $\text{Depreciation} = \dfrac{\text{Cost of Asset - Salvage Value}}{\text{Estimated Life}} = \dfrac{4,00,000 - 40,000}{4} = ₹\ 90,000$

(*ii*) **Calculation of Profit/Loss on Sale**

Book value in the beginning of the year	1,30,000
(–) Depreciation	90,000
Book value of asset on the date of sale	40,000
Sale Proceeds	50,000
Profit on Sale (50,000 – 40,000)	₹ 10,000

ILLUSTRATION |13| (Depreciation is charged by WDV method) TU Limited purchased a crane for ₹ 11,75,000 and spend ₹ 50,000 for its registration on 1st January, 2014. Depreciation is charged @ 10% per annum, WDV method. The crane is sold for ₹ 7,00,000 on 31st March, 2016. Assuming that TU Limited follows the financial year, prepare crane account for the relevant period.

Sol. Dr **Crane Account** Cr

Date	Particulars	JF	Amt (₹)	Date	Particulars	JF	Amt (₹)
2014 Apr 1	To Bank A/c (11,75,000 + 50,000)		12,25,000	2014 Mar 31	By Depreciation A/c		30,625
					By Balance c/d		11,94,375
			12,25,000				12,25,000
2014 Apr 1	To Balance b/d		11,94,375	2015 Mar 31	By Depreciation A/c		1,19,437.5
					By Balance c/d		10,74,937.5
			11,94,375				1194,375
2015 Apr 1	To Balance b/d		10,74,937.5	2016 Mar 31	By Depreciation A/c		1,07,493.75
				Mar 31	By Bank A/c		7,00,000
				Mar 31	(Loss on sale)		2,67,443.75
			10,74,937.5				10,74,937.5

Working Note

Depreciation for the year 2014-15 $= 12,25,000 \times \dfrac{10}{100} \times \dfrac{3}{12} = ₹\ 30,625$

2. IF THE ASSET IS SOLD/DISCARDED IN THE MIDDLE OF THE YEAR

In this case, the depreciation to be charged should be calculated upto the date of sale of asset. Rest of the treatment is similar to that already discussed in the previous case.

ILLUSTRATION |14| Madhukar Ltd. purchased a truck for ₹ 7,50,000 on 1st July, 2014. Depreciation is charged on truck @ 15% per annum on straight line method. On 1st October, 2016, the truck met with an accident. It was sold for ₹ 2,00,000. Prepare truck account for three years assuming that the company closes its books on 31st December every year.

Sol. Dr **Truck Account** Cr

Date	Particulars	JF	Amt (₹)	Date	Particulars	JF	Amt (₹)
2014 July 1	To Bank A/c		7,50,000	2014 Dec 31	By Depreciation A/c (W.NI)		56,250
				Dec 31	By Balance c/d		6,93,750
			7,50,000				7,50,000
2015 Jan 1	To Balance b/d		6,93,750	2015 Dec 31	By Depreciation A/c		1,12,500
					By Balance c/d		5,81,250
			6,93,750				6,93,750

Date	Particulars	JF	Amt (₹)	Date	Particulars	JF	Amt (₹)
2016 Jan 1	To Balance b/d		5,81,250	2016 Oct 1	By Bank A/c		2,00,000
				Oct 1	By Depreciation A/c (W.N 2)		84,375
				Oct 1	By Profit and Loss A/c (Loss on sale)		2,96,875
			5,81,250				5,81,250

Working Notes

W.N.1

Depreciation on truck for the year 2014 will be calculated for a period of 6 months, *i.e.,* from 1st July to 31st December.

$\therefore$ Depreciation $= 7{,}50{,}000 \times \frac{15}{100} \times \frac{6}{12} =$ ₹ 56,250

W.N.2

Depreciation on truck for the year 2016 will be calculated for a period of 9 months, *i.e.,* from 1st January to 30th September.

$\therefore$ Depreciation $= 7{,}50{,}000 \times \frac{15}{100} \times \frac{9}{12} =$ ₹ 84,375

W.N.3

Book value of truck on 1st January, 2016	5,81,250
(–)Depreciation upto the date of sale	84,375
Book value on the date of sale	4,96,875
(–) Sale proceeds	2,00,000
∴ Loss on sale of asset	2,96,875

ILLUSTRATION |15| On 1st October, 2010 a truck was purchased for ₹ 8,00,000 by Laxmi Transport Ltd. Depreciation was provided at 15% per annum on the diminishing balance basis on this truck. On 31st December, 2013 this truck was sold for ₹ 5,00,000. Accounts are closed on 31st March, every year. Prepare a truck account for the 4 years. **NCERT**

Sol. Dr **Truck Account** Cr

Date	Particulars	JF	Amt (₹)	Date	Particulars	JF	Amt (₹)
2012 Oct 1	To Bank A/c		8,00,000	2013 Mar 31	By Depreciation A/c $\left(8{,}00{,}000 \times \frac{15}{100} \times \frac{6}{12}\right)$		60,000
				Mar 31	By Balance c/d		7,40,000
			8,00,000				8,00,000
2013 Apr 1	To Balance b/d		7,40,000	2014 Mar 31	By Depreciation A/c $\left(7{,}40{,}000 \times \frac{15}{100}\right)$		1,11,000
					By Balance c/d		6,29,000
			7,40,000				7,40,000
2014 Apr 1	To Balance b/d		6,29,000	2015 Mar 31	By Depreciation A/c $\left(6{,}29{,}000 \times \frac{15}{100}\right)$		94,350
					By Balance c/d		5,34,650
			6,29,000				6,29,000
2015 Apr 1	To Balance b/d		5,34,650	2016 Dec 31	By Depreciation A/c $\left(5{,}34{,}650 \times \frac{15}{100} \times \frac{9}{12}\right)$		60,148
Dec 31	To Profit and Loss A/c (Profit)		25,498	Dec 31	By Bank A/c (Sale proceed)		5,00,000
			5,60,148				5,60,148

Working Note

Calculation of Profit/Loss on Sale

Book Value as on 1st April, 2015	5,34,650
(–) Depreciation	60,148
	4,74,502
(–) Sale Proceeds	5,00,000
Profit on Sale	₹ 25,498

3. IF A PART OF ASSET IS SOLD/DISCARDED DURING A YEAR

If a part of asset is sold/discarded during a year, then it is advisable that the students split the asset in two parts from the date of purchase itself. Depreciation should be provided on each part separately. In the year in which the part is sold/discarded, following points should be kept in mind.

(*i*) For the part discarded, depreciation should be computed upto the date of sale.

(*ii*) For the part not discarded, depreciation should be computed for the whole year.

ILLUSTRATION |16| (When a part of machinery is sold.) A company whose accounting year is the calendar year, purchased on 1st April, 2014 machinery costing ₹ 30,000. On 1st June, 2016 one third of the machinery which was installed on 1st April, 2014 became obsolete and was sold for ₹ 3,000.

Show how the machine account would appear in the books of the company, it being given that machinery was depreciated by fixed installment at 10% per annum.

Sol. Dr Machinery A/c Cr

Date	Particulars		JF	Amt (₹)	Date	Particulars		JF	Amt (₹)
2014 Apr 1	To Bank A/c (W.N.1)				2014 Dec 31	By Depreciation A/c (W.N.2)			
	A	20,000				A	1,500		
	B	10,000		30,000		B	750		2,250
					Dec 31	By Balance c/d			
						A	18,500		
						B	9,250		27,750
				30,000					30,000
2015 Jan 1	To Balance b/d				2015 Dec 31	By Depreciation A/c			
	A	18,500				A	2,000		
	B	9,250		27,750		B	1,000		3000
						By Balance c/d			
						A	16,500		
						B	8,250		24,750
				27,750					27,750
2016 Jan 1	To Balance b/d				2016 June 1	By Bank A/c (B)			3,000
	A	16,500			June 1	By Depreciation A/c (W.N.3)			417
	B	8,250		24,750	June 1	By Profit and Loss A/c (W.N.4)			4,833
					Dec 31	By Deprecation A/c (A)			2,000
					Dec 31	By Balance c/d (A)			14,500
				24,750					24,750

Working Notes

W.N.1

Cost of machine = ₹ 30,000 Part of machinery sold = 1/3rd

∴ Cost of part of machinery sold = $30{,}000 \times \frac{1}{3}$ = ₹ 10,000

So, machinery has been split in two parts

30,000 → 20,000 (A) and 10,000 (B)

W.N.2

Depreciation on parts of machinery for a period of nine months, *i.e.* from 1st April to 31st December.

Depreciation on 'A' part = $20{,}000 \times \frac{10}{100} \times \frac{9}{12}$ = ₹ 1,500

Depreciation on 'B' part = $10{,}000 \times \frac{10}{100} \times \frac{9}{12}$ = ₹ 750

W.N.3

Depreciation on part sold for a period of 5 months, *i.e.* from 1st January to 31st May.

$= 10{,}000 \times \frac{10}{100} \times \frac{5}{12}$ = ₹ 417

W.N.4

Book value of asset as on1st January, 2016	8,250
(–) Depreciation upto the date of sale	417
Book value on the date of sale	7,833
(–) Sale proceeds	3,000
Loss on sale of asset transferred to profit and loss account	4,833

4. IF MORE THAN ONE ASSET IS PURCHASED AND SOLD DURING A YEAR

If more than one asset is purchased and sold during the year, then the following points should be kept in mind

(*i*) Each asset purchased should be recorded separately in the account.

(*ii*) The date of purchase of each asset should be carefully noted. Depreciation should be provided, in the year of purchase, from the date of purchase to the year end.

(*iii*) Depreciation on each asset should be shown separately.

(*iv*) Balance of each asset should be shown individually.

(*v*) Date of sale of each asset should also be noted carefully. In the year of sale, depreciation should be provided upto the date of sale.

(*vi*) For assets not sold, depreciation should be provided for the whole year.

ILLUSTRATION |17| A firm purchased on 1st January, 2013 a second-hand machinery for ₹ 36,000 and spent ₹ 4,000 on its installation.

On 1st July in the same year, another machinery costing ₹ 20,000 was purchased. On 1st July, 2015 machinery brought on 1st January, 2013 was sold for ₹ 12,000 and a new machine purchased for ₹ 64,000 on the same date. Depreciation is provided annually on 31st December @ 10% per annum on the written down value method. Show the machinery account from 2013 to 2015.

Sol. Dr **Machinery Account** Cr

Date	Particulars	JF	Amt (₹)	Date	Particulars		JF	Amt (₹)
2013				2013				
Jan 1	To Bank A/c (Machine I)		40,000	Dec 31	By Depreciations A/c			
	(₹ 36,000 + ₹ 4,000)				Machine I	4,000		
Jul 1	To Bank A/c (Machine II)		20,000		Machine II	1,000		5,000
				Dec 31	By Balance c/d			
					Machine I	36,000		

Date	Particulars		JF	Amt (₹)	Date	Particulars		JF	Amt (₹)
						Machine II	19,000		55,000
				60,000					60,000
2014					2014				
Jan 1	To Balance b/d				Dec 31	By Depreciation A/c			
	Machine I	36,000				Machine I	3,600		
	Machine II	19,000		55,000		Machine II	1,900		5,500
					Dec 31	By Balance c/d			
						Machine I	32,400		
						Machine II	17,100		49,500
				55,000					55,000
2015					2015				
Jan 1	To Balance b/d				Jul 1	By Depreciation A/c (Machine I) $\left(32{,}400\times\frac{10}{100}\times\frac{6}{12}\right)$			1,620
	Machine I	32,400				By Bank A/c			12,000
	Machine II	17,100		49,500		By Profit and Loss A/c (Loss)			18,780
Jul 1	To Bank A/c (Machine III)			64,000					
					Dec 31	By Depreciation A/c			
						Machine II	1,710		
						Machine III	3,200		4,910
					Dec 31	By Balance c/d			
						Machine II	15,390		
						Machine III	60,800		76,190
				1,13,500					1,13,500
2016									
Jan 1	To Balance b/d								
	(Machine II)	15,390							
	(Machine III)	60,800		76,190					

Working Note

Calculation of Profit/Loss on Sale of Machine I

Book Value as on 1st January, 2015	32,400
(–) Depreciation	1,620
	30,780
(–) Sale Proceeds	12,000
Loss on Sale	₹ 18,780

Comprehensive Illustrations

ILLUSTRATION |18| **(When assets are purchased and sold on different dates and depreciation is charged on straight line method.) On 1st April, 2012 Manas Ltd purchased 10 machines of ₹ 30,000 each. On 30th June, 2013. 1 machine out of the 10 machines purchased on 1st April, 2012 was sold for ₹ 24,000 and on 31st December, 2014 one more machine was sold for ₹ 22,500. A new machine was purchased on 30th September, 2015 for ₹ 32,000. The company has adopted the practice of providing depreciation at 10% per annum on original cost of machine. The company closes its books on 31st March, every year. You are required to prepare machinery account upto 31st March, 2016.**

Sol. Dr **Machinery Account** Cr

Date	Particulars	JF	Amt (₹)	Date	Particulars	JF	Amt (₹)
2012				2013			
Apr 1	To Bank A/c (₹ 30,000 × 10)		3,00,000	Mar 31	By Depreciation A/c (3,00,000 × 10%)		30,000
				Mar 31	By Balance c/d		2,70,000
			3,00,000				3,00,000
2013				2013			
Apr 1	To Balance b/d		2,70,000	Jun 30	By Depreciation A/c $\left(30{,}000 \times \frac{10}{100} \times \frac{3}{12}\right)$		750
				Jun 30	By Bank A/c		24,000
				Jun 30	By Profit and Loss A/c (WN1)		2,250
				2014			
				Mar 31	By Depreciation A/c (₹ 2,70,000 × 10%)		27,000
				Mar 31	By Balance c/d		2,16,000
			2,70,000				2,70,000
2014				2014			
Apr 1	To Balance b/d		2,16,000	Dec 31	By Depreciation A/c $\left(30{,}000 \times \frac{10}{100} \times \frac{9}{12}\right)$		2,250
Dec 31	To Profit and Loss A/c (WN2)		750	Dec 31	By Bank A/c		22,500
				2015			
				Mar 31	By Depreciation A/c (₹ 2,40,000 × 10%)		24,000
				Mar 31	By Balance c/d		1,68,000
			2,16,750				2,16,750
2015				2016			
Apr 1	To Balance b/d		1,68,000	Mar 31	By Depreciation A/c (WN3)		25,600
Sep 30	To Bank A/c		32,000	Mar 31	By Balance c/d		1,74,400
			2,00,000				2,00,000

Working Note

(i) Calculation of Gain or Loss on Sale on 30th June, 2012

Original cost of machine sold		30,000
(–) Depreciation provided upto date of sale		
On 31st March, 2013 (On ₹ 30,000 @ 10% for 1 year)	3,000	
On 30th June, 2013 (On ₹ 30,000 @ 10% for 3 months)	750	3,750
Book value on date of sale		26,250
(–) Selling price		24,000
Loss on sale		₹ 2,250

(ii) Calculation of Gain or Loss on Sale on 31st December, 2014

Original cost of machine sold		30,000
(–) Depreciation provided upto date of sale		
On 31st March, 2013 (On ₹ 30,000 @ 10% for 1 year)	3,000	
On 31st March, 2014 (On ₹ 30,000 @ 10% for 1 year)	3,000	
On 31st December, 2014 (On ₹ 30,000 @ 10% for 9 months)	2,250	8,250
Book value on date of sale		21,750
(–) Selling price		22,500
Profit on sale		₹ 750

(iii) Depreciation Provided on 31st March, 2016

On ₹ 2,40,000 @ 10% for 1 year	24,000
On ₹ 32,000 @ 10% for 6 months	1,600
	₹ 25,600

ILLUSTRATION |19| (When a part of machinery gets damaged) On 1st January, 2013 A Ltd company purchased machinery for ₹ 20,00,000. Depreciation is provided @ 15% per annum on diminishing balance method. On 1st March, 2015 1/4 of machinery was damaged by fire and ₹ 40,000 were received from the insurance company in full settlement. On 1st September, 2015 another machinery was purchased by the company for ₹ 15,00,000.

Write up the machinery account from 2015 to 2016. Books are closed on 31st December, every year.

NCERT

Sol. Dr **Machinery Account** Cr

Date	Particulars		JF	Amt (₹)	Date	Particulars		JF	Amt (₹)
2015					2015				
Jan 1	To Balance b/d (W.N.1)				Mar 1	By Bank A/c (Insurance)			40,000
	A	10,83,750							
	B	3,61,250		14,45,000		By Depreciation A/c (B)(W.N.2)			9,031
Sep 1	To Bank A/c (C)			15,00,000		By Profit and loss A/c			3,12,219
					Dec 31	By Depreciation A/c			
						A	1,62,562		
						C	75,000		2,37,562
					Dec 31	By Balance c/d			
						A	9,21,188		
						C	14,25,000		23,46,188
				29,45,000					29,45,000
2016					2016				
Jan 1	To Balance b/d				Dec 31	By Depreciation A/c			
	A	9,21,188				A	1,38,178		
	C	14,25,000		23,46,188		C	2,13,750		3,51,928
					Dec 31	By Balance c/d			
						A	7,83,010		
						C	12,11,250		19,94,260
				23,46,188					23,46,188

Working Notes

W.N.1

Cost of Machinery purchased on 1st January, 2013 = ₹ 20,00,000

One fourth part of Machinery = ₹ 5,00,000

So, the machinery is split into two parts;	Part A	Part B
	15,00,000	₹5,00,000
(–) Dep. for 2013	2,25,000	75,000
WDv	12,75,000	4,25,000
(–) Dep. for 2014	1,91,250	63,750
WDv	10,83,750	3,61,250

W.N.2.

Depreciation on Part B in 2015 $= 3{,}61{,}250 \times \frac{15}{100} \times \frac{2}{12} =$ ₹ 9,031

ILLUSTRATION |20| In Mr Hayat's ledger, the written down value of a machine as on 1st April, 2015 is ₹ 70,000. The rate of depreciation is 15% per annum on the written down value method.

The machine is under an annual repairs and maintenance contract with Mr Swami who charge ₹ 1,250 per quarter. A new machine was bought and the cheque issued for ₹ 97,500 and the cash paid ₹ 2,500 for its immediate erection and subsequent use on 1st July, 2015.

The annual maintenance contract of the new machine bought was to be signed after the one year guarantee period was over. Show the machinery account, as it would appear in the ledger for the year ended 31st March, 2016.

Sol. Dr **Machinery Account** Cr

Date	Particulars	JF	Amt (₹)	Date	Particulars	JF	Amt (₹)
2015				2016			
Apr 1	To Balance b/d		70,000	Mar 31	By Depreciation A/c (WN 1)		21,750
Jul 1	To Bank A/c		97,500	Mar 31	By Balance c/d		1,48,250
Jul 1	To Cash A/c		2,500				
			1,70,000				1,70,000

Working Note

(i) Calculation of Depreciation

On old machine @ 15% on ₹ 70,000 for 1 year (70,000 × 15 / 100)	10,500
On new machine @ 15% on ₹ 1,00,000 for 9 months (₹ 1,00,000 × 15 / 100 × 9/12)	11,250
	₹ 21,750

(ii) Repairs and maintenance charges are revenue expenses so they are charged to the profit and loss account.

ILLUSTRATION |21| A company had bought machinery for ₹ 5,00,000 including a boiler worth ₹ 50,000. The machinery account had been credited for depreciation on the reducing instalment system for the past 4 years @ 10%. In the beginning of the 5th year, the boiler became useless on account of damage to some of its vital parts and the damaged boiler is sold for ₹ 10,000. Write up the machinery account.

Sol. Dr **Machinery Account** Cr

Date	Particulars		JF	Amt (₹)	Date	Particulars		JF	Amt (₹)
Ist Year	To Bank A/c				Ist year	By Depreciation A/c			
	A	4,50,000				A	45,000		
	B	50,000		5,00,000		B	5,000		50,000
						By Balance c/d			
						A	4,05,000		
						B	45,000		4,50,000
				5,00,000					5,00,000
IInd Year	To Balance b/d				IInd Year	By Depreciation A/c			
	A	4,05,000				A	40,500		
	B	45,000		4,50,000		B	4,500		45,000
						By Balance c/d			
						A	3,64,500		
						B	40,500		4,05,000
				4,50,000					4,50,000
IIIrd Year	To Balance b/d				IIIrd Year	By Pepreciation A/c			
	A	3,64,500				A	36,450		
	B	40,500		4,05,000		B	4,050		40,500
						By Balance c/d			
						A	3,28,050		
						B	36,450		3,64,500
				4,05,000					4,05,000

Date	Particulars		JF	Amt (₹)	Date	Particulars		JF	Amt (₹)
IVth Year	To Balance b/d				IVth Year	By Depreciation A/c			
	A	3,28,050				A	32,805		
	B	36,450		3,64,500		B	3,645		36,450
						By Balance c/d			
						A	2,95,245		
						B	32,805		3,28,050
				3,64,500					3,64,500
Vth Year	To Balance b/d				Vth Year	By Bank (B)			10,000
	A	2,95,245				By Profit and Loss A/c			22,805
	B	32,805		3,28,050		(32,805-10,000)			
						By Depreciation A/c (A)			29,525
						By Balance c/d			2,65,720
				3,28,050					3,28,050

ILLUSTRATION |22| **On 1st January, 2013, Satkar Transport Ltd purchased 3 buses for ₹ 10,00,000 each. On 1st July, 2015 one bus was involved in an accident and was completely destroyed and ₹ 7,00,000 were received from the insurance company in full settlement. Depreciation is written-off @ 15% per annum on diminishing balance method. Prepare bus account from 2013 to 2016. Books are closed on 31st December, every year.** **NCERT**

Sol. Dr **Bus Account** Cr

Date	Particulars		JF	Amt (₹)	Date	Particulars		JF	Amt (₹)
2013 Jan 1	To Bank A/c				2013 Dec 31	By Depreciation A/c			
	Bus 1	10,00,000				Bus 1	1,50,000		
	Bus 2	10,00,000				Bus 2	1,50,000		
	Bus 3	10,00,000		30,00,000		Bus 3	1,50,000		4,50,000
					Dec. 31	By Balance c/d			
						Bus 1	8,50,000		
						Bus 2	8,50,000		
						Bus 3	8,50,000		25,50,000
				30,00,000					30,00,000
2014 Jan 1	To Balance b/d				2014 Dec 31	By Depreciation A/c			
	Bus 1	8,50,000				Bus 1	1,27,500		
	Bus 2	8,50,000				Bus 2	1,27,500		
	Bus 3	8,50,000		25,50,000		Bus 3	1,27,500		3,82,500
					Dec 31	By Balance c/d			
						Bus 1	7,22,500		
						Bus 2	7,22,500		
						Bus 3	7,22,500		21,67,500
				25,50,000					25,50,000
2015 Jan 1	To Balance b/d				2015 Jul 1	By Bank A/c (Insurance)			7,00,000
	Bus 1	7,22,500			Jul 1	By Depreciation A/c			54,188
	Bus 2	7,22,500				(Bus 1) $\left(7{,}22{,}500\times\frac{15}{100}\times\frac{6}{12}\right)$			
	Bus 3	7,22,500		21,67,500					
Jul 1	To Profit and Loss A/c (W.N.)			31,688					
					Dec 31	By Depreciation A/c			
						Bus 2	1,08,375		
						Bus 3	1,08,375		2,16,750
					Dec 31	By Balance c/d			
						Bus 2	6,14,125		
						Bus 3	6,14,125		12,28,250
				21,99,188					21,99,188

Date	Particulars		JF	Amt (₹)	Date	Particulars		JF	Amt (₹)
2016					2016				
Jan 1	To Balance b/d				Dec 31	By Depreciation A/c			
	Bus 2	6,14,125				Bus 2	9,2,119		
	Bus 3	6,14,125		12,28,250		Bus 3	92,119		1,84,238
					Dec 31	By Balance c/d			
						Bus 2	5,22,006		
						Bus 3	5,22,006		10,44,012
				12,28,250					12,28,250

ILLUSTRATION |23| On 1st January, 2014, Z Ltd purchased machinery for ₹ 1,20,000 and on 30th June, 2015 it acquired additional machinery at a cost ₹ 20,000. On 31st March, 2016, one of the original machine (purchased on 1st January, 2014) which had cost of ₹ 5,000 was found to have become obsolete and was sold as scrap for ₹ 500. It was replaced on that date by a new machine costing ₹ 8,000. Depreciation is to be provided @ 15% per annum on the written down value. Accounts are closed on 31st December, each year. Show the machinery account for the first 3 years.

Sol. Dr **Machinery Account** Cr

Date	Particulars		JF	Amt (₹)	Date	Particulars		JF	Amt (₹)
2014					2014				
Jan 1	To Bank A/c				Dec 31	By Depreciation			
	A	1,15,000				A	17,250		
	B	5,000		1,20,000		B	750		18,000
					Dec 31	By Balance c/d			
						A	97,750		
						B	4,250		1,02,000
				1,20,000					1,20,000
2015					2015				
Jan 1	To Balance b/d				Dec 31	By Depreciation A/c			
	A	97,750				A	14,663		
	B	4,250		1,02,000		B	638		
						C	1,500		16,801
					Dec 31	By Balance c/d			
Jun 30	To Bank A/c (C)			20,000		A	83,087		
						B	3,612		
						C	18,500		1,05,199
				1,22,000					1,22,000
2016					2016				
Jan 1	To Balance b/d				Mar 31	By Bank A/c (B)			500
	A	83,087			Mar 31	By Depreciation A/c (B) $\left(3612 \times \frac{15}{100} \times \frac{3}{12}\right)$			135
	B	3,612							
	C	18,500		1,05,199					
Mar 31	To Bank A/c (D)			8,000	Mar 31	By Profit and Loss A/c			2,977
					Dec 31	By Depreciation A/c			
						A	12,463		
						C	2,775		
						D	900		16,138
					Dec 31	By Balance c/d			
						A	70,624		
						C	15,725		
						D	7,100		93,449
				1,13,199					1,13,199

NUMERICAL Questions for Practice

1 M/s Lokesh Fabrics purchased a textile machine on 1st April, 2011 for ₹ 1,00,000. On 1st July, 2012 another machine costing ₹ 2,50,000 was purchased. The machine purchased on 1st April, 2011 was sold for ₹ 25,000 on 1st October, 2015. The company charges depreciation @ 15% per annum on straight line method. Prepare machinery account for the year ended 31st March, 2016.

Ans Balance in Machinery Account = ₹ 1,09,375

2 Rohini Cement Ltd purchased on 1st January, 2014 a plant for ₹ 80,000. On 1st April, 2015, it purchased additional plant costing ₹ 48,000. On 1st September, 2016 the plant purchased on 1st January, 2014 was sold off for ₹ 42, 000 and on the same date fresh plant was purchased at the cost of ₹ 75,000.

Depreciation is provided at 10% per annum on the diminishing balance method every year. Accounts are closed each year on 31st December. Show the plant account for 3 year.

Ans Balance in Plant Account = ₹ 1,12,460.

3 A company purchased machinery for ₹ 1,00,000 on 1st January, 2014. The machinery is depreciated at 10% per annum on the original cost. On 1st July, 2016 the machinery was sold for ₹ 60,000. Give the machinery account, assuming that the books are closed on 31st December, each year.

Ans Balance of Machinery = ₹ 80,000; Loss on Sale of Machinery = ₹ 15,000

4 A company purchased on 1st July, 2014 machinery costing ₹ 30,000. It further purchased machinery on 1st January, 2015 costing ₹ 20,000 and on 1st October, 2015 costing ₹ 10,000. On 1st April, 2016 one-third of the machinery installed on 1st July, 2014 became obsolete and was sold for ₹ 3,000.

The company follows financial year as the accounting year.

Show how the machinery account would appear in the books of company if depreciation is charged @ 10% per annum on written down value method.

Ans Balance of Machinery Account—₹ 39,330 (Mach. I: ₹ 14,985; Mach. II: ₹ 15,795; Mach. III: ₹ 8,550); Loss on Sale of Machine (Mach. I) (1/3): ₹ 5,325]

[***Hint***: Balance on 1st April, 2016: Mach. I (2/3)— ₹ 16,650 and Mach. I (1/3)—₹ 8,325; Mach. II—₹ 17,550; Mach. III—₹ 9,500. Depreciation (2014-15)—Mach. I (2/3) ₹ 1,665; Mach. II ₹ 1,755; Mach. III ₹ 950.]

5 On 1st July, 2012, A Co Ltd purchased second-hand machinery for ₹ 20,000 and spend ₹ 3,000 on reconditioning and installing it. On 1st January, 2013, the firm purchased new machinery worth ₹ 12,000. On 30th June, 2014, the machinery purchased on 1st January, 2013, was sold for ₹ 8,000 and on 1st July, 2014, a fresh plant was installed. Payment for this plant was to be made as follows

1st July, 2014	₹ 5,000
30th June, 2015	₹ 6,000
30th June, 2016	₹ 5,500

Payments in 2015 and 2016 include interest of ₹ 1,000 and ₹ 500 respectively.

The company writes off 10% per annum on the original cost. The accounts are closed every year on 31st March. Show the machinery account for the year ended 31st March, 2015.

Ans Balance in Machinery Account = ₹ 30,550

[***Hint***: Cost of plant purchased on 1st July, 2014 = ₹ 5,000 + (₹ 6,000— ₹ 1,000 interest) + (₹ 5,500 –₹ 500 for interest) = ₹ 15,000. Interest expenses are of revenue nature and not of capital nature and hence not debited to machinery account.]

|TOPIC 3|
Creating Provision for Depreciation Account/Accumulated Depreciation Account

Under this method, a separate account named as 'provision for depreciation' or 'accumulated depreciation' account is created and the depreciation is transferred to this account. There are some basic characteristic of this method of recording depreciation, which are given below

(*a*) Asset account continues to appear at its original cost year after year over its entire life.

(*b*) Depreciation is accumulated in a separate account instead of being adjusted into the asset account at the end of each accounting period.

The following journal entries are passed in this method to record purchase of asset and to provide for depreciation.

Journal Entries

(i) For Recording Purchase of Asset	Asset A/c To Bank/Cash/Vendor A/c	Dr
(ii) For Providing Depreciation	Depreciation A/c To Provision for Depreciation A/c	Dr
(iii) For Closure of Depreciation Account	Profit and Loss A/c To Depreciation A/c	Dr

BALANCE SHEET TREATMENT

In the balance sheet, the fixed asset continues to appear as its original cost on the asset side. The depreciation charged till that date appears in the provision for depreciation account, which is shown either on the 'liabilities side' of the balance sheet or by way of deduction from the original cost of the asset concerned on the asset side of the balance sheet.

Balance Sheet

Liabilities	Amt (₹)	Assets		Amt (₹)
		Asset	...	
		(–) Provision for Depreciation	(...)	...

or

Balance Sheet

Liabilities	Amt (₹)	Assets	Amt (₹)
Provision for Depreciation	...	Asset	...

ILLUSTRATION |24| (When depreciation is charged as per fixed instalment method and provision for depreciation account is maintained.) On 1st April, 2012, Bajrang Marbles purchased a Machine for ₹ 2,80,000 and spent ₹ 10,000 on its carriage and ₹ 10,000 on its installation. It is estimated that its working life is 10 years and after 10 years its scrap value will be ₹ 20,000.

Prepare machine account, depreciation account and provision for depreciation account (or accumulated depreciation account) for the first four years by providing depreciation using straight line method. Accounts are closed on 31st March every year.

Sol. Dr **Machinery Account** Cr

Date	Particulars	JF	Amt (₹)	Date	Particulars	JF	Amt (₹)
2012 Apr 1	To Bank A/c (2,80,000 + 10,000 + 10,000)		3,00,000	2013 Mar 31	By Balance c/d		3,00,000
			3,00,000				3,00,000
2013 Apr 1	To Balance b/d		3,00,000	2014 Mar 31	By Balance c/d		3,00,000

Date	Particulars	JF	Amt (₹)	Date	Particulars	JF	Amt (₹)
			3,00,000				3,00,000
2014 Apr 1	To Balance b/d		3,00,000	2015 Mar 31	By Balance c/d		3,00,000
			3,00,000				3,00,000
2015 Apr 1	To Balance b/d		3,00,000	2016 Mar 31	By Balance c/d		3,00,000
			3,00,000				3,00,000

Dr **Depreciation Account** Cr

Date	Particulars	JF	Amt (₹)	Date	Particulars	JF	Amt (₹)
2013 Mar 31	To Provision for Depreciation A/c		28,000	2013 Mar 31	By Profit and Loss A/c		28,000
			28,000				28,000
2014 Mar 31	To Provision for Depreciation A/c		28,000	2014 Mar 31	By Profit and Loss A/c		28,000
			28,000				28,000
2015 Mar 31	To Provision for Depreciation A/c		28,000	2015 Mar 31	By Profit and Loss A/c		28,000
			28,000				28,000
2015 Mar 31	To Provision for Depreciation A/c		28,000	2016 Mar 31	By Profit and Loss A/c		28,000
			28,000				28,000

Dr **Provision for Depreciation Account** Cr

Date	Particulars	JF	Amt (₹)	Date	Particulars	JF	Amt (₹)
2013 Mar 31	To Balance c/d		28,000	2013 Mar 31	By Depreciation A/c		28,000
			28,000				28,000
2014 Mar 31	To Balance c/d		56,000	2013 Apr 1	By Balance b/d		28,000
				2014 Mar 31	By Depreciation A/c		28,000
			56,000				56,000
2015 Mar 31	To Balance c/d		84,000	2014 Apr 1	By Balance b/d		56,000
				2014 Mar 31	By Depreciation A/c		28,000
			84,000				84,000
2016 Mar 31	To Balance c/d		1,12,000	Apr 1	By Balance b/d		84,000
				2016 Mar 31	By Depreciation A/c		28,000
			1,12,000				1,12,000

Working Note

$$\text{Depreciation} = \frac{\text{Cost of Asset} - \text{Salvage Value}}{\text{Estimated Life of Assets}} = \frac{3{,}00{,}000 - 20{,}000}{10} = ₹\ 28{,}000$$

ILLUSTRATION |25| (When depreciation is charged as per WDV method and provision for depreciation account is maintained) Kamal Bros purchased a machine on 1st April, 2012 at a cost ₹ 6,000 and spent ₹ 4,000 on its installation. The firm writes off depreciation @ 10% per annum by written down value method. The scrap value of the machine at the end of its economic life of 4 years is expected to be ₹ 13,122.

Show the machine account, depreciation account and provision for depreciation account for 4 years in the books Kamal Bros. The book are closed on 31st March every year.

Sol. Dr **Machinery Account** Cr

Date	Particulars	JF	Amt (₹)	Date	Particulars	JF	Amt (₹)
2012 Apr 1	To Bank A/c (16,000 + 4,000)		20,000	2013 Mar 31	By Balance c/d		20,000
			20,000				20,000
2013 Apr 1	To Balance b/d		20,000	2014 Mar 31	By Balance c/d		20,000
			20,000				20,000
2014 Apr 1	To Balance b/d		20,000	2015 Mar 31	By Balance c/d		20,000
			20,000				20,000
2015 Apr 1	To Balance b/d		20,000	2016 Mar 31	By Balance c/d		20,000
			20,000				20,000

Dr **Depreciation Account** Cr

Date	Particulars	JF	Amt (₹)	Date	Particulars	JF	Amt (₹)
2013 Mar 31	To Provision for Depreciation A/c		2,000	2013 Mar 31	By Profit and Loss A/c		2,000
			2,000				2,000
2014 Mar 31	To Provision for Depreciation A/c		1,800	2014 Mar 31	By Profit and Loss A/c		1,800
			1,800				1,800
2015 Mar 31	To Provision for Depreciation A/c		1,620	2015 Mar 31	By Profit and Loss A/c		1,620
			1,620				1,620
2016 Mar 31	To Provision for Depreciation A/c		1,458	2016 Mar 31	By Profit and Loss A/c		1,458
			1,458				1,458

Dr **Provision for Depreciation Account** Cr

Date	Particulars	JF	Amt (₹)	Date	Particulars	JF	Amt (₹)
2013 Mar 31	To Balance c/d		2,000	2013 Mar 31	By Depreciation A/c		2,000
			2,000				2,000
2014 Mar 31	To Balance c/d		3,800	2013 Apr 1	By Balance b/d		2,000
				2014 Mar 31	By Depreciation A/c		1,800
			3,800				3,800

Date	Particulars	JF	Amt (₹)	Date	Particulars	JF	Amt (₹)
2015 Mar 31	To Balance c/d		5,420	2014 Apr 1	By Balance b/d		3,800
				2015 Mar 31	By Depreciation A/c		1,620
			5,420				5,420
2016 Mar 31	To Balance c/d		6,878	2015 Apr 1	By Balance b/d		5,420
				2016 Mar 31	By Depreciation A/c		1,458
			6,878				6,878

ILLUSTRATION |26| Reliance Ltd purchased a second hand machine for ₹ 56,000 on 1st October, 2014 and spent ₹ 28,000 on its overhaul and installation before putting it to operation. It is expected that the machine can be sold for ₹ 6,000 at the end of its useful life of 15 years. Moreover, an estimated cost of ₹ 1,000 is expected to be incurred to recover the salvage value of ₹ 6,000. Prepare machine account and provision for depreciation account for the first 3 years charging depreciation by fixed instalment method. Accounts are closed on 31st December, every year. **NCERT**

Sol. Dr **Machinery Account** Cr

Date	Particulars	JF	Amt (₹)	Date	Particulars	JF	Amt (₹)
2014 Oct 1	To Bank A/c (56,000 + 28,000)		84,000	2014 Dec 31	By Balance c/d		84,000
			84,000				84,000
2015 Jan 1	To Balance b/d		84,000	2015 Dec 31	By Balance c/d		84,000
			84,000				84,000
2016 Jan 1	To Balance b/d		84,000	2016 Dec 31	By Balance c/d		84,000
			84,000				84,000

Dr **Provision for Depreciation Account** Cr

Date	Particulars	JF	Amt (₹)	Date	Particulars	JF	Amt (₹)
2014 Dec 31	To Balance c/d		1,317	2014 Dec 31	By Deprecation A/c (5,267 × 3/12)		1,317
			1,317				1,317
2015 Dec 31	To Balance c/d		6,584	2015 Jan 1	By Balance b/d		1,317
				Dec 31	By Depreciation A/c		5,267
			6,584				6,584
2016 Dec 31	To Balance c/d		11,851	2016 Jan 1	By Balance b/d		6,584
				Dec 31	By Depreciation A/c		5,267
			11,851				11,851
				2017 Jan 1	By Balance b/d		11,851

Working Note

Computation of Depreciation $= \frac{56{,}000 + 28{,}000 - 5{,}000}{15} =$ ₹ 5,267

Disposal of Asset

When the asset has been sold off or is disposed, and provision of depreciation account is maintained, then the sale of the asset is recorded through 'Asset Disposal Account'. The following journal entries are passed in this regard

(i) For Transfer of Original Cost of Asset Disposed off	Asset Disposal A/c To Asset A/c	Dr
(ii) For Transfer of Accumulated Depreciation on Asset Disposed off	Provision for Depreciation A/c To Asset Disposal A/c	Dr
(iii) For Recording Sale Proceeds	Cash/Bank A/c To Asset Disposal A/c	Dr
(iv) For Transfer of the Balance in Asset Disposal Account (a) In Case of Profit	Asset Disposal A/c To Profit and Loss A/c	Dr
(b) In Case of Loss	Profit and Loss A/c To Asset Disposal A/c	Dr

Asset Disposal Account

The original cost of the asset being sold is debited to the asset disposal account and accumulated depreciation amount appearing in provision for depreciation account relating to that asset till the date of disposal is credited to the asset disposal account. The net amount realised from the sale of the asset is also credited to this account. The balance of asset disposal account shows profit or loss which is transferred to profit and loss account. Asset disposal account may ultimately show a debit or credit balance. The debit balance indicates loss on disposal and the credit balance indicates profit on disposal.

Dr **Asset Disposal Account** Cr

Date	Particulars	Amt (₹)	Date	Particulars	Amt (₹)
	To Asset A/c	...		By Provision for Depreciation A/c	...
	To Profit and Loss A/c * [Balancing figure (Profit)]	...		By Bank A/c (Sale)	...
				By Profit and Loss A/c * [Balancing figure (Loss)]	...

* Any one will appear

ILLUSTRATION |27| **(When machinery is sold at the end of the year and provision for depreciation account is maintained.) Sunny Ltd purchased a vehicle for ₹ 4,00,000. After 4 years its salvage value is estimated at ₹ 40,000. Find out the amount of depreciation to be charged every year based on straight line basis and show how the vehicle account would appear for 4 years assuming, it is sold for ₹ 50,000 at the end, when provision for depreciation account is maintained.**

Sol. Dr **Vehicle Account** Cr

Date	Particulars	JF	Amt (₹)	Date	Particulars	JF	Amt (₹)
I year	To Bank A/c		4,00,000	End of the year	By Balance c/d		4,00,000
			4,00,000				4,00,000
II year	To Balance b/d		4,00,000	End of the year	By Balance c/d		4,00,000
			4,00,000				4,00,000
III year	To Balance b/d		4,00,000	End of the year	By Balance c/d		4,00,000
			4,00,000				4,00,000
IV year	To Balance b/d		4,00,000	End of the year	By Asset Disposal A/c		4,00,000
			4,00,000				4,00,000

Dr **Provision for Depreciation Account** Cr

Date	Particulars	JF	Amt (₹)	Date	Particulars	JF	Amt (₹)
I year	To Balance c/d		90,000	End of the year	By Depreciation A/c		90,000
			90,000				90,000
II year	To Balanced c/d		1,80,000	End of the year	By Balance b/d		90,000
					By Depreciation A/c		90,000
			1,80,000				1,80,000
III year	To Balance c/d		2,70,000	End of the year	By Balance b/d		1,80,000
					By Depreciation A/c		90,000
			2,70,000				2,70,000
IV year	To Asset Disposal A/c		3,60,000	End of the year	By Balance b/d		2,70,000
					By Depreciation A/c		90,000
			3,60,000				3,60,000

Dr Asset Disposal Account Cr

Date	Particulars	JF	Amt (₹)	Date	Particulars	JF	Amt (₹)
End of IVth year	To Machinery A/c		4,00,000	End of IVth year	By Provision for Depreciation A/c		3,60,000
	To Profit and Loss A/c		10,000		By Bank A/c		50,000
			4,10,000				4,10,000

Working Note

1. Depreciation $= \frac{\text{Cost of Asset} - \text{NRV}}{\text{Life of Asset}} = \frac{4{,}00{,}000 - 40{,}000}{4} =$ ₹ 90,000
2. Calculation of Profit/Loss on Sale

Book Value as on Date of Sale	4,00,000
(–) Provision for Depreciation	3,60,000
	40,000
(–) Sale Proceeds	50,000
Profit	₹ 10,000

ILLUSTRATION |28| **(When one machinery is purchased and sold in the middle of the year and provision for depreciation account is maintained.) On 1st April, 2013 a firm purchased a machinery for ₹ 1,00,000. On 1st July, 2016 the machinery became obsolete and was sold for ₹ 40,000. The firm charges depreciation on its machinery @ 10% per annum on written down value method. The books are closed on 31st March of every year. Prepare necessary ledger accounts assuming that provision for depreciation account is maintained.**

Sol. Dr **Machinery Account** Cr

Date	Particulars	Amt (₹)	Date	Particulars	Amt (₹)
2013 Apr 1	To Bank A/c	1,00,000	2014 Mar 31	By Balance c/d	1,00,000
		1,00,000			1,00,000
2014 Apr 1	To Balance b/d	1,00,000	2015 Mar 31	By Balance c/d	1,00,000
		1,00,000			1,00,000
2015 Apr 1	To Balance b/d	1,00,000	2016 Mar 31	By Balance c/d	1,00,000
		1,00,000			1,00,000
2016 Apr 1	To Balance b/d	1,00,000	2016 July 1	By Asset Disposal A/c	1,00,000
		1,00,000			1,00,000

Dr **Provision For Depreciation Account** Cr

Date	Particulars	Amt (₹)	Date	Particulars	Amt (₹)
2014			2014		
Mar 31	To Balance c/d	10,000	Mar 31	By Depreciation A/c (1,00,000 × 10%)	10,000
		10,000			10,000
2015			2014		
Mar 31	To Balance c/d	19,000	Apr 1	By Balance b/d	10,000
			2015		
			Mar 31	By Depreciation A/c (1,00,000 −10,000 × 10%)	9,000
		19,000			19,000
2016			2016		
Mar 31	To Balance c/d	27,100	Apr 1	By Balance b/d	19,000
			2003		
			Mar 31	By Depreciation A/c (90,000 − 9,000 × 10%)	8,100
		27,100			27,100
2016			2016		
July 1	To Asset Disposal A/c	28,922.50	Apr 1	By Balance b/d	27,100
			July 1	By Depreciation A/c $\left[(81{,}000 - 8{,}100) \times 10\% \times \frac{3}{12}\right]$	1,822.50
		28,922.50			28,922.50

Asset Disposal A/c

Date	Particulars	JF	Amt (₹)	Date	Particulars	JF	Amt (₹)
2016				2016			
July 1	To Machinery A/c		1,00,000	July 1	By Provision for Depreciation A/c		28,922.50
				July 1	By Bank A/c		40,000
				July 1	By Profit and Loss A/c		3,10,77.50
			1,00,000				1,00,000

Comprehensive Illustrations

ILLUSTRATION |29| (When assets are purchased and sold on different dates and depreciation is charged on written down value basis, when provision for depreciation account is maintained.) On 1st April, 2014, X Ltd purchased a machinery for ₹ 12,00,000. On 1st October, 2013 a part of the machinery purchased on 1st April, 2014 for ₹ 80,000 was sold for ₹ 45,000 and a new machinery at the cost of ₹ 1,58,000 was purchased and installed on the same date. The company has adopted the method of providing 10% per annum depreciation on the diminishing balance of the machinery.

Show the necessary ledger accounts assuming that provision for depreciation account and machinery disposal account is maintained. The accounting year ends on 31st March.

Sol. Dr **Machinery Account** (At original cost) Cr

Date	Particulars	JF	Amt (₹)	Data	Particulars	JF	Amt (₹)
2014				2015			
Apr 1	To Bank A/c			Mar 31	By Balance c/d		
	A 11,20,000				A 11,20,000		
	B 80,000		12,00,000		B 80,000		12,00,000
2015			12,00,000	2016			12,00,000
Apr1	To Balance b/d			Mar 31	By Balance c/d		
	A 11,20,000				A 11,20,000		
	B 80,000		12,00,000		B 80,000		12,00,000
			12,00,000				12,00,000
2016				2016			
Apr 1	To Balance b/d			Oct 1	By Machinery Disposal A/c		80,000
	A 11,20,000						
	B 80,000		12,00,000	2017			
Oct 1	To Bank A/c (c)		1,58,000	Mar 31	By Balance c/d		
					A 11,20,000		
					C 1,58,000		12,78,000
			13,58,000				13,58,000

Dr **Provision for Depreciation Account** Cr

Date	Particulars	JF	Amt (₹)	Date	Particulars	JF	Amt (₹)
2015				2015			
Mar 31	To Balance c/d			Mar 31	By Depreciation A/c		
	A 1,12,000				A 1,12,000		
	B 8,000		1,20,000		B 8,000		1,20,000
			1,20,000				1,20,000
2016				2015			
Mar 31	To Balance c/d			Apr 1	By Balance C/d		
	A 2,12,800				A 11,20,000		
	B 1,520		2,28,000		B 80,000		12,00,000
				2016			
				Mar 31	By Depreciation A/c		
					A 1,00,800		
					B 7,200		1,08,000
			2,28,000				2,28,000
2016				2016			
Oct 1	To Machinery Disposal A/c (B) (15,200+3,240)		18,440	Apr 1	By Balance b/d		
					A 2,12,800		
					B 15,200		2,28,000
2017				Oct 1	By Depreciation A/c (B) (W.N)		3,240
Mar 31	To Balance c/d						
	A 3,03,520			2017			
	C 7,900		3,11,420	Mar 31	By Depreciation A/c		
					A 90,720		
					C 7,900		98,620
			3,29,860				3,29,860

Dr **Machinery Disposal Account** Cr

Date	Particulars	JF	Amt (₹)	Date	Particulars	JF	Amt (₹)
2016 Oct 1	To Machinery A/c		80,000	2016 Oct 1	By Provision for Depreciation A/c		18,440
					By Bank A/c		45,000
					By Profit and Loss A/c (Loss on sale) (WN 1)		16,560
			80,000				80,000

Working Note

(i) Calculation of Profit/Loss on Sale of Machinery

Original cost as on 1st April, 2014	80,000
(–) Depreciation @ 10% per annum for 2014-15	8,000
Book value as on 1st April, 2015	72,000
(–) Depreciation @ 10% per annum for 2015-16	7,200
Book value as on 1st April, 2016	64,800
(–) Depreciation @ 10% per annum upto date of sale (₹ 64,800 × 10/100 × 6/12)	3,240
Book value as on 1st October, 2016	61,560
(–) Sale proceeds	45,000
Loss on sale of machinery	₹ 16,560

ILLUSTRATION |30| **(When assets are purchased and sold on different dates and depreciation is charged on original cost basis, when provision for depreciation account is maintained) Bansal Construction Ltd purchased a machine on 1st October, 2010 for ₹ 6,55,000. On 1st March, 2011, it purchased another machine for ₹ 2,40,000. On 1st July, 2012 it sold off the first machine purchased in 2010, for ₹ 5,24,000. Accumulated depreciation account is maintained charging depreciation at 10% per annum on straight line method. Accounts are closed each year on 31st March, prepare machinery account and accumulated depreciation account for the year ended on 31st March, 2011, 2012 and 2013. Also prepare machinery disposal account.**

Sol. Dr **Machinery Account** Cr

Date	Particulars		JF	Amt (₹)	Date	Particulars		JF	Amt (₹)
2010 Oct 1	To Bank A/c (A)			6,55,000	2011 Mar 31	By Balance c/d			
						A	6,55,000		
						B	2,40,000		8,95,000
2011 Mar 1	To Bank A/c (B)			2,40,000					
				8,95,000					8,95,000
2011 Apr 1	To Balance b/d				2012 Mar 31	By Balance c/d			
	A	6,55,000				A	6,55,000		
	B	2,40,000		8,95,000		B	2,40,000		8,95,000
				8,95,000					8,95,000
2012 Apr 1	To Balance b/d				2012 Jul 1	By Machinery Disposal A/c (A)			6,55,000
	A	6,55,000							
	B	2,40,000		8,95,000	2013 Mar 31	By Balance c/d (B)			2,40,000
				8,95,000					8,95,000
2013 Apr 1	To Balance b/d			2,40,000					

Dr — Provision for Depreciation Account — Cr

Date	Particulars		JF	Amt	Data	Particulars		JF	Amt
2011 Mar 31	To Balance c/d				2011 Mar 31	By Depreciation A/c			
	A	32,750				A	32,750		
	B	2,000		34,750		B	2,000		34,750
				34,750					34,750
2012 Mar 31	To Balance c/d				2011 Apr 1	By Balance b/d			
	A	98,250				A	32,750		
	B	26,000		1,24,250		B	2,000		34,750
					2012 Mar 31	By Depreciation A/c			
						A	65,500		
						B	24,000		89,500
				1,24,250					1,24,250
2012 Jul 1	To Machinery Disposal A/c			1,14,625	2012 Apr 1	By Balance b/d			
						A	98,250		
2013						B	26,000		1,24,250
Mar 31	To Balance c/d (B)			50,000	Jul 1	By Depreciation A/c (A)			16,375
					2013 Mar 31	By Depreciation A/c (B)			24,000
				1,64,625					1,64,625

Dr — Machinery Disposal Account — Cr

Date	Particulars	Amt (₹)	Date	Particulars	Amt (₹)
2015 Jul 1	To Machinery A/c	6,55,000	2015 Jul 1	By Provision for Depreciation A/c	1,14,625
			Jul 1	By Bank A/c	5,24,000
			Jul 1	By Profit and Loss A/c (Loss)	16,375
		6,55,000			6,55,000

Working Note

Original cost on 1st October, 2013		6,55,000
(–) Depreciation for 6 months provided on 31st March, 2011	32,750	
Depreciation for 1 year provided on 31st March, 2012	65,500	
Depreciation for 3 months provided on 31st July, 2013	16,375	1,14,625
Book value as on July, 2015		5,40,375
(–) Sale proceeds		5,24,000
Loss on sale of machinery		16,375

ILLUSTRATION |31| **The following balances appear in the books of Crystal Ltd on 1st January, 2016.**

Items	Amt (₹)
Machinery account	15,00,000
Provision for depreciation account	5,50,000

On 1st April, 2016, a machinery which was purchased on 1st January, 2013 for ₹ 2,00,000 was sold for ₹75,000. A new machine was purchased on 1st July, 2016 for ₹ 6,00,000. Depreciation is provided on machinery at 20% per annum on straight line method and books are closed on 31st December every year. Prepare the machinery account and provision for depreciation account for the year ending 31st December, 2016.

NCERT

Sol. Dr **Machinery Account** Cr

Date	Particulars	JF	Amt (₹)	Date	Particulars	JF	Amt (₹)
2016				2016			
Jan 1	To Balance b/d (13,00,000 + 2,00,000)		15,00,000	Apr 1	By Machinery Disposal A/c		2,00,000
Jul 1	To Bank A/c		6,00,000	Dec 1	By Balance c/d		19,00,000
			21,00,000				21,00,000

Dr **Provision for Depreciation Account** Cr

Date	Particulars	JF	Amt (₹)	Date	Particulars	JF	Amt (₹)
2016				2016			
Apr 1	To Machinery Disposal A/c		1,30,000	Jan 1	By Balance b/d		5,50,000
				Apr 1	By Depreciation A/c		10,000
Dec 31	To Balance c/d		7,50,000	Dec 31	By Depreciation A/c 2,60,000 +60,000		3,20,000
			8,80,000				8,80,000

Dr **Machinery Disposal Account** Cr

Date	Particulars	JF	Amt (₹)	Date	Particulars	JF	Amt (₹)
2016				2016			
Apr 1	To Machinery A/c		2,00,000	Apr 1	By Provision for Depreciation A/c		1,30,000
Apr 1	To Profit and Loss A/c (Profit)		5,000	Apr 1	By Bank A/c		75,000
			2,05,000				2,05,000

Working Note

Depreciation charged on Machinery costing ₹ 2,00,000 in past 3 years

2013 @ 20% = ₹40,000

2014 @ 20% = ₹40,000

2015 @ 20% = ₹40,000

2016 @ 20% = ₹10,000 (for 3 months)

Total depreciation charged = ₹ 1,30,000

ILLUSTRATION |32| On 1st January, 2013 *X* Ltd purchased for *Y* Ltd a plant costing ₹ 4,00,000 on instalment basis payable as follows

	Amt (₹)
On 1st January, 2013	1,00,000
On 1st July, 2013	1,00,000
On 1st January, 2014	1,00,000
On 1st January, 2014	1,00,000

The company spent ₹ 10,000 on transportation and instalation of the plant. It was decided to provide for depreciation on the straight line method. Useful life of the plant was estimated at 5 years. It was also estimated that at the end of the useful life, realisable value of the plant would be ₹ 12,000 (gross) and dismantling cost of plant to be paid by company was estimated at ₹ 2,000. The plant was destroyed by fire on 31st December, 2016 and an insurance claim of ₹ 50,000 was admitted by the insurance company. Prepare the plant account, accumulated depreciation account and plant disposal account assuming that the company closes its books on 31st December, every year.

Sol. Calculation of Depreciation $= \dfrac{\text{Total Cost} - \text{Net Scrap Value}}{\text{Estimated Useful Life of Plant (in years)}}$

$$= \frac{4{,}00{,}000 + 10{,}000 - (12{,}000 - 2{,}000)}{5 \text{ Years}} = \frac{4{,}00{,}000}{5} = ₹\ 80{,}000 \text{ per year}$$

Dr **Plant Account** Cr

Date	Particulars		JF	Amt (₹)	Date	Particulars	JF	Amt (₹)
2013					2013			
Jan 1	To Bank A/c	1,00,000			Dec 31	By Balance c/d		4,10,000
	To Bank A/c	10,000						
	To Supplier A/c	3,00,000		4,10,000				
				4,10,000				4,10,000
2014					2014			
Jan 1	To Balance b/d			4,10,000	Dec 31	By Balance c/d		4,10,000
				4,10,000				4,10,000
2015					2015			
Jan 1	To Balance b/d			4,10,000	Dec 31	By Balance c/d		4,10,000
				4,10,000				4,10,000
2016					2016			
Jan 1	To Balance b/d			4,10,000	Dec 31	By Plant Disposal A/c (Transfer)		4,10,000
				4,10,000				4,10,000

Dr **Provision for Depreciation Account** Cr

Date	Particulars	Amt (₹)	Date	Particulars	Amt (₹)
2013			2013		
Dec 31	To Balance c/d	80,000	Dec 31	By Depreciation A/c	80,000
		80,000			80,000
2014			2014		
Dec 31	To Balance c/d	1,60,000	Jan 1	By Balance b/d	80,000
			Dec 31	By Depreciation A/c	80,000
		1,60,000			1,60,000
2015			2015		
Dec 31	To Balance c/d	2,40,000	Jan 1	By Balance b/d	1,60,000
			Dec 31	By Depreciation A/c	80,000
		2,40,000			2,40,000
2016			2016		
Dec 31	To Plant Disposal A/c	3,20,000	Jan 1	By Balance b/d	2,40,000
			Dec 31	By Depreciation A/c	80,000
		3,20,000			3,20,000

Dr **Plant Disposal Account** Cr

Date	Particulars	Amt (₹)	Date	Particulars	Amt (₹)
2016			2016		
Dec 31	To Plant A/c	4,10,000	Dec 31	By Provision for Depreciation A/c	3,20,000
			Dec 31	By Bank A/c (Insurance claim)	50,000
			Dec 31	By Profit and Loss A/c (Loss) (Balancing figure)	40,000
		4,10,000			4,10,000

NUMERICAL Questions for Practice

1 Karan Enterprises has the following balances in its books as on 31st March, 2015.

Machinery (gross value) ₹ 6,00,000

Provision for depreciation ₹ 2,50,000

A machine purchased for ₹ 1,00,000 on 1st November, 2016 having accumulated depreciation amounting to ₹ 60,000 was sold on 1st April, 2016 for ₹ 35,000. Prepare machinery account, provision for depreciation account and machinery disposal account.

Ans Balance in Machinery Account = ₹ 5,00,000; Loss on Sale = ₹ 5,000

2 Prominent Ltd purchased on 1st April, 2013 a plant for ₹ 5,00,000. On 1st October, 2013 an additional plant was purchased costing ₹ 2,50,000. On 1st October, 2015 the plant purchased on 1st April, 2013 having become obsolete, was sold for ₹ 2,00,000. Depreciation is provided @ 10% per annum on the original cost on 31st March, every year. Show the machinery, machinery diposal and posivion for depreciation accounts for the year, 2014-15 and 2015-16.

Ans Balance in Machinery Account = ₹ 2,50,000, Balance in Provision for Depreciation Account = ₹ 37,500, Loss on Sale = ₹ 2,25,000.

3 On 1st April, 2014, X Ltd. purchased a machinery for ₹ 12,00,000. On 1st October, 2016, a part of the machinery purchased on 1st April, 2014 for ₹ 80,000 was sold for ₹ 45,000 and a new machinery at the cost of ₹ 1,58,000 was purchased and installed on the same date. The company has adopted the method of providing 10% per annum depreciation on the diminishing balance of the machinery.

Show the necessary ledger accounts assuming that provision for depreciation account is maintained, the accounting year ends on 31st March.

Ans Balance in Machinery Account = ₹ 12,78,000, Balance in Provision for Depreciation Account = ₹ 3,11,420, Loss on Sale = ₹ 16,560.

4 Aakash Ltd purchased on 1st January, 2013 a second hand machinery for ₹ 2,00,000 and immediately spent ₹ 50,000 for its overhauling and installation. On 1st July, 2016, the plant become obsolete and was sold for ₹ 90,000. Depreciation is provided @ 10% per annum on original cost basis. Books are closed on 31st December every year. Show the necessary ledger account assuming that (a) provision for depreciation is maintained (b) Provision for depreciation account is maintained.

Ans (a) Balance in Machinery Account = ₹ 1,75,000.
(b) Balance in Machinery Account = ₹ 2,50,000; Balance in Provision for Depreciation Account = ₹ 87,500.

5 On 1st April, 2013 a firm purchased a machinery for ₹ 1,00,000. On 1st July, 2016 the machinery became obsolete and was sold for ₹ 40,000.

The firm charges depreciation on its machinery @ 10% per annum on written down value method. The books are closed on 31st March of every year. Prepare necessary ledger accounts assuming that

(a) Provision for depreciation account is not maintained.
(b) Provision for depreciation account is maintained.

Ans (*a*) Balance in Machinery Account = ₹ 72,900, Loss on Sale = ₹ 31,077.50.
(*b*) Balance in Machinery Account = ₹ 1,00,000, Balance in Provision for Depreciation Account = ₹ 28,922.50.

6 Kaushik Ltd purchased a vehicle for ₹ 4,00,000. After 4 year its salvage value is estimated at ₹ 40,000. To find out the amount of depreciation to be charged every year based on straight line basis, and also to show the vehicle account as would appear for 4 years, assuming it is sold for ₹ 50,000 at the end when

(a) Depreciation is charged to asset account.
(b) Provision for depreciation accout is maintained.

Prepare the ledger in the books of accounts of Kaushik Ltd. by both the above methods.

Ans (a) Balance in Vehicle Account = ₹ 1,30,000, Profit on Sale = ₹ 10,000.
(b) Balance in Vehicle Account = ₹ 4,00,000.

|TOPIC 4|
Provisions and Reserves

PROVISIONS

The amount set aside for the purpose of providing for any known liability, uncertain loss or expense, the amount of which cannot be ascertained with reasonable accuracy, is referred to as provision.

In other words, provision means providing for a liability on the basis of estimation. It means liability is certain but amount is not. It should be noted that if the liability and amount are certain it will be an outright liability and not a provision.

Examples of provisions are

(*i*) Provision for depreciation
(*ii*) Provision for repairs and renewals
(*iii*) Provision for taxation
(*iv*) Provision for bad and doubtful debts
(*v*) Provision for discount on debtors.

Objectives of Provision

Points highlighting the objectives of provision are as follows

(*i*) **To Meet Anticipated Losses and Liabilities** Provisions are created for meeting anticipated losses and liabilities such as provision for doubtful debts, provision for discount on debtors and provision for taxation.

(*ii*) **To Meet Known Losses and Liabilities** Provisions are created for meeting known losses and liabilities such as provision for repairs and renewals.

(*iii*) **To Present Correct Financial Statements** In order to present correct financial statements and to report true profit and financial position, the business must maintain provision for known liabilities and losses.

Accounting Treatment and Disclosure of Provision

Provision is a charge against the profits and is created by debiting profit and loss account. In the balance sheet, the amount of provision may be shown either

(*i*) on the assets side, by way of deduction from the concerned asset.

For example, provision for doubtful debts is shown as deduction from the amount of sundry debtors and provision for depreciation as a deduction from the concerned fixed assets.

(*ii*) on the liability side along with the current liabilities.

For example, provision for taxes and provision for repairs and renewals.

RESERVES

Reserves are referred to as the amount set aside from profits or surpluses and retained in the business to provide for certain future needs like growth and expansion or to meet future contingencies.

Examples of reserves are

(*i*) General reserve
(*ii*) Workmen compensation fund
(*iii*) Investment fluctuation fund
(*iv*) Capital reserve
(*v*) Dividend equalisation reserve.

Reserves are not a charge against profit, but are the appropriations of profit and therefore not shown in the profit and loss account.

Retention of profits in the form of reserves reduces the amount of profits available for distribution among the owners of the business.

Objectives of Reserves

The objectives of creating the reserves includes the following

(*i*) To strengthen the financial position of an enterprise.
(*ii*) To meet a future contingency.
(*iii*) To expand the business operations and to bring uniformity in distribution of dividends.
(*iv*) To redeem a long-term liability like debentures etc.

Types of Reserves

Reserves are generally classified into

1. **REVENUE RESERVES**

The reserves created from revenue profits which arise out of the normal operating activities of the business and are otherwise freely available for distribution as dividend, are known as revenue reserves.

Revenue reserves can be classified into

(i) General Reserve

The reserve which is not created for a specific purpose is general reserve. It strengthens the financial position of the business. It is also known as **free reserve or contingency reserve.**

(ii) Specific Reserves

As the name suggests, these are the reserves that are created for some specific purpose and can be utilised only for that purpose.

Examples of specific reserves are given below

(*a*) **Dividend Equalisation Reserve** This reserve is created to stabilise or maintain dividend rate. In the year of high profit, amount is transferred to dividend equalisation reserve. In the year of low profit, this reserve amount is used to maintain the rate of dividend.

(*b*) **Workmen Compensation Fund** It is created to provide for claims of the workers due to accident, etc.

(*c*) **Investment Fluctuation Fund** It is created to provide for decline in the value of investment due to market fluctuation.

(*d*) **Debenture Redemption Reserve** It is created to provide funds for redemption of debentures.

Secret Reserve

It has been defined as any reserve which does not appear in the balance sheet. It is also called as inner reserve or internal reserve or hidden reserve. Secret reserves are a result of understatement of assets or overstatement of liabilities and corresponding understatement of capital. With the existence of secret reserves, the finanical position of the company is better than it appears from the balance sheet. Creation of secret reserve is prohibited as per Companies Act.

Secret reserve is created by the following methods

(*i*) By including fictitious assets.
(*ii*) By writing down the value of goodwill to a nominal value.
(*iii*) By showing an asset as a contingent asset.
(*iv*) By providing excess depreciation on fixed assets.
(*v*) By charging capital expenditure to revenue account.
(*vi*) By completely omitting some of the assets from the balance sheet.
(*vii*) By writing down the asset much below their cost or market value, etc.

2. **CAPITAL RESERVE**

The reserves created out of capital profits and not available for distribution as dividend are known as capital reserves. Capital reserves can be used for writing off capital losses or for issue of bonus shares in case of a company.

Examples of capital reserves are given below

(*i*) Premium on issue of shares or debentures.
(*ii*) Profit on sale of fixed assets.
(*iii*) Profit on redemption of debentures.
(*iv*) Profit on revaluation of fixed assets and liabilities.
(*v*) Profits prior to incorporation.
(*vi*) Profit on re-issue of forfeited shares.
(*vii*) Capital redemption reserve.
(*viii*) Profit on forfeiture of shares.

Accounting Treatment and Disclosure

Reserves are not a charge against profit, but are the appropriation of profits. Hence, reserves are created through profit and loss appropriation account.

Reserves are shown under the head reserves and surplus on the liabilities side of the balance sheet.

Differences between Provision and Reserves

The differences between provision and reserves are stated in the table given below

Basis	*Provision*	*Reserves*
Basic Nature	Provisions are Charge against profit.	Reserves are appropriation of profits.
Meaning	It is created to meet known liability.	It is created to meet unknown liability.
Effects on Taxable Profits	It reduces taxable profits.	It has no effect on taxable profit.
Presentation in Balance Sheet	It is shown either (i) by way of deduction from the item on the assets side for which it is created, (ii) in the liabilities side along with current liabilities.	It is shown on the liabilities side after capital amount.
Element of Compulsion	Creation of provision is necessary. It must be made even if there are no profits.	Generally, creation of a reserve is at the discretion of management. Reserves cannot be created unless there are profits.
Use for the Payment of Dividend	It can not be used for dividend distribution.	It can be used for dividend distribution.
Investment, Outside, the Business	Provisions are never invested outside the business.	Reserves may be invested outside the business.'
Purpose	It is created for a specific liability.	It is created for strengthening the financial position.
Mode of Creation	It is created by debiting the profit and loss account.	It is created by debiting the profit and loss appropriation account.

CHAPTER PRACTICE

OBJECTIVE TYPE Questions

Multiple Choice Questions

1 Depreciation is a/an .... cost.

(a) current (b) sequence
(c) expired (d) matured

Ans (c) Depreciation cost is reduced or deducted before calculating taxable profits. It is an expired cost on which assets value has been decreased.

2 Which of the following is not depreciable?

(a) Plant (b) Machinery
(c) Land (d) Building

Ans (c) There is no depreciation charged on land, because land price get increased year on year and land price becomes high.

3 ...... refers to reduction in value or expiration of cost of asset resulting from production.

(a) Depletion (b) Depreciation
(c) Amortisation (d) None of these

Ans (a) Depletion

4 Balance sheet will not show the correct financial position of the business, if depreciation is not provided on assets, as the assets

(a) will remain overvalued
(b) will remain undervalued
(c) will remain cost effective
(d) None of the above

Ans (a) It is necessary for the business to show true and fair financial position. Hence, depreciation should be reduced from assets to present them on correct value.

5 Decline in the economic value of the assets due to innovation or improved technique and change in taste and fashion is

(a) original assets value
(b) obsolescence
(c) correct cost value
(d) variable assets and cost

Ans (b) When new technology replaces the older one, this process of replacement is called obsolescence. It can be due to change in market demand, change in taste and fashion, etc.

6 Apart from the tax regulation, it is necessary to charge depreciation to comply with the provisions of

(a) Partnership Act (b) Companies Act, 2013
(c) Labour Law Act (d) All of these

Ans (b) Companies Act, 2013

7 A machinery for packing processed food products is claimed to have a useful life of 10 years by the manufacturer but the buyer company fears that the machine will be obsolete in the next 5 years. What is the useful life of assets for charging depreciation?

(a) Useful life will be of 10 years
(b) Useful life will be of 5 years
(c) Useful life can be of 10 or 5 years
(d) None of the above

Ans (b) Useful life will be of 5 years

8 Reserves are created for

(a) growth (b) expansion
(c) income (d) Both (a) and (b)

Ans (d) Reserves are referred as the amount set aside from profits and retained in the business to provide for certain future needs like growth and expansion or to meet future contingencies.

9 What kind of reserves are not created for a specific purpose in the business, which is a part of revenue reserve?

(a) Specific reserve (b) General reserve
(c) Revenue reserve (d) None of these

Ans (b) General reserves are created from retained earnings which are kept aside out of company's profit. These reserves are not created for any specific purpose.

10 Due to the presence of ......, the financial position of the company is better than it appears from the balance sheet.

(a) retained earnings (b) depreciation
(c) secret reserves (d) amortisation

Ans (c) Secret reserves are a result of understatement of assets or overstatement of liabilities and corresponding understatement of capital.

11 Provision is a charge against the profits and is created by debiting profit and loss account. In balance sheet, amount may be shown

(a) on assets side (b) profit and loss account
(c) trading account (d) None of these

Ans (a) on assets side

12 **On 1st April, 2017 a plant was purchased by Mohit Ltd for ₹ 2,00,000. The rate of depreciation was charged at 40%. Under diminishing balance method, calculate the depreciation amount for 31st March, 2018.**

(a) ₹ 40,000 (b) ₹ 80,000
(c) ₹ 1,20,000 (d) ₹ 48,000

Ans (b) Machine cost = ₹ 2,00,000, Depreciation rate = 40%
Hence, depreciation amount for Ist year will be

$$2{,}00{,}000 \times \frac{40}{100} = ₹\ 80{,}000$$

13 **Original cost of an asset is ₹ 2,00,000 and depreciation is charged @ 10% per annum at written down value. Calculate the amount of depreciation charged in 2nd year?**

(a) ₹ 20,000 (b) ₹ 18,000
(c) ₹ 16,200 (d) ₹ 14,580

Ans (b) Depreciation for first year

$$= 2{,}00{,}000 \times \frac{10}{100} = ₹\ 20{,}000$$

$$\text{Depreciation for second year} = (2{,}00{,}000 - 20{,}000) \times \frac{10}{100}$$

$$= 1{,}80{,}000 \times \frac{10}{100} = ₹18{,}000$$

14 **Original cost of machine is ₹ 4,00,000 with a scrap value of ₹ 25,000 after 4 years. What will be the rate of depreciation as per written down value method?**

(a) 100% (b) 25% (c) 50% (d) 75%

Ans (c) Rate of depreciation $= \left[1 - \sqrt[n]{\frac{s}{c}}\right] \times 100$

Where, n = Expected useful life
s = Scrap value
c = Cost of an asset

$$= \left[1 - \sqrt[4]{\frac{25{,}000}{4{,}00{,}000}}\right] \times 100$$

$$= [1 - 0.5] \times 100 = 50\% \text{ per annum}$$

15 **Ramesh purchased a machinery for ₹ 50,000 by cheque on 1st July, 2011. Another machine was purchased for ₹ 30,000 by cheque on 1st January, 2013. Depreciation is charged at 10% per annum by the straight line method. Accounts are closed each year on 31st December. What will be the journal entry for depreciation on 1st machinery on 31st December, 2013?**

		Dr	Cr
(a)	Depreciation A/c Dr	5,000	
	To Accumulated Depreciation A/c		5,000
(b)	Bank A/c Dr	5,000	
	To Depreciation A/c		5,000
(c)	Accumulated Depreciation A/c Dr	5,000	
	To Depreciation A/c		5,000
(d)	Depreciation A/c Dr	5,000	
	To Bank A/c		5,000

Ans (a) In journal entry of depreciation, depreciation account is debited to reduce asset value, *i.e.* indirectly saving money for new purchase in future after machine become scrap and accumulated depreciation is credited to create business liability to pay for replacement of fixed asset.

16 **A company bought a machine for ₹ 90,000 on credit. Another ₹ 10,000 is spent on its installation. If the estimated useful life is 5 years and scrap value of the end was ₹ 5,000. What will be the rate of depreciation?**

(a) 17% (b) 18% (c) 19% (d) 20%

Ans (c) Depreciation $= \frac{\text{Cost} - \text{Estimated Scrap Value}}{\text{Expected Useful Life}}$

$$= \frac{(90{,}000 + 10{,}000) - 5{,}000}{5} = ₹\ 19{,}000$$

$$\text{Rate of depreciation} = \frac{\text{Annual Depreciation}}{\text{Cost of Assets}} \times 100$$

$$= \frac{19{,}000}{1{,}00{,}000} \times 100$$

$$= 19\% \text{ per annum}$$

17 **Book value of machine as on 31st March, 2013 is ₹ 2,91,600. This machine was purchased on 1st April, 2010. Depreciation is charged at 10% on written down value method. What will be the cost of machine?**

(a) ₹ 1,00,000 (b) ₹2,00,000
(c) ₹ 3,00,000 (d) ₹4,00,000

Ans (d)

	Let cost of machine on 1st April, 2010	100.00
∴	Depreciation for Ist year (2010-11)	10.00
	Written Down Value (WDV)	90.00
	Depreciation for IInd year (2011-12)	(9.00)
	Written Down value	81.00
	Depreciation for IIIrd year (2012-13)	(8.10)
	Written down value 31st March, 2013	72.90

When WDV is 72.9 cost = 100

$$\text{When WDV is ₹ 2,91,600, cost is} = \frac{100}{72.9} \times 2{,}91{,}600$$

$$= ₹\ 4{,}00{,}000$$

Fill in the Blanks

18 **Depreciation represents a .... in the value of fixed assets.**

Ans decrease

19 Estimated sale value of an asset after its useful life is called ....

Ans scrap value

20 .... is the decrease in the value of wasting assets.

Ans Depletion

21 Depreciation under written down value method is computed on .... of fixed asset.

Ans book value

22 Scrap value of the asset means value of asset realised after the expiry of its ....

Ans useful life

State True or False

23 Amount of depreciation remains constant under written down value method.

Ans False. Amount of depreciation remains constant under straight line method.

24 Depreciation is not to be charged on land.

Ans True

25 Depreciation cannot be provided if there is a loss in a financial year.

Ans False. Depreciation is a charge against profit. So, it is to be provided in case of loss in a financial year.

26 Provisions are made to meet the unforeseen liability.

Ans False. Provisions means an amount set aside to meet a future expense or loss whose exact amount is uncertain.

27 If the amount of reserve is invested in ...., it is termed as reserve fund.

Ans outside securities

Match the Following

28

	Column I		*Column II*
1.	Related to natural resources or wasting assets	(a)	Amortisation
2.	Write-off the cost of an intangible asset	(b)	Debenture redemption reserve
3.	Reserve created for redemption of debentures	(c)	Depreciation
4.	Decline in the value of fixed assets	(d)	Depletion

Ans 1-(d), 2-(a), 3-(b), 4-(c)

Journalise the Following

29 For providing depreciation at the end of each year.

Ans

Depreciation A/c To Asset A/c (Being depreciation charged)	Dr	—	—

30 There is a loss on sale of asset.

Ans

Profit and Loss A/c To Asset A/c (Being loss on sale of asset charged from Profit and Loss A/c)	Dr	—	—

31 Provision for depreciation account is maintained.

Ans

Depreciation A/c To Provision for Depreciation A/c (Being depreciation charged to provision for Depreciation A/c)	Dr	—	—

32 For transferring amount of depreciation.

Ans

Profit and Loss A/c To Depreciation A/c (Being depreciation amount transferred to profit and loss account)	Dr	—	—

VERY SHORT ANSWER Type Questions

33 What is depreciation? **NCERT**

Ans Depreciation means decline in the value of fixed assets on account of usage and various other factors, such as passage of time or obsolescence.

34 Is depreciation the result of fluctuations in the value of fixed asset?

Ans No, depreciation is not the result of fluctuations becuase fluctuations affect the market value of the asset whereas depreciation is not concerned with the market value. It is a gradual and permanent decrease in the value of the asset.

35 Should depreciation be provided even if there is a loss in financial year?

Ans Yes, depreciation is a charge against profit and must be provided even if there is loss in a financial year. If it is not charged, the financial statements will show lower loss and higher value of assets. This is because depreciation is not related to the market value.

36 Why depreciation is not charged on land?

Ans Depreciaton is not charged on land because its life is not limited to few years.

37 **Depletion method for charging depreciation is used for which assets?**

Ans Depletion method for charging depreciation is used for wasting assets like mines and quarries.

38 **For which type of assets is the straight line method considered suitable?**

Ans Straight line method is suitable for those assets in which repair charges are less and the possibility of obsolescence is low.

39 **Under which method the value of an asset can never be completely extinguished?**

Ans Diminishing balance method

40 **For which type of assets is the written down value method considered suitable?**

Ans *This method is suitable for those assets in relation to which*

(*i*) The amount of repairs and renewals goes on increasing as the asset grows older.

(*ii*) The possibilities of obsolescence are more.

41 **What is the portion of the acquisition cost of the asset, yet to be allocated known as?**

Ans Written down value

42 **In case of a long-term asset, repair and maintenance expenses are expected to rise in later years than in earlier years. Which method is suitable for charging depreciation if the management does not want to increase burden on profit and loss account on account of depreciation and repair.** **NCERT**

Ans The company should charge depreciation as per written down value method because under this method depreciation charge declines in later years. Hence, the total of depreciation and repair expense remains similar year after year.

43 **Give four examples each of 'provision' and 'reserves'.** **NCERT**

Ans Examples of provisions are provision for doubtful debts, provision for taxation, provision for repairs and renewals and provision for depreciation.

Examples of reserves are general reserve, workmen compensation fund, investment fluctuation fund and capital reserve.

44 **Give four examples each of 'revenue reserve' and 'capital reserve'.** **NCERT**

Ans Examples of revenue reserve are general reserve, investment fluctuation fund, dividend equalisation fund and debenture redemption fund, etc.

Examples of capital reserve are premium on issue of shares or debentures, profit on redemption of debentures, profit on re-issue of forfeited shares and profit on sale of fixed assets, etc.

45 **Name reserves which are generally not distributed as dividend.**

Ans Capital reserve

46 **Which reserves are created for maintaining a stable rate of dividend?**

Ans Dividend equalisation reserve

47 **Is reserve a charge against profit or a appropriation of profit?**

Ans Reserves are created after the calculation of net profit by debiting profit and loss appropriation account. Hence, it is an appropriation of profit.

48 **A company has incurred losses in the current year and has not provided for depreciation. Is the action of company correct?**

Ans No, the company is not correct since ignoring depreciation expenses would not result in true and fair position of the financial statements.

49 **An asset can be obsolete while it is not fully depreciated. Comment.**

Ans The statement is correct as an asset can be obsolete even when if it is capable of being used and is not fully depreciated. It is due to the technological innovation or change in market demand for the product.

SHORT ANSWER Type Questions

50 **State briefly the needs for providing depreciation.** **NCERT**

Ans Refer to text on page no. 228

51 **What are the causes of depreciation?** **NCERT**

Ans Refer to text on page no. 228

52 **What are the effects of depreciation on profit and loss account and balance sheet?** **NCERT**

Ans Depreciation is charged as expenditure in profit and loss account and the depreciation figure is deducted from the value of concerned asset on the assets side of the balance sheet.

In that case on one hand, it reduces the profit of the concern, on the other hand, it reduces the assets side in the balance sheet. Here, it is worth mentioning that depreciation is non-cash expenditure.

53 **What are provisions? How are they created? Give accounting treatment in case of provision for doubtful debts.** **NCERT**

Ans The amount set aside for the purpose of providing for any known liability, uncertain loss or expense, the amount of which cannot be ascertained with reasonable accuracy, is referred to as provision.

Provision is a charge against the profits and is created by debiting profit and loss account.

In the balance sheet, the amount of provision may be shown either

(*i*) on the assets side, by way of deduction from the concerned asset.

(*ii*) on the liabilities side along with the current liability.

54 Give the features of provision.

Ans *Features of provision are as follows*

(*i*) It is created to meet a known liability.

(*ii*) Provision is a charge to profit and loss account.

(*iii*) The liability is known but the amount of such liability cannot be ascertained with reasonable accuracy.

(*iv*) Creation of provision ensures proper matching of revenue and expenses.

55 Explain the concept of secret reserves. **NCERT**

Ans Reserves that are created by overstating liabilities or understanding assets are known as secret reserves. They are not shown in the balance sheet. It is created by the management to avoid competition by reducing profit. Creation of secret reserve is not allowed by Companies Act which requires full disclosure of all material facts and accounting policies.

56 Distinguish between 'revenue reserve' and 'capital reserve'. **NCERT**

Ans *The differences between revenue reserve and capital reserve*

Basis	*Revenue Reserve*	*Capital Reserve*
Source of Creation	It is created out of revenue profits which arise out of normal operating activities of the business.	It is created primarily out of capital profits which do not arise out of the normal operating activities of the business.
Purpose	It is created for strengthening the financial position of the business.	It is created for the purpose laid down in companies act.
Usage	A specific revenue reserve can be utilised only for the earmarked purpose.	It can be utilised for specific purposes as provided in the law in force e.g. to write-off capital losses or issue of bonus shares.
Dividend	It can be used for dividend.	It cannot be used for dividend.

57 Distinguish between general reserve and specific reserve. **NCERT**

Ans *The differences between general reserve and specific reserve are*

Basis	*General Reserve*	*Specific Reserve*
Meaning	The reserves which is not created for a specific purpose is general reserve.	The reserves which are created for a specific purpose are known as specific reserves.
Usage	It can be used for any purpose.	It cannot be used for any purpose other than the specified purpose for which it is created.
Examples	Retained earnings, reserve funds etc.	Debenture redemption reserve, dividend equalisation reserve, etc.

58 Depreciation is a non-cash expense which should not be provided for in the profit and loss account. Comment.

Ans It is not correct to say that depreciation being a non-cash expense should not be allowed for in the books. If depreciation is not provided for, it will result in overstatement of assets and profits. It is also not in agreement with the matching principle which says that expenses for a period should be matched with the revenues.

LONG ANSWER Type Questions

59 Explain the determinants of the amount of depreciation.

Or Explain basic factors affecting the amount of depreciation. **NCERT**

Ans (*i*) **Original** (Historical) **Cost of the Assets** It includes all the cost incurred on acquisition, installation, freight and transportation, insurance charges, etc up to the point the asset is ready for use. In case a second hand asset is purchased, it will include the initial repair cost to put the asset in a workable condition.

(*ii*) **Estimated Net Residual Value/Scrap Value/Salvage Value** It is estimated sale value of asset at the end of its useful life. This residual value is net of expenses for disposal/sale *i.e.* net residual value is the value arrived at after deducting the expenses necessary for disposal of asset.

For example, if scrap value of an asset after 10 years is ₹ 10,000 but expenses relating to disposal/sale of asset are ₹ 2,000 then net residual value will be ₹ 8,000.

(*iii*) **Expected Useful Life** Useful life of an asset is the estimated economic or commercial life of an asset. Generally, it is expressed in number of years but can also be expressed in other units. *For example,* number of units of output (in case of mines) or number of working hours.

(*iv*) **Depreciable Cost** Depreciable cost of an asset is equal to its cost less net scrap value. It is the depreciable cost which is distributed and charged as depreciation expense over the useful life.

60 Discuss in detail the straight line method and written down value method of depreciation. Distinguish between the two and also give situations where they are useful. **NCERT**

Ans (*i*) **Straight Line Method** Under this method, a fixed and equal amount in the form of depreciation is charged every year during the life time of the asset. It is also known as original cost method. As the amount of depreciation remains equal from year to year, it is also called as fixed or equal instalment method.

Suitability This method of depreciation is suitable for assets in which the repair charges are less and the possibility of obsolescence is less and expiration cost depends upon time period involved.

(*ii*) **Written Down Value Method** Under this method, depreciation is charged on the book value of the asset rather than original cost. It involves charging a fixed rate on the written down value. The amount of depreciation goes on reducing, year after year. As the book value keeps on reducing, it is also known as **reducing balance method or diminishing balance method.**

Suitability This method of depreciation is suitable for those assets that have a long life and require more repair with passage of time.

The difference between straight line method and written down value method as given below

Basis	*Straight Line Method*	*Written Down Value Method*
Basis of Charging Depreciation	Depreciation is calculated on the original cost.	Depreciation is calculated on the book value.
Annual Depreciation Charge	The amount of depreciation is fixed (constant) for all years.	The amount of depreciation declines year after year.
Recognition by Income Tax Law	It is not recognised by Income Tax Law.	It is recognised by Income Tax Law.
Book Value of the Asset	It becomes zero at the end of its effective life.	It can never be zero.
Effect of Depreciation and Repair on Profit and Loss Account	Unequal effect over the life of the asset, as depreciation remains same over the year but repair cost increase in the later years.	Equal effect over the life of the asset, as depreciation cost is high and repairs are less in the initial years but in the later years the repair cost increase and depreciation cost decreases.

61 Name and explain different type of reserves in details. **NCERT**

Ans *Reserves are generally classified into*

(*i*) **Revenue Reserves** The reserves created from revenue profits which arise out of the normal operating activities of the business and are otherwise freely available for distribution as dividend are known as revenue reserves.

Revenue reserves can be classified into

(*a*) **General Reserve** The reserves which are not created for a specific purpose are general reserve. They strengthen the financial position of the business and are also known as **free reserve or contingency reserve.**

(*b*) **Specific Reserve** As the name suggest, these are the reserves that are created for some specific purpose and can be utilised only for that purpose.

Examples of specific reserve are given below

- **Dividend Equalisation Reserve** This reserve is created to stabilise or maintain dividend rate. In the year of high profit, amount is transferred to dividend equalisation reserve. In the year of low profit, this reserve amount is used to maintain the rate of dividend.
- **Workmen Compensation Fund** It is created to provide for claims of the workers due to accident, etc.
- **Investment Fluctuation Fund** It is created to make for decline in the value of investment due to market fluctuation.
- **Debenture Redemption Reserve** It is created to provide funds for redemption of debentures.

(*ii*) **Capital Reserve** The reserves created out of capital profits and not available for distribution as dividend are known as capital reserve. Capital reserves can be used for writing off capital losses or issue of bonus shares in case of a company. *Examples of capital profits are given below*

(*a*) Premium on issue of shares or debentures.
(*b*) Profit on sale of fixed assets.
(*c*) Profit on redemption of debentures.
(*d*) Profit on revaluation of fixed assets and liabilities.
(*e*) Profits prior to incorporation.
(*f*) Profit on re-issue of forfeited shares.
(*g*) Capital redemption reserve.
(*h*) Profit on forfeiture of shares.

NUMERICAL Questions

1 Cost of a machine is ₹ 4,20,000 with salvage value ₹ 20,000. What is the depreciation amount for second year as per written down value method. Charge depreciation @ 10% per annum.

Ans Depreciation for IInd year $= (4,20,000 - 42,000) \times \frac{10}{100}$
$= ₹\ 37,800$

2 An asset was purchased for ₹ 5,00,000. Another ₹ 5,000 were incurred for freight and transportation. Installation expenses amounted to ₹ 20,000 and commission paid on purchases to agent 5% of cost of asset. What is the cost to be recognised in books for the purpose of depreciation?

Ans Cost of assets = ₹ 5,50,000

3 A company bought a machine for ₹ 90,000 on credit. Another ₹ 10,000 is spent on its installation. If the estimated useful life is 5 years and scrap value at the end was ₹ 5,000. Calculate the amount and rate of depreciation.

Ans Depreciation = ₹ 19,000
Rate of depreciation 19% per annum

4 Original cost of a machinery ₹ 10,00,000; Salvage value ₹ 40,000; Expected useful life 10 years. What will be the amount of depreciation for the fourth year according to original cost method? Also specify the rate of depreciation.

Ans Depreciation = ₹ 96,000 each year
Rate of depreciation = 9.6%

5 On 1st April, 2016, X Ltd acquired a machine for ₹ 12,00,000. Installation expenses were ₹ 80,000. Residual value after 5 years ₹ 2,00,000. On 1st October, 2016 it incurred repair expenses of ₹ 40,000. What will be the annual depreciation under straight line method?

Ans Annual depreciation = ₹ 2,16,000

Note *Repairs will not be added to the cost of machinery since it is a revenue expenditure.*

6 Singhania Industries purchased a second hand machine for ₹ 56,00,000 on 1st July, 2013 and spent ₹ 24,00,000 on its repair and installation and ₹ 5,00,000 for its carriage. On 1st September, 2014, it purchased another machine for ₹ 2,50,00,000 and spent ₹ 10,00,000 on its installation. Depreciation in provided on machinery @ 10% per annum on original cost method annually on 31st December . Prepare machinery account and depreciation account from the year 2013 to 2016.

Ans Balance of Machinery Account :
Machine I = ₹ 55,25,000; Machine II = ₹ 1,99,33,333

7 Parul Ltd purchased a machinery on 1st January, 2013 for ₹ 11,00,000 and spent ₹ 1,00,000 on its installation. On 1st September, 2013 it purchased another machine for ₹ 7,40,000. On 1st May, 2014 it purchased another machine for ₹ 16,80,000 (including installation expenses). Depreciation was provided on machinery @ 10% per annum on original cost method annually on 31st December. Prepare machine account and provision for depreciation account for the years 2013, 2014, 2015 and 2016.

Ans Balance of Machinery Account on 31st March, 2016 = ₹ 36,20,000, Provision for Depreciation Account on 31st March, 2016 = ₹ 11,74,666

8 You are given the following balance on 1st April, 2015.

Machinery Account	₹ 5,00,000
Provision for Depreciation Account	₹ 1,16,000

Depreciation is charged on machinery @ 20% per annum by the diminishing balance method. A piece of machinery purchased on 1st April, 2013 for ₹ 1,00,000 was sold on 1st October, 2015 for ₹ 60,000. Prepare the machinery account and provision for depreciation account for the year ended 31st March, 2016. Also prepare the machinery disposal account.

Ans Profit on Sale of Machinery = ₹ 2,400.
Balance in Machinery Account = ₹ 4,00,000
Provision for Depreciation Account = ₹ 1,44,000

9 Modern Ltd purchased a machinery on 1st May, 2014 for ₹ 60,000. On 1st July, 2015, it purchased another machine for ₹ 20,000. On 31st March, 2016 it sold the first machine purchased in 2014 for ₹ 38,500. Depreciation is provided @ 20% per annum on the original cost each year. Accounts are closed on 31st December every year. Prepare the machinery account for 3 years.

Ans Profit on Sale of Machinery = ₹ 1,500;
Balance of Machinery Account = ₹ 14,000

10 On 1st April, 2014 Prerna Ltd purchased a second hand machine for ₹ 1,16,000 and spent ₹ 4,000 on its erection. On 1st October, 2016 this machine was sold for ₹ 57,200. Prepare the machinery account for the first 3 years according to written down value, taking rate of depreciation @ 10% per

annum. Accounts are closed on 31st March, each year.

Ans Loss on Sale of Machine = ₹ 35,140.

11 Adhikari Ltd purchased on 1st January, 2012 a machine for ₹ 1,20,000. On 1st July, 2015 he also purchased another machine for ₹ 1,00,000. On 1st July, 2016 he sold the machine purchased on 1st January, 2015 for ₹ 80,000. It was decided that depreciation @ 10% was to be written-off every year under diminishing balance method. Assuming the accounts were closed on 31st December every year, show the machine account for the years 2015 and 2016.

Ans Balance on 31st December, 2016 = ₹ 85,500; Loss on Sales of Machine = ₹ 22,600

12 M/s P and Q purchased machinery for ₹ 40,000 on 1st July, 2014. Depreciation is provided @ 10% per annum on the diminishing balance. On 31st October, 2016, one-fourth of the machinery was found unsuitable and disposed off for ₹ 5,600. On the same date new machinery at a cost of ₹ 15,000 was purchased. Write up the machinery account from 2014 to 2016. The accounts are closed on 31st December.

Ans Loss on Sale of Machinery = ₹ 2,237; Balance in Machinery Account = ₹ 37,835

13 A firm purchased on 1st January, 2014 certain machinery for ₹ 5,82,000 and spent ₹ 18,000 on its erection. On 1st July, 2014 additional machinery costing ₹ 2,00,000 was purchased. On 1st July, 2016 the machinery purchased on 1st January, 2014 auctioned for ₹ 2,86,000 and a new machinery for ₹ 4,00,000 was purchased on the same date. Depreciation was provided annually on 31st December, at the rate of 10% on the written down value method. Prepare the machinery account from 2014 to 2016.

Ans Balance of Machinery Account = ₹ 5,33,900; Loss on Sale of Machinery = ₹ 1,75,700

14 A limited company purchased on 1st January, 2014 a plant for ₹ 38,000 and spent ₹ 2,000 for carriage and brokerage. On 1st April, 2015 it purchased additional plant costing ₹ 20,000. On 1st August, 2016 the plant purchased on 1st January, 2014 was sold for ₹ 25,000. On the same date, the plant purchased on 1st April, 2015 was sold at a profit of ₹ 2,800. Depreciation is provided @ 10% per annum on diminishing balance method every year. Accounts are closed on 31st December every year. Show the plant account for 3 years.

Ans Loss on Sale of Plant I = ₹ 5,510; Sale of Plant II = ₹ 20,220

15 Modi Industries purchased 10 machines for ₹ 2,25,000 each on 1st July, 2013. On 1st October, 2015 one of the machines got destroyed by fire and an insurance claim of ₹ 1,35,000 was admitted by the company.
On the same date, another machine is purchased by the company for ₹ 3,75,000.
The company writes off 15% per annum depreciation on written down value basis. The company maintains the calendar year as its financial year. Prepare the machinery account from 2013 to 2016.

Ans Balance of Machinery Account ₹ 7,66,866 (Old), ₹ 2,04,530 (New)

16 The following balances appear in the books of M/s. Amrit as on 1st April

	₹
Machinery Account	60,000
Provision for Depreciation Account	36,000

On 1st April, 2015, they decided to dispose off a machinery for ₹ 8,400 which was purchased on 1st April, 2011 for ₹ 16,000.
You are required to prepare the machinery account, provision for depreciation account and machinery disposal account for 2015-16. Depreciation was charged at 10% on original cost method.

Ans Balance of Machinery Account (31st March, 2016) = ₹ 44,000; Provision for Depreciation Account (31st March, 2016) = ₹ 34,000; Loss on Sale of Machinery = ₹ 1,200

17 On 1st October, 2013, X Ltd. Purchased a machinery for ₹ 2,50,000. A part of machinery which was purchased for ₹ 20,000 on 1st October, 2013 became obsolete and was disposed off on 1st January, 2016 (having a book value ₹ 17,100 on 1st April, 2015) for ₹ 2,000. Depreciation is charged @ 10% annually on written down value. Prepare machinery disposal account and also show your workings. The books being closed on 31st March of every year.

Hint: Loss on Sale of Machinery = ₹ 13,817, Loss on Sale of Machine = ₹ 17,100 (1st April, 2015) = ₹ 1,283 (Depreciation upto 1st January, 2014)— ₹ 2,000 (Sale value) = ₹ 13,817

09

After studying this chapter, the students will become familiarise with the different types of errors, steps involved in locating errors, how to rectify errors before the preparation of trial balance and after the preparation of trial balance but before preparing the final accounts.

RECTIFICATION OF ERRORS

INTRODUCTION TO ERRORS

Errors are unintentional mistakes which are commonly committed while recording transactions in the books of accounts. These errors may be committed in the journal, ledger or trial balance or any financial statements.

Some common errors include the following

(*i*) Error in totalling of the debit and credit balances in the trial balance.

(*ii*) Error in totalling of subsidiary books.

(*iii*) Error in posting of the total of subsidiary books.

(*iv*) Error in showing account balances in wrong column of the trial balance, or with the wrong amount.

(*v*) Omission in showing an account balance in the trial balance.

(*vi*) Error in the calculation of a ledger account balance.

(*vii*) Error while posting a journal entry *i.e.*, a journal entry may not have been posted properly to the ledger, *i.e.*, posting made either with wrong amount or on the wrong side of the account or in the wrong account.

(*viii*) Error in recording a transaction in the journal by making a reverse entry, *i.e.*, account to be debited is credited and account to be credited is debited, or an entry with the wrong amount.

(*ix*) Error in recording a transaction in subsidiary book with wrong name or wrong amount.

CHAPTER CHECKLIST

CLASSIFICATION OF ERRORS

Keeping in view the nature of errors, errors can be classified into the following four categories

1. Errors of Commission

When a transaction is recorded wrongly in the books of accounts, it is called error of commission. It includes wrong posting of transactions, wrong totalling or wrong balancing of the accounts, wrong casting of the subsidiary books or wrong recording of amount in the books of original entry. Errors of commission can be classified into the following

(*i*) **Error of Recording** This error arises when any transaction is incorrectly recorded in the books of original entry. This error will not affect the trial balance.

For example, goods purchased from Ravi for ₹ 450, recorded as ₹ 540, in the purchase book.

It will not affect the trial balance as same amount will be posted in both the accounts *i.e.* purchases account and Ravi's account.

(*ii*) **Error of Casting** This error arises when a mistake is committed in totalling. This error affects the trial balance.

For example, sales book is totalled as ₹ 1,000 instead of ₹ 10,000.

(*iii*) **Error of Carrying Forward** It is an error which arises when a mistake is committed in carrying forward a total of one page to the next page. This error affects the trial balance.

For example, total of sales book is carried forward as ₹ 10,000 instead of ₹ 1,000

(*iv*) **Error of Posting** When the information recorded in the books of original entry is incorrectly entered in the ledger, it is an error of posting.

(*a*) Posting with wrong amount (This error will affect the trial balance).

For example, posting the total of purchase book ₹ 11,500 as ₹ 11,550 in the purchase account.

(*b*) Posting to the wrong side but correct account (This error will affect the trial balance)

For example, goods sold to X for ₹ 550, entered to the credit of X's account instead of posting to the debit side of his account.

(*c*) Posting twice in an account (This error will affect the trial balance).

(*d*) Errors in posting to the wrong account but correct side (This error will not affect the trial balance).

2. Errors of Omission

This kind of error arises when a transaction is partially or completely omitted (left out) to be recorded in the books of accounts. These can be of two types

(*i*) **Error of Complete Omission** When a transaction is completely omitted from recording in the books of original record, it is an error of complete omission. This error does not affect the trial balance.

For example, credit sales to Shyam for ₹ 10,000, omitted to be recorded in books.

(*ii*) **Error of Partial Omission** When a transaction is partially omitted from recording in the books, it is an error of partial omission. This error affects the trial balance.

For example, credit sales recorded in the sales book but not posted into debtor's account.

3. Errors of Principle

When a transaction is recorded in the books of accounts violating the accounting principles, *i.e.*, allocation between capital and revenue items, it is known as errors of principle. These errors do not affect the trial balance.

(*i*) **Treating Capital Items as Revenue Items** *For example*, wages paid for installation of new machinery charged to wages account instead of machinery account.

(*ii*) **Treating Revenue Items as Capital Items** *For example*, ₹ 200 paid for the repair of an existing machinery but debited to machinery accout instead of repairs account.

4. Compensating Errors

When two or more errors are committed in such a way that the net effect of these errors on the debits and credits of accounts is nil, such errors are called compensating errors. These errors do not affect the tallying of trial balance.

For example, If the total of purchase book is posted in the ledger as ₹ 10,000 instead of ₹ 1,000 and at the same time Varsha's account is credited in the ledger as ₹ 10,000 instead of ₹ 1,000. As a result of these errors, there is an excess credit of ₹ 9,000 in Varsha's account and an excess debit of ₹ 9,000 in purchases account. Thus, these two errors nullify the effects of each other.

SEARCHING OF ERRORS

The following steps will be useful in searching errors

Step 1 The two columns of the trial balance should be totalled again. If in place of a number of accounts, only one account has been written in the trial balance, then the list of such accounts should be checked and totalled again.

Step 2 It should be seen that the cash and bank balances have been written in the trial balance.

Step 3 The exact difference in the trial balance should be determined. The ledger should be properly checked, it is possible that a balance equal to the difference has been omitted from the trial balance. The difference should also be halved; it is possible that balance equal to half the difference has been written in the wrong column.

Step 4 The ledger accounts should be balanced again.

Step 5 The totalling of subsidiary books should be checked again, especially if the difference is ₹1, ₹100 etc.

Step 6 If the difference is very big, the balance in various accounts should be compared with the corresponding accounts in the previous period. If the figures differ materially, the respective accounts should be checked again.

Step 7 Postings of the amounts equal to the difference or half the difference should be checked. It is possible that an amount has been omitted to be posted or has been posted on the wrong side.

Step 8 If there is still a difference in the trial balance, a complete checking will be necessary. The posting of all the entries including the opening entry should be checked. It may be better to begin with the nominal accounts.

RECTIFICATION OF ERRORS

Rectification of errors is the procedure of rectifying the errors committed and to set right the accounting records. These errors may affect or may not affect the trial balance but they must be detected and corrected.

There are various objectives or reasons for which the errors are rectified, they are as follows

(*i*) For the preparation of correct accounting records.

(*ii*) For determining the correct net profit or loss by preparing the profit and loss account with correct figures.

(*iii*) To find out the true financial position of the firm by preparing the balance sheet with correct data.

From the point of view of rectification, the errors may be classified into the following two categories

1. Errors which do not Affect the Agreement of Trial Balance

These errors are the two-sided errors and are not disclosed by the trial balance. Trial balance tallies even if these errors are made. These errors are made in two or more accounts and can be rectified by recording a journal entry by way of giving the correct debit and credit to the concerned accounts. Following errors do not affect the agreement of trial balance

(*i*) Errors of complete omission.

(*ii*) Error of recording

(*iii*) Errors of principle

(*iv*) Compensating errors

(*v*) Error of posting to the wrong account but on the correct side

Note *For the above errors, the rectifying entry will be same whether the error is depicted before preparing trial balance or after the preparation of trial balance but before the final accounts are prepared.*

The rectification process involves the following steps

Step 1 **Wrong Entry** Write the entry which has already been passed in the books i.e. the wrong entry.

Step 2 **Correct Entry** Write the entry which should have been passed i.e. the correct entry.

Step 3 *Rectifying Entry Write the net effect of entries in step 1 and step 2 in the following form*

Debit of correct entry
Credit of wrong entry } will be debited

Credit of correct entry
Debit of wrong entry } will be credited

The given steps can be better explained with the help of following illustrations

ILLUSTRATION |1| Rectify the following errors

(i) Cash received from Karim ₹ 6,000 posted to Nadeem.

(ii) Cash sales to Radhika ₹ 15,000 was shown as receipt of commission in the cash book.

(iii) Furniture purchased from M/s Rao Furniture for ₹ 8,000 was entered into the purchases book.

(iv) Credit sales to Rajni ₹ 5,000 recorded in purchases book.

Sol. (*i*) Cash received from Karim ₹ 6,000 posted to Nadeem.

This is an error of commission.

Wrong entry

	Particulars		Dr (₹)	Cr (₹)
Step 1 ⟶	Cash A/c	Dr	6,000	
	To Nadeem			6,000

Correct entry

	Particulars		Dr (₹)	Cr (₹)
Step 2 ⟶	Cash A/c	Dr	6,000	
	To Karim			6,000

Rectification entry

	Particulars		Dr (₹)	Cr (₹)
Step 3 ⟶	Nadeem	Dr	6,000	
	To Karim			6,000

Note : *Nadeem has been wrongly credited. Therefore, he will be debited. Karim will be credited, to give effect to the correct entry. Cash has been rightfully debited.*

(*ii*) Cash sales to Radhika ₹ 15,000 was shown as receipt of commission in the cash book.

This is an error of commission.

Wrong entry

	Particulars		Dr (₹)	Cr (₹)
Step 1 ⟶	Cash A/c	Dr	15,000	
	To Commission A/c			15,000

Correct entry

	Particulars		Dr (₹)	Cr (₹)
Step 2 ⟶	Cash A/c	Dr	15,000	
	To Sales A/c			15,000

Rectification entry

	Particulars		Dr (₹)	Cr (₹)
Step 3 ⟶	Commission A/c	Dr	15,000	
	To Sales A/c			15,000

(*iii*) Furniture purchased from M/s Rao Furniture for ₹ 8,000 was entered into the purchases book.

This is an error of principle.

Wrong entry

	Particulars		Dr (₹)	Cr (₹)
Step 1 ⟶	Purchases A/c	Dr	8,000	
	To M/s Rao Furniture			8,000

Correct entry

	Particulars		Dr (₹)	Cr (₹)
Step 2 ⟶	Furniture A/c	Dr	8,000	
	To Ms Rao Furniture			8,000

Rectification entry

	Particulars		Dr (₹)	Cr (₹)
Step 3 ⟶	Furniture A/c	Dr	8,000	
	To Purchases A/c			8,000

(*iv*) Credit sales to Rajni ₹ 5,000 recorded in purchases book.

This is an error of commission.

Wrong entry

Step 1 ⟶	Purchases A/c	Dr	5,000	
	To Rajni			5,000

Correct entry

Step 2 ⟶	Rajni	Dr	5,000	
	To Sales A/c			5,000

Rectification entry

Step 3 ⟶	Rajni	Dr	10,000	
	To Sales A/c			5,000
	To Purchases A/c			5,000

ILLUSTRATION |2| Pass the necessary journal entries to rectify the following errors

(i) Credit sale of ₹ 1,700 to Raj was recorded as sales to Aryan.

(ii) Credit sale of old machinery to Sohan for ₹ 1,700 was entered in the sales book for ₹ 7,100.

(iii) Credit sales to Mohan ₹ 7,000 were not recorded.

(iv) Credit purchase from Rohan ₹ 9,000 were not recorded.

(v) Goods returned to Rakesh ₹ 4,000 were not recorded.

(vi) Goods returned from Mahesh ₹ 1,000 were not recorded. **NCERT**

Sol. **Rectification Entries in Journal**

Date	Particulars		LF	Amt (Dr)	Amt (Cr)
(i)	Raj	Dr		1,700	
	To Aryan				1,700
	(Being the credit sale of ₹ 1,700 to Raj recorded as sales to Aryan, now rectified)				
(ii)	Sales A/c	Dr		7,100	
	To Sohan				5,400
	To Machinery A/c				1,700
	(Being the credit sale of machinery to Sohan for ₹ 1,700 entered in the sales book as ₹ 7,100, now rectified)				
(iii)	Mohan	Dr		7,000	
	To Sales A/c				7,000
	(Being goods sold to Mohan not recorded, now rectified)				
(iv)	Purchases A/c	Dr		9,000	
	To Rohan				9,000
	(Being goods purchased from Rohan on credit not recorded, now rectified)				
(v)	Rakesh	Dr		4,000	
	To Purchases Return A/c				4,000
	(Being goods returned to Rakesh not recorded, now rectified)				
(vi)	Sales Return A/c	Dr		1,000	
	To Mahesh				1,000
	(Being goods returned by Mahesh not recorded, now rectified)				

ILLUSTRATION |3| Rectify the following errors

(i) Credit sales to Mohan ₹ 7,000 were recorded as ₹ 700.
(ii) Credit purchase from Rohan ₹ 9,000 were recorded as ₹ 900.
(iii) Goods returned to Rakesh ₹ 4,000 were recorded as ₹ 400.
(iv) Goods returned from Mahesh ₹ 1,000 were recorded as ₹ 100.
(v) Furniture purchased on credit from Kartik for ₹ 60,000 posted as ₹ 6,000.
(vi) Furniture purchased on credit from Kartik for ₹ 60,000 posted to Jatin's account.
(vii) Furniture purchased on credit from Kartik for ₹ 60,000 posted to machinery account. **NCERT**

Sol.

Rectification Entries in Journal

Date	Particulars	LF	Amt (Dr)	Amt (Cr)
(i)	Mohan Dr		6,300	
	To Sales A/c			6,300
	(Being goods sold to Mohan for ₹ 7,000 recorded as ₹ 700, now rectified)			
(ii)	Purchases A/c Dr		8,100	
	To Rohan			8,100
	(Being goods purchased from Rohan on credit for ₹ 9,000 recorded as ₹ 900, now rectified)			
(iii)	Rakesh Dr		3,600	
	To Purchases Return A/c			3,600
	(Being goods returned to Rakesh ₹ 4,000 recorded as ₹ 400, now rectified)			
(iv)	Sales Return A/c Dr		900	
	To Mahesh			900
	(Being goods returned by Mahesh ₹ 1,000 recorded as ₹ 100, now rectified)			
(v)	Furniture A/c Dr		54,000	
	To Kartik			54,000
	(Being the error in posting of amount, now rectified)			
(vi)	Jatin Dr		60,000	
	To Kartik			60,000
	(Being the error in posting to wrong account, now rectified)			
(vii)	Furniture A/c Dr		60,000	
	To Machinery A/c			60,000
	(Being the error in posting furniture to wrong account, now rectified)			

ILLUSTRATION |4| Rectify the following errors

(i) Credit sales to Mohan ₹ 7,000 were recorded as ₹ 7,200.
(ii) Credit purchase from Rohan ₹ 9,000 were recorded as ₹ 9,900.
(iii) Goods returned to Rakesh ₹ 4,000 were recorded as ₹ 4,040.
(iv) Goods returned from Mahesh ₹ 1,000 were recorded as ₹ 1,600.
(v) Cash sale of ₹ 3,400 to Aroha was posted to the credit of Aroha.
(vi) Credit sale of old furniture to X for ₹ 3,400 was credited to the sales account.
(vii) Credit sale of old furniture to Vishal for ₹ 1,700 was posted as ₹ 7,100. **NCERT**

Sol. **Rectification Entries in Journal**

Date	Particulars	LF	Amt (Dr)	Amt (Cr)
(i)	Sales A/c Dr		200	
	To Mohan			200
	(Being goods sold to Mohan for ₹ 7,000 were recorded as ₹ 7,200, now rectified)			
(ii)	Rohan Dr		900	
	To Purchases A/c			900
	(Being goods purchased from Rohan for ₹ 9,000 recorded as ₹ 9,900, now rectified)			
(iii)	Purchases Return A/c Dr		40	
	To Rakesh			40
	(Being goods returned to Rakesh ₹ 4,000 recorded as ₹ 4,040, now rectified)			
(iv)	Mahesh Dr		600	
	To Sales Return A/c			600
	(Being goods returned by Mahesh for ₹ 1,000 recorded as ₹ 1,600, now rectified)			
(v)	Aroha Dr		3,400	
	To Sales A/c			3,400
	(Being the cash sale posted to the credit of Aroha, now rectified)			
(vi)	Sales A/c Dr		3,400	
	To Furniture A/c			3,400
	(Being the credit sale of old furniture credited to sales account, now rectified)			
(vii)	Furniture A/c Dr		5,400	
	To Vishal			5,400
	(Being the credit sale of old furniture to Vishal for ₹ 1,700 posted as ₹ 7,100, now rectified)			

ILLUSTRATION |5| Rectify the following errors

(i) Salary paid ₹ 5,000 was debited to employee's personal account.

(ii) Rent paid ₹ 4,000 was posted to landlord's personal account.

(iii) Goods withdrawn by proprietor for personal use ₹ 1,000 were debited to sundry expenses account.

(iv) Cash received from Kohli ₹ 2,000 was posted to Kapur's account.

(v) Cash paid to Babu ₹ 1,500 was posted to Sabu's account.

(vi) Goods sold to Rohan on credit amounting to ₹ 700 were omitted from the accounts although cash received subsequently from him stands posted to his credit.

(vii) On 31st March, goods of the value of ₹ 6,000 were returned by Rohan and were taken into stock on the same date but entry was not passed in the books. **NCERT**

Sol. **Rectification Entries in Journal**

Date	Particulars		LF	Amt (Dr)	Amt (Cr)
(i)	Salaries A/c	Dr		5,000	
	To Employee A/c				5,000
	(Being salary paid to employee ₹ 5,000, wrongly debited to employee's personal account, now rectified)				
(ii)	Rent A/c	Dr		4,000	
	To Landlord A/c				4,000
	(Being rent paid to landlord ₹ 4,000, wrongly posted to landlord's personal account, now rectified)				
(iii)	Drawings A/c	Dr		1,000	
	To Sundry Expenses A/c				1,000
	(Being goods withdrawn by proprietor for his personal use ₹ 1,000 were wrongly recorded as sundry expenses, now rectified)				
(iv)	Kapur	Dr		2,000	
	To Kohli				2,000
	(Being cash received from Kohli, recorded in Kapur's account, now rectified)				
(v)	Babu	Dr		1,500	
	To Sabu				1,500
	(Being cash paid to Babu was posted wrongly to Sabu's account, now rectified)				
(vi)	Rohan	Dr		700	
	To Sales A/c				700
	(Being the rectification of goods sold to Rohan not recorded in the books)				
(vii)	Return Inwards A/c	Dr		6,000	
	To Rohan				6,000
	(Being the entry of goods returned by Rohan and taken into stock omitted from records)				

ILLUSTRATION |6| Rectify the following errors

(i) Credit purchase from Rohan ₹ 9,000 were recorded in sales book.

(ii) Goods returned to Rakesh ₹ 4,000 were recorded in the sales return book.

(iii) Good returned from Mahesh ₹ 1,000 were recorded in purchases return book.

(iv) Goods returned from Mahesh ₹ 2,000 were recorded in purchases book. **NCERT**

Sol. **Rectification Entries in Journal**

Date	Particulars		LF	Amt (Dr)	Amt (Cr)
(i)	Sales A/c	Dr		9,000	
	Purchases A/c	Dr		9,000	
	To Rohan				18,000
	(Being goods purchased from Rohan on credit were recorded in sales book, now rectified)				
(ii)	Rakesh	Dr		8,000	
	To Purchases Return A/c				4,000
	To Sales Return A/c				4,000
	(Being goods returned to Rakesh, wrongly recorded in sales return book, now rectified)				
(iii)	Sales Return A/c	Dr		1,000	
	Purchases Return A/c	Dr		1,000	
	To Mahesh				2,000
	(Being goods returned by Mahesh were recorded in purchases return book, now rectified)				
(iv)	Sales Return A/c	Dr		2,000	
	To Purchases A/c				2,000
	(Being goods returned from Mahesh, recorded in purchases book, now rectified)				

ILLUSTRATION |7| Rectify the following errors

(i) A credit purchases of ₹ 3,120 from Vihan was passed in the books as ₹ 4,200.

(ii) Goods (cost ₹ 2,500 sales price ₹ 3,000) distributed as free samples among prospective customers were not recorded.

(iii) Wages paid to the firm's workmen for making additions to machinery amounting to ₹ 1,050 were debited to the wages account.

Sol. **Rectification Entries in Journal**

Date	Particulars	LF	Amt (Dr)	Amt (Cr)
(i)	Vihan Dr		1,080	
	To Purchases A/c			1,080
	(Being the rectification of a purchase of ₹ 3,120 from Vihan passed as ₹ 4,200)			
(ii)	Free Samples A/c Dr		2,500	
	To Purchases A/c			2,500
	(Being the goods distributed as free samples omitted to be recorded, now recorded)			
(iii)	Plant and Machinery A/c Dr		1,050	
	To Wages A/c			1,050
	(Being the wages for additions to machinery wrongly treated as revenue expenditure, now rectified by capitalising the same)			

ILLUSTRATION |8| The following errors, affecting the account for the year 2013 were detected in the books of Raj Brothers, Meerut.

(i) Sale of old furniture ₹ 300 treated as sale of goods.

(ii) Receipt of ₹ 1,000 from A credited to B.

(iii) Goods worth ₹ 200 bought from Z have remained unrecorded so far.

(iv) Rent of proprietor, ₹ 1,200 debited to rent account.

Sol. **Rectification Entries in Journal**

Date	Particulars	LF	Amt (Dr)	Amt (Cr)
(i)	Sales A/c Dr		300	
	To Furniture A/c			300
	(Being rectification of sales of furniture treated as sales of goods)			
(ii)	B Dr		1,000	
	To A			1,000
	(Being rectification of a receipt from A credited to B)			
(iii)	Purchases A/c Dr		200	
	To Z			200
	(Being purchases of goods from Z unrecorded)			
(iv)	Drawings A/c Dr		1,200	
	To Rent A/c			1,200
	(Being rectification of payment of rent of proprietor's residence treated as payment of office rent)			

ILLUSTRATION |9| Give journal entries to rectify the following

(i) A purchase of goods from Varun amounting to ₹ 300 has been wrongly entered through the sales book.

(ii) On 31st December, goods of the value of ₹ 600 were returned by X and were taken into stock on the same date but no entry was passed in the books.

(iii) An amount of ₹ 400 due from Y which had been written-off as a bad debt in a previous year, was unexpectedly recovered, and had been posted to the personal account of Y.

(iv) A cheque for ₹ 200 received from Z was dishonoured and had been posted to the debit of sales returns account.

(v) Depreciation provided on machinery ₹ 4,000 was posted as ₹ 400.

(vi) Bad debts written-off ₹ 5,000 were posted as ₹ 6,000.

(vii) Discount allowed to a debtor ₹ 100 on receiving cash from him was posted as ₹ 60.

(viii) Goods withdrawn by proprietor for personal use ₹ 800 were posted as ₹ 300.

(ix) Bills receivable for ₹ 2,000 received from a debtor was posted as ₹ 3,000. **NCERT**

Sol.

Rectification Entries in Journal

Date	Particulars		LF	Amt (Dr)	Amt (Cr)
(i)	Purchases A/c	Dr		300	
	Sales A/c	Dr		300	
	To Varun				600
	(Being correction of wrong entry in the sales book for a purchases of goods from Varun)				
(ii)	Returns Inwards A/c	Dr		600	
	To X				600
	(Being entry of goods returned by him and taken in stock omitted from records)				
(iii)	Y	Dr		400	
	To Bad Debts Recovered A/c				400
	(Being correction of wrong credit to personal account in respect of recovery of previously written-off bad debts)				
(iv)	Z	Dr		200	
	To Sales Return A/c				200
	(Being correction of wrong debit to sales return account for dishonour of cheque received from Z).				
(v)	Depreciation A/c	Dr		3,600	
	To Machinery A/c				3,600
	(Being depreciation charged on machinery ₹ 4,000, wrongly posted as ₹ 400, now rectified)				
(vi)	Debtor's A/c	Dr		1,000	
	To Bad Debts A/c				1,000
	(Being bad debts of ₹ 5,000, wrongly charged as ₹ 6,000, now rectified)				
(vii)	Discount Allowed A/c	Dr		40	
	To Debtor's A/c				40
	(Being discount allowed to debtors ₹ 100, wrongly posted as ₹ 60, now rectified)				
(viii)	Drawings A/c	Dr		500	
	To Purchases A/c				500
	(Being drawings of ₹ 800 wrongly recorded in the books as ₹ 300, now rectified)				
(ix)	Debtor's A/c	Dr		1,000	
	To Bills Receivable A/c				1,000
	(Being bills receivable for ₹ 2,000 received from debtor, wrongly posted as ₹ 3,000, now rectified)				

ILLUSTRATION |10| The following errors were found in the book of Rajan & Sons. Give the necessary entries to correct them.

(i) Repairs made were debited to building account ₹ 100.
(ii) ₹ 200 paid for rent, debited to landlord's account.
(iii) Salary ₹ 250 paid to a clerk due to him has been debited to his personal account.
(iv) ₹ 200 received from Rina & Co has been wrongly entered as from Reena & Co.
(v) ₹ 1400 paid in cash for a typewriter was charged to office expenses account.
(vi) Credit sales to Mohan ₹ 7,000 were posted to Karan.
(vii) Credit purchase from Rohan ₹ 9,000 were posted to Gobind.
(viii) Goods returned to Rakesh ₹ 4,000 were posted to Naresh.
(ix) Goods returned from Mahesh ₹ 1,000 were posted to Manish.
(x) Cash sales ₹ 2,000 were posted to commission account. **NCERT**

Sol.

Rectification Entries in Journal

Date	Particulars		LF	Amt (Dr)	Amt (Cr)
(i)	Repairs A/c	Dr		100	
	To Building A/c				100
	(Being correction of wrong debit to building account for repairs made)				
(ii)	Rent A/c	Dr		200	
	To Landlord's Personal A/c				200
	(Being correction of wrong debit to landlord's account for rent paid)				
(iii)	Salaries A/c	Dr		250	
	To Clerk's (Personal) A/c				250
	(Being correction of wrong debit to clerk's personal account for salaries paid)				
(iv)	Reena & Co.	Dr		200	
	To Rina & Co.				200
	(Being correction of wrong credit to Reena & Co. instead of Rina & Co.)				
(v)	Typewriter A/c	Dr		1,400	
	To Office Expenses A/c				1,400
	(Being correction of wrong debit to office expenses account for purchases of typewriter)				
(vi)	Mohan	Dr		7,000	
	To Karan				7,000
	(Being goods sold to Mohan, wrongly posted to Karan's account, now rectified)				
(vii)	Gobind	Dr		9,000	
	To Rohan				9,000
	(Being credit purchase from Rohan, wrongly posted to Gobind's account, now rectified)				
(viii)	Rakesh	Dr		4,000	
	To Naresh				4,000
	(Being goods returned to Rakesh, wrongly posted in Naresh's account, now rectified)				
(ix)	Manish	Dr		1,000	
	To Mahesh				1,000
	(Being goods returned by Mahesh, wrongly posted in Manish's account, now rectified)				
(x)	Commission A/c	Dr		2,000	
	To Sales A/c				2,000
	(Being cash sales wrongly posted to commission account, now rectified)				

ILLUSTRATION |11| Rectify the following errors

(i) Depreciation provided on machinery ₹ 4,000 was not recorded.
(ii) Bad debts written-off ₹ 5,000 were not recorded.
(iii) Discount allowed to a debtor ₹ 100 on receiving cash from him was not recorded.
(iv) Bills receivable for ₹ 2,000 received from a debtor was not recorded. **NCERT**

Sol.

Rectification Entries in Journal

Date	Particulars		LF	Amt (Dr)	Amt (Cr)
(i)	Depreciation A/c	Dr		4,000	
	To Machinery A/c				4,000
	(Being depreciation charged on machinery not recorded now rectified)				
(ii)	Bad Debts A/c	Dr		5,000	
	To Debtor's A/c				5,000
	(Being bad debts written-off on debtors were not recorded, now rectified)				
(iii)	Discount Allowed A/c	Dr		100	
	To Debtor's A/c				100
	(Being discount allowed to debtor was not recorded, now rectified)				
(iv)	Bills Receivable A/c	Dr		2,000	
	To Debtor's A/c				2,000
	(Being bills receivable received from debtors not recorded, now rectified)				

ILLUSTRATION |12| Pass journal entries to rectify the following errors

(i) Credit purchase of goods of ₹ 3,000 from Viraj & Co. was not recorded in the books although the goods were taken into stock.
(ii) Credit sale of goods to Harish amounting to ₹ 10,000 was posted to the account of Haneef.
(iii) Acquisition charges on the purchase of a new building amounting of ₹ 10,000 were debited to the sundry expenses account.
(iv) Outstanding telephone charges of ₹ 6,000 had been completely omitted.
(v) Material from store ₹ 15,000 and wages ₹ 6,000 had been used in making tools and implements for use in own factory, but no adjustments were made in the books.

Sol.

Rectification Entries in Journal

Date	Particulars		LF	Amt (Dr)	Amt (Cr)
(i)	Purchases A/c	Dr		3,000	
	To Viraj & Co				3,000
	(Being the rectification of purchase of goods from Viraj & Co omitted from books)				
(ii)	Harish	Dr		10,000	
	To Haneef				10,000
	(Being the sale made on credit to Harish posted wrongly to the debit of Haneef, now rectified)				
(iii)	Building A/c	Dr		10,000	
	To Sundry Expenses A/c				10,000
	(Being the rectification of wrong debit to sundry expenses account for acquisition charges on purchases of new building)				
(iv)	Telephone Charges A/c	Dr		6,000	
	To Outstanding Telephone Charges A/c				6,000
	(Being the outstanding telephone charges omitted to be recorded, now recorded)				
(v)	Tools and Implements A/c	Dr		21,000	
	To Purchases A/c				15,000
	To Wages A/c				6,000
	(Being materials and wages used for tools and implements not recorded in the books)				

NUMERICAL Questions for Practice

1 Pass journal entries to rectify the following errors

(i) Machinery purchased for ₹ 10,000 has been debited to purchases account.

(ii) ₹ 1,400 paid to Mr W as legal charges were debited to his personal account.

(iii) ₹ 20,000 paid to X & Y Company for machinery purchased stands debited to company account.

(iv) Typewriter purchased for ₹ 12,000 was wrongly passed through purchases book.

(v) ₹ 40,000 paid for the purchase of motor cycle for proprietor has been charged to general expenses account.

(vi) ₹ 30,000 paid for the purchase of 'gas engine' were debited to purchases account.

(vii) Cash paid to Ram ₹ 800 was debited to the account of M.

2 Pass rectifying entries

(i) ₹ 10,000 being the cost of a radio purchased for the personal use of the proprietor has been debited to radio account in the ledger.

(ii) Goods taken by the proprietor for ₹ 2,000, has not been entered in the books at all.

(iii) A cheque of ₹ 1,000 received from Vishu was credited to the account of Abhi and debited to cash instead of bank account.

(iv) A cheque of ₹ 2,600 received from Raman was dishonoured and debited to general expenses account.

(v) A sum of ₹ 6,000 drawn by the proprietor for his private travel was debited to travelling expenses account.

(vi) Credit purchase of ₹ ,1000 from Akshay was posted to the credit of Veer's account.

(vii) An amount of ₹ 3,200 due from Chetan, written off as 'bad-debt' in previous year, was unexpectedly received this year, and has been credited to the account of Chetan.

3 Rectify the following errors

(i) ₹ 9,000 spent on the extension of buildings were debited to repairs account.

(ii) Wages paid to the firm's own workmen ₹ 7,200 for the installation of a new machinery were posted to wages account.

(iii) Contractor's bill for the construction of a godown at a cost of ₹ 20,000 has been charged to repairs account.

(iv) ₹ 3,000 paid as wages to a worker, Bahadur Singh, have been debited to his personal account.

(v) Old furniture sold for ₹ 1,000 has been credited to sales account.

(vi) A cheque of ₹ 1,240 received from Ram, has been wrongly credited to Shyam.

4 Give rectifying entries for the following

(i) A credit sale of goods to Ram ₹ 5,000 has been wrongly passed through the purchases book.

(ii) A credit purchase of goods from Shyam amounting to ₹ 2,000 has been wrongly passed through the sales book.

(iii) A return of goods worth ₹ 2,200 to Mohan was passed through the sales return book.

(iv) A return of goods worth ₹ 1,000 by Ganesh were entered in purchases return book.

(v) Goods for ₹ 11,000 were purchased from Modern Traders on credit, but no entry has yet been passed.

(vi) Purchases return for ₹ 3,000 not recorded in the books.

(vii) Goods for ₹ 1,4,000 sold to Zee Traders on credit were entered in the sales book as ₹ 200 only.

(viii) Goods of the value of ₹ 3,600 returned by Kamal Co. were included in stock, but no entry was passed in the books.

(ix) Goods purchased for ₹ 1,800 were entered in the purchases book as ₹ 18,000.

(x) An invoice for goods sold to X was overcast by ₹ 200.

5 Give journal entries to rectify the following errors

(i) Goods purchased from A for ₹ 2,600 were recorded in sales book by mistake.

(ii) Goods for ₹ 4,400 sold to B were passed through purchases book.

(iii) A customer returned goods worth ₹ 1,000. It was recorded in purchases return book.

(iv) A credit sale of ₹ 126 to D was entered in the books as ₹ 162.

(v) Sale of old chairs and table for ₹ 700 was treated as sale of goods.

(vi) Rent of proprietor's residence, ₹ 800, debited to rent account.

(vii) A sale of goods to E for ₹ 2,500 was passed through the purchases book.

(viii) Salary of ₹ 800 paid to F was wrongly debited to his personal account.

2. Errors which Affect the Agreement of Trial Balance

These errors are the one-sided errors and are disclosed by the trial balance. Trial balance does not tally if these errors are made. These errors are made only in one account and cannot be rectified by recording a journal entry unless a suspense account is opened. Following are the errors which affect the agreement of trial balance

(*i*) Error of casting
(*ii*) Error in carrying forward
(*iii*) Error of posting to the wrong side but in correct account
(*iv*) Posting twice in an account
(*v*) Error in posting with wrong amount
(*vi*) Error of partial omission
(*vii*) Error in totalling or balancing of an account.

Rectification of these errors depends on the stage at which the errors are located. The stages can be as follows

- Before preparing the trial balance
- After preparing the trial balance

I. BEFORE PREPARATION OF TRIAL BALANCE

When errors are rectified before preparation of trial balance rectification is done, by debiting or crediting the respective accounts with the required amount by giving an explanatory note in the particulars column.

Effect of Errors and their Rectification

Effect of Error	*Rectification*
Excess debit	It is to be made on the credit side by the difference
Excess credit	It is to be made on the debit side by the difference.
Less debit	It is to be made on the debit side by the difference
Less credit	It is to be made on the credit side by the difference.
Debit omitted	It is to be made on the debit side by the amount omitted.
Credit omitted	It is to be made on the credit side by the amount omitted.
A debit item wrongly credited in the account	It is to be made on the debit side by the amount to be debited plus amount credited.
A credit item wrongly debited in the account.	It is to be made on the credit side by the amount to be credited plus amount debited.

The above effects of errors and their rectification can be better understood with the help of an example.

ILLUSTRATION |13| How would you rectify the following errors before trial balance has been prepared?

(i) Total of purchases book has been undercast by ₹ 100.

Purchases book has been undercast by ₹ 100. It means that purchases account has been less debited by ₹ 100. Total of the purchases book is debited to purchases account in the ledger. The rectification will be made by writing the following words on the debit of purchases account. "To undercasting of purchases book ...100".

Dr **Purchases Account** Cr

Date	Particulars	Amt (₹)	Date	Particulars	Amt (₹)
	To Undercasting of Purchases Book	100			

(ii) Purchase from X for ₹ 15,000 has been omitted to be posted to his account.

Posting to the purchases account will be correct. The mistake will affect only X's account where ₹ 15,000 has not been posted to the credit side. Hence, the rectification will be made by writing the following words on the credit side of X's account.

"By omission in posting ...... ₹ 15,000."

Dr **X's Account** Cr

Date	Particulars	Amt (₹)	Date	Particulars	Amt (₹)
				By Omission in Posting	15,000

(iii) Purchase from Z for ₹ 40,000 has been posted to the wrong side of his account

Posting to the purchases account will be correct. The mistake will affect only Z's account. Z's account has been wrongly debited with ₹ 40,000 whereas his account should have been credited with this amount. Hence, the rectification will be made by double the amount of entry. As such, ₹ 80,000 will be written on the credit side of Z's account.

"By error in posting to the wrong side ...... ₹ 80,000."

Dr **Z's Account** Cr

Date	Particulars	Amt (₹)	Date	Particulars	Amt (₹)
				By Error in Posting to the Wrong Side	80,000

(iv) An amount of ₹ 151 for a credit sale to Hari, although correctly entered in the sales books, has been posted as ₹ 115 in Hari's account.

The mistake will only affect Hari's account which has been less debited by ₹ 36 (151 – 115). The rectification will be made in Hari's account by writing the following words on the debit side of Hari's account.

"To difference in amount posted on the debit side ...... 36."

Dr **Hari's Account** Cr

Date	Particulars	Amt (₹)	Date	Particulars	Amt (₹)
	To Difference in Amount	36			

(v) A payment of ₹ 75 for salaries to P has been posted twice to salaries account.

Excess debit will be removed by a credit in the salaries account by writing the following words.

"By double posting .... 75"

Dr **Salaries Account** Cr

Date	Particulars	Amt (₹)	Date	Particulars	Amt (₹)
				By Double Posting	75

II. AFTER PREPARING THE TRIAL BALANCE BUT BEFORE PREPARING FINAL ACCOUNTS

At this stage, the errors are rectified after the preparation of trial balance and transfer of difference in trial balance to the suspense account. The errors at this stage are rectified by passing a journal entry with the respective account or accounts affected by error and suspense account.

It should be noted that errors, unless stated otherwise are normally rectified with the help of suspense account.

SUSPENSE ACCOUNT

Suspense account is a temporary account which is opened to balance the trial balance.

If the debit side of the trial balance exceeds the credit side, the difference is put on the credit side of the trial balance. In this case, 'suspense account' will show a credit balance. If the credit side of the trial balance exceeds the debit side, the difference is put on the debit side of trial balance. In this case, 'suspense account' will show a debit balance. Errors which affect the trial balance are rectified with the help of suspense account. When all the errors which affect the equality of trial balance are located and rectified with the help of the suspense account, the suspense account stands balanced. However, if the suspense account shows a balance even after the errors have been rectified, then this means that there are certain errors which are yet to be rectified.

Such balance in the suspense account is taken to the balance sheet on the assets side if there is a debit balance or the liabilities side if there is a credit balance.

Following points should be kept in mind while rectifying one sided errors using suspense account

→ For short debit in one account → Debit that account and credit the suspense account

→ Excess credit in one account → Debit that account and credit the suspense account

→ Short credit in one account → Credit that account and debit the suspense account

→ Excess debit in one account → Credit that account and debit the suspense account

The process of rectification using suspense account can be better explained with the help of following illustration

ILLUSTRATION |14| Rectify the following errors

(i) Sales returns from Megha ₹ 1,600 was posted to her account as ₹ 1,000.

(ii) Cash paid to Neha ₹ 2,000 was not posted to her account.

(iii) Depreciation written-off on furniture ₹ 1,500 was not posted to depreciation account.

(iv) Credit sales to Mohan ₹ 10,000 were to his account as ₹ 12,000.

Sol. (*i*) Sales returns from Megha ₹ 1,600 were posted to her account as ₹ 1,000. This error results in short credit in Megha's account.

Rectification entry

Suspense A/c	Dr	600	
To Megha			600

(*ii*) Cash paid to Neha ₹ 2,000 was not posted to her account. This error results in omission of entry in the debit of Neha's account.

Rectification entry

Neha	Dr	2,000	
To Suspense A/c			2,000

(*iii*) Depreciation written-off on furniture ₹ 1,500 was not posted to depreciation account.
This error results in omission of posting of amount to th debit of depreciation account.

Rectification entry

Depreciation A/c	Dr	1,500	
To Suspense A/c			1,500

(*iv*) Credit sales to Mohan ₹ 10,000 were posted to his account as ₹ 12,000.
This error results in excess debit in the account of Mohan.

Rectification entry

Suspense A/c	Dr	2,000	
To Mohan			2,000

Guiding Principles of Rectification of Errors

(*i*) If error is committed in **books of original entry** then assume that all postings are done accordingly.

(*ii*) If error is at the **posting stage** then assume that recording in the subsidiary books has been done correctly.

(*iii*) If error is in **posting to a wrong account** (without mentioning side and amount of posting) then assume that posting has been done on the right side and with the right amount.

(*iv*) If **posting is done to a correct account but with wrong amount** (without mentioning side of posting) then assume that posting has been done on the right side and with the right amount.

(*v*) If error is in **posting to a wrong account on the wrong side** (without mentioning side of posting) then assume that posting has been done with the amount as per the original recording of the transaction.

(*vi*) If error is of **posting to a wrong account with wrong amount** (without mentioning the side of posting) then assume that posting has been done on the right side.

(*vii*) If **posting is done to a correct account on the wrong side** (without mentioning amount of posting) then assume that posting has been done with correct amount as per original recording.

(*viii*) When the word **'debited'** is used, it implies the posting on debit side of an account to which an individual item is posted.

(*ix*) When the word **'credited'** is used, it implies the posting on credit side of an account to which an individual item is posted.

(*x*) Any error in **posting of individual transactions** in subsidiary books relates to individual account only, the sales account, purchases account, sales return account or purchases return account are not involved.

(*xi*) If a transaction is recorded in cash book, then the error in posting relates to the other affected account, not to cash account/bank account.

(*xii*) If a transaction is recorded through journal proper, then the phrase 'transaction was not posted' indicates error in both the accounts involved, unless stated otherwise.

(*xiii*) Error in **casting of subsidiary books** will affect only that account where total of the particular book is posted leaving the individual personal accounts unaffected.

ILLUSTRATION |15| Rectify the following errors

(i) Sales book overcast by ₹ 700.
(ii) Purchase book overcast by ₹ 500.
(iii) Sales return book overcast by ₹ 300.
(iv) Purchase return book overcast by ₹ 200.
(v) Sales book undercast by ₹ 300.
(vi) Purchase book undercast by ₹ 400.
(vii) Return inwards book undercast by ₹ 200.
(viii) Return outwards book undercast by ₹ 100.

Sol.

Rectification Entries in Journal

Date	Particulars		LF	Amt (Dr)	Amt (Cr)
(i)	Sales A/c	Dr		700	
	To Suspense A/c				700
	(Being sales books overcast by ₹ 700, now rectified)				
(ii)	Suspense A/c	Dr		500	
	To Purchases A/c				500
	(Being purchases book overcast by ₹ 500, now rectified)				
(iii)	Suspense A/c	Dr		300	
	To Sales Return A/c				300
	(Being sales return book overcast by ₹300, now rectified)				
(iv)	Purchases Return A/c	Dr		200	
	To Suspense A/c				200
	(Being purchases return book overcast by ₹ 200, now rectified)				
(v)	Suspense A/c	Dr		300	
	To Sales A/c				300
	(Being sales book undercast by ₹ 300, now rectified)				

Date	Particulars		LF	Amt (Dr)	Amt (Cr)
(vi)	Purchases A/c	Dr		400	
	To Suspense A/c				400
	(Being purchases book undercast by ₹ 400, now rectified)				
(vii)	Return Inwards A/c	Dr		200	
	To Suspense A/c				200
	(Being sales return book undercast by ₹ 200, now rectified)				
(viii)	Suspense A/c	Dr		100	
	To Return Outwards A/c				100
	(Being return outwards book undercast by ₹ 100, now rectified)				

Note *Errors in subsidiary books are rectified through respective accounts.*

ILLUSTRATION |16| Rectify the following errors assuming that suspense account was opened. Ascertain the difference in trial balance.

(i) Depreciation provided on machinery ₹ 4,000 was not posted to depreciation account.

(ii) Bad debts written-off ₹ 5,000 were not posted to debtor's account.

(iii) Discount allowed to a debtor ₹ 100 on receiving cash from him was not posted to discount allowed account.

(iv) Goods withdrawn by proprietor for personal use ₹ 800 were not posted to drawings account.

(v) Bills receivable for ₹ 2,000 received from a debtor was not posted to bills receivable account.

NCERT

Sol.

Rectification Entries in Journal

Date	Particulars		LF	Amt (Dr)	Amt (Cr)
(i)	Depreciation A/c	Dr		4,000	
	To Suspense A/c				4,000
	(Being depreciation on machinery was not posted to depreciation account, now rectified)				
(ii)	Suspense A/c	Dr		5,000	
	To Debtor's A/c				5,000
	(Being bad debts written-off were not posted to debtor's account, now rectified)				
(iii)	Discount Allowed A/c	Dr		100	
	To Suspense A/c				100
	(Being discount allowed to customer, not posted to discount account, now rectified)				
(iv)	Drawings A/c	Dr		800	
	To Suspense A/c				800
	(Being goods withdrawn for personal use, not recorded in drawings account, now rectified)				
(v)	Bills Receivable A/c	Dr		2,000	
	To Suspense A/c				2,000
	(Being bills receivable received from a debtor was not recorded in bills receivable account, now rectified)				

Suspense Account

Dr Date	Particulars	JF	Amt (₹)	Date	Particulars	JF	Amt (₹) Cr
	To Debtor's A/c		5,000		By Depreciation A/c		4,000
	To Balance b/d		1,900		By Discount Allowed A/c		100
					By Drawings A/c		800
					By Bills Receivable A/c		2,000
			6,900				6,900

Note *The difference between the totals of debit and credit side represents the opening balance of suspense account.*

ILLUSTRATION |17| A book-keeper of a trading concern having failed to agree the trial balance, opened a suspense account and entered the difference in the trial balance.

The following errors were subsequently discovered

(i) Goods sold to Manohar for ₹ 550 was posted as ₹ 5,500.

(ii) Purchases return book was carried forward as ₹ 1,220 instead of ₹ 1,120.

You are required to pass the journal entries for rectification of the above errors.

Sol.

Rectification Entries in Journal

Date	Particulars		LF	Amt (Dr)	Amt (Cr)
(i)	Suspense A/c	Dr		4,950	
	To Manohar				4,950
	(Being the sales of goods wrongly over-debited to customer, now rectified)				
(ii)	Purchases Return A/c	Dr		100	
	To Suspense A/c				100
	(Being the error in carrying forward of total of purchases return book, now rectified)				

ILLUSTRATION |18| Write out the journal entries to rectify the following errors, using a suspense account.

(i) Goods of the value of ₹ 1,000 returned by P were entered in the sales daybook and posted there from to the credit of his account.

(ii) An amount of ₹ 1,500 entered in the sales returns book, has been posted to the debit of Q who returned the goods.

(iii) A sale of ₹ 2,000 made to R was correctly entered in the sales day book but wrongly posted to the debit of S as ₹ 200.

(iv) Bad debts aggregating ₹ 4,500 were written-off during the year in the sales ledger but were not adjusted in the general ledger.

(v) The total of 'discount allowed' column in the cash book for the month of September, 2016 amounting to ₹ 2,500 was not posted.

Sol.

Rectification Entries in Journal

Date	Particulars		LF	Amt (Dr)	Amt (Cr)
(i)	Sales A/c	Dr		1,000	
	Sales Returns A/c	Dr		1,000	
	To Suspense A/c				2,000
	(Being the value of goods returned by P wrongly posted to sales and omission of debit to sales returns account, now rectified)				
(ii)	Suspense A/c	Dr		3,000	
	To Q				3,000
	(Being wrong debit to Q for goods returned by him, now rectified)				

Date	Particulars	LF	Amt (Dr)	Amt (Cr)
(iii)	R Dr		2,000	
	To S			200
	To Suspense A/c			1,800
	(Being omission of debit to R and wrong credit to S ₹ 200, for sale of ₹ 2,000, now rectified)			
(iv)	Bad Debts A/c Dr		4,500	
	To Suspense A/c			4,500
	(Being the amount of bad debts written-off not adjusted in general ledger, now rectified)			
(v)	Discount Allowed A/c Dr		2,500	
	To Suspense A/c			2,500
	(Being the total of discount allowed during September, 2013 not posted from the cash book, now rectified)			

ILLUSTRATION |19| An accountant, while balancing his books found that there was a difference of ₹ 85.95 in the trial balance. Being required to prepare the final accounts, he placed this difference to a newly opened suspense account which was carried forward to the next year, when the following errors were discovered.

(i) Goods bought from a merchant for ₹ 5.50 had been posted to the credit of his account as ₹ 55.
(ii) An item of ₹10.62 entered in the sales return book had been posted to the debit of the customer who returned the goods.
(iii) ₹ 60 owing by a customer had been omitted from the schedule of sundry debtors.
(iv) ₹ 2.31 discount received from a creditor had been duly entered in his account but not posted to discount received account.

Give journal entries necessary to correct these errors and prepare the suspense account.

Sol.

Rectification Entries in Journal

Date	Particulars	LF	Amt (Dr)	Amt (Cr)
(i)	Merchant A/c Dr		49.50	
	To Suspense A/c			49.50
	(Being excess amount posted to the credit of a merchant account)			
(ii)	Suspense A/c Dr		21.24	
	To Customer A/c			21.24
	(Being amount wrongly debited instead of being credited in the customer account)			
(iii)	Sundry Debtors A/c Dr		60.00	
	To Suspense A/c			60.00
	(Being customer's account not recorded in the list of sundry debtors)			
(iv)	Suspense A/c Dr		2.31	
	To Discount Received A/c			2.31
	(Being discount received not posted to the credit of discount received account)			

Suspense Account

Dr Date	Particulars	JF	Amt (₹)	Date	Particulars	JF	Cr Amt (₹)
	To Balance b/d		85.95		By Merchant A/c		49.50
	To Customer A/c		21.24		By Sundry Debtors A/c		60.00
	To Discount Received A/c		2.31				
			109.50				109.50

Note *After passing all the rectifying entries, it is ascertained that the credit side of the suspense account exceeds the debit by ₹ 85.95. As such it will be treated as the opening balance of suspense account and will be written on the debit side.*

ILLUSTRATION |20| Trial balance of Kohli did not agree and showed an excess debit of ₹ 16,300. He put the difference to a suspense account and discovered the following errors.

(i) Cash received from Rajat ₹ 5,000 was posted to the debit of Kamal as ₹ 6,000.

(ii) Salary paid to an employee ₹ 2,000 was debited to his personal account as ₹ 1,200.

(iii) Goods withdrawn by proprietor for personal use ₹ 1,000 were credited to sales account as ₹ 1,600.

(iv) Depreciation provided on machinery ₹ 3,000 was posted to machinery account as ₹ 300.

(v) Sale of old car for ₹ 10,000 was credited to sales account as ₹ 6,000.

Rectify the errors and prepare suspense account. **NCERT**

Sol.

Rectification Entries in Journal

Date	Particulars		LF	Amt (Dr)	Amt (Cr)
(i)	Suspense A/c	Dr		11,000	
	To Rajat				5,000
	To Kamal				6,000
	(Being cash received from Rajat ₹ 5,000, wrongly debited to Kamal's account as ₹ 6,000, now rectified)				
(ii)	Salaries A/c	Dr		2,000	
	To Employee's A/c				1,200
	To Suspense A/c				800
	(Being salary paid ₹ 2,000, wrongly entered in employee's personal account as ₹ 1,200, now rectified)				
(iii)	Sales A/c	Dr		1,600	
	To Purchases A/c				1,000
	To Suspense A/c				600
	(Being goods withdrawn by proprietor ₹ 1,000 wrongly credited to sales account as ₹ 1,600, now rectified)				
(iv)	Suspense A/c	Dr		2,700	
	To Machinery A/c				2,700
	(Being depreciation charged on machinery ₹ 3,000 wrongly credited to machinery accounts ₹ 300, now rectified).				
(v)	Sales A/c	Dr		6,000	
	Suspense A/c	Dr		4,000	
	To Car A/c				10,000
	(Being sale of old car for ₹ 10,000 wrongly posted in sales account as ₹ 6,000, now rectified)				

Dr **Suspense Account** Cr

Date	Particulars	JF	Amt (₹)	Date	Particulars	JF	Amt (₹)
	To Rajat		5,000		By Balance b/d		16,300
	To Kamal		6,000		By Salaries A/c		800
	To Machinery A/c		2,700		By Sales A/c		600
	To Car A/c		4,000				
			17,700				17,700

ILLUSTRATION |21| Trial balance of Anuj did not agree. It showed an excess credit ₹ 6,000. He put the difference to suspense account. He discovered the following errors.

(i) Cash received from Ravish ₹ 8,000 posted to his account as ₹ 6,000.
(ii) Return inwards book overcast by ₹ 1,000.
(iii) Total of sales book ₹ 10,000 was not posted to sales account.
(iv) Credit purchases from Nanak ₹ 7,000 were recorded in sales book. However, Nanak's account was correctly credited .
(v) Machinery purchased for ₹ 10,000 was posted to purchase account as ₹ 5,000.

Rectify the errors and prepare suspense account. **NCERT**

Sol. **Rectification Entries in Journal**

Date	Particulars		LF	Amt (Dr)	Amt (Cr)
(i)	Suspense A/c	Dr		2,000	
	To Ravish				2,000
	(Being cash received from Ravish ₹ 8,000 wrongly posted to Ravish account as ₹ 6,000, now rectified)				
(ii)	Suspense A/c	Dr		1,000	
	To Return Inwards A/c				1,000
	(Being return inwards book overcast by ₹ 1,000, now rectified)				
(iii)	Suspense A/c	Dr		10,000	
	To Sales A/c				10,000
	(Beings sales of ₹ 10,000 was not posted to sales account, now rectified)				
(iv)	Purchases A/c	Dr		7,000	
	Sales A/c	Dr		7,000	
	To Suspense A/c				14,000
	(Being purchase figure of ₹ 7,000 was wrongly posted in sales book, now rectified)				
(v)	Machinery A/c	Dr		10,000	
	To Purchases A/c				5,000
	To Suspense A/c				5,000
	(Being purchases of machinery for ₹ 10,000 recorded through purchase account as ₹ 5,000 now rectified.				

Dr **Suspense Account** Cr

Date	Particulars	JF	Amt (₹)	Date	Particulars	JF	Amt (₹)
	To Balance b/d		6,000		By Purchases A/c		7,000
	To Ravish		2,000		By Sales A/c		7,000
	To Return Inwards A/c		1,000		By Machinery A/c		5,000
	To Sales A/c		10,000				
			19,000				19,000

ILLUSTRATION |22| Trial balance of Madan did not agree and he put the difference to suspense account. He discovered the following errors.

(i) Sales return book overcast by ₹ 800.

(ii) Purchases return to Sahu ₹ 2,000 was not posted.

(iii) Installation charges on new machinery purchased ₹ 500 were debited to sundry expenses account as ₹ 50.

(iv) Rent paid for residential accommodation of Madan (the proprietor) ₹ 1,400 was debited to rent account as ₹ 1,000.

Rectify the errors and prepare suspense account to ascertain the difference in trial balance. **NCERT**

Sol.

Rectification Entries in Journal

Date	Particulars		LF	Amt (Dr)	Amt (Cr)
(i)	Suspense A/c	Dr		800	
	To Sales Return A/c				800
	(Being sales return book overcast by ₹ 800, now rectified)				
(ii)	Sahu	Dr		2,000	
	To Suspense A/c				2,000
	(Being purchases return to Sahu was not recorded in his personal account, now rectified)				
(iii)	Machinery A/c	Dr		500	
	To Sundry Expenses A/c				50
	To Suspense A/c				450
	(Being installation charges on machinery ₹ 500, wrongly debited to machinery account ₹ 50, now rectified)				
(iv)	Drawings A/c	Dr		1,400	
	To Rent A/c				1,000
	To Suspense A/c				400
	(Being rent paid for proprietor's residence ₹ 1,400, recorded as rent expenses for ₹ 1,000, now rectified)				

Suspense Account

Dr Cr

Date	Particulars	JF	Amt (₹)	Date	Particulars	JF	Amt (₹)
	To Sales Return A/c		800		By Sahu		2,000
	To Balance b/d		2,050		By Machinery A/c		450
					By Drawings A/c		400
			2,850				2,850

ILLUSTRATION |23| Rectify the following errors and ascertain the amount of difference in trial balance by preparing suspense account.

(i) Credit sales to Mohan ₹ 7,000 were not posted.
(ii) Credit purchase from Rohan ₹ 9,000 were not posted.
(iii) Goods returned to Rakesh ₹ 4,000 were not posted.
(iv) Goods returned from Mahesh ₹ 1,000 were not posted.
(v) Cash paid to Ganesh ₹ 3,000 was not posted.
(vi) Cash sales ₹ 2,000 were not posted. **NCERT**

Sol.

Rectification Entries in Journal

Date	Particulars	LF	Amt (Dr)	Amt (Cr)
(i)	Mohan Dr		7,000	
	To Suspense A/c			7,000
	(Being goods sold to Mohan on credit were not posted in his personal account, now rectified)			
(ii)	Suspense A/c Dr		9,000	
	To Rohan			9,000
	(Being goods purchased from Rohan were not posted in his personal account, now rectified)			
(iii)	Rakesh Dr		4,000	
	To Suspense A/c			4,000
	(Being goods returned to Rakesh were not posted to his personal account, now rectified)			
(iv)	Suspense A/c Dr		1,000	
	To Mahesh			1,000
	(Being goods returned by Mahesh were not posted to his personal account, now rectified)			
(v)	Ganesh Dr		3,000	
	To Suspense A/c			3,000
	(Being cash paid to Ganesh was not posted to his personal account, now rectified)			
(vi)	Suspense A/c Dr		2,000	
	To Sales A/c			2,000
	(Being cash sales was not posted to sales account, now rectified)			

Note *In errors relating to posting, it is assumed that the entry is correctly recorded in subsidiary books.*

Dr **Suspense Account** Cr

Date	Particulars	JF	Amt (₹)	Date	Particulars	JF	Amt (₹)
	To Rohan		9,000		By Mohan		7,000
	To Mahesh		1,000		By Rakesh		4,000
	To Sales A/c		2,000		By Ganesh		3,000
	To Balance b/d		2,000				
			14,000				14,000

ILLUSTRATION |24| Rectify the following errors and ascertain the amount of difference in trial balance by preparing suspense account.

(i) Credit sales to Mohan ₹ 7,000 were posted as ₹ 9,000.
(ii) Credit purchase from Rohan ₹ 9,000 were posted as ₹ 6,000.
(iii) Goods returned to Rakesh ₹ 4,000 were posted as ₹ 5,000.
(iv) Goods returned from Mahesh ₹ 1,000 were posted as ₹ 3,000.
(v) Cash sales ₹ 2,000 were posted as ₹ 200. **NCERT**

Sol.

Rectification Entries in Journal

Date	Particulars		LF	Amt (Dr)	Amt (Cr)
(i)	Suspense A/c	Dr		2,000	
	To Mohan				2,000
	(Being credit sales to Mohan for ₹ 7,000, wrongly posted in his personal account as ₹ 9,000, now rectified)				
(ii)	Suspense A/c	Dr		3,000	
	To Rohan				3,000
	(Being credit purchase from Rohan for ₹ 9,000, wrongly posted in his personal account as 6,000, now rectified)				
(iii)	Suspense A/c	Dr		1,000	
	To Rakesh				1,000
	(Being goods returned to Rakesh ₹ 4,000, wrongly posted as ₹ 5,000, now rectified)				
(iv)	Mahesh	Dr		2,000	
	To Suspense A/c				2,000
	(Being goods returned from Mahesh for ₹ 1,000, wrongly posted as ₹ 3,000, now rectified)				
(v)	Suspense A/c	Dr		1,800	
	To Sales A/c				1,800
	(Being cash sales for ₹ 2,000 wrongly posted as ₹ 200, now rectified)				

Dr **Suspense Account** Cr

Date	Particulars	JF	Amt (₹)	Date	Particulars	JF	Amt (₹)
	To Mohan		2,000		By Mahesh		2,000
	To Rohan		3,000		By Balance b/d		5,800
	To Rakesh		1,000				
	To Sales A/c		1,800				
			7,800				7,800

ILLUSTRATION |25| Rectify the following errors assuming that a suspense account was opened. Ascertain the difference in trial balance.

(i) Credit sales to Mohan ₹ 7,000 were posted to the credit of his account.
(ii) Credit purchase from Rohan ₹ 9,000 were posted to the debit of his account as ₹ 6,000.
(iii) Goods returned to Rakesh ₹ 4,000 were posted to the credit of his account.
(iv) Goods returned from Mahesh ₹ 1,000 were posted to the debit of his account as ₹ 2,000.
(v) Cash sales ₹ 2,000 were posted to the debit of sales account as ₹ 5,000. **NCERT**

Sol. **Rectification Entries in Journal**

Date	Particulars	LF	Amt (Dr)	Amt (Cr)
(i)	Mohan Dr		14,000	
	To Suspense A/c			14,000
	(Being goods sold to Mohan wrongly credited to his account, now rectified)			
(ii)	Suspense A/c Dr		15,000	
	To Rohan			15,000
	(Being goods purchased from Rohan for ₹ 9,000, wrongly debited to his account ₹ 6,000, now rectified)			
(iii)	Rakesh Dr		8,000	
	To Suspense A/c			8,000
	(Being goods returned to Rakesh wrongly posted to credit in his account, now rectified)			
(iv)	Suspense A/c Dr		3,000	
	To Mahesh			3,000
	(Being goods returned by Mahesh for ₹ 1,000, wrongly debited to his account ₹ 2,000, now rectified)			
(v)	Suspense A/c Dr		7,000	
	To Sales A/c			7,000
	(Being cash sales of ₹ 2,000, wrongly debited of sales account as 5,000, now rectified)			

Dr **Suspense Account** Cr

Date	Particulars	JF	Amt (₹)	Date	Particulars	JF	Amt (₹)
	To Rohan		15,000		By Mohan		14,000
	To Mahesh		3,000		By Rakesh		8,000
	To Sales A/c		7,000		By Balance b/d		3,000
			25,000				25,000

ILLUSTRATION |26| Rectify the following errors assuming that suspense account was opened. Ascertain the difference in trial balance.

(i) Furniture purchased for ₹ 10,000 wrongly debited to purchases account as ₹ 4,000.

(ii) Repair on machinery ₹ 1,400 debited to machinery account as ₹ 2,400.

(iii) Repair on overhauling of secondhand machinery purchased ₹ 2,000 was debited to repair account as ₹ 200.

(iv) Sale of old machinery at book value ₹ 3,000 was credited to sales account as ₹ 5,000. **NCERT**

Sol. **Rectification Entries in Journal**

Date	Particulars	LF	Amt (Dr)	Amt (Cr)
(i)	Furniture A/c Dr		10,000	
	To Purchases A/c			4,000
	To Suspense A/c			6,000
	(Being purchase of furniture for ₹ 10,000 entered wrongly in purchases book ₹ 4,000, now rectified)			
(ii)	Repairs A/c Dr		1,400	
	Suspense A/c Dr		1,000	
	To Machinery A/c			2,400
	(Being repair of machinery ₹ 1,400 wrongly debited to machinery account ₹ 2,400 now rectified)			

Date	Particulars		LF	Amt (Dr)	Amt (Cr)
(iii)	Machinery A/c	Dr		2,000	
	To Repairs A/c				200
	To Suspense A/c				1,800
	(Being overhauling of secondhand machine ₹ 2,000, wrongly debited to repair account as ₹ 200, now rectified)				
(iv)	Sales A/c	Dr		5,000	
	To Machinery A/c				3,000
	To Suspense A/c				2,000
	(Being sales of machinery for ₹ 3,000, wrongly credited to sales account as ₹ 5,000, now rectified)				

Dr **Suspense Account** Cr

Date	Particulars	JF	Amt (₹)	Date	Particulars	JF	Amt (₹)
	To Machinery A/c		1,000		By Furniture A/c		6,000
	To Balance b/d		8,800		By Machinery A/c		1,800
					By Sales A/c		2,000
			9,800				9,800

ILLUSTRATION |27| Rectify the following errors assuming that a suspense account was opened. Ascertain the difference in trial balance.

(i) Credit sales to Mohan ₹ 7,000 were posted to Karan as ₹ 5,000.
(ii) Credit purchase from Rohan ₹ 9,000 were posted to the debit of Gobind as ₹ 10,000.
(iii) Goods returned to Rakesh ₹ 4,000 were posted to the credit of Naresh as ₹ 3,000.
(iv) Goods returned from Mahesh ₹ 1,000 were posted to the debit of Manish as ₹ 2,000.
(v) Cash sales ₹ 2,000 were posted to commission account as ₹ 200. **NCERT**

Sol.

Rectification Entries in Journal

Date	Particulars		LF	Amt (Dr)	Amt (Cr)
(i)	Mohan	Dr		7,000	
	To Karan				5,000
	To Suspense A/c				2,000
	(Being goods sold to Mohan for ₹ 7,000, wrongly posted to Karan's account as ₹ 5,000, now rectified)				
(ii)	Suspense A/c	Dr		19,000	
	To Rohan				9,000
	To Gobind				10,000
	(Being goods returned by Rohan ₹ 9,000, wrongly posted to Gobind's account ₹ 10,000, now rectified)				
(iii)	Rakesh	Dr		4,000	
	Naresh	Dr		3,000	
	To Suspense A/c				7,000
	(Being goods returned to Rakesh ₹ 4,000, posted wrongly to Naresh's account ₹ 3,000, now rectified)				
(iv)	Suspense A/c	Dr		3,000	
	To Mahesh				1,000
	To Manish				2,000
	(Being goods returned by Mahesh ₹ 1,000, wrongly posted to Manish's account ₹ 2,000, now rectified)				
(v)	Commission A/c	Dr		200	
	Suspense A/c	Dr		1,800	
	To Sales A/c				2,000
	(Being cash sales for ₹ 2,000, wrongly posted to the commission account ₹ 200, now rectified)				

Dr			Suspense Account				Cr
Date	Particulars	JF	Amt (₹)	Date	Particulars	JF	Amt (₹)
	To Rohan		9,000		By Mohan		2,000
	To Gobind		10,000		By Rakesh		4,000
	To Mahesh		1,000		By Naresh		3,000
	To Manish		2,000		By Balance b/d		14,800
	To Sales A/c		1,800				
			23,800				23,800

ILLUSTRATION |28| Rectify the following errors assuming that suspense account was opened. Ascertain the difference in trial balance.

(i) Credit sales to Mohan ₹ 7,000 were recorded in purchases book. However, Mohan's account was correctly debited.

(ii) Credit purchase from Rohan ₹ 9,000 were recorded in sales book. However, Rohan's account was correctly credited.

(iii) Goods returned to Rakesh ₹ 4,000 were recorded in sales return book. However, Rakesh's account was correctly debited.

(iv) Goods returned from Mahesh ₹ 1,000 were recorded through purchases return book. However, Mahesh's account was correctly credited.

(v) Goods returned to Naresh ₹ 2,000 were recorded through purchases book. However, Naresh's account was correctly debited. **NCERT**

Sol. **Rectification Entries in Journal**

Date	Particulars		LF	Amt (Dr)	Amt (Cr)
(i)	Suspense A/c	Dr		14,000	
	To Sales A/c				7,000
	To Purchases A/c				7,000
	(Being goods sold to Mohan wrongly entered through purchases book, now rectified)				
(ii)	Purchases A/c	Dr		9,000	
	Sales A/c	Dr		9,000	
	To Suspense A/c				18,000
	(Being goods purchased from Rohan, wrongly entered in sales book, now rectified)				
(iii)	Suspense A/c	Dr		8,000	
	To Purchases Return A/c				4,000
	To Sales Return A/c				4,000
	(Being purchases return wrongly entered through sales return book, now rectified)				
(iv)	Sales Return A/c	Dr		1,000	
	Purchases Return A/c	Dr		1,000	
	To Suspense A/c				2,000
	(Being sales return from Mahesh, wrongly entered through sales return book, now rectified)				
(v)	Suspense A/c	Dr		4,000	
	To Purchases Return A/c				2,000
	To Purchases A/c				2,000
	(Being purchases return wrongly entered through purchases account, now rectified)				

Dr			Suspense Account				Cr
Date	Particulars	JF	Amt (₹)	Date	Particulars	JF	Amt (₹)
	To Sales A/c		7,000		By Purchases A/c		9,000
	To Purchases A/c		7,000		By Sales A/c		9,000
	To Purchases Return A/c		4,000		By Sales Return A/c		1,000
	To Sales Return A/c		4,000		By Purchases Return A/c		1,000
	To Purchases Return A/c		2,000		By Balance b/d		6,000
	To Purchases A/c		2,000				
			26,000				26,000

ILLUSTRATION |29| On going through the trial balance of Vardhman Ltd., you find that the debit is in excess by ₹ 150. This was credited to suspense account. On a close scrutiny of the books, the following mistakes were noticed.

(i) The total of debit side of expenses account has been cast in excess by ₹ 50.
(ii) The sales account has been totalled in short by ₹ 100.
(iii) One item of purchase of ₹ 25 has been posted from the day book to ledger as ₹ 250.
(iv) The sales return of ₹ 100 from a party has not been posted to that account though the party's account has been credited.
(v) A credit sale of ₹ 50 has been credited to the sales and also to the sundry debtors' account.

Pass necessary journal entries for correcting the above and prepare the 'suspense account' as it would appear in the ledger.

Sol. *(a)* **Rectification Entries in Journal**

Date	Particulars		LF	Amt (Dr)	Amt (Cr)
(i)	Suspense A/c	Dr		50	
	To Expenses A/c				50
	(Being the mistake in totalling of expenses account, now rectified)				
(ii)	Suspense A/c	Dr		100	
	To Sales A/c				100
	(Being the mistake in totalling of sales accounts, now rectified)				
(iii)	Supplier's/Creditor	Dr		225	
	To Suspense A/c				225
	(Being the mistake in posting from day book to ledger, now rectified)				
(iv)	Sales Returns A/c	Dr		100	
	To Suspense A/c				100
	(Being the sales return from a party not posted to 'sales returns', now rectified)				
(v)	Sundry Debtors	Dr		100	
	To Suspense A/c				100
	(Being the sales wrongly credited to customer's account, now rectified)				

(b)

Dr			Suspense Account				Cr
Date	Particulars	JF	Amt (₹)	Date	Particulars	JF	Amt (₹)
	To Expenses A/c		50		By Balance b/d		150
	To Sales A/c		100		By Sundry Creditors/Suppliers		225
	To Balance c/d		425		By Sales Returns A/c		100
					By Sundry Debtors		100
			575				575

Note *Suspense account exhibits a closing balance. This indicates that there are certain other errors which are not yet rectified.*

ILLUSTRATION |30| Give the journal entries to rectify the following error using suspense account, where necessary.

(i) Goods of the value of ₹ 2,000 returned by Mr Gupta were entered in the sales book and posted therefrom to the credit of his account.

(ii) Goods worth ₹ 1,500 bought by the proprietor for his personal use without any payment being made as yet, were wrongly entered in the purchases book.

(iii) A cheque for ₹ 500 received from Ashok was dishonoured and has been posted to the debit of sales return account.

(iv) The total of one page of the sales book was carried forward to the next page as ₹ 680 instead of ₹ 860.

(v) An item of ₹ 500 relating to prepaid insurance account was omitted to be brought forward from the previous year's books.

Sol. **Rectification Entries in Journal**

Date	Particulars		LF	Amt (Dr)	Amt (Cr)
(i)	Sales Return A/c	Dr		2,000	
	Sales A/c	Dr		2,000	
	To Suspense A/c				4,000
	(Being the goods returned wongly entered in the sales book, now rectified)				
(ii)	Drawings A/c	Dr		1,500	
	To Purchases A/c				1,500
	(Being the goods taken for personal use wrongly entered in purchases book, now rectified)				
(iii)	Ashok	Dr		500	
	To Sales Return A/c				500
	(Being the dishonour of cheque debited to sales return account, now rectified)				
(iv)	Suspense A/c	Dr		180	
	To Sales A/c				180
	(Being the wrong carried forward of total of sales book, now rectified)				
(v)	Prepaid Insurance A/c	Dr		500	
	To Suspense A/c				500
	(Being the prepaid insurance premium was omitted to be brought forward, now rectified)				

ILLUSTRATION |31| Trial balance of Khatau did not agree. He put the difference to suspense account and discovered the following errors.

(i) Credit sales to Manas ₹ 16,000 were recorded in the purchases book as ₹ 10,000 and posted to the debit of Manas as ₹ 1,000.

(ii) Furniture purchased from Noor ₹ 6,000 was recorded through purchases book as ₹ 5,000 and posted to the debit of Noor ₹ 2,000.

(iii) Goods returned to Rai ₹ 3,000 recorded through the sales book as ₹ 1,000.

(iv) Old machinery sold for ₹ 2,000 to Maneesh recorded through sales book as ₹ 1,800 and posted to the credit of Manish as ₹ 1,200.

(v) Total of return inwards book ₹ 2,800 posted to purchases account.

Rectify the above errors and prepare suspense account to ascertain the difference in trial balance. **NCERT**

Sol. **Rectification Entries in Journal**

Date	Particulars		LF	Amt (Dr)	Amt (Cr)
(i)	Suspense A/c	Dr		11,000	
	Manas	Dr		15,000	
	To Purchases A/c				10,000
	To Sales A/c				16,000
	(Being goods sold to Manas ₹ 16,000, wrongly recorded in purchases book as ₹ 10,000 and debited to his account as ₹ 1,000, now rectified)				
(ii)	Furniture A/c	Dr		6,000	
	Suspense A/c	Dr		7,000	
	To Noor				8,000
	To Purchases A/c				5,000
	(Being furniture purchased ₹ 6,000, wrongly recorded in purchases account as ₹ 5,000 and debited to Noor's account as ₹ 2,000, now rectified)				
(iii)	Sales A/c	Dr		1,000	
	Rai	Dr		2,000	
	To Return Outwards A/c				3,000
	(Being goods returned to Rai, ₹ 3,000 wrongly recorded in sales book as ₹ 1,000, now rectified)				
(iv)	Manish	Dr		1,200	
	Sales A/c	Dr		1,800	
	Maneesh	Dr		2,000	
	To Machinery A/c				2,000
	To Suspense A/c				3,000
	(Being old machinery sold to Maneesh ₹ 2,000, wrongly recorded in sales account as ₹ 1,800 and credited to Manish's account as ₹ 1,200, now rectified)				
(v)	Return Inwards A/c	Dr		2,800	
	To Purchases A/c				2,800
	(Being total of return inward book, wrongly posted to purchases book, now rectified)				

Dr **Suspense Account** Cr

Date	Particulars	JF	Amt (₹)	Date	Particulars	JF	Amt (₹)
	To Purchases A/c		10,000		By Manish		1,200
	To Sales A/c		1,000		By Sales A/c		1,800
	To Purchases A/c		5,000		By Balance b/d		15,000
	To Noor		2,000				
			18,000				18,000

ILLUSTRATION |32| Pass the journal entries to rectify the following errors detected during preparation of the trial balance.

(i) Purchases book is undercast by ₹ 1,000.
(ii) Wages paid for construction of office debited to wages account ₹ 20,000.
(iii) A credit sale of goods ₹ 1,200 to Ramesh has been wrongly passed through the purchases book.
(iv) Goods purchased for ₹ 5,000 were posted as ₹ 500 to the purchases account.
(v) An amount of ₹ 2,000 due from Mahesh Chand which had been written-off as a bad debt in previous year was unexpectedly recovered has been posted to the personal account of Mahesh Chand.
(vi) A credit purchase of ₹ 1,040 from Ramesh was passed in the books as ₹ 1,400.
(vii) Goods (cost ₹ 5,000, sales price ₹ 6,000) distributed as free samples among prospective customers were not recorded anywhere.
(viii) Goods worth ₹ 1,500 returned by Green & Co. have not been recorded anywhere.

Sol.

Rectification Entries in Journal

Date	Particulars		LF	Amt (Dr)	Amt (Cr)
(i)	Purchases A/c	Dr		1,000	
	To Suspense A/c				1,000
	(Being the purchases book undercast, now rectified)				
(ii)	Building A/c	Dr		20,000	
	To Wages A/c				20,000
	(Being the wages for construction of building wrongly debited to wages account, now rectified)				
(iii)	Ramesh	Dr		2,400	
	To Sales A/c				1,200
	To Purchases A/c				1,200
	(Being the wrong recording of sales in purchases book, now rectified)				
(iv)	Purchases A/c	Dr		4,500	
	To Suspense A/c				4,500
	(Being the short posting in purchases account, now rectified)				
(v)	Mahesh Chand	Dr		2,000	
	To Bad Debts Recovered A/c				2,000
	(Being the bad debts recovered wrongly credited to Mahesh Chand, now rectified)				
(vi)	Ramesh	Dr		360	
	To Purchases A/c				360
	(Being the credit purchases of ₹ 1,040 was passed in the books as ₹ 1,400, now rectified)				
vii)	Free Sample or Advertising A/c	Dr		5,000	
	To Purchases A/c				5,000
	(Being the distribution of sample recorded)				
(viii)	Sales Return A/c	Dr		1,500	
	To Green & Co.				1,500
	(Being the sales return recorded)				

ILLUSTRATION |33| Trial balance of Raju showed an excess debit of ₹ 10,000. He put the difference to suspense account and discovered the following errors.

(i) Depreciation written-off the furniture ₹ 6,000 was not posted to furniture account.
(ii) Credit sales to Rupam ₹ 10,000 were recorded as ₹ 7,000.
(iii) Purchases book undercast by ₹ 2,000.
(iv) Cash sales to Rana ₹ 5,000 were not posted.
(v) Old machinery sold for ₹ 7,000 was credited to sales account.
(vi) Discount received ₹ 800 from Kanan on paying cash to him was not posted.

Rectify the errors and prepare suspense account.

Sol. **Rectification Entries in Journal**

Date	Particulars	LF	Amt (Dr)	Amt (Cr)
(i)	Suspense A/c Dr To Furniture A/c (Being depreciation on furniture was not posted to furniture account, now rectified)		6,000	6,000
(ii)	Rupam Dr To Sales A/c (Being sales of ₹ 10,000 to Rupam, recorded as ₹ 7,000, now rectified)		3,000	3,000
(iii)	Purchases A/c Dr To Suspense A/c (Being purchase book undercast by ₹ 2,000, now rectified)		2,000	2,000
(iv)	Suspense A/c Dr To Sales A/c (Being cash sales to Rana was not recorded, now rectified)		5,000	5,000
(v)	Sales A/c Dr To Machinery A/c (Being sales of old machinery, wrongly credited to sales account, now rectified)		7,000	7,000
(vi)	Kanan Dr To Discount Received A/c (Being discount received from Kanan not recorded, now rectified)		800	800

Dr **Suspense Account** Cr

Date	Particulars	JF	Amt (₹)	Date	Particulars	JF	Amt (₹)
	To Furniture A/c		6,000		By Balance b/d		10,000
	To Sales A/c		5,000		By Purchases A/c		2,000
	To Balance c/d		1,000				
			12,000				12,000

ILLUSTRATION |34| Give journal entries to rectify the following errors assuming that suspense account had been opened.

(i) Goods distributed as free sample ₹ 5,000 were not recorded in the books.
(ii) Goods withdrawn for personal use by the proprietor ₹ 2,000 were not recorded in the books.
(iii) Bills receivable received from a debtor ₹ 6,000 was not posted to his account.
(iv) Total of return inwards book ₹ 1,200 was posted to return outwards account.
(v) Discount allowed to Reema ₹ 700 on receiving cash from her was recorded in the books as ₹ 70.

NCERT

Sol.

Rectification Entries in Journal

Date	Particulars		LF	Amt (Dr)	Amt (Cr)
(i)	Free Samples or Advertising A/c	Dr		5,000	
	To Purchases A/c				5,000
	(Being goods distributed as free samples ₹ 5,000 were not recorded in the books, now rectified)				
(ii)	Drawings A/c	Dr		2,000	
	To Purchases A/c				2,000
	(Being goods withdrawn for personal use were not recorded, now rectified).				
(iii)	Suspense A/c	Dr		6,000	
	To Debtor's A/c				6,000
	(Being bills receivable received from debtors ₹ 6,000 was not posted to his account, now rectified)				
(iv)	Return Inwards A/c	Dr		1,200	
	Return Outwards A/c	Dr		1,200	
	To Suspense A/c				2,400
	(Being total of return inward book, posted to return outward book, now rectified)				
(v)	Discount Allowed A/c	Dr		630	
	To Reema				630
	(Being discount allowed to Reema ₹ 700, wrongly recorded as ₹ 70 only, now rectified)				

Suspense Account

Dr | Cr

Date	Particulars	JF	Amt (₹)	Date	Particulars	JF	Amt (₹)
	To Debtor's A/c		6,000		By Return Inwards A/c		1,200
					By Return Outwards A/c		1,200
					By Balance b/d		3,600
			6,000				6,000

ILLUSTRATION |35| Correct the following errors by opening a suspense account.

(i) The sales book has been totalled ₹ 100 short.

(ii) Goods worth ₹ 150 returned by Vishal & Co have not been recorded anywhere.

(iii) Goods purchased ₹ 250 have been posted to the debit of the supplier Raja & Co.

(iv) Furniture purchased from Narayan & Brothers ₹ 1,000 has been entered in purchases day book.

(v) Discount received from Monu & Sonu ₹ 15 has not been entered in the discount column of the cash book.

(vi) Discount allowed to Naveen & Co. ₹ 18 has not been entered in the discount column of the cash book. The account of Naveen & Co has, however, been correctly posted.

Sol. **Rectification Entries in Journal**

Date	Particulars		LF	Amt (Dr)	Amt (Cr)
(i)	Suspense A/c	Dr		100	
	To Sales A/c				100
	(Being the correction arising from undercasting of sales day book)				
(ii)	Return Inward A/c	Dr		150	
	To Vishal & Co.				150
	(Being the recording of unrecorded returns)				
(iii)	Suspense A/c	Dr		500	
	To Raja & Co.				500
	(Being the correction of the error by which Raja & Co. was debited instead of being credited by ₹ 250)				
(iv)	Furniture A/c	Dr		1,000	
	To Purchases A/c				1,000
	(Being the correction of recording purchase of furniture of ordinary purchases)				
(v)	Monu & Sonu	Dr		15	
	To Discount A/c				15
	(Being the recording of discount omitted to be recorded)				
(vi)	Discount Allowed A/c	Dr		18	
	To Suspense A/c				18
	(Being the correction of omission of the discount allowed from cash book customer's account already posted correctly.				

Dr **Suspense Account** Cr

Date	Particulars	JF	Amt (₹)	Date	Particulars	JF	Amt (₹)
	To Sales A/c		100		By Balance b/d		582
	To Raja & Co		500		By Discount Allowed A/c		18
			600				600

Note (*i*) *It should be noted that opening balance in the suspense account will be equal to the difference in the trial balance.*

(*ii*) *If the question is silent as to whether a suspense account has been opened, the student should make his assumption, state it clearly and then proceed.*

ILLUSTRATION |36| Correct the following errors found in the books of Siddharth. The trial balance was out by ₹ 493 excess credit. The difference thus has been posted to a suspense account.

(i) An amount of ₹ 100 was received from Parth on 31st December, 2011 but has been omitted to enter in the cash book.

(ii) The total of returns inward book for December has been cast ₹ 100 short.

(iii) The purchase of an office table costing ₹ 300 has been passed through the purchases day book.

(iv) ₹ 375 paid for wages to workmen for making show-cases had been charged to wages account.

(v) A purchase of ₹ 67 had been posted to the creditors account as ₹ 60.

(vi) A cheque for ₹ 200 received from Kanav had been dishonoured and was passed to the debit of 'allowances account'.

(vii) ₹ 1,000 paid for the purchase of a motor cycle for Siddharth had been charged to 'miscellaneous expenses account'.

(viii) Good amounting to ₹ 100 had been returned by customer and were taken into stock, but no entry in respect thereof, was made into the books.

(ix) A sale of ₹ 200 to Rahul & Co. was wrongly credited to their account.

Sol. **Rectification Entries in Journal**

Date	Particulars		LF	Amt (Dr)	Amt (Cr)
(i)	Cash A/c	Dr		100	
	To Parth				100
	(Being the amount received)				
(ii)	Returns Inward A/c	Dr		100	
	To Suspense A/c				100
	(Being the mistake in totalling the returns inward book, now rectified)				
(iii)	Furniture A/c	Dr		300	
	To Purchases A/c				300
	(Being the rectification of mistake by which purchase of furniture was entered in purchases book and hence, debited to purchases account)				
(iv)	Furniture A/c	Dr		375	
	To Wages A/c				375
	(Being the wages paid to workmen for making showcases which should be capitalised and not to be charged to wages account)				
(v)	Suspense A/c	Dr		7	
	To Creditor's (Personal) A/c				7
	(Being the mistake in crediting the creditor's account less by ₹ 7, now rectified)				
(vi)	Kanav	Dr		200	
	To Allowances A/c				200
	(Being the cheque of Kanav dishonoured, previously debited to allowance account)				
(vii)	Drawings A/c	Dr		1,000	
	To Miscellaneous Expenses				1,000
	(Being the motor cycle purchased for Siddharth debited to his drawings account instead of miscellaneous expenses account as previously done by mistake)				
(viii)	Returns Inward A/c	Dr		100	
	To Customer's (Personal) A/c				100
	(Being correction of the omission to record return of goods by customers)				
(ix)	Rahul & Co.	Dr		400	
	To Suspense A/c				400
	(Being the correction of mistake by which the account of Rahul & Co was credited by ₹ 200 instead of being debited)				

Dr **Suspense Account** Cr

Date	Particulars	JF	Amt (₹)	Date	Particulars	JF	Amt (₹)
2011				2011			
Dec 31	To Balance b/d		493	Dec 31	By Returns Inward A/c		100
Dec 31	To Creditor's A/c		7		By Rahul & Co		400
			500				500

NUMERICAL Questions for Practice

1 Rectify the following errors assuming that a suspense account has been opened.

(i) Goods costing ₹ 800 purchased from T on credit were omitted to be credited to his account.

(ii) Goods costing ₹ 800 purchased from T on credit were credited to his account as ₹ 80.

(iii) Goods costing ₹ 800 purchased from T on credit were credited to his account as ₹ 880.

(iv) Goods costing ₹ 800 purchased from T on credit were posted to the debit of his account.

(v) Goods costing ₹ 800 purchased from T on credit were posted to the debit of his account as ₹ 80.

2 Rectify the following errors assuming that suspense account was opened. Ascertain the difference in trial balance.

(i) Credit sales to R ₹ 7,000 were recorded in purchases book. However, R's account was correctly debited.

(ii) Credit purchases from P ₹ 9,000 were recorded in sales book. However, P's account was correctly credited.

(iii) Goods returned to Z ₹ 4,000 were recorded in sales returns book. However, Z's account was correctly debited.

(iv) Goods returned from X ₹ 1,000 were recorded through purchases returns book. However, X's account was correctly credited.

(v) Goods returned to Y ₹ 2,000 were recorded through purchases book. However, Y's account was correctly debited.

Ans Opening Credit Balance of Suspense Account = ₹ 6,000, Total of Suspense Account = ₹ 26,000

3 Rectify the following errors by means of journal entries

(i) A cheque of ₹ 10,000 received from L was dishonoured and was debited to discount account.

(ii) Purchase of ₹ 1,080 from R was written in sales day book, but was correctly posted to correct side of R's account.

(iii) Salary paid to S ₹ 2,000 was debited to his personal account as ₹ 1,800.

(iv) Furniture costing ₹ 1,000, purchased from K was wrongly entered in purchases book as ₹ 900.

4 Pass journal entries to rectify the following errors detected during preparation of trial balance.

(i) Purchases book is undercast by ₹ 2,000.

(ii) Wages paid for construction of office debited to wages account ₹ 40,000.

(iii) A credit sale of goods ₹ 2,400 to Q has been wrongly passed through the purchases book.

(iv) Goods purchased for ₹ 10,000 were posted as ₹ 1,000 to the purchases account.

(v) An amount of ₹ 4,000 due from RP Sharma which had been written-off as a bad-debt in a previous year was unexpectedly recovered and has been posted to the personal account of RP Sharma.

(vi) A credit purchase of ₹ 2,080 from Q was passed in the books as ₹ 2,800.

(vii) Goods (Cost ₹ 10,000, Sales Price ₹ 12,000) distributed as free samples among prospective customers was not recorded anywhere.

(viii) Goods worth ₹ 3,000 returned by X and Co. have not been recorded anywhere.

5 Give rectifying journal entries for the following errors

(i) Sale of goods to X ₹ 16,000 was entered in the sales book as ₹ 1,600.

(ii) A credit purchase of ₹ 3,000 from W has been wrongly passed through the sales book.

(iii) Repairs to building ₹ 1,200 were debited to building account.

(iv) ₹ 4,100 paid to Ashu is posted to the debit of Vishu's account as ₹ 10,040.

(v) Purchases return book is overcast by ₹ 1,600.

6 Rectify the following errors

(i) The sales book has been totalled ₹ 2,000 short.

(ii) Goods worth ₹ 3,000 returned by Z and Co. have not been recorded anywhere.

(iii) Goods purchased worth ₹ 5,000 have been posted to the debit of the supplier, X and Co.

(iv) Furniture purchased from G and Co. worth ₹ 20,000 has been entered in purchases day book.

(v) Cash received from A ₹ 5,000 has not been posted in his account.

7 In taking out the trial balance, a book-keeper finds excess debit of ₹ 3,809. Being desirous of closing his books, he places the difference to a newly opened suspense account which is carried forward. In the next period, he discovered that

(i) ₹ 17,715 received from Raj have not been posted to his account.
(ii) A sum of ₹ 9,500 written off as depreciation on fixtures has not been posted to the depreciation account.
(iii) ₹ 1,50,000 paid for furniture purchased have been charged to ordinary purchases account.
(iv) A discount of ₹ 3,742 allowed to a customer has been credited to him as ₹ 3,648.
(v) The total of the inwards return has been added ₹ 900 short.
(vi) An item of sales for ₹ 5,900 was posted as ₹ 9,500 the sales account.

Give the rectifying entries and prepare the suspense account.

Ans Total of Suspense Account = ₹ 17,809

8 A book-keeper failed to balance his trial balance, the credit side exceeding the debit side by ₹ 175. This amount was entered in a suspense account. Later on, the under mentioned errors were discovered

(i) Goods amounting to ₹ 620 sold to Kartik & Co. were correctly entered in the sales book, but posted to the company's account as ₹ 260.
(ii) A credit balance of ₹ 755 of rent received account was shown as ₹ 570.
(iii) The total of returns outwards book amounting to ₹ 200 was not posted to the ledger.
(iv) Goods worth ₹ 100 were purchased from Aakash but the amount was entered in the sales book. The account of Aakash was correctly credited.
(v) Sales book was undercast by ₹ 100.
(vi) The total of the credit side of Rohan's account was overcast by ₹ 100.

Give journal entries to rectify these errors and prepare the suspense account.

Ans Total of Suspense Account = ₹ 660

9 Rectify the following entries giving suitable narrations

(i) A sale of ₹ 800 has been passed through the purchases day book. The customer account has however been correctly debited.
(ii) A bill receivable from Vikas has been dishonoured on maturity and was posted to the debit of bills receivable ₹ 260.
(iii) Goods returned by A ₹ 160 have not been recorded in the return inward book.

10 The trial balance prepared by a book-keeper showed a difference of ₹ 1,006 which was placed in a newly opened suspense account and carried forward to the next year, when the following errors were discovered

(i) Goods purchased for ₹ 99 had been posted to the credit of the supplier as ₹ 990.
(ii) ₹ 75 received as discount from a creditor was duly entered in his account but it was omitted to be posted to discount account.
(iii) Sale of furniture for ₹ 1,400 had been entered in sales book.
(iv) ₹ 900 due from a customer were omitted to be taken to the schedule of sundry debtors.
(v) Goods of the value of ₹ 3,000 returned by a customer were taken into the stock but no entry was made in the books.
(vi) ₹ 335 entered in the sales returns book had been posted to the debit of the customer who returned the goods.

Give necessary journal entries to rectify the above errors and prepare suspense account.

Ans Opening Debit Balance of Suspense Account = ₹ 1,006. Total of Suspense Account = ₹ 1,791.

11 A book-keeper finds that the debit side of the trial balance is short of ₹ 308 and so far the time being, he balances the side by putting the difference to suspense account. Subsequently, the following errors were disclosed.

(i) An entry for goods for ₹ 102 to X was posted to his account as ₹ 120.
(ii) ₹ 100 being the monthly total of discount allowed to customers were credited to discount account in the ledger.
(iii) ₹ 275 paid by X were credited to X's account.
(iv) ₹ 26 appearing in the cash book as paid for the purchase of stationery for office use have not been posted to ledger.
(v) The debit of purchases account was undercast by ₹ 100.

You are required to make the necessary journal entries and the suspense account.

Ans Suspense Account Tallies, Total of Suspense Account = ₹ 326

CHAPTER PRACTICE

OBJECTIVE TYPE Questions

Multiple Choice Questions

1 Error in which effect of one error is nullified by the effect of another error is called ....

(a) error of commission (b) compensating error
(c) error of omission (d) None of these

Ans (b) compensating error

2 Which error(s) does/do not affect the trial balance?

(a) Error of commission
(b) Error of principle
(c) Error of complete omission
(d) Both (b) and (c)

Ans (d) Both (b) and (c)

3 If wages paid for installation of new machinery is debited to wages account, it is **NCERT**

(a) an error of commission
(b) an error of principle
(c) a compensating error
(d) an error of omission

Ans (b) an error of principle

4 Which of the following is not an error of commission? **NCERT**

(a) Overcasting of sales book
(b) Credit sales to Ramesh ₹ 5,000 credited to his account
(c) Wrong balancing of machinery account
(d) Cash sales not recorded in cash book

Ans (d) Cash sales not recorded in cash book

5 Undercasting of sales book is corrected by ...... sales account.

(a) debiting (b) crediting
(c) both debit/credit (d) None of these

Ans (b) Suspense account will be made to debit and sales account will be made to credit with the same amount.

6 Goods of ₹ 1,000 purchased on credit from Mr 'A' are recorded in purchases book for ₹ 10,000. Which type of error is this?

(a) Error of casting
(b) Error of recording
(c) Error of carrying forward
(d) Error of posting

Ans (b) Error of recording

7 An item of ₹ 53 has been debited to a personal account as ₹ 35. It is an error of

(a) commission (b) omission
(c) complete error (d) principle

Ans (a) commission

8 Suspense account is used to rectify

(a) one sided errors
(b) two sided errors
(c) Both (a) and (b)
(d) suspense account cannot be used to rectify errors

Ans (a) one sided errors

9 If suspense account shows a credit balance, it will be taken to

(a) liability side of balance sheet
(b) assets side of balance sheet
(c) capital side of balance sheet
(d) credit side of profit and loss account

Ans (a) Suspense account is opened to tally the trial balance, its credit balance will be taken to liability side of balance sheet and debit balance will be taken to assets side of balance sheet.

10 If suspense account does not balance off even after rectification of errors, it implies that **NCERT**

(a) there are some one sided errors only in the books yet to be located
(b) there are no more errors yet to be located
(c) there are some two sided errors only yet to be located
(d) there may be both one sided errors and two sided errors yet to be located

Ans (a) there are some one sided errors only in the books yet to be located

11 Which of these errors will be rectified through suspense account? **NCERT**

(a) Sales return book undercast by ₹ 1,000
(b) Sales return by Madhu ₹ 1,000
(c) Sales return by Madhu ₹ 1,000 recorded as ₹ 100
(d) Sales return by Madhu ₹ 1,000 recorded through purchase return account

Ans (a) Sales return book undercast by ₹ 1,000

12 Credit purchase from Rohan ₹ 9,000 was posted to the debit of Gobind as ₹ 10,000. In this case, suspense account will be debited with

(a) ₹ 9,000 (b) ₹ 10,000
(c) ₹ 19,000 (d) None of these

Ans (c) This is the double amount error, in this Rohan will be credited with ₹ 9,000 and Gobind with ₹ 10,000 and suspense account will be debited with ₹ 19,000 (9,000 + 10,000).

13 Preeti was paid cash ₹ 2,800 but Jyoti was debited by ₹ 2,000. In rectifying entry, suspense account will be

(a) debited ₹ 2,800
(b) credited ₹ 2,000
(c) credited ₹ 800
(d) debited ₹ 800

Ans (c) Cash paid to Preeti wrongly debited to Jyoti, so Jyoti will be credited with ₹ 2,000 and Preeti will be debited with ₹ 2,800. Difference (2,800 – 2,000) = ₹ 800 will be put in credit side of suspense account.

14 Which of these is not an error of principle? **NCERT**

(a) Purchase of furniture debited to purchases account
(b) Repairs on the overhauling of second hand machinery purchased debited to repairs account
(c) Cash received from Manoj posted to Saroj
(d) Sale of old car credited to sales account

Ans (c) Cash received from Manoj posted to Saroj

15 Material ₹ 10,000 and wages ₹ 3,000 were used for construction of building. No adjustment entry was made in the books. Rectifying entry will be

(a)	Wages A/c	Dr	10,000	
	To Building A/c			10,000
(b)	Material A/c	Dr	10,000	
	Building A/c	Dr	3,000	
	To Cash A/c			13,000
(c)	Building A/c	Dr	13,000	
	To Purchases A/c			10,000
	To Wages A/c			3,000

(d) None of the above

Ans (c) Building is a fixed asset and all the expenses regarding its construction should be added to it, as these all are capital expenditure in nature.
So, building account will be debited with ₹ 13,000 (10,000 + 3,000).

Fill in the Blanks

16 To make the trial balance equal or balanced, the difference may be transferred to .... account.

Ans suspense

17 Rectifying entries are passed in ....

Ans journal proper

18 If a transaction is omitted to be recoreded in the books of accounts, it is an error of ....

Ans omission

19 .... error arises when any transaction is incorrectly recorded in the books of original entry.

Ans Recording

20 Error of carrying forward arises when a mistake is committed in carrying forward a .... of one page to the next page.

Ans total

State True or False

21 Amount posted in the wrong account or written on the wrong side of an account is called error of omission.

Ans False. Amount posted on the wrong side or to a wrong account is called error of commission.

22 Errors of omission will not affect the agreement of trial balance.

Ans True

23 Wrong casting of subsidiary books does not affect the trial balance.

Ans False. Trial balance is affected by the wrong casting of subsidiary books.

24 Errors of principle arise when a transaction is recorded in the books of accounts violating the accounting principles.

Ans True

25 Errors which do not affect the agreement of trial balance are two-sided errors.

Ans True

Match the Following

26

	Column I		*Column II*
1.	One error neutralise other	(a)	Error of principle
2.	Purchase account is debited in case of furniture purchased	(b)	Error of ommission
3.	Transactions completely ommitted in recording	(c)	Compensatory error

Ans 1-(c), 2-(a), 3-(b)

27

	Column I		*Column II*
1.	Do not affect the trial balance	(a)	Suspense account
2.	Affect the trial balance	(b)	Errors
3.	Imaginary account	(c)	Two-sided errors
4.	Unintentional mistake	(d)	One-sided errors

Ans 1-(c), 2-(d), 3-(a), 4-(b)

Journalise the Following

28 Pass a rectified journal entry if machinery purchased for ₹ 40,000 has been debited to purchase account.

Ans

Machinery A/c	Dr	40,000	
To Purchase A/c			40,000
(Being machinery purchased wrongly debited to Purchase A/c, now rectified)			

29 Pass a rectified journal entry if goods returned to X ₹ 2,000 were recorded in the sales return book.

Ans

X's A/	Dr	4,000	
To Purchase Return A/c			2,000
To Sales Return A/c			2,000
(Being goods returned to X wrongly recorded in sales return book, now rectified)			

30 Pass a rectified journal entry in case an amount of ₹ 2,000 collected from Riddhi, a debtor which were already written-off as bad debts, were posted to the credit of Riddhi's Account.

Ans

Riddhi	Dr	2,000	
To Bad Debts Recovered A/c			2,000
(Being amount previously written-off as bad debts now recovered but credited to Riddhi's A/c, now rectified)			

31 Pass a rectified journal entry if credit purchase from Ronit for ₹ 81,000 was not recorded.

Ans

Purchases A/c	Dr	81,000	
To Ronit			81,000
(Being goods purchased from Ronit on credit not recorded, now rectified)			

32 Pass a rectified journal entry if furniture purchased on credit from Krishna for ₹ 1,20,000 posted as ₹ 12,000.

Ans

Furniture A/c	Dr	1,08,000	
To Krishna			1,08,000
(Being the error in posting of amount, now rectified)			

VERY SHORT ANSWER Type Questions

33 What is meant by a rectifying entry?

Ans Rectifying entry means an entry passed to correct the error committed.

34 Give two examples of two-sided error.

Ans (*i*) Machinery purchased recorded in the purchases book.
(*ii*) Old furniture sold recorded as sales of goods.

35 Name two types of errors with example which do not affect the trial balance.

Ans (*i*) **Error of Principle** *e.g.*, recording of machinery purchased as purchases.
(*ii*) **Error of Complete Omission** *e.g.*, goods purchased from Ram of ₹ 10,000 but not recorded in the books of accounts.

36 What is meant by error of principle?

Ans Error of principle means recording a transaction in contravention of accounting principles.

37 Give two examples of error of principle. **NCERT**

Ans (*i*) Recording freight on purchase of fixed asset as a revenue expenditure.
(*ii*) Wages paid to a worker for making additions to machinery debited to wages account.

38 A machine is purchased for ₹ 10,000 and is wrongly recorded in purchases account. What will be the errors effect on trial balance?

Ans Trial balance will not show any difference.

39 Why is a compensating error not disclosed by trial balance?

Ans A compensating error is not disclosed by the trial balance as one error is nullified by another error.

40 Give two examples of compensating error.

Ans (*i*) Sales of ₹ 10,000 recorded as ₹ 1,000.
(*ii*) Purchases of ₹ 10,000 recorded as ₹ 1,000.

41 Goods were sold to Abhi for ₹ 2,000 and to Zen for ₹ 1,000. The transactions were recorded properly in the sales book, but ₹ 1,000 was posted to Abhi, while ₹ 2,000 was posted to Zen. Identify the type of error.

Ans Compensating error

42 Will the transaction that is correctly recorded in the journal proper but not posted in the ledger at all, effect the trial balance?

Ans No, such error of posting has the same effect on both the debit and credit aspects of a transaction as posting has not been done in both the accounts.

43 Will the transaction that is recorded in wrong book of original entry with wrong amount, affect the trial balance?

Ans No, error of recording has the same effect on both the debit and credit aspects of a transaction.

44 Will the trial balance agree in case of errors of partial omission? Why?

Ans No, the trial balance will not agree. Because a trial balance will agree only if both the aspects of a transaction are posted into ledger accounts with correct amount.

45 Give two examples of errors of commission. **NCERT**

Ans (*i*) Recording purchases of goods for ₹ 5,000 as ₹ 50,000.

(*ii*) Cash balance of ₹ 1,000 carried forward as ₹ 10,000.

46 Give two examples of one-sided error.

Ans (*i*) Depreciation on computers not posted to depreciation account.

(*ii*) Purchase of stationery of ₹ 1,000 posted twice to stationery account.

47 If suspense account does not balance off even after rectification of errors, what does it imply?

Ans There are some one-sided errors in the books yet to be located.

SHORT ANSWER Type Questions

48 Explain the errors of commission and give two examples with measures to rectify them. **NCERT**

Ans For errors of commission, refer to text on page no. 276.

Example 1 Sales made to X of ₹ 10,000 recorded as ₹ 1,000.

In this case X's account has been debited with ₹ 1,000 instead of ₹ 10,000. This will be rectified by passing the following entry

X	Dr	9,000	
To Sales A/c			9,000

Example 2 Cash received from Karim ₹ 60,000 posted to Nadim.

In this case cash received from Karim has been wrongly posted to Nadim. Hence Nadim's account has been wrongly credited.

In order to rectify the error, Nadim's account should be debited as it is wrongly credited, and Karim's account should be credited as it is not recorded. Thus, the rectifying entry will be

Nadim	Dr	60,000	
To Karim			60,000

49 Explain errors of omission and give atleast two examples of such errors.

Ans For errors of omission, refer to text on page no. 276.

50 Explain errors of principle and give two examples with measures to rectify them. **NCERT**

Ans For error of principle, refer to text on page no. 276.

Example 1 Wages paid for construction of building are debited to wages account.

In this case, wages paid for the construction of building should be treated as a capital expenditure and accordingly should be debited to the building account. However, the wages account is wrongly debited.

In order to rectify this error, wages account will be credited as it is wrongly debited, and building account will be debited, as it is not recorded. Thus, the rectifying entry will be

Building A/c	Dr
To Wages A/c	

Example 2 Sale of old machinery recorded as sales

In this case, the sale of old machinery should not be recorded as sales and the machinery account should have been credited.

In order to rectify this error, sales account will be debited, as it is wrongly credited and machinery will be credited, as it is not recorded in the books. Thus, the rectifying entry will be

Sales A/c	Dr
To Machinery A/c	

51 Explain compensating errors and give atleast one example of such errors.

Ans For compensating errors refer to text on page no. 276.

52 Name the errors, which do not affect the trial balance.

Ans Refer to page no. 277.

53 What is a suspense account ? Is it necessary that a suspense account will balance off after rectification of the errors detected by the accountant? If not, then what happens to the balance still remaining in suspense account? **NCERT**

Ans Suspense account is an account which is opened on a temporary basis to balance the trial balance.

No, it is not necessary that a suspense account will balance after rectification of the errors detected by the accountant.

Suspense account can remain unbalanced if all the errors are not detected. Balance remaining in the suspense account is transferred to the balance sheet on the assets side, if there is a debit balance, or the liabilities side if there is a credit balance.

LONG ANSWER Type Questions

54 What are different types of errors that are usually committed in recording business transaction? **NCERT**

Ans *Keeping in view the nature of errors, errors can be classified into the following four categories*

(*i*) **Errors of Commission**

When a transaction is recorded wrongly in the books of accounts, it is called error of commission.

Errors of commission can be classified into the following

(*a*) **Error of Recording** This error arises when any transaction is incorrectly recorded in the books of original entry. This error will not affect the trial balance.

(*b*) **Error of Casting** This error arises when a mistake is committed in totalling. This error affects the trial balance.

(*c*) **Error of Carrying Forward** It is an error which arises when a mistake is committed in carrying forward a total of one page on the next page. This error affects the trial balance.

(*d*) **Error of Posting** When the information recorded in the books of original entry are incorrectly entered in the ledger, it is an error of posting.

(*ii*) **Errors of Omission**

This kind of error arises when a transaction is partially or completely omitted (left out) to be recorded in the books of accounts. *These can be of two types*

(*a*) **Error of Complete Omission** When a transaction is completely omitted from recording in the books of original record, it is an error of complete omission. This error does not affect the trial balance.

(*b*) **Error of Partial Omission** When a transaction is partially omitted from recording in the books, it is an error of partial omission. This error affects the trial balance.

(*iii*) **Errors of Principle**

When a transaction is recorded in the books of accounts violating the accounting principles, *i.e.,* treating capital as revenue or *vice-versa* it is known as errors of principle. These errors do not affect the trial balance.

(*iv*) **Compensating Errors**

When two or more errors are committed in such a way that the net effect of these errors on the debits and credits of accounts is nil, such errors are called compensating errors. These errors do not affect the tallying of trial balance.

55 What kinds of errors would cause difference in the trial balance? Also list examples that would not be revealed by a trial balance. **NCERT**

Ans The errors that lead to the differences in the trial balance are termed as one-sided errors. These are those errors that affect only one account.

Below are given the errors that cause differences in the trial balance

(*i*) Wrong casting of any account, this is termed as the error of casting.

(*ii*) Wrong carrying forward of the balances from previous year's books or from one end of page to another. These types of errors are termed as the errors in carrying forward.

(*iii*) If entries are posted in the wrong side of accounts.

(*iv*) Posting of a wrong amount in account, this is termed as the error of posting.

(*v*) If entries are recorded partially, *i.e.,* the entries are not recorded completely, then due to the error of partial omission, trial balance does not agree.

(*vi*) Examples of errors that would not be revealed in a trial balance.

(*vii*) Sales to Mr X, omitted to be recorded in the sales day book.

56 Give the stages of errors and what errors occur at those stages.

Ans Error may occur at any of the following stages of the accounting process.

At the stage of recording transactions in the journal

(*i*) Error of principle
(*ii*) Error of omission
(*iii*) Error of commission

At the stage of posting the entries in the ledger

(*i*) Error of omission
  (*a*) Partial omission
  (*b*) Complete omission
(*ii*) Error of commission
  (*a*) Posting to wrong account
  (*b*) Posting on the wrong side
  (*c*) Posting of wrong amount

At the stage of the balancing the ledger accounts

(*i*) Wrong totalling of accounts
(*ii*) Wrong balancing of accounts

At the stage of preparing the trial balance

(*i*) Error of omission
(*ii*) Error of commission
  (*a*) Recording in the wrong account
  (*b*) Recording the wrong amount
  (*c*) Recording in the wrong side

57 What are the steps taken by an accountant to locate the errors in trial balance? **NCERT**

Ans *The following steps will be useful in locating errors*

Step 1 The two columns of the trial balance should be totalled again. If in place of a number of accounts, only one account has been written in the trial balance, then the list of such accounts should be checked and totalled again.

Step 2 It should be seen that the cash and bank balances have been written in the trial balance.

Step 3 The exact difference in the trial balance should be determined. The ledger should be properly checked as it is possible that a balance equal to the difference has been omitted from the trial balance. The difference should also be halved; it is possible that balance equal to half the difference has been written in the wrong column.

Step 4 The ledger accounts should be balanced again.

Step 5 The totalling of subsidiary books should be checked again, especially if the difference is ₹ 1, ₹ 100 etc.

Step 6 If the difference is very big, the balance in various accounts should be compared with the corresponding accounts in the previous period. If the figures differ materially, the respective accounts should be checked again.

Step 7 Postings of the amounts equal to the difference or half the difference should be checked. It is possible that an amount has been omitted to be posted or has been posted on the wrong side.

Step 8 If there is still a difference in the trial balance, a complete checking will be necessary. The posting of all the entries including the opening entry should be checked. It may be better to begin with the nominal accounts.

NUMERICAL Questions

1 Rectify the following errors

(i) Furniture purchased for ₹ 10,000 was wrongly debited to purchases account.
(ii) Machinery purchased on credit from G for ₹ 20,000 was recorded through purchases book.
(iii) Repairs on machinery ₹ 1,400 debited to machinery account.

(iv) Repairs on overhauling of secondhand machinery purchased ₹ 2,000 was debited to repairs account.

(v) Sale of old machinery at book value of ₹ 3,000 was credited to sales account.

(vi) Furniture purchased on credit from H for ₹ 1,000 was entered in the purchases book.

(vii) ₹ 5,000 spent on the extension of buildings was debited to buildings repairs account.

(viii) Goods returned by B ₹ 1,200 were entered in the returns outwards book.

2 Pass journal entries to rectify the following errors

(i) A builder's bill for ₹ 10,000 for erection of a small cycle shed was debited to repair account.

(ii) A cheque of ₹ 3,400 received from Vihan was dishonoured and had been posted to the debit side of allowance account.

(iii) ₹ 1,600 paid for the newly purchased fan posted to purchases account.

(iv) ₹ 8,000 the amount of sale of an old machinery has been credited to sales account.

(v) ₹ 2,000 received from Z has been credited to M's account.

3 Pass journal entries to rectify the following errors

(i) Sales of ₹ 200 to X were recorded as ₹ 2,000 in the sales book.

(ii) Goods of ₹ 300 taken by the proprietor have not been entered in the books at all.

(iii) Goods of the value of ₹ 400 returned to Y, but no entry was made in the books.

(iv) A cheque of ₹ 400 received from Z was dishonoured and debited to discount allowed account.

4 Rectify the following errors

(i) An amount of ₹ 2,500 spent for the extension of machinery has been debited to wages account.

(ii) ₹ 100 paid as cartage for the newly purchased furniture, posted to cartage account.

(iii) An amount of ₹ 600 due from Narayan, which has been written-off as bad-debt in previous year, was unexpectedly recovered, and has been credited to the personal account of Narayan.

(iv) Bill for ₹ 820 received from Kartik for repairs to machinery was entered in the purchases book as ₹ 720.

5 Pass journal entries to rectify the following errors

(i) Goods amounting to ₹ 4,000 have been sold on credit, but no entry has been made in the books.

(ii) No entry has been made for sales return of ₹ 450.

(iii) Goods purchased from A on credit for ₹ 5,000 was recorded in purchases book as ₹ 500.

(iv) Sales of ₹ 600 to B were recorded as ₹ 60 in the sales book.

(v) Goods purchased on credit from C for ₹ 400 was recorded as ₹ 4,000 in purchases book.

(vi) Goods costing ₹ 1,000 have been purchased on credit from D, but no entry has been made in the books, although the goods were taken into stock.

6 Pass the rectifying entries for the following

(i) Sale of goods ₹ 6,000 to W were recorded as ₹ 600 in the sales book.

(ii) Credit purchase of goods from W amounting to ₹ 2,000 has been wrongly passed through the sales book.

(iii) Return of goods worth ₹ 500 by a customer was entered in purchases return book.

(iv) Cheque of ₹ 400 received from X was dishonoured and debited to the discount account.

7 Give rectifying journal entries for the following errors

(i) Sales of goods to Madan ₹ 6,000 were entered in the sales book as ₹ 600.

(ii) Credit purchase of ₹ 1,500 from M has been wrongly passed through the sales book.

(iii) Repairs to building ₹ 300 were debited to building account.

(iv) ₹ 2,050 paid to N is posted to the debit of M's account as ₹ 5,020.

(v) Purchases return book is overcast by ₹ 400.

8 Give rectifying entries for the following

(i) ₹ 5,400 received from Mr A was posted to the debit of his account.

(ii) The total of sales return book overcast by ₹ 800.

(iii) ₹ 2,740 paid for repairs to motor car was debited to motor car account as ₹ 1,740.

(iv) Returned goods to Shyam ₹ 1,500 were passed through returns inward book.

9 There was a difference of ₹ 8,595 in a trial balance. It has been transferred to debit side of suspense account. Later on following errors were discovered. Pass the rectifying entries and prepare the suspense account.

(i) ₹ 283 discount received from a creditor had been duly entered in his account but not posted to discount account.

(ii) Goods bought from a merchant for ₹ 770 had been posted to the credit of his account as ₹ 7,700.

(iii) ₹ 6,000 owing by a customer had been omitted from the schedule of sundry debtors.

(iv) An item of ₹ 2,026 entered in the sales return book had been posted to the debit of the customer who returned the goods.

Ans Suspense Account Total = ₹ 12,930

10 Pass the rectification entries and show the suspense account in the books of a partnership firm, from the following particulars

(i) The total of sales return day book was overcast by ₹ 1,000.

(ii) Purchase of equipment, from Veer & Co worth ₹ 2,000, in cash, was entered through the purchases day book and accordingly, credited to the supplier's account.

(iii) Discount ₹ 500 allowed by Nimish, a creditor, not been entered in the books of account.

(iv) ₹ 350 paid for carriage on sale of goods was credited to carriage inward account when posted from the cash book.

(v) Bill receivable worth ₹ 1,800 received from a debtor was entered in the bills payable book though correctly entered in the debtor's account.

(vi) A sum of ₹ 2,500 collected from Harish, a debtor, whose dues were already written-off as bad debt, was posted to the credit side of Harish account.

(vii) Goods worth ₹ 1,500 bought by the partner Kunal for his personal use without any payment being made as yet, was wrongly entered in the purchases day book.

Ans Balance in Suspense Account = ₹ 3,300

11 A book-keeper prepared a trial balance on 31st March, 2013, which showed a difference of ₹2,715.53. The difference was placed to the debit of a suspense account. The undermentioned errors were subsequently discovered.

(i) ₹ 710, the total of sales return book has been posted to the credit of the purchases return account.

(ii) An item of ₹ 626 written-off as a bad-debt from C has not been debited to bad debts account.

(iii) Goods sold to W and X for ₹ 1,600 and ₹ 1,200 respectively, but were recorded in the sales book as to W ₹ 1,200 and X as ₹ 1,600.

(iv) Goods of ₹ 850 were returned to B. It was recorded in purchases book as ₹ 580.

(v) An amount of ₹ 675.25 for a credit sale to Govind, although correctly entered in the sales book, has been wrongly posted as ₹ 756.52.

(vi) A sum of ₹ 375.40 owed by Y has been included in the list of sundry creditors.

(vii) An amount of ₹ 750 spent on the repairs of an old machinery has been debited to repairs account.

Pass journal entries to rectify the errors and prepare a suspense account.

Ans Suspense Account Total = ₹ 2,796

12 You are presented with a trial balance showing a difference, which has been carried to suspense account and the following errors are revealed

(i) ₹ 350 paid in cash for a typewriter was charged to office expenses account.

(ii) Goods amounting to ₹ 660 sold to Arun, were correctly entered in the sales book but posted to Arun's account as ₹ 760. The total sales for the month were overcast by ₹ 1,000.

(iii) Goods worth ₹ 130 returned by Monu, were entered in the sales book and posted therefrom to the credit of Monu's personal account.

(iv) Goods sold for ₹ 1,240 and debited on 20th December to Naina, were returned by him on 23rd and taken into stock on 31st December, no entries being made in the books for return.

(v) Sales return book was overcast by ₹ 100.

Journalise the necessary corrections and raise suspense account, assuming that there are no other errors.

Ans Suspense Account Total = ₹ 1,260

PART B

FINANCIAL ACCOUNTING-II

10

After studying this chapter, the students will be able to understand the concept of financial statements—its meaning, objectives, importance and users of financial statements. Students will further learn the meaning, objectives and preparation of trading and profit and loss account, and balance sheet.

FINANCIAL STATEMENTS-I (WITHOUT ADJUSTMENT)

|TOPIC 1|

Introduction to Financial Statements

Financial statements are the final/end products of an accounting process. These statements are prepared at the end of accounting period and give information about the financial position and performance of an enterprise.

A complete set of financial statements includes

(*i*) **Trading and profit and loss account (or income statement)** which shows the profitability of business operations during an accounting period.

(*ii*) **Balance sheet (or position statement)** which shows the financial position of an enterprise at a particular date.

(*iii*) **Schedules and notes to accounts** forming part of balance sheet and profit and loss account, containing detailed information about certain transactions and events.

CHAPTER CHECKLIST

- Introduction to Financial Statements
- Trading and Profit and Loss Account
- Balance Sheet

Objectives of Financial Statements

The basic objectives of preparing financial statements are

(*i*) To present a true and fair view of the working of the business.

(*ii*) To help to judge the effectiveness of the management.

(*iii*) To provide sufficient and reliable information to various persons interested in financial statements.

(*iv*) To facilitate efficient allocation of resources.

(*v*) To disclose various accounting policies.

(*vi*) To provide information about the cash flows.

(*vii*) To provide information about the earning capacity.

(*viii*) To provide financial data on assets and liabilities of an enterprise.

Importance of Financial Statements

The financial statements are important due to the following reasons

(*i*) Trading account helps in knowing the gross profit earned or gross loss incurred by the business during the accounting period.

(*ii*) The net profit earned or net loss incurred by the business during the accounting period can be known by preparing profit and loss account.

(*iii*) Balance sheet provides complete information related to the assets, liabilities and capital of the business at a particular date.

(*iv*) The profit calculated and various items of balance sheet can be compared with that of previous years. It helps to ascertain whether the business is progressing and whether the financial performance and position of the business has improved or not.

(*v*) The profit and loss account and balance sheet enables the calculation of various ratios. The analysis of various ratios helps in taking appropriate decisions for the business.

(*vi*) It helps in the creation of various provisions and reserves to meet future uncertainties and to strengthen the financial position of the firm.

Users of Financial Statements

The various internal and external users and their need for information are as follows

1. INTERNAL USERS

Internal users may be categorised as follows

(*i*) **Owners** They are interested in financial statements as they want to know the profit earned or loss incurred by the business. Also they are concerned regarding the safety of their capital.

(*ii*) **Management** Management is interested in financial statements as these statements help them to make various decisions such as determination of selling price, cost controls and reduction, investment into new projects, etc.

(*iii*) **Employees and Workers** Employees are interested in financial statements as they want to know about the stability and profitability of the business. It is on the basis of financial statements only that employees decide whether they should demand for bonus or wage hike or not.

2. EXTERNAL USERS

External users may be categorised as follows

(*i*) **Creditors** As the creditors give credit to the business, they are interested to know whether the business will be able to pay their interest regularly, and repay their debts when due.

(*ii*) **Investors** Investors (including shareholders) are the suppliers of funds to run the firm. They are interested in the profitability, dividends declared, market value of their investment and long-term solvency of the business firm, and this information can be availed through financial statements. Potential investors are interested in financial statements as it helps them to know about the earning capacity of the business and its prospects for future growth and returns.

(*iii*) **Banks and Financial Institutions** Banks and financial institutions are interested in financial statements as they provide loans to the business and are interested to know whether the business is capable of returning the loan along with the interest.

(*iv*) **Government and its Authorities** They are interested in financial statements as it helps them to determine taxation policies and for assessing national income and similar statistics.

(*v*) **Other Parties** Some other parties may also be interested in the financial statements from their own point of view such as trade associations, newspapers, economists, etc.

(*vi*) **Researchers** The information contained in the financial statements helps researchers to make various surveys/studies related to a particular firm or industry.

Preparation of Financial Statements

Financial statements are prepared from trial balance following the accounting concepts and conventions. Preparation of financial statements requires clear understanding of capital and revenue items.

Capital and Revenue Items

It is important to make a clear distinction between items of capital nature and revenue nature for the preparation of trading and profit and loss account and the balance sheet. If any item is wrongly classified *i.e.*, if any item of revenue nature is treated as capital item or *vice-versa*, the ascertainment of profit or loss will be incorrect.

The various capital and revenue items are explained below.

(i) Capital Expenditure

It is an expenditure which is incurred in acquiring or increasing the value of fixed assets or repayment of a long-term liability. It yields benefits which extend to more than one accounting period.

e.g., purchase of fixed assets, material for construction of building, installation charges of plant and machinery, etc.

The effect of capital expenditure is shown in the balance sheet.

(ii) Revenue Expenditure

These are the expenditures which are incurred for the day-to-day conduct of the business. Its benefits extend up to one accounting period.

e.g., purchase of goods, whitewash of building, payment of wages and salaries, etc.

Revenue expenditures are shown in trading and profit and loss account.

(iii) Deferred Revenue Expenditure

It is a revenue expenditure that is incurred during an accounting period but its benefit extends beyond that accounting period. Such expenditure is normally written off over a period of 3 to 5 years.

e.g., heavy advertising to launch a new product etc.

The part of deferred revenue expenditure written off is shown in profit and loss account and the balance part is shown in the balance sheet as fictitious asset.

(iv) Capital Receipts

These are those receipts which are received once in a while. It is the amount received by the business on account of capital, loans or sale proceeds of fixed assets.

e.g., sale of a fixed asset like old machinery, loan taken from a bank etc.

The effect of capital receipts is shown in the balance sheet.

(v) Revenue Receipts

These are those receipts which arise in the normal course of business.

e.g., Interest on investment, sales made by the firm, etc.

These receipts are shown in trading account and profit and loss account.

ILLUSTRATION |1| State whether the following expenditures are capital or revenue in nature.

(*i*) A second-hand machine was purchased for ₹ 1,75,000 and ₹ 25,000 was spent on the repairs of the machine to bring it to a workable condition.
(*ii*) ₹ 10,000 was spent on installing the machine.
(*iii*) ₹ 5,000 were spent as annual repair charges on machines.
(*iv*) Insurance premium paid on machine ₹ 2,000.
(*v*) ₹ 20,000 is the cost of air-conditioning of the office of General Manager.

Sol. (*i*) ₹ 2,00,000 (1,75,000 + 25,000) is capital expenditure as it relates to purchase of a capital asset and making it ready for use.
(*ii*) ₹ 10,000 is also capital expenditure, as it is also related to making an asset ready for use.
(*iii*) ₹ 5,000 spent on annual repair charges are revenue expenditure as they are incurred on maintenance of an asset and not for improving its performance.
(*iv*) Insurance premium paid is also a revenue expenditure as its benefit will expire within a year.
(*v*) ₹ 20,000 is capital expenditure because its benefit will extend to a number of years.

ILLUSTRATION |2| State with reasons whether following are capital or revenue expenditures

(*i*) Custom duty paid on import of a machinery.
(*ii*) Wages paid in connection with the erection of a new machinery.
(*iii*) ₹ 5000 spent on repainting the factory.
(*iv*) Repairs for ₹ 2000 necessiated by negligence of an operator of machine.
(*v*) ₹ 10,000 paid for electricity bill (2007).

Sol. (*i*) Custom duty paid is capital expenditure becauses it relates to acquisition of asset.
(*ii*) Wages paid for erection of a new machinery is also capital expenditure because it is related to a new asset.
(*iii*) ₹ 5000 spent on repainting is revenue expenditure as it is related to maintenance cost of factory.
(*iv*) It is a revenue expenditure because repair charges will not improve the working of the machine.
(*v*) It is also a revenue expenditure because it is a part of operating cost.

|TOPIC 2|
Trading and Profit and Loss Account

TRADING ACCOUNT

Trading account is the first stage in the preparation of the final accounts.

It is prepared to ascertain whether the selling of goods and/or rendering of services to customers have proved profitable for the business or not.

Trading account is a nominal account and is based on matching and accrual concept. Trading account relates to a particular period and is prepared at the end of that period.

Need and Importance of Trading Account

Need and importance of trading account are as follows

(*i*) The main objective of preparing trading account is to know the gross profit or gross loss.

(*ii*) Trading account provides information about those expenses which are directly related with purchasing goods. This enables the management to control such expenses.

(*iii*) Trading account helps to compare closing stock of current year with that of previous years. In case closing stock shows an increasing trend, reasons must be found out, as more the stock, lesser the selling efficiency of the firm.

(*iv*) The gross profit ratio is compared with the desired ratios or with the ratio of previous years to evaluate the performance. It enables the businessman to take effective measures to safeguard himself against future losses.

Preparation of Trading Account

Trading account consists of two sides *viz.* debit and credit. Entries or items of **debit side** are opening stock, purchases and other direct expenses and on **credit side** sales and closing stock are recorded.

The preparation of trading account requires the following steps

STEP I WRITE THE FOLLOWING ITEMS ON THE DEBIT SIDE OF TRADING ACCOUNT

(*i*) **Opening Stock** It is the stock of goods in hand at the beginning of the accounting year.

(*ii*) **Purchases and Deductions Therefrom** Goods, which have been bought for resale, appear as purchases on the debit side of the trading account. They include both cash as well as credit purchases.

Following items are deducted from purchases

- Purchase Return
- Goods taken by the proprietor for his personal use.
- Goods given as charity.
- Goods given by way of samples.

Note *Goods which are returned to suppliers are termed as purchases return or return outwards.*

(*iii*) **Direct Expenses** These are those expenses which are incurred in purchasing and transporting the goods till they are brought to the place of business for sale.

These include the following

- **Wages** It refers to remuneration paid to workers who are directly engaged for loading and unloading of goods.

  Note *'Wages and salaries' account is treated as a direct expense.*

- **Factory Lighting** It is the electricity consumed for providing light for running the factory.
- **Carriage Inwards/Freight Inwards** These expenses are the items of transport expenses, which are incurred on bringing materials/goods purchased to the place of business.
- **Factory Rent and Rates** It is the rent paid for the factory premises as well as the municipal taxes or charges for water, etc.
- **Fuel/Water/Power/Gas** These items are used in the production process and hence are part of expenses.

- **Dock Charges** Dock charges are the charges levied on ships and their cargo while entering or leaving docks.
- **Duty on Purchases** Any duty paid on purchases of goods is debited to trading account.
- **Octroi** It is levied by the municipal committee when the goods enter the city.
- **Royalty** These are the payments which are made for acquiring the right to use patents.
- **Consumable Stores** These are incurred to keep the machine in right condition and includes engine oil, cotton waste, soft soap, oil grease and waste, consumed in a factory. The amount to be shown can be calculated with the help of the given formula.

The closing entry for transferring the above accounts is as follows

Trading A/c	Dr
To Opening Stock A/c	
To Purchases A/c	
To Wages A/c	
To Carriage Inwards A/c	
To Sales Returns A/c	
To All Other Direct Expenses A/c	

Note *Alternatively sales return account can be closed by transferring its balance to sales account.*

STEP 2 WRITE THE FOLLOWING ITEMS ON THE CREDIT SIDE OF TRADING ACCOUNT

(*i*) **Sales** It is the main item of revenue for the business. Sales account in trial balance shows gross total sales (cash as well as credit) made during the year.

(*ii*) **Sales Return** Goods returned by customers are called sales return or return inwards. These are shown as deduction from total sales and the computed amount is known as net sales.

(*iii*) **Closing Stock** It refers to the stock of unsold goods at the end of the current accounting period. According to the convention of conservatism, stock is valued at cost or net realisable value, whichever is lower. Following points related to closing stock should be kept in mind

- If closing stock appears outside the trial balance then it will be shown in trading account.
- If closing stock appears in trial balance, then it will not be shown in trading account.

The closing entry for transferring the above accounts is as follows

Sales A/c	Dr
Closing Stock A/c	Dr
Purchase Returns A/c	Dr
To Trading A/c	

Note *Alternatively purchases return account can be closed by transferring its balance to purchases account.*

At a glance : Relevant Items in Trading Account

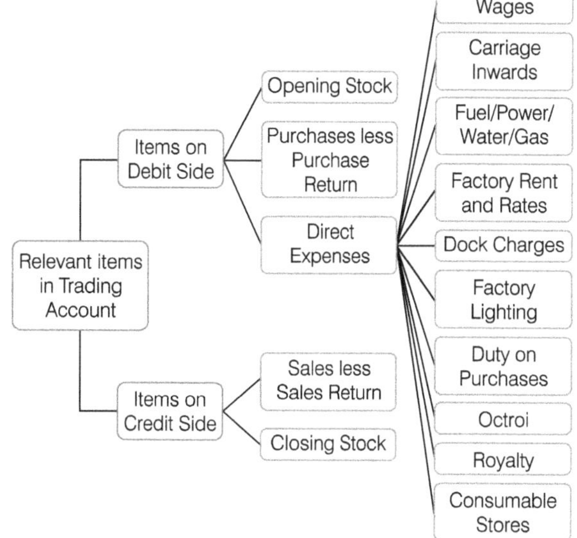

STEP 3 CLOSURE OF TRADING ACCOUNT

Trading account is closed by transferring its balance to profit and loss account by passing the following entry

(*i*) **In Case of Gross Profit** If the credit side of the trading account exceeds the debit side, the difference will be the gross profit. It signifies excess of sales over purchases and direct expenses.

Trading A/c	Dr
To Profit and Loss A/c	

(*ii*) **In Case of Gross Loss** If the debit side of the trading account exceeds the credit side, the difference will be gross loss. It signifies that the amount of purchases including direct expenses is more than the sales.

Profit and Loss A/c	Dr
To Trading A/c	

FORMAT OF A TRADING ACCOUNT

Trading Account
Dr — for the year ended ... — Cr

Particulars		Amt (₹)	Particulars		Amt (₹)
To Opening Stock		...	By Sales	...	
To Purchases	...		(–) Return Inwards	(...)	...
(–) Return Outwards	(...)	...	By Closing Stock		...
To Direct Expenses		...	By Abnormal Loss of Stock		...
To Wages and Salaries		...	By Gross Loss Transferred to Profit and Loss A/c*		...
To Freight Inwards		...			
To Carriage Inwards		...			
To Gross Profit Transferred to Profit and Loss A/c*		...			
		...			...

* Either gross profit or gross loss shall appear.

Formulae Related to Trading Account

The formulae related to trading account are used frequently. Some important formulae are given below

(*i*) Net Sales = Total Sales (Cash and Credit) – Sales Return

(*ii*) Net Purchases = Total Purchases (Cash and Credit) – Purchases Return

(*iii*) Adjusted Purchases = Net Purchases + Opening Stock – Closing Stock

Note *If adjusted purchases is given in the trial balance, then opening stock is not shown in the trading account. Adjusted purchases shown on the debit side of trading account and closing stock is shown on the credit side of trading account.*

(*iv*) Cost of Goods Sold = Opening Stock + Net Purchases + Direct Expenses – Closing Stock

or

Cost of Goods Sold = Cost of Production – Closing Stock

(*v*) Cost of Production or Cost of Goods available for Sale = Opening Stock + Net Purchases + Wages – Purchases Return.

(*vi*) Gross Profit = Net Sales – Cost of Goods Sold.

Note *A negative figure implies gross loss.*

(*vii*) Operating Profit = Gross Profit – Operating Expenses + Operating Income

(*viii*) Operating Expenses = Administration Expenses + Selling and Distribution Expenses

(*ix*) Stores Consumed During the Year = Opening Balance in Stores + Purchases of Stores During the Year – Closing Balance of Stores.

ILLUSTRATION |3| Prepare a trading account of M/s Anjali from the following information related to 31st March, 2016.

Opening stock	60,000
Purchases	3,00,000
Sales	7,50,000
Purchases return	18,000
Sales return	30,000
Carriage on purchases	12,000
Carriage on sales	15,000
Factory rent	18,000
Office rent	18,000
Dock and clearing charges	48,000
Freight and octroi	6,500
Coal, gas and water	10,000

Sol.

Trading Account

Dr for the year ended 31st March, 2016 Cr

Particulars		Amt (₹)	Particulars		Amt (₹)
To Opening Stock		60,000	By Sales	7,50,000	
To Purchases	3,00,000		(–) Sales Return	30,000	7,20,000
(–) Purchases Return	18,000	2,82,000			
To Carriage on Purchases		12,000			
To Factory Rent		18,000			
To Dock and Clearing Charges		48,000			
To Freight and Octroi		6,500			
To Coal, Gas and Water		10,000			
To Gross Profit Transferred to Profit and Loss A/c		2,83,500			
		7,20,000			7,20,000

Note *Carriage on sales and office rent will not be debited to trading account as they are not direct expenses. It will appear in the profit and loss account as it is indirect expenses.*

ILLUSTRATION |4| From the following information, prepare trading account for the year ended 31st March, 2016, cash purchases ₹ 4,50,000; credit purchases ₹ 27,00,000; return inwards ₹ 60,000; cash sales ₹ 4,80,000; credit sales ₹ 33,00,000; return outwards ₹ 30,000; freight inwards ₹ 9,000; carriage inwards ₹ 9,000; wages and salaries ₹ 12,000; opening stock ₹ 4,50,000; closing stock ₹ 2,64,000 but its market value is ₹ 2,52,000.

Sol.

Trading Account

Dr for the year ended 31st March, 2016 Cr

Particulars		Amt (₹)	Particulars		Amt (₹)
To Opening Stock		4,50,000	By Sales		
To Purchases			Cash Sales	4,80,000	
Cash Purchases	4,50,000		Credit Sales	33,00,000	
Credit Purchases	27,00,000			37,80,000	
	31,50,000		(–) Return Inwards	60,000	37,20,000
(–) Return Outwards	30,000	31,20,000	By Closing Stock (Valued at cost or market value whichever is less)		2,52,000
To Freight Inwards		9,000			
To Carriage Inwards		9,000			
To Wages and Salaries		12,000			
To Gross Profit transferred to Profit and Loss A/c		3,72,000			
		39,72,000			39,72,000

ILLUSTRATION |5| Prepare a trading account for the year ended 31st March, 2016 from the following balances.

	Amt (₹)		Amt (₹)
Opening stock	80,000	Purchases return	24,000
Purchases	4,00,000	Sales return	40,000
Sales	10,00,000	Carriage on purchases	16,000
Freight and octroi	13,000	Carriage on sales	20,000
Wages	60,000	Factory rent	24,000
Factory lighting	21,600	Office rent	15,000
Coal, gas and water	4,400	Import duty	64,000

Closing stock is valued at ₹ 1,20,000.

Sol.

Trading Account

Dr for the year ended 31st March, 2016 Cr

Particulars		Amt (₹)	Particulars		Amt (₹)
To Opening Stock		80,000	By Sales	10,00,000	
To Purchases	4,00,000		(–) Sales Return	40,000	9,60,000
(–) Purchases Return	24,000	3,76,000	By Closing Stock		1,20,000
To Freight and Octroi		13,000			
To Wages		60,000			
To Factory Lighting		21,600			
To Coal, Gas and Water		4,400			
To Carriage on Purchases		16,000			
To Factory Rent		24,000			
To Import Duty		64,000			
To Gross Profit transferred to Profit and Loss A/c		4,21,000			
		10,80,000			10,80,000

ILLUSTRATION |6| Following balances appeared in the trial balance of a firm as on 31st March, 2016.

		Amt (₹)
Opening stock	Raw material	80,000
	Finished goods	1,40,000
Purchases		3,60,000
Sales		7,00,000
Returns	Purchases	10,000
	Sales	6,000
Wages		1,30,000
Factory expenses		90,000
Freight	Inwards	20,000
	Outwards	30,000

At the end of the concerned period, the stocks at hand were

Raw material	70,000
Work-in-progress	20,000
Finished goods	1,10,000

Prepare the trading account of the firm.

Sol.

Trading Account
for the year ended 31st March, 2016

Dr Particulars		Amt (₹)	Particulars		Cr Amt (₹)
To Opening Stock			By Sales	7,00,000	
Raw Material	80,000		(–) Returns	6,000	6,94,000
Finished Goods	1,40,000	2,20,000	By Closing Stock		
To Purchases	3,60,000		Raw Material	70,000	
(–) Returns	10,000	3,50,000	Work-in-progress	20,000	
To Wages		1,30,000	Finished Goods	1,10,000	2,00,000
To Factory Expenses		90,000			
To Freight Inwards		20,000			
To Gross Profit transferred to Profit and Loss A/c		84,000			
		8,94,000			8,94,000

Note *Freight outwards is not shown in the trading account, it will appear in the profit and loss account, as it is an indirect expense.*

ILLUSTRATION |7| In a burglary at the godown of Bharat Goel on the night of 14th July, 2016 part of the stock was stolen.

From the following particulars, find out the estimated value of loss of stock by theft.

	₹
Stock on 1st April, 2016	1,20,000
Purchases from 1st April to 14th July, 2016	8,20,000
Sales from 1st April to 14th July, 2016	12,00,000
Stock remaining after burglary	24,000

The normal rate of gross profit for his business is 30% of selling price.

Sol.

Trading Account
for the period 1st April to 14th July, 2016

Dr Particulars	Amt (₹)	Particulars	Cr Amt (₹)
To Opening Stock	1,20,000	By Sales	12,00,000
To Purchases	8,20,000	By Closing Stock (Balancing figure)	1,00,000
To Gross Profit @ 30% on Sales	3,60,000		
	13,00,000		13,00,000

	₹
Stock on 14th July, 2016 as calculated above	1,00,000
Less: Stock remaining after burglary	24,000
Value of stock stolen	76,000

ILLUSTRATION |8| From the following information, prepare a trading account for the year ending 31st March, 2016.

	₹
Opening stock	80,000
Purchases	8,40,000
Expenses on purchases	16,000
Expenses on sales	30,000
Wages	60,000
Sales	12,00,000
Closing stock	1,04,000

Sol.

Trading Account

Dr for the year ended 31st March, 2016 Cr

Particulars	Amt (₹)	Particulars	Amt (₹)
To Opening Stock	80,000	By Sales	12,00,000
To Purchases	8,40,000	By Closing Stock	1,04,000
To Expenses on Purchases	16,000		
To Wages	60,000		
To Gross Profit transferred to Profit and Loss A/c	3,08,000		
	13,04,000		13,04,000

Note *Expenses on sales will not be considered while preparing trading account or while computing the cost of goods sold.*

ILLUSTRATION |9| From the following information, prepare trading account for the year ended 31st March, 2016

	Amt (₹)
Cost of goods sold	45,00,000
Sales	72,00,000
Closing stock	2,40,000
Wages	25,000

Sol.

Trading Account

Dr for the year ended 31st March, 2016 Cr

Particulars	Amt (₹)	Particulars	Amt (₹)
To Cost of Goods Sold	45,00,000	By Sales	72,00,000
To Gross Profit Transferred to Profit and Loss A/c	27,00,000		
	72,00,000		72,00,000

Note *Wages has not been shown on the debit side and closing stock has not been shown on the credit side of the trading account because it has already been adjusted while calculating the cost of goods sold.*

ILLUSTRATION |10| From the following information, prepare the trading account for the year ended 31st March, 2016 Adjusted purchases ₹ 48,00,000; freight and carriage inwards ₹ 40,000; freight and carriage outwards ₹ 30,000; wages ₹ 3,36,000; octroi charges ₹ 4,000; fuel and power ₹ 60,000; office rent ₹ 36,000; trade expenses ₹ 20,000; sales ₹ 60,00,000; closing stock ₹ 3,00,000.

Sol.

Trading Account

Dr for the year ended 31st March, 2016 Cr

Particulars	Amt (₹)	Particulars	Amt (₹)
To Adjusted Purchases	48,00,000	By Sales	60,00,000
To Freight and Carriage Inwards	40,000		
To Wages	3,36,000		
To Octroi Charges	4,000		
To Fuel and Power	60,000		
To Gross Profit transferred to Profit and Loss A/c	7,60,000		
	60,00,000		60,00,000

Note *(i) Adjusted Purchases = Net Purchases + Opening Stock – Closing Stock*

(ii) Closing stock has not been shown on the credit side of trading account since it has already been adjusted while computing the adjusted purchases.

(iii) Following items are not entered in the trading account because they are indirect expenses and will appear in the profit and loss account.

(a) Freight and carriage outwards; (b) Office rent; (c) Trade expenses.

ILLUSTRATION |11| Trading account of M/s Silverline Technologies is given below.

Trading Account
for the year ended 31st March, 2016

Dr Particulars	Amt (₹)	Particulars	Amt (₹) Cr
To Opening Stock	6,75,000	By Net Sales	25,65,000
To Net Purchases	10,25,000	By Closing Stock	5,35,000
To Wages and Salaries	3,15,000		
To Freight Inwards	67,000		
To Other Direct Expenses	1,20,000		
To Gross Profit Transferred to Profit and Loss A/c	8,98,000		
	31,00,000		31,00,000

Pass closing journal entries on the basis of the above trading account. Also transfer the gross profit to profit and loss account.

Sol.

JOURNAL

Date	Particulars		LF	Amt (Dr)	Amt (Cr)
	Trading A/c	Dr		22,02,000	
	To Opening Stock A/c				6,75,000
	To Net Purchases A/c				10,25,000
	To Wages and Salaries A/c				3,15,000
	To Freight Inwards A/c				67,000
	To Other Direct Expenses A/c				1,20,000
	(Being opening stock, net purchases, wages and salaries, freight inwards and other direct expenses transferred to trading account)				
	Net Sales A/c	Dr		25,65,000	
	Closing Stock A/c	Dr		5,35,000	
	To Trading A/c				31,00,000
	(Being net sales and closing stock transferred to trading account)				
	Trading A/c	Dr		8,98,000	
	To Profit and Loss A/c				8,98,000
	(Being gross profit transferred to profit and loss account)				

ILLUSTRATION |12| Net sales during the year, 2016 is ₹ 2,85,000. Gross profit is 25% on sales. Find out cost of goods sold.

Sol. Gross profit = ₹ 2,85,000 × 25 / 100 = ₹ 71, 250.

Cost of Goods Sold = Sales − Gross Profit = 2,85,000 − 71,250 = ₹ 2,13,750.

ILLUSTRATION |13| Opening stock ₹ 30,000, purchases ₹ 54,600, expenses on purchases ₹ 6,000, sales ₹ 90,000, expenses on sales ₹ 3,000, closing stock ₹ 36,600. Calculate cost of goods sold and gross profit.

Sol. Cost of Goods Sold = Opening Stock + Purchases + Expenses on Purchases − Closing Stock

= 30,000 + 54,600 + 6,000 − 36,600 = ₹ 54,000

Gross Profit = Net Sales − Cost of Goods Sold = 90,000 − 54,000 = ₹ 36,000

ILLUSTRATION |14| Net sales during the year 2016 is ₹ 3,00,000, gross profit is 25% on cost. Find out gross profit and cost of goods sold.

Sol. Gross profit is 25% on cost

Hence, if cost is ₹ 100, gross profit will be ₹ 25, and sales will be ₹ 125

Thus, if sales is 125, gross profit will be ₹ 25

If sale is ₹ 3,00,000, gross profit will be $3{,}00{,}000 \times \frac{25}{125} =$ ₹ 60,000

Cost of Goods Sold = Sales – Gross Profit = 3,00,000 – 60,000 = ₹ 2,40, 000

ILLUSTRATION |15| Calculate net sales and gross profit from the following information. Cost of goods sold ₹ 2,00,000 gross profit 20% on sales.

Sol. If sale is ₹ 100, gross profit will be ₹ 20 and cost =100 – 20=₹80

Hence, if cost of goods sold is ₹ 80, sale will be ₹100

if cost of goods sold is ₹2,00,000, sale will be $\frac{100}{80} \times 2{,}00{,}000 =$ ₹ 2,50,000

Gross Profit = Sales – Cost of Goods Sold = ₹ 2,50,000 – ₹ 2,00,000 = ₹ 50,000

ILLUSTRATION |16| Calculate closing stock and cost of goods sold. Opening stock ₹ 5,000 ; sales ₹ 16,000; carriage inwards ₹ 1,000, sales return ₹ 1,000; gross profit ₹ 6,000; purchases ₹ 10,000; purchases return ₹ 900.

Sol. Cost of Goods Sold = Net Sales (Sales – Sales Return) – Gross Profit = 15,000 – 6,000 = ₹ 9,000.

Closing Stock = Opening Stock + Net Purchases (Purchases-Purchases Return) + Carriage Inwards- Cost of Goods Sold

= 5,000+9,100+1000-9000 = ₹ 6,100

ILLUSTRATION |17| From the following information, find cost of goods sold and net sales

	Amt (₹)		Amt (₹)
Opening stock	3,00,000	Wages	6,000
Purchases	8,40,000	Freight	10,800
Closing stock	2,40,000	Carriage inwards	3,000

The percentage of gross profit on sales is 20%.

Sol. **Calculation of Cost of Goods Sold**

Opening Stock	3,00,000
(+) Purchases	8,40,000
Wages	6,000
Freight	10,800
Carriage Inwards	3,000
	11,59,800
(–) Closing Stock	2,40,000
Cost of Goods Sold	₹ 9,19,800

Calculation of Net Sales

Let sales = 100, gross profit will be = 20.

Therefore, cost of sales will be = 100 – 20 = 80.

When cost of sales is 80, then sales = 100.

When cost of sales is 1, then sales = 100/ 80.

When cost of sales is ₹ 9,19,800, then sales = 100 / 80 × 9,19,800 = ₹ 11,49,750.

ILLUSTRATION |18| Ascertain cost of goods sold from the following

	Amt (₹)
Indirect expenses	30,400
Direct expenses	37,200
Sales	2,40,000
Net purchases	1,44,000
Return inwards	24,000
Return outwards	16,000
Closing inventory	56,000
Opening inventory	32,000

Sol. Cost of Goods Sold = Direct Expenses + Net Purchases + Opening Inventory − Closing Inventory
= 37,200 + 1,44,000 + 32,000 − 56,000 = ₹ 1,57,200

ILLUSTRATION |19| From the following balances extracted from the books of M/s Ahuja and Nanda. Calculate the amount of

(i) Cost of goods available for sale (ii) Cost of goods sold during the year
(iii) Gross profit

	Amt (₹)
Opening stock	25,000
Credit purchases	7,50,000
Cash purchases	3,00,000
Credit sales	12,00,000
Cash sales	4,00,000
Wages	1,00,000
Salaries	1,40,000
Closing stock	30,000
Sales return	50,000
Purchases return	10,000

Sol. (*i*) Cost of goods available for sale means total goods produced during the year.
Cost of Production = (Opening Stock + Purchases + Wages − Purchases Return)
= 25,000 + (7,50,000 + 3,00,000) + 1,00,000 − 10,000 = ₹ 11,65,000

(*ii*) Cost of Goods Sold = Cost of Production − Closing Stock
= 11,65,000 − 30,000 = ₹ 11,35,000

(*iii*) Gross Profit = Net Sales − Cost of Goods Sold
= 15,50,000−11,35,000 = ₹ 4,15,000

ILLUSTRATION |20| Calculate the amount of gross profit and operating profit on the basis of the following balances extracted from the books of M/s Rajiv & Sons for the year ended 31st March, 2016

NCERT

	Amt (₹)
Opening stock	50,000
Net sales	11,00,000
Net purchases	6,00,000
Direct expenses	60,000
Administration expenses	45,000
Selling and distribution expenses	65,000
Loss due to fire	20,000
Closing stock	70,000

Sol. Computation of gross profit

Trading Account

Dr — for the year ended 31st March, 2016 — Cr

Particulars	Amt (₹)	Particulars	Amt (₹)
To Opening Stock A/c	50,000	By Sales A/c	11,00,000
To Purchases A/c	6,00,000	By Closing Stock A/c	70,000
To Direct Expenses A/c	60,000		
To Gross Profit Transferred to Profit and Loss A/c	4,60,000		
	11,70,000		11,70,000

Operating Profit = Gross Profit − (Operating Expenses + Operating Income)

= 4,60,000 − (1,10,000 + 0) = ₹ 3,50,000.

Note *(i) Loss due to fire is a non-operating expenses.*

(ii) Operating Expenses = Administration Expenses + Selling and Distribution Expenses

= 45,000 + 65,000 = ₹ 1,10,000

ILLUSTRATION |21| Calculate gross profit when total purchases during the year are ₹ 8,00,000; return outwards ₹ 20,000; direct expenses ₹ 60,000 and 2/3rd of the goods are sold for ₹ 6,10,000.

Sol. Cost of Goods Sold = Total Purchases − Return Outwards + Direct Expenses

= 8,00,000 − 20,000 + 60,000 = 8,40,000

A. 2/3rd goods sold for ₹ 6,10,000

B. Cost of 2/3rd goods = 8,40,000 × 2/3 = ₹ 5,60,000

C. Gross profit = A − B = 6,10,000 − 5,60,000 = ₹ 50,000

ILLUSTRATION |22| Calculate closing stock from the following details opening stock ₹ 20,000; cash sales ₹ 60,000; credit sales ₹ 40,000; purchases ₹ 70,000. Rate of gross profit on cost $33\frac{1}{3}$%.

Sol. Total Sales = Cash Sales + Credit Sales = 60,000 + 40,000 = ₹ 1,00,000

Let cost = ₹ 100, Gross profit = $33\frac{1}{3}$% on cost, Sales = $133\frac{1}{3}$

Gross Profit on Sales = $33\frac{1}{3}/133\frac{1}{3} = \frac{1}{4}$%

Gross Profit = ₹ 1,00,000 × $\frac{1}{4}$ = ₹ 25,000

Cost of Goods Sold = Sales − Gross Profit = 1,00,000 − 25,000 = ₹ 75,000

Cost of Goods Sold = Opening Stock + Purchases − Closing Stock

75,000 = 20,000 + 70,000 − Closing stock

Closing stock = 20,000 + 70,000 − 75,000 = ₹ 15,000.

NUMERICAL Questions for Practice

1 Ascertain the value of closing stock from the following.

Particulars	Amt (₹)
Opening stock	2,40,000
Purchases during the Year	18,60,000
Sales during the Year	31,20,000
Rate of gross profit	40% on sales

Ans Closing Stock = ₹ 2,28,000.

2 Calculate net sales and gross profit from the following.

Cost of goods sold ₹ 9,00,000

gross profit 25% on sales

Ans Net Sales = ₹ 12,00,000; Gross Profit = ₹ 3,00,000

3 Ascertain cost of goods sold and gross profit from the following.

Particulars	Amt (₹)
Opening Stock	64,000
Purchases	5,60,000
Direct Expenses	40,000
Indirect Expenses	90,000
Closing Stock	1,00,000
Sales	8,00,000
Sales Return	16,000

Ans Cost of Goods Sold = ₹ 5,64,000; Gross Profit = ₹ 2,20,000.

4 Prepare a trading account from the following particulars for the year ended 31st March, 2016.

Particulars	Amt (₹)	Particulars	Amt (₹)
Opening Stock	5,00,000	Purchases Return	44,000
Purchases	14,00,000	Sales Return	72,000
Sales	36,00,000	Custom Duty	30,000
Wages	4,12,000	Gas, Fuel and Power	1,20,000
Carriage Inwards	68,000	Dock Charges	16,000
Carriage Outwards	40,000	Factory Lighting	1,92,000
Manufacturing Expenses	4,96,000	Office Lighting	10,000

Closing stock is valued at ₹ 12,00,000.

Ans Gross Profit = ₹ 15,38,000

5 From the following information, prepare trading account for the year ended 31st March, 2016.

Particulars	Amt (₹)	Particulars	Amt (₹)
Stock (As on 1st April,.2015)	80,000	Return Outwards	1,60,000
Purchases	8,00,000	Wages and Salaries	1,00,000
Sales	7,60,000	Return Inwards	40,000
Carriage Inwards	40,000	Stock (31st March, 2016)	2,60,000

Ans Gross Profit = ₹ 1,00,000

Note *The net realisable value (market value) of stock as on 31st March, 2016 was ₹ 2,40,000.*

6 **Calculate gross profit on the basis of the following information.**

Particulars	Amt (₹)
Purchases	13,60,000
Return Outwards	60,000
Carriage Inwards	40,000
Carriage Outwards	30,000
Wages	1,00,000

3/4 of the goods are sold for ₹ 12,00,000.

Ans Gross Profit = ₹ 1,20,000.

7 **From the following figures, ascertain the gross profit for the year ended 31st March, 2016.**

Particulars	Amt (₹)	Particulars	Amt (₹)
Opening Stock (1st April, 2015)	50,000	Goods Purchased during the year	2,80,000
Freight and Packing	20,000	Closing Stock (31st March, 2016)	60,000
Sales	3,80,000	Packing Expenses on Sales	12,000

Ans Gross Profit = ₹ 90,000

PROFIT AND LOSS ACCOUNT

Profit and loss account is prepared after the preparation of trading account. It is prepared to ascertain the net profit earned or net loss incurred by the business entity during an accounting period.

Profit and loss account is prepared following accrual basis of accounting. It relates to a particular accounting period and is prepared at the end of that period.

Need and Importance of Profit and Loss Account

Need and importance of profit and loss account are as follows

(*i*) Profit and loss account discloses the net profit earned or net loss suffered by an enterprise during an accounting period.

(*ii*) The net profit of the current year can be compared with that of the previous years, to know whether the business is making progress or not.

(*iii*) It helps in comparing various expenses with the expenses of the previous year which inturn enables to take steps for controlling the unnecessary expenses.

(*iv*) A balance sheet can only be prepared after ascertaining the net profit through the preparation of profit and loss account.

Preparation of Profit and loss Account

Profit and loss account also consists of two sides *viz.* debit and credit. The indirect expenses are transferred to the debit side of the profit and loss account. All revenues/gains other than sales are transferred to the credit side of the profit and loss account.

The preparation of proift and loss account requires the following steps

STEP 1 WRITE THE FOLLOWING ITEMS OT THE DEBIT SIDE OF PROFIT AND LOSS ACCOUNT

(*i*) **Gross Loss** If the trading account discloses gross loss, it is shown on the debit side of profit and loss account.

(*ii*) **Office and Administrative Expenses** Office and administrative expenses include the following

- Salaries ('Salaries and wages' account is also treated as an indirect expense)
- Rent and rates for the office premises (It includes office and godown rent, municipal rates and taxes)
- Lighting in the office
- Printing and stationery
- Postage, telegrams and telephone charges
- Legal expenses
- Audit fees
- Repairs and small renewals/replacements relating to plants and machinery, furniture, fixtures and fittings, etc at office

(*iii*) **Selling and Distribution Expenses**

The selling and distribution expenses will comprise of the following

- Salesmen's salaries and commission
- Commission to agents paid or payable on business transactions
- Advertising
- Warehousing expenses
- Packing expenses
- Freight and carriage on sales or carriage outwards
- Export duties
- Sales tax to the extent, it cannot be recovered from the customers
- Maintenance of vehicles for distribution of goods and their running expenses
- Insurance of finished goods in inventory and goods in transit
- Bad debts

(*iv*) **Finance Expenses** Expenses incurred in respect of arranging finance for business are known as finance expenses. Finance expenses normally include

- Interest paid on loan
- Discount on bills discounted
- Discount allowed to customers
- Interest on capital

(*v*) **Abnormal Loss** These are extraordinary expenses that may occur during the accounting period and are debited and shown separately in profit and loss account. Such as loss by theft, loss on sale of fixed assets, loss of stock by fire not covered by insurance, etc.

(*vi*) **Depreciation and Repairs on Fixed Assets** Depreciation on fixed assets and repairs on fixed assets are treated as a business expense and debited to the profit and loss account.

- *Domestic expenses of the proprietor, drawings whether in the form of cash or goods, personal income tax and life insurance premium paid by the firm on behalf of the proprietor or partners are not shown in profit and loss account if appearing in trial balance.*

The closing entries for transferring the above accounts is as follows

Profit and Loss A/c	Dr
To Salaries A/c	
To Rent, Rates and Taxes A/c	
To Interest A/c	
To Other Expenses A/c	

STEP 2 WRITE THE FOLLOWING ITEMS ON THE CREDIT SIDE OF PROFIT AND LOSS ACCOUNT

(*i*) **Gross Profit** If the trading account discloses gross profit, it is shown on the credit side of profit and loss account.

(*ii*) **Other Incomes and Gains** All items of incomes and gains are shown on the credit side of the profit and loss account such as

- income from investments
- commission earned
- dividend received
- rent received
- interest received
- discount received

(*iii*) **Abnormal Gains** There may be capital gains during the year *e.g.*, profit arising on sale of fixed assets. The profit is shown as a separate income on the credit side of profit and loss account.

The closing entries for transferring the above accounts is as follows

Commission Received A/c	Dr
Interest Received A/c	Dr
Discount Received A/c	Dr
Bad Debts Recovered A/c	Dr
To Profit and Loss A/c	

At a Glance : Relevant Items in Profit and Loss Account

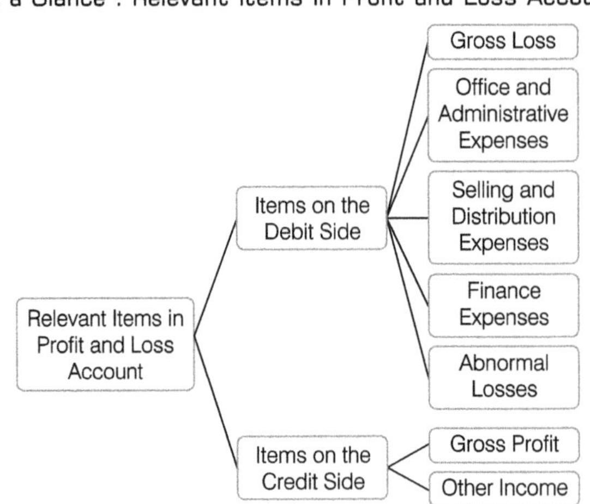

STEP 3 CLOSURE OF PROFIT AND LOSS ACCOUNT

Profit and loss account is closed by transferring its balance to the capital account of proprietor.

(*i*) **In Case of Net Profit** If the credit side of the profit and loss account exceeds that of debit side, the difference is termed as net profit.

Profit and Loss A/c	Dr
To Capital A/c	

(*ii*) **In Case of Net Loss** If the debit side of the profit and loss account exceeds that of credit side, the difference is termed as net loss.

Capital A/c	Dr
To Profit and Loss A/c	

FORMAT OF PROFIT AND LOSS ACCOUNT

Profit and Loss Account

Dr for the year ended... Cr

Particulars	Amt (₹)	Particulars	Amt (₹)
To Gross Loss Transferred from Trading A/c*	...	By Gross Profit Transferred from Trading A/c*	...
To Salaries	...	By Rent Received	...
To Rent, Rates and Taxes	...	By Discount Received	...
To Stationery and Printing	...	By Commission Earned	...
To Postage and Telegrams	...	By Interest	...
To Audit Fees	...	By Bad Debts Recovered	...
To Legal Charges	...	By Income from Investment	...
To Telephone Expenses	...	By Dividend on Shares	...
To Insurance Premium	...	By Miscellaneous Revenue Gains	...
To Business Promotion Expenses	...	By Income from Any Other Source	...
To Repairs and Renewals	...	By Net Loss Transferred to Capital A/c**	...
To Depreciation	...		
To Interest	...		
To Sundry Expenses	...		
To Conveyance	...		
To Bank Charges	...		

Particulars	Amt (₹)	Particulars	Amt (₹)
To Establishment Expenses	...		
To General Expenses	...		
To Car Running and Maintenance	...		
To Electricity Expenses	...		
To Loss by Fire, Theft	...		
To Commission	...		
To Advertisement	...		
To Freight and Carriage Outwards	...		
To Discount Allowed	...		
To Travelling Expenses	...		
To Bad Debts	...		
To Net Profit transferred to Capital A/c**	...		
	...		...

* Either of the two will appear.
** Either of the two will appear.

Formulae Related to Profit and Loss Account

The following formulae relate to profit and loss account

(*i*) Net Profit = Gross Profit + Other Incomes – Indirect Expenses

or

Net Profit = Operating Profit – Non-operating Expenses + Non-operating Incomes

(*ii*) Operating Profit/Earning Before Interest and Tax (EBIT) = Net Sales – Operating Cost

- *Operating activities are the principal revenue producing activities of the enterprise and other activities that are not investing or financing activities.*
- *Operating expenses Include office and administrative expenses, selling and distribution expenses, cash discount allowed, interest on bills payable and other short-term debts, bad debts and so on.*

(*iii*) Operating Cost = Cost of Goods Sold + Administration and Office Expenses + Selling and Distribution Expenses

* *Non-operating expenses are expenses which are incidental or indirect to the main operations of the business. They include interest on loan, charities and donation, loss on sale of fixed assets, extraordinary losses due to theft, loss by fire and so on.*

** *Non-operating incomes include receipt of interest, rent, dividend, profit on sale of fixed assets, etc.*

ILLUSTRATION |23| From the following information, prepare the profit and loss account for the year ending on 31st March, 2016

	Amt (₹)		Amt (₹)
Gross profit	62,00,000	Salaries and wages	20,00,000
Discount received	1,00,000	Discount allowed	2,00,000
Interest on loan paid	2,50,000	Interest received	3,00,000
Commission received	2,00,000	Commission to salesmen	1,50,000
Rent, rates and taxes	4,00,000	Rent received	1,00,000
Fire insurance premium	3,60,000	Carriage outwards	1,00,000
Freight outwards	50,000	Repairs and maintenance	60,000
Printing and stationery	60,000	Travelling expenses	1,60,000
Entertainment expenses	1,20,000	Water and electricity	1,20,000
Postage and telegram	50,000	Advertising and publicity	4,00,000
Sales promotion expenses	40,000	Telephone expenses	1,00,000
Bad debts	1,00,000	Packing expenses	50,000

	Amt (₹)		Amt (₹)
Audit fees	2,00,000	Bank charges	40,000
Depreciation on furniture		Legal charges	1,00,000
Sales office	1,00,000	Miscellaneous expenses	1,00,000
Administrative office	2,00,000	Loss on sale of fixed assets	50,000
Miscellaneous incomes	2,00,000	Loss by theft	5,00,000
Profit on sale of fixed assets	8,50,000	Dividend received on shares	30,000
Loss by fire	1,00,000	Income from investments	20,000
Loss by embezzlement	1,00,000		

Sol.

Profit and Loss Account

Dr for the year ended 31st March, 2016 Cr

Particulars	Amt (₹)	Particulars	Amt (₹)
To Salaries and Wages	20,00,000	By Gross Profit b/d	62,00,000
To Rent, Rates and Taxes	4,00,000	By Discount Received	1,00,000
To Fire Insurance Premium	3,60,000	By Interest Received	3,00,000
To Repairs and Maintenance	60,000	By Commission Received	2,00,000
To Printing and Stationery	60,000	By Rent Received	1,00,000
To Water and Electricity	1,20,000	By Profit on Sale of Fixed Assets	8,50,000
To Postage and Telegram	50,000	By Income from Investments	20,000
To Telephone Expenses	1,00,000	By Miscellaneous incomes	2,00,000
To Depreciation on Furniture	3,00,000	By Dividend on Shares	30,000
To Audit Fees	2,00,000		
To Bank Charges	40,000		
To Legal Charges	1,00,000		
To Miscellaneous Expenses	1,00,000		
To Discount Allowed	2,00,000		
To Carriage Outwards	1,00,000		
To Freight Outwards	50,000		
To Commission to Salesmen	1,50,000		
To Travelling Expenses	1,60,000		
To Entertainment Expenses	1,20,000		
To Sales Promotion Expenses	40,000		
To Advertising and Publicity	4,00,000		
To Bad Debts	1,00,000		
To Packing Expenses	50,000		
To Interest on Loan	2,50,000		
To Loss on Sale of Fixed Assets	50,000		
To Loss by Fire	1,00,000		
To Loss by Theft	5,00,000		
To Loss by Embezzlement	1,00,000		
To Net Profit transferred to Capital A/c	17,40,000		
	80,00,000		80,00,000

ILLUSTRATION |24| Calculate gross profit, operating profit and net profit from the following.

Particulars	Amt (₹)	Particulars	Amt (₹)
Opening Stock	4,00,000	Commission Paid	4,800
Purchases	38,00,000	Commission Received	12,000
Sales	50,00,000	Travelling Expenses	9,600
Purchases Return	1,40,000	Office Expenses	7,000
Sales Return	2,00,000	Interest on Long-term Loans	44,000
Wages	1,60,000	Dividend on Investments	5,600
Advertising	24,000	Printing and Stationery	7,200
Salaries	3,56,000	Loss on Sale of Machinery	70,000
Rent and Taxes	1,24,000	Carriage Outwards	2,800
Lighting	30,000	Loss by Theft	50,200
		Gain on Sale of Building	1,00,000

Closing stock was valued at ₹ 5,00,000

Sol.

Trading and Profit and Loss Account

Dr for the year ended .... Cr

Particulars		Amt (₹)	Particulars		Amt (₹)
To Opening Stock		4,00,000	By Sales	50,00,000	
To Purchases	38,00,000		(–) Sales Return	2,00,000	48,00,000
(–) Purchases Return	1,40,000	36,60,000	By Closing Stock		5,00,000
To Wages		1,60,000			
To Gross Profit Transferred to Profit and Loss A/c		10,80,000			
		53,00,000			53,00,000
To Advertising		24,000	By Gross profit b/d		10,80,000
To Salaries		3,56,000	By Commission Received		12,000
To Rent and Taxes		1,24,000			
To Lighting		30,000			
To Commission Paid		4,800			
To Travelling Expenses		9,600			
To Office Expenses		7,000			
To Printing and Stationery		7,200			
To Carriage Outwards		2,800			
To Operating Profit c/d		5,26,600			
		10,92,000			10,92,000
To Interest on Long-term Loans		44,000	By Operating Profit b/d		5,26,600
To Loss on Sale of Machinery		70,000	By Dividend on Investments		5,600
To Loss by Theft		50,200	By Gain on Sale of Building		1,00,000
To Net Profit Transferred to Capital A/c		4,68,000			
		6,32,200			6,32,200

ILLUSTRATION |25| Following is the trial balance of J Subramanium on 31st March, 2016. Pass the closing entries and prepare the trading and profit and loss account for the year ended 31st March, 2016.

Trial Balance
as on 31st March, 2016

Name of Account	Debit (₹)	Credit (₹)
Capital A/c		30,000
Stock A/c (1st April, 2015)	6,000	
Cash at Bank	3,000	
Cash in Hand	1,320	
Machinery A/c	18,000	
Furniture and Fittings A/c	4,080	
Purchases A/c	45,000	
Wages A/c	30,000	
Fuel and Power A/c	9,000	
Factory Lighting A/c	600	
Salaries A/c	21,000	
Discount Allowed A/c	1,500	
Discount Received A/c		900
Advertising A/c	15,000	
Sundry Office Expenses A/c	12,000	
Sales A/c		1,50,000
Sundry Debtors	25,500	
Sundry Creditors		11,100
	1,92,000	1,92,000

Value of closing stock as on 31st March, 2016 was ₹ 8,100.

Sol.

JOURNAL

Date	Particulars		LF	Amt (Dr)	Amt (Cr)
2016					
Mar 31	Trading A/c	Dr		90,600	
	To Stock A/c				6,000
	To Purchases A/c				45,000
	To Wages A/c				30,000
	To Fuel and Power A/c				9,000
	To Factory Lighting A/c				600
	(Being the accounts in the trial balance which have to be transferred to the trading account, debit side are transferred)				
Mar 31	Sales A/c	Dr		1,50,000	
	To Trading A/c				1,50,000
	(Being the amount of sales transferred to the credit of the trading account)				
Mar 31	Closing Stock A/c	Dr		8,100	
	To Trading A/c				8,100
	(Being the value of stock on hand on 31st March, 2016)				
Mar 31	Trading A/c	Dr		67,500	
	To Profit and Loss A/c				67,500
	(Being the transfer of gross profit)				
Mar 31	Profit and Loss A/c	Dr		49,500	
	To Discount Allowed A/c				1,500
	To Salaries A/c				21,000

Date	Particulars	LF	Amt (Dr)	Amt (Cr)
	To Advertising A/c			15,000
	To Sundry Office Expenses A/c			12,000
	(Being the various expenses accounts transferred to the debit of the profit and loss account)			
Mar 31	Discount Received A/c Dr		900	
	To Profit and Loss A/c			900
	(Being the credit balance of discount received transferred to the profit and loss account)			
Mar 31	Profit and Loss A/c Dr		18,900	
	To Capital A/c			18,900
	(Being the net profit transferred to the capital account)			

Trading and Profit and Loss Account
for the year ended 31st March, 2016

Dr Cr

Particulars	Amt (₹)	Particulars	Amt (₹)
To Stock	6,000	By Sales	1,50,000
To Purchases	45,000	By Closing Stock	8,100
To Wages	30,000		
To Fuel and Power	9,000		
To Factory Lighting	600		
To Gross Profit transferred to Profit and Loss A/c	67,500		
	1,58,100		1,58,100
To Salaries	21,000	By Gross Profit transferred from Trading A/c	67,500
To Discount Allowed	1,500	By Discount Received	900
To Advertising	15,000		
To Sundry Office Expenses	12,000		
To Net Profit transferred to Capital A/c	18,900		
	68,400		68,400

]ILLUSTRATION |26| Operating profit earned by M/s Arora & Sachdeva in 2015-16 was ₹ 17,00,000. Its non-operating incomes were ₹ 1,50,000 and non-operating expenses were ₹ 3,75,000. Calculate the amount of net profit earned by the firm. **NCERT**

Sol. Operating Profit = Net Profit + Non-operating Expenses – Non-operating Income

Hence, Net Profit = Operating Profit + Non-operating Income – Non-operating Expenditure

Operating profit (Given) = 17,00,000

Non-operating income = 1,50,000

Non-operating expenses = 3,75,000

Hence, Net profit = 17,00,000 + 1,50,000 – 3,75,000 = ₹ 14,75,000.

ILLUSTRATION |27| From the following figures, calculate operating profit.

	Amt (₹)
Net profit	1,00,000
Rent received	10,000
Gain on sale of machine	15,000
Interest on loan	20,000
Donation	2,000

Sol. Operating Profit = Net Profit – Non-operating Income + Non-operating Expenses

= 1,00,000 – 25,000 + 22,000 = ₹ 97,000

Non-operating Income = Rent Received + Gain on Sale of Machine = 10,000 + 15,000 = ₹ 25,000

Non-operating Expenses = Interest on Loan + Donation = 20,000 + 2,000 = ₹ 22,000

ILLUSTRATION |28| Cash sales ₹ 29,000, credit sales ₹ 31,000, cost of goods sold ₹ 52,000, expenses on purchases ₹ 3,000, expenses on sales ₹ 6,700. Find out gross profit and net profit.

Sol. Gross Profit = Net Sales − Cost of Goods Sold

= (₹ 29,000+ ₹ 31,000) − ₹ 52,000 = ₹ 8,000

Net Profit = Gross Profit − Indirect Expenses = ₹ 8,000 − ₹ 6,700 = ₹ 1,300

NUMERICAL Questions for Practice

1 Prepare profit and loss account for the year ended 31st March, 2016 from the following particulars.

Particulars	Amt (₹)	Particulars	Amt (₹)
General Expenses	24,000	Gross Profit	15,38,000
Charity	6,000	Carriage Outwards	40,000
Office Lighting	10,000	Office Expenses	32,000
Legal Charges	11,600	Fire Insurance Premium	36,000
Advertisement	28,400	Telephone Expenses	27,000
Bank Charges	2400	Establishment Expenses	5,000
Commission	14,000	Miscellaneous Expenses	14,200
Rent, Rates and Taxes	60,000	Discount Received	12,400
Interest on investments	24,000	Traveller's Salary	1,20,000
Sundry Receipts	12,000	Repair	8,600
Indirect Expenses	42,100	Commission Received	4,000
Printing and Stationery	3,000		

Ans Net Profit = ₹ 11,44,000

2 Calculate operating profit from the following.

Net Profit ₹ 10,00,000, dividend received ₹ 12,000, loss on sale of furniture ₹ 24,000, loss by fire ₹ 1,00,000, salaries ₹ 2,40,000, interest on loan from bank ₹ 20,000, rent received ₹ 48,000, donation 10,200

Ans Operating Profit = ₹ 10,94,200

3 Calculate the amount of gross profit, operating profit and net profit on the basis of the following balances extracted from the books of M/s Vishal and Sons for the year ended March 31, 2016.

Opening stock ₹ 1,00,000, net sales ₹ 22,00,000, net purchases ₹ 12,00,000, direct expenses ₹ 1,20,000, administration expenses ₹ 90,000, selling and distribution expenses ₹ 1,30,000, loss due to fire ₹ 40,000, closing stock ₹ 1,40,000

Ans Gross Profit = ₹ 9,20,000; Operating Profit = ₹ 7,00,000; Net Profit = ₹ 6,60,000.

4 From the following information, prepare a profit and loss account for the year ending 31st March, 2016.

Gross profit ₹ 60,000, rent ₹ 5,000, salary ₹ 15,000, commission paid ₹ 7,000, interest paid on loan ₹ 5,000, advertising ₹ 4,000, discount received ₹ 3,000, printings and stationary ₹ 2,000, legal charges ₹ 5,000, bad debts ₹ 1,000, depreciation ₹ 2,000, interest received ₹ 4,000, loss by fire ₹ 3,000

Ans Net Profit = ₹ 18,000

|TOPIC 3|
Balance Sheet

The balance sheet is a statement prepared for showing the financial position of the business summarising its assets and liabilities at a given date. It is prepared at the end of the accounting period after the trading and profit and loss account have been prepared. It is called a balance sheet because it is a statement of balances of ledger accounts which have not been closed even after the preparation of the trading and profit and loss account.

Need and Importance of Preparation of Balance Sheet

The need and importance of preparing a balance sheet is stated in the following points

(*i*) It helps to ascertain the true financial position of the business at a particular point of time.

(*ii*) It helps in ascertaining the nature and cost of various assets of the business such as the amount of closing stock, amount owing from debtors, amount of fictitious assets, etc.

(*iii*) It helps in determining the nature and amount of various liabilities of the business.

(*iv*) It gives information about the exact amount of capital at the end of the year and the addition or deduction made from it during the course of the current year.

(*v*) It helps in finding out whether the firm is solvent or not. The firm is solvent if the assets exceed the external liabilities. It would be insolvent in opposite case.

(*vi*) It helps in preparing the opening entries in the beginning of the next year.

Preparation of Balance Sheet

All the account of assets, liabilities and capital are shown in the balance sheet. Accounts of capital and liabilities are shown on the left hand side, known as **liabilities.** Assets and other debit balances are shown on the right hand side, known as **assets.**

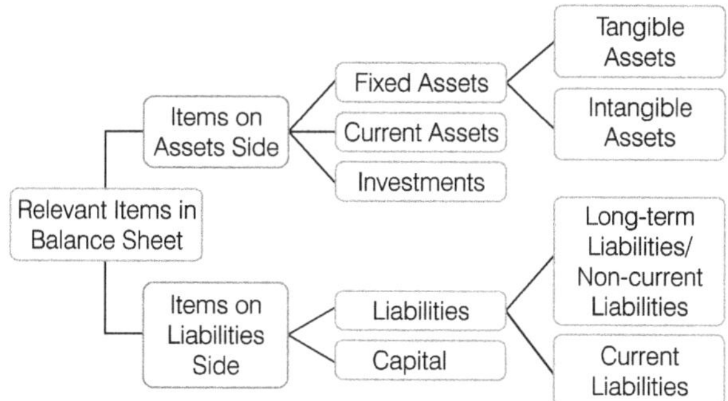

Relevant Items in Balance Sheet

The preparation of Balance Sheet requires the following steps

STEP 1 WRITE THE FOLLOWING ITEMS ON THE ASSETS SIDE OF BALANCE SHEET

(*i*) **Fixed Assets** These are those assets, which are held on a long-term basis in the business. Such assets are not acquired for the purpose of resale. *e.g.*, land, building, plant and machinery, furniture and fixtures, goodwill, patents, etc. Fixed assests can be of following two types.

- **Tangible Assets** These are those fixed assets which can be seen and touched *e.g.*, land and building, plant and machinery, furniture and fixtures, etc.
- **Intangible Assets** These are those assets which cannot be seen or touched. These assets are not in physical form. *e.g.*, goodwill, patents, trademarks.
  - *Fixed assets are valued at cost less depreciation.*

(*ii*) **Current Assets** These are those assets which are either in the form of cash or can be converted into cash within a year or are held for their consumption in the production of goods or rendering of services in the normal course of business.

The examples of such assets are cash in hand, cash at bank, bills receivable, stock of raw materials, semi-finished goods and finished goods, sundry debtors, short-term investments, prepaid expenses, etc.

These assets are temporary. These are also referred to as **floating or circulating assets.**

(*iii*) **Investments** Investments represent capital expenditure on purchase of shares, debentures, bonds, etc. to earn interest, dividend and other benefits.

STEP 2 WRITE THE FOLLOWING ITEMS ON THE LIABILITIES SIDE OF BALANCE SHEET

(*i*) **Liabilities**

- **Current Liabilities** These are those liabilities which are expected to be paid within a year. The examples of such liabilities are bank overdraft, bills payable, sundry creditors, short-term loans, outstanding expenses, etc.
- **Non-current Liabilities/Fixed Liabilities/ Long-term Liabilities** These are those liabilities which are usually payable after a year from the date of balance sheet. In other words, all liabilities other than the current liabilities are known as long-term liabilities. They mainly include long-term loans, borrowings or debentures, etc.

(*ii*) **Capital** It is the excess of assets over liabilities due to outsiders. It represents the amount originally contributed by the proprietor/partners as increased by profits and interest on capital and decreased by losses, drawings and interest on drawings.

The total of both the liabilities and assets side will tally.

Contingent Liabilities

These are the liabilities which will become payable only on the happening of some specific event, otherwise these are not paid. Such as

(i) **Liabilities for Bill Discounted** In case a bill discounted from the bank is dishonoured by the acceptor on the due date, the firm will become liable to the bank.

(ii) **Liability is Respect of a Suit Pending in a Court of Law** This would become an actual liability if the suit is decided against the firm.

(iii) **Liability in Respect of a Guarantee Given for Another Person** The firm would become liable to pay the amount
if the person for whom guarantee is given fails to meet his obligation.

Contingent liabilities are not shown in the balance sheet. They are shown as a footnote just below the balance sheet so that their existence may be revealed.

FORMAT OF BALANCE SHEET

There is no prescribed format of balance sheet, for a proprietary and partnership firms. However, Schedule III Part I of the Companies Act, 2013 prescribes the format and the order in which the assets and liabilities of a company should be shown.

That format is out of scope of the current syllabus. However, we will study the format of balance sheet derived on the basis of grouping and marshalling of assets and liabilities.

GROUPING AND MARSHALLING OF ASSETS AND LIABILITIES

A major concern of accounting is about preparing and presenting the financial statements in a manner that is useful to the users for decision-making. Therefore, it becomes necessary that the items appearing in the balance sheet should be properly grouped and presented in a particular order.

Grouping of Assets and Liabilities

The term grouping means putting together items of similar nature under a common heading. The various items appearing in the balance sheet can also be properly grouped.

For example, the balance of accounts of cash, bank, debtors, etc can be grouped and shown under the heading of 'current assets'.

Marshalling of Assets and Liabilities

Marshalling refers to the arrangement of assets and liabilities in a particular order.

In a balance sheet, the assets and liabilities are arranged either in the order of liquidity or permanence.

Order of Permanence

In case of permanence, the most permanent assets or liabilities are put on the top in a balance sheet and thereafter they are arranged in their reducing level of permanence.

General format of balance sheet in order of permanence is given below

Balance Sheet
as at...

Liabilities		Amt (₹)	Assets	Amt (₹)
Capital			**Fixed Assets**	
Opening Balance	...		Goodwill	...
(+) Net Profit	...		Land and Building	...
	...		Plant and Machinery	...
(–) Drawings	(...)	...	Furniture	...
Long-term Liabilities			Investments	...
Loans		...	**Current Assets**	
Current Liabilities			Closing Stock	...
Bank Overdraft		...	Debtors	...
Sundry Creditors		...	Bills Receivable	...
Bills Payable			Cash at Bank	...
			Cash in Hand	...
		...		...

Contingent Liabilities

Order of liquidity

Liquidity means the ease with which the assets may be converted into cash. In case of liquidity, the order is reversed. The liquid items are written first, followed by permanent items. The general format of balance sheet in order of liquidity is given below

Balance Sheet
as at...

Liabilities		Amt (₹)	Assets	Amt (₹)
Current Liabilities			**Current Assets**	
Bills Payable		...	Cash in Hand	...
Sundry Creditors		...	Cash at Bank	...
Bank Overdraft		...	Bills Receivable	...
Long-term Liabilities			Debtors	...
Loans		...	Closing Stock	...
Capital		...	Investments	...
Opening Balance	...		**Fixed Assets**	
(+) Net Profit	...		Furniture	...
	...		Plant and Machinery	...
(–) Drawings	(...)		Land and Building	...
		...	Goodwill	...
		...		...

Contingent Liabilities

ILLUSTRATION |29| From the following information, prepare a balance sheet of Mr Raghav as at 31st March, 2016. (i) in order of permanence. (ii) in order of liquidity.

Particulars	Amt (₹)	Particulars	Amt (₹)
Plant and Machinery	2,00,000	Furniture and Fixtures	40,000
Prepaid Expenses	2,000	Accrued Income	4,000
Income Received in Advance	4,000	Outstanding Expenses	2,000
Bills Payable	6,000	Bills Receivables	4,000
Sundry Debtors	2,00,000	Sundry Creditors	1,98,000
Bank Overdraft	20,000	Investments in Shares of X Ltd	20,000
Long-term Loan from Bank	2,00,000	Closing Stock	1,70,000
Capital	4,00,000	Building	2,00,000
Land	20,000	Goodwill	20,000
Drawings	20,000	Net Profit	1,20,000
Cash in Hand	10,000	Cash at Bank	38,000
Income Tax Paid	2,000		

Sol. (*i*)

Balance Sheet
as at 31st March, 2016

Liabilities		Amt (₹)	Assets	Amt (₹)
Capital			**Fixed Assets**	
Opening Balance	4,00,000		Goodwill	20,000
(+) Net Profit	1,20,000		Land	20,000
	5,20,000		Building	2,00,000
(−) Drawings	20,000		Plant and Machinery	2,00,000
(−) Income Tax	2,000	4,98,000	Furniture and Fixtures	40,000
Long-term Liabilities			**Investments**	
Long-term Loan		2,00,000	Shares of Raghav Ltd	20,000
Current Liabilities			**Current Assets**	
Income Received-in-Advance		4,000	Closing Stock	1,70,000
Sundry Creditors		1,98,000	Accrued Income	4,000
Outstanding Expenses		2,000	Prepaid Expenses	2,000
Bills Payable		6,000	Sundry Debtors	2,00,000
Bank Overdraft		20,000	Bills Receivable	4,000
			Cash at Bank	38,000
			Cash in Hand	10,000
		9,28,000		9,28,000

(*ii*)

Balance Sheet
as at 31st March, 2016

Liabilities	Amt (₹)	Assets	Amt (₹)
Current Liabilities		**Current Assets**	
Bank Overdraft	20,000	Cash in Hand	10,000
Bills Payable	6,000	Cash at Bank	38,000
Outstanding Expenses	2,000	Bills Receivable	4,000
Sundry Creditors	1,98,000	Sundry Debtors	2,00,000
Income Received in Advance	4,000	Prepaid Expenses	2,000
Long-term Liabilities		Accrued Income	4,000
Long-term Loan	2,00,000	Closing Stock	1,70,000

Liabilities		Amt (₹)	Assets	Amt (₹)
Capital			**Investments**	
Opening Balance	4,00,000		Shares of Raghav Ltd	20,000
(+) Net Profit	1,20,000		**Fixed Assets**	
	5,20,000		Furniture and Fixtures	40,000
(–) Drawings	20,000		Plant and Machinery	2,00,000
(–) Income Tax	2,000	4,98,000	Building	2,00,000
			Land	20,000
			Goodwill	20,000
		9,28,000		9,28,000

Opening Journal Entry

The balances of various accounts in balance sheet are carried forward from one accounting period to another accounting period. In fact, the balance sheet of an accounting period becomes the opening trial balance of the next accounting period. Next year, an opening entry is made which opens the accounts contained in the balance sheet.

While passing an opening entry, all assets account are debited and all liabilities accounts are credited.

ILLUSTRATION |30| Following balances appear in the books of Aviral as on 31st December, 2021.

Assets

Debtors ₹ 31,000; Bank ₹ 10,000; Cash ₹ 2,000; Furniture ₹ 30,000

Liabilities and Capital

Capital ₹ 33,000; Long-term Loan ₹ 10,000; Creditors ₹ 30,000

Pass opening entry as on 1st January, 2022.

Sol.

JOURNAL

Date	Particulars		LF	Amt (Dr)	Amt (Cr)
2022					
Jan 1	Debtors A/c	Dr		31,000	
	Bank A/c	Dr		10,000	
	Cash A/c	Dr		2,000	
	Furniture A/c	Dr		30,000	
	To Capital A/c				33,000
	To Long-term Loan A/c				10,000
	To Creditors A/c				30,000
	(Being the balance brought forward)				

Comprehensive Illustrations

ILLUSTRATION |31| The following trial balance is extracted from the books of M/s Ram on 31st March, 2016. You are required to prepare trading and profit and loss account and the balance sheet as on date. **NCERT**

Name of Account	Debit Balance (₹)	Name of Account	Credit Balance (₹)
Debtors	12,000	Apprenticeship Premium	5,000
Purchases	50,000	Loan	10,000
Coal, Gas and Water	6,000	Bank Overdraft	1,000
Factory Wages	11,000	Sales	80,000
Salaries	9,000	Creditors	13,000

Name of Account	Debit Balance (₹)	Name of Account	Credit Balance (₹)
Rent	4,000	Capital	20,000
Discount	3,000		
Advertisement	500		
Drawings	1,000		
Loan	6,000		
Petty Cash	500		
Sales Return	1,000		
Machinery	5,000		
Land and Building	10,000		
Income Tax	100		
Furniture	9,900		

Sol.

Trading and Profit and Loss Account
for the year ended 31st March, 2016

Dr | Cr

Particulars	Amt (₹)	Particulars		Amt (₹)
To Purchases	50,000	By Sales	80,000	
To Coal, Gas and Water	6,000	(–) Sales Return	1,000	79,000
To Factory Wages	11,000			
To Gross Profit Transferred to Profit and Loss A/c	12,000			
	79,000			79,000
To Salaries	9,000	By Gross Profit b/d		12,000
To Rent	4,000	By Apprenticeship Premium		5,000
To Discount	3,000			
To Advertisement	500			
To Net Profit transferred to Capital A/c	500			
	17,000			17,000

Balance Sheet
as at 31st March, 2016

Liabilities		Amt (₹)	Assets	Amt (₹)
Capital	20,000		Machinery	5,000
(+) Net Profit	500		Land and Building	10,000
	20,500		Furniture	9,900
(–) Drawings	1,000		Loan and Advances	6,000
(–) Income Tax	100	19,400	Debtors	12,000
Creditors		13,000	Petty Cash	500
Loan		10,000		
Bank Overdraft		1,000		
		43,400		43,400

ILLUSTRATION |32| The following is the trial balance of Manju Chawla on 31st March, 2016. You are required to prepare trading and profit and loss account and a balance sheet as on date. **NCERT**

Name of Account	Debit Balance (₹)	Credit Balance (₹)
Opening Stock	10,000	—
Purchases and Sales	40,000	80,000
Returns	200	600
Productive Wages	6,000	—
Dock and Clearing Charges	4,000	—

Name of Account	Debit Balance (₹)	Credit Balance (₹)
Donation and Charity	600	—
Delivery Van Expenses	6,000	—
Lighting	500	—
Sales Tax Collected	—	1,000
Bad Debts	600	—
Miscellaneous Incomes	—	6,000
Rent from Tenants	—	2,000
Royalty	4,000	—
Capital	—	40,000
Drawings	2,000	—
Debtors and Creditors	6,000	7,000
Cash	3,000	—
Investment	6,000	—
Patents	4,000	—
Land and Machinery	43,000	—

Closing stock ₹ 2,000.

Sol.

Trading and Profit and Loss Account
for the year ended 31st March, 2016

Dr | | | | | Cr

Particulars		Amt (₹)	Particulars		Amt (₹)
To Opening Stock		10,000	By Sales	80,000	
To Purchases	40,000		(–) Sales Return	200	79,800
(–) Purchases Return	600	39,400	By Closing Stock		2,000
To Productive Wages		6,000			
To Dock and Clearing Charges		4,000			
To Royalty		4,000			
To Gross Profit Transferred to Profit and Loss A/c		18,400			
		81,800			81,800
To Donation and Charity		600	By Gross Profit b/d		18,400
To Delivery Van Expenses		6,000	By Rent From Tenants		2,000
To Lighting		500	By Miscellaneous Incomes		6,000
To Bad Debts		600			
To Net Profit transferred to Capital A/c		18,700			
		26,400			26,400

Balance Sheet
as at 31st March, 2016

Liabilities		Amt (₹)	Assets	Amt (₹)
Capital	40,000		Investment	6,000
(+) Net Profit	18,700		Patents	4,000
	58,700		Land and Machinery	43,000
(–) Drawings	2,000	56,700	Cash	3,000
Creditors		7,000	Debtors	6,000
Sales Tax Collected		1,000	Suspense Account	700
			Closing Stock	2,000
		64,700		64,700

Note *There is a difference of ₹ 700 in debit side of trial balance, so it will be shown in the assets side of the balance sheet.*

ILLUSTRATION |33| From the following balances of M/s Nilu Sarees as on 31st March, 2016. Prepare trading and profit and loss account and balance sheet as on date. **NCERT**

Particulars	Amt (₹)	Particulars	Amt (₹)
Opening Stock	10,000	Sales	2,28,000
Purchases	78,000	Capital	70,000
Carriage Inwards	2,500	Interest	7,000
Salaries	30,000	Commission	8,000
Commission	10,000	Creditors	28,000
Wages	11,000	Bills Payable	2,370
Rent and Taxes	2,800		
Repair	5,000		
Telephone Expenses	1,400		
Legal Charges	1,500		
Sundry Expenses	2,500		
Cash in Hand	12,000		
Debtors	30,000		
Machinery	60,000		
Investments	90,000		
Drawings	18,000		

Closing stock as on 31st March, 2016 ₹ 22,000.

Sol.

Trading and Profit and Loss Account

Dr for the year ended 31st March, 2016 Cr

Particulars	Amt (₹)	Particulars	Amt (₹)
To Opening Stock	10,000	By Sales	2,28,000
To Purchases	78,000	By Closing Stock	22,000
To Carriage Inwards	2,500		
To Wages	11,000		
To Gross Profit Transferred to Profit and Loss A/c	1,48,500		
	2,50,000		2,50,000
To Salaries	30,000	By Gross Profit Transferred from Trading A/c	1,48,500
To Commission	10,000	By Interest	7,000
To Rent and Taxes	2,800	By Commission	8,000
To Repair	5,000		
To Telephone Expenses	1,400		
To Legal Charges	1,500		
To Sundry Expenses	2,500		
To Net Profit transferred to Capital A/c	1,10,300		
	1,63,500		1,63,500

Balance Sheet

as at 31st March, 2016

Liabilities		Amt (₹)	Assets	Amt (₹)
Capital	70,000		Machinery	60,000
(+) Net Profit	1,10,300		Investment	90,000
	1,80,300		Debtors	30,000
(–) Drawings	18,000	1,62,300	Cash in Hand	12,000
Creditors		28,000	Closing Stock	22,000
Bills Payable		2,370		
Suspense Account		21,330		
		2,14,000		2,14,000

Note *(i) Total of debit side of trial balance is ₹ 3,64,700 and total of credit side of trial balance is ₹ 3,43,370. The difference in credit side is ₹ 21,330.*

(ii) Difference in credit side of trial balance ₹ 21,330 will be treated as liabilities and posted in liabilities side of balance sheet.

NUMERICAL Questions for Practice

1 **From the following particulars, prepare balance sheet as at 31st March, 2016.**

Particulars	Debit (₹)	Credit (₹)
Capital		80,000
Drawings	8,800	
Debtors and Creditors	12,800	8,400
Cash in Hand	720	
Cash at Bank	14,400	
Plant	20,000	
Furniture	7,400	
Net Profit		3,320
General Reserve		2,000
Closing Stock	29,600	
	93,720	93,720

Ans Balance Sheet Total = ₹ 84,920

2 **From the following information, prepare balance sheet of a trader as at 31st March, 2016 arranging the assets and liabilities–(i) in order of permanence and (ii) in order of liquidity.**

Particulars	Amt (₹)	Particulars	Amt (₹)
Goodwill	40,000	Bank	40,000
Capital	3,60,000	Sundry Creditors	1,26,000
Liabilities for Expenses	2,400	Bills Receivable	26,000
Cash in Hand	2,000	Plant and Machinery	80,000
Investment	40,000	Provision for Doubtful Debts	5000
Bills Payable	21,400	Closing Stock	1,60,000
Net Profit	1,85,200	Furniture	32,000
Sundry Debtors	1,00,000	Drawings	60,000
Land and Building	1,20,000		

Ans Balance Sheet Total = ₹ 6,35,000

3 **From the following balances, as on 31st March, 2016, prepare trading and profit and loss account and balance sheet.**

Particulars	Amt (₹)	Particulars	Amt (₹)
Capital Account	20,000	Return Outwards	1000
Plant and Machinery	8,000	Rent	800
Sundry Debtors	4,800	Sales	32,800
Sundry Creditors	2,400	Manufacturing Expenses	1,600
Drawings	2,400	Trade Expenses	1,400
Purchases	21,000	Bad Debts	400
Wages	10,000	Carriage	300
Bank	2,000	Bills Payable	1,400
Repairs	100	Return Inwards	800
Stock (1st April, 2015)	4,000		

Closing stock (31st March, 2016) was valued at ₹ 2,900.

Ans Gross Loss = ₹ 1,000; Net Loss = ₹ 3,700 ; Balance Sheet Total = ₹ 17,700

4 From the following balances prepare final accounts as at 31st March 2016.

Particulars	Amt (₹)	Particulars	Amt (₹)
Stock 1st April, 2015	47,000	Freight Inwards	2,200
Purchases	93,600	Freight Outwards	6,000
Sales	2,60,000	Rent (Factory 1/3, Office 2/3)	15,000
Productive Expenses	54,000	Legal Expenses	1,600
Unproductive Expenses	11,600	Miscellaneous Receipts	1000
Trade Expenses	2400	Sundry Debtors	60,000
Return Inwards	13,200	Sundry Creditors	32,200
Return Outwards	5600	Donation	1,200
Loose Tools	14,400	Bad Debts	9,500
Trademarks	10,000	Bad Debts Recovered	8,000
Discount (Cr)	4,200	Bank Charges	5,600
Salaries	19,200	Loan on Mortgage	40,000
Fixed Deposit with Punjab National Bank	20,000	Interest on Loan	4,800
Cash in Hand	2600		
Motor Vehicles	1,00,000		
Leasehold Land	1,20,000		
Capital	2,74,900		
Life Insurance Premium	12,000		

Value of closing stock, was ₹ 73,000 on 31 st March, 2016.

Ans Gross Profit = ₹ 1,23,600, Net Profit = ₹ 64,900; Balance Sheet Total = ₹ 4,00,000.

5 Following trial balance is extracted from the books of a merchant on 31st March, 2016.

Particulars	Amt (₹)	Particulars	Amt (₹)
Debit Balance		Taxes and Insurance	2,500
Furniture and Fittings	1,280	General Charges	1,564
Motor Vehicles	12,500	Salaries	6,600
Building	15,180	**Credit Balances**	
Bad Debts	250	Capital	25,780
Sundry Debtors	7,600	Bills Payable	400
Stock on 1st April, 2015	6,920	Sundry Creditors	5,000
Purchases	11,150	Sales	30,900
Sales Return	400	Bank Overdraft	5,700
Advertising	900	Purchases Return	250
Interest	236	Commission	350
Cash in Hand	1,300		

Stock in hand on 31st March, 2016 was ₹ 6,500.

From the above, prepare trading and profit and loss account for the year ended 31st March, 2016 and balance sheet as at that date.

Ans Gross Profit = ₹ 19,180; Net Profit = ₹ 7,480, Balance Sheet Total = ₹ 44,360

6 From the following balances, prepare final accounts of M/s Goel and Sons for the year ended 31st March, 2016.

Salary ₹ 10,800; Insurance ₹ 5000; Cash ₹ 800; Purchases ₹ 1,68,340; Rent received ₹ 6,300; Drawings ₹ 4,200; Bills payable ₹ 7,800; Debtors ₹ 76,160; Stock (1st April, 2015) ₹ 59,000; Bank overdraft ₹ 19,400; Carriage ₹ 4,400; Creditors ₹ 8,400, Trade expenses ₹ 9,800; Sales return ₹ 9,400; Machinery ₹ 24,000; Wages ₹ 90,000; Sales ₹ 2,94,400; Purchases return ₹ 7,800; Capital ₹ 1,17,800; Closing stock (31st March, 2016) ₹ 72,400.

Ans Gross Profit = ₹ 43,460; Net Profit = ₹ 24,160; Balance Sheet Total = ₹ 1,73,360.

CHAPTER PRACTICE

OBJECTIVE TYPE Questions

Multiple Choice Questions

1 The financial statements consist of
(a) Trial balance
(b) Profit and loss account
(c) Balance sheet
(d) Both (b) and (c)

Ans (d) Both (b) and (c)

2 Income statement includes
(a) Trading account (b) Profit and loss account
(c) Both (a) and (b) (d) Balance sheet

Ans (c) Both (a) and (b)

3 Ram is the owner of a firm. He brought additional capital of ₹ 1,00,000 to the firm. The receipt of money in business is
(a) revenue receipt
(b) capital receipt
(c) revenue expenditure
(d) capital expenditure

Ans (b) If the receipts imply an obligation to return the money, these are capital receipt.

4 Profit and loss account is prepared
(a) for the whole year
(b) for a particular period
(c) on a particular date
(d) None of the above

Ans (b) for a particular period

5 Choose the correct chronological order of ascertainment of the following profits from the profit and loss **NCERT**
(a) Operating Profit, Net Profit, Gross Profit
(b) Operating Profit, Gross Profit, Net Profit
(c) Gross Profit, Net Profit, Operating Profit
(d) Gross Profit, Net Profit, Operating Profit

Ans (c) Gross Profit, Net Profit, Operating Profit

6 Liability which is payable on the happening of an event is
(a) contingent liabilities
(b) fluctuating liabilities
(c) current liabilities
(d) None of the above

Ans (a) Liabilities in respect of bill discounted, guarantee for a loan or disputed claims are the examples of contingent liabilities. These liabilities are payable on the happening of an event or contingency in future.

7 Capital expenditure .... the earning capacity or .... the operating expenses of a business.
(a) increases, reduces (b) reduces, increases
(c) maintain, reduces (d) reduces, maintain

Ans (a) increases, reduces

8 Depreciation or the expired cost of fixed assets will be
(a) revenue expenditure
(b) capital expenditure
(c) deferred revenue expenditure
(d) None of the above

Ans (a) Revenue expenditure is an expenditure, the benefit of which is consumed within the accounting period. It is treated as an expense of the current year.

9 On which assumption the expenditure is classified as capital and revenue expenditure?
(a) Going concern assumption
(b) Accrual assumption
(c) Money measurement assumption
(d) Consistency assumption

Ans (a) Going concern assumption

10 While calculating operating profit, the following are not taken into account **NCERT**
(a) Normal transactions
(b) Abnormal items
(c) Expenses of a purely financial nature
(d) Both (b) and (c)

Ans (d) Both (b) and (c)

11 'Capital gains' are those profits
(a) which are earned as interest on investments
(b) which are earned by selling of goods
(c) which are earned by selling fixed assets of the business
(d) which are related to discounts received from creditors

Ans (c) which are earned by selling fixed assets of the business

12 In which of the following cases, closing stock will not be shown in the trading account?
(a) When valuation of closing stock is on FIFO method
(b) When closing stock is not ascertained accurately

(c) When closing stock is adjusted in the purchases
(d) When it is appearing outside the trial balance

Ans (c) When closing stock is adjusted in the purchases

13 Which of the following is correct?

(a) Net Sales = Cash Sales + Credit Sales – Sales Return
(b) Net Sales = Cash Sales + Credit Sales + Sales Return
(c) Net Sales = Total Sales – Credit Sales
(d) Net Sales = Sales + Credit Sales

Ans (a) Net Sales = Cash Sales + Credit Sales – Sales Return

14 Consider the following statement.

I. Balance sheet contains only the balances of personal and real accounts.
II. Assets side of balance sheet is always equal to capital side.
III. Drawings are not shown in the balance sheet as it is a personal expense of the owner.

Choose the correct option.

(a) All are correct (b) All are incorrect
(c) Only I is correct (d) Only II and III is correct

Ans (c) Only I is correct

15 Which of the following statement(s) is/are true?

I. Revenue expenditure gives benefit within the accounting period.
II. Revenue expenditures are non-recurring in nature.

Choose the correct option.

(a) Both I and II (b) Only I
(c) Only II (d) Neither I nor II

Ans (b) Only I

16 Which of the following is correct?

(a) Operating Profit = Operating Profit – Non-operating expenses - Non-operating incomes
(b) Operating Profit = Net Profit + Non-operating expenses + Non-operating incomes
(c) Operating Profit = Net Profit + Net-operating expenses – Non-operating incomes
(d) Operating Profit = Net Profit – Non-operating expenses + Non-operating incomes

Ans (c) Operating Profit = Net Profit + Net-operating expenses – Non-operating incomes

17 Match the following and tick the correct option.

I. Trading account	(i) Net purchase + opening stock – closing stock
II. Cost of goods sold	(ii) Debit side of trading account
III. Adjusted purchases	(iii) For the year ended
IV. Wages	(iv) Opening stock + purchases + direct expenses – closing stock

Codes

	I	II	III	IV
(a)	(iv)	(ii)	(iii)	(i)
(b)	(i)	(ii)	(iii)	(iv)
(c)	(iii)	(iv)	(i)	(ii)
(d)	(iii)	(iv)	(ii)	(i)

Ans (c) (iii) (iv) (i) (ii)

18 Net sales during the year, 2017 is ₹ 2,85,000. Gross profit is 25% on sales. Find out cost of goods sold.

(a) ₹ 2,85,000 (b) ₹ 2,13,750
(c) ₹ 71,250 (d) Zero

Ans (b) Gross Profit $= ₹\ 2{,}85{,}000 \times \frac{25}{100} = ₹\ 71{,}250$

So, Cost of Goods Sold = Net Sales – Gross Profit
= 2,85,000 – 71,250
= ₹ 2,13,750

19 Calculate the gross profit and choose the correct option, if rate of gross profit is 25% on sales and cost of goods sold is ₹ 1,80,000.

(a) ₹ 60,000 (b) ₹ 36,000
(c) ₹ 45,000 (d) ₹ 30,000

Ans (a) Gross profit will be 25% on sales.

So, profit % on cost $= \frac{25}{75}$ or $\frac{1}{3}$ cost.

Hence, $\frac{1{,}80{,}000 \times 1}{3} = ₹ 60{,}000$

20 Find out the closing stock from the following Opening Stock = ₹ 20,000, Sales = ₹ 1,00,000, Purchases = ₹ 70,000

Rate of gross profit on cost $= 33\frac{1}{3}\%$

(a) ₹ 20,000 (b) ₹ 35,000
(c) ₹ 15,000 (d) ₹ 45,000

Ans (c) Rate of gross profit on cost $= 33\frac{1}{3}\%$. But sales is given. So, gross profit on sales will be 25%.

∴ Gross Profit $= \frac{1{,}00{,}000 \times 25}{100} = ₹\ 25{,}000$

Cost of goods sold = 1,00,000 – 25,000 = ₹ 75,000

∴ Closing stock
= Opening Stock + Purchases – Cost of goods sold
= 20,000 + 70,000 – 75,000 = ₹ 15,000

Fill in the Blanks

21 Interest on drawings is .... to Profit and Loss account.

Ans credited

22 Income earned but not received is shown in ....

Ans assets

23 'Carriage on Sale' is shown in ....

Ans profit and loss account

24 Any expenditure intended to benefit the current period is ....

Ans revenue expenditure

25 The information contained in the financial statements helps .... to make various surveys/studies related to a particular firm or industry.

Ans researchers

State True or False

26 Revenue expenditure is usually a recurring item.

Ans True

27 Net profit increase the capital.

Ans True

28 Balance sheet is prepared on a particular date.

Ans True

29 Assets side of balance sheet represents credit balance.

Ans False. Assets side represents debit balance.

30 Balance sheet is a statement.

Ans True

Match the Following

31

Column I	Column II
1. Trading and Profit & Loss	(a) Balance sheet
2. Balance sheet	(b) Tangible Assets
3. Physical existence	(c) Statement
4. Financial position	(d) Account

Ans 1-(d), 2-(c), 3-(b), 4-(a)

32

Column I	Column II
1. Paid to workers	(a) Carriage inwards
2. Incurred on bringing material/goods purchased	(b) Fuel
3. Paid for factory premises	(c) Wages
4. Used in production process	(d) Rent

Ans 1-(c), 2-(a), 3-(d), 4-(b)

Journalise the Following

33 To incorporate closing stock in the books.

Ans

Particulars		Dr	Cr
Closing Stock A/c	Dr	—	
To Trading A/c			—
(Being closing stock transferred to Trading A/c)			

34 To close purchase return account.

Ans

Particulars		Dr	Cr
Purchase Return A/c	Dr	—	
To Purchase A/c			—
(Being amount of purchase return transferred to Purchase A/c)			

35 To transfer Gross Profit to Profit and Loss account.

Ans

Particulars		Dr	Cr
Trading A/c	Dr	—	
To Profit and Loss A/c			—
(Being amount of gross profit transferred to Profit and Loss A/c)			

36 To transfer debit balance of Profit and Loss Account.

Ans

Particulars		Dr	Cr
Capital A/c	Dr	—	
To Profit and Loss A/c			—
(Being net loss transferred to Capital A/c)			

VERY SHORT ANSWER Type Questions

37 State what is the end product of financial accounting.

Ans The end product of financial accounting is the preparation of financial statements *i.e.*, trading and profit and loss account, balance sheet and notes to accounts.

38 Name the two basic financial statements.

Ans (*i*) Trading and profit and loss account
(*ii*) Balance sheet

39 What is the use of financial statements for management?

Ans Management is interested in financial statements to make various decisions such as determination of selling price, cost controls and reduction, investment into new projects, etc.

40 What is the use of financial statements for employees and trade unions?

Ans They are interested in financial statements as they want to know about the stability and profitability of the business. It is on the basis of financial statements only that employees decide wheter they should demand for bonus or wage hike or not.

41 **What is capital expenditure? Give two examples of capital expenditure.**

Ans Expenditure which is incurred in acquiring and increasing the value of fixed assets or for repayment of long-term liability is known as capital expenditure.

e.g., Purchases of fixed asset, expenditure incurred on improvement of existing asset.

42 **What is a revenue expenditure? Give two examples of revenue expenditure.**

Ans Those expenditures which are incurred for the day to day conduct of the business are referred to as revenue expenditure. *e.g.*, expenditure on repairs and maintenance of assets, payment of rent.

43 **Explain the term deferred revenue expenditure with the help of an example.**

Ans Deferred revenue expenditure is that expenditure which is revenue in nature but the benefit of which extends beyond the accounting year in which it is incurred. *e.g.*, Large expenditure incurred on advertising to introduce a new product in the market.

44 **What is capital receipt?**

Ans Capital receipts are those receipts which are received by the business on account of capital, loans or sale proceeds of fixed assets.

45 **What is a revenue receipt?**

Ans Revenue receipt is the amount received by the business in normal course of business.

46 **What is gross profit?**

Ans It is the excess of selling price of the goods over the cost of goods sold.

47 **Name any two items that are credited to trading account?**

Ans Closing stock and sales

48 **How is return inwards shown in the trading account?**

Ans Return inwards is shown on the credit side of the trading account by way of deduction from sales. Alternatively, it can also be shown as a separate item on the debit side of the account.

49 **If total of credit side of a trading account is more than the debit side, does it mean the enterprise has incurred loss or earned profit? Why?**

Ans It means the business has earned profits as revenues are credited whereas expenses are debited.

50 **What are direct expenses? Give two examples of direct expenses.**

Ans Direct expenses are those expenses which are incurred on purchases of goods upto the point of bringing them to the place of business.

e.g., freight inwards, manufacturing wages.

51 **What is profit and loss account?**

Ans Profit and loss account shows the financial performance of a business during an accounting period. It is prepared to ascertain the net profit or net loss incurred by the business entity during an accounting period.

52 **What is net profit?**

Ans Net profit is the excess of all revenue over all expenses and losses of a business enterprise.

53 **Where is apprenticeship premium received, appearing in the trial balance shown?**

Ans On the credit side of profit and loss account.

54 **Give any two items that are debited to profit and loss account.**

Ans (*i*) Business promotion expenses

(*ii*) Insurance premium

55 **If total of debit side of profit and loss account is more than the credit side, does it mean net profit or net loss? Why?**

Ans It means net loss. It is so because all incomes and gains are credited while all expenses and losses are debited. If total of debit side (expenses) is more than the total of credit side (incomes), it will result in net loss.

56 **What is meant by indirect expenses? Give two examples.**

Ans Indirect expenses are those expenses which are incurred and are not directly associated with the purchases of goods or manufacture of goods. *e.g.*, salaries, printing and stationery expenses.

57 **What is an operating profit?** **NCERT**

Ans Operating profit means the excess of operating revenue over operating expenses.

58 **Give the formula to calculate operating profit from net profit.**

Ans Operating Profit = Net Profit + Non-operating Expenses − Non-operating Incomes.

59 **Operating profit earned by Heer Mehta in 2016-17 was ₹ 8,50,000. Her non-operating incomes were ₹ 75,000 and non-operating expenses were ₹ 1,87,500. Calculate the profit earned during the year.**

Ans Net Profit = Operating profit + Non-operating incomes − Non-operating Expenses
= ₹ 8,50,000 + ₹ 75,000 − ₹ 1,87,500
= ₹ 7,37,500

60 What do you understand by fixed assets?

Ans Fixed assets are those assets that are acquired for continued use and not for resale.

61 What do you understand by current assets?

Ans Current assets are those assets of business that are kept temporarily for resale or for converting into cash.

62 Give any two examples of intangible assets.

Ans *The two examples of intangible assets are*
(*i*) Goodwill (*ii*) Patents

63 Give any two examples of fictitious assets.

Ans *The two examples of fictitious assets are*
(*i*) Debit balance of profit and loss account.
(*ii*) Advertisement expenses not yet written-off.

64 What is meant by marshalling of assets and liabilities?

Ans Marshalling is the arrangement of assets and liabilities in particular order in the balance sheet.
There are two ways of marshalling
(*i*) Order of liquidity (*ii*) Order of permanence

65 When assets are listed in order of liquidity in a balance sheet in which order following shall appear?

Land and building, cash in hand, machinery, bills receivable

Ans Cash in hand, bills receivable, machinery, land and building.

66 How is income tax paid by a sole trader shown in the balance sheet?

Ans By way of deduction from capital

67 Where is the closing stock appearing in the trial balance shown?

Ans On the assets side of the balance sheet

68 If 'adjusted purchases' and 'closing stock' are given in the trial balance, will you transfer 'closing stock' to trading account? Give reason.

Ans No, closing stock will not be transferred to trading account because it already stands credited to trading account as adjusted purchases mean opening stock + purchases − closing stock.

69 Is it true that profit and loss account shows the financial position of the enterprise?

Ans No, it does not show the financial position of the enterprise. It shows the financial performance *i.e.*, profit or loss of an enterprise for a particular period.

70 Debit balance in the profit and loss account is a profit. Comment.

Ans Debit balance in the profit and loss account is a loss because expenses are more than revenue.

71 Cost of obtaining license to carry out business is a capital expenditure or revenue expenditure?

Ans It is a capital expenditure.

72 Is it true that under the liquidity approach, assets which are most liquid are presented at the bottom of the balance sheet?

Ans No, under the liquidity approach, assets which are most liquid are presented at the top of the balance sheet.

73 Godrej Ltd imported from Germany one machinery for sale in India and another machinery for production purpose. Will you treat them as goods or fixed assets?

Ans Machinery imported for sale in India will be treated as goods. Machinery purchased for production will be treated as fixed assets.

74 When liabilities are listed in order of liquidity in a balance sheet, which should be listed first–capital or creditors?

Ans Creditors

SHORT ANSWER Type Questions

75 What are financial statements and what information is provided by them? **NCERT**

Ans Financial statements are the final/end products of an accounting process, which begins with the identification of accounting information and recording it in the books of primary entry.

Financial statements are prepared following the accounting concepts and conventions. These statements are prepared at the end of accounting period and give information about the financial position and performance of an enterprise.

Trading and profit and loss account present a true and fair view of the financial performance of the business in the form of profit and loss during the year. Balance sheet presents a true and fair view of the financial position of the business.

76 What are the objectives of preparing financial statements? **NCERT**

Ans *The basic objectives of preparing financial statements are*

(*i*) To present a true and fair view of the working of the business.

(*ii*) To help to judge the effectiveness of the management.

(*iii*) To provide sufficient and reliable information to various persons interested in financial statements.

(*iv*) To facilitate efficient allocation of resources.

(*v*) To disclose various accounting policies.

(*vi*) To provide information about the cash flows.

(*vii*) To provide information about the earning capacity.

(*viii*) To provide financial data on assets (economic resources) and liabilities (obligations) of an enterprise.

77 Give examples of capital expenditure.

Ans *The examples of capital expenditure are*

(*i*) Payment of wages for construction or extension of building.

(*ii*) Payment of wages for addition of rooms or erection of sheds in the building.

(*iii*) Carriage, cartage and freight paid on acquiring assets such as plant and machinery, furniture, etc.

(*iv*) Repairs of assets, purchased second hand.

(*v*) Payment for goodwill.

78 Give examples of revenue expenditure.

Ans Payment of expenses in acquiring or manufacturing goods *i.e.,* carriage and wages, etc. Payment of selling and distribution expenses. *i.e.* Repairs and maintenance of plant, machines, furniture, equipment, etc.

79 What is the purpose of preparing trading and profit and loss account? **NCERT**

Ans Trading account is prepared to know the amount of gross profit or gross loss. It also provides information about those expenses which are directly related with purchasing goods. This enables the management to control such expenses. Trading account also helps to compare closing stock of current year with that of the previous years. This helps to assess the growth in sales over the year.

80 Explain the concept of cost of goods sold. **NCERT**

Ans Cost of goods sold is the production cost of the goods sold. *Cost of goods sold is ascertained as follows*

Cost of Goods Sold = Opening Stock + Net Purchases − Closing Stock + Direct Labour/Expenses

81 What are closing entries? Give examples of closing entries of trading account. **NCERT**

Ans The preparation of trading and profit and loss account requires that the balances of accounts of all concerned items are transferred to it for its compilation. The entries which are passed for closing these accounts are known as closing entries.

Closing entries of trading account are

Trading A/c	Dr
To Opening Stock A/c	
To Purchases A/c	
To Wages A/c	
To Carriage Inwards A/c	
To All Other Direct Expenses A/c	
Sales A/c	Dr
Closing Stock A/c	Dr
To Trading A/c	

82 What are the features of a trading account?

Ans *Features of trading account are*

(*i*) Trading account is the first stage in the preparation of final accounts.

(*ii*) It provides information about gross profit and gross loss.

(*iii*) Balance of trading account is transferred to profit and loss account.

(*iv*) Trading account is a nominal account.

(*v*) Trading account relates to a particular accounting period and is prepared at the end of that period.

(*vi*) Trading account records only revenue items and not capital items.

83 What are the features of profit and loss account?

Ans *Features of profit and loss account are*

(*i*) It is prepared after preparing the trading account.

(*ii*) While preparing profit and loss account, accrual basis of accounting is followed.

(*iii*) Profit and loss account relates to a particular accounting period and is prepared at the end of that period.

(*iv*) It provides information about the net profit or net loss.

84 Discuss the need of preparing a balance sheet. **NCERT**

Ans *The need and importance of preparing a balance sheet is stated in the following points*

(*i*) It helps to ascertain the true financial position of the business at a particular point of time.

(*ii*) It helps in ascertaining the nature and cost of various assets of the business such as the amount of closing stock, amount owing from debtors, amount of fictitious assets, etc.

(*iii*) It helps in determining the nature and amount of various liabilities of the business.

(*iv*) It gives information about the exact amount of capital at the end of the year and the addition or deduction made into it in the current year.

(*v*) It helps in finding out whether the firm is solvent or not. The firm is solvent if the assets exceed the external liabilities. It would be insolvent if opposite is the case.

(*vi*) It helps in preparing the opening entries at the beginning of the next year.

85 Distinguish between capital receipts and revenue receipts.

Ans *The differences between capital receipts and revenue receipts are*

Basis	*Capital Receipts*	*Revenue Receipts*
Meaning	The amount received in form of capital introduced, loans taken and sale proceeds of the fixed assets is known as capital receipts.	The amount received mainly by selling of goods and serivces is known as revenue receipts.
Nature	Capital receipts are capital in nature.	Revenue receipts are revenue (*i.e.,* day-to-day activities) in nature.
Shown	Capital receipts are shown on the liabilities side of balance sheet.	Revenue receipts are shown at the credit of either trading account or profit and loss account.
Examples	Sale of fixed assets, capital contribution and loans taken, etc., are some example of capital receipts.	Profit on sale of assets, sale of goods, interest received on loans (advanced), royalty, etc., are some examples of revenue receipts.

86 Distinguish between tangible assets and intangible assets.

Ans *The differences between tangible assets and intangible assets are*

Basis	*Tangible Assets*	*Intangible Assets*
Physical Existence	These assets have physical identity *e.g.,* land, building, plant, etc.	These assets do not have physical existence *e.g.,* goodwill, patent, trademarks, etc.
Depreciation or Amortisation	Fixed tangible assets are depreciated.	Intangible assets are amortised.
Fixed vs Current	Tangible assets can be fixed or current *e.g.,* stock.	Intangible assets usually fall in the category of fixed assets.
Acceptance in Security	Lenders accept such assets as security for a loan given.	Lenders usually do not accept such assets as security for a loan given.
Risk of Loss Due to Fire	The assets may be lost due to fire.	These assets cannot be lost due to fire.

87 Distinguish between fixed assets and current assets.

Ans *The differences between fixed assets and current assets are*

Basis	*Fixed Assets*	*Current Assets*
Purpose of Holding	These assets are used to earn profits and operate the business.	These assets are consumed during the normal operating cycle of the business or are realised in cash.
Valuation	These assets are valued at cost less depreciation.	Current assets are valued at cost or market price whichever is lower.
Sources of Finance	Fixed assets are financed out of the long-term funds.	Current assets are mainly acquired out of the short-term funds.
Subject to Change	Fixed assets are usually not subject to change.	Current assets are usually subject to change.
Nature of Profit on Sale	Profit on sale of these assets is of capital nature *i.e.,* capital profit.	Profit on sale of current assets is of revenue nature *i.e.,* revenue profit.

88 **Give four points of difference between trading and profit and loss account.**

Ans *The differences between trading account and profit and loss account*

Basis	*Trading Account*	*Profit and Loss Account*
Relation	Trading account is a part of profit and loss account.	Profit and loss account is the main account.
Purpose	The gross profit or gross loss is ascertained from the trading account.	The profit and loss account is prepared to ascertain the net profit or net loss of the business.
Transfer of Balance	The balance of the trading account is transferred to the profit and loss account.	The balance of the profit and loss account is transferred to the capital account of the proprietor.
Items	Items shown in the trading account are purchases, sales, stock, direct expenses, etc.	Items like indirect expenses related to sales, distribution, administration, finance, etc., are shown in the profit and loss account.

89 **Distinguish between a balance sheet and trial balance.**

Ans *The differences between balance sheet and trial balance are*

Basis	*Trial Balance*	*Balance Sheet*
Object	It is prepared to check the arithmetical accuracy of the books of accounts.	It is prepared to known the true financial position of the firm.
Contents	All the ledger accounts are shown in the trial balance.	The balances of only those ledger accounts which have not been closed till the preparation of trading and profit and loss account are shown in the balance sheet.
Headings	The headings of its two columns are debit and credit.	The headings of its two sides are assets and liabilities.
Closing Stock	Normally, a closing stock does not figure in the trial balance.	This account appears in the balance sheet.
Period	Normally, it is prepared every month and whenever desired.	Normally, it is prepared only at the end of the trading period.
Accounts	All accounts must be written in the trial balance.	Only real and personal accounts appear in balance sheet.
Necessity	Though desirable, its preparation is not necessary.	It is necessary to prepare a balance sheet.

LONG ANSWER Type Questions

90 **Briefly explain the limitations of financial statements.**

Ans *Limitations of financial statements are as follows*

(*i*) **Historical in nature** The information given in financial statements is historical in nature and does not reflect the future.

(*ii*) **Affected by personal judgements** Financial statements are affected by personal judgement of the accountant. Stock valuation, provision for depreciation, etc are based on personal judgement and therefore are not free from bias.

(*iii*) **Different accounting practices** The financial statements can be drawn up on the basis of different accounting practices. *e.g.*, depreciation can be provided either on straight line basis or on written down value basis. Profit earned or loss suffered will be different under different assumptions.

(*iv*) **Ignorance of qualitative or non-monetary elements** Financial statements ignore the qualitative elements like quality of management, quality of labour force, public relations, etc.

(*v*) **Ignorance of price level changes** It ignores the price level changes of present market value of the assets as assets are shown at the historical cost.

91 What is a balance sheet? What are its characteristics? **NCERT**

Ans The balance sheet is a statement prepared for showing the financial position of the business summarising its assets and liabilities at a given date. It is prepared at the end of the accounting period after the trading and profit and loss account have been prepared. The assets reflect debit balances and liabilities (including capital) reflect credit balances.

It is called a balance sheet because it is a statement of balances of ledger accounts which have not been closed till the preparation of the trading and profit and loss account.

Features/Characteristics of balance sheet are as follows

(*i*) Balance sheet is prepared at a particular point of time and not for a particular period.
(*ii*) It is only a statement and not an account.
(*iii*) It is prepared after the preparation of trading and profit and loss account.
(*iv*) It shows the financial position of the business.
(*v*) It is a summary of balances of those ledger accounts which have not been closed by transferring to the trading and profit and loss account.
(*vi*) It shows the nature and value of assets.
(*vii*) It shows the nature and amount of liabilities.
(*viii*) The total of assets side must be equal to the liabilities side.

92 **Distinguish between capital expenditure and revenue expenditure and state whether the following statements are items of capital or revenue expenditure.**

(i) Expenditure incurred on repairs and whitewashing at the time of purchase of an old building in order to make it usable.
(ii) Expenditure incurred to provide one more exit in a cinema hall in compliance with a government order.
(iii) Registration fees paid at the time of purchase of a building.
(iv) Expenditure incurred in the maintenance of a tea garden which will produce tea after 4 years.
(v) Depreciation charged on a plant.
(vi) The expenditure incurred in erecting a platform on which a machine will be fixed.
(vii) Advertising expenditure, the benefits of which will last for 4 years. **NCERT**

Ans *The differences between capital expenditure and revenue expenditure are*

Basis	*Capital Expenditure*	*Revenue Expenditure*
Effect on Earning Capacity	Capital expenditure increases the earning capacity of business.	Revenue expenditure is incurred to maintain the earning capacity.
Purpose	It is incurred to acquire fixed assets for operation of business.	It is incurred on day-to-day conduct of business.
Nature	Capital expenditure is non-recurring in nature.	Revenue expenditure is generally recurring in nature.,
Period	Its benefit extend to more than one accounting year.	Its benefit normally extend to one accounting year.
Recorded	Capital expenditure (subject to depreciation) is recorded in balance sheet.	Revenue expenditure (subject to adjustment for outstanding and prepaid amount) is transferred to trading and profit and loss account.

(*i*) Expenditure incurred on repairs and whitewashing at the time of purchase of an old building in order to make it usable – Capital Expenditure

(*ii*) Expenditure incurred to provide one more exit in a cinema hall in compliance with a government order – Capital Expenditure

(*iii*) Registration fees paid at the time of purchase of a building – Capital Expenditure

(*iv*) Expenditure incurred in the maintenance of a tea garden which will produce tea after 4 years – Revenue Expenditure

(v) Depreciation charged on a plant – Revenue Expenditure

(vi) The expenditure incurred in erecting a platform on which a machine will be fixed – Capital Expenditure

(vii) Advertising expenditure, the benefits of which will last for 4 years–Deferred Revenue Expenditure.

93 **Distinguish between profit and loss account and balance sheet.**

Ans *The differences between profit and loss account and balance sheet are*

Basis	*Profit and Loss Account*	*Balance Sheet*
Types of Account	Only nominal accounts are entered in profit and loss account.	It records personal and real accounts.
Objective	The objective of preparing profit and loss account is to ascertain the net profit or loss of the business.	The purpose of preparing balance sheet is to understand the financial position of the firm.
Sides	The left hand side of the profit and loss account is the debit and the right hand side is credit.	It has liabilities at its left hand side and assets at right hand side.
Nature	Profit and loss account is an account. We use the word 'To' before accounts at the debit side and 'By' at the credit side.	Balance sheet is not an account, it is a statement. We do not use 'To' or 'By' in it.
Specific Date/Period	Profit and loss account shows the performance of the accounting period, generally a year.	Balance sheet shows the position of assets and liabilities on a particular date.
Types of Expenditure	Revenue expenditure are recorded in the profit and loss account.	Capital expenditure are entered at the assets side of the balance sheet.

NUMERICAL Questions

1 **From the following information, prepare the trading account for the year ended 31st March, 2016.**

Particulars	Amt (₹)
Cost of Goods Sold	24,20,000
Opening Stock	1,00,000
Closing Stock	1,60,000
Carriage Inwards	30,000
Sales	30,00,000

2 **Calculate closing stock from the following details.**

Particulars	Amt (₹)
Opening Stock	9,60,000
Purchases	27,20,000
Sales	39,00,000

Gross profit is 30% on cost.

Ans Closing Stock = ₹ 6,80,000

3 **Calculate gross profit and cost of goods sold from the following information.**

Net sales ₹ 24,00,000

Gross profit $33\frac{1}{3}$% on sales

Ans Gross Profit = ₹ 8,00,000; Cost of Goods Sold = ₹ 16,00,000

4 **Calculate closing stock and cost of goods sold:**
Opening stock ₹ 10,000; Sales ₹ 32,000; Carriage inwards ₹ 2,000; Sales return ₹ 2,000; Gross profit ₹ 12,000; Purchase ₹ 20,000; Purchase returns ₹ 1800.

Ans Cost of Goods Sold = ₹ 18,000; Closing Stock = ₹ 12,200

5 From the following information, prepare the trading account for the year ended 31st March, 2016.
Adjusted purchases ₹ 30,00,000; Sales ₹ 42,80,000; Return inwards ₹ 80,000; Freight and packing ₹ 30,000; Packing expenses on sales ₹ 40,000; Depreciation ₹ 72,000; Factory expenses ₹ 1,20,000; Closing stock ₹ 2,40,000.

Ans Gross Profit = ₹ 10,50,000

6 From the following figures, prepare profit and loss account of Sohan Lal, as it would appear in the year that ended 31st March, 2016.

Particulars	Amt (₹)	Particulars	Amt (₹)
Salaries and Wages	6,000	Advertising	2,000
Commission Paid	400	Discount allowed	3600
Postage and Telegram	300	Rent Received	3400
Insurance	600	Interest on Investment	3,000
Interest Paid	800	Bad Debts	1,800
Carriage Outwards	1000	Brokerage Paid	190

The gross profit was 45% of sales, which amounted to ₹ 130,000.

Ans Net Profit = ₹ 48,210

7 From the following balance of the ledger of Sh Gajendra Singh, prepare trading and profit and loss account and balance sheet.

Particulars	Debit (₹)	Credit (₹)
Stock on 1st April, 2015	90,000	
Stock on 31st March, 2016	1,38,600	
Purchases and Sales	6,90,000	10,37,400
Returns	37,500	45,600
Commission on Purchases	3,600	
Freight, Octroi and Carriage	78,000	
Wages and Salary	32,400	
Fire Insurance Premium	2,460	
Business Premises	1,20,000	
Sundry Debtors	78,300	
Sundry Creditors		80,100
Goodwill	24,000	
Patents	25,200	
Coal, Gas and Power	22,800	
Printing and Stationery	6,300	
Postage and Telegram	2,130	
Travelling Expenses	12,750	
Drawings	21,600	
Depreciation	3,000	
General Expenses	25,050	
Capital		2,69,280
Investments	24,000	
Interest on Investments		2,400
Custom Duty on Imported Goods	13,500	
Cash in Hand	7,710	
Banker's Account		15,600
Commission	13,800	13,200
Loan on Mortgage		90,000
Interest on Loan	9,000	

Particulars	Debit (₹)	Credit (₹)
Bills Payable		6,840
Bills Receivable	13,620	
Income Tax	9,000	
Horses and Carts	60,900	
Discount on Purchases		4,800
	15,65,220	15,65,220

Ans Gross Profit = ₹ 1,15,200 ; Net Profit = ₹ 61,110; Balance Sheet Total = ₹ 4,92,330

8 **Following is the trial balance of PC Mukherjee as at 31st March, 2016.**

Debit Balances	Amt (₹)	Credit Balances	Amt (₹)
Stock [1st April, 2015]	20,000	Discount Received	1,500
Purchases	1,16,000	Return Outwards	5,200
Wages	4,000	Sales	1,97,300
Return Inwards	7,040	Bills Payable	6,000
Carriage on Purchases	4,720	Sundry Creditors	11,200
Carriage on Sales	1,420	Creditors for Rent	1000
Office Salaries	9,600	Capital	80,000
Duty on Imported Goods	5,400	Loan from Damodar	20,000
Rent and Taxes	4,800	Commission	2,400
Cash	2,200		
Bank Balance	15,640		
Bad Debts	1,200		
Discount Allowed	1,280		
Land and Building	40,000		
Scooter	13,200		
Scooter Repairs	1,700		
Bills Receivable	7,000		
Commission	3,600		
Sundry Debtors	50,800		
Interest on Damodar 's Loan	3,000		
Drawings	12,000		
	3,24,600		3,24,600

Prepare a trading and profit and loss account of for the year ended on 31st March 2016 and the balance sheet as at that date. The stock on 31st March, 2016 was ₹ 44,000.

Ans Gross Profit = ₹ 89,340, Net Profit = ₹ 66,640; Balance Sheet Total = ₹ 1,72,840

9 **From the following balances, prepare trading and profit and loss account and balance sheet.**

Debit Balances	Amt (₹)	Credit Balances	Amt (₹)
Machinery	7,000	Capital Account	20,000
Debtors	5,400	Creditors	2,800
Drawings	1,800	Sales	29,000
Purchases	19,000		
Wages	10,000		
Bank	3,000		
Opening Stock	4,000		
Rent	900		
Sundry Expenses	400		
Carriage	300		

Closing stock was ₹ 600

Ans Gross Loss = ₹ 3,700; Net Loss = ₹ 5,000; Balance Sheet Total = ₹ 16,000

10 **From the following trial balance and additional information of Mr Rajesh Ahuja, a proprietor, prepare trading and profit and loss account for the year ended 31st March, 2016 and balance sheet as at that date.**

Particulars	Dr Balance (₹)	Cr Balance (₹)
Building	3,20,000	
Wages	52,000	
Machinery	32,000	
Salaries and Wages	83,200	
Debtors	67,400	
Capital		4,46,200
Purchases and Sales	1,13,000	2,01,400
Creditors		25,000
Income Tax	4,000	
Drawings	1,000	
Total	6,72,600	6,72,600

Closing stock at cost ₹ 2,00,000 but at market price ₹ 1,77,000

Ans Gross Profit = ₹ 2,13,400; Net Profit = ₹ 1,30,200; Balance Sheet Total = ₹ 5,96,400

11 **From the following trial balance, prepare the trading and profit and loss account for the year ended 31st March, 2016 and the balance sheet as at that date.**

Name of Account	Debit Balance (₹)	Name of Account	Credit Balance (₹)
Debit balances		**Debit balances**	
Sundry Debtors	1,500	Rent, Rates and Taxes	800
Stock on 1st April, 2015	5,000	Salaries	2,000
Land and Building	10,000	Drawings	2,000
Cash in Hand	1,600	Purchases	10,000
Cash at Bank	4,000	Office Expenses	2,500
Wages	3,000	Plant and Machinery	5,700
Bills Receivable	2,000	**Credit balances**	
Interest	200	Capital	25,000
Bad Debts	500	Interest	600
Repairs	300	Sundry Creditors	7,000
Furniture and Fixtures	1,500	Sales	17,000
Depreciation	1,000	Bills Payable	400

On 31st March, 2016 the stock was valued at ₹ 10,000.

Ans Gross Profit = ₹ 9,000; Net Profit = ₹ 3,200; Balance Sheet Total = ₹ 33,600

12 **From the following balances, as on 31st March, 2016, prepare trading and profit and loss account and the balance sheet.**

Capital account	50,000	Return outwards	2,500
Plant and machinery	20,000	Rent	2,000
Sundry debtors	12,000	Sales	82,000
Sundry creditors	6,000	Manufacturing expenses	4,000
Drawings	6,000	Trade expenses	3,500
Purchases	52,500	Bad debts	1,000
Wages	25,000	Carriage	750
Bank	5,000	Bills payable	3,500
Repairs	250	Return inwards	2,000
Stock (1st April, 2015)	10,000		

Closing stock (31st March, 2016) was valued at ₹ 7,250.

Ans Gross Loss = ₹ 2,500; Net Loss = ₹ 9,250; Balance Sheet Total = ₹ 44,250

13 **Following is the trial balance of Vandana Vohra on 31st March, 2016. Draw the final accounts from the balances therefrom.**

Name of Account	Debit Balance (₹)	Credit Balance (₹)
Capital		3,00,000
Stock on 1st April, 2015	60,000	
Cash at Bank	20,000	
Cash in Hand	10,000	
Machinery	2,00,000	
Furniture	26,000	
Purchases	4,00,000	
Wages	1,00,000	
Carriage Inwards	66,000	
Salaries	1,40,000	
Discount Allowed	8,000	
Discount Received		10,000
Advertising	1,00,000	
Office Expenses	80,000	
Sales		10,00,000
Sundry Debtors	1,80,000	
Sundry Creditors		80,000
	13,90,000	13,90,000

Value of closing stock as on 31st March, 2016 was ₹ 1,00,000.

Ans Gross Profit = ₹ 4,74,000; Net Profit = ₹1,56,000; Balance Sheet Total = ₹ 5,36,000

14 **The following balances were extracted from the books of Garima Aggarwal on 31st March, 2016.**

Capital	98,000	Loan	31,520
Drawings	8,000	Sales	2,61,440
General expenses	10,000	Purchases	1,88,000
Building	44,000	Motor car	8,000
Machinery	37,360	Reserve fund	3,600
Stock	64,800	Commission (Credit)	5,280
Power	8,960	Car expenses	7,200
Taxes and insurance	5,260	Bills payable	15,400
Wages	28,800	Cash	320
Debtors	25,120	Bank overdraft	13,200
Creditors	10,000	Charity	420
Bad debts	2,200		

Stock on 31st March, 2016 was valued at ₹ 23,500. Prepare the final accounts for the year ended 31st March, 2016.

Ans Gross Profit = ₹ 64,880; Net Profit = ₹ 45,080; Balance Sheet Total = ₹ 2,08,800

15 **Following is the trial balance of Kartik Makkar as on 31st March, 2016.**

Name of Accounts	Debit Balance (₹)	Name of Accounts	Credit Balance (₹)
Stock on 1st April, 2015	20,000	Discount Received	1,500
Purchases	1,16,000	Return Outwards	5,200
Wages	4,000	Sales	1,97,300
Return Inwards	7,040	Bills Payable	6,000
Carriage on Purchases	4,720	Sundry Creditors	11,200
Carriage on Sales	1,420	Creditors for Rent	1,000
Office Salaries	9,600	Capital	80,000
Duty on Imported Goods	5,400	Loan from Raj	20,000
Rent and Taxes	4,800	Commission	2,400
Cash	2,200		

Name of Accounts	Debit Balance (₹)	Name of Accounts	Credit Balance (₹)
Bank Balance	15,640		
Bad Debts	1,200		
Discount Allowed	1,280		
Land and Building	40,000		
Scooter	13,200		
Scooter Repairs	1,700		
Bills Receivable	7,000		
Commission	3,600		
Sundry Debtors	50,800		
Interest on Raj's Loan	3,000		
Drawings	12,000		
	3,24,600		3,24,600

Prepare a trading and profit and loss account for the year ended on 31st March, 2016 and the balance sheet as at that date. The stock on 31st March, 2010 was ₹ 44,000.

Ans Gross Profit = ₹ 89,340; Net Profit = ₹ 66,640; Balance Sheet Total = ₹ 1,72,840

16 **From the following trial balance of Mr A Lal, prepare trading and profit and loss account and balance sheet as on 31st March, 2014.** **NCERT**

Name of Account	Debit Balance (₹)	Credit Balance (₹)
Stock as on 1st April, 2011	16,000	
Purchases and sales	67,600	1,12,000
Return inwards and outwards	4,600	3,200
Carriage inwards	1,400	
General expenses	2,400	
Bad debts	600	
Discount received		1,400
Bank overdraft		10,000
Interest on bank overdraft	600	
Commission received		1,800
Insurance and taxes	4,000	
Scooter expenses	200	
Salaries	8,800	
Cash in hand	4,000	
Scooter	8,000	
Furniture	5,200	
Building	65,000	
Debtors and creditors	6,000	16,000
Capital		50,000

Closing stock ₹ 15,000.

11

After studying this chapter the students will understand the need for adjustments in preparing financial statements.
The students will further learn the various items which usually need adjustments in preparing final accounts and their accounting treatment, *i.e.,* the adjusting entry to be passed, and how will the adjustments appear in the final accounts *i.e.,* trading and profit and loss account and balance sheet.

FINANCIAL STATEMENTS-II (WITH ADJUSTMENTS)

In the last chapter we have learnt to prepare final accounts in the form of trading and profit and loss account and balance sheet without adjustments. Sometimes it is noticed that after preparation of trial balance, but before final accounts are prepared, some business transactions have been completely or partially omitted or are wrongly recorded.

Besides this, there are some incomes or expenses, which relate to the next year, but have been received or paid in the current year. Therefore, it is necessary to incorporate these adjustments while preparing final accounts.

CHAPTER CHECKLIST

- Need for Adjustment in Preparing the Final Accounts
- Adjustment in Preparation of Financial Statement

Need for Adjustments in Preparing the Final Accounts

In order to ascertain true profit or loss of a business for a particular year, it is necessary that all expenses and incomes related to that period should be taken into consideration. The need of making various adjustments are stated below

(*i*) To ascertain the true profit or loss of the business.
(*ii*) To determine the true financial position of the business.
(*iii*) To make a record of the transactions earlier omitted in the books.
(*iv*) To rectify the errors committed in the books.
(*v*) To complete the incomplete transactions.
(*vi*) To make a record of accrued income (*i.e.,* income which have been accrued but have not been received).
(*vii*) To make a record of outstanding expenses (*i.e.,* expenses which are due but have not been paid).
(*viii*) To make adjustment for prepaid expenses (*i.e.,* expenses which have been paid in advance).
(*ix*) To make adjustment for unearned income (*i.e.,* income which have been received in advance).
(*x*) To provide for other reserves and provisions, depreciation, etc.

ADJUSTMENTS IN PREPARATION OF FINANCIAL STATEMENTS

All such items which need to be brought into books of accounts at the time of preparing the final accounts are referred to as 'adjustments'.

Some common adjustments relate to

(*i*) Closing stock
(*ii*) Outstanding expenses
(*iii*) Prepaid/Unexpired expenses
(*iv*) Depreciation
(*v*) Accrued income
(*vi*) Income received in advance
(*vii*) Bad debts
(*viii*) Provision for doubtful debts
(*ix*) Provision for discount on debtors
(*x*) Manager's commission
(*xi*) Interest on capital
(*xii*) Interest on drawings
(*xiii*) Interest on loan
(*xiv*) Abnormal or accidental losses
(*xv*) Goods taken for personal use
(*xvi*) Goods distributed as free samples

Journal entries which are recorded to give effect to these adjustments are known as **adjusting entries.** All adjustments are reflected in the final accounts at two places to complete the double entry.

Note *Interest on drawings and interest on loan are not in syllabus however, they have been given for the knowledge of the students as these are basic adjustments.*

1. Closing Stock

Closing stock implies the value of unsold goods at the end of an accounting period. Closing stock is valued at cost or net realisable value, whichever is lower.

If Given in Adjustment

Accounting Treatment

Adjusting Entry		Trading Account	Balance Sheet
Closing Stock A/c To Trading A/c (Being the closing stock recorded in the books)	Dr	Shown on the credit side.	Shown on the assets side under current assets.

If Given in Trial Balance

Accounting Treatment

Trading Account	Balance Sheet
Nil	Shown on the assets side under current assets.

EXAMPLE Suppose the value of closing stock shown outside the trial balance on 31st March, 2016 is ₹ 1,00,000. Pass an adjusting entry and show how will this appear in final accounts.

Sol. **Adjusting Entry**

JOURNAL

Closing Stock A/c To Trading A/c (Being closing stock recorded)	Dr	1,00,000	 1,00,000

Effect on Final Accouts

Trading Account

Dr — for the year ended 31st March, 2016 — Cr

Particulars	Amt (₹)	Particulars	Amt (₹)
		By Closing Stock	1,00,000

Balance Sheet
as at 31st March, 2016

Liabilities	Amt (₹)	Assets	Amt (₹)
		Closing Stock	1,00,000

2. Outstanding Expenses

(Expenses Due but Not Paid or Expenses Unpaid or Due)

There are certain business expenses which become due during the current accounting period but are actually paid in the next accounting period. Such expenses are termed as outstanding expenses. Such items usually are outstanding wages, salaries, etc.

If Given in Adjustment

Accounting Treatment

Adjusting Entry		Trading Account	Profit and Loss Account	Balance Sheet
Concerned Expenses A/c To Outstanding Expenses A/c (Being the unpaid expenses provided)	Dr	If it is a direct expense *e.g.*, wages Added to the related expense on the debit side.	If it is an indirect expense *e.g.*, salaries Added to the related expense on the debit side.	Shown on the liabilities side as a current liability.

If Given in Trial Balance

Accounting Treatment

Trading Account	Profit and Loss Account	Balance Sheet
Nil	Nil	Shown on the liabilities side as a current liability.

EXAMPLE

Extract of Trial Balance
as on 31st March, 2016

Name of Accounts	Debit Balance (₹)	Credit Balance (₹)
Wages paid	66,000	
Salary paid	16,500	

Additional Information

Wages ₹ 6,000 and salary ₹ 1,500 are outstanding.

Pass an adjustment entry and show how will this appear in final accounts.

Sol. **Adjustment Entries**

JOURNAL

(i) Wages A/c	Dr	6,000	
To Outstanding Wages A/c			6,000
(Being wages due)			
(ii) Salary A/c	Dr	1,500	
To Oustanding Salary A/c			1,500
(Being salary due)			

Effect on Final Accounts

Trading Account

Dr for the year ended 31st March, 2016 Cr

Particulars		Amt (₹)	Particulars	Amt (₹)
To Wages A/c	66,000			
(+) Outstanding Wages	6,000	72,000		

Profit and Loss Account

Dr for the year ended 31st March, 2016 Cr

Particulars		Amt (₹)	Particulars	Amt (₹)
To Salary A/c	16,500			
(+) Outstanding Salary	1,500	18,000		

Balance Sheet
as at 31st March, 2016

Liabilities	Amt (₹)	Assets	Amt (₹)
Outstanding Wages	6,000		
Outstanding Salary	1,500		

3. Prepaid Expenses

(Expenses Paid in Advance or Unexpired Expenses)

There may be certain business expenses, the payment of which might have been made in the current accounting year but which relate of the next accounting year. Such expenses are called prepaid expenses. Such items usually are unexpired insurance, interest paid in advance, etc.

If Given in Adjustment

Accounting Treatment

Adjusting Entry	Trading Account	Profits and Loss Account	Balance Sheet
Prepaid Expenses A/c Dr To Concerned Expenses A/c (Being concerned expenses paid in advance)	(If it is a direct expense *e.g.*, wages) Deducted from the related expense on the debit side.	(If it is an indirect expense *e.g.*, insurance premium) Deducted from the related expense, on the debit side.	Shown on the assets side as current assets.

If Given in Trial Balance

Accounting Treatment

Trading Account	Profit and Loss Account	Balance Sheet
Nil	Nil	Shown on the assets side as a current asset.

EXAMPLE

Extract of Trial Balance
as on 31st March, 2016

Name of Accounts	Debit Balance (₹)	Credit Balance (₹)
Insurance Account	8,000	

Additional Information

Prepaid insurance amounted to ₹ 2,000.

Pass an adjusting entry and show how will this appear in final accounts.

Sol. **Adjustment Entry**

JOURNAL

Prepaid Insurance A/c	Dr	2,000	
To Insurance A/c			2,000
(Being insurance paid in advance)			

Effect on Final Accounts

Profit and Loss Account
Dr for the year ended 31st March, 2016 Cr

Particulars		Amt (₹)	Particulars	Amt (₹)
To Insurance	8,000			
(–) Prepaid Insurance	2,000	6,000		

Balance Sheet
as at 31st March, 2016

Liabilities	Amt (₹)	Assets	Amt (₹)
		Prepaid Insurance	2,000

4. Depreciation

Depreciation refers to the decrease in the value of assets on account of wear and tear and passage of time.

If Given in Adjustment

Accounting Treatment

Adjusting Entry	Profit and Loss Account	Balance Sheet
Depreciation A/c Dr To Concerned Asset A/c/Provision for Depreciation A/c (Being depreciation charged)	Shown on the debit side as a separate item.	Shown on the assets side by way of deduction from the value of concerned fixed assets. If provision for depreciation account is maintained, amount of depreciation is added to provision for depreciation account and the total accumulated depreciation is shown on the asset side by way of deduction from the original cost of the asset.

If Given in Trial Balance

Accounting Treatment

Profit and Loss Account	Balance Sheet
Shown on the debit side	Nil

EXAMPLE

Extract of Trial Balance
as on 31st March, 2016

Name of Accounts	Debit Balance (₹)	Credit Balance (₹)
Machinery	1,00,000	
Furniture	16,000	

Additional Information

Machinery is to be depreciated @ 10% per annum and furniture @ 20% per annum.
Pass an adjusting entry and show how will this appear in final accounts.

***Sol.* Adjustment Entry**

JOURNAL

Depreciation A/c	Dr	13,200	
To Machinery A/c (1,00,000 × 10%)			10,000
To Furniture A/c (16,000 × 20%)			3,200
(Being depreciation charged)			

Effect on Final Accounts

Profit and Loss Account
for the year ended 31st March, 2016

Dr | Cr

Particulars	Amt (₹)	Particulars	Amt (₹)
To Depreciation			
Machinery	10,000		
Furniture	3,200		

Balance Sheet
as at 31st March, 2016

Liabilities	Amt (₹)	Assets		Amt (₹)
		Machinery	1,00,000	
		(–) Depreciation	10,000	90,000
		Furniture	16,000	
		(–) Depreciation	3,200	12,800

EXAMPLE Following is the extract from a trial balance.

Trial Balance
as on ...

	(₹)	(₹)
Machinery A/c	4,00,000	
Furniture A/c	2,00,000	
Provision for Depreciation : On Machinery		1,20,000
On Furniture		54,200

Additional Information

Depreciation is to be charged on machinery at 10% per annum on original cost and on furniture at 10% per annum by the diminishing balance method. Show the effect in financial statements.

Sol.

Profit and Loss Account

for the year ended ...

Dr | | | | Cr

Particulars		Amt (₹)	Particulars	Amt (₹)
To Depreciation				
On Machinery (10% on ₹ 4,00,000)	40,000			
On Furniture 10/100 × (₹ 2,00,000 – ₹ 54,200)	14,580	54,580		

Balance Sheet

as at 31st March, 2016

Liabilities	Amt (₹)	Assets		Amt (₹)
		Machinery A/c	4,00,000	
		(–) Provision for Depreciation (1,20,000 + 40,000)	1,60,000	2,40,000
		Furniture	2,00,000	
		(–) Provision for Depreciation (54,200 + 14,580)	68,780	1,31,220

ILLUSTRATION |1| (Based on adjustments from 1 to 4) From the following trial balance of Hanif Lal , prepare trading and profit and loss account for the year ended 31st March, 2016 and a balance sheet as on that date.

Particulars	Amt (₹)	Particulars	Amt (₹)
Opening Stock	40,000	Sales	5,40,000
Purchases	1,60,000	Purchase Return	8,000
Sales Return	12,000	Discount	10,400
Carriage Inwards	7,200	Sundry Creditors	50,000
Carriage Outwards	1,600	Bills Payable	3,600
Wages	84,000	Capital	1,50,000
Salaries	55,000		
Plant and Machinery	1,80,000		
Furniture	16,000		
Sundry Debtors	1,04,000		
Bills Receivable	5,000		
Cash in Hand	12,600		
Travelling Expenses	7,400		
Lighting (Factory)	2,800		
Rent and Taxes	14,400		
General Expenses	21,000		
Insurance	3,000		
Drawings	36,000		
	7,62,000		7,62,000

Adjustments

(i) Stock on 31st March, 2016 was valued at ₹ 48,000 (market value ₹ 60,000).
(ii) Wages outstanding for March, 2016 amounted to ₹ 6,000.
(iii) Salaries outstanding for March, 2016 amounted to ₹ 5,000.
(iv) Prepaid insurance amounted to ₹ 600.
(v) Provide depreciation on plant and machinery at 5% and on furniture at 20%.

Sol.

Trading and Profit and Loss Account
for the year ending 31st March, 2016

Dr Particulars		Amt (₹)	Particulars		Cr Amt (₹)
To Opening Stock		40,000	By Sales	5,40,000	
To Purchases	1,60,000		(–) Sales Return	12,000	5,28,000
(–) Purchases Return	8,000	1,52,000	By Closing Stock		48,000
To Carriage Inwards		7,200			
To Wages	84,000				
(+) Outstanding Wages	6,000	90,000			
To Factory Lighting		2,800			
To Gross Profit c/d		2,84,000			
		5,76,000			5,76,000
To Carriage Outwards		1,600	By Gross Profit b/d		2,84,000
To Salaries	55,000		By Discount Received		10,400
(+) Outstanding Salaries	5,000	60,000			
To Travelling Expenses		7,400			
To Rent and Taxes		14,400			
To General Expenses		21,000			
To Insurance	3,000				
(–) Prepaid Insurance	600	2,400			
To Depreciation on					
Plant and Machinery	9,000				
Furniture	3,200	12,200			
To Net Profit Transferred to Capital A/c		1,75,400			
		2,94,400			2,94,400

Balance Sheet
as at 31st March, 2016

Liabilities		Amt (₹)	Assets		Amt (₹)
Bills Payable		3,600	Cash in Hand		12,600
Sundry Creditors		50,000	Bills Receivable		5,000
Outstanding Wages		6,000	Sundry Debtors		1,04,000
Outstanding Salaries		5,000	Closing Stock		48,000
Capital	1,50,000		Prepaid Insurance		600
(+) Net Profit	1,75,400		Furniture	16,000	
	3,25,400		(–) Depreciation	3,200	12,800
(–) Drawings	36,000	2,89,400	Plant and Machinery	1,80,000	
			(–) Depreciation	9,000	1,71,000
		3,54,000			3,54,000

Working Note

1. Closing stock is valued at cost or realisable value, whichever is less.
2. Depreciation on plant and machinery $= 1,80,000 \times \frac{5}{100} =$ ₹ 9,000

   Depreciation on furniture $= 16,000 \times \frac{20}{100} =$ ₹ 3,200

5. Accrued Income (Outstanding Income or Income Receivable)

It refers to the income which has been earned but not received during the current accounting period. *e.g.*, interest on investment due but not yet received, commission receivable, rent, etc.

If Given in Adjustment

Accounting Treatment

Adjusting Entry		Profit and Loss Account	Balance Sheet
Accrued Income A/c To Concerned Income A/c (Being concerned income receivable)	Dr	Added to the respective income on the credit side.	Shown on the asset side as a current asset.

If Given in Trial Balance

Accounting Treatment

Profit and Loss Account	Balance Sheet
Nil	Shown on the assets side as a current asset.

EXAMPLE

Extract of Trial Balance
as on 31st March, 2016

Name of Accounts	Debit Balance (₹)	Credit Balance (₹)
Commission received		9,000

Additional Information

Commission earned but not received ₹ 1,800.

Pass an adjusting entry and show how will this appear in final accounts.

***Sol.* Adjustment Entry**

JOURNAL

Particulars		Dr	Cr
Accrued Commission A/c	Dr	1,800	
To Commission A/c			1,800
(Being commission receivable)			

Effect on Final Accounts

Profit and Loss Account
Dr for the year ended 31st March, 2016 Cr

Particulars	Amt (₹)	Particulars		Amt (₹)
		By Commission	9,000	
		(+) Accrued Commission	1,800	10,800

Balance Sheet
as at 31st March, 2016

Liabilities	Amt (₹)	Assets	Amt (₹)
		Accrued Commission	1,800

6. Income Received in Advance
(Unearned Income or Unaccrued Income)

The income or portion of income which is received during the current accounting year but it has not been earned, is called unearned income.

If Given in Adjustment

Accounting Treatment

Adjusting Entry		Profit and Loss Account	Balance Sheet
Concerned Income A/c To Income Received in Advance A/c (Being adjustment for unearned income)	Dr	Deducted from the concerned income on the credit side.	Shown on the liabilities side.

If Given in Trial Balance

Accounting Treatment

Profit and Loss Account	Balance Sheet
Nil	Shown on the liabilities side.

EXAMPLE

Extract of Trial Balance
as at 31st March, 2016

Name of Accounts	Debit Balance (₹)	Credit Balance (₹)
Rent Received		15,600

Additional Information

Rent received but not earned ₹ 1,200.

Pass an adjusting entry and show how will this appear in final accounts.

Sol. **Adjustment Entry**

JOURNAL

Particulars		Dr (₹)	Cr (₹)
Rent A/c To Rent Received in Advance A/c (Being adjustment entry for unearned rent)	Dr	1,200	1,200

Effect on Final Accounts

Profit and Loss Account
for the year ended 31st March, 2016

Dr | Cr

Particulars	Amt (₹)	Particulars		Amt (₹)
		By Rent	15,600	
		(–) Unearned Rent	1,200	14,400

Balance Sheet
as at 31st March, 2016

Liabilities	Amt (₹)	Assets	Amt (₹)
Unearned Rent	1,200		

ILLUSTRATION |2| (Based on adjustment 5 and 6) From the following trial balance of Varshney and Sons, prepare trading account and profit and loss account for the year ending 31st December, 2016 and a balance sheet as on that date.

Particulars	Amt (₹)	Particulars	Amt (₹)
Opening Stock	10,400	Capital	32,000
Purchases	31,000	Creditors	4,000
Sales Returns	600	Sales	40,000
Debtors	8,000	Commission	5,480
Building	10,000	Rent	4,000
Machinery	7,200		
Furniture	3,200		
Bills Receivable	4,000		
Salaries	3,200		
Tax	400		
Insurance	600		
Carriage on Purchases	1,800		
Trade Expenses	600		
Travelling Expenses	880		
Wages	2,000		
Cash	1,600		
	85,480		85,480

Adjustments

(*i*) Closing stock ₹ 24,000. (*ii*) Rent due but not received ₹ 200.

(*iii*) Commission to the extent of ₹ 280 received in advance.

Sol.

Trading and Profit and Loss Account

Dr for the year ended 31st December, 2016 Cr

Particulars	Amt (₹)	Particulars		Amt (₹)
To Opening Stock	10,400	By Sales	40,000	
To Purchases	31,000	(–) Sales Returns	600	39,400
To Carriage on Purchases	1,800	By Closing Stock		24,000
To Wages	2,000			
To Gross Profit c/d	18,200			
	63,400			63,400
To Salaries	3,200	By Gross Profit b/d		18,200
To Tax	400	By Commission	5,480	
To Insurance	600	(–) Unearned Commission	280	5,200
To Trade Expenses	600	By Rent	4,000	
To Travelling Expenses	880	(+) Accrued Rent	200	4,200
To Net Profit Transferred to Capital A/c	21,920			
	27,600			27,600

Balance Sheet
as at 31st December, 2016

Liabilities		Amt (₹)	Assets	Amt (₹)
Creditors		4,000	Cash	1,600
Unearned Commission		280	Bills Receivable	4,000
Capital	32,000		Debtors	8,000
(+) Net Profit	21,920	53,920	Closing Stock	24,000
			Accrued Rent	200
			Furniture	3,200
			Machinery	7,200
			Building	10,000
		58,200		58,200

7. Bad Debts

The amount which cannot recovered from the debtors is known as bad debts. It refers to a debt, which became irrecoverable.

If Given in Adjustment

Accounting Treatment

Adjusting Entries		Profit and Loss Account	Balance Sheet
Bad Debts A/c To Debtors A/c (Being bad debts written-off)	Dr	Shown on the debit side as a separate item, or as a addition to the bad debts already written off.	Shown on the assets side by way of deduction from the debtors.
Profit and Loss A/c To Bad Debts A/c (Being the bad debts transferred to profit and loss account)	Dr		

If Given in Trial Balance

Accounting Treatment

Profit and Loss Account	Balance Sheet
Shown on the debit side	Nil

It is to be noted that both type of bad debts i.e., appearing in trial balance and outside the trial balance are charged to profit and loss account but only those bad debts which are given outside the trial balance are deducted from debtors.

EXAMPLE

Extract of Trial Balance
as on 31st March, 2016

Name of Accounts	Debit Balance (₹)	Credit Balance (₹)
Bad debts	2,400	
Sundry debtors	60,000	

Additional Information

Write-off further bad debts ₹ 3,000.

Pass an adjusting entry and show how will this appear in final accounts.

Sol. Adjustment Entry

JOURNAL

Bad Debts A/c	Dr	3,000	
To Sundry Debtors A/c			3,000
(Being further bad debts written-off)			

Effect on Final Accounts

Profit and Loss Account

Dr for the year ended 31st March, 2016 Cr

Particulars		Amt (₹)	Particulars	Amt (₹)
To Bad Debts	2,400			
(+) Further Bad Debts	3,000	5,400		

Balance Sheet

as at 31st March, 2016

Liabilities	Amt (₹)	Assets		Amt (₹)
		Sundry Debtors	60,000	
		(–) Bad Debts	3,000	57,000

8. Provision for Doubtful Debts

A provision for bad debts is created in accordance to convention of conservatism to cover any possible loss on account of bad debts likely to occur in future. Generally such a provision is created at a fixed percentage on debtors at the end of every year.

If Given in Adjustment

Accounting Treatment

Adjusting Entry		Profit and Loss Account	Balance Sheet
Profit and Loss A/c To Provision for Doubtful Debts A/c (Being adjustment for provision for doubtful debt)	Dr	Shown as a separate item or added to the bad debts on the debit side	Shown on the assets side by way of deduction from the amount of sundry debtors

If Given in Trial Balance

Profit and Loss Account	Balance Sheet
Shown as a deduction from total of bad debts and new provision	Nil

Note

- *The provision appearing in the trial balance is referred to as 'old provision'.*
- *The provision appearing in adjustments is referred to as 'new provision'.*
- *If old provision exceeds the total of bad debts and new provision, then in this case, the balance will be shown on the credit side of profit and loss account. The new provision will, however, be deducted from debtors in the balance sheet.*

EXAMPLE

Extract of Trial Balance

as on 31st March, 2016

Name of Accounts	Debit Balance Amt (₹)	Credit Balance Amt (₹)
Debtors	30,000	

Additional Information

Create a provision for bad and doubtful debts @ 5% on debtors.

Sol. **Adjustment Entry**

JOURNAL

Particulars			
Profit and Loss A/c	Dr	1,500	
To Provision for Bad and Doubtful Debts A/c			1,500
(Being creation of provision at 5% on debtors)			

Effect on Final Accounts

Profit and Loss Account
Dr for the year ended 31st March, 2016 Cr

Particulars	Amt (₹)	Particulars	Amt (₹)
To Provision for Doubtful Debts	1,500		

Balance Sheet
as at 31st March, 2016

Liabilities	Amt (₹)	Assets		Amt (₹)
		Debtors	30,000	
		(–) Provision for Doubtful Debts	1,500	28,500

EXAMPLE

Extract of Trial Balance
as on 31st March, 2016

Name of Accounts	Debit Balance (₹)	Credit Balance (₹)
Sundry debtors	32,000	
Bad debts	2,000	
Provision for doubtful debts		3,500

Additional Information

Write-off further bad debts ₹ 1,000 and create a provision for doubtful debts @ 5% on debtors.
Pass necessary journal entries and show relevant accounts (including final accounts)

Sol.

JOURNAL

Date	Particulars		LF	Amt (Dr)	Amt (Cr)
	Bad Debts A/c	Dr		1,000	
	To Sundry Debtors A/c				1,000
	(Being further bad debts)				
	Provision for Doubtful Debts A/c	Dr		3,000	
	To Bad Debts A/c				3,000
	(Being bad debts (2,000 + 1,000) adjusted against the provision)				
	Profit and Loss A/c	Dr		1,050	
	To Provision for Doubtful Debts A/c				1,050
	(Being amount charged from profit and loss account)				

Dr Sundry Debtors Account Cr

Date	Particulars	LF	Amt (₹)	Date	Particulars	LF	Amt (₹)
	To Balance b/d		32,000		By Bad Debts A/c		1,000
					By Balance c/d		31,000
			32,000				32,000

Dr Bad Debts Account Cr

Date	Particulars	LF	Amt (₹)	Date	Particulars	LF	Amt (₹)
	To Balance b/d		2,000		By Provision for Doubtful Debts A/c		3,000
	To Sundry Debtors A/c		1,000				
			3,000				3,000

Dr Provision for Doubtful Debts Account Cr

Date	Particulars	LF	Amt (₹)	Date	Particulars	LF	Amt (₹)
	To Bad Debts A/c		3,000		By Balance b/d		3,500
	To Balance c/d (5% of 32,000–1,000)		1,550		By Profit and Loss A/c (Balancing Figure)		1,050
			4,550				4,550

Profit and Loss Account
Dr for the year ended 31st March, 2016 Cr

Particulars		Amt (₹)	Particulars	Amt (₹)
To Provision for Doubtful Debts A/c				
Bad Debts	2,000			
(+) Further Bad Debts	1,000			
(+) New Provision	1,550			
	4,550			
(–) Old Provision	3,500	1,050		

Balance Sheet
as at 31st March, 2016

Liabilities	Amt (₹)	Assets		Amt (₹)
		Sundry Debtors	32,000	
		(–) Further Bad Debts	1,000	
			31,000	
		(–) Provision for Doubtful Debts (31,000 × 5 / 100 = ₹ 1,550)	1,550	29,450

EXAMPLE An extract of trial balance is given as

	Amt (₹)
Debtors	1,60,000
Bad debts	4,000
Provision for bad debts	10,000

Additional Information

Bad debts ₹ 1,000, provision on debtors @ 3%. Pass adjusting entries and show the relevant extracts of final accounts.

Sol. **JOURNAL**

Date	Particulars		LF	Amt (Dr)	Amt (Cr)
	Bad Debts A/c	Dr		1,000	
	To Debtors A/c				1,000
	(Being further bad debts)				

Date	Particulars		LF	Amt (Dr)	Amt (Cr)
	Provision for Doubtful Debts A/c	Dr		5,000	
	To Bad Debts A/c				5,000
	(Being bad debts adjusted against the provision)				
	Provision for Doubtful Debts A/c	Dr		230	
	To Profit and Loss A/c				230
	(Being excess provision credited to profit and loss account)				

Profit and Loss Account
for the year ended 31st March, 2016

Dr | Cr

Particulars	Amt (₹)	Particulars	Amt (₹)
		By Provision for Doubtful Debts	230

Balance Sheet
as at 31st March, 2016

Liabilities	Amt (₹)	Assets		Amt (₹)
		Debtors	1,60,000	
		(–) Further Bad Debts	1,000	
			1,59,000	
		(–) New Provision	4,770	1,54,230
		(3% on 1,59,000)		

Working Note

Provision for Doubtful Debts

Old Bad Debts	4,000
(+) Further Bad Debts	1,000
	5,000
(+) New Provision on Debtors	4,770
	9,770
(–) Old Provision on Debtors	10,000
	(230)

Since the old provision is in excess of new provision, the difference *i.e.*, 230 will be transferred to the credit side of profit and loss account.

9. Provision for Discount on Debtors

Generally, business allows cash discount to those debtors from whom the payment is received within a fixed period. Therefore a provision for such discount is made in the current year, for those debtors who will make early payment in the next accounting period.

If Given in Adjustment

Accounting Treatment

Adjusting Entry		Profit and Loss Account	Balance Sheet
Profit and Loss A/c To Provision for Discount on Debtors A/c (Being adjustment of discount on debtors adjusted)	Dr	Shown on debit side as a separate item.	Shown on the assets side by way of deduction from sundry debtors.

If Given in Trial Balance

Accounting Treatment

Profit and Loss Account	Balance Sheet
Shown as a deduction from total of bad debts and provision for bad debts	Nil

Note *Provision for discount on creditors is computed on creditors and is shown on the credit side of profit and loss account and as a deduction from creditors, in the balance sheet.*

EXAMPLE

Extract of Trial Balance
as on 31st March, 2016

Name of Accounts	Debit Balance (₹)	Credit Balance (₹)
Bad debts	10,800	
Provision for bad and doubtful debts (1st April, 2015)		22,500
Sundry debtors	6,00,000	

Additional Information

(*i*) Write-off further bad debts ₹ 6,000.
(*ii*) Provision for doubtful debts to be maintained at 5% on sundry debtors.
(*iii*) Create a provision for discount on sundry debtors at 3%.

Show effect on profit and loss account and balance sheet.

Sol. **Effect on Final Acccounts**

Profit and Loss Account
Dr for the year ended 31st March, 2016 Cr

Particulars		Amt (₹)	Particulars	Amt (₹)
To Bad Debts	10,800			
(+) Further Bad Debts	6,000			
	16,800			
(+) New Provision	29,700			
	46,500			
(–) Old Provision	22,500	24,000		
To Provision for Discount on Debtors		16,929		

Balance Sheet
as at 31st March, 2016

Liabilities	Amt (₹)	Assets		Amt (₹)
		Sundry Debtors	6,00,000	
		(–) Further Bad Debts	6,000	
			5,94,000	
		(–) New Provision for Doubtful Debts (5% on 5,94,000)	29,700	
			5,64,300	
		(–) Provision for Discount on Debtors (3% on 5,64,300)	16,929	5,47,371

ILLUSTRATION |3| (Based on adjustments 7, 8, 9)

From the following trial balance prepare trading account, profit and loss account and balance sheet for the year ended 31st December, 2016.

Particulars	Amt (₹)	Particulars	Amt (₹)
Opening Stock	10,000	Sales	5,20,000
Purchases	3,00,000	Purchases Returns	10,000
Debtors	1,40,000	Creditors	1,00,000
Drawings	20,000	Provision for Bad Debts	4,000
Sales Returns	16,000	Bills Payable	30,000
Wages	24,000	Bank Overdraft	20,000
Salaries	40,000	Capital	7,20,000

Particulars	Amt (₹)	Particulars	Amt (₹)
Repairs	12,000		
Bad Debts	8,000		
Carriage	4,000		
Discount	6,000		
Land and Building	4,00,000		
Plant and Machinery	3,00,000		
Furniture and Fixtures	80,000		
Cash	4,000		
Goodwill	40,000		
	14,04,000		14,04,000

Adjustments

(i) Closing stock ₹ 40,000.
(ii) Further bad debts ₹ 6,000.
(iii) Create a reserve for doubtful debts @ 5%.
(iv) Create a provision for discount on debtors and creditors @ 2%.
(v) Charge depreciation on plant and machinery and furniture and fixtures @ 10% per annum.

Sol.

Trading and Profit and Loss Account
for the year ended 31st December, 2016

Dr | Cr

Particulars		Amt (₹)	Particulars		Amt (₹)
To Opening Stock		10,000	By Sales	5,20,000	
To Purchases	3,00,000		(−) Sales Returns	16,000	5,04,000
(−) Purchases Returns	10,000	2,90,000	By Closing Stock		40,000
To Wages		24,000			
To Carriage		4,000			
To Gross Profit c/d		2,16,000			
		5,44,000			5,44,000
To Salaries		40,000	By Gross Profit b/d		2,16,000
To Repairs		12,000	By Provision for Discount on Creditors		2,000
To Discount Allowed		6,000			
To Bad Debts	8,000				
(+) Further Bad Debts	6,000				
	14,000				
(+) Provision for	6,700				
Doubtful Debts	20,700				
(−) Old Provision	(4,000)	16,700			
To Provision for Discount on Debtors		2,546			
To Depreciation on Plant and Machinery		30,000			
To Depreciation on Furniture and Fixtures		8,000			
To Net Profit Carried to Capital A/c		1,02,754			
		2,18,000			2,18,000

Balance Sheet
as at 31st December, 2016

Liabilities		Amt (₹)	Assets		Amt (₹)
Creditors	1,00,000		Cash		4,000
(−) Provision for Discount @ 2%	2,000	98,000	Goodwill		40,000
Bils Payable		30,000	Land and Building		4,00,000
Bank Overdraft		20,000	Plant and Machinery	3,00,000	
Capital	7,20,000		(−) Depreciation	30,000	2,70,000
(+) Net Profit	1,02,754		Furniture and Fixtures	80,000	
	8,22,754		(−) Depreciation	8,000	72,000
(−) Drawings	20,000	8,02,754	Debtors	1,40,000	
			(−) Further Bad Debts	6,000	
				1,34,000	
			(−) Provision for Bad Debts 5%	6,700	
				1,27,300	
			(−) Provision for Discount @ 2%	2,546	1,24,754
			Closing Stock		40,000
		9,50,754			9,50,754

10. Manager's Commission

Sometimes, the manager is entitled to commission on profits in addition to salary. Such commission is calculated at the end of the accounting period and is always given as an adjustment. It is calculated as a fixed percentage of the profits.

Such profits may be either before or after charging such commission. In case, it is not mentioned, the commission should be allowed as a percentage of net profit before charging such commission.

Commission payable can be calculated as follows

(*i*) **When commission is paid at a fixed percentage of net profit before charging such commission**

In this case, commission will be calculated as

Commission = Net Profit before Commission × Rate of Commission

(*ii*) **When commission is paid at a fixed percentage of net profit after charging such commission**

In this case, commission is calculated as

$$\text{Commission} = \text{Net Profit before Such Commission} \times \frac{\text{Rate of Commission}}{100 + \text{Rate of Commission}}$$

Accounting Treatment

Adjusting Entry		Profit and Loss Account	Balance Sheet
Manager's Commission A/c To Commission Payable/Outstanding Commission A/c (Being manager commission adjusted)	Dr	Shown on the debit side as a separate item.	Commission payable is shown on the liabilities side.
Profit and Loss A/c To Manager's Commission A/c (Being the commission payable to manager transferred to profit and loss account)	Dr		

EXAMPLE The net profit of a firm amounts to ₹ 31,500 before charging commission. The manager of the firm is entitled to a commission of 5% on the net profits. Calculate the commission payable to the manager in each of the following alternative cases and also show its effect on final accounts.

(i) If the manager is allowed commission on the net profit before charging such commission.

(ii) If the manager is allowed commission on the net profit after charging such commission. Also show its treatment in final accounts ending on 31st March, 2016.

Sol. (*i*) Commission = Net Profit before Charging such Commission $\times \frac{\text{Rate of Commission}}{100}$

$$= 31{,}500 \times \frac{5}{100} = ₹1{,}575$$

(*ii*) Commission = Net Profit before Charging such Commission $\times \frac{\text{Rate of Commission}}{100 + \text{Rate of Commission}}$

$$= 31{,}500 \times \frac{5}{105} = ₹1{,}500$$

Effect on Final Accounts

Profit and Loss Account
for the year ended 31st March, 2016

Dr Cr

Particulars	Amt (₹)	Particulars	Amt (₹)
To Manager's Commission	1,575		

Balance Sheet
as at 31st March, 2016

Liabilities	Amt (₹)	Assets	Amt (₹)
Current Liabilities			
Manager's Commission Outstanding	1,575		

11. Interest on Capital

The cost of using the capital invested by the proprietor/partner in an enterprise is interest on capital.

Interest is calculated at a given rate of interest on capital as at the beginning of the accounting year. If any additional capital is brought during the year, the interest may also be computed on such amount from the date on which it was brought into the business.

If Given in Adjustment

Accounting Treatment

Adjusting Entries		Profit and Loss Account	Balance Sheet
Interest on Capital A/c To Capital A/c (Being interest on capital provided)	Dr	Shown as an expense on the debit side as a separate item.	Shown on the liabilities side by way of addition to the capital.
Profit and Loss A/c To Interest on Capital A/c (Being interest on capital transferred to profit and loss account)	Dr		

If Given in Trial Balance

Accounting Treatment

Profit and Loss Account	Balance Sheet
It will be shown on the debit side of profit and loss account.	Nil

EXAMPLE

Extract of Trial Balance
as on 31st March, 2016

Particulars	Debit Balance (₹)	Credit Balance (₹)
Capital		10,000

Additional Information

Interest on capital to be allowed @ 12% per annum.

Sol. **Adjusting Entries**

JOURNAL

Interest on Capital A/c (10,000 × 12 / 100) Dr			1,200	
To Capital				1,200
(Being interest on capital provided)				
Profit and Loss A/c Dr			1,200	
To Interest on Capital A/c				1,200
(Being interest on capital transferred to profit and loss account)				

Effect on Final Accounts

Profit and Loss Account
Dr for the year ended 31st March, 2016 Cr

Particulars	Amt (₹)	Particulars	Amt (₹)
To Interest on Capital A/c	1,200		

Balance Sheet
as at 31st March, 2016

Liabilities		Amt (₹)	Assets	Amt (₹)
Capital				
Opening Balance	10,000			
(+) Interest on Capital	1,200	11,200		

12. Interest on Drawings

When the owner/proprietor withdraws money for his personal use, it is termed as drawings.

Interest on drawings is charged from the owner for the withdrawals made by him. Therefore, it is an expense for the owner and an income for the business.

If Given in Adjustments

Accounting Treatment

Adjusting Entries	Profit and Loss Account	Balance Sheet
Drawings A/c Dr To Interest on Drawings A/c (Being interest on drawings adjusted)	Shown as a gain on the credit side.	Shown by way of deduction from capital on the liabilities side.
Interest on Drawings A/c Dr To Profit and Loss A/c (Being interest on drawings transferred to profit and loss account)		

If Given in Trial Balance

Accounting Treatment

Profit and Loss Account	Balance Sheet
It will be shown in the credit side of profit and loss account.	Nil

EXAMPLE

Extracts of Trial Balance
as at 31st March, 2016

Particulars	Debit Balance (₹)	Credit Balance (₹)
Capital A/c		10,00,000
Drawings A/c	1,60,000	

Adjustment : Charge ₹ 6,000 as interest on drawings.

***Sol.* Adjustment Entries**

JOURNAL

Particulars		Dr (₹)	Cr (₹)
Drawings A/c	Dr	6,000	
To Interest on Drawings A/c			6,000
(Being interest charged on drawings)			
Interest on Drawings A/c	Dr	6,000	
To Profit and Loss A/c			6,000
(Being interest on drawings credited to profit and loss account)			

Dr **Profit and Loss Account** Cr

Particulars	Amt (₹)	Particulars	Amt (₹)
		By Interest on Drawings	6,000

Balance Sheet

Liabilities		Amt (₹)	Assets	Amt (₹)
Capital	10,00,000			
(–) Drawings	1,60,000			
	8,40,000			
(–) Interest on Drawings	6,000	8,34,000		

13. Interest on Loan

If the business has taken a loan, then interest on such loan will be an expense for the firm.

If Given in Adjustment

Accounting Treatment

Adjusting Entries	Profit and Loss Account	Balance Sheet
Interest on Loan A/c Dr To Loan A/c (Being interest on loan provided)	Shown on the debit side as a separate item.	Outstanding amount of interest will be added to loan account on the liability side.
Profit and Loss A/c Dr To Interest on Loan A/c (Being interest on loan debited to profit and loss account)		

If Given in Trial Balance

Accounting Treatment

Profit and Loss Account	Balance Sheet
Shown on the debit side	Nil

EXAMPLE

Extract of Trial Balance
as on 31st December, 2016

Loan from Vishal		10,000

Adjustment: Interest on Vishal's loan is to be given @ 5% per annum for the whole year.

Sol. **Adjustment Entries**

JOURNAL

Interest on Loan A/c To Vishal's Loan A/c (Being interest on Vishal's loan provided @ 5% per annum)	Dr	500	 500
Profit and Loss A/c To Interest on Loan A/c (Being interest on loan debited to profit and loss account)	Dr	500	 500

Effect on Final Accounts

Profit and Loss Account
Dr for the year ended 31st December, 2016 Cr

Particulars	Amt (₹)	Particulars	Amt (₹)
To Interest on Loan	500		

Balance Sheet
as at 31st December, 2016

Liabilities		Amt (₹)	Assets	Amt (₹)
Vishal's Loan	10,000			
(+) Interest	500	10,500		

Interest on Loan Given

When loan appears on the debit side of trial balance, it means the amount has been lend to outsiders. It is an asset for the firm and interest on such loan will be an income for the firm.

If Given in Adjustment

Accounting Treatment

Adjusting Entries	Profit and Loss Account	Balance Sheet
Loan A/c Dr To Interest on Loan A/c (Being interest on loan due to be received)	Shown on the credit side as a separate item.	Accrued interest on such loan will be added to loan account on the assets side.
Interest on Loan A/c Dr To Profit and Loss A/c (Being interest on loan given credited to profit and loss account)		

If Given in Trial Balance

Accounting Treatment

Profit and Loss Account	Balance Sheet
Shown on the credit side	Nil

EXAMPLE

Extract of the Trial Balance
as on 31st December, 2016

Loan to Kartik	16,000	

Adjustment Interest on Kartik's loan is due to be received @ 12% per annum for the whole year.

Sol. **Adjustment Entries**

JOURNAL

Kartik's Loan A/c	Dr	1,920	
To Interest on Loan A/c			1,920
(Being interest on Kartik's loan due to be received)			
Interest on Loan A/c	Dr	1,920	
To Profit and Loss A/c			1,920
(Being interest on loan credited to profit and loss account)			

Effect on Final Accounts

Profit and Loss Account
Dr for the year ended 31st December, 2016 Cr

Particulars	Amt (₹)	Particulars	Amt (₹)
		By Interest on Loan	1,920

Balance Sheet
as at 31st December, 2016

Liabilities	Amt (₹)	Assets		Amt (₹)
		Kartik's Loan	16,000	
		(+) Interest	1,920	17,920

ILLUSTRATION |4| (Based on adjustments from 7 to 13) Prepare trading account, profit and loss account and balance sheet from the following particulars for the year ended 31st December, 2015.

Particulars	Amt (Dr)	Amt (Cr)
Cash in Hand	7,600	
Cash at Bank	16,218	
Purchases and Sales	3,16,000	6,50,000
Return Inwards	5,000	
Return Outwards		3,600
Carriage on Purchases	2,000	
Carriage on Sales	600	
Fuel and Power	7,800	
Stock 1.1.2015	56,420	
Building	1,64,000	
Machinery	2,25,000	
Debtors and Creditors	1,44,000	44,000
Investments	1,00,000	
Interest on Investments		2,000

Particulars	Amt (Dr)	Amt (Cr)
Loan from Narayan on 1.7.2015 @ 10% per annum		40,000
Repairs	8,562	
General Expenses	40,800	
Provision for Bad Debts		4,200
Wages and Salaries	39,440	
Miscellaneous Receipts		9,040
Interest on Mr Narayan's Loan	1,400	
Capital		4,00,000
Drawings	18,000	
	11,52,840	11,52,840

Adjustments

(i) Bad debts ₹ 2,000.

(ii) Provision for doubtful debts is to be maintained at 5% on sundry debtors.

(iii) Provision for 2% discount on debtors and creditors.

(iv) Manager is entitled to get the commission at 10% on net profit after charging such commission.

(v) Closing stock was valued at ₹ 60,000.

(vi) Allow interest on capital @ 10%.

(vii) Charge ₹ 1,000 as interest on drawings.

Sol.

Trading and Profit and Loss Account

Dr — for the year ending 31st December, 2015 — Cr

Particulars		Amt (₹)	Particulars		Amt (₹)
To Opening Stock		56,420	By Sales	6,50,000	
To Purchases	3,16,000		(–) Return Inwards	5,000	6,45,000
(–) Return Outwards	3,600	3,12,400	By Closing Stock		60,000
To Carriage on Purchases		2,000			
To Fuel and Power		7,800			
To Wages and Salaries		39,440			
To Gross Profit c/d		2,86,940			
		7,05,000			7,05,000
To Carriage on Sales		600	By Gross Profit b/d		2,86,940
To Repairs		8,562	By Interest on Investments		2,000
To General Expenses		40,800	By Miscellaneous Receipts		9,040
To Further Bad Debts	2,000		By Provision for Discount on Creditors		880
(+) New Provision	7,100		By Interest on Drawings		1,000
	9,100				
(–) Old Provision	4,200	4,900			
To Interest on Narayan's Loan	1,400				
(+) Outstanding Interest	600	2,000			
To Provision for Discount on Debtors		2,698			
To Interest on Capital (4,00,000×10%)		40,000			
To Manager's Commission (Outstanding)		18,209			
To Net Profit Transferred to Capital A/c		1,82,091			
		2,99,860			2,99,860

Balance Sheet
as on 31st December, 2015

Liabilities		Amt (₹)	Assets		Amt (₹)
Sundry Creditors	44,000		Cash in Hand		7,600
(–) Provision for Discount			Cash at Bank		16,218
On Creditors @ 2%	880	43,120	Sundry Debtors	1,44,000	
Narayan's Loan	40,000		(–) Bad Debts	2,000	
(+) Outstanding Interest	600	40,600		1,42,000	
Manager's Commission		18,209	(–) Provision for Bad		
Capital	4,00,000		Debts @ 5%	7,100	
(+) Interest on Capital	40,000		(–) Provision for	1,34,900	
	4,40,000		Discount on Debtors @ 2%	2,698	1,32,202
(+) Net Profit	1,82,091		Closing Stock		60,000
	6,22,091		Investments		1,00,000
(–) Drawings	18,000		Machinery		2,25,000
	6,04,091		Building		1,64,000
(–) Interest on Drawings	1,000	6,03,091			
		7,05,020			7,05,020

Working Note

- Manager's commission = $(2{,}99{,}860 - 99{,}560) = 2{,}00{,}300 \times \frac{10}{110} = ₹\ 18{,}209$
- Interest on loan = $40{,}000 \times \frac{10}{100} \times \frac{6}{12} = ₹\ 2{,}000$

(–) Already paid = 1,400
Outstanding = ₹ 600

14. Abnormal or Accidental Losses

Sometimes losses occur due to some abnormal circumstances such as fire, theft, earthquake, accidents, abnormal spoilage/leakage/breakages/pilferage, etc. such losses are called abnormal losses.

In this case, trading account will be credited with the cost of the goods destroyed.

If the goods destroyed are not insured, the cost of goods destroyed is debited to profit and loss account.

In case the goods are insured, the claim admitted by the insurance company is deducted and the claim not admitted, is debited to profit and loss account.

Insurance company's account will be shown as an asset in the balance sheet.

If Given in Adjustment

Accounting Treatment

Adjusting Entries		Trading Account	Profit and Loss Account	Balance Sheet
Loss of Stock A/c To Trading A/c (Being the loss of stock by fire)	Dr	The total value of abnormal loss is shown on the credit side as a separate item, whether recovered or not.	The total value of irrecovered loss of stock, is shown on the debit side as a separate item. Irrecovered Loss = (Total Loss – Amount Recovered from Insurance Company)	Any amount, which is due from the insurance company is shown on the assets side.
Insurance Claim/Insurance Company A/c Profit and Loss A/c To Loss of Stock A/c (Being the insurance company admitted a partial claim only)	Dr Dr			

If given in Trial Balance

Accounting Treatment

Trading A/c	Profit and Loss Account	Balance Sheet
—	Shown on the debit side	—

EXAMPLE On 28th March, 2016 stock worth ₹ 80,000 were destroyed by fire. The stock was insured and the insurance company admitted a claim of ₹ 60,000 only. Give the necessary journal entries and show how it will be treated in the final accounts.

Sol. **Adjustment Entries**

JOURNAL

Date	Particulars		LF	Amt (Dr)	Amt (Cr)
2016					
Mar 31	Loss by Fire A/c	Dr		80,000	
	To Trading A/c				80,000
	(Being the loss of stock by fire)				
Mar 31	Insurance Company A/c	Dr		60,000	
	Profit and Loss A/c	Dr		20,000	
	To Loss by Fire A/c				80,000
	(Being the insurance company admitted a partial claim only)				

Effect on Final Accounts

Trading Account
Dr for the year ended 31st March, 2016 Cr

Particulars	Amt (₹)	Particulars	Amt (₹)
		By Loss by Fire A/c	80,000

Profit and Loss Account
Dr for the year ended 31st March, 2016 Cr

Particulars		Amt (₹)	Particulars	Amt (₹)
To Loss by Fire A/c	80,000			
(–) Insurance Claim	60,000	20,000		

Balance Sheet
as at 31 March, 2016

Liabilities	Amt (₹)	Assets	Amt (₹)
		Claim Due from Insurance Company	60,000

15. Goods Taken for Personal Use

When the goods are taken by the proprietor for his personal use from the business, it is treated as drawings.

If Given in Adjustment

Accounting Treatment

Adjusting Entry		Trading Account	Balance Sheet
Drawings A/c To Purchases A/c	Dr	Deduct drawings of goods (cost) from purchases on the debit side.	Deduct it from capital on the liabilities side.

If Given in Trial Balance

Accounting Treatment

Trading A/c	Balance Sheet
—	Deduct it from capital

EXAMPLE

Extract of Trial Balance
as at 31st March, 2016

Name of Accounts	Debit Balance (₹)	Credit Balance (₹)
Purchases	1,00,000	
Capital		3,00,000

Additional Information

During the year, the proprietor, Mr Rajesh withdrew goods worth ₹ 5,000.

Pass an adjusting entry and show effect on financial statements.

***Sol.* Adjusting Entry**

JOURNAL

Date	Particulars		LF	Amt (Dr)	Amt (Cr)
	Drawings A/c	Dr		5,000	
	To Purchases A/c				5,000

Effect on Financial Statements

Trading Account
Dr — for the year ended 31st March, 2016 — Cr

Particulars		Amt (₹)	Particulars	Amt (₹)
To Purchases	1,00,000			
(–) Goods withdrawn by Proprietor	5,000	95,000		

Balance Sheet
as at 31st March, 2016

Liabilities		Amt (₹)	Assets	Amt (₹)
Capital	3,00,000			
(–) Goods Withdrawn by Proprietor	5,000	2,95,000		

16. Goods Distributed as Free Samples

With a view to promote sales, goods are distributed as free samples. When goods are distributed as free samples, the stock gets reduced.

If Given in Adjustment

Accounting Treatment

Adjusting Entry		Trading Account	Profit and Loss Account
Advertisement A/c To Purchases A/c (Being goods distributed as free sample)	Dr	Cost of goods distributed as free samples will be deducted from purchases on the debit side.	Shown on the debit side as advertisement expenses.

If Given in Trial Balance

Accounting Treatment

Trading Account	Profit and Loss Account
—	Shown on the debit side as advertisement expenses

ILLUSTRATION |5|

Extract of Trial Balance
as at 31st March, 2016

Name of Accounts	Debit Balance (₹)	Credit Balance (₹)
Purchases	1,00,000	

Additional Information

During the year the proprietor, Mr Rohan distributed goods worth ₹ 10,000 as free samples.
Pass an adjusting entry and show effect on financial statements.

Sol. **Adjusting Entry**

JOURNAL

Date	Particulars		LF	Amt (Dr)	Amt (Cr)
	Advertisement A/c	Dr		10,000	
	To Purchases A/c				10,000

Effect on Financial Statements

Trading Account
Dr for the year ended 31st March, 2016 Cr

Particulars		Amt (₹)	Particulars	Amt (₹)
To Purchases	1,00,000			
(–) Goods Distributed as Free Sample	10,000	90,000		

Profit and Loss Account
Dr for the year ended 31st March, 2016 Cr

Particulars	Amt (₹)	Particulars	Amt (₹)
To Avertisement Expenses	10,000		

ILLUSTRATION |6| (Based on adjustments 14 to 16)

From the following trial balance prepare trading account, profit and loss account and balance sheet for the year ended 31st December, 2016.

Account Title	Amt (₹)	Account Title	Amt (₹)
Capital	10,00,000	Sundry Creditors	97,000
Life Insurance Premium	8,000	Sales	12,00,000
Plant and Machinery	2,50,000	Returns Outwards	10,000
Stock in the Beginning	1,50,000	Discount (Dr)	8,000
Purchases	8,72,000	Discount (Cr)	12,000
Return Inwards	20,000	Rent for Premises Sublet	10,000
Sundry Debtors	2,10,000	Lighting	5,000
Furniture	92,000	Salaries	2,13,000
Freehold Property	4,00,000	Cash	1,58,000
Freight and Duty	20,000	Loan from Bank at 10% per annum on 1.1.2016	1,00,000
Carriage Inwards	8,000		
Carriage Outwards	2,000	Bank Interest (Dr)	9,000
Trade Expenses	4,000		

Adjustments

(i) Stock on 31st December, 2016 was valued at ₹ 3,00,000.

(ii) Stock for ₹ 50,000 was burnt by fire on 25th December, 2016 and the Insurance Company admitted the claim of ₹ 30,000.

(iii) Good worth ₹ 15,000 were distributed as free samples, goods worth ₹ 12,000 were used for personal purposes by the proprietor and goods worth ₹ 8,000 were given away as charity.

(iv) Use of goods in business worth ₹ 20,000.

(v) Machine worth ₹ 50,000 burnt by fire on 30th December, 2016 which was not insured.

Sol.

Trading and Profit and Loss Account

for the year ending 31st December, 2016

Dr Particulars		Amt (₹)	Particulars		Amt (₹) Cr
To Opening Stock		1,50,000	By Sales	12,00,000	
To Purchases	8,72,000		(−) Return Inwards	20,000	11,80,000
(−) Return Outwards	10,000		By Closing Stock		3,00,000
	8,62,000				
(−) Loss by Fire	50,000				
	8,12,000				
(−) Free Samples	15,000				
	7,97,000				
(−) Drawings in Goods	12,000				
	7,85,000				
(−) Charity in Goods	8,000				
	7,77,000				
(−) Use in Business	20,000	7,57,000			
To Freight and Duty		20,000			
To Carriage Inwards		8,000			
To Gross Profit c/d		5,45,000			
		14,80,000			14,80,000
To Carriage Outwards		2,000	By Gross Profit b/d		5,45,000
To Trade Expenses		4,000	By Discount Received		12,000
To Discount Allowed		8,000	By Rent		10,000
To Lighting		5,000			
To Salaries		2,13,000			
To Bank Interest	9,000				
(+) Interest Outstanding	1,000	10,000			
To Loss by Accident		20,000			
To Free Samples		15,000			
To Charity		8,000			
To Loss of Machine by Fire		50,000			
To Net Profit Transferred to Capital A/c		2,32,000			
		5,67,000			5,67,000

Balance Sheet
as at 31st December, 2016

Liabilities		Amt (₹)	Assets		Amt (₹)
Bank Loan	1,00,000		Cash		1,58,000
(+) Outstanding Interest	1,000	1,01,000	Sundry Debtors		2,10,000
Sundry Creditors		97,000	Closing Stock		3,00,000
Capital	10,00,000		Insurance Company		30,000
(+) Net Profit	2,32,000		Furniture		92,000
	12,32,000		Plant and Machinery	2,50,000	
(−) Life Insurance			(−) Loss by Fire	50,000	2,00,000
Premium (Drawings)	8,000		Freehold Property		4,00,000
	12,24,000		Use of Goods in Business		20,000
(−) Drawing in Goods	12,000	12,12,000			
		14,10,000			14,10,000

Working Note

$$\text{Interest on loan} = 1{,}00{,}000 \times \frac{10}{100} = ₹\,10{,}000$$

Already paid = ₹ 9,000

Outstanding = ₹ 1,000

17. Implied Adjustments

Like other adjustments, discussed earlier, the implied adjustment must also be adjusted at the time of preparing final accounts. Sometimes, a loan account is noticed in the trial balance, carrying a specific rate of interest. In such case, it is necessary to ascertain whether the full amount of interest due on the loan has been paid or not. Thus, interest is calculated even if nothing is mentioned in the adjustment about the interest. If no amount of interest is shown in the trial balance, the full amount of interest will be treated as outstanding. In case some amount of interest is shown in the trial balance, compare the amount of interest calculated with the amount of interest given in the trial balance and the difference if any, will be treated as outstanding interest.

Comprehensive Illustrations

ILLUSTRATION |7| From the following trial balance, prepare the trading and profit and loss account for the year ended 31st March, 2016 and the balance sheet as at that date.

Name of Accounts	Amt (₹)	Name of Accounts	Amt (₹)
Salaries	20,446	Sales	1,32,840
Bills Receivable	12,754	Capital	1,00,000
Investments	80,000	Provision for Doubtful Debts	5,000
Furniture	24,000	10% Loan (1st October, 2015)	20,000
Opening Stock	9,000	Discount Received	800
Purchases	60,000	Sundry Creditors	18,600
Sundry Debtors	40,000	Bills Payable	10,000
Interest on Loan	800	Outstanding Salaries	1,000
Insurance Premium	1,800	Bad debts Recovered	400
Wages	9,200	Interest on Investments	4,000
Rent	3,040	Trading Commission	14,000
Bad Debts	2,400		
Carriage Outwards	1,200		
Cash at Bank	20,000		

Name of Accounts	Amt (₹)	Name of Accounts	Amt (₹)
Depreciation on Furniture	5,000		
Accrued Commission	2,000		
Advertisement	15,000		
	3,06,640		3,06,640

Additional Information

(i) Closing stock ₹ 12,000.

(ii) Goods costing ₹ 2,000 were distributed as free samples while goods costing ₹ 1,000 were taken by the proprietor for personal use.

(iii) A credit sale of ₹ 4,000 was not recorded in the sales book.

(iv) Closing stock included goods costing ₹ 2,000 which were sold and recorded as sales but not delivered to the customer.

(v) Maintain provision for doubtful debts @ 5%.

Sol.

Trading and Profit and Loss Account
for the year ended 31st March, 2016

Dr | Cr

Particulars		Amt (₹)	Particulars		Amt (₹)
To Opening Stock		9,000	By Sales	1,32,840	
To Purchases	60,000		(+) Credit Sales	4,000	1,36,840
(–) Free Samples	2,000		By Closing Stock	12,000	
	58,000		(–) Cost of Goods Sold		
(–) Drawings of Goods	1,000	57,000	but not Delivered	2,000	10,000
To Wages		9,200			
To Gross Profit c/d		71,640			
		1,46,840			1,46,840
To Salaries		20,446	By Gross Profit b/d		71,640
To Interest on Loan	800		By Provision for Doubtful Debts		400
(+) Outstanding Interest on Loan	200	1,000	By Discount Received		800
To Insurance Premium		1,800	By Bad Debts Recovered		400
To Rent		3,040	By Interest on Investment		4,000
To Carriage Outwards		1,200	By Trading Commission		14,000
To Depreciation on Furniture		5,000			
To Advertisement		15,000			
To Free Samples		2,000			
To Net Profit Transferred to Capital A/c		41,754			
		91,240			91,240

Balance Sheet
as at 31st March, 2016

Liabilities		Amt (₹)	Assets		Amt (₹)
10% Loan		20,000	Bill Receivable		12,754
Outstanding Interest on Loan		200	Investments		80,000
Creditors		18,600	Furniture		24,000
Bills Payable		10,000	Debtors	40,000	
Outstanding Salaries		1,000	(+) Credit Sales not Recorded	4,000	
Capital	1,00,000			44,000	
(+) Net Profit	41,754		(–) New Provision	2,200	41,800
	1,41,754		Accrued Commission		2,000
(–) Drawings of Goods	1,000	1,40,754	Closing Stock		10,000
			Bank		20,000
		1,90,554			1,90,554

Working Note Interest on loan $= 20,000 \times \frac{10}{100} \times \frac{6}{12} =$ ₹ 1,000

(–) Already paid = ₹ (800)

Outstanding = ₹ 200

Calculation of Provision for Doubtful Debts

To Bad Debts	2,400
(+) New Provision	2,200
	4,600
(–) Old Provision	5,000
	(400)

Since the old provision is in excess of new provision the difference *i.e.*, 400 will be shown the credit side of profit and loss account.

ILLUSTRATION |8| The trial balance of Ramesh Vyas as on 31st March, 2016 was as follows

Name of Accounts	Debit Balance (₹)	Credit Balance (₹)
Purchases/Sales	81,25,250	1,26,20,000
Provision for Doubtful Debts		2,60,000
Sundry Debtors/Sundry Creditors	25,10,000	15,26,300
Bills Payable		1,97,500
Opening Stock	13,36,250	
Wages	11,56,850	
Salaries	2,78,750	
Furniture	3,62,500	
Postage	2,11,300	
Power and Fuel	67,500	
Trade Expenses	2,91,550	
Bad Debts	26,250	
Loan to Ram @ 10% (1st December, 2015)	1,50,000	
Cash in Hand and at Bank	5,00,000	
Trade Expenses Accrued but Not Paid		35,000
Drawings/Capital A/c	2,22,600	5,00,000
Outstanding Wages		1,00,000
	1,52,38,800	1,52,38,800

Prepare the trading and profit and loss account for the year ended 31st March, 2016 and the balance sheet as at that date after taking into consideration the following information.

(i) Stock on 31st March, 2016 was ₹ 6,27,500.

(ii) Depreciation on furniture is to be charged @ 10%.

(iii) Provision for doubtful debts is to be maintained @ 5% on sundry debtors.

(iv) Sundry debtors include an item of ₹ 25,000 due from a customer who has become insolvent.

(v) Goods of the value of ₹ 75,000 have been destroyed by fire and insurance company admitted a claim for ₹ 50,000

(vi) Received ₹ 60,000 worth of goods on 27th March, 2016 but the invoice of purchases was not recorded in purchases book.

Sol.

Trading and Profit and Loss Account
for the year ended 31st March, 2016

Dr Particulars		Amt (₹)	Particulars	Cr Amt (₹)
To Opening Stock		13,36,250	By Sales	1,26,20,000
To Purchases	81,25,250		By Abnormal Loss of goods by Fire	75,000
(+) Omitted Purchases	60,000	81,85,250	By Closing Stock	6,27,500
To Wages		11,56,850		
To Power and Fuel		67,500		
To Gross Profit c/d		25,76,650		
		1,33,22,500		1,33,22,500
To Loss by Fire	75,000		By Gross Profit b/d	25,76,650
(–) Insurance Claim	50,000	25,000	By Provision for Doubtful Debts	84,500
To Salaries		2,78,750	By Accrued Interest on Loan	5,000
To Postage		2,11,300		
To Trade Expenses		2,91,550		
To Depreication on Furniture		36,250		
To Net Profit Transferred to Capital A/c		18,23,300		
		26,66,150		26,66,150

Balance Sheet
as at 31st March, 2016

Liabilities		Amt (₹)	Assets		Amt (₹)
Creditors	15,26,300		Claim from Insurance Company		50,000
(+) Omitted Purchases	60,000	15,86,300	Cash in Hand and at Bank		5,00,000
Bills Payable		1,97,500	Closing Stock		6,27,500
Outstanding Wages		1,00,000	Sundry Debtors	25,10,000	
Trade Expenses Accrued		35,000	(–) Bad Debts	25,000	
Capital	5,00,000			24,85,000	
(–) Drawings	2,22,600		(–) Provision for Doubtful Debts	1,24,250	23,60,750
	2,77,400		Loan to Ram	1,50,000	
(+) Net Profit	18,23,300		(+) Accrued Interest	5,000	1,55,000
		21,00,700	Furniture	3,62,500	
			(–) Depreciation	36,250	3,26,250
		40,19,500			40,19,500

Working Note

1. Depreciation on furniture $= 3{,}62{,}500 \times \frac{10}{100} = 36{,}250$
2. Interest on loan $= 1{,}50{,}000 \times \frac{10}{100} \times \frac{4}{12} = 5{,}000$
3.

Bad Debts	26,250
(+) Further Bad Debts	25,000
	51,250
(+) New Provision	1,24,250
	1,75,500
(–) Old Provision	2,60,000
	(84,500)

4. Purchases were omitted to be recorded in purchases book, implying that it was a credit transaction.

ILLUSTRATION |9| From the following trial balance extracted from the books of MMN, prepare the trading and profit and loss account for the year ended 31st December, 2016 and the balance sheet as at that date.

Name of Accounts	Debit Balance (₹)	Credit Balance (₹)
Capital		90,000
Drawings	6,480	
Land and Buiding	25,000	
Plant and Machinery	14,270	
Furniture and Fixtures	1,250	
Carriage Inwards	4,370	
Wages	21,470	
Salaries	4,670	
Provision for Bad Debts		2,470
Sales		91,230
Sales Return	1,760	
Bank Charges	140	
Coal, Gas and Water	720	
Rates and Taxes	840	
Discount		120
Purchases	42,160	
Purchases Return		8,460
Bills Receivable	1,270	
Trade Expenses	1,990	
Sundry Debtors	37,800	
Sundry Creditors		12,170
Stock (1st January, 2016)	26,420	
Apprentice Premium		500
Fire Insurance	490	
Cash at Bank	13,000	
Cash in Hand	850	
Total	2,04,950	2,04,950

Additional Adjustments

Charge depreciation on land and building at $2\frac{1}{2}\%$, on plant and machinery account at 10% and on furniture and fixtures at 10%. Make a provision of 5% on debtors for doubtful debts. Carry forward the following unexpired amounts.

(i) Fire insurance ₹ 125
(ii) Rates and taxes ₹ 240
(iii) Apprentice premium ₹ 400
(iv) Closing stock ₹ 29,390

Sol.

Trading and Profit and Loss Account

Dr   for the year ended 31st December, 2016   Cr

Particulars		Amt (₹)	Particulars		Amt (₹)
To Opening Stock		26,420	By Sales	91,230	
To Purchases	42,160		(–) Sales Return	1,760	89,470
(–) Purchases Return	8,460	33,700	By Closing Stock		29,390
To Wages		21,470			
To Carriage Inwards		4,370			

Particulars		Amt (₹)	Particulars		Amt (₹)
To Coal, Gas and Water		720			
To Gross Profit c/d		32,180			
		1,18,860			1,18,860
To Salaries		4,670	By Gross Profit b/d		32,180
To Bank Charges		140	By Discount Received		120
To Rates and Taxes	840		By Apprentice Premium	500	
(–) Prepaid	240	600	(–) Unexpired	400	100
To Trade Expenses		1,990	By Old Provision for Doubtful Debts		2,470
To Fire Insurance	490				
(–) Prepaid	125	365			
To Provision for Doubtful Debts		1,890			
To Depreciation on					
Land and Building	625				
Plant and Machinery	1,427				
Furniture and Fixtures	125	2,177			
To Net Profit Transferred to Capital A/c		23,038			
		34,870			34,870

Balance Sheet
as at 31st December, 2016

Liabilities		Amt (₹)	Assets		Amt (₹)
Sundry Creditors		12,170	Land and Building	25,000	
Apprentice Premium Received in Advance		400	(–) Depreciation	625	24,375
Capital	90,000		Plant and Machinery	14,270	
(+) Net Profit	23,038		(–) Depreciation	1,427	12,843
	1,13,038		Furniture and Fixtures	1,250	
(–) Drawings	6,480	1,06,558	(–) Depreciation	125	1,125
			Sundry Debtors	37,800	
			(–) Provision for Doubtful Debts	1,890	35,910
			Bills Receivable		1,270
			Closing Stock		29,390
			Cash at Bank		13,000
			Cash in Hand		850
			Prepaid Fire Insurance		125
			Prepaid Rates and Taxes		240
		1,19,128			1,19,128

Working Note

1. Depreciation on land and building $= 25{,}000 \times \frac{2.5}{100} =$ ₹ 625
2. Depreciation on plant and machinery $= 14{,}270 \times \frac{10}{100} =$ ₹ 1,427
3. Depreciation on furniture and fixtures $= 1{,}250 \times \frac{10}{100} =$ ₹ 125
4. Provision for doubtful debts $= 37{,}800 \times \frac{5}{100} =$ ₹ 1,890

ILLUSTRATION |10| The following were the balances extracted from the books of Yogita as on 31st March, 2016.

Debit Balances	Amt (₹)	Credit Balances	Amt (₹)
Cash in Hand	540	Sales	98,780
Cash at Bank	2,630	Returns Outward	500
Purchases	40,675	Capital Account	62,000
Returns Inward	680	Sundry Creditors	6,300
Wages	8,480	Rent	9,000
Fuel and Power	4,730		
Carriage on Sales	3,200		
Carriage on Purchases	2,040		
Opening Stock	5,760		
Building	32,000		
Freehold Land	10,000		
Machinery	20,000		
Salaries	15,000		
Patents	7,500		
General Expenses	3,000		
Insurance	600		
Drawings	5,245		
Sundry Debtors	14,500		

Taking into account the following adjusments, prepare the trading and profit and loss account and balance sheet as at 31st March, 2016 .

(i) Stock in hand on 31st March, 2016 was ₹ 6,800.
(ii) Machinery is to be depreciated @ 10% and patents @ 20%.
(iii) Salaries for the month of March, 2013 amounting to ₹ 1,500 were outstanding.
(iv) Insurance includes an annual premium of ₹ 170 on a policy expiring on 30th September, 2016.
(v) Further bad debts are ₹725. Create a provision of 5% on debtors.
(vi) Rent receivable ₹ 1,000.

Sol.

Trading and Profit and Loss Account

Dr — for the year ended 31st March, 2016 — Cr

Particulars		Amt (₹)	Particulars		Amt (₹)
To Opening Stock		5,760	By Sales	98,780	
To Purchases	40,675		(–) Returns Inward	680	98,100
(–) Returns Outward	500	40,175	By Closing Stock		6,800
To Wages		8,480			
To Fuel and Power		4,730			
To Carriage on Purchases		2,040			
To Gross Profit c/d		43,715			
		1,04,900			1,04,900
To Carriage on Sales		3,200	By Gross Profit b/d		43,715
To Salaries	15,000		By Rent	9,000	
(+) Outstanding Salaries	1,500	16,500	(+) Rent Receivable	1,000	10,000
To General Expenses		3,000			
To Insurance	600				
(–) Unexpired Insurance	85	515			

Particulars		Amt (₹)	Particulars	Amt (₹)
To Further Bad Debts	725			
(+) New Provision	689	1,414		
To Depreciation on Machinery		2,000		
To Depreciation on Patents		1,500		
To Net Profit Transferred to Capital A/c		25,586		
		53,715		53,715

Balance Sheet
as at 31st March, 2016

Liabilities		Amt (₹)	Assets		Amt (₹)
Creditors		6,300	Cash in Hand		540
Salaries Outstanding		1,500	Cash at Bank		2,630
Capital	62,000		Closing Stock		6,800
(+) Net Profit	25,586		Sundry Debtors	14,500	
	87,586		(–) Further Bad Debts	725	
(–) Drawings	5,245	82,341		13,775	
			(–) Provision for Bad Debts	689	13,086
			Rent Receivable		1,000
			Prepaid Insurance		85
			Patents	7,500	
			(–) Depreciation	1,500	6,000
			Freehold Land		10,000
			Building		32,000
			Machinery	20,000	
			(–) Depreciation	2,000	18,000
		90,141			90,141

Working Note

1. Depreciation on machinery $= 20{,}000 \times \frac{10}{100} =$ ₹ 2,000
2. Depreciation on patents $= 7{,}500 \times \frac{20}{100} =$ ₹ 1,500
3. Prepaid insurance $= 170 \times \frac{6}{12} = 85$ (from April to September 2016)
4. Provision for doubtful debts $= (14{,}500 - 725) \times \frac{5}{100} =$ ₹ 689

ILLUSTRATION |11| Suresh started buisness on 1st April, 2015 with a capital of ₹ 30,000. The following trial balance was drawn up from his books at the end of the year.

Name of Accounts	Amt (₹)	Name of Accounts	Amt (₹)
Drawings	4,500	Capital	40,000
Plant and Fixtures	8,000	Sales	1,60,000
Purchases	1,16,000	Creditors	12,000
Carriage Inwards	2,000	Bills Payable	9,000
Wages	8,000		
Return Inwards	4,000		
Salaries	10,000		
Printing	800		
Advertisement	1,200		

Name of Accounts	Amt (₹)	Name of Accounts	Amt (₹)
Trade Charges	600		
Rent	1,400		
Debtors	25,000		
Bills Receivable	5,000		
Investments	15,000		
Discount	500		
Cash at Bank	16,000		
Cash in Hand	3,000		
	2,21,000		2,21,000

The value of stock as at 31st March, 2016 was ₹ 26,000. You are required to prepare his trading and profit and loss account for the year ended 31st March, 2016 and a balance sheet as on the date after taking the following facts into account.

(i) Interest on capital is to be provided at 6% per annum.
(ii) An additional capital of ₹ 10,000 was introduced by Suresh on 1st October, 2016.
(iii) Plant and fixtures are to be depreciated by 10% per annum.
(iv) Salaries outstanding on 31st March, 2014 amounted to ₹ 500.
(v) Accrued interest on investment amounted to ₹ 750.
(vi) ₹ 500 are bad debts and provision for doubtful debts is to be created at 5% on the balance of debtors.

Sol.

Trading and Profit and Loss Account
for the year ended 31st March, 2016

Dr | | | | | Cr

Particulars		Amt (₹)	Particulars		Amt (₹)
To Purchases		1,16,000	By Sales	1,60,000	
To Wages		8,000	(–) Return Inwards	4,000	1,56,000
To Carriage Inwards		2,000	By Closing Stock		26,000
To Gross Profit c/d		56,000			
		1,82,000			1,82,000
To Salaries	10,000		By Gross Profit b/d		56,000
(+) Outstanding Salaries	500	10,500	By Accrued Interest on Investment		750
To Printing		800			
To Advertisement		1,200			
To Trade Charges		600			
To Rent		1,400			
To Discount Allowed		500			
To Interest on Capital (W.N.)		2,100			
To Depreciation on Plant and Fixtures		800			
To Further Bad Debts	500				
(+) New Provision	1,225	1,725			
To Net Profit Transferred to Capital A/c		37,125			
		56,750			56,750

Balance Sheet
as at 31st March, 2016

Liabilities		Amt (₹)	Assets		Amt (₹)
Bills Payable		9,000	Cash in Hand		3,000
Creditors		12,000	Cash at Bank		16,000
Outstanding Salary		500	Bills Receivable		5,000
Capital	40,000		Debtors	25,000	
(+) Interest on Capital	2,100		(–) Bad Debts	500	
(+) Net Profit	37,125			24,500	
	79,225		(–) Provision for Doubtful Debts	1,225	23,275
(–) Drawings	4,500	74,725	Closing Stock		26,000
			Investments	15,000	
			(+) Accrued Interest	750	15,750
			Plant and Fixtures	8,000	
			(–) Depreciation	800	7,200
		96,225			96,225

Working Note

1. Interest on capital is calculated as follows

	Amt (₹)
On ₹ 30,000 @ 6% per annum for 1 year	1,800
On ₹ 10,000 @ 6% per annum for 6 months	300
	₹ 2,100

2. Depreciation on Plant and fixtures $= 8{,}000 \times \frac{10}{100} =$ ₹ 800

3. Provision for doubtful debts $= (25{,}000 - 500) \times \frac{5}{100} =$ ₹ 1,225

ILLUSTRATION |12| From the following trial balance of M/s Arjun & Sons as at 31st December, 2016 prepare trading and profit and loss account and balance sheet.

Name of Accounts	Debit Balance (₹)	Credit Balance (₹)
Drawings and Capital	18,000	80,000
Purchases and Sales	82,600	1,55,000
Stock (1st January, 2016)	42,000	
Returns Outward		1,600
Carriage Inward	1,200	
Wages	4,000	
Power	6,000	
Machinery	50,000	
Furniture	14,000	
Rent	22,000	
Salary	15,000	
Insurance	3,600	
8% Bank Loan		25,000
Debtors	20,600	
Creditors		18,900
Cash in Hand	1,500	
	2,80,500	2,80,500

Additional Information

(i) Closing stock ₹ 64,000. (ii) Wages outstanding ₹ 2,400.

(iii) Bad debts ₹ 600 and provision for bad doubtful debts to be 5% on debtors.

(iv) Rent is paid for 11 months. (v) Loan from the bank was taken on 1st July, 2016.

(vi) Provide depreciation on machinery @ 10% per annum.

(vii) Provide manager's commission at 10% on net profit after charging such commission.

Sol.

Trading and Profit and Loss Account
for the year ended 31st December, 2016

Dr | | | | | Cr

Particulars		Amt (₹)	Particulars	Amt (₹)
To Opening Stock		42,000	By Sales	1,55,000
To Purchases	82,600		By Closing Stock	64,000
(–) Returns Outwards	1,600	81,000		
To Carriage Inwards		1,200		
To Wages	4,000			
(+) Outstanding Wages	2,400	6,400		
To Power		6,000		
To Gross Profit c/d		82,400		
		2,19,000		2,19,000
To Rent	22,000		By Gross Profit b/d	82,400
(+) Outstanding Rent	2,000	24,000		
To Salary		15,000		
To Insurance		3,600		
To Outstanding Interest on Bank Loan		1,000		
To Further Bad Debts	600			
(+) New Provision	1,000	1,600		
To Depreciation on Machinery		5,000		
To Manager's Commission		2,927		
To Net Profit Transferred to Capital A/c		29,273		
		82,400		82,400

Balance Sheet
as at 31st December 2016

Liabilities		Amt (₹)	Assets		Amt (₹)
Bank Loan	25,000		Cash in Hand		1,500
(+) Outstanding Interest	1,000	26,000	Debtors	20,600	
Creditors		18,900	(–) Further Bad Debts	600	
Outstanding Wages		2,400		20,000	
Outstanding Rent		2,000	(–) Provision for Doubtful Debts	1,000	19,000
Manager's Commission		2,927	Closing Stock		64,000
Capital			Furniture		14,000
(+) Net Profit	80,000		Machinery	50,000	
(–) Drawings	29,273		(–) Depreciation	5,000	45,000
	1,09,273				
(–) Drawings	18,000	91,273			
		1,43,500			1,43,500

Working Note

1. Interest on bank loan will be calculated for 6 months i.e. from July to December. $25{,}000 \times \frac{8}{100} \times \frac{6}{12} = ₹1{,}000$
2. Rent per month $= \frac{22{,}000}{11} = 2{,}000$, $\therefore$ 2,000 will be the outstanding rent.
3. Depreciation on Machinery $= 50{,}000 \times \frac{10}{100} = ₹\,5{,}000$
4. Provision for Doubtful Debts $= (20{,}600 - 600) \times \frac{5}{100} = ₹\,1{,}000$
5. Manager's commission $= 82{,}400 - 50{,}200 = 32{,}200 \times \frac{10}{110} = 2{,}927$

ILLUSTRATION |13| The following is the trial balance of Ram Krishan Vyas on 31st March, 2016. Prepare trading and profit and loss account and balance sheet after making the following adjustments.

(i) Value of closing stock ₹ 29,638.

(ii) Depreciate plant and machinery @ 10%, furniture @ 5% and horses and carts by ₹ 1,000. Also write-off goodwill by ₹ 3,000.

(iii) Provide 5% for doubtful debts on debtors.

(iv) Prepaid expenses : Insurance ₹ 300 and taxes ₹ 190.

(v) $\frac{3}{5}$th of insurance and taxes, rent and general expenses to be charged to factory and the balance to the office.

(vi) Advertising is to be written-off over 3 years.

(vii) Commission to manager @ 10% on net profit after changing such commission.

Name of Accounts	Amt (₹)	Name of Accounts	Amt (₹)
Plant and Machinery	19,720	Capital	80,000
Manufacturing Wages	34,965	Creditors	50,160
Salaries	10,135	Bank Loan	10,000
Furniture	9,480	Purchases Return	1,140
Freight on Purchases	1,980	Sales	2,46,850
Freight on Sales	2,150	Provision for Bad Debts	6,000
Building	25,000		
Manufacturing Expenses	9,455		
Fuel and Power	1,276		
Electricity (Factory)	986		
Insurance and Taxes	4,175		
Goodwill	30,000		
Rent	2,400		
Debtors	78,140		
Stable Expenses	2,473		
Opening Stock	34,170		
Horses and Carts	5,165		
Purchases	97,165		
Sales Returns	3,170		
General Expenses	8,000		
Bad Debts	1,485		

Name of Accounts	Amt (₹)	Name of Accounts	Amt (₹)
Interest and Bank Charges	475		
Advertising	4,500		
Bank Balance	7,540		
Cash	145		
	3,94,150		3,94,150

Sol.

Trading and Profit and Loss Account
for the year ended 31st March, 2016

Dr | Cr

Particulars		Amt (₹)	Particulars		Amt (₹)
To Opening Stock		34,170	By Sales	2,46,850	
To Purchases	97,165		(–) Sales Return	3,170	2,43,680
(–) Purchases Return	1,140	96,025	By Closing Stock		29,638
To Manufacturing Wages		34,965			
To Freight on Purchases		1,980			
To Manufacturing Expenses		9,455			
To Fuel and Power		1,276			
To Electricity (Factory)		986			
To Insurance and Taxes		2,211			
To Rent		1,440			
To General Expenses		4,800			
To Gross Profit c/d		86,010			
		2,73,318			2,73,318
To Salaries		10,135	By Gross Profit b/d		86,010
To Freight on Sales		2,150	By Old Provision for Doubtful Debts		608
To Insurance and Taxes		1,474			
To Rent		960			
To Stable Expenses		2,473			
To General Expenses		3,200			
To Interest and Bank Charges		475			
To Advertising		1,500			
To Depreciation on					
Plant and Machinery	1,972				
Furniture	474				
Horses and Carts	1,000	3,446			
To Goodwill		3,000			
To Manager's Commission		5,255			
To Net Profit Transferred to Capital A/c		52,550			
		86,618			86,618

Balance Sheet
as at 31st March, 2016

Liabilities		Amt (₹)	Assets		Amt (₹)
Bank Loan		10,000	Cash		145
Creditors		50,160	Bank Balance		7,540
Manager's Commission		5,255	Debtors	78,140	
Capital	80,000		(–) New Provision for Doubtful Debts	3,907	74,233
(+) Net Profit	52,550	1,32,550	Closing Stock		29,638

Liabilities	Amt (₹)	Assets		Amt (₹)
		Prepaid Insurance and Taxes		490
		Furniture	9,480	
		(–) Depreciation	474	9,006
		Horses and Carts	5,165	
		(–) Depreciation	1,000	4,165
		Plant and Machinery	19,720	
		(–) Depreciation	1,972	17,748
		Buildings		25,000
		Advertising		3,000
		Goodwill		27,000
	1,97,965			1,97,965

Working Notes

1. Rent to be debited

   (i) in trading account $= 2{,}400 \times \frac{3}{5} =$ ₹ 1,440 (ii) in profit and loss account $= 2{,}400 \times \frac{2}{5} =$ ₹ 960

2. General expenses to be debited

   (i) in trading account $= 8{,}000 \times \frac{3}{5} =$ ₹ 4,800 (ii) in profit and loss account $= 8{,}000 \times \frac{2}{5} =$ ₹ 3,200

3. Insurance and taxes to be debited

   (i) in trading account $= (4{,}175 - 490) \times \frac{3}{5} =$ ₹ 2,211

   (ii) in profit and loss account $= (4{,}175 - 490) \times \frac{2}{5} =$ ₹ 1,474

4. Depreciation on

   (i) Plant and machinery $= 19{,}720 \times \frac{10}{100} =$ ₹ 1,972 (ii) Furniture $= 9{,}480 \times \frac{5}{100} =$ ₹ 474

5. Advertising to be debited to

   Profit and loss account $= 4{,}500 \times \frac{1}{3} =$ ₹ 1500

6. Manager's commission $= 86{,}618 - 28{,}813 = 57{,}805 \times \frac{10}{110} =$ ₹ 5,255

7. Calculation of Provision for Doubtful Debts

To Bad Debts	1,485
(+) New Provision	3,907
	5,392
(–) Old Provision	6,000
	(608)

When the resultant figure is negative, it will be shown on the credit side of profit and loss account.

ILLUSTRATION |14| Prepare trading, profit and loss account and balance sheet from the following particulars as on 31st March, 2016.

Name of Accounts	Debit Balance (₹)	Credit Balance (₹)
Cash in Hand	20,000	
Cash at Bank	1,80,000	
Purchase and Sales	22,00,000	35,00,000
Return Inwards	60,000	
Return Outwards		75,000
Carriage on Purchases	44,000	
Carriage on Sales	21,000	
Fuel and Power	1,55,000	
Stock (1st April, 2015)	3,60,000	
Bad Debts	62,000	
Bad Debts Provision		25,000
Debtors and Creditors	8,20,000	3,00,000
Capital		21,70,000
Investments	2,00,000	
Interest on Investments		20,000
Loan from X (@ 18% per annum)		1,00,000
Repairs	15,200	
General Expenses	1,06,000	
Land and Buildings	18,00,000	
Wages and Salaries	1,80,000	
Miscellaneous Receipts		1,200
Bills Payable		52,000
Stationery	20,000	
	62,43,200	62,43,200

Additional Information

(i) Written-off ₹ 20,000 as bad debts and provision for doubtful debts is to be maintained at 5% on debtors.

(ii) Loan from X was taken on 1st August, 2015. No interest has been paid so far.

(iii) Included in general expenses is insurance premium ₹ 12,000, paid for one year ending 30th June, 2016.

(iv) 1/3 of wages and salaries is to be charged to trading account and the balance to profit and loss account.

(v) Entire stationery was used by the proprietor for his personal own purpose.

(vi) Closing stock was valued at ₹ 5,00,000.

Sol.

Trading and Profit and Loss Account

for the year ended 31st March, 2016

Dr | Cr

Particulars		Amt (₹)	Particulars		Amt (₹)
To Stock 1st April, 2015		3,60,000	By Sales	35,00,000	
To Purchases	22,00,000		(–) Return inwards	60,000	34,40,000
(–) Return Outwards	75,000	21,25,000	By Closing Stock		5,00,000
To Carriage on Purchases		44,000			
To Fuel and Power		1,55,000			
To Wages and Salaries		60,000			
To Gross Profit c/d		11,96,000			
		39,40,000			39,40,000

Particulars		Amt (₹)	Particulars	Amt (₹)
To Carriage on Sales		21,000	By Gross Profit b/d	11,96,000
To Wages and Salaries		1,20,000	By Interest on Investments	20,000
To Repairs		15,200	By Miscellaneous Receipts	1,200
To General Expenses	1,06,000			
(–) Prepaid Insurance	3,000	1,03,000		
To Bad Debts	62,000			
(+) Further Bad Debts	20,000			
(+) New Provision for Doubtful Debts	40,000			
	1,22,000			
(–) Old Provision	25,000	97,000		
To Outstanding Interest		12,000		
To Net Profit Transferred to Capital A/c		8,49,000		
		12,17,200		12,17,200

Balance Sheet
as at 31st March, 2016

Liabilities		Amt (₹)	Assets		Amt (₹)
Bills Payable		52,000	Cash in Hand		20,000
Creditors		3,00,000	Cash at Bank		1,80,000
Loan from X	1,00,000		Debtors	8,20,000	
(+) Outstanding Interest	12,000	1,12,000	(–) Further Bad Debts	20,000	
Capital	21,70,000			8,00,000	
(+) Net Profit	8,49,000		(–) Provision for Doubtful Debts	40,000	7,60,000
	30,19,000		Closing Stock		5,00,000
(–) Drawings (Stationery used)	20,000	29,99,000	Prepaid Insurance		3,000
			Investments		2,00,000
			Land and Buildings		18,00,000
		34,63,000			34,63,000

Working Notes

1. Provision for Doubtful Debts

$$= (8{,}20{,}000 - 20{,}000) \times \frac{5}{100} = 40{,}000$$

2. Interest on loan (from August, 2015 to March, 2016)

$$= 1{,}00{,}000 \times \frac{18}{100} \times \frac{8}{12} = ₹\ 12{,}000$$

3. Prepaid Insurance Premium

$$= 12{,}000 \times \frac{3}{12} = 3{,}000$$

4. Wages and Salaries to be debited

(i) in trading account $= 1{,}80{,}000 \times \frac{1}{3} = 60{,}000$ (ii) in profit and loss account $= 1{,}80{,}000 \times \frac{2}{3} = 1{,}20{,}000$

ILLUSTRATION |15| Prepare trading and profit and loss account for the year ended 31st March, 2016 and a balance sheet as on that date from the following trial balance.

Name of Accounts	Amt (₹)	Name of Accounts	Amt (₹)
Stock on 1st April, 2015	16,000	Sales Less Returns	1,10,000
Purchases Less Returns	38,000	Sundry Creditors	15,000
SP Kumar	1,500	Capital	33,900
Wages	7,700	Mortgage and Interest to Date	7,800
Carriage Inwards	1,300	Rent Outstanding	500
Carriage Outwards	750		
Salaries	20,000		
Advertisements	4,500		
Trade Expenses	2,400		
Rent	6,000		
Establishment	2,700		
Stable Expenses	1,050		
Mortgage Interest	300		
Sundry Debtors	20,000		
Cash in Hand	1,250		
Machinery	43,750		
	1,67,200		1,67,200

Additional Adjustments

(i) Closing stock was ₹ 23,000.

(ii) Provision for doubtful debts be created on sundry debtors @ 5% and a provision for discount on sundry debtors at 2%.

(iii) Salary of ₹ 1,500 paid to SP Kumar an employee of the firm, stands debited to his personal account and it is to be corrected.

(iv) A stationery bill for ₹ 100 remains unpaid and unrecorded.

(v) Write-off one-third of advertisement expenses.

(vi) Sundry creditors include ₹ 5,000 loan taken from Mr Sudhir on 1st September, 2015 bearing interest @ 12% per annum.

Sol.

Trading and Profit and Loss Account

Dr for the year ending 31st March, 2016 Cr

Particulars		Amt (₹)	Particulars	Amt (₹)
To Opening Stock		16,000	By Sales Less Returns	1,10,000
To Purchases Less Returns		38,000	By Closing Stock	23,000
To Wages		7,700		
To Carriage Inwards		1,300		
To Gross Profit c/d		70,000		
		1,33,000		1,33,000
To Carriage Outwards		750	By Gross Profit b/d	70,000
To Salaries	20,000			
(+) Salary to P Kumar	1,500	21,500		
To Advertisements		1,500		
To Trade Expenses		2,400		
To Rent		6,000		

Particulars	Amt (₹)	Particulars	Amt (₹)
To Establishment	2,700		
To Stable Expenses	1,050		
To Mortgage Interest	300		
To Provision for Doubtful Debts	1,000		
To Provision for Discount on Debtors	380		
To Stationery	100		
To Outstanding Interest On Sudhir's Loan	350		
To Net Profit Transferred to Capital A/c	31,970		
	70,000		70,000

ILLUSTRATION |16| Given below is the trial balance of M/s Kartik and Sons as on 31st March, 2016.

Name of Accounts	Debit Balance (₹)	Credit Balance (₹)
Capital		14,40,000
Drawings	80,000	
Sales		20,30,000
Purchases	12,40,000	
Stock-in-Trade (1st April, 2015)	40,000	
Sales Return	24,000	
Purchases Return		30,000
Sundry Debtors	1,60,000	
Sundry Creditors		60,000
Rent	44,000	
Electricity	32,000	
Other Expenses	64,000	
Wages	2,24,000	
Cash in Hand	2,44,000	
Cash at Bank	12,64,000	
Advance to Supplier	1,44,000	
	35,60,000	35,60,000

Additional Information

(i) On scrutiny it is found that bank balance as per current account statement on 31st March, 2016 was ₹ 11,56,000. A cheque of ₹ 1,40,000 was collected from a debtor returned dishonoured and a cheque of ₹ 32,000 was deposited by another debtor directly.

(ii) Closing stock as on 31st March, 2016 was ₹ 80,000.

(iii) Purchases return ₹ 4,000 was wrongly posted as sales return but correctly debited to supplier's account.

(iv) Purchases day book is found overcast by ₹ 12,000.

(v) Sales day book is found undercast by ₹ 4,000.

You are required to (1) redraft the trial balance and (2) prepare the final accounts of M/s Kartik and Sons.

Sol.

Rectification Entries

Date	Particulars		LF	Amt (Dr)	Amt (Cr)
(i)	Debtors	Dr		1,40,000	
	To Bank A/c				1,40,000
	(Being the cheque dishonoured)				
(ii)	Bank A/c	Dr		32,000	
	To Debtors				32,000
	(Being the amount deposited into bank directly by debtor)				
(iii)	Suspense A/c	Dr		8,000	
	To Purchases Return A/c				4,000
	To Sales Return A/c				4,000
	(Being the purchases return wrongly recorded as sales return, now rectified)				
(iv)	Suspense A/c	Dr		12,000	
	To Purchases A/c				12,000
	(Being the overcasting in purchases book, now rectified)				
(v)	Suspense A/c	Dr		4,000	
	To Sales A/c				4,000
	(Being the undercasting of sales book, now rectified)				

Trial Balance (Redrafted)
as on 31st March, 2016

Name of Accounts	Debit Balance (₹)	Credit Balance (₹)
Capital		14,40,000
Drawings	80,000	
Sales (20,30,000 + 4,000)		20,34,000
Purchases (12,40,000 – 12,000)	12,28,000	
Stock-in-Trade (1st April, 2015)	40,000	
Sales Return (24,000 – 4,000)	20,000	
Purchases Return (30,000 + 4,000)		34,000
Sundry Debtors (1,60,000 + 1,40,000 – 32,000)	2,68,000	
Sundry Creditors		60,000
Rent	44,000	
Electricity	32,000	
Other Expenses	64,000	
Wages	2,24,000	
Cash in Hand	2,44,000	
Cash at Bank (12,64,000 – 1,40,000 + 32,000)	11,56,000	
Advance to Supplier	1,44,000	
Suspense A/c	24,000	
	35,68,000	35,68,000

Note *The existence of suspense account in the rectified trial balance implies that errors still exist.*

Trading and Profit and Loss Account
for the year ended 31st March, 2016

Dr | | | | | Cr

Particulars		Amt (₹)	Particulars		Amt (₹)
To Opening Stock		40,000	By Sales	20,34,000	
To Purchases	12,28,000		(–) Sales Return	20,000	20,14,000
(–) Purchases Return	34,000	11,94,000	By Closing Stock		80,000
To Wages		2,24,000			
To Gross Profit c/d		6,36,000			
		20,94,000			20,94,000
To Rent		44,000	By Gross Profit b/d		6,36,000
To Electricity		32,000			
To Other Expenses		64,000			
To Net Profit Transferred to Capital A/c		4,96,000			
		6,36,000			6,36,000

Balance Sheet
as at 31st March, 2016

Liabilities		Amt (₹)	Assets	Amt (₹)
Sundry Creditors		60,000	Cash in Hand	2,44,000
Capital	14,40,000		Cash at Bank	11,56,000
(+) Net Profit	4,96,000		Sundry Debtors	2,68,000
	19,36,000		Closing Stock	80,000
(–) Drawings	80,000	18,56,000	Advance to Supplier	1,44,000
			Suspense A/c	24,000
		19,16,000		19,16,000

Balance Sheet
as at 31st March, 2016

Liabilities		Amt (₹)	Assets		Amt (₹)
Sundry Creditors	15,000		Cash in Hand		1,250
(–) Loan from Sudhir	5,000	10,000	Sundry Debtors	20,000	
Outstanding Rent		500	(–) Provision for Doubtful Debts		
Outstanding Stationery		100		1,000	
Mortgage and Interest		7,800	(–) Provision for Discount	19,000	
Loan from Sudhir	5,000			380	18,620
(+) Outstanding Interest	350	5,350	Closing Stock		23,000
Capital	33,900		Machinery		43,750
(+) Net Profit	31,970	65,870	Advertisement Expenses		3,000
		89,620			89,620

Working Note

Interest on Sudhir's loan is outstanding for 7 months.

$$5{,}000 \times \frac{12}{100} \times \frac{7}{12} = ₹\ 350$$

ILLUSTRATION |17| From the following trial balance of Monika Textiles as at 31st March, 2016, prepare, trading and profit and loss account and balance sheet. Also pass the necessary adjustment entries.

Name of Accounts	Debit Balance (₹)	Credit Balance (₹)
Stock at Commencement	15,00,000	
Purchases and Sales	1,09,00,000	1,80,00,000
Manufacturing Wages	8,00,000	
Fuel, Power and Lighting	12,00,000	
Salaries	11,00,000	
Income Tax	5,50,000	
Loan to X @ (10% per annum)	5,00,000	
Interest on X's Loan		30,000
Apprentice Premium		4,50,000
Rent	4,00,000	
Rent Owing		60,000
Furniture (Includes furniture of 1,00,000 purchased on 1st October, 2015)	5,00,000	
Bills Receivable and Bills Payable	6,00,000	1,60,000
Plant	72,00,000	
Debtors and Creditors	28,00,000	13,00,000
Capital		1,00,00,000
Cash	19,50,000	
	3,00,00,000	3,00,00,000

Additional Information

(i) Closing stock was valued at ₹ 30,00,000.

(ii) Goods worth ₹ 5,00,000 were sold and despatched on 28th March, 2016 but no entry was passed to this effect.

(iii) Goods costing ₹ 7,00,000 were purchased and included into stock but no entry was passed to record the purchases.

(iv) Create a provision of 2% for discount on debtors.

(v) Apprentice premium received on 1st April, 2015 was for 3 years.

(vi) Depreciate furniture by 10% per annum.

(vii) Salaries for the month of March, 2016 are still outstanding.

Sol.

JOURNAL

Date	Particulars		LF	Amt (Dr)	Amt (Cr)
(i)	Closing Stock A/c	Dr		30,00,000	
	To Trading A/c				30,00,000
	(Being closing stock transferred to trading account)				
(ii)	Debtors A/c	Dr		5,00,000	
	To Sales A/c				5,00,000
	(Being goods sold but omitted to be recorded)				
(iii)	Purchase A/c	Dr		7,00,000	
	To Creditors A/c				7,00,000
	(Being goods purchased but omitted to be recorded)				
(iv)	Profit and Loss A/c	Dr		66,000	
	To Provision for Discount on Debtors A/c				66,000
	(Being provision for discount charged from profit and loss account)				

Date	Particulars		LF	Amt (Dr)	Amt (Cr)
(v)	Apprentice Premium A/c	Dr		3,00,000	
	To Apprentice Premium Received in Advance A/c				3,00,000
	(Being apprentice premium received in advance)				
(vi)	Depreciation A/c	Dr		45,000	
	To Furniture A/c				45,000
	(Being depreciation charged on furniture)				
(vii)	Salary A/c	Dr		1,00,000	
	To Salary Outstanding A/c				1,00,000
	(Being salary outstanding)				

Trading and Profit and Loss Account
for the year ending 31st March, 2016

Dr Cr

Particulars		Amt (₹)	Particulars		Amt (₹)
To Opening Stock		15,00,000	By Sales	1,80,00,000	
To Purchases	1,09,00,000		(+) Debtors	5,00,000	1,85,00,000
(+) Creditors	7,00,000	1,16,00,000	By Closing Stock		30,00,000
To Manufacturing Wages		8,00,000			
To Fuel, Power and Lighting		12,00,000			
To Gross Profit c/d		64,00,000			
		2,15,00,000			2,15,00,000
To Rent		4,00,000	By Gross Profit b/d		64,00,000
To Provision for Discount on Debtors		66,000	By Interest on X's Loan	30,000	
To Depreciation on Furniture (W.N)			(+) Accrued Interest	20,000	50,000
To Salaries	11,00,000	45,000	By Apprentice Premium	4,50,000	
(+) Outstanding Salaries	1,00,000	12,00,000	(−) Received in Advance	3,00,000	1,50,000
To Net Profit Transferred to Capital A/c		48,89,000			
		66,00,000			66,00,000

Balance Sheet
as at 31st March, 2016

Liabilities		Amt (₹)	Assets		Amt (₹)
Bills Payable		1,60,000	Cash		19,50,000
Creditors	13,00,000		Bills Receivable		6,00,000
(+) Purchases	7,00,000	20,00,000	Debtors	28,00,000	
Rent Owing		60,000	(+) Sales	5,00,000	
Apprentice Premium Received in Advance		3,00,000		33,00,000	
Salary Outstanding		1,00,000	(−) Provision for Discount	66,000	32,34,000
Capital	1,00,00,000		Closing Stock		30,00,000
(+) Net Profit	48,89,000		Loan to X		5,00,000
	1,48,89,000		Accrued Interest on X's Loan		20,000
(−) Drawings (Income Tax)	5,50,000	1,43,39,000	Furniture	5,00,000	
			(−) Depreciation	45,000	4,55,000
			Plant		72,00,000
		1,69,59,000			1,69,59,000

Working Note

(i) Calculation of depreciation on furniture is as follows

	Amt (₹)
Depreciation on 4,00,000 for 1 year	40,000
Depreciation on 1,00,000 for 6 months	5,000
	₹ 45,000

(ii) Income tax will be treated as drawings.

(iii) Salaries ₹11,00,000 given in trial balance are for 11 months. Therefore, 1 month salary ₹ 1,00,000 is outstanding.

(iv) Interest on loan $= 5{,}00{,}000 \times \frac{10}{100} = 50{,}000$

$= 30{,}000$

Accrued Interest $= 20{,}000$

ILLUSTRATION |18| **The following is the trial balance of Swati on 31st March, 2016.**

Name of Accounts	Debit Balance (₹)	Credit Balance (₹)
Purchases	3,00,000	
Debtors	4,00,000	
Interest Earned		8,000
Salaries	60,000	
Sales		6,42,000
Purchases Return		10,000
Wages	40,000	
Rent	30,000	
Sales Return	20,000	
Bad Debts Written-off	14,000	
Creditors		2,40,000
Capital		2,00,000
Drawings	48,000	
Provision for Doubtful Debts		12,000
Printing and Stationery	16,000	
Insurance	24,000	
Opening Stock	1,00,000	
Office Expenses	24,000	
Furniture and Fittings	40,000	
Provision for Depreciation		4,000
	11,16,000	11,16,000

Prepare the trading and profit and loss account for the year ended 31st March, 2016 and the balance sheet as at that date for making the following adjustments.

(i) Depreciate furniture and fittings by 10% on original cost.

(ii) Make a provision for doubtful debts equal to 5% of debtors.

(iii) Salaries for the month of March amounted to ₹ 6,000 were unpaid which must be provided for. The balance in the account includes ₹ 4,000 paid in advance.

(iv) Insurance is prepaid to the extent of ₹ 4,000.

(v) Provide ₹ 16,000 for office expenses.

(vi) Stock valued at ₹ 12,000 were put up by Swati for her personal use, the cost of which has not been adjusted in the books of accounts.

(vii) Closing stock valued at ₹ 1,36,000 (net realisable value ₹ 1,20,000).

Sol.

Trading and Profit and Loss Account
for the year ended 31st March, 2016

Dr Particulars		Amt (₹)	Particulars		Cr Amt (₹)
To Opening Stock		1,00,000	By Sales	6,42,000	
To Purchases	3,00,000		(–) Sales Return	20,000	6,22,000
(–) Purchases Return	10,000		By Closing Stock		1,20,000
	2,90,000				
(–) For Personal Use	12,000	2,78,000			
To Wages		40,000			
To Gross Profit c/d		3,24,000			
		7,42,000			7,42,000
To Salaries	60,000		By Gross Profit b/d		3,24,000
(+) Outstanding Salaries	6,000		By Interest Earned		8,000
	66,000				
(–) Paid in Advance	4,000	62,000			
To Rent		30,000			
To Bad Debts	14,000				
(+) New Provision	20,000				
	34,000				
(–) Old Provision	12,000	22,000			
To Printing and Stationery		16,000			
To Insurance	24,000				
(–) Prepaid	4,000	20,000			
To Office Expenses	24,000				
(+) Outstanding	16,000	40,000			
To Provision for Depreciation On Furniture and Fittings		4,000			
To Net Profit Transferred to Capital A/c		1,38,000			
		3,32,000			3,32,000

Balance Sheet
as at 31st March, 2016

Liabilities			Amt (₹)	Assets		Amt (₹)
Sundry Creditors			2,40,000	Stock		1,20,000
Outstanding Salaries			6,000	Debtors	4,00,000	
Outstanding Office Expenses			16,000	(–) Provision for Doubtful Debts	20,000	3,80,000
Capital		2,00,000		Prepaid Salaries		4,000
(+) Net Profit		1,38,000		Prepaid Insurance		4,000
		3,38,000		Furniture and Fittings	40,000	
(–) Drawings	48,000			(–) Provision for Depreciation	8,000	32,000
Stock for Personal Use	12,000	60,000	2,78,000			
			5,40,000			5,40,000

Working Note

1. Depreciation on Furniture & Fittings = $40,000 \times \frac{10}{100} = 4,000$
2. Balance in Provision for Depreciation Account = 4,000 + 4,000 = 8,000
3. Provision for Doubtful Debts = $4,00,000 \times \frac{5}{100} = 20,000$

CHAPTER PRACTICE

OBJECTIVE TYPE Questions

Multiple Choice Questions

1 Need or objective for adjustments in preparation of final accounts is
(a) to know the correct financial position
(b) to provide for all losses
(c) to reduce the liability
(d) to increase the assets

Ans (a) to know the correct financial position

2 Entries which need to be accounted for in the books of accounts at the time of preparing final accounts are called
(a) opening entries
(b) closing entries
(c) adjustment entries
(d) final account entry

Ans (c) adjustment entries

3 In case of sole proprietor business, income tax is considered as
(a) business expense (b) proprietor's expense
(c) capital expense (d) All of these

Ans (b) Income tax is considered as personal expense of the owner in business, so income tax will be added to drawings and subtracted from capital.

4 If the rent of one month is still to be paid the adjustment entry will be **NCERT**
(a) debit outstanding rent account and credit rent account
(b) debit profit and loss account and credit rent account
(c) debit rent account and credit profit and loss account
(d) debit rent account and credit outstanding rent account

Ans (d) debit rent account and credit outstanding rent account

5 If the rent received in advance ₹ 2,000. The adjustment entry will be **NCERT**
(a) debit profit and loss account and credit rent account
(b) debit rent account and credit rent received in advance account
(c) debit rent received in advance account and credit rent account
(d) None of the above

Ans (b) debit rent account and credit rent received in advance account

6 Goods distributed as free sample. The effect of this entry will be
(a) it is the proprietor drawings
(b) it is deducted from purchases in the trading account
(c) it will be shown on the debit side of the profit and loss account
(d) Both (b) and (c)

Ans (d) Both (b) and (c)

7 Manager's commission is always treated as .... expenses.
(a) outstanding (b) accrued
(c) unearned (d) prepaid

Ans (a) Manager commission is calculated on net profit of the firm. It is considered as an outstanding expense for the firm, so it is transferred to liabilities side of balance sheet.

8 If the insurance premium paid ₹ 1,000 and pre-paid insurance ₹ 300. The amount of insurance premium shown in profit and loss account will be **NCERT**
(a) ₹ 1,300 (b) ₹ 1,000
(c) ₹ 300 (d) ₹ 700

Ans (d) Total amount of insurance premium paid = ₹100
(−) Prepaid insurance =(₹300)
₹700

9 Consider the following statement.
I. Interest on capital is an expense for the proprietor.
II. Interest on capital is shown on the debit side of profit and loss account.
III. It is added to the capital in the balance sheet.

Choose the correct option.
(a) I, II, III are correct
(b) Both I and II are correct
(c) Both II and III are correct
(d) I, II, III are incorrect

Ans (c) Both II and III are correct

10 Loan from bank @ 12% per annum is ₹ 8,00,000. Interest on loan is due for the whole year.

Amount shown on liabilities side of balance sheet will be

(a) ₹ 8,00,000 (b) ₹8,12,000
(c) ₹ 8,90,000 (d) ₹8,96,000

Ans (d) *Amount transferred to liability side will be as follows*

$$\text{Interest} = \left(\frac{8{,}00{,}000 \times 12}{100}\right) = ₹\ 96{,}000$$

Total amount = 8,00,000 + 96,000 = ₹ 8,96,000

11 If the opening capital is ₹ 50,000 as on 1st April, 2016 and additional capital introduced ₹ 10,000 on 1st January, 2017. Interest charge on capital 10% p.a. The amount of interest on capital shown in profit and loss account as on 31st March, 2017 will be

(a) ₹ 5,250 (b) ₹ 6,000
(c) ₹ 4,000 (d) ₹ 3,000

Ans (a) Interest on Capital

10% p.a. on ₹ 50,000 on 12 months

$$= 50{,}000 \times \frac{10}{100} \times \frac{12}{12} = ₹5{,}000$$

10% on ₹ 10,000 on 3 months

$$= 10{,}000 \times \frac{10}{100} \times \frac{3}{12} = ₹\ 250$$

Total interest = 5,000 + 250 = ₹ 5,250

12 Consider the following information.

Cost of New Machine Purchased = ₹ 1,20,000

Installation Expenses = ₹ 30,000

Estimated Life of Machine = 5 years

Residual Value after 5 years = ₹ 25,000

Company started the production with this machine from 1st October, 2017. Assuming that the firm closes its accounts on 31st December every year, find the adjusted value of machine on 31st December, 2017?

(a) ₹ 1,43,750 (b) ₹ 1,25,000
(c) ₹ 1,75,000 (d) None of these

Ans (a) Value of machine = Depreciation on machine

$$= \left(\frac{1{,}20{,}000 + 30{,}000 - 25{,}000}{5}\right) \times \frac{3}{12} = ₹\ 6{,}250$$

So, adjusted value of machine = (Purchase value + Installation expenses − Depreciation)

$$= (1{,}20{,}000 + 30{,}000 - 6{,}250) = ₹\ 1{,}43{,}750$$

13 If capital of a firm = ₹ 5,00,000

Rate of interest @ 10%

Drawings = ₹ 30,000

What will be the net capital?

(a) ₹ 5,30,000 (b) ₹5,80,000
(c) ₹ 5,00,000 (d) ₹5,20,000

Ans (d) Interest on capital $= \frac{5{,}00{,}000 \times 10}{100} = ₹\ 50{,}000$

Net capital = (Capital + Interest on capital − Drawings)

$= 5{,}00{,}000 + 50{,}000 - 30{,}000 = ₹\ 5{,}20{,}000$

14 Rahul's trial balance provide you the following information.

Debtors	₹ 80,000
Bad debts	₹ 2,000
Provision for doubtful debts	₹ 4,000

It is desired to maintain a provision for bad debts of ₹ 1,000 state the amount to be debited/credited in profit and loss account. **NCERT**

(a) ₹ 5,000 (Debit) (b) ₹ 3,000 (Debit)
(c) ₹ 1,000 (Credit) (d) None of these

Ans (c)

Bad debts	= ₹ 2,000
New Provision	= ₹ 1,000
	₹ 3,000
(−) Old Provision	= (₹4,000)
	(₹ 1,000)

Fill in the Blanks

15 .... implies the value of unsold goods at the end of an accounting period.

Ans Closing stock

16 Depreciation refers to the decrease in the value of assets on account of wear and tear and ....

Ans passage of time

17 The income which is received during the current accounting year but it has not been earned, is called ....

Ans Unearned income

18 The amount which cannot be recovered from the .... is known as bad debts.

Ans debtors

19 If nothing is mentioned, the manager's commission should be allowed as a percentage of net profit .... charging such commission.

Ans before

State True or False

20 The cost of using the capital invested by the proprietor in an enterprise is interest on drawings.

Ans False. The cost of using the capital invested by the proprietor in an enterprise is interest on capital.

21 If the goods destroyed are not insured, the cost of goods destroyed is debited to profit and loss account.

Ans True

22 When the goods are taken by the proprietor for his personal use from the business, it is treated as sales.

Ans False. When the goods are taken by the proprietor for his personal use from the business, it is treated as drawings.

23 The expenses which become due during the current accounting period but are actually paid in the next accounting period are termed as outstanding expenses.

Ans True

Match the Following

24

Column I	Column II
1. Expenses due but not paid	(a) Unaccrued
2. Expenses paid but not due	(b) Accrued
3. Income due but not received	(c) Prepaid
4. Income received but not due	(d) Outstanding

Ans 1-(d), 2-(c), 3-(b), 4-(a)

25

Column I	Column II
1. Closing stock	(a) Current liability
2. Manager commission	(b) A court case
3. Depreciation	(c) Valued at cost or market price, whichever is low
4. Contingent liability	(d) Allocation of cost

Ans 1-(c), 2-(a), 3-(d), 4-(b)

Journalise the Following

26 **For prepaid insurance amounted to ₹ 200.**

Ans

Particulars		Dr	Cr
Prepaid Insurance A/c	Dr	200	
To Insurance A/c			200
(Being amount of prepaid insurance adjusted)			

27 **For interest on capital to be allowed.**

Ans

Particulars		Dr	Cr
Interest on Capital A/c	Dr	—	
To Capital A/c			—
(Being interest on capital allowed)			

28 **Interest on loan @ 6% p.a. is due for the whole year for a loan of ₹ 50,000.**

Ans

Particulars		Dr	Cr
Interest on Loan A/c	Dr	3,000	
To Outstanding Interest A/c			3,000
(Being interest on loan due)			

29 **To write-off further bad debts of ₹ 1,000.**

Ans

Particulars		Dr	Cr
Bad Debts A/c	Dr	1,000	
To Debtors A/c			1,000
(Being further bad debts written-off)			

30 **Goods worth ₹ 40,000 were burnt by fire and a claim of 80% has been accepted by the insurance company.**

Ans

Particulars		Dr	Cr
Insurance Claim A/c	Dr	32,000	
Profit and Loss A/c	Dr	8,000	
To Loss by Fire A/c			40,000
(Being goods lost by fire and 80% claim accepted by the insurance company)			

VERY SHORT ANSWER Type Questions

31 **If closing stock is given outside the trial balance, where will you show it in the final account?**

Ans If closing stock is given outside the trial balance it will be shown on the credit side of the trading account and also on the assets side of the balance sheet under the main head current assets.

32 **Why is closing stock valued at lower of cost or realisable value by accountants?**

Ans It is based on the principle of prudence (or conservatism) according to which all anticipated losses should be taken into account but all unrealised gains should be ignored.

33 **State the need for providing outstanding expenses in final accounts.**

Ans Outstanding expenses are provided as per the accrual concept of accounting according to which all expenses for the year, whether paid or not, should be recorded.

34 **Why are prepaid expenses segregated from the current year's expenses and taken to the balance sheet as a current asset?**

Ans Prepaid expenses are segregated from the current year's expenses and taken to the balance sheet as a current asset because such expenses relate to the next year.

35 **Rent paid on 1st October, 2014 for the year upto 30th September, 2015 was ₹ 1,200 and rent paid on 1st October, 2015 for the year up to 30th September, 2016 was ₹1,600. Find the rent payable, as shown in the profit and loss**

account for the year ended 31st December, 2015.

Ans ₹ 1,300 $\left(1,200\times\frac{9}{12}\right)+\left(1,600\times\frac{3}{12}\right)$

36 Net profit before the following adjustments ₹ 1,80,000
Outstanding salary ₹ 10,000
Prepaid insurance ₹ 13,000

Calculate profit after adjustments.

Ans 1,80,000 + 13,000 − 10,000 = ₹ 1,83,000

37 Following information is given in trial balance.

Bad debt	₹ 3,000
Provision for bad debts	₹ 3,500
Debtors	₹ 40,000

Additional information

It is desired to make a provision for doubtful debts @ of 10% on debtors. Find the amount to be debited to profit and loss account.

Ans ₹ 3,500

Provision for Doubtful Debts

Bad Debts	3,000
(+) New Provision @ 10%	4,000
	7,000
(−) Old Provision	(3,500)
	3,500

38 What is meant by provision for discount on debtors? **NCERT**

Ans It refers to the provision which is created to provide for discount to be allowed to good debtors (*i.e.*, sundry debtors less bad debts and the provision for doubtful debts).

39 Is provision for discount on debtors made before making provision for doubtful debts?

Ans No, provision for discount on debtors is made after making provision for doubtful debts from debtors.

40 By providing for discount on debtors and making provision for doubtful debts, which accounting concept is followed?

Ans Prudence or conservatism concept

41 Goods distributed as free samples are recorded at which value and why?

Ans Goods distributed as free samples are recorded at purchase cost because it is not a sale but advertisement expense.

42 Net profit of a firm before charging manager's commission is ₹ 21,000. If the manager is entitled to 5% commission after charging such commission, how much manager will get as commission?

Ans $21{,}000\times\frac{5}{105}$ = ₹ 1,000

43 Goods worth ₹ 3,00,000 were burnt by fire and claim of ₹ 1,80,000 has been accepted by the insurance company. How it will be recorded in final accounts?

Ans ₹ 3,00,000 will be deducted from purchases on the debit side of trading account, ₹ 1,20,000 will, be shown on the debit side of profit and loss account and ₹ 1,80,000 will be shown on the assets side of the balance sheet.

44 If depreciation reduces profits, reduces value of assets and also reduces capital of the proprietor, then why do enterprises provide for depreciation?

Ans Financial statements must show a true and fair view of the financial performance and position of the business. If depreciation is not provided, both fixed asset and profit will be shown at inflated amounts.

45 Accrued income is credited to the profit and loss account and shown in the balance sheet as a current asset. Why?

Ans Under the accrual concept of accounting, income is recognised when goods or services have been sold, whether the amount has been received or not. Since, it is income, it is credited to the profit and loss account. And since the amount is due to the enterprise, it is shown as a current asset in the balance sheet.

SHORT ANSWER Type Questions

46 What are the adjusting entries? Why are they necessary for preparing final accounts?

Or

Why is it necessary to record the adjusting entries in the preparation of final accounts? **NCERT**

Ans It is the entry passed to record expenses and incomes that relate to the accounting period but are yet to be paid or received.

The need of making various adjustments are stated below

(*i*) To ascertain the true profit or loss of the business.

(*ii*) To determine the true financial position of the business.

(*iii*) To make a record of the transactions earlier omitted in the books.

(*iv*) To rectify the errors committed in the books.

(*v*) To complete the incomplete transactions.

47 What is meant by closing stock? Show its treatment in final accounts. **NCERT**

Ans Closing stock implies the value of unsold goods at the end of an accounting period. Closing stock is valued at cost or net realisable value, whichever is lower.

If closing stock is given in adjustment it with be shown on the credit side of trading account and will also be shown on the assets side of balance sheet under current assets. If closing stock is given in trial balance, it will only be shown on the assets side of balance sheet under current assets.

48 State the meaning of **NCERT**

(i) Outstanding expenses
(ii) Prepaid expenses
(iii) Income received in advance
(iv) Accrued income

Ans (*i*) **Outstanding Expenses** Those expenses whose benefit have been derived during the current year but payment is not made at the end of the year are known as outstanding expenses.

(*ii*) **Prepaid Expenses** Those expenses which have been paid in current year but the benefit of which will be available in the next accounting year are known as prepaid expenses.

(*iii*) **Income Received in Advance** The income or portion of income which is received during the current accounting year but has not been earned is called unearned income.

(*iv*) **Accrued Income** It refers to the income which has been earned but not received during the current accounting period.

49 What is meant by provision for doubtful debts? What relevant accounts are prepared and what journal entries are recorded in final accounts? How is the amount for provision for doubtful debts calculated? **NCERT**

Ans The provision for doubtful debts is the estimated amount of bad debts that will arise from amount receivable from debtors.

A provision is created to cover possible loss on account of bad debts likely to occur in future. The relevant account prepared is 'provision for doubtful debts account'.

The following journal entry is recorded in the books of account.

Profit and Loss A/c Dr
To Provision for Doubtful Debts A/c
(Being adjustment for provision for doubtful debts)

The amount of provision for doubtful debts is calculated in the following manner

$$\text{(Debtors—Further Bad Debts)} \times \frac{\text{Percentage of Provision}}{100}$$

50 Show the treatment of prepaid expenses and depreciation, at the time of preparation of final accounts?

(i) When given inside the trial balance.
(ii) When given outside the trial balance. **NCERT**

Ans (*i*) **Prepaid Expenses**

If Given Outside the Trial Balance If the given expense is a direct expense it will be deducted from the related expense on the debit side of trading account.

If the given expense is a indirect expense it will be deducted from the related expense on the debit side of profit and loss account and it will be shown on the asset side of balance sheet under current assets.

If Given in Trial Balance In case prepaid expense is given outside the trial balance it will only be shown on the assets side as current asset.

(*ii*) **Depreciation**

If Given Outside the Trial Balance
Depreciation is shown as a separate item on the debit side of profit and loss account and is shown on the assets side of balance sheet by way of deduction from the value of concerned fixed assets.

If Given in Trial Balance It depreciation appears in the trial balance, it will only be shown on the debit side of profit and loss account.

51 Why is it necessary to create a provision for doubtful debts at the time of preparation of final accounts? **NCERT**

Ans In order to bring an element of certainty in amount of bad debts, a provision for doubtful debts is created to cover the loss of possible bad debts, as per the convention of conservatism.

52 What adjusting entries would you record for the following? **NCERT**

(i) Depreciation
(ii) Discount on debtors
(iii) Interest on capital
(iv) Manager's commission

Ans (*i*) **Depreciation–Adjusting Entry**

Depreciation A/c Dr

To Concerned Asset A/c *or*

To Provision for

Depreciation A/c

(Being depreciation charged)

(*ii*) **Discount on Debtors–Adjusting Entry**

Profit and Loss A/c Dr

To Provision for Discount on Debtors A/c

(Being adjustment of discount on debtors adjusted)

(*iii*) **Interest on Capital–Adjusting Entry**

Interest on Capital A/c Dr

To Capital A/c

(Being interest on capital adjusted)

(*iv*) **Manager's Commission–Adjusting Entry**

Manager's Commission A/c Dr

To Commission Payable/Outstanding Commission A/c

(Being manager commission adjusted)

NUMERICAL Questions

1 From the following balances, prepare trading, profit and loss account and a balance sheet as on 31st March, 2016.

Particulars	Amt (₹)	Particulars	Amt (₹)
Capital	1,64,000	Sundry Creditors	18,000
Life Insurance Premium	56,000	Sales	2,48,000
Plant and Machinery	10,000	Returns Outwards	2,000
Stock in the Beginning	30,000	Special Rebates (Debit)	1,600
Purchases	1,74,400	Special Rebates (Credit)	2,400
Return Inwards	12,000	Rent for Premises Sublet	2,000
Sundry Debtors	42,000	Lighting	800
Furniture	18,200	Motor Car Expenses	12,600
Motor Car	80,000	Bank Balance	30,400
Freight and Duty	4,000	Loan from Suresh at 12% per annum	20,000
Carriage Inwards	1,600	Interest on Loan from Suresh (Debit)	1,800
Carriage Outwards	600		
Trade Expenses	30,800		

Additional Information

(i) Stock on 31st March, 2016 was valued at 50,000 (realisable value ₹ 64,000).

(ii) Stock of ₹ 12,000 was burnt by fire on 25th March. It was fully insured and the insurance company admitted the claim in full.

(iii) Goods worth ₹ 3,600 were distributed as free sample. Goods worth ₹ 3,000 were used for personal purposes by the proprietor and goods worth ₹ 1,000 were given away as charity.

(iv) Depreciate motor car by 15%.

(v) Included in trade expenses is insurance premium of ₹ 4,800 paid for the year ending 30th June, 2016.

Ans Gross Profit = ₹ 97,600, Net Profit = ₹ 37,800, Balance Sheet Total = ₹ 2,31,800

2 From the following balances extracted from the books of Karan and the additional information, prepare the trading and profit and loss account for the year ended 31st March, 2016 and also show the balance sheet as on that date.

Name of Accounts	Debit Balance (₹)	Credit Balance (₹)
Stock on 1st April, 2015	6,25,000	
Purchases and Sales	9,03,000	13,72,000
Returns	22,000	13,000
Capital A/c		3,00,000
Drawings	45,000	
Land and Buildings	3,00,000	
Furniture and Fittings	80,000	
Trade Debtors and Trade Creditors	2,50,000	4,50,000
Cash in Hand	35,000	
Investments	1,00,000	
Interest		5,000
Commission		30,000
Direct Expenses	75,000	
Postage, Stationery and Telephone	25,000	
Fire Insurance Premium	20,000	
Salaries	90,000	
Bank Overdraft		4,00,000
	25,70,000	25,70,000

Additional Information

(i) Closing stock on 31st March, 2016 is valued at ₹ 6,50,000. Goods worth ₹ 5,000 are reported to have been taken away by the proprietor for his personal use at home during the year.

(ii) Interest on investments ₹ 5,000 is yet to be received while ₹ 10,000 of the commission received is yet to be earned.

(iii) ₹ 5,000 of the fire insurance premium paid is in respect of the quarter ending 30th June, 2016.

(iv) Salaries ₹ 10,000 for March, 2016 and bank overdraft interest estimated at ₹ 20,000 are yet to be recorded as outstanding charges.

(v) Depreciation is to be provided on land and buildings @ 5% per annum and on funiture and fittings @ 10% per annum.

(vi) Make a provision for doubtful debts @ 5% of trade debtors.

Ans. Gross Profit = ₹ 4,15,000, Net Profit = ₹ 2,49,500, Balance Sheet Total = ₹ 13,89,500

3 From the following trial balance extracted from the books of Sanchit, prepare a trading and profit and loss account for the year ended 31st March, 2016 and a balance sheet as on that date.

Name of Accounts	Debit Balance (₹)	Credit Balance (₹)
Capital		90,000
Drawings	6,480	
Land and Buildings	25,000	
Plant and Machinery	14,270	
Furniture and Fixtures	1,250	

Name of Accounts	Debit Balance (₹)	Credit Balance (₹)
Carriage Inwards	4,370	
Wages	21,470	
Salaries	4,670	
Bad Debts Provision (as on 1st April, 2015)		2,470
Sales		91,230
Sales Returns	1,760	
Bank Charges	140	
Coal, Gas and Water	720	
Rates and Taxes	840	
Discount A/c		120
Purchases	42,160	
Purchases Returns		8,460
Bills Receivable	1,270	
Trade Expenses	1,990	
Sundry Debtors	37,800	
Sundry Creditors		12,170
Stock (1st April, 2015)	26,420	
Apprentice Premium (paid by an apprentice in factory)		500
Fire Insurance	490	
Cash at Bank	13,000	
Cash in Hand	850	
	2,04,950	2,04,950

Additional Information

(i) Carry forward the following unexpired amounts.

- (a) Fire Insurance ₹ 125
- (b) Rates and Taxes ₹ 240
- (c) Apprentice Premium ₹ 400

(ii) Transfer to building account ₹ 3,000 from purchases and ₹ 2,000 from wages, representing cost of material and labour spent on additions to building made during the year.

(iii) Charge depreciation on land and buildings @ 2.5% and on plant and machinery @ 10%.

(iv) Make a provision @ 5% on sundry debtors for bad debts.

(v) Charge 5% interest on capital.

(vi) The value of stock as on 31st March, 2016 was ₹ 29,390.

Ans Gross Profit = ₹ 37,180, Net Profit = ₹ 23,538, Balance Sheet Total = ₹ 1,24,128

4 Following is the trial balance of Vikas as on 31st March, 2016.

Name of Account	Debit Balance (₹)	Credit Balance (₹)
Capital		16,00,000
Drawings	1,20,000	
Stock (1st April, 2015)	9,00,000	
Purchases	52,00,000	
Sales		62,00,000
Furniture	2,00,000	
Sundry Debtors	8,00,000	
Freight and Octroi	92,000	
Trade Expenses	10,000	
Salaries	1,10,000	
Rent	48,000	
Advertising Expenses	1,00,000	
Insurance Premium	8,000	
Commission		26,000
Discount	4,000	
Bad Debts	32,000	
Provision for Doubtful Debts		18,000
Creditors		4,00,000
Cash in Hand	1,04,000	
Bank	1,16,000	
Land and Building	4,00,000	
	82,44,000	82,44,000

Additional Information

(i) Stock on 31st March, 2016 was valued at ₹ 10,60,000.

(ii) Salaries have been paid so far for 11 months only.

(iii) Unexpired insurance included in the figure of ₹ 8,000 appearing in the trial balance is ₹ 2,000.

(iv) Commission earned but not yet received amounted to ₹ 2,440 is to be recorded in the books of accounts.

(v) Provision for doubtful debts is to be brought up to 3% of sundry debtors.

(vi) Manager is to be allowed a commission @ 10% of net profit after charging such commission.

(vii) Furniture is depreciated @ 10% per annum.

Prepare the trading and profit and loss account for the year ended 31st March, 2016 and the balance sheet as at that date.

Ans Gross Profit = ₹ 10,68,000, Net Profit = ₹ 6,75,400, Balance Sheet Total = ₹ 26,40,440

5 **The following balances were extracted from the books of Siddarth on 31st December, 2016.**

Name of Account	Amt (₹)	Name of Account	Amt (₹)
Stock at the Beginning	82,000	Purchases	4,40,000
Rent	19,200	Sales	5,60,000
Salary	40,000	Returns (Debit)	12,000
Bad Debts	800	Returns (Credit)	4,000
Provision for Doubtful Debts	6,000	Carriage Inward	7,000
Travelling Expenses	2,800	Carriage Outward	1,000
Insurance Premium	3,600	Capital	3,50,000
Proprietor's Withdrawals	8,000	Loan (Credit)	40,000
Telephone Charges	14,600	Sales Tax Collected	6,000
Printing and Advertising	10,000	Debtors	80,000
Commission (Credit)	12,000	Creditors	48,000
Rent from Sublet	9,600	Investment	10,000
Land and Building	2,80,000	Interest on Investments	1,200
Furniture	20,000		
Cash	5,800		

Prepare trading and profit and loss account for the year and a balance sheet as on 31st December, 2016 after taking into account the following.

(i) **Stock was valued at ₹ 1,50,000 on 31st December, 2016. You are informed that a fire occurred on 28th December, 2016 in the godown and stock of the value of ₹ 20,000 was destroyed. Insurance company admitted a claim of 75%.**

(ii) **One-third of the commission received is in respect of work to be done next year.**

(iii) **Create a provision @ 5% for doubtful debts.**

(iv) **50% of printing and advertising is to be carried forward as a charge in the following year.**

(v) **₹ 1,800 is due for interest on loan.**

(vi) **Provide for manger's commission @ 10% on net profit before charging such commission.**

Ans Gross Profit = ₹ 1,93,000, Net Profit = ₹ 1,08,000, Balance Sheet Total = ₹ 5,61,800.

Hint: Manager's commission = ₹ 12,000.

Provision for doubtful debts will be shown on the credit side of profit and loss account at ₹ 2,000.

6 **From the following particulars taken out from the books of Anand, prepare trading and profit and loss account for the year ended 31st March, 2016 and balance sheet as on that date.**

Name of Accounts	Amt (₹)	Name of Accounts	Amt (₹)
Plant and Machinery on 1st April, 2015	16,00,00	Rent	24,000
Plant and Machinery Purchased (1st July, 2015)	40,000	Insurance Premium Paid (From 1st January, 2016 to 31st December, 2016)	2,400
Sundry Debtors	2,40,000	Cash at Bank	10,800
Creditors	64,000	Wages	40,000
Furniture	10,000	Octroi	800
Motor Car	1,40,000	Advertising	9,600
Purchases	3,20,000	Carriage Inwards	20,400

Name of Accounts	Amt (₹)	Name of Accounts	Amt (₹)
Sales	5,60,000	Carriage Outwards	4,000
Sales Returns	30,000	Fuel and Power	31,400
Salaries	72,000	Anand's Capital	7,00,000
Opening Stock	1,20,000	Anand's Drawings	24,000
Motor Car Expenses	12,000	Brokerage	1,400
Stationery	1,000	Donation	10,200

Additional Information

(i) Closing stock ₹ 1,10,000 stock valued at ₹ 20,000 was destroyed by fire on 18th March, 2016 but the insurance company admitted a claim of ₹ 13,600 only which was received in April, 2016.

(ii) Stationery for ₹ 300 was used by the proprietor.

(iii) Goods costing ₹ 2,400 were given away as charity.

(iv) A new signboard costing ₹ 3,000 is included in advertising.

(v) Rent is to be allocated 2/3rd to factory and 1/3rd to office.

(vi) Depreciate machinery by 10% and motor car by 20%.

Ans Gross Profit = ₹ 1,13,800, Net Loss = ₹ 57,500, Balance Sheet Total = ₹ 6,82,200

7 From the following figures prepare the trading and profit and loss account for the year ended 31st March, 2016 and the balance sheet as at that date.

Particulars	Amt (₹)	Particulars	Amt (₹)
Stock (1st April, 2015)	1,50,000	Sundry Debtors	1,64,000
Purchases	16,00,000	Loan from Vishal	20,000
Sales	24,00,000	Interest on Vishal's Loan	3,000
Motor Car	3,00,000	Furniture	40,000
Car Expenses	84,000	Land and Building	4,00,000
Rent	11,000	Capital	5,00,000
Salaries	70,400	Sundry Creditors	1,82,600
Bad Debts	3,000	Returns Inward	15,000
Provision for Bad Debts	16,200	Returns Outward	12,000
Commission (Cr)	9,200	Cash in Hand	32,800
Wages	2,50,000		
Insurance	16,800		

Additional Information

(i) Commission include ₹ 3,200 being commission received in advance.

(ii) Write off ₹ 4,000 as further bad debts and maintain bad debts provision at 5% on debtors.

(iii) Expenses paid in advance are : Wages ₹ 10,000 and insurance ₹ 2,400.

(iv) Rent and salaries have been paid for 11 months.

(v) Loan from Vishal has been taken at 18% per annum interest.

(vi) Depreciate furniture by 15% per annum and motor car by 20% per annum.

(vii) Closing stock was valued at ₹ 1,20,000.

Ans Gross Profit = ₹ 5,27,000, Net Profit = ₹ 2,77,400 and Balance Sheet Total = ₹ 9,91,200

8 Following are balances from the trial balance of Dharmesh Traders as at 31st March, 2016.

Particulars	Amt (₹)	Particulars	Amt (₹)
Opening Stock	11,240	Interest on Securities	12,800
Purchases	3,08,400	Land and Building	20,00,000
Sales	7,49,600	Securities	12,00,000
Wages	2,52,000	Cash in Hand	51,200
Carriage Inward	1,800	Bank Overdraft	6,80,000
Freight on Purchase	1,400	Discount Allowed	3,000
Salaries	16,000	Discount Received	840
Insurance	5,600	Bills Payable	8,000
Duty on Import of Goods	8,400	Loan (Cr)	22,000
Repair to Machinery	2,800	Bills Receivable	14,000
Drawings	11,200	Capital A/c	26,95,200
Customer's A/c	31,600	Suppliers A/c	80,000
Postage	1,000	Kabir's Loan (Cr)	37,200
Trade Expenses	2,000	Plant and Machinery	3,64,000

Prepare trading and profit and loss account for the year ended 31st March, 2016 and balance sheet as at that date after taking into account the following adjustments

(i) Closing stock was valued at ₹ 38,000.

(ii) Depreciation to be provided on land and building @ 5% per annum and on plant and machinery @ 10% per annum.

(iii) Write off ₹ 4,000 as bad debt.

(iv) Insurance was prepaid ₹ 1,400.

(v) Create provision for doubtful debts @ 5% on debtors.

(vi) Wages include ₹ 9,600 for installation of a new machinery.

Ans Gross Profit = ₹ 2,13,960, Net Profit = 55,860, Balance Sheet Total = ₹ 35,67,060.

9 From the following information prepare financial statements of M/S Rajan and Bros for the year ending 31st March, 2016.

Particulars	Amt (₹)	Particulars	Amt (₹)
Stock (1-4-2015)	33,600	Capital	1,56,000
Sales Returns	16,000	Sales	6,18,000
Purchases	4,86,000	Return Outward	11,400
Freight Inwards	17,200	Trade Creditors	9,600
Rent and Taxes	11,400	10% Bank Loan (1-7-2015)	48,000
Salaries	18,600	Income From Investment	7,200
Trade Debtors	48,000	Discount Received	4,500
Bank Interest	2,000		
Printing and Advertising	29,200		
Cash at Bank	36,600		
Discount Allowed	2,680		
Investment	50,000		
Furniture	7,600		
General Expenses	7,220		
Audit Fees	1,000		
Insurance	1,600		

Particulars	Amt (₹)	Particulars	Amt (₹)
Travelling Expenses	6,000		
Plant and Machinery	60,000		
Drawings	20,000		
	8,54,700		8,54,700

Additional Information

(i) Depreciation on plant and machinery @ 10% per annum, a machine has been purchased on 1st July, 2015 for ₹ 24,000.

(ii) The manager is entitled to a commission of 10% of the net profit before charging such commission.

(iii) Closing stock in trade is valued at ₹ 12,000 (cost), ₹ 12,400 (Market Price)

(iv) Rent outstanding ₹ 10,000.

Ans Gross Profit = ₹ 88,600, Net Profit = ₹ 3,240, Balance Sheet Total = ₹ 2,08,800

10 From the following trial balance extracted from the books of Gopichand, prepare trading and profit and loss account for the year ending 31st March, 2016 and a balance sheet as at that date.

Particulars	Debit Balance (₹)	Credit Balance (₹)
Furniture	6,400	
Loose Tools	62,500	
Buildings	75,000	
Capital Account		1,25,000
Bad Debts	1,250	
Provision for Bad Debts		2,000
Sundry Debtors and Creditors	38,000	25,000
Stock (on 1st April, 2015)	34,600	
Purchases and Sales	54,750	1,54,500
Bank Overdraft		28,500
Sales Return and Purchases Return	2,000	1,250
Stationary	4,500	
Interest A/c	1,180	
Commission		3,750
Cash in Hand	6,500	
Taxes and Insurance	12,500	
General Expenses	7,820	
Salaries	33,000	
	3,40,000	3,40,000

The following adjustments are to be made

(i) Stock in hand on 31st March, 2016 was ₹ 32,500.

(ii) Depreciate building @ 5% and furniture @ 10%. Loose tools are revalued at ₹ 50,000 at the end of the year.

(iii) Salaries ₹ 3,000 and taxes ₹ 1,200 are outstanding.

(iv) Insurance amounting to ₹ 1,000 is prepaid.

(v) Write off a further ₹ 1,000 as bad debts and provision for doubtful debts is to be made equal to 5% on sundry debtors.

(vi) Half of the stationary was used by the proprietor for his personal purposes.

Ans Gross Profit = ₹ 96,900, Net Profit = ₹ 21,710 and Balance Sheet Total = ₹ 2,02,160

11 **The following is the trial balance of Ram Kishan on 31st December, 2016.**

Name of Account	Debit Balance (₹)	Credit Balance (₹)
Cash in Hand	1,080	
Cash at Bank	5,260	
Purchases	81,350	
Return Outwards		1,000
Sales		1,97,560
Return Inwards	1,360	
Wages	20,960	
Fuel and Power	9,460	
Carriage on Sales	6,400	
Carriage on Purchases	4,080	
Stock (1st January, 2016)	11,520	
Building	60,000	
Freehold Land	20,000	
Machinery	40,000	
Salaries	30,000	
Patents	15,000	
General Expenses	6,000	
Insurance	1,200	
Capital		1,42,000
Drawings	10,490	
Sundry Debtors	29,000	
Sundry Creditors		12,600
	3,53,160	3,53,160

Taking into account the following adjustments, pass the necessary journal entries and prepare the trading and profit and loss account and the balance sheet.

(i) Stock in hand on 31st December, 2016 is ₹ 13,600.

(ii) Machinery is to be depreciated @ 10% and patents @ 20%.

(iii) Salaries for the month of December, 2016 amounted to ₹ 3,000 were unpaid.

(iv) Insurance included a premium of ₹ 170 for next year.

(v) Wages include a sum of ₹ 4,000 spend on the erection of a cycle shed for employees and customers.

(vi) A provision for doubtful debts is to be created to the extent of 5% on sundry debtors.

Ans Gross Profit = ₹ 87,430; Net Profit = ₹ 32,550; Balance Sheet Total = ₹ 1,79,660.

12 **Following is the trial balance of Shri Paras on 31st March, 2016. You are required to prepare final accounts after giving effects to the adjustments.**

Particulars	Amt (₹)	Particulars	Amt (₹)
Sundry Debtors	2,90,000	Sundry Creditors	1,26,000
Drawings	1,04,900	Capital A/c	14,20,000
Insurance	12,000	Returns Outward	10,000
General Expenses	60,000	Sales	19,75,600
Salaries	3,00,000		
Patents	1,50,000		
Machinery	4,00,000		
Freehold Land	2,00,000		

Particulars	Amt (₹)	Particulars	Amt (₹)
Building	6,00,000		
Stock (1st April, 2015)	1,15,200		
Cash at Bank	52,600		
Carriage on Purchases	40,800		
Carriage on Sales	64,000		
Fuel and Power	94,600		
Wages	2,09,600		
Returns Inward	13,600		
Purchases	8,13,500		
Cash in Hand	10,800		
	35,31,600		35,31,600

Following adjustments are made

(i) Stock on 31st March, 2016 was valued at ₹ 1,36,000.

(ii) A provision for bad and doubtful debts is to be made to the extent of 5% on sundry debtors.

(iii) Depreciate machinery by 10%, patents by 20% and building by 5%.

(iv) Wages include a sum of ₹ 40,000 spent on construction of a cycle shed.

(v) Salaries for the month of February and March, 2016 were not paid.

(vi) Insurance includes a premium of ₹ 3,400 on a policy expiring on 30th September, 2016.

(vii) General manager is entitled to a commission of 10% on the net profit after charging his commission.

Ans Gross Profit = ₹ 8,74,300; Net Profit= ₹ 2,39,546; Balance Sheet Total = ₹ 17,64,600.

13 Prepare trading and profit and loss account for the year ended 31st March, 2016 and balance sheet as at that date from the following trial balance.

Heads of Accounts	Debit Balance (₹)	Credit Balance (₹)
Capital		20,000
Cash	3,000	
Bank Overdraft		4,000
Purchases	24,000	
Sales		30,000
Sales Return	2,000	
Purchases Return		4,000
Establishment Expenses	4,400	
Taxes and Insurance	1,000	
Bad Debts	1,000	
Provision for Doubtful Debts		1,400
Debtors	10,000	
Creditors		4,000
Commission		1,000
Deposits	8,000	
Opening Stock	6,000	
Drawings	2,800	
Furniture	1,200	
Bills Receivable	6,000	
Bills Payable		5,000
Total	69,400	69,400

Additional Information

(i) Salaries ₹ 200 and taxes ₹ 400 are outstanding but insurance ₹ 100 is prepaid.
(ii) Commission ₹ 200 received in advance for the next year.
(iii) Interest ₹ 420 is to be received on deposits and interest on bank overdraft ₹ 600 is to be paid.
(iv) Provision for doubtful debts to be maintained at ₹ 2,000.
(v) Depreciate furniture by 10%.
(vi) Stock on 31st March, 2016 is ₹ 9,000.
(vii) A fire occurred on 1st April, 2015 destroying goods costing ₹ 2,000.

Ans Gross Profit = ₹ 11,000; Net Profit = ₹ 4,000; Balance Sheet Total = ₹ 35,600

14 From the following balances, prepare trading, profit and loss account and a balance sheet as at 31st March, 2016.

Particulars	Amt (₹)	Particulars	Amt (₹)
Stock (1st April 2015)	40,000	Goodwill	32,000
Purchases	5,84,000	Furniture and Fittings	1,16,000
Duty and Clearing Charges	68,000	Repair Charges	5,800
Capital	3,20,000	Bank	48,000
Sales	11,80,000	Salaries	2,20,000
Rent	20,000	General Expenses	36,000
Returns Inwards	32,000	Debtors	4,60,000
Cash Discount Allowed	30,000	Creditors	2,70,000
Cash Discount Received	38,000		
Drawings	1,16,200		

Take the following adjustments into account

(i) General expenses include ₹ 10,000 chargeable to furniture purchased on 1st October, 2015.
(ii) Create a reserve of 5% on debtors for bad and doubtful debts after treating ₹ 60,000 as a bad debt.
(iii) Rent for two months is outstanding.
(iv) Depreciation on furniture and fittings for the year is to be at the rate of 10% per annum.
(v) Closing stock was ₹ 80,000, but there was a loss by fire on 20th March to the extent of ₹ 16,000. Insurance company admitted the claim in full.
(vi) Goods costing ₹ 5,000 were used by the proprietor.
(vii) Goods costing ₹ 3,000 were distributed as free samples.

Ans Gross Profit = ₹ 5,60,000; Net Profit = ₹ 1,97,100; Balance Sheet Total = ₹ 6,69,900

15 Following is the trial balance of Mr Ishan Rajput as at 31st March, 2016.

Particulars	Amt (₹)	Particulars	Amt (₹)
Goodwill	3,00,000	Purchases Returns	26,500
Land and Buildings	6,00,000	Capital A/c	20,30,000
Plant and Machinery	4,00,000	Bills Payable	1,38,000
Loose Tools	30,000	Sundry Creditors	3,00,000
Bills Receivable	20,000	Sales	11,50,000
Stock (1st April, 2015)	4,00,000		
Purchases	5,10,000		
Wages	2,00,000		
Carriage Inwards	12,000		

Particulars	Amt (₹)	Particulars	Amt (₹)
Coal and Gas	56,000		
Salaries	40,000		
Rent	27,000		
Discount Allowed	15,000		
Cash at Bank	2,50,000		
Cash in Hand	14,000		
Sundry Debtors	4,50,000		
Repairs	18,000		
Printing and Stationery	6,000		
Bad Debts	12,000		
Advertisements	35,000		
Furniture and Fixtures	12,000		
General Expenses	2,500		
Investments	50,000		
Drawings	1,50,000		
Carriage Outwards	15,000		
Sales Returns	20,000		
	36,44,500		36,44,500

You are required to prepare final accounts after taking into account the following adjustments

(i) Closing stock on 31st March, 2016 was ₹ 6,00,000.

(ii) Depreciate plant and machinery at 5%, loose tools at 15% and furniture and fixtures at 5%.

(iii) Provide $2\frac{1}{2}$% for discount on sundry debtors and also provide 5% for bad and doubtful debts on sundry debtors.

(iv) Only three quarter's rent has been paid, the last quarter's rent being outstanding.

(v) Interest earned but not received ₹ 6,000.

(vi) Write off $\frac{1}{4}$th of advertisement expenses.

Ans Gross Profit = ₹ 5,78,500; Net Profit = ₹ 3,72,960; Total of Balance Sheet = ₹ 26,99,960

16 From the following trial balance of Sh. Balraj Singh, prepare trading and profit and loss account for the year ending 31st March, 2016 and a balance sheet as at that date.

Particulars	Amt (₹)	Particulars	Amt (₹)
Stock at Commencement	80,000	Sales	10,20,000
Purchases	6,40,000	Loan from Vipul @ 15% per annum	80,000
Returns Inward	14,000	Returns Outwards	16,000
Sundry Debtors	1,60,000	Bank	48,400
Cash	18,800	Provision for Doubtful Debts	5,000
Manufacturing Expenses	88,000	Discount	3,600
Trade Expenses	14,400	Rent of Premises sublet, for the	
Carriage	7,000	year to 30th September, 2016	8,000
Salaries and Wages	31,600	Capital	2,40,000
Postage and Telegrams	3,000	Sundry Creditors	94,000
Stationery	1,600		
Freight Inwards	8,600		

Particulars	Amt (₹)	Particulars	Amt (₹)
Land and Building	4,00,000		
Patents	16,000		
Furniture	20,000		
Insurance Premium	12,000		
	15,15,000		15,15,000

Additional Information

(i) Closing stock was valued at ₹ 1,20,000. You are informed that goods valued ₹ 24,000 were sold and despatched on 29th March, 2016, but no entry was passed to this effect.

(ii) Insurance premium include ₹ 2,400 paid on 1st October, 2015 to run for one year from 1st October, 2015 to 30th September, 2016.

(iii) Loan from Vipul was taken on 1st July, 2015. Interest has not been paid so far.

(iv) Create provision for doubtful debts at 5% on sundry debtors after writing off ₹ 1,200 as bad debts during the year.

(v) A bill of ₹ 6,400 for advertisement in newspaper remained unpaid at the end of the year.

(vi) Purchases include furniture costing ₹ 10,000 purchased on 1st April, 2015.

(vii) Charge 10% per annum depreciation on furniture and write off $\frac{1}{5}$th of patents.

Ans Gross Profit = ₹ 3,52,400; Net Profit = ₹ 2,71,660; Balance Sheet Total = ₹ 7,53,460

Hint: Rent shown in trial balance is for 3 quarters or 9 months. As such rent outstanding for the remaining 3 months will be $\frac{27,000}{9} \times 3 =$ ₹ 9,000

17 From the following balances extracted from the books of Sharma, prepare the trading and profit and loss account for the year ended 31st March, 2016 and balance sheet as at that date after taking into consideration the adjustments given below.

Trial Balance
as at 31st March, 2016

Particulars	Debit Balance (₹)	Credit Balance (₹)
Drawing and Capital	15,000	1,00,000
Purchases and Sales	1,44,200	1,90,000
Returns	2,600	5,400
Sundry Debtors and Creditors	36,400	71,500
Stock (1.04.2015)	39,600	
Bad Debts	6,000	
Bill Receivable and Payable	24,000	46,000
Cash in Hand	600	
Office Expenses	12,420	
Sales Van	30,000	
Sales Van Expenses	2,800	
Discount		5,820
Rent and Taxes	21,400	
Telephone Charges	2,100	
Postage and Telegram	1,900	
Furniture	10,000	
Printing and Stationery	5,500	
Commission	16,800	
Carriage Inwards	6,400	
Salaries and Wages	41,000	
	4,18,720	4,18,720

Additional Information

(i) Closing stock was valued at ₹ 1,23,400.

(ii) Depreciate furniture and machinery @ 10% per annum and sales van @ 20% per annum.

(iii) Outstanding rent amounted to ₹ 1,800.

(iv) Bad debts ₹ 400.

(v) Make a provision for doubtful debts @ 5% on debtors.

(vi) Charge one-fourth of salaries and wages to the trading account.

(vii) A new machinery was purchased on credit and installed on 31st December, 2015 costing ₹ 30,000. No entry for the same has yet been passed in the books.

Ans Gross Profit = ₹ 1,26,000; Net Profit = ₹ 10,150; Balance Sheet Total = ₹ 2,44,450

18 Prepare trading and profit and loss account and balance sheet as at 31st March, 2016, from the following balances.

Particulars	Amt (₹)	Particulars	Amt (₹)
Capital A/c	10,00,000	Stock (on 1.04.2015)	1,34,000
Drawings A/c	72,000	Salaries and Wages	48,000
Bills Receivable	11,600	Outstanding Salaries and Wages	4,000
Plant and Machinery	7,60,000	Insurance (including premium	
Sundry Debtors	1,16,000	of ₹ 2,000 per annum paid	
Loan A/c (Cr) at 12% per annum	40,000	upto 30.9.2016)	5,200
Manufacturing Wages	80,000	Cash	93,200
Returns Inwards	6,000	Bank Overdraft	30,000
Purchases	2,40,000	Repairs and Renewals	3,200
Sales	5,20,000	Interest and Discount (Dr)	8,800
Rent	56,000	Bad Debts	8,000
Commission Received	12,000	Sundry Creditors	60,000
		Fixtures and Fittings	24,000

Additional Information

(i) Stock on hand on 31st March, 2016 was ₹ 1,60,000.

(ii) Further bad debts written off ₹ 4,000 and create a provision of 5% on sundry debtors.

(iii) Rent has been paid up to 31st May, 2016.

(iv) Manufacturing wages include ₹ 20,000 of a new machinery purchased on 1st October, 2015.

(v) Depreciate plant and machinery by 10% per annum and fixtures and fittings by 20% per annum.

(vi) Commission earned but not received ₹ 2,000.

(vii) Interest on loan for the last two months is not paid.

(viii) Goods worth ₹ 8,000 were distributed as free samples.

Ans Gross Profit = ₹ 2,48,000; Net Profit = ₹ 41,600; Balance Sheet Total = ₹ 11,04,400

19 Following trial balance as on 31st March, 2016 extracted from the books of Kartik Makkar.

Name of Accounts	Debit Balance (₹)	Credit Balance (₹)
Kartik's Capital A/c		6,00,000
Kartik's Drawings	25,000	
Furniture	1,00,000	
Plant and Machinery	1,40,000	
Stock (1st April, 2015)	90,000	

Name of Accounts	Debit Balance (₹)	Credit Balance (₹)
Bills Receivable and Payable	20,000	30,000
Sundry Debtors and Creditors	2,80,000	3,20,000
Purchases and Sales	4,00,000	7,50,000
Carriage Inwards	5,000	
Carriage Outwards	2,500	
Freight	6,000	
Manufacturing Wages	1,10,000	
Fuel and Power	4,000	
Factory Expenses	27,000	
Salaries	90,000	
Rent	30,000	
Prepaid Rent	12,000	
Outstanding Salaries		10,000
Discount	2,000	4,000
Printing and Stationery	3,000	
General Expenses	9,000	
Cash in Hand	21,500	
Cash at Bank	3,37,000	
Provision for Doubtful Debts		4,000
Provision for Discount on Debtors		2,000
Bad Debts	6,000	
	17,20,000	17,20,000

Errors

(i) Purchases include sales return of ₹ 10,000 and sales include purchases return of ₹ 8,000.

(ii) Goods withdrawn by the proprietor for own consumption ₹ 4,000 were included in purchases.

(iii) Wages paid for installation of plant and machinery amounted to ₹ 4,000 were included in wages account.

(iv) Free samples distributed for publicity costing ₹ 5,000 but not recorded in the books.

(v) An advance of ₹ 10,000 to a supplier was wrongly included in the list of sundry debtors.

(vi) A dishonored bill receivable for ₹ 4,000 returned by the bank with whom it had been discounted, had been credited to bank account and debited to bills receivable account.

Additional Information

(i) Charge depreciation on plant and machinery at 15% and on furniture at 10%.

(ii) Create a provision for doubtful debts @ 5% and provision for discount on debtors at 2%.

(iii) Closing stock is valued at ₹ 160,000.

Prepare the trading and profit and loss account for the year ended 31st March, 2016.

Ans Gross Profit = ₹ 2,81,000; Net Profit = ₹ 92,994; Balance Sheet Total = ₹ 10,23,994

20 Prepare the trading and profit and loss account and a balance sheet of M/s Shine Ltd from the following particulars.

Name of Accounts	Amt (₹)	Name of Accounts	Amt (₹)
Sundry Debtors	1,00,000	Bills Payable	85,550
Bad Debts	3,000	Sundry Creditors	25,000
Trade Expenses	2,500	Provision for Bad Debts	1,500
Printing and Stationery	5,000	Return Outwards	4,500

Name of Accounts	Amt (₹)	Name of Accounts	Amt (₹)
Rent, Rates and Taxes	3,450	Capital	2,50,000
Freight	2,250	Discount Received	3,500
Sales Return	6,000	Interest Received	11,260
Motor Car	25,000	Sales	1,00,000
Opening Stock	75,550		
Furniture and Fixtures	15,500		
Purchases	75,000		
Drawings	13,560		
Investments	65,500		
Cash in Hand	36,000		
Cash at Bank	53,000		
	4,81,310		4,81,310

Additional Information

(i) Closing stock was valued ₹ 35,000.
(ii) Depreciation charged on furniture and fixtures @ 5%.
(iii) Further bad debts ₹ 1,000. Make a provision for bad debts @ 5% on sundry debtors.
(iv) Depreciation charged on motor car @ 10%.
(v) Interest on drawings @ 6%.
(vi) Rent, rates and taxes was outstanding ₹ 200.
(vii) Discount on debtors 2%.

Ans Gross Loss = ₹ 19,300; Net Loss = ₹ 27,482; Balance Sheet Total = ₹ 3,18,894

21 The trial balance of M/s Taj & Co as on 31st December, 2016 was as follows

Name of Accounts	Amt (₹)	Name of Accounts	Amt (₹)
Purchases	1,62,505	Sales	2,52,400
Sundry Debtors	50,200	Provision for Doubtful Debts	5,200
Opening Stock	26,725	Sundry Creditors	30,526
Wages	23,137	Bills Payable	3,950
Salaries	5,575	Outstanding Wages	2,000
Furniture	7,250	Trade Expenses Accrued but not Paid	700
Postage	4,226	Capital A/c	10,000
Power and Fuel	1,350		
Trade Expenses	5,831		
Bad Debts	525		
Loan to Suraj @ 10% per annum (1st September, 2016)	3,000		
Cash at Bank	10,000		
Drawings A/c	4,452		
	3,04,776		3,04,776

Prepare the trading and profit and loss account for the year ended 31st December, 2016 and the balance sheet after considering the following information.

(i) Depreciation on Furniture to be charged @ 10% .
(ii) Debtors include an item of ₹ 500 due from a customer who has become insolvent.
(iii) Provision for doubtful debts @ 5% on sundry debtors is to be maintained.
(iv) Goods valued at ₹ 1,500 destroyed by fire and insurance company admitted a claim for ₹ 1,000.
(v) Stock on 31st December, 2016 was ₹ 12,550.

Ans Gross Profit = ₹ 52,733; Net Profit = ₹ 37,666; Balance Sheet Total = ₹ 80,390

SAMPLE PROJECT REPORTS

Project 1 **Collection of Source Documents, Preparation of Vouchers**

Project 2 **Preparation of Bank Reconciliation Statement**

Project 3 **Comprehensive**
Case Study of a Sole Proprietor Willing to Start a Driving School and also to Sell Car Accessories

PROJECT REPORT

A project report is a written statement of what the analyser analyses in his/her evaluation. The project report needs to be prepared with great care and consideration.

A project report should

- be handwritten
- be concise
- be clear
- have diagrammatic presentation
- have topics with suitable headings
- end up with conclusion

ELEMENTS

Try to ensure that your report contains the following elements

Title Page

This should include the project title, name of the company on which you are conducting your research and name of the student. You can also list the name of your school, class and subject teacher.

Acknowledgement

It is usual to thank those individuals, who have particularly provided useful assistance, technical or otherwise, during your project. In this, you praise your supervisor as he/she will have invested quite a lot of time in overseeing your progress. You can also give a note of thank to the department of the company, which provides you a relevant data.

Content Page

This should list the main sections and sub-sections of your report. Choose self-explanatory titles with their respective pages and use double spacing for clarity. Content should be impressive and explanatory so that the reader would clearly understand the motto of the project.

Try to avoid too many levels of sub-heading.

Introduction

This is one of the most important component of the project report. It should begin with a clear statement of what the project is about, so that the nature and scope of the project can be understood by a reader. It should summarise everything which you set out to achieve and provide a clear summary of the project's background, relevance and main contributions. The introduction should set the context for the project and should provide the reader with a summary of the key things to look out for in, the remainder of the report. It is useful in stating the main objectives of the project as part of the introduction.

Background

The background section of the report should set the project into action, it specifies the problem of the company, what remedial actions were taken by the company, what are its effects. It gives the layout of the whole project.

Body of Report

The central part of the report usually consists of three or four sections detailing the technical work undertaken during the project. The structure of these sections is highly project dependent. They can reflect the chronological development of the project. It includes the detailed description regarding the matter of the project.

Evaluation

This might involve quantitative and qualitative evaluation such as expressibility, functionality, ease-of-use, etc of a product. At some point, you should also evaluate the strengths and weaknesses of what you have done. It includes certain questionnaires, sampling test which help in evaluating the result on the basis of truths and facts.

Conclusion

The conclusion should list the things, which have been learnt as a result of the work you have done. It shows the ultimate response of the project undertaken by a student. It should be expressive and impressive so that a reader would clearly evaluate the result and rate you on the basis of your presentation.

PROJECT WORK

Title of the Project	:	....
		....
Company Chosen for the Project	:	....
		....
		....
Name	:	....
School	:	....
Year	:	2022-23
Class	:	XI
Submitted To	:	....

I would like to extend my sincere and heartfelt gratitude to my Accounts Teacher Mr/Ms............................ who have helped me in this endeavor and has always been very cooperative and without his/her help, cooperation, guidance and encouragement the project couldn't have been what it evolved to be.

I extend my heartfelt thanks to my faculty for their guidance and constant supervision as well as for providing me the necessary information regarding the project.

I am also thankful to my parents for their cooperation and encouragement.

Last but not the least, gratitute to all my friends who helped me (directly or indirectly) to complete this project within a limited time frame.

Thanks again to all who helped me.

Name of the Student ....

Roll No. ....

Certificate

This is to Certify that the project work ....

is the bonafide work of .... (Name of the student) who carried out the work under my supervision

....

____

(Name and Signature of Teacher/Supervisor)

INDEX

S.No.	Title of Project Work	Page No.	Remarks	Teacher's Signature
1.				
2.				
3.	Comprehensive			

Project I Collection of Source Documents, Preparation of Vouchers, Recording of Transactions with the Help of Vouchers

SITUATION

Mr Kartik Makkar, M.Com, started his own business under the name of Kartik Makkar & Sons, at Abulane, Meerut on 1st January, 2016, to deal in a variety of electronic goods.

He introduced ₹ 6,00,000 as capital out of which ₹ 1,00,000 was in cash and balance by cheque. Enclosed herewith are the original papers relating to his business transactions for the month of January 2016. You are required to prepare voucher for each finanacial transaction and record the transactions with the help of vouchers.

Transaction 1

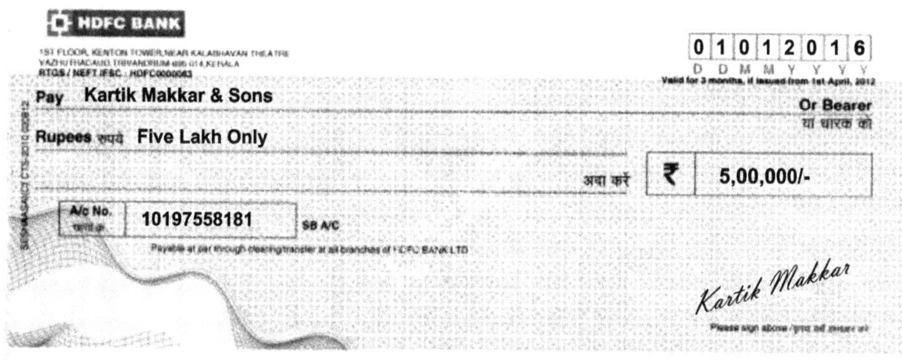

Transaction 2

Ram & Co
Furnishers and Decorators
Begum Bridge, Meerut

M/s Kartik Makkar & Sons, Abulane, Meerut

Bill No. 426 | 2nd Jan, 2016

S. No.	Particulars	Quantity	Rate (₹)	Amount (₹)
1.	Shelves	20	2,200	44,000
2.	Chairs	18	400	7,200
3.	Tables	9	600	5,400
4.	Cabinets	8	3,800	30,400
5.	Show Case	3	11,000	33,000
				1,20,000
		Less 5%		6,000
				1,14,000
	Rupees One Lakh Fourteen Thousand Only			

E & O E | For Ram & Co.

Transaction 3

Ordeal Store Greater Kailash, Delhi **M/s Kartik Makkar & Sons** Meerut	3rd Jan, 2016
Particulars	Amount (₹)
15 Ceiling Fans @ 6,000 each	90,000
28 Electric Irons @ 2,000 each	56,000
Rupees One Lakh Forty Six Thousand Only	1,46,000
Received by Cheque No. 13551 on AXIS Bank Ltd.	
	For Ordeal Stores

Transaction 4

RAJ & BROS. Shastri Nagar, Meerut **Cash Memo** (Original) **M/s Kartik Makkar & Sons** Meerut	4th Jan, 2016
S.No. Particulars	Amount (₹)
1. One Compuer and Printer	74,000
2. One Billing Machine	16,000
Rupees Ninty Thousand Only	90,000
Received in full vide Cheque No. 13552 on AXIS Bank Ltd., Meerut	
	For Raj & Bros.

Transaction 5

Vishal Electronics & Co. 14, Nehru Place, Delhi **M/s Kartik Makkar and Sons** Abulane, Meerut Order No. 6	Invoice No. 536 5th Jan, 2016
Particulars	Amount (₹)
4 Water Heaters @ 8,000 each	32,000
1 Air Conditioner @ 40,000 each	40,000
	72,000
Less : 10% Discount	7,200
	64,800
Rupees Sixty Four Thousand Eight Hundred Only R/R enclosed	
E. & O.E For Vishal Electronics & Co.	

Transaction 6

Kartik Makkar & Sons Abulane, Meerut Cash Memo	6th Jan, 2016
Particulars	Amount (₹)
5 Ceiling Fans @ 6,000 each	30,000
Less : Cash Discount	2,000
	28,000
Rupees Twenty Eight Thousand Only Received-Vide cheque No. 43525 on Punjab National Bank	
	For Kartik Makkar & Sons

Transaction 7 : On 8th Jan, 2016

Cash paid ₹ 5,000 for advertisement in newspaper

Transaction 8

Kartik Makkar & Sons Abulane, Meerut **M/s Gaur & Sons,** Meerut Order No. 48	Invoice No. 1 9th Jan, 2016
Particulars	Amount (₹)
4 Water Heaters @ 15,000 each	60,000
5 Ceiling Fans @ 8,000 each	40,000
28 Electric Irons @ 5,000 each	1,40,000
2 Air Conditioner @ 47,000 each	94,000
	3,34,000
Rupees Three Lakhs Thirty Four Thousand Only	
E. & O.E.	For Kartik Makkar & Sons

Transaction 9

Raj & Co.

No. 1234 | Begum Bridge, Meerut | 10th Jan, 2016

Receipt (Original)

Received with thanks form M/s Kartik Makkar & Sons, Meerut sum of Rupees Fifty Thousand Only, as part payment of Bill No. 426 dated 2nd January, 2016 through cheque No. 13553 on AXIS Bank Ltd., Meerut

₹ 50,000/-

For Raj & Co.

Transaction 10

Kartik Makkar & Sons Abulane, Meerut M/s Veenu Bros, Haryana Series No. 72	Invoice No. 2 11th Jan, 2016
Particulars	Amount (₹)
5 Ceiling Fans 10,000 each	50,000
Less : Trade Discount	6,000
	44,000
Rupeese Forty Four Thousand Only Goods Sent by Transport	
	For Kartik Makkar & Sons

Transaction 11 : On 12 Jan, 2016

Received ₹ 2,00,000 as part payment against Bill No. 1, dated 9th January, 2016 vide cheque no. 43557 on the Union Bank, Meerut

Transaction 12

Vishal Electronics 14, Nehru Place, Delhi **M/s Kartik Makkar and Sons** Abulane, Meerut Order No. 21	Invoice No. 247 13th Jan, 2016
Particulars	Amount (₹)
3 Mini TVS @ 5,000 each	15,000
	15,000
Rupees Fifteen Thousand Only	
E. & O. E.	For Vishal Electronics

Transaction 13

Manohar & Sons Valley Bazar, Meerut Cash Memo (Duplicate)	15th Jan, 2016
Particulars	Amount (₹)
1 Air Conditioner @ 30,000 each	30,000
	30,000
Rupees Thirty Thousand Only Received Cash	
	For Manohar & Sons

Transaction 14

Bill of Exchange

Meerut 16th Jan, 2016

Stamp

One month after date pay M/s Kartik Makkar & Sons or order the sum of Rupees Twenty Two Thousand Only, value received

For Kartik Makkar & Sons

Kartik Makkar

₹ 22,000

To

M/s Veenu Bros, Haryana

In addition to the above allowed M/s Veenu Brothers a discount of ₹ 2,000.

Transaction 15 : Only 24 Jan, 2016

Mr Kartik Makkar withdrew ₹ 6,000 from bank account for personal use vide cheque no. 13554.

Transaction 16 : On 25 Jan, 2016

Premium paid ₹ 7,000/- for fire and burglary insurance for the year by cheque no. 13555.

Transaction 17

Promissory Note		
₹ 15,000	Meerut	25th Jan, 2016
Two months after date, I/We promise to pay Ms Vishal Electronics or order sum of Rupees Fifteen Thousand Only for the value received.		
		For Kartik Makkar & Sons
		Kartik Makkar

Transaction 18 : On 30 Jan, 2016

Amount paid by cheque numbered 13556, ₹ 3,000 for printing of receipt books, cash memos and letter-heads.

Transaction 19 : On 30 Jan, 2016

Salary of ₹ 12,000 paid to salesman for the month of January, by cheque numbered 13557.

Event as on 30 Jan, 2016

Inventory was counted and valued ₹ 1,61,800.

Solution. Project is to prepare vouchers with the help of source documents and record transactions with the help of vouchers.

Voucher for Transaction 1

Kartik Makkar & Sons, Abulane, Meerut No. : 1 **Receipt Voucher**	Date 1st Jan, 2016
Particulars	Amount (₹)
Bank Account	5,00,000 (Dr)
Capital Account	5,00,000 (Cr)
Amounts (in words) Rupees Five Lakhs Only	
(Being capital introduced through cheque)	
	Authorised Signatory

Kartik Makkar & Sons, Abulane, Meerut No. : 2 **Receipt Voucher**	Date 1st Jan, 2016
Particulars	Amount (₹)
Cash Account	1,00,000 (Dr)
Capital Account	1,00,000 (Cr)
Amounts (in words) Rupees One Lakh Only	
(Being business started with cash)	
	Authorised Signatory

Voucher for Transaction 2

Kartik Makkar & Sons, Abulane, Meerut No. : 1 **Journal Voucher**	Date 2nd Jan, 2016
Particulars	Amount (₹)
Furniture and Fixtures Account	1,14,000 (Dr)
Ram & Co.	1,14,000 (Cr)
Amounts (in words) Rupees One Lakh Fourteen Thousand Only	
(Being furniture purchased from Ram Co. Bill No. 426)	
	Authorised Signatory

Note ₹ 6,000 being trade discount has not been recorded.

Voucher for Transaction 3

No. 1	**Kartik Makkar & Sons**, Abulane, Meerut **Payment Voucher**	Date 3rd Jan, 2016

Particulars	Amount (₹)
Purchases Account	1,46,000 (Dr)
Bank Account	1,46,000 (Cr)
Amount (in words) Rupees One Lakh Forty Six Thousand Only	
Received with thanks Rupees One Lakh Forty Six Thousand vide Cheque No. 13551	
Receiver's Signature	**Authorised Signatory**

Voucher for Transaction 4

No. : 2	**Kartik Makkar & Sons**, Abulane, Meerut **Payment Voucher**	Date 4th Jan, 2016

Particulars	Amount (₹)
Office Equipments	
Computer and Printer	74,000 (Dr)
Billing Machine	16,000 (Dr)
Bank Account	90,000 (Cr)
Amount (in words) Rupees Ninty Thousand Only	
Received with thanks Rupees Ninty Thousand Only vide Cheque No. 13552.	
Receiver's Signature	**Authorised Signatory**

Voucher for Transaction 5

No. : 1	**Kartik Makkar & Sons**, Abulane, Meerut **Purchase Voucher**	Date 5th Jan, 2016

Particulars	Amount (₹)
Purchases Account	64,800 (Dr)
Vishal Electronics	64,800 (Cr)
Amounts (in words) Rupees Sixty Four Thousand Eight Hundred Only	
Being water heaters and air conditioner purchased vide Invoice No. 536	
	Authorised Signatory

Voucher for Transaction 6

No. : 3	**Kartik Makkar & Sons**, Abulane Meerut **Receipt Voucher**	Date 6th Jan, 2016

Particulars	Amount (₹)
Bank Account	28,000 (Dr)
Discount Allowed	2,000 (Cr)
Sales	30,000 (Cr)
Amounts (in words) Rupees Thirty Thousand Only	
Being ceiling fans sold vide Cheque No. 43525 on PNB	
	Authorised Signatory

Voucher for Transaction 7

Kartik Makkar & Sons, Abulane, Meerut No. : 3 **Payment Voucher**	Date 8th Jan, 2016
Particulars	Amount (₹)
Advertisement Expense	5,000 (Dr)
Cash Account	5,000 (Cr)
Amount (in words) Rupees Five Thousand Only	
Received with thanks Rupees Five Thousand in Cash. **Receiver's Signature**	**Authorised Signatory**

Voucher for Transaction 8

Kartik Makkar & Sons, Abulane, Meerut No. : 1 **Sales Voucher**	Date 9th Jan, 2016
Particulars	Amount (₹)
Gaur & Sons	3,34,000 (Dr)
Sales Account	3,34,000 (Cr)
Amounts (in words) Rupees Three Lakhs Thirty Four Thousand Only	
(Being water heaters, etc., sold vide Bill No. 1)	**Authorised Signatory**

Voucher for Transaction 9

Kartik Makkar & Sons, Abulane, Meerut No. : 4 **Payment Voucher**	Date 10th Jan, 2016
Particulars	Amount (₹)
Ram & Co.	50,000 (Dr)
Bank Account	50,000 (Cr)
Amounts (in words) Rupees Fifty Thousand Only	
Received Rupees Fifty Thousand Only against Bill No. 426 dated 2nd January, 2016 through Cheque No. 13553. **Receiver's Signature**	**Authorised Signatory**

Voucher for Transaction 10

Kartik Makkar & Sons, Abulane, Meerut No. : 2 **Sales Voucher**	Date 11th Jan, 2016
Particulars	Amount (₹)
M/s Veenu Bros.	44,000 (Dr)
Sales Account	44,000 (Cr)
Amounts (in words) Rupees Forty Four Thousand Only	
(Being ceiling fans sold vide Bill No. 2)	**Authorised Signatory**

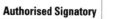

Voucher for Transaction 11

Kartik Makkar & Sons, Abulane Meerut No. : 4 Receipt Voucher	Date 12th Jan, 2016
Particulars	Amount (₹)
Bank Account	2,00,000 (Dr)
Gaur & Sons	2,00,000 (Cr)
Amounts (in words) Rupees Two Lakhs Only	
(Being part payment received against Bill No. 1 dated 9th January, 2016 vide Cheque. No. 43557 drawn on Union Bank, Meerut) **Authorised Signatory**	

Voucher for Transaction 12

Kartik Makkar & Sons, Abulane, Meerut No. : 2 Purchase Voucher	Date 13th Jan, 2016
Particulars	Amount (₹)
Purchases Account	15,000 (Dr)
Vishal Electronics	15,000 (Cr)
Amounts (in words) Rupees Fifteen Thousand Only	
(Being mini TVs purchased vide Bill No. 247 dated 13th January, 2016) **Authorised Signatory**	

Voucher for Transaction 13

Kartik Makkar & Sons, Abulane, Meerut No. : 5 Payment Voucher	Date 15th Jan, 2016
Particulars	Amount (₹)
Purchases Account	30,000 (Dr)
Cash Account	30,000 (Cr)
Amounts (in words) Rupees Thirty Thousand Only	
Received with thanks Rupees Thirty Thousand in Cash against vide Bill No. 213 Dated 15th January, 2016 **Receiver's Signature** **Authorised Signatory**	

Voucher for Transaction 14

Kartik Makkar & Sons, Abulane, Meerut No. : 2 Journal Voucher	Date 16th Jan, 2016
Particulars	Amount (₹)
Bills Receivable Account	22,000 (Dr)
Discount Allowed	2,000 (Dr)
M/s Veenu Bros.	24,000 (Cr)
Amounts (in words) Rupees Twenty Two Thousand Only	
(Being bills receivable received and discount allowed against Bill No. 2 dated 11th January, 2016) **Authorised Signatory**	

Voucher for Transaction 15

Kartik Makkar & Sons, Abulane, Meerut No. : 6 **Payment Voucher**	Date 24th Jan, 2016
Particulars	Amount (₹)
Drawings Account	6,000 (Dr)
Bank	6,000 (Cr)
Amounts (in words) Rupees Six Thousand Only	
Received with thanks Rupees Six Thousand Only vide Cheque No. 13554. **Receiver's Signature** **Authorised Signatory**	

Voucher for Transaction 16

Kartik Makkar & Sons, Abulane, Meerut No. : 7 **Payment Voucher**	Date 25th Jan, 2016
Particulars	Amount (₹)
Insurance Account	7,000 (Dr)
Bank Account	7,000 (Cr)
Amounts (in words) Rupees Seven Thousand Only	
Received with thanks Rupees Seven Thousand Only Cheque No. 13555. **Receiver's Signature** **Authorised Signatory**	

Voucher for Transaction 17

Kartik Makkar & Sons, Abulane, Meerut No. : 3 **Journal Voucher**	Date 25th Jan, 2016
Particulars	Amount (₹)
M/s Vishal Electronics	15,000 (Dr)
Promissory Note Two Months after Date	15,000 (Cr)
Amounts (in words) Rupees Fifteen Thousand Only	
Being promissory note issued, two months after date. **Authorised Signatory**	

Voucher for Transaction 18

Kartik Makkar & Sons, Abulane, Meerut No. : 8 **Payment Voucher**	Date 30th Jan, 2016
Particulars	Amount (₹)
Printing and Stationery Account	3,000 (Dr)
Bank Account	3,000 (Cr)
Amounts (in words) Rupees Three Thousand Only	
Received with thanks Rupees Three Thousand Only vide Cheque No. 13556. **Receiver's Signature** **Authorised Signatory**	

Voucher for Transaction 19

No. : 9	**Kartik Makkar & Sons**, Abulane, Meerut **Payment Voucher**	Date 30th Jan, 2016
	Particulars	Amount (₹)
Salary Account		12,000 (Dr)
Bank Account		12,000 (Cr)
Amounts (in words) Rupees Twelve Thousand Only		
Received with thanks Rupees Twelve Thousand Only vide Cheque No. 13557.		
Receiver's Signature		**Authorised Signatory**

Memorandum for event on 30th January, 2016.

Kartik Makkar & Sons

Memorandum

Enclosed is a list of unsold goods in stock on 30th January, 2016. Worth ₹ 1,61,800/- only.

Dated : 30th January, 2016 **Signature of Valuer**

JOURNAL

(In the Books of Kartik Makkar & Sons)

Date	Particulars		LF	Amt (Dr)	Amt (Cr)
2016					
Jan 2	Furniture and Fixtures A/c	Dr		1,14,000	
	To Ram & Co				1,14,000
	(Being furniture and fixtures purchased on credit vide bill no. 426)				
Jan 6	Discount Allowed A/c	Dr		2,000	
	To Sales A/c				2,000
	(Being goods sold and cheque no. 43525 on PNB is received, allowed discount)				
Jan 16	Discount Allowed A/c	Dr		2,000	
	To Veenu Bros				2,000
	(Being bill of exchange written on received and allowed them discount for ₹ 2,000)				

(In the Books of Kartik Makkar & Sons)

Dr **Cash Book** Cr

Date	Particulars	LF	Cash (₹)	Bank (₹)	Date	Particulars	LF	Cash (₹)	Bank (₹)
2016					2016				
Jan 1	To Capital A/c		1,00,000	5,00,000	Jan 3	By Purchases A/c			1,46,000
Jan 6	To Sales A/c			28,000	Jan 4	By Office Equip. A/c			90,000
Jan 12	To Gaur & Sons			2,00,000	Jan 8	By Advertisement A/c		5,000	
					Jan 10	By Ram & Co			50,000
					Jan 15	By Purchases A/c		30,000	
					Jan 24	By Drawings A/c			6,000
					Jan 25	By Insurance A/c			7,000
					Jan 30	By Printing & Stationery A/c			3,000
					Jan 30	By Salary A/c			12,000
					Jan 30	By Balance c/d		65,000	4,14,000
			1,00,000	7,28,000				1,00,000	7,28,000
2016									
Feb 1	To Balance b/d		65,000	4,14,000					

Purchase Book

Date	Particulars		Invoice No.	LF	Details	Total Amt (₹)
2016						
Jan 5	**Vishal Electronics**		536			
	4 Water Heaters @ 8,000 each				32,000	
	1 Air Conditioners @ 40,000 each				40,000	
					72,000	
	(–) Trade Discount (10%)				7,200	64,800
Jan 15	**Vishal Electronics**		247			
	3 Mini TVs @ 5,000 each				15,000	15,000
Jan 31	**Purchase A/c**	**Dr**				79,800

Sales Book

Date	Particulars		LF	Details	Total Amt (₹)
2016					
Jan 9	**M/s Gaur & Sons**				
	4 Water Heaters @ 15,000 each			60,000	
	5 Ceiling Fans @ 8,000 each			40,000	
	28 Electric Irons @ 5,000 each			1,40,000	
	2 Air Conditioners @ 47,000 each			94,000	3,34,000
Jan 11	**M/s Veenu Bros**				
	5 Ceiling Fans @ 10,000 each			50,000	
	(–) Trade Discount			6,000	44,000
2016					
Jan 3	**Sales A/c**	**Cr**			3,78,000

Bills Receivable Book

S.No.	From whom Received	Acceptor	Date of	Term Bill	Date of Maturity	Amount (₹)	How Disposed
1	Veenu Bros	Veenu Bros	16th Jan, 2016	1 Month	19th Feb, 2016	22,000	

Bills Payable Book

S.No.	Date of Bill	Name of Drawer	Payee	Term	Date of Maturity	Amount (₹)	Remarks
1	25th Jan, 2016	Kartik Makkar & Sons	Kartik Makkar & Sons	2 Months	28th March, 2016	15,000	

Project 2 Preparation of Bank Reconciliation Statement with the given Cash Book and the Pass Book

Vardhman & Co Bank Reconciliation Statement

SITUATION

Ankit Jain works as a cashier for Vardhman & Co, his responsibilities include entering and maintaining the firm's cash book and preparing a bank reconciliation statement at the end of the month.

The firm's cash book for March 2016 which Ankit has just finished entering and balancing for the month end is shown below. A copy of the firm's bank statement from the ICICI Bank Ltd. dated 31st March, 2016 has just been received and is also illustrated.

You are to make the entries necessary to update the cash book and reconcile the cash book with Bank Statement.

Vardhman & Co.

Cash Book

Receipts			Payments		
Date	Details	Bank	Date	Details	Bank
2016			2016		
1 Mar	Balance b/d	✓ 12,60,500	1 Mar	Munjal & Co Rent	✓ 2,00,000
4 Mar	Raja Ltd	✓ 3,10,000	4 Mar	S.Subbu 210725	✓ 1,83,500
8 Mar	Vishal Bros	✓ 13,500	5 Mar	RK & Co 210726	✓ 5,54,000
11 Mar	Neha Limited	24,000	8 Mar	Bata & Son 210727	✓ 1,60,000
11 Mar	Nayyar & Sons	53,000	13 Mar	K.Mohan 210728	16,000
12 Mar	V.Parikh	✓ 1,50,500	14 Mar	N.Laxmi 210729	14,000
13 Mar	Vipul Shah	1,000	15 Mar	Ravish & Co 210730	500
14 Mar	Rajesh Ltd	1,000	16 Mar	Oprah Instruments 210731	1,000
15 Mar	Sky Automation Pvt Ltd	11,000	17 Mar	Fashion Stores 210732	10,000
16 Mar	City Ventures	4,200	18 Mar	Swaroop Garage 210733	5,000
17 Mar	Spencer Partners	4,550	19 Mar	Jason Ltd 210734	2,000
18 Mar	Reliance Communication	4,000	20 Mar	Sharda Gandhi 210735	1,250
19 Mar	Bindals Store	1,500	21 Mar	Maruti Ltd 210736	7,500
20 Mar	Mona & Co	29,000	22 Mar	Max Insurance (DD)	✓ 69,500
25 Mar	A.Varmani	1,04,500	25 Mar	Vijay Computers 210737	✓ 9,00,000
31 Mar	Balance c/d	3,02,000	30 Mar	Rates (DD)	✓ 1,50,000
		22,74,250			22,74,250
			1 Apr	Balance b/d	3,02,000

Vardhman & Co

Pass Book

ICICI Bank				STATEMENT
3F, Sector 3, Shastri Nagar, Meerut				
Account	Vardhman & Co		**Account No.**	24569810
Date	31st March, 2016			

Date	Details	Debit	Credit	Balance
2016				
1 Mar	Balance			✓ 12,60,500 Cr
1 Mar	Munjal & Co	✓ 2,00,000		10,60,500 Cr
4 Mar	Raja Ltd		✓ 3,10,000	13,70,500 Cr
7 Mar	210725	✓ 1,83,500		11,87,000 Cr
11 Mar	Ronak Ltd		77,000	12,64,000 Cr
13 Mar	V.Parikh		✓ 1,50,500	14,14,500 Cr
15 Mar	Cheques		✓ 13,500	14,28,000 Cr
18 Mar	210727	✓ 1,60,000		12,68,000 Cr
18 Mar	210726	✓ 5,54,000		7,14,000 Cr
22 Mar	Max Insurance (DD)	✓ 69,500		6,44,500 Cr
27 Mar	210720	✓ 9,00,000		2,55,500 Dr
28 Mar	Mahonar's		57,000	1,98,500 Dr
29 Mar	Rates	✓ 1,50,000		3,48,500 Dr
29 Mar	Bank Interest	26,500		3,75,000 Dr
29 Mar	Bank Charges	22,500		3,97,500 Dr

The numerical difference between the pass book and cash book is ₹ 3,97,500 (–) ₹ 3,02,000 = ₹ 95,500. This is the difference which Ankit will have to reconcile.

Solution

To reconcile the cash book with the bank pass book following five steps are taken in practical.

Step 1. *Tick off the items which are found both in cash book and bank statement. Put (✓) sign before such items.*

Items ticked (✓) will neither be recorded in amended cash book nor in bank reconciliation statement.

Step 2. *Update the cash book from the bank statement.*

The unticked items on the bank statement indicate items that have gone through the bank account but have not yet been entered in Vardhman & Co's cash book. *These are*

			Amt (₹)
Receipt	11 Mar	Ronak	77,000
Receipt	28 Mar	Manohar	57,000
Payment	29 Mar	Bank Interest	26,500
Payment	29 Mar	Bank Charges	22,500

These items now need to be entered in the cash book to update it.

Step 3. *Balance the cash book bank columns to produce an updated balance*

Amended Cash Book

Dr	Receipts			Payments	Cr
Date	Details	Bank (₹)	Date	Details	Bank (₹)
2016			2016		
	To Ronak Ltd	77,000	31 Mar	By balance b/d	3,02,000
	To Manohar's	57,000		By Bank Interest	26,500
	To balance c/d	2,17,000		By Bank Charges	22,500
		3,51,000			3,51,000
				By balance b/d	2,17,000

The balance of bank column of cash book stands at ₹ 2,17,000 (overdraft) but the bank statement shows a balance of ₹ 3,97,500 (overdraft). Thus, a difference of ₹ 1,80,500 (*i.e.,* 3,97,500 – 2,17,000) still exist.

The remaining difference is dealt with in the Bank Reconciliation Statement.

Step 4. *Identify the remaining unticked items from the cash book. These are*

		Amt (₹)
Receipt	11 Mar	24,000
Receipt	11 Mar	53,000
Receipt	13 Mar	1,000
Receipt	14 Mar	1,000
Receipt	15 Mar	11,000
Receipt	16 Mar	4,200
Receipt	17 Mar	4,550
Receipt	18 Mar	4,000
Receipt	19 Mar	1,500
Receipt	20 Mar	29,000
Receipt	25 Mar	1,04,500
Payments	13 Mar	16,000
Payments	14 Mar	14,000
Payments	15 Mar	500
Payments	16 Mar	1,000
Payments	17 Mar	10,000
Payments	18 Mar	5,000
Payments	19 Mar	2,000
Payments	20 Mar	1,250
Payments	21 Mar	7,500

These items should appear on next month's bank statement and are timing differences. These are the items which will be required in the preparation of the bank reconciliation statement.

Step 5. *Preparation of Bank Reconciliation Statement.*

(*i*) Enter the Cash book Balance - The balance figure to use, as 'per the cash book' is the revised cash book balance after entering the items that appeared on the bank statement which had not previously been entered.

(*ii*) Add cheques issued but not presented for payment *i.e.,* unpresented cheques. *They are*

		Amt (₹)
K. Mohan	(Cheque No. 210728)	16,000
N. Mohan	(Cheque No. 210729)	14,000
Ravish & Co	(Cheque No 210730)	500
Oprah Instruments	(Cheque No 210731)	1,000
Fashion Stores	(Cheque No 210732)	10,000
Swaroop Garage	(Cheque No 210733)	5,000
Jason Ltd	(Cheque No 210734)	2,000
Sharda Ltd	(Cheque No 210735)	1,250
Maruti Ltd	(Cheque No 210736)	7,500
		57,250

(*iii*) Deduct cheques paid into the bank for collection but not yet collected. *They are*

	Amt (₹)
Neha Ltd	24,000
Nayyar & Sons	53,000
Vipul Shah	1,000
Rajesh Ltd	1,000
Sky Automation Pvt Ltd	11,000
City Ventures	4,200
Spencer Partners	4,550
Reliance Communication	4,000
Bindals Store	1,500
Mona & Co	29,000
A. Varmani	1,04,500
	2,37,750

(*iv*) Completing the Reconciliation - Now that all the outstanding items have been added or deducted, the recalculated balance on the bank reconciliation statement should be the same as the final bank statement balance.

Bank Reconciliation Statement
as on 31st March, 2016

Particulars			Plus Items (₹)	Minus Items (₹)
Overdraft (Cr. Balance) as per Cash Book				2,17,000
Add	Cheques issued but not presented for payment			
	K.Mohan (Ch. No. 210728)	16,000		
	N.Laxmi (Ch. No. 210729)	14,000		
	Ravish & Co (Ch. No. 210730)	500		
	Oprah Instruments (Ch. No. 210731)	1,000		
	Fashion Stores (Ch. No. 210732)	10,000		
	Swaroop Garage (Ch. No. 210733)	5,000		
	Jason Ltd (Ch. No. 210734)	2,000		
	Sharda Ltd (Ch. No. 210735)	1,250		
	Maruti Ltd (Ch. No. 210736)	7,500	57,250	
Less	Cheques paid into bank for collection but not yet collected			
	Neha Ltd.	24,000		
	Nayyar & Sons	53,000		
	Vipul Shah	1,000		
	Rajesh Ltd	1,000		
	Sky Automation Pvt Ltd	11,000		
	City Ventures	4,200		
	Sencer Partners	4,550		
	Reliance Communication	4,000		
	Bindals Store	1,500		
	Mona & Co.	29,000		
	A Varmani	1,04,500		2,37,750
	Overdraft (Dr. Balance) as per Pass Book		3,97,500	
			4,54,750	4,54,750

PROJECT REPORT

Project 3 Comprehensive

Case Study of a Sole Proprietor, willing to Start a Driving School and also to Sell Car Accessories

SITUATION

On 1st January, 2016 Mr Veer Das decided to start a driving school and also to sell car accessories through same place. For this purpose he bought a workshop at a cost of ₹ 20,00,000 and decided to invest ₹ 7,50,000 as a further capital in the proposed business. He employed assistants and training staff for this purpose. He wants to start with 5 second hand cars. For further funds he approached Punjab National Bank and secured a loan of 18,00,000 @ 10% per annum. The loan was payable in 4 instalments along with interest due.

	Amt (₹)
Purchased cars	13,00,000
Security depsoited for electricity connection with electricity board	60,000
Security deposited with BSNL for telephone and Internet connection	1,50,000
Purchased furniture	1,20,000
Fees received from students	19,50,000
Bought car accessories	3,30,000
Sale of car accessories	4,80,000
Wages paid	2,70,000
Salaries paid	3,75,000
Electricity charges	1,42,500
Advertisement	66,000
Postage and call	28,500
General expenses	18,000
Insurance premium	13,800
Bought laptop and printer	90,000

He withdrew ₹ 36,000 per month as drawings and repaid the annual instalment of bank loan along with interest due to 31st December, 2016. Assume all transactions took place through Punjab National Bank.

You are required to

(1) Journalise these transactions after considering the following information
   - (i) Depreciate building by 5% and cars and furniture @ 10% per annum
   - (ii) Stationery unpaid ₹ 27,000
   - (iii) Advertisement include unissued material worth ₹ 12,000.
   - (iv) Insurance prepaid ₹ 4,500
   - (v) Stock of car accessories ₹ 58,500.

(2) Post them into ledger and prepare trial balance.

(3) Prepare financial statements for the year ended 31st December, 2016.

Solution

Project is to record the transactions in journal book, post them into ledger accounts, draw a trial balance and to prepare the trading and profit and loss account and balance sheet.

(1) JOURNAL

Date	Particulars		LF	Amt (Dr)	Amt (Cr)
2016					
Jan 01	Building A/c	Dr		20,00,000	
	Bank A/c	Dr		7,50,000	
	To Capital A/c				27,50,000
	(Being capital invested in business)				
Jan 01	Bank A/c	Dr		18,00,000	
	To Bank Loan A/c				18,00,000
	(Being loan taken from PNB *i.e.,* 80% of ₹ 22,50,000)				
	Cars A/c	Dr		13,00,000	
	To Bank A/c				13,00,000
	(Being cars purchased)				
Jan 01	Electricity Board A/c	Dr		60,000	
	BSNL A/c	Dr		1,50,000	
	To Bank A/c				2,10,000
	(Being security deposited)				
	Furniture A/c	Dr		1,20,000	
	To Bank A/c				1,20,000
	(Being furniture purchased)				
	Bank A/c	Dr		19,50,000	
	To Fees from Students A/c				19,50,000
	(Being fees received from driving school during year)				
	Purchases A/c	Dr		3,30,000	
	To Bank A/c				3,30,000
	(Being accessories purchased for cars)				
	Bank A/c	Dr		4,80,000	
	To Sales A/c				4,80,000
	(Being cars accessories sold)				
	Wages A/c	Dr		2,70,000	
	Salaries A/c	Dr		3,75,000	
	Electricity Charges A/c	Dr		1,42,500	
	Advertisement A/c	Dr		66,000	
	Stationery A/c	Dr		28,500	
	General Expenses A/c	Dr		18,000	
	Insurance A/c	Dr		13,800	
	To Bank A/c				9,13,800
	(Being expenses paid)				
	Laptop and Printer A/c	Dr		90,000	
	To Bank A/c				90,000
	(Being printer purchased)				
	Drawings A/c (36,000 × 12)	Dr		4,32,000	
	To Bank A/c				4,32,000
	(Being drawings made during year)				
	Interest on Bank Loan A/c	Dr		1,80,000	
	To Bank Loan A/c				1,80,000
	(Being interest due as bank loan *i.e.,* 10% ₹ 18,00,000)				
	Bank Loan A/c	Dr		6,30,000	
	To Bank A/c				6,30,000
	(Being first instalment on loan paid along with interest @ 10% on loan *i.e.,* ₹ 4,50,000 + ₹ 1,80,000)				

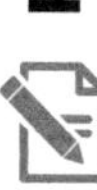

Date	Particulars		LF	Amt (Dr)	Amt (Cr)
2016 Dec. 31	Depreciation A/c To Building A/c To Cars A/c To Furniture A/c (Being depreciation provided on tangible fixed assets)	Dr		2,42,000	 1,00,000 1,30,000 12,000
	Stationery A/c To Stationery Outstanding A/c (Being stationery due but not paid)	Dr		27,000	 27,000
	Stock of Advertisement A/c To Advertisement A/c (Being stock of advertisement material)	Dr		12,000	 12,000
	Prepaid Insurance A/c To Insurance A/c (Being insurance prepaid)	Dr		4,500	 4,500
	Closing Stock A/c To Purchases A/c (Being stock of accessories purchased for cars left)	Dr		58,500	 58,500
	Total			1,15,29,800	1,15,29,800

(2)

Ledger Accounts

Building Account

Dr | Cr

Date	Particulars	JF	Amt (₹)	Date	Particulars	JF	Amt (₹)
2016 Jan 01	To Capital A/c		20,00,000	2016 Dec 31 Dec 31	By Depreciation A/c By Balance c/d		1,00,000 19,00,000
			20,00,000				20,00,000
2017 Jan 01	To Balance b/d		19,00,000				

Bank Account

Dr | Cr

Date	Particulars	JF	Amt (₹)	Date	Particulars	JF	Amt (₹)
2016 Jan 01	To Capital A/c To Bank Loan A/c To Fees from Students A/c To Sales A/c		7,50,000 18,00,000 19,50,000 4,80,000	2016 Dec 31	By Cars A/c By Electricity Board (Security) By BSNL (Security) By Furniture A/c By Purchases A/c By Wages A/c By Salaries A/c By Electricity Charges A/c By Advertisement A/c By Stationery A/c By General Expenses A/c By Insurance A/c By Laptop and Printer A/c By Drawings A/c By Bank Loan A/c By Balance c/d		13,00,000 60,000 1,50,000 1,20,000 3,30,000 2,70,000 3,75,000 1,42,500 66,000 28,500 18,000 13,800 90,000 4,32,000 6,30,000 9,54,200
			49,80,000				49,80,000
2017 Jan 01	To Balance b/d		9,54,200				

Dr **Capital Account** Cr

Date	Particulars	JF	Amt (₹)	Date	Particulars	JF	Amt (₹)
2016				2016			
Dec 31	By Balance c/d		27,50,000	Jan 01	By Building A/c		20,00,000
					By Bank A/c		7,50,000
			27,50,000				27,50,000
				2017			
				Jan 01	By Balance b/d		27,50,000

Dr **Bank Loan Account** Cr

Date	Particulars	JF	Amt (₹)	Date	Particulars	JF	Amt (₹)
2016				2016			
Dec 31	To Bank A/c		6,30,000	Jan 01	By Bank A/c		18,00,000
Dec 31	To Balance c/d		13,50,000	Dec 31	By Interest A/c		1,80,000
			19,80,000				19,80,000
				2017			
				Jan 01	By Balance b/d		13,50,000

Dr **Cars Account** Cr

Date	Particulars	JF	Amt (₹)	Date	Particulars	JF	Amt (₹)
2016				2016			
Jan 01	To Bank A/c		13,00,000	Dec 31	By Depreciation A/c		1,30,000
				Dec 31	By Balance c/d		11,70,000
			13,00,000				13,00,000
2017							
Jan 01	To Balance b/d		11,70,000				

Dr **Electricity Board Account** Cr

Date	Particulars	JF	Amt (₹)	Date	Particulars	JF	Amt (₹)
2016				2016			
Jan 01	To Bank A/c		60,000	Dec 31	By Balance c/d		60,000
			60,000				60,000
2017							
Jan 01	To Balance b/d		60,000				

Dr **BSNL Account** Cr

Date	Particulars	JF	Amt (₹)	Date	Particulars	JF	Amt (₹)
2016				2016			
Jan 01	To Bank A/c		1,50,000	Dec 31	By Balance c/d		1,50,000
			1,50,000				1,50,000
2017							
Jan 01	To Balance b/d		1,50,000				

Dr **Furniture Account** Cr

Date	Particulars	JF	Amt (₹)	Date	Particulars	JF	Amt (₹)
2016				2016			
Jan 01	To Bank A/c		1,20,000	Dec 31	By Depreciation A/c		12,000
				Dec 31	By Balance c/d		1,08,000
			1,20,000				1,20,000
2017							
Jan 01	To Balance b/d		1,08,000				

Dr **Fees from Students Account** Cr

Date	Particulars	JF	Amt (₹)	Date	Particulars	JF	Amt (₹)
2016 Dec. 31	To Trading A/c		19,50,000	2016	By Bank A/c		19,50,000
			19,50,000				19,50,000

Dr **Purchases Account** Cr

Date	Particulars	JF	Amt (₹)	Date	Particulars	JF	Amt (₹)
2016	To Bank A/c		3,30,000	2016 Dec 31 Dec 31	By Closing Stock A/c By Trading A/c		58,500 2,71,500
			3,30,000				3,30,000

Dr **Sales Account** Cr

Date	Particulars	JF	Amt (₹)	Date	Particulars	JF	Amt (₹)
2016 Dec 31	To Trading A/c		4,80,000	2016	By Bank A/c		4,80,000
			4,80,000				4,80,000

Dr **Wages Account** Cr

Date	Particulars	JF	Amt (₹)	Date	Particulars	JF	Amt (₹)
2016 Dec 31	To Bank A/c		2,70,000	2016 Dec 31	By Trading A/c		2,70,000
			2,70,000				2,70,000

Dr **Salaries Account** Cr

Date	Particulars	JF	Amt (₹)	Date	Particulars	JF	Amt (₹)
2016	To Bank A/c		3,75,000	2016 Dec 31	By Profit and Loss A/c		3,75,000
			3,75,000				3,75,000

Dr **Electricity Charges Account** Cr

Date	Particulars	JF	Amt (₹)	Date	Particulars	JF	Amt (₹)
2016	To Bank A/c		1,42,500	2016 Dec 31	By Profit and Loss A/c		1,42,500
			1,42,500				1,42,500

Dr **Advertisement Account** Cr

Date	Particulars	JF	Amt (₹)	Date	Particulars	JF	Amt (₹)
2016	To Bank A/c		66,000	2016 Dec 31 Dec 31	By Stock of Advertisement A/c By Profit and Loss A/c		12,000 54,000
			66,000				66,000

Dr **Stationery Account** Cr

Date	Particulars	JF	Amt (₹)	Date	Particulars	JF	Amt (₹)
2016	To Bank A/c To Stationery Outstanding A/c		28,500 27,000	2016 Dec 31	By Profit and Loss A/c		55,500
			55,500				55,500

Dr **General Expenses Account** Cr

Date	Particulars	JF	Amt (₹)	Date	Particulars	JF	Amt (₹)
2016				2016			
	To Bank A/c		18,000	Dec 31	By Profit and Loss A/c		18,000
			18,000				18,000

Dr **Insurance Account** Cr

Date	Particulars	JF	Amt (₹)	Date	Particulars	JF	Amt (₹)
2016				2016			
	To Bank A/c		13,800	Dec 31	By Prepaid Insurance A/c		4,500
				Dec 31	By Profit and Loss A/c		9,300
			13,800				13,800

Dr **Laptop and Printer Account** Cr

Date	Particulars	JF	Amt (₹)	Date	Particulars	JF	Amt (₹)
2016				2016			
Jan 01	To Bank A/c		90,000	Dec 31	By Balance c/d		90,000
			90,000				90,000
2017							
Jan 01	To Balance b/d		90,000				

Dr **Drawings Account** Cr

Date	Particulars	JF	Amt (₹)	Date	Particulars	JF	Amt (₹)
2016				2016			
	To Bank A/c		4,32,000	Dec 31	By Balance c/d		4,32,000
			4,32,000				4,32,000
2017							
Jan 01	To Balance b/d		4,32,000				

Dr **Interest on Bank Loan Account** Cr

Date	Particulars	JF	Amt (₹)	Date	Particulars	JF	Amt (₹)
2016				2016			
Dec 31	To Bank Loan A/c		1,80,000	Dec 31	By Profit and Loss A/c		1,80,000
			1,80,000				1,80,000

Dr **Stationery Outstanding Account** Cr

Date	Particulars	JF	Amt (₹)	Date	Particulars	JF	Amt (₹)
2016				2016			
Dec 31	To Balance c/d		27,000	Dec 31	By Stationery A/c		27,000
			27,000				27,000
				2017			
				Jan 01	By Balance b/d		27,000

Dr **Stock of Advertisement Account** Cr

Date	Particulars	JF	Amt (₹)	Date	Particulars	JF	Amt (₹)
2016				2016			
Dec 31	To Advertisement A/c		12,000	Dec 31	By Balance c/d		12,000
			12,000				12,000
2017							
Jan 01	To Balance b/d		12,000				

Dr **Prepaid Insurance Account** Cr

Date	Particulars	JF	Amt (₹)	Date	Particulars	JF	Amt (₹)
2016 Dec 31	To Insurance A/c		4,500	2016 Dec 31	By Balance c/d		4,500
			4,500				4,500
2017 Jan 01	To Balance b/d		4,500				

Dr **Closing Stock Account** Cr

Date	Particulars	JF	Amt (₹)	Date	Particulars	JF	Amt (₹)
2016 Dec 31	To Purchases A/c		58,500	2016 Dec 31	By Balance c/d		58,500
			58,500				58,500
2017 Jan 01	To Balance b/d		58,500				

Dr **Depreciation Account** Cr

Date	Particulars	JF	Amt (₹)	Date	Particulars	JF	Amt (₹)
2016 Dec 31	To Building A/c		1,00,000	2016 Dec 31	By Profit and Loss A/c		2,42,000
Dec 31	To Cars A/c		1,30,000				
Dec 31	To Furniture A/c		12,000				
			2,42,000				2,42,000

Trial Balance
as on 31st December, 2016

S. No.	Name of Accounts	Debit Balance (₹)	Credit Balance (₹)
1.	Building	19,00,000	—
2.	Bank	9,54,200	—
3.	Capital	—	27,50,000
4.	Bank Loan	—	13,50,000
5.	Cars	11,70,000	—
6.	Electricity Board	60,000	—
7.	BSNL	1,50,000	—
8.	Furniture	1,08,000	—
9.	Fees from Students	—	19,50,000
10.	Purchases	2,71,500	—
11.	Sales	—	4,80,000
12.	Wages	2,70,000	—
13.	Salaries	3,75,000	—
14.	Electricity Charges	1,42,500	—
15.	Advertisement	54,000	—
16.	Postage and Call	55,500	—
17.	General Expenses	18,000	—
18.	Insurance	9,300	—
19.	Laptop and Printer	90,000	—
20.	Drawings	4,32,000	—
21.	Interest on Bank Loan	1,80,000	—
22.	Depreciation	2,42,000	—
23.	Salaries Outstanding	—	27,000
24.	Stock of Advertisement	12,000	—
25.	Prepaid Insurance	4,500	—
26.	Closing Stock of Goods (31st December, 2016)	58,500	—
	Total	65,57,000	65,57,000

(3) Financial Statements

Trading and Profit and Loss A/c
for the year ending 31st December, 2016

Dr | | | | | Cr

Particulars		Amt (₹)	Particulars	Amt (₹)
To Purchases		2,71,500	By Sales A/c	4,80,000
To Wages		2,70,000	By Fees from Students	19,50,000
To Gross Profit c/d		18,88,500		
		24,30,000		24,30,000
To Salaries		3,75,000	By Gross Profit b/d	18,88,500
To Electricity Charges		1,42,500		
To Advertisement		54,000		
To Stationery		55,500		
To General Expenses		18,000		
To Insurance		9,300		
To Interest on Bank Loan		1,80,000		
To Depreciation				
Building	1,00,000			
Cars	1,30,000			
Furniture	12,000	2,42,000		
To Net Profit Transferred to Capital A/c		8,12,200		
		18,88,500		18,88,500

Balance Sheet
as at 31st December, 2016

Liabilities		Amt (₹)	Assets		Amt (₹)
Stationery Outstanding		27,000	Bank		9,54,200
Bank Loan		13,50,000	Prepaid Insurance		4,500
Capital	27,50,000		Closing Sock		58,500
(+) Net Profit	8,12,200		Stock of Advertisement		12,000
	35,62,200		Building	20,00,000	
(–) Drawings	4,32,000	31,30,200	(–) Depreciation	1,00,000	19,00,000
			Cars	13,00,000	
			(–) Depreciation	1,30,000	11,70,000
			Furniture	1,20,000	
			(–) Depreciation	12,000	1,08,000
			Laptop and Printer		90,000
			Electricity Board (Security Deposit)		60,000
			BSNL (Security Deposit)		1,50,000
		45,07,200			45,07,200

BAR DIAGRAMS and PIE CHARTS FOR EXPENSES

Bar Diagram of Indirect Expenses

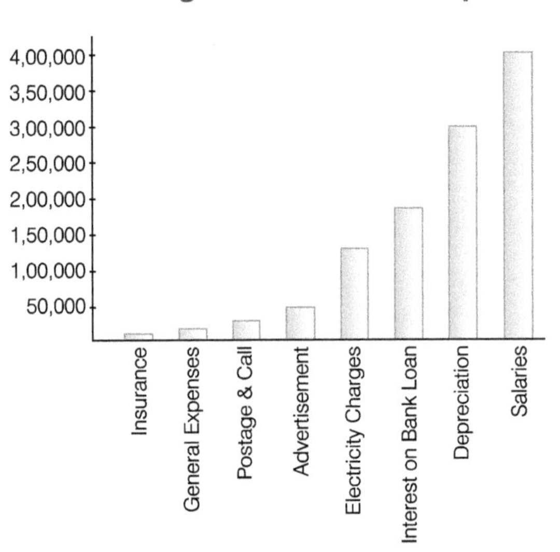

Pie Chart of Indirect Expenses

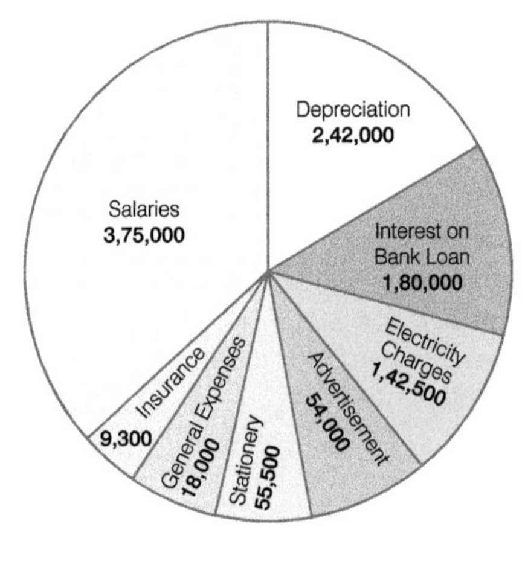

Bar Diagram of Direct and Indirect Expenses

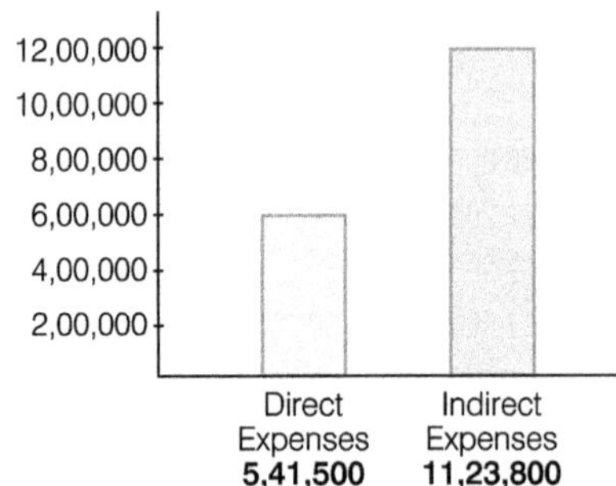

Pie Chart of Direct and Indirect Expenses

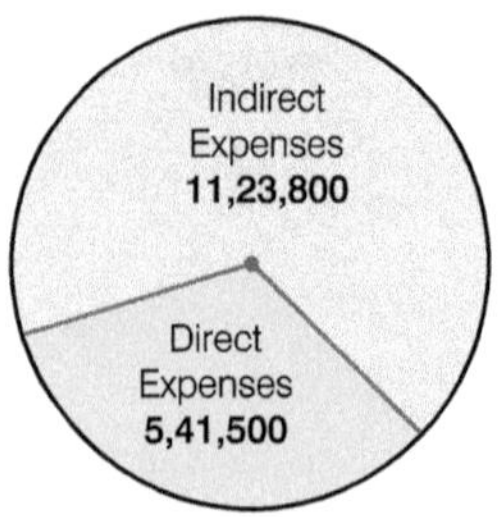

BAR DIAGRAMS and PIE CHARTS FOR LIABILITIES

Bar Diagram of Liabilities

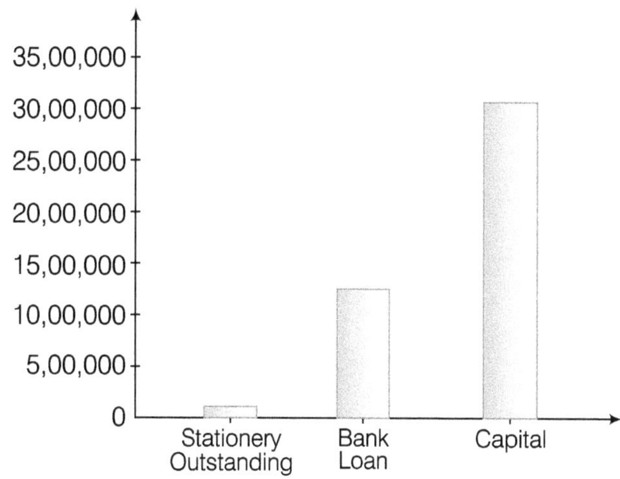

Pie Chart of Liabilities

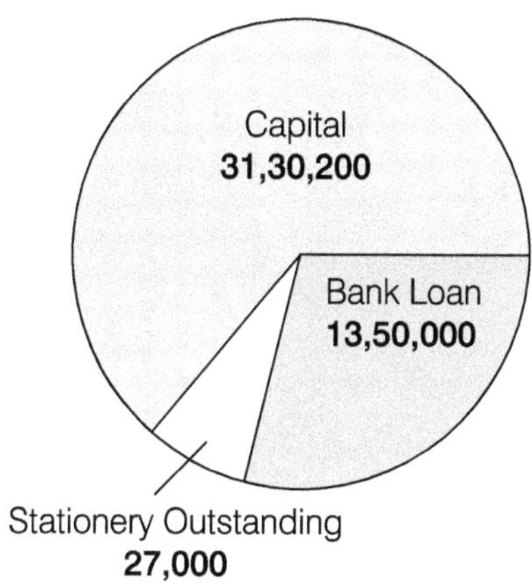

BAR DIAGRAMS and PIE CHARTS FOR ASSETS

Bar Diagram of Assets

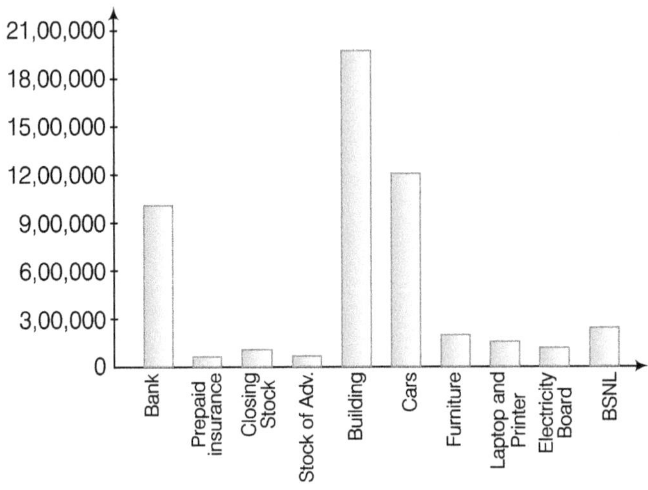

Pie Chart of Assets

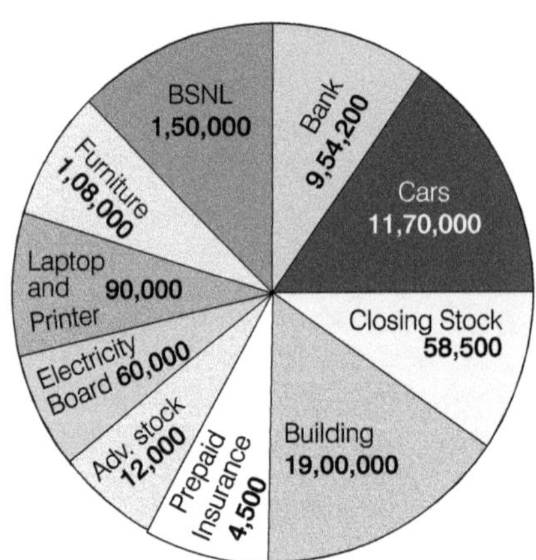

SAMPLE QUESTION PAPER 1

A Highly Simulated Sample Question Paper for CBSE Class XI Examinations

ACCOUNTANCY

GENERAL INSTRUCTIONS

1. This question paper contains two parts A and B.
2. All questions in both the parts are compulsory.
3. All parts of questions should be attempted at one place.
4. Marks for questions are indicated against each questions.
5. Answers should be brief and to the point.

TIME : 3 HOURS **MAX. MARKS : 80**

UNSOLVED

Part A

1. If total assets of the business are ₹ 4,50,000 and outside liabilities are ₹ 2,00,000, calculate owner's equity. (1)

(a) ₹ 6,50,000 (b) ₹ 2,50,000 (c) ₹ 4,50,000 (d) ₹ 2,00,000

2. Which of the following are two sided errors? (1)

(a) Machinery purchased recorded in purchase book
(b) Old furniture sold recorded as sale of goods
(c) Both (a) and (b)
(d) None of the above

3. Purchase of office furniture of ₹ 10,000 has been debited to general expense account. Which type of error is it? (1)

(a) Error of Omission (b) Error of Commission
(c) Error of Principle (d) Compensating error

4. Debtors are included under (1)

(a) Bills receivable (b) Fixed assets (c) Trade receivables (d) Trading account

5. Sales return is also called (1)

(a) return outward (b) return inward (c) bills payable (d) goods return

6. How many categories are there in GST for accounting purpose? (1)

(a) 5 (b) 6 (c) 7 (d) 4

7. Which of the following is a business transaction? (1)

(a) Goods worth ₹ 10,000 purchased on credit
(b) Purchasing air conditioner ₹ 15,000 for cash for personal use
(c) Owner not keeping good health
(d) Owner purchased a car of ₹ 5,00,000 for his son

8. Date of purchase 1st January, 2019, purchase price ₹ 1,00,000. On 30th September, 2020, this machine was sold for ₹ 50,000. Depreciation is provided on straight line method basis. The loss on sale will be (1)
(a) ₹ 10,000 (b) ₹ 15,000 (c) ₹ 0 (d) ₹ 20,000

9. The amount due from customers which could not be recovered and requires to be written-off is booked into
(a) bad debt recovered account (b) cash withdrawal
(c) goods withdrawn (d) bad debts account (1)

10. Goods costing ₹ 50,000 (selling price ₹ 60,000) were destroyed by fire. What will be the journal entry? (1)
(a) Loss by Fire A/c Dr 50,000
To Purchases A/c 50,000
(b) Purchases A/c Dr 50,000
To Loss by Fire A/c 50,000
(c) Cash A/c Dr 50,000
To Loss by Fire A/c 50,000
(d) Loss by Fire A/c Dr 50,000
To Cash A/c 50,000

UNSOLVED

11. According to .... principle, there should be reporting of all the significant information relating to the economic affairs of the business. (1)

12. While preparing BRS, a cheque of ₹ 1,000 received from a debtor recorded in Cash book but omitted to be banked. When balance as per cash book is the starting point, it will be .... (1)

13. Give an example of each of provision and reserves. (1)

14. Briefly define the following terms (3)
(i) Liabilities (ii) Purchases (iii) Sales

Or Write any three points of difference between cash basis of accounting and accrual basis of accounting.

15. Complete the missing journal entries. (4)

JOURNAL

Date	Particulars		LF	Amt (Dr)	Amt (Cr)
2020					
Jul 1	Richa	Dr		1,00,000	
	To Cash A/c				...
	To Discount Received A/c				...
	(Being ₹ 95,000 paid to Richa in full settlement of her account of ₹ 1,00,000)				
Jul 5	....	Dr		2,00,000	
	....				80,000
	....				1,20,000
	(Being goods purchased for cash ₹ 80,000 and on credit from Hritik Roshan for ₹ 1,20,000)				
Jul 18	Furniture A/c	Dr		1,00,000	
	To				1,00,000
	(Being furniture worth ₹ 1,00,000 bought and paid by cheque)				

Date	Particulars		LF	Amt (Dr)	Amt (Cr)
Jul 30	....	Dr		2,000	
	To				2,000
	(Being rent ₹ 2,000 due but not paid)				

16. Rectify the following errors and use suspense account where necessary. **(4)**

(i) ₹ 2,500 paid for office furniture was debited to office expenses account.

(ii) A cash sale of ₹ 7,500 to Saksham was correctly entered in the cash book but was posted to the credit of Saksham's account.

(iii) Goods amounting to ₹ 1,800, returned by Aryan, were entered in the sales book and posted therefrom to the credit of Aryan's account.

(iv) Bills receivable received from Sangeet for ₹ 5,000 was posted to the credit of bills payable account and credited to Sangeet's account.

Or From the following information, draw up a trial balance in the books of Ramesh Kumar as on 31st March, 2020.

Capital ₹ 2,80,000; purchases ₹ 72,000; discount allowed ₹ 2,400; carriage inwards ₹ 17,400; carriage outwards ₹ 4,600; sales ₹ 1,20,000; return inward ₹ 600; return outward ₹ 1,400; rent and taxes ₹ 2,400; plant and machinery ₹ 1,61,400; stock on 1st April, 2018 ₹ 31,000; sundry debtors ₹ 40,400; sundry creditors ₹ 24,000; investments ₹ 7,200; commission received ₹ 3,600; cash in hand ₹ 200; cash at bank ₹ 20,200; motor cycle ₹ 69,200 and stock on 31st March, 2019 (not adjusted) ₹ 41,000.

17. Briefly explain the historical cost concept. **(4)**

18. Enter the following transactions in the purchase book of M/s Shyam Book Store, Meerut. **(6)**

2020

Jan 4 Purchased from Vikas Book Store on credit, Meerut, vide Invoice No. 221
200 Business Studies Books @ ₹ 150 each, paid GST @ 12%
100 Economics Books @ ₹ 100 each, paid GST @ 12%

Jan 8 Purchased goods from Mayur Book Store on credit, Delhi, vide Invoice No. 231
150 Accountancy Books @ 250 each, paid GST @ 12%
50 Biology Books @ 350 each, paid GST @ 12%

Jan 13 Purchased goods from Nanak Book Store, Delhi, vide Invoice No. 239
20 Arihant Economics Class 12th @400 each, plus GST @12%
10 Arihant Political Class 12th @400 each, plus GST @12%
Less 20% trade discount on total purchases.

19. From the following particulars, prepare a bank reconciliation statement as on 31st March, 2016.

(i) Bank balance as per cash book is ₹ 1,00,000.

(ii) A cheque for ₹ 10,000 deposited but not recorded in the cash book. Bank has collected and credited this cheque.

(iii) A bank deposit of ₹ 2,000 was recorded in the cash book as if there is no bank column therein.

(iv) A cheque issued for ₹ 2,500 was recorded as ₹ 2,050 in the cash column. Bank has made the payment of this cheque.

(v) The debit balance of ₹ 15,000 as on the previous day was brought forward as a credit balance.

(vi) The payment side of the cash book (bank column) was undercast by ₹ 1,000.

(vii) A cash discount allowed of ₹ 1,120 was recorded as ₹ 1,210 in the bank column.

(viii) A cheque of ₹ 5,000 received from a debtor was recorded in the cash book but not deposited in the bank for collection.

(ix) One outgoing cheque of ₹ 3,000 was recorded twice in the cash book. **(6)**

20. A firm purchased on 1st January, 2017 a second hand plant for ₹ 72,000 and spent ₹ 8,000 on its installation.

On 1st July in the same year, another plant costing ₹ 40,000 was purchased. On 1st July, 2019 plant brought on 1st January, 2017 was sold for ₹ 24,000 and a new plant purchased for ₹ 1,28,000 on the same date. Depreciation is provided annually on 31st December @ 10% p.a. on the written down value method. Show the plant account from 2017 to 2019. (8)

Or

(i) What do you understand by historical cost of an assets?

(ii) Following balances appear in the books of Mukesh Sharma, as on 1st April, 2020

Machinery Account	₹ 80,000
Provision for Depreciation Account	₹ 31,000

On 1st July, 2020, a machinery which was purchased on 1st April, 2017 for ₹ 12,000 was sold for ₹ 5,000 plus CGST and SGST @ 6% each and on the same date another machinery was purchased for ₹ 3,200 plus CGST and SGST @ 6% each. The firm charges depreciation @ 15% p.a. by fixed installment method and followed financial year.

Prepare machinery account and provision for depreciation account for the year 2020-21. Also, pass journal entry for the sale of machinery.

UNSOLVED

21. Analyse the effect of each transaction and prove that the accounting equation (A = L + C) always remains balanced. (8)

(i) Introduced ₹ 4,00,000 as cash and ₹ 25,000 by stock.

(ii) Purchased plant for ₹ 1,50,000 by paying ₹ 7,500 in cash and balance at a later date.

(iii) Deposited ₹ 3,00,000 into the bank.

(iv) Purchased office furniture for ₹ 50,000 and made payment by cheque.

(v) Purchased goods worth ₹ 40,000 for cash and for ₹ 17,500 on credit.

(vi) Goods amounting to ₹ 22,500 was sold for ₹ 30,000 on cash basis.

(vii) Goods costing to ₹ 40,000 was sold for ₹ 62,500 on credit basis.

(viii) Cheque issued to the supplier of goods worth ₹ 17,500.

(ix) Cheque received from customer amounting to ₹ 37,500.

(x) Withdrawn by owner for personal use ₹ 12,500.

Or

Journalise the following transactions in the books of M/s. Chandra Mohan.

(i) Vishal who owed ₹ 5,000 was declared insolvent and 60 paise in a rupee are received as final compensation.

(ii) Out of insurance paid this year, ₹ 3,000 is related to next year.

(iii) Provide depreciation @ 10% on furniture costing ₹ 10,000 for 9 months.

(iv) Paid customs duty ₹ 11,000 in cash on import of a new machinery.

(v) Goods sold costing ₹ 10,000 to M/s. Bhardwaj & Sons at a invoice price 10% above cost less 10% trade discount.

(vi) Received a cheque from Rajesh ₹ 5,450. Allowed him discount ₹ 150.

(vii) Returned goods to Simran of the value of ₹ 350.

(viii) Issued a cheque in favour of M/s. Rajveer Timber Company on account of the purchase of timber worth ₹ 7,500.

(ix) Sold goods to Sunny, list price ₹ 4,000, trade discount 10% and cash discount 5%. He paid the amount on the same day and availed the cash discount.

(x) Received an order from Gauri & Co. for supply of goods of the list price ₹ 1,00,000 with an advance of 10% of list price.

(xi) Received commission ₹ 5,000 half of which is in advance.

(xii) Cash embezzled by an employee ₹ 1,000.

Part B

22. Which of the following is correct? (1)
 (a) Gross Profit = Net Profit – Other Income + Indirect Expenses
 (b) Gross Profit = Net Profit – Indirect Expenses + Other Incomes
 (c) Gross Profit = Net Profit + Cost of Goods Sold
 (d) Gross Profit = Net Profit – Cost of Goods Sold

23. Ankit is the owner of a firm. He brought additional capital of ₹ 8,00,000 to the firm. The receipt of money in business is (1)
 (a) revenue receipt (b) capital receipt
 (c) revenue expenditure (d) capital expenditure

24. Loan from bank @ 12% per annum is ₹ 8,00,000. Interest on loan is due for the whole year. Amount shown on liabilities side of balance sheet will be (1)
 (a) ₹ 8,00,000 (b) ₹ 8,12,000 (c) ₹ 8,90,000 (d) ₹ 8,96,000

UNSOLVED

25. Which of the following is the journal entry for unsold stock at the end of the accounting year 31st March, 2020 of ₹ 40,500? (1)

(a) Closing Stock A/c	Dr	40,500	
To Profit and Loss A/c			40,500
(b) Trading A/c	Dr	40,500	
To Profit and Loss A/c			40,500
(c) Closing Stock A/c	Dr	40,500	
To Trading A/c			40,500
(d) Trading A/c	Dr	40,500	
To Closing Stock A/c			40,500

26. Goods distributed as free sample. The effect of this entry will be (1)
 (a) it is the proprietor drawings
 (b) it is deducted from purchases in the trading account
 (c) it will be shown on the debit side of the profit and loss account
 (d) Both (b) and (c)

27. Any expenditure intended to benefit the current period is .... (1)

28. Where is apprenticeship premium received, appearing in the trial balance shown? (1)

29. Operating profit earned by Ashima Grewal a sole proprietor, in 2019-20 was ₹ 17,00,000. Her non-operating incomes were ₹ 1,50,000 and non-operating expenses were ₹ 3,75,000. Calculate the net profit earned during the year. (3)

Or Calculate net purchases from the following details

Particulars	Amt (₹)
Gross Profit	90,000
Net Profit	48,000
Net Sales	3,00,000

Particulars	Amt (₹)
Return Inward	10,000
Return Outward	20,000
Freight Inward	5,000
Wages	10,000
Lighting	15,000
Closing Stock	20,000

Opening stock is one and half times of closing stock.

30. Distinguish between capital receipts and revenue receipts. **(4)**

Or

Define closing entries. Give examples of closing entries of trading account.

31. From the following ledger balances of Mr Navjot Singh, prepare the trading and profit and loss account for the year ended 31st March, 2020 after making the necessary adjustments. **(4)**

Particulars	Amt (₹)	Particulars	Amt (₹)
Trade expenses	1,600	Purchases	1,64,000
Freight and duty	4,000	Stock (1st April, 2019)	30,000
Carriage outwards	1,000	Plant and machinery (1st April, 2019)	40,000
Sundry debtors	41,200	Plant and machinery	10,000
Furniture and fixtures	10,000	(additions on 1st October, 2019)	
Return inwards	4,000	Drawings	12,000
Printing and stationery	800	Capital	1,60,000
Rent, rates and taxes	9,200	Provision for doubtful debts	1,600
Sundry creditors	20,000	Rent for premises sublet	3,200
Sales	2,40,000	Insurance charges	1,400
Return outwards	2,000	Salaries and wages	42,600
Postage and telegraphs	1,600	Cash in hand	12,400
		Cash at bank	41,000

Additional Information

(i) Stock on 31st March, 2020 was ₹ 28,000.

(ii) Write-off ₹ 1,200 as bad debts.

(iii) Provision for doubtful debts is to be maintained @ 5%.

(iv) Provision for depreciation on furniture and fixtures at 5% p.a. and on plant and machinery at 20% p.a.

(v) Insurance prepaid was ₹ 200.

(vi) A fire occurred in the godown and stock of the value of ₹ 10,000 was destroyed. It was insured and the insurance company admitted full claim.

32. From the following trial balance of Sh. Prakash, prepare trading and profit and loss account for the year ended 31st March, 2020 and balance sheet as at that date. **(6)**

Particulars	Amt (Dr)	Amt (Cr)
Purchases and Sales	5,50,000	10,40,000
Return Inwards	30,000	—
Return Outwards	—	18,000
Carriage	24,800	—
Wages and Salaries	1,17,200	—

UNSOLVED

Particulars	Amt (Dr)	Amt (Cr)
Trade Expenses	4,400	—
Rent	—	26,000
Insurance	4,000	—
Audit Fees	2,400	—
Debtors and Creditors	2,20,000	1,24,200
Bills Receivable and Bills Payable	6,600	4,400
Printing and Advertising	11,000	—
Commission	—	2,000
Opening Stock	72,000	—
Cash-in-Hand	25,600	—
Cash-at-Bank	53,600	—
Bank Loan	—	40,000
Interest on Loan	3,000	—
Capital	—	5,00,000
Drawings	30,000	—
Fixed Assets	6,00,000	—
	17,54,600	17,54,600

Additional Information

(i) Stock at the end ₹ 1,20,000.
(ii) Depreciation to be charged on fixed assets @ 10%.
(iii) Commission earned but not received amounting to ₹ 800.
(iv) Rent received in advance ₹ 2,000.
(v) 8% interest to be allowed on capital and ₹ 1,800 to be charged as interest on drawings.

UNSOLVED

Answers

1. (b) **2.** (c) **3.** (c) **4.** (c) **5.** (b) **6.** (b) **7.** (a)
8. (b) **9.** (d) **10.** (a)
11. full disclosure **12.** subtracted **16.** *Or* Total of trial balance = ₹ 4,29,000
18. Purchases account debited by ₹ 1,17,152 **19.** Credit Balance as per Pass book = ₹ 1,35,290

20. Balance of plant account
2017 = ₹ 72,000 (Plant I), ₹ 38,000 (Plant II)
2018 = ₹ 64,800 (Plant I), ₹ 34,200 (Plant II)
2019 = ₹ 30,780 (Plant II), ₹ 1,21,600 (Plant III)
(Brought down to 2020)
Loss on sale of plant = ₹ 37,560

Or

(ii) Balance of machinery on 31st March, 2021 ₹ 71,200, loss on sale of machinery is ₹ 1,150.

21. Assets = Liabilities + Capital ⇒ ₹ 5,97,500 = ₹ 1,42,500 + ₹ 4,55,000
22. (a) **23.** (b) **24.** (d) **25.** (c) **26.** (d) **27.** revenue expenditure
29. Net profit is ₹ 14,75,000 *Or* Net purchases is ₹ 1,70,000
31. Gross profit = ₹ 78,000
Net profit = ₹ 12,100
32. Gross profit = ₹ 3,84,000
Net profit = ₹ 2,87,800
Total of balance sheet = ₹ 9,66,600

SAMPLE QUESTION PAPER 2

A Highly Simulated Sample Question Paper for CBSE Class XI Examinations

ACCOUNTANCY

GENERAL INSTRUCTIONS

1. This question paper contains two parts A and B.
2. All questions in both the parts are compulsory.
3. All parts of questions should be attempted at one place.
4. Marks for questions are indicated against each questions.
5. Answers should be brief and to the point.

TIME : 3 HOURS **MAX. MARKS : 80**

UNSOLVED

Part A

1. The last step of accounting process is (1)
   (a) communicating (b) indentifying (c) summarising (d) interpreting result
2. Which of these is not a business transaction? (1)
   (a) Bought furniture of ₹ 10,000 for business.
   (b) Paid for salaries of employees ₹ 5,000.
   (c) Paid son's fees from her personal bank account ₹ 20,000.
   (d) Paid son's fees from business ₹ 2,000.
3. Identify the incorrect statement. (1)
   (a) India has followed dual GST model, i.e. Central (GST) and State (GST).
   (b) Goods and services tax is a value added tax.
   (c) An integrated tax (GST) would be levied and collected by the centre on interstate supply of goods and services.
   (d) The list of exempted goods and services are different for the centre and the state.
4. Which source document is prepared by the seller for goods sold against cash? (1)
   (a) Pay-in-slip (b) Receipt (c) Cash memo (d) Invoice
5. Which of the following accounts are related to expenses, losses, revenue, gain, etc like salary account? (1)
   (a) Real (b) Nominal (c) Assets (c) Liabilities
6. During the year, Z had cash sales of ₹ 1,95,000 and credit sales of ₹ 80,000. His expenses for the year were ₹ 1,35,000 out of which ₹ 40,000 are still to be paid. Find out Z's income following accrual basis of accounting. (1)
   (a) ₹ 1,00,000 (b) ₹ 1,80,000 (c) ₹ 1,40,000 (d) ₹ 1,30,000
7. When there is return of goods in a journal, then a debit note is prepared and sent to supplier, what type of journal is used for this purpose? (1)

(a) Sale return journal
(b) Purchase return journal
(c) Cash sale journal
(d) Cash purchase journal

8. A cheque of ₹ 2,345 issued by Z was recorded in deposit column as ₹ 2,435. To ascertain the balance as cash book of Z. (1)

(a) ₹ 2,345 should be added to the balance as per pass book.
(b) ₹ 2,435 should be subtracted from the balance as per pass book.
(c) ₹ 4,780 should be subtracted from the balance as per pass book.
(d) ₹ 10 should be added to the balance as per pass book.

9. An asset was purchased ₹ 5,00,000, ₹ 5,000 were incurred for freight and transportation ₹ 20,000 spent on installation expenses and commission paid on purchase to agent 5% of cost of asset. Pass the necessary journal entry. (1)

(a) Cash A/c Dr 5,50,000
To Asset A/c 5,50,000

(b) Asset A/c Dr 5,50,000
To Purchases A/c 5,50,000

(c) Asset A/c Dr 5,50,000
To Cash A/c 5,50,000

(d) Purchases A/c Dr 5,50,000
To Asset A/c 5,50,000

10. What will be the journal entry to record transfer of asset sold to a asset disposal account? (1)

(a) Asset A/c Dr
To Asset Disposal A/c

(b) Asset Disposal A/c Dr
To Cash A/c

(c) Cash A/c Dr
To Asset Disposal A/c

(d) Asset Disposal A/c Dr
To Asset A/c

11. When discount is allowed to customers for making prompt payment, it is called .... discount. (1)

12. .... is an example of source documents which is used by the purchaser for returning the purchased goods. (1)

13. Do you think that a transaction can break the accounting equation? (1)

14. State the advantages offered by accrual basis of accounting. (3)

Or Give any three points of difference between book-keeping and accounting.

15. Record the following transactions during the week ending 30th December, 2019 with a weekly imprest of ₹ 500. (4)

Date	Particulars	Amt (₹)
Dec 24	Stationery	100
Dec 25	Bus fare	12
Dec 25	Cartage	40
Dec 26	Taxi fare	80
Dec 27	Wages to casual labour	90
Dec 29	Postage	80

16. Prepare bank reconciliation statement of Shri Subhash Bhalla as on 31st December, 2019. (4)

(i) The payment of a cheque for ₹ 550 was recorded twice in the pass book.
(ii) Withdrawal column of the pass book was undercast by ₹ 200.

UNSOLVED

(iii) A cheque of ₹ 200 has been debited in the bank column of the cash book but it was not sent to bank at all.

(iv) Interest on bank overdraft ₹ 300 charged by the bank.

(v) ₹ 500 in respect of dishonoured bill were entered in the pass book but not in the cash book.

(vi) Overdraft as per pass book is ₹ 20,000.

17. "IFRS are very useful for multinational or global business enterprises." In the light of this statement, give any four such benefits of IFRS. (4)

Or

When should revenue be recognised as per revenue recognition principle? Are there exceptions to the general rule?

18. In taking out a trial balance, a book-keeper finds that debit total exceeds the credit total by ₹ 7,040. The amount is placed to the credit of a newly opened suspense account. Subsequently, the following mistakes were discovered. You are required to pass the necessary entries for rectifying the mistakes and show the suspense account. (6)

(i) Sales day book was overcast by ₹ 2,000.

(ii) A sale of ₹ 1,000 to Gokul Prasad was wrongly debited to Kanti Prasad.

(iii) General expenses ₹ 360 was posted as ₹ 1,600.

(iv) Cash received from Shanti Prasad was debited to his account ₹ 3,000.

(v) While carrying forward the total of one page of the purchase book to the next, the amount of ₹ 24,700 was entered as ₹ 26,500.

UNSOLVED

19. Pass the journal entries for the following transactions (6)

(i) Purchased goods from Sangeet of ₹ 80,000; plus SGST 6% and CGST 6%.

(ii) Hemant who owed to Manu ₹ 10,000 is declared insolvent and 55 paise in a rupee is received from his estate.

(iii) Sold goods to Amitoj at the list price of ₹ 75,000 less 20% trade discount; plus SGST 6% and CGST 6%.

(iv) Purchased machinery from Atul for ₹ 40,000 and paid him by means of bank draft purchased from bank for ₹ 40,040.

20. Tata Ltd purchased a machinery on 1st April, 2017 for ₹ 1,20,000. It bought another machinery on 1st July, 2018 for ₹ 80,000. On 1st January, 2020, machinery bought on 1st April, 2017 was sold for ₹ 80,000 and a fresh plant was purchased on the same date for ₹ 60,000. Depreciation is charged at 10% p.a. on diminishing balance method. Show the machinery account for 3 years assuming that accounts are closed on 31st March each year. (8)

Or MJ Ltd purchased a second hand plant for ₹ 1,80,000 and spent ₹ 20,000 on its installation and freight on 1st July, 2016. Depreciation was provided @ 10% p.a. on reducing balance method. On 31st December, 2018, 1/5th of the plant was damaged due to fire and scrap was sold for ₹ 10,000. It was decided to buy a new plant for ₹ 60,000 on 1st January, 2019.

Prepare plant account for 3 years assuming that books were closed on 31st March every year.

21. Write a two-column cash book with cash and bank columns from the following transactions and post them into ledger. Also pass necessary journal entries related to discount allowed and discount received. (8)

2022

Mar 1	Cash in hand ₹ 30,000
Mar 3	Purchased goods for cash ₹ 12,000
Mar 5	Deposited in bank ₹ 10,000

Mar 8	Cash sales ₹ 20,000
Mar 10	Cash withdrew from bank for office use ₹ 4,000
Mar 12	Received cash from Daksh ₹ 6,000 and allowed him discount of ₹ 200
Mar 15	Received cheque from Kanika ₹ 4,000 and deposited in the bank on the same day, allowed her discount ₹ 150
Mar 18	Received cheque from Sakshi for ₹ 10,000 (not banked)
Mar 19	Cheque received from Sakshi deposited in the bank
Mar 24	Paid to Simran by cheque ₹ 5,000, she allowed discount ₹ 250
Mar 27	Withdrew from bank for personal use ₹ 3,000
Mar 28	Sold goods on credit to Deeksha ₹ 8,000
Mar 30	Purchased goods on credit from Simran ₹ 10,000
Mar 31	Received cheque from Deeksha ₹ 4,000 and deposited in the bank
Mar 31	Bank charges for the month ₹ 200

Or Following is the trial balance of Raj Nayak as on 31st March, 2016.

Name of Accounts	LF	Debit Balance (₹)	Credit Balance (₹)
Capital			6,40,000
Fixed Assets		3,60,000	
Drawings		1,20,000	
Debtors		4,80,000	
Creditors			3,60,000
Purchases		14,20,000	
Sales			21,00,000
Bank Balance		90,000	
Cash in Hand		60,000	
Salaries		3,30,000	
Rent		2,40,000	
Total		31,00,000	31,00,000

Having prepared the trial balance, it was discovered that following transactions remained unrecorded

(i) Goods were sold on credit amounting to ₹ 80,000.

(ii) Paid to creditors ₹ 44,000 by cheque.

(iii) Goods worth ₹ 14,000 were returned to a supplier.

(iv) Paid salary ₹ 30,000 by cheque.

Required

(i) Pass journal entries for the above mentioned transactions and post them into ledger.

(ii) Redraft the trial balance.

UNSOLVED

Part B

22. Which of the following is correct? (1)
    (a) Net sales = Cash sales + Credit sales – Sales return
    (b) Net sales = Cash sales + Credit sales + Sales return
    (c) Net sales = Total sales – Credit sales (d) Net sales = Sales + Credit sales

23. In which of the following cases, closing stock will not be shown in the trading account? (1)
    (a) When valuation of closing stock is on FIFO method
    (b) When closing stock is not ascertained accurately
    (c) When closing stock is adjusted in the purchases
    (d) When it is appearing outside the trial balance

24. Consider the following statement. (1)
    I. Balance sheet contains only the balances of personal and real accounts.
    II. Assets side of balance sheet is always equal to capital side.
    III. Drawings are not shown in the balance sheet as it is a personal expense of the owner.
    Choose the correct option.
    (a) All are correct (b) All are incorrect (c) Only I is correct (d) Only II and III is correct

25. Find out the closing stock from the following Opening Stock = ₹ 20,000, Sales = ₹ 1,00,000, Purchases = ₹ 70,000, Rate of gross profit on cost = $33\frac{1}{3}\%$ (1)
    (a) ₹ 20,000 (b) ₹ 35,000 (c) ₹ 15,000 (d) ₹ 45,000

26. **Extract of Trial Balance**
as on 31st March, 2020

Name of Accounts	Debit Balance (₹)	Credit Balance (₹)
Bad Debt	3,000	
Provision for Bad Debts		3,500
Debtors	40,000	

It is desired to maintain a provision for doubtful debts @ 10% on debtors. The amount debited to profit and loss account is (1)
    (a) ₹ 4,000 (b) ₹ 5,000 (c) ₹ 6,500 (d) ₹ 3,500

27. Liability which is payable on the happening of an event is .... (1)

28. Name any two items that are credited to trading account? (1)

29. Calculate closing stock from the following details (3)

Opening stock	₹ 20,000
Cash sales	₹ 60,000
Purchases	₹ 70,000
Credit sales	₹ 40,000

Rate of gross profit on cost $33\frac{1}{3}\%$.

Or Calculate opening stock from the following details

Closing stock	₹ 20,000
Cash sales	₹ 60,000
Net purchases	₹ 70,000
Net credit sales	₹ 40,000
Return outward	₹ 5,000
Return inward	₹ 7,000

Rate of gross profit on cost $33\frac{1}{3}\%$.

30. State the objectives of preparing financial statements. (4)

Or Differentiate between a balance sheet and trial balance.

31. The following trial balance is extracted from the books of a Rama Enterprises on 31st Decemeber, 2019 (4)

Particulars	Debit Balance (₹)	Credit Balance (₹)
Furniture	6,400	—
Vehicles	62,500	—
Buildings	75,000	—
Capital	—	1,25,000
Bad debts	1,250	—
Provision for doubtful debts	—	2,000
Sundry debtors and creditors	38,000	25,000
Stock on 1st January, 2019	34,600	—
Purchases and sales	54,750	1,54,500
Bank overdraft	—	28,500
Sales and purchases returns	2,000	1,250
Advertising	4,500	—
Interest on bank overdraft	1,180	—
Commission	—	3,750
Cash	6,500	—
Taxes and insurance	12,500	—
General expenses	7,820	—
Salaries	33,000	—
	3,40,000	3,40,000

The following adjustments are to be made

(i) Stock in hand on 31st December, 2019 was ₹ 32,500.

(ii) Depreciate buildings at the rate of 5%, furniture and fittings at the rate of 10% and motor vehicles at the rate of 20%.

(iii) ₹ 850 is due for interest on bank overdraft.

(iv) Salaries ₹ 3,000 and taxes ₹ 1,200 are outstanding.

(v) Insurance amounting to ₹ 1,000 is prepaid.

(vi) $\frac{1}{3}$rd of the commission received is in respect of work to be done next year.

(vii) Write-off a further sum of ₹ 1,000 as bad debts and provision for doubtful debts is to be made equal to 10% on sundry debtors.

Prepare a trading and profit and loss account for the year ending 31st December, 2019.

32. The following balances have been extracted from the trial balance of M/s Runway Shine Ltd. Prepare a trading and profit and loss account and a balance sheet as on 31st December, 2019. (6)

Name of Accounts	Amt (₹)	Name of Accounts	Amt (₹)
Purchases	1,50,000	Sales	2,50,000
Opening stock	50,000	Return outwards	4,500
Return inwards	2,000	Interest received	3,500
Carriage inwards	4,500	Discount received	400
Cash-in-hand	77,800	Creditors	1,25,000

UNSOLVED

Name of Accounts	Amt (₹)	Name of Accounts	Amt (₹)
Cash-at-bank	60,800	Bills payable	6,040
Wages	2,400	Capital	1,00,000
Printing and stationery	4,500		
Discount	400		
Bad debts	1,500		
Insurance	2,500		
Investment	32,000		
Debtors	53,000		
Bills receivable	20,000		
Postage and telegraph	400		
Commission	200		
Interest	1,000		
Repair	440		
Lighting charges	500		
Telephone charges	100		
Carriage outwards	400		
Motor car	25,000		
	4,89,440		4,89,440

UNSOLVED

Additional Information

(i) Further bad debts ₹ 1,000, Discount on debtors ₹ 500 and make a provision on debtors @ 5%.
(ii) Interest received on investment @ 5%.
(iii) Wages and interest outstanding ₹ 100 and ₹ 200 respectively.
(iv) Depreciation charged on motor car @ 5% p.a.
(v) Closing stock ₹ 32,500.

Answers

1. (a) **2.** (c) **3.** (d) **4.** (c) **5.** (b) **6.** (c) **7.** (b)
8. (b) **9.** (c) **10.** (d) **11.** trade **12.** Debit note

15. Balance of petty cash book = ₹ 98

16. Credit balance as per cash book = ₹ 18,650

20. Balance of machinery account
2017-18 = ₹ 1,08,000; 2018-19 = ₹ 1,71,200; 2019-20 = ₹ 1,25,100
Loss on sale of machinery = ₹ 9,910
Or
Balance of plant account
2016-17 = ₹ 1,85,000; 2017-18 = ₹1,66,500
Loss on sale of plant = ₹ 20,802
2018-19 = ₹ 1,78,380

21. Cash Balance = ₹ 38,000; Bank Balance = ₹15,800
Or
Trial Balance Total = ₹ 31,36,000

22. (a) **23.** (c) **24.** (c) **25.** (c) **26.** (d) **27.** contingent liabilities

29. Closing stock = ₹ 15,000 *Or* Opening stock = ₹ 25,000

31. Net profit = ₹ 15,510

32. Net profit = ₹ 66,010; Total of balance sheet = ₹ 2,97,350

SAMPLE QUESTION PAPER 3

A Highly Simulated Sample Question Paper for CBSE Class XI Examinations

ACCOUNTANCY

GENERAL INSTRUCTIONS

1. This question paper contains two parts A and B.
2. All questions in both the parts are compulsory.
3. All parts of questions should be attempted at one place.
4. Marks for questions are indicated against each questions.
5. Answers should be brief and to the point.

TIME : 3 HOURS **MAX. MARKS : 80**

UNSOLVED

Part A

1. Which of the following is not the qualitative characteristic of accounting information? (1)
   (a) Reliability (b) Relevance (c) Comparability (d) Simple
2. Credit purchase from Rohan ₹ 9,000 was posted to the debit of Gobind as ₹ 10,000. In this case, suspense account will be debited with (1)
   (a) ₹ 9,000 (b) ₹ 10,000 (c) ₹ 19,000 (d) None of these
3. Which of the following is/are the limitation(s) of accounting? (1)
   (a) It relates to the past transactions
   (b) It is quantitative and financial in nature
   (c) Both (a) and (b)
   (d) It does not act as an evidence
4. Financial transactions in the books of accounts are recorded on the basis of (1)
   (a) voucher (b) cash memo (c) debit note (d) None of these
5. What adjustment entry is passed at the end of the year for outstanding expenses? (1)
   (a) Expenses A/c Dr
   To Outstanding Expenses A/c
   (b) Outstanding Expenses A/c Dr
   To Expenses A/c
   (c) Outstanding Expenses A/c Dr
   To Cash A/c
   (d) Expenses A/c Dr
   To Cash A/c
6. While doing balancing of accounts, personal and real accounts are balanced and nominal accounts are (1)
   (a) taken to profit and loss account.
   (b) closed by transferring to trading and profit and loss account.
   (c) left with balancing figure.
   (d) two-sided entry is passed.
7. Written down value of an asset after 3 years of depreciation on reducing balance method @ 15% p.a. is ₹ 49,130. What was its original value? (1)
   (a) ₹ 40,000 (b) ₹ 80,000 (c) ₹ 45,000 (d) ₹ 70,200

8. The credit balance as per cashbook is ₹ 1,500. Cheques for ₹ 400 were deposited but were not collected. The cheques issued but not presented were ₹ 100, ₹ 125, ₹ 50. Balance as per pass book will be (1)
(a) ₹ 1,625 (b) ₹ 2,175 (c) ₹ 1,375 (d) ₹ 825

9. Paid to Z ₹ 11,500 in full settlement of ₹ 12,000. Posting will be made in Z's account as (1)
(a) ₹ 12,000 on debit side (b) ₹ 12,000 on credit side
(c) ₹ 11,500 on debit side (d) ₹ 11,500 on credit side

10. What will be the journal entry for 'wages paid ₹ 5,000' for installation of machinery? (1)

(a) Machinery A/c	Dr	5,000	
To Cash A/c			5,000
(b) Machinery A/c	Dr	5,000	
To Wages A/c			5,000
(c) Cash A/c	Dr	5,000	
To Machinery A/c			5,000
(d) Wages A/c	Dr	5,000	
To Machinery A/c			5,000

11. The disagreement of trial balance indicates that an .... has been committed. (1)

12. Undercasting of sales book is corrected by .... sales account. (1)

13. Why cash column of the cash book always have a debit balance? (1)

14. Define briefly management accounting, social responsibility accounting and human resource accounting. (3)

Or Goods & Services Tax (GST) can be classified under these given categories.
(i) CGST (ii) SGST (iii) UTGST (iv) IGST
Explain any two.

UNSOLVED

15. Prepare a bank reconciliation statement from the following particulars. (4)
On the 31st December, 2018, I had an overdraft of ₹ 7,500 as shown by my pass book.
(i) I have issued cheques amounting to ₹ 2,500 of which cheques worth ₹ 2,000 only seem to have been presented for payment.
(ii) Cheques amounting to ₹ 1,000 have been paid in by me on 30th December but out of those, only ₹ 750 were credited in the pass book.
(iii) I also find that a cheque for ₹ 100 which I had debited to bank account in my books has been omitted to be banked.
(iv) There is debit in my pass book of ₹ 250 for interest.
(v) An entry of ₹ 300 of a payment by a customer directly into the bank appears in the pass book.
(vi) My pass book also shows a credit of ₹ 600 to my account being interest on my investments collected directly by my bankers.

16. From the following information, draw up a trial balance in the books of Shri Manmohan as on 31st March, 2019 Capital ₹ 1,12,000; purchases ₹ 28,800; discount allowed ₹ 960; carriage inwards ₹ 6,960; carriage outwards ₹ 1,840; sales ₹ 48,000; return inwards ₹ 240; return outwards ₹ 560; rent and taxes ₹ 960; plant and machinery ₹ 64,560; stock on 1st April, 2018 ₹ 12,400; sundry debtors ₹ 16,160; sundry creditors ₹ 9,600; investments ₹ 2,880; commission received ₹ 1,440; cash in hand ₹ 80; cash at bank ₹ 8,080; motor cycle ₹ 27,680 and stock on 31st March, 2019 (not adjusted) ₹ 16,400. (4)

17. Enter the following transactions in a simple cash book for December 2019. **(4)**

Date	Particulars	Amt (₹)
Dec 1	Cash in hand	48,000
Dec 4	Cash received from Ram	16,000
Dec 8	Rent paid	8,000
Dec 11	Purchased goods for cash	24,000
Dec 17	Cash sales	36,000
Dec 20	Stationery purchased	1,200
Dec 23	Cash paid to Ramesh	8,000
Dec 27	Paid salary	4,000
Dec 29	Paid wages	2,000

Or Trial balance of Anita did not agree and she put the difference to suspense account. She discovered the following errors

(i) Sales return book overcast by ₹ 8,175.

(ii) Purchase return to Arpit ₹ 3,125 was not posted to his account.

(iii) Installation charges on new machinery purchased ₹ 1,750 were debited to sundry expenses account as ₹ 175.

(iv) Rent paid for residential accommodation of Anita (the proprietor) ₹ 5,200 was debited to rent account as ₹ 5,000.

Rectify the errors and prepare suspense account to ascertain the difference in trial balance.

18. Explain full disclosure principle. **(6)**

19. From the following information, complete the following journal entries **(6)**

Date	Particulars		LF	Amt (Dr)	Amt (Cr)
(i)	Purchases A/c	Dr		1,60,000	
	Input CGST A/c (6%)	Dr		...	
	Input SGST A/c (6%)	Dr		...	
	To Ramesh				...
	(Being goods purchased from Ramesh worth ₹ 1,60,000 on credit, plus CGST and SGST of 6% each)				
(ii)	Cash A/c	Dr		...	
	Bad Debts A/c	Dr		...	
	To Ramdas				20,000
	(Being Ramdas as who received ₹ 20,000 was declared final payment of 60 paisa received from Ramdas)				
(iii)	Sita	Dr		1,12,000	
	To Sales A/c				...
	To Output CGST A/c (6%)				...
	To Output SGST A/c (6%)				...
	(Being goods sold to Sita for ₹ 1,00,000 on credit, plus CGST and SGST of 6% each)				
(iv)	Interest on Capital A/c	Dr		...	
	To Capital A/c				...
	(Being 10% interest due on capital ₹ 10,00,000 for 6 months)				
(v)	....	Dr		10,000	
	To				10,000
	(Being salary ₹ 10,000 due but not paid)				
(vi)	Cash A/c	Dr		...	
	Discount Allowed A/c	Dr		...	
	To Sanjeev				30,000
	(Being cash received ₹ 29,800 from Sanjeev in full settlement ₹ 30,000)				

UNSOLVED

20. On 1st January, 2016, Satkar Transport Ltd purchased 3 buses for ₹ 10,00,000 each. On 1st July, 2018, one bus was involved in an accident and was completely destroyed and ₹ 7,00,000 were received from the insurance company in full settlement. Depreciation is written-off @ 15% p.a. on diminishing balance method. Prepare bus account from 2016 to 2019. Books are closed on 31st December, every year. (8)

Or A company purchased on 1st July, 2014 machinery costing ₹ 30,000. It further purchased machinery on 1st January, 2015 costing ₹ 20,000 and on 1st October, 2015 costing ₹ 10,000. On 1st April, 2016 one-third of the machinery installed on 1st July, 2014 became obsolete and was sold for ₹ 3,000.

The company follows financial year as the accounting year.

Show how the machinery account would appear in the books of company if depreciation is charged @ 10% per annum on written down value method.

21. Enter the following transactions in proper subsidiary books of Balram. (8)

2016		Amt (₹)
Jan 1	Sold goods to Ramesh	21,000
	Bought from Hari Ram	31,200
Jan 2	Ramesh returned goods	3,000
	Sold to Dina Nath	22,000
Jan 2	Purchased goods from Mangal	28,000
Jan 4	Returned goods to Mangal	4,000
Jan 4	Bought from Devi Dayal	13,000
Jan 4	Sold to Zakir Hussain	14,000
Jan 5	Zakir Hussain returned goods	1,800
Jan 6	Sold to Ram Saran	20,000
Jan 6	Sold to Ghanshyam	12,000
Jan 7	Ram Saran returned goods	2,000
Jan 7	Bought from Devi Dayal	28,000
Jan 8	Returned goods to Devi Dayal	3,000
Jan 9	Purchased goods from Raghu Nath subject to a trade discount of 10%	40,000
Jan 10	Sold to Raja Ram goods subject to trade discount of 5%	20,000

Or Give rectifying entries for the following

(i) A credit sale of goods to Ram ₹ 5,000 has been wrongly passed through the purchases book.

(ii) A credit purchase of goods from Shyam amounting to ₹ 2,000 has been wrongly passed through the sales book.

(iii) A return of goods worth ₹ 2,200 to Mohan was passed through the sales return book.

(iv) A return of goods worth ₹ 1,000 by Ganesh were entered in purchases return book.

(v) Goods for ₹ 11,000 were purchased from Modern Traders on credit, but no entry has yet been passed.

(vi) Purchases return for ₹ 3,000 not recorded in the books.

(vii) Goods for ₹ 1,4,000 sold to Zee Traders on credit were entered in the sales book as ₹ 200 only.

(viii) Goods of the value of ₹ 3,600 returned by Kamal Co. were included in stock, but no entry was passed in the books.

(ix) Goods purchased for ₹ 1,800 were entered in the purchases book as ₹ 18,000.

(x) An invoice for goods sold to X was overcast by ₹ 200.

UNSOLVED

Part B

22. What is prepared in sole-proprietorship business with the objective of calculating gross profit or gross loss of the business? (1)

(a) Trading account (b) Profit and Loss account (c) Balance sheet (d) None of these

23. Choose the correct chronological order of ascertainment of the following profits from the profit and loss (1)

(a) Operating Profit, Net Profit, Gross Profit (b) Operating Profit, Gross Profit, Net Profit
(c) Gross Profit, Net Profit, Operating Profit (d) Gross Profit, Net Profit, Operating Profit

24. In case of sole proprietor business, income tax is considered as (1)

(a) business expense (b) proprietor's expense (c) capital expense (d) All of these

25. Calculate net sales from the following information (1)

Cost of Goods Sold = ₹ 1,00,000; Gross profit 20% on sales

(a) ₹ 1,00,000 (b) ₹ 1,25,000 (c) ₹ 25,000 (d) ₹ 75,000

26. Identify the principle/convention involved in making provision for doubtful debts in profit and loss account. (1)

(a) Convention of conservatism (b) Convention of consistency
(c) Convention of disclosure (d) None of these

27. Manager's Commission is always treated as .... expenses. (1)

28. Goods distributed as free samples are recorded at which value and why? (1)

29. Calculate operating profit from the following.

Net Profit ₹ 10,00,000, dividend received ₹ 12,000, loss on sale of furniture ₹ 24,000, loss by fire ₹ 1,00,000, salaries ₹ 2,40,000, interest on loan from bank ₹ 20,000, rent received ₹ 48,000, donation 10,200 (3)

Or Calculate the amount of gross profit, operating profit and net profit on the basis of the following balances extracted from the books of M/s Vishal and Sons for the year ended March 31, 2016.

Opening stock ₹ 1,00,000, net sales ₹ 22,00,000, net purchases ₹ 12,00,000, direct expenses ₹ 1,20,000, administration expenses ₹ 90,000, selling and distribution expenses ₹ 1,30,000, loss due to fire ₹ 40,000, closing stock ₹ 1,40,000

30. Why is it necessary to record the adjusting entries in the preparation of final accounts? (4)

Or Why is it necessary to create a provision for doubtful debts at the time of preparation of final accounts?

31. The following balances have been extracted from the trial balance of M/s Haryana Chemical Ltd. You are required to prepare a trading and profit and loss account for the year ended 31st December, 2019 from the given information. (4)

Name of Accounts	Amt (₹)	Name of Accounts	Amt (₹)
Opening stock	50,000	Sales	3,50,000
Purchases	1,25,500	Purchase return	2,500
Sales return	2,000	Creditors	25,000
Cash in hand	21,200	Rent	5,000
Cash at bank	12,000	Interest	2,000
Carriage	100	Bills payable	1,71,700
Freehold land	3,20,000	Capital	3,00,000
Patents	1,20,000		
General expenses	2,000		

Name of Accounts	Amt (₹)	Name of Accounts	Amt (₹)
Sundry debtors	32,500		
Building	86,000		
Machinery	34,500		
Insurance	12,400		
Drawings	10,000		
Motor vehicle	10,500		
Bad debts	2,000		
Light and water	1,200		
Trade expenses	2,000		
Power	3,900		
Salary and Wages	5,400		
Loan 15% (1st September, 2018)	3,000		
	8,56,200		8,56,200

Adjustments

(i) Closing stock was valued at the end of the year ₹ 40,000.

(ii) Salary amounting ₹ 500 and trade expenses ₹ 300 are due.

(iii) Depreciation charged on building and machinery are @ 4% and @ 5% respectively.

(iv) Make a provision of 5% on sundry debtors.

UNSOLVED

32. Prepare trading and profit and loss account and balance sheet from the trial balance given of Joe Textiles as at 31st March, 2020. **(6)**

Name of Accounts	Debit Balance (₹)	Credit Balance (₹)
Stock at Commencement	30,00,000	—
Purchases and Sales	2,18,00,000	3,60,00,000
Manufacturing Wages	16,00,000	—
Fuel, Power and Lighting	24,00,000	—
Salaries	22,00,000	—
Income Tax	11,00,000	—
Loan to X @ (10% per annum)	10,00,000	—
Interest on X's Loan	—	60,000
Apprentice Premium	—	9,00,000
Rent	8,00,000	—
Rent Owing	—	1,20,000
Furniture (includes furniture of ₹ 2,00,000 purchased on 1st Oct, 2019)	10,00,000	—
B/R and B/P	12,00,000	3,20,000
Plant	1,44,00,000	—
Debtors and Creditors	56,00,000	26,00,000
Capital	—	2,00,00,000
Cash	39,00,000	—
	6,00,00,000	6,00,00,000

Additional Information

(i) Closing stock was valued at ₹ 60,00,000.

(ii) Goods worth ₹ 10,00,000 were sold and dispatched on 28th March, 2020 but not recorded.

(iii) Goods costing ₹ 14,00,000 were purchased but no entry passed.

(iv) Create a provision of 2% for discount on debtors.

(v) Apprentice premium received on 1st April, 2019 was for 3 years.

(vi) Depreciate furniture by 10% per annum.

(vii) Salaries for March, 2020 were outstanding.

Answers

1. (d) **2.** (c) **3.** (c) **4.** (a) **5.** (a) **6.** (b)
7. (b) **8.** (a) **9.** (a) **10.** (a) **11.** error
12. crediting **15.** Overdraft as per Cash Book = ₹ 8300
16. Total of Trial Balance = ₹ 1,71,600 **17.** Cash Balance = ₹ 52,800 *Or* Total of Suspense Account = ₹ 8,175
19. Input CGST, SGST = ₹ 9,600; Output CGST, SGST = ₹ 6,000; Cash = ₹ 29,800; Discount allowed = ₹ 200
20. Balance of Bus account = ₹ 10,44,013; Profit on accidental bus = ₹ 31,688; Depreciation on accidental bus = ₹ 54,188

Or

Balance of Machinery Account—₹ 39,330 (Mach. I: ₹ 14,985; Mach. II: ₹ 15,795; Mach. III: ₹ 8,550); Loss on Sale of Machine (Mach. I) (1/3): ₹ 5,325
21. Total of Purchases Book = ₹ 1,36,200, Total of Sales Book = ₹ 1,08,000, Total of Purchases Return Book = ₹ 7,000
Total of Sales Return Book = ₹ 6,800
22. (a) **23.** (c) **24.** (b) **25.** (b) **26.** (a)
27. Outstanding **29.** Operating Profit = ₹ 10,94,200 *Or* Gross Profit = ₹ 9,20,000; Operating Profit = ₹ 7,00,000; Net Profit = ₹ 6,60,000.
31. Net Profit = ₹ 1,85,560; Gross Profit = ₹ 2,11,000
32. Gross Profit = ₹ 1,28,00,000; Net Profit = ₹ 97,78,000; Balance Sheet Total = ₹ 3,39,18,000

SAMPLE QUESTION PAPER 4

A Highly Simulated Sample Question Paper for CBSE Class XI Examinations

ACCOUNTANCY

GENERAL INSTRUCTIONS

1. This question paper contains two parts A and B.
2. All questions in both the parts are compulsory.
3. All parts of questions should be attempted at one place.
4. Marks for questions are indicated against each questions.
5. Answers should be brief and to the point.

TIME : 3 HOURS **MAX. MARKS : 80**

UNSOLVED

Part A

1. Goods sold for cash ₹ 20,000, plus 12% IGST. Sales account will be credited by (1)
(a) ₹ 17,600 (b) ₹ 20,000 (c) ₹ 22,400 (d) ₹ 12,600

2. IGST is levied on (1)
(a) Intra-state sale (b) Inter-state sale (c) International sale (d) Credit sale

3. Accounting is considered as .... (1)
(a) an art (b) a science (c) both art and science (d) a study

4. If the amount is posted in the wrong account or it is written on the wrong side of an account, what error is it? (1)
(a) Error of Principle (b) Error of Commission
(c) Error of Omission (d) Compensating Errors

5. Which qualitative characteristic of accounting information is reflected when accounting information is clearly presented? (1)
(a) Reliability (b) Relevance (c) Understandability (d) Comparability

6. A machinery was purchased on 1st April, 2019 for ₹ 5,00,000 and on 1st October, 2020, a new machine is added for ₹ 2,00,000. Calculate the balance of machine account, if depreciation is charged at 20% per annum on written down value method for the year ending 31st March, 2020.
(a) ₹ 6,00,000 (b) ₹ 5,60,000 (c) ₹ 6,60,000 (d) ₹ 5,80,000 (1)

7. Which of the following errors will be rectified through suspense account? (1)
(a) Sales return book undercast by ₹ 1,000 (b) Sales return by Z ₹ 1,000 not recorded
(c) Sales return by Z recorded as ₹ 100
(d) Sales return by Z ₹ 1,000 recorded through purchase return book.

8. Where would a second hand motor car purchased on credit from Mr XYZ be recorded? (1)
(a) Purchase return book (b) Purchase book
(c) Journal proper (d) Cash book

9. If the business's owner wtihdraws cash for his/her personal use, what will be the effect on capital? (1)
(a) Increase in capital (b) Remain the same (c) Decrease in capital (d) No effect on capital

10. Which of the following is the journal for cash and goods given as charity? (1)
(a) Cash A/c Dr
To Charity A/c
To Purchases A/c
(b) Purchases A/c Dr
To Cash A/c
To Charity A/c
(c) Charity A/c Dr
To Cash A/c
To Purchases A/c
(d) Cash A/c Dr
Purchases A/c Dr
To Charity A/c

11. AS-26 is titled as .... (1)

12. .... of accounting are like the foundation pillars on which the structure of accounting is based. (1)

13. Name the basis of accounting which is recognised under the Companies Act, 2013. (1)

14. "Accounting information should be comparable". Do you agree with this statement ? Give reasons. (3)

Or Explain any three objectives of accounting.

15. Enter the following transactions in a two column cash book. (4)

Date	Particulars	Amt (₹)
2019		
Jul 1	Cash in hand	3,50,000
Jul 3	Cash deposited into bank	40,000
Jul 5	Paid to Mahima	30,000
Jul 8	Goods purchased	40,000
Jul 10	Received from Sohan Lal	98,000
Jul 16	Goods sold	40,000
Jul 21	Paid to Sawant	29,500
Jul 28	Paid wages for the month	50,000
	Paid in full settlement of ₹ 40,000 to Sushil	39,000
Jul 29	Cash withdrawn from bank for office use	4,000
Jul 30	Salary paid through cheque	15,000

Or Differentiate between trade discount and cash discount.

16. "Business units last indefinitely." Mention and explain the concept on which the above statement is based. (4)

17. Prepare accounting equation from the following information (4)
(i) Rama started business with cash ₹ 1,00,000; machinery ₹ 50,000 and goods ₹ 50,000.
(ii) Sold 1/2 of above stock (goods) at 10% profit for cash.
(iii) Rent paid ₹ 500; Outstanding salary ₹ 1,500.
(iv) Remaining goods sold to Suman at 10% profit on cost at 5% cash discount.

18. On 31st March, 2016 passbook of Shri Rajendra shows a debit balance of ₹ 10,000. From the following, prepare a bank reconciliation statement. (6)
(i) Cheques amounting to ₹ 8,000 drawn on 25th March, 2016 of which cheques of ₹ 5,000 were encashed on 2nd April, 2016.
(ii) Cheques paid into the bank for collection ₹ 5,000 but cheques of ₹ 2,200 could only be collected in March, 2016.
(iii) Bank charges ₹ 25 and dividend of ₹ 350 on investments collected by the bank could not be shown in the cash book.

UNSOLVED

(iv) A bill of ₹ 10,000 was retired by the bank under rebate of ₹ 150 but the full amount was credited in the cash book.

(v) The payment of a cheque for ₹ 550 was recorded twice in the passbook.

(vi) Withdrawal column of the passbook undercast by ₹ 200.

(vii) ₹ 500 in respect of dishonoured cheque were entered in the passbook but not in the cash book.

19. Journalise the following transactions of Anjuman Gupta. (6)

2016	Particulars	Amt (₹)
Dec 1	Kunal Gupta started business with cash	1,00,000
Dec 2	Paid into bank	60,000
Dec 3	Bought goods from M/s. Gaurav & Co. on credit	20,000
Dec 4	Purchased furniture	2,000
Dec 4	Purchased adding machine	8,000
Dec 4	Purchased typewriter	6,000
	(Payment in all cases made by cheque)	
Dec 6	Paid for postage	150
Dec 8	Sold goods for cash	4,000
Dec 9	Sold goods on credit to M/s. Rastogi & Co.	10,000
Dec 15	Paid to M/s Gaurav & Co.	19,500
	Discount allowed by them	500
Dec 25	Sold goods to M/s. Singh & Co.	5,600
Dec 27	Received cheque from M/s Rastogi & Co. in full settlement of amount due from them	9,750
Dec 31	Paid for electricity charges	100
Dec 31	Paid salary	1,500
Dec 31	Paid rent of building by cheque, half of the building is used by the proprietor for residential use	5,000
Dec 31	Drew for private use	3,500

UNSOLVED

20. The trial balance of Murari Ltd shows a difference of ₹ 6,000, the credit side being excess. The difference is subsequently found due to the following mistakes

(i) The purchase of an office table costing ₹ 40,000 had been passed through the purchase day book.

(ii) A motor car had been purchased for ₹ 68,000. Cash had been correctly credited but the motor car account had been debited with ₹ 62,800 only.

(iii) Interest on deposits received ₹ 1,200 had been debited in the cash account but had not been credited to the interest account.

(iv) The balance in the account of Mr Rahim ₹ 2,000 had been written-off as bad debt but no other account had been debited.

Give the necessary entries for rectification of errors and prepare suspense account. (8)

Or

Priya Gold has purchased a machinery for ₹ 10,00,000 on 1st October, 2016. Another machine was purchased for ₹ 6,00,000 plus IGST @ 12% in cash on 1st April, 2018. Depreciation is charged @ 10% p.a. by the straight line method. Accounts are closed every year on 31st March. You are required to show machinery account on 31st March, 2019 in both the cases

(i) When provision for depreciation account is not maintained.

(ii) When provision for depreciation account is maintained.

21. From the following list of balances extracted from the books of Kumar prepare a trial balance as on 31st March, 2016. The amount required to balance should be entered as capital. (8)

Name of Accounts	Amt (₹)	Name of Accounts	Amt (₹)
Purchases	3,64,000	Proprietor's Withdrawals	12,000
Stock on 1st April, 2015	70,000	Sundry Debtors	72,000
Sales	8,00,000	Sundry Creditors	24,000
Sundry Expenses	3,000	Bad Debts	2,000
Leasehold Premises	1,00,000	Investment @ 10%	40,000
Freehold Premises	3,60,000	Interest on Investment	4,000
Return Inwards	5,000	Long-term Borrowings	1,20,000
Furniture and Fixtures	58,000	Loan from SBI	1,60,000
Equipment	1,60,000	Interest on Loan	13,000
Repairs to Equipment	1,000	Petty Cash Account	80
Depreciation	16,000	Balance at Bank	6,920
		Stock on 31st March, 2016 (not adjusted)	92,000

Or Kaushik Ltd purchased a vehicle for ₹ 4,00,000. After 4 year its salvage value is estimated at ₹ 40,000. To find out the amount of depreciation to be charged every year based on straight line basis, and also to show the vehicle account as would appear for 4 years, assuming it is sold for ₹ 50,000 at the end when

(i) Depreciation is charged to asset account.

(ii) Provision for depreciation accout is maintained.

Prepare the ledger in the books of accounts of Kaushik Ltd. by both the above methods.

UNSOLVED

Part B

22. Freight inward of ₹ 4,000 is outstanding at the end of the year. Where it is recordable in final accounts? (1)

(a) Trading account and Balance sheet
(b) Profit and loss account and Balance sheet
(c) Trading account and Profit and loss account
(d) Trading account (Debit) and Balance sheet (Assets)

23. Consider the following statement. (1)

I. Interest on capital is an expense for the proprietor.

II. Interest on capital is shown on the debit side of profit and loss account.

III. It is added to the capital in the balance sheet.

Choose the correct option.

(a) I, II, III are correct
(b) Both I and II are correct
(c) Both II and III are correct
(d) I, II, III are incorrect

24. Opening capital at ₹ 60,000, drawings ₹ 5,000, capital added during the year ₹ 10,000, closing capital ₹ 90,000. Calculate profit. (1)

(a) ₹ 1,55,000
(b) ₹ 25,000
(c) ₹ 45,000
(d) ₹ 1,35,000

25. Which of the following is the journal entry to record the creation for provision for bad debts account? (1)

(a) Profit and Loss A/c Dr
To Provision for Bad Debts A/c

(b) Provision for Bad Debts A/c Dr
To Profit and Loss A/c

(c) Trading A/c Dr
To Provision for Bad Debts A/c

(d) Trading A/c Dr
To Provision for Bad Debts A/c

26. Rahul's trial balance provide you the following information. (1)

Debtors ₹ 80,000

Bad debts ₹ 2,000

Provision for doubtful debts ₹ 4,000

It is desired to maintain a provision for bad debts of ₹ 1,000 state the amount to be debited/credited in profit and loss account.

(a) ₹ 5,000 (Debit) (d) ₹ 3,000 (Debit) (c) ₹ 1,000 (Credit) (b) None of these

27. The amount which cannot be recovered from the debtors is known as .... (1)

28. What is meant by indirect expenses? Give two examples. (1)

29. State whether the following statements are items of capital or revenue expenditure, with reason. (3)

(i) Expenditure incurred on repairs and white washing at the time of purchase of an old building in order to make it usable.

(ii) Registration fees paid at the time of purchase of a building.

(iii) Depreciation on plant and machinery.

Or Calculate the gross profit from the following for 50% goods sold.

Total purchases during the current year are ₹ 9,00,000, Return outward ₹ 50,000, Lighting ₹ 30,000, Wages ₹ 80,000 and Electricity ₹ 8,000 and 1/2nd goods are sold for ₹ 8,00,000.

30. What is the need of preparing a balance sheet? (4)

Or Define closing stock. Show its treatment in final accounts.

31. Following balances have been extracted from the trial balance of M/s Keshav Electronics Ltd. You are required to prepare the trading and profit and loss account for the year ended 31st December, 2019. (4)

Particulars	Amt (₹)	Particulars	Amt (₹)
Opening stock	2,26,000	Sales	6,80,000
Purchases	4,40,000	Return outwards	15,000
Drawings	75,000	Creditors	50,000
Buildings	1,00,000	Bills payable	63,700
Motor van	30,000	Interest received	20,000
Freight inwards	3,400	Capital	3,50,000
Sales return	10,000		
Trade expenses	3,300		
Heat and power	8,000		
Salary and wages	5,000		
Legal expenses	3,000		
Postage and telegram	1,000		
Bad debts	6,500		
Cash-in-hand	79,000		
Cash-at-bank	98,000		
Sundry debtors	25,000		
Investments	40,000		
Insurance	3,500		
Machinery	22,000		
	11,78,700		11,78,700

UNSOLVED

The following additional information is available

(i) Stock on 31st December, 2019 was ₹ 30,000.

(ii) Depreciation is to be charged on building @ 5% and motor van @ 10%.

(iii) Provision for doubtful debts is to be maintained @ 5% on sundry debtors.

(iv) Unexpired insurance was ₹ 600.

(v) The manager is entitled to a commission @ 5% on net profit after charging such commission.

32. From the following trial balance, extracted from the books, prepare trading and profit and loss account for the year ended 31st March, 2020 and balance sheet as at that date. **(6)**

Name of Accounts	Amt (Dr)	Amt (Cr)
Capital	—	2,70,000
Drawings	19,440	—
Land and building	75,000	—
Plant and machinery	42,810	—
Furniture and fixtures	3,750	—
Carriage inwards	13,110	—
Wages	64,410	—
Salaries	14,010	—
Provision for bad debts	—	7,410
Sales	—	2,73,690
Sales return	5,280	—
Bank charges	420	—
Gas and water	2,160	—
Rates and taxes	2,520	—
Discount	—	360
Purchases	1,26,480	—
Purchases return	—	25,380
Bills receivable	3,810	—
Trade expenses	5,970	—
Sundry debtors	1,13,400	—
Sundry creditors	—	36,510
Stock (1st April, 2019)	79,260	—
Apprentice premium	—	1,500
Fire insurance	1,470	—
Cash-at-bank	39,000	—
Cash-in-hand	2,550	—
Total	6,14,850	6,14,850

UNSOLVED

Adjustments

Charge depreciation on land and building at $2\frac{1}{2}$%, on plant and machinery at 10% and on furniture and fixtures at 10%. Make provision of 5% on debtors for doubtful debts. Carry forward the following unexpired amounts

(i) Fire insurance ₹ 375

(ii) Rates and taxes ₹ 720

(iii) Apprentice premium ₹ 1,200

(iv) Closing stock ₹ 88,170

Answers

1. (b) **2.** (b) **3.** (c) **4.** (b) **5.** (c) **6.** (d)
7. (a) **8.** (c) **9.** (c) **10.** (c) **11.** intangible assets
12. Basic assumptions
15. Cash Balance = ₹ 2,63,500; Bank Balance = ₹ 21,000
17. Assets = Liabilities + Capital
₹ 2,03,125 = ₹ 1,500 + ₹ 2,01,625
18. Credit balance as per Cash Book = ₹ 11,825
20. Total of Suspense Account = ₹ 7,200
Or (i) Balance in Machinery A/c I = ₹ 7,50,000; II = ₹ 5,40,000
(ii) Balance in Machinery A/c = ₹ 16,00,000; Balance in provision for depreciation A/c = ₹ 3,10,000
21. Trial Balance Total = ₹ 12,83,000; Capital = ₹ 1,75,000
Or (i) Balance inVehicle Account = ₹ 1,30,000, Profit on Sale = ₹ 10,000
(ii) Balance in Vehicle Account = ₹ 4,00,000.
22. (a) **23.** (c) **24.** (b) **25.** (a) **26.** (c)
27. bad debts **29.** *Or* Gross Profit = ₹ 3,20,000
31. Gross Profit = ₹ 37,600; Net Profit = ₹ 25,381
32. Gross Profit = ₹ 96,540; Net Profit = ₹ 69,114; Balance Sheet Total = ₹ 3,57,384

SAMPLE QUESTION PAPER 5

A Highly Simulated Sample Question Paper for CBSE Class XI Examinations

ACCOUNTANCY

GENERAL INSTRUCTIONS

1. This question paper contains two parts A and B.
2. All questions in both the parts are compulsory.
3. All parts of questions should be attempted at one place.
4. Marks for questions are indicated against each questions.
5. Answers should be brief and to the point.

TIME : 3 HOURS **MAX. MARKS : 80**

UNSOLVED

Part A

1. If a transaction is properly analysed and recorded (1)

(a) only two accounts will be used to record the transaction
(b) one account will be used to record transaction
(c) one account balance will increase and another will decrease
(d) total amount debited will equals total amount credited

2. A company bought a machine for ₹ 90,000 on credit. Another ₹ 10,000 is spent on its installation. If the estimated useful life is 5 years and scrap value at the end was ₹ 5,000, calculate the rate of depreciation. (1)

(a) 18% (b) 19% (c) 17% (d) 20%

3. If the amount is posted in the wrong account or if it is written on the wrong side of the account, what is the error called? (1)

(a) Error of Principle (b) Compensating Error
(c) Error of omission (d) Error of Commission

4. The debit notes issued are used to prepare which book? (1)

(a) Purchase return book (b) Sales return book
(c) Sales book (d) Purchase book

5. The amount of money that is owed by an outsider is a/an (1)

(a) asset (b) liability
(c) expense (d) capital

6. Fixed assets and current assets are categorised as per the concept of (1)

(a) going concern (b) separate entity
(c) consistency (d) conservatism

7. Sudesh's salary is ₹ 10,000 per month. During a month, he withdrew goods worth ₹ 2,500 for personal use and also got ₹ 9,500 in cash. The excess payment of ₹ 2,000 will be debited to (1)
   (a) Salary A/c
   (b) Purchases A/c
   (c) Salary-in-advance A/c
   (d) Sales A/c

8. Sales book records .... (1)
   (a) cash sales
   (b) credit sales
   (c) Both cash and credit sales
   (d) None of these

9. Overdraft as per cash book is ₹ 10,000, cheques deposited but not credited is ₹ 2,500. What is balance as per pass book? (1)
   (a) ₹ 11,000
   (b) ₹ 4,000
   (c) ₹ 9,000
   (d) ₹ 16,000

10. Journal entry for debts which were written-off as bad but are subsequently recovered will be (1)
   (a) Bad Debts A/c Dr
   To Bad Debts Recovered A/c
   (b) Cash/Bank A/c Dr
   To Bad Debts A/c
   (c) Cash/Bank A/c Dr
   To Bad Debts Recovered A/c
   (d) Bad Debts Recovered A/c Dr
   To Cash/Bank A/c

11. Journal is prepared in .... order. (1)

12. The amount of capital will be .... when cash is ₹ 5,000, furniture is ₹ 12,000, stock is ₹ 30,000 and creditors are ₹ 6,000. (1)

13. What will be the effect on the trial balance if ₹ 5,000 are received as rent and correctly entered in the books but not posted to rent account? (1)

14. What do you understand by cash basis of accounting? Give any two advantages of cash basis of accounting. (3)

Or Explain the dual aspect principle with the help of an example.

UNSOLVED

15. Prepare accounting equation from the following (4)

	Amt (₹)
(i) Darshan started business with cash	2,50,000
(ii) He purchased furniture for cash	35,000
(iii) He paid commission	2,000
(iv) He purchased goods on credit	40,000
(v) He sold goods (costing ₹ 20,000) for cash	26,000

16. On 31st December, 2019, the cash book of Rohan showed an overdraft of ₹ 56,000. From the following particulars, make out a bank reconciliation statement. (4)
   (i) Cheques drawn but not cashed before 31st December, 2019 amounted to ₹ 39,460.
   (ii) Cheques paid into the bank but not credited before 31st December, 2019 amounted to ₹ 48,910.
   (iii) A bill receivable for ₹ 5,200 previously discounted with the bank had been dishonoured and bank charges debited in the pass book amounted to ₹ 550.
   (iv) Debit is made in the pass book for ₹ 1,200 on account of interest on overdraft.
   (v) The bank has collected interest on investment and credited ₹ 7,600 in the pass book.

17. From the following list of balances extracted from the books of Shri Mohan Prasad, prepare a trial balance as at 31st March, 2019. **(4)**

Name of Accounts	Amt (₹)	Name of Accounts	Amt (₹)
Stock on 1st April, 2018	22,000	Investments	30,000
Purchases	2,57,500	Interest on investments	2,700
Sales	3,61,800	Cash and bank balance	1,240
Carriage inwards	300	Premises	60,000
Carriage outwards	120	Fixtures	14,000
Return inwards	8,500	Miscellaneous expenses	520
Return outwards	2,000	Miscellaneous income	140
Debtors	32,000	Loan from PNB	25,000
Creditors	17,400	Interest on above loan	3,000
Bad debts	600	Capital	70,000
Stationery	420	Proprietor's withdrawal	6,000
Insurance	340	Computers	9,000
Wages and salaries	18,500	Goodwill	15,000
		Stock on 31st March, 2019 (not adjusted)	31,000

Or

Record the following transactions in a journal.

(i) Received cash from Lipakshi for a bad debts written-off last year ₹ 800.

(ii) Bought goods at the list price of ₹ 2,00,000 from Ipshita less 20% trade discount and 2% cash discount and paid 40% by cheque.

(iii) Sold goods to Ishaan at the list price of ₹ 4,00,000 less 20% trade discount and 2% cash discount. Ishaan paid 50% by cheque.

18. List the points highlighting the nature of accounting standards. **(6)**

19. From the following information, complete the missing information using a suspense account. **(6)**

Date	Particulars		LF	Amt (Dr)	Amt (Cr)
(i)	....	Dr		...	
	Sales A/c	Dr		...	
	To Suspense A/c				...
	(Being purchase of ₹ 4,000 from Bheem was entered in sales book but Bheem's personal account was rightly credited, now rectified)				
(ii)	Nakul	Dr		...	
	To Suspense A/c				...
	(Being sales to Nakul of ₹ 4,300 credited to his account as ₹ 3,400, now rectified)				
(iii)	Sales A/c	Dr		...	
	....	Dr		...	
	To Furniture A/c				...
	(Being sale of old furniture of ₹ 5,400 was credited to sales account as ₹ 4,500 now rectified)				
(iv)	Drawings A/c	Dr		1,000	
	To				1,000
	(Being goods worth ₹ 1,000 taken by proprietor for personal use was not recorded)				

Date	Particulars		LF	Amt (Dr)	Amt (Cr)
(v)	Suspense A/c	Dr		...	
	To Sales A/c				...
	(Being sale of ₹ 2,960 to Arjun was entered in sales book as ₹ 2,690, now rectified)				
(vi)	Sales Return A/c	Dr		2,100	
	To Suspense A/c				2,100
	(Being sales return book balance of ₹ 2,100 not included in books, now included)				

20. On 1st April, 2013 a firm purchased a machinery for ₹ 1,00,000. On 1st July, 2016 the machinery became obsolete and was sold for ₹ 40,000.

The firm charges depreciation on its machinery @ 10% per annum on written down value method. The books are closed on 31st March of every year. Prepare necessary ledger accounts assuming that

(i) Provision for depreciation account is not maintained.

(ii) Provision for depreciation account is maintained. **(8)**

Or

A truck was purchased on 1st April, 2018 for ₹ 10,00,000. On 1st October, 2018, another truck was purchased for ₹ 6,00,000. Estimated scrap values were ₹ 40,000 and ₹ 20,000 respectively. Depreciation is to be provided @ 10% p.a. on the trucks under the reducing balance system.

(i) Show the truck account for the year ended 31st March, 2019 and 2020.

(ii) Show how the truck account will appear in the balance sheet as at 31st March, 2020.

21. From the following cash and bank transactions of Mr Pulkit, owner of Pulkit Stationery House, prepare a two column cash book and post them into ledger. **(8)**

Date	Particulars	Amt (₹)
2016		
Apr 1	Cash in hand	22,000
	Cash at bank	27,500
Apr 3	Purchased goods from M/s Arun for ₹ 3,500 and paid by cheque GST applicable is 6%	
Apr 9	Cash purchases ₹ 4,000 less trade discount 5%	
Apr 10	Purchased postage stamps	250
Apr 12	Proceeds of cash sales of ₹ 25,000 deposited into bank	
Apr 14	Drew cash for personal use	2,050
Apr 15	Received from Manan cash ₹ 1,500 and cheque ₹ 2,500, both deposited into bank allowed ₹ 250 as cash discount	
Apr 15	Withdrew from bank for office use	4,000
Apr 16	Paid wages ₹ 1,500 and rent ₹ 2,500	
Apr 19	Paid M/s Vrijesh by cheque, cash discount allowed by him ₹ 500	12,000
Apr 23	Received a cheque from Nitin for sale of old goods	4,000
Apr 25	Paid M/s Arun cash ₹ 3,750 and ₹ 1,800 by a cheque, received cash discount ₹ 125	
Apr 26	Karan, a customer, deposited into bank	3,000
Apr 29	Withdrew from bank for personal use	1,000
Apr 30	Bank charged commission	500
Apr 30	Withdrew from bank for paying income tax	2,500

Or Vishwas of Delhi started business on 1st April, 2019 with building of ₹ 12,00,000 and machinery of ₹ 3,00,000. He purchased these assets from Delhi and paid by cheque from his savings account. He introduced capital of ₹ 3,00,000 in cash. Journalise the following transactions for the month of April, prepare the ledger accounts and balance them

UNSOLVED

Date	Particulars	Amt (₹)
2019		
Apr 1	Purchased goods for cash from Ram, Delhi	55,000
Apr 4	Purchased goods from Naresh, Gurugram (Haryana)	40,000
Apr 5	Sold goods for cash	70,000
Apr 12	Cash depoisted into bank*	80,000
Apr 14	Purchased machinery costing ₹ 10,000 for cash	
Apr 15	Solds goods to Garg Bros., Delhi	30,000
Apr 16	Returned goods to Naresh	2,000
Apr 28	Paid salary for the month of April*	10,000
Apr 30	Received bank interest*	400
Apr 30	Paid for courier charges	1,000

CGST and SGST is levied @ 6% each on intra-state transactions and @ 12% on inter-state transactions excepts transactions marked with (*).

Part B

UNSOLVED

22. Cost of goods purchased for resale is an example of (1)

(a) capital expenditure
(b) revenue expenditure
(c) deferred revenue expenditure
(d) None of these

23. Trading account is a (1)

(a) personal account (b) nominal account (c) real account (d) asset account

24. Rent paid during the year @ ₹ 1,000 p.m., amounts to ₹ 11,000 and some part of rent is outstanding. Pass the journal entry to record the outstanding rent. (1)

(a) Outstanding Rent A/c Dr 1,000
To Rent A/c 1,000

(b) Rent A/c Dr 1,000
To Outstanding Rent A/c 1,000

(c) Cash A/c Dr 1,000
To Rent A/c 1,000

(d) None of the above

25. Calculate Cost of Goods Sold (COGS), if opening stock = ₹ 8,500, purchases = ₹ 30,700, direct wages = ₹ 4,800, interest on loan = ₹ 2,800, closing stock = ₹ 9,000. (1)

(a) ₹ 30,000 (b) ₹ 32,000 (c) ₹ 35,000 (d) ₹ 40,000

26. While calculating operating profit, the following are not taken into account. (1)

(a) Normal transactions
(b) Abnormal items
(c) Expenses of a purely financial nature
(d) Both (b) and (c)

27. Capital expenditure .... the earning capacity. (1)

28. Why is closing stock valued at lower of cost or realisable value by accountants? (1)

29. State the purpose of preparing trading and profit and loss account. (3)

Or Write the features of a trading account.

30. Give four points of difference between trading and profit and loss account. (4)

Or Explain any four limitations of financial statements.

31. From the following trial balance and additional information of Mr Amit Sharma, a proprietor, prepare trading and profit and loss account for the year ended 31st March, 2022.

Name of Accounts	Ddebit Balance (₹)	Credit Balance (₹)
Building	3,20,000	—
Wages	52,000	—
Machinery	32,000	—
Salaries and Wages	83,200	—
Debtors	67,400	—
Capital	—	4,46,200
Purchases and Sales	1,13,000	2,01,400
Creditors	—	25,000
Income Tax	4,000	—
Drawings	1,000	—
Total	6,72,600	6,72,600

Closing stock at cost ₹ 2,00,000 but at market price ₹ 1,77,000 **(4)**

32. From the following balances, prepare trading and profit and loss account and a balance sheet as on 31st March, 2019.

Particulars	Amt (₹)	Particulars	Amt (₹)
Capital	16,40,000	Sundry creditors	1,80,000
Life insurance premium	56,000	Sales	24,80,000
Plant and machinery	1,00,000	Return outwards	20,000
Stock in the beginning	3,00,000	Special rebates (debit)	16,000
Purchases	17,44,000	Special rebates (credit)	24,000
Return inwards	1,20,000	Rent for premises sublet	20,000
Sundry debtors	4,20,000	Lighting	8,000
Furniture	1,82,000	Motor car expenses	1,26,000
Motor car	8,00,000	Bank balance	3,04,000
Freight and duty	40,000	Loan from Vishal @ 12% p.a.	2,00,000
Carriage inward	16,000	Interest on loan from Vishal (debit)	18,000
Carriage outward	6,000		
Trade expenses	3,08,000		

Additional Information

(i) Stock on 31st March, 2019 was valued at ₹ 5,00,000 (realisable value ₹ 6,40,000).

(ii) Stock of ₹ 1,20,000 was burnt by fire on 25th March. It was fully insured and the insurance company admitted the claim in full.

(iii) Goods worth ₹ 36,000 were distributed as free samples. Goods worth ₹ 30,000 were used for personal purposes by the proprietor and goods worth ₹ 10,000 were given away as charity.

(iv) Depreciate motor car by 15%.

(v) Included in trade expenses is insurance premium of ₹ 48,000 paid for the year ending 30th June, 2019. **(6)**

UNSOLVED

Answers

1. (d)	**2.** (b)	**3.** (d)	**4.** (a)	**5.** (a)
6. (a)	**7.** (c)	**8.** (b)	**9.** (c)	**10.** (c)

11. chronological

12. ₹ 41,000

15. Assets = Liabilities + Capital
₹ 2,94,000 = ₹ 40,000 + ₹ 2,54,000

16. Debit Balance as per Pass Book = ₹ 64,800

17. Trial Balance Total = ₹ 4,79,040

20. (i) Balance in Machinery Account = ₹ 72,900, Loss on Sale = ₹ 31,077.50
(ii) Balance in Machinery Account = ₹ 1,00,000, Balance in Provision for Depreciation Account = ₹ 28,922.50

Or Balance of Truck Account 2018-2019 = ₹ 14,70,000; 2019-2020 = ₹ 13,23,000

21. Cash Balance = ₹ 12,150, Bank Balance = ₹ 38,200

22. (b)	**23.** (b)	**24.** (b)	**25.** (c)	**26.** (d)

27. increases

31. Gross Profit = ₹ 2,13,400; Net Profit = ₹ 1,30,200

32. Gross Profit = ₹ 9,76,000; Net Profit = ₹ 3,78,000; Balance Sheet Total = ₹ 23,18,000

Lightning Source UK Ltd.
Milton Keynes UK
UKHW050748261022
411115UK00004B/7